Aggregation Functions

Aggregation is the process of combining several numerical values into a single representative value, and an aggregation function performs this operation. These functions arise wherever aggregating information is important: applied and pure mathematics (probability, statistics, decision theory, functional equations), operations research, computer science, and many applied fields (economics and finance, pattern recognition and image processing, data fusion, etc.).

This readable book provides a comprehensive, rigorous and self-contained exposition of aggregation functions. Classes of aggregation functions covered include triangular norms and conorms, copulas, means and averages, and those based on nonadditive integrals. The properties of each method, as well as their interpretation and analysis, are studied in depth, together with construction methods and practical identification methods. Special attention is given to the nature of scales on which values to be aggregated are defined (ordinal, interval, ratio, bipolar). It is an ideal introduction for graduate students and a unique resource for researchers.

All the titles listed below can be obtained from good booksellers or from Cambridge University Press. For a complete series listing visit

http://www.cambridge.org/uk/series/sSeries.asp?code=EOM

ENCYCLOPEDIA OF MATHEMATICS AND ITS APPLICATIONS

Aggregation Functions

MICHEL GRABISCH

University of Panthéon-Sorbonne
Paris, France

JEAN-LUC MARICHAL

University of Luxembourg
Luxembourg

RADKO MESIAR

Slovak University of Technology
Bratislava, Slovakia

ENDRE PAP

University of Novi Sad
Novi Sad, Serbia

CAMBRIDGE
UNIVERSITY PRESS

CAMBRIDGE UNIVERSITY PRESS
Cambridge, New York, Melbourne, Madrid, Cape Town,
Singapore, São Paulo, Delhi, Tokyo, Mexico City

Cambridge University Press
The Edinburgh Building, Cambridge CB2 8RU, UK

Published in the United States of America by
Cambridge University Press, New York

www.cambridge.org
Information on this title: www.cambridge.org/9780521519267

© M. Grabisch, J.-L. Marichal, R. Mesiar and E. Pap 2009

First published 2009

A catalogue record for this publication is available from the British Library

ISBN 978-0-521-51926-7 Hardback

To Agnieszka, Francis, Raphaëlle, and Rémi
M.G.

To Pascale, Olivia, Jean-Philippe, and Claudia
J.-L.M.

To Anka, Janka, and Andrejka
R.M.

To Darinka and Danijela
E.P.

Contents

Figures

x

Tables

Preface

The process of combining several numerical values into a single representative one is called *aggregation*, and the numerical function performing this process is called an *aggregation function*. This simple definition demonstrates the size of the field of application of aggregation: applied mathematics (e.g., probability, statistics, decision theory), computer sciences (e.g., artificial intelligence, operations research), as well as many applied fields (economics and finance, pattern recognition and image processing, data fusion, multicriteria decision aid, automated reasoning, etc.).

Although the history of aggregation is probably as old as mathematics (think of the arithmetic mean), its existence has remained underground till only recently, and its utilization rather intuitive and hardly formalized. The rapid growth of the above-mentioned application fields, largely due to the arrival of computers, has made necessary the establishment of a sound theoretical basis for aggregation functions. Hence, since the 1980s, aggregation functions have become a genuine research field, rapidly developing, but in a rather scattered way since aggregation functions are rooted in many different fields. Indeed, most of the results were disseminated in various journals or specialized books, where usually only one specific class of aggregation functions devoted to one specific domain is discussed.

Actually, in these early years of the twenty-first century, a substantial amount of literature is already available, many significant results have been found (such as characterizations of various families of aggregation functions), and many connections have been made with either related fields or former work (such as triangular norms in probabilistic metric spaces, theory of means and averages, etc.). Yet for the researcher as well as for the practitioner, this abundance of literature, because it is scattered in many domains, is more a handicap than an advantage, and there is a real lack of a unified and complete view of aggregation functions, where one could find the most important concepts and results presented in a clear and rigorous way.

This book has been written with the intention of filling this gap: it offers a full, comprehensive, rigorous, and unified treatment of aggregation functions. Our main motivation has been to bring a unified viewpoint of the aggregation problem, and to provide an abstract mathematical presentation and analysis of aggregation functions used in various disciplines, without referring explicitly to a given domain. The book also provides a unified terminology and notation.

To reach this aim, we have tried to follow as closely as possible the following guidelines. First, by contrast to the style of many handbooks, the chapters are not a collection of definitions, facts and assertions without proof, but we have maintained a straight, visible and logical line in our discourse, avoiding anecdotal details. Second, our aim was not to be exhaustive, citing every latest advance in the field, but to be selective, and put material into a historical perspective. As far as possible, we have tried to provide the original references. Third, the presentation is mathematical and rigorous, avoiding jargon and inherent imprecision from the various applied domains where aggregation functions are used (often under different names such as aggregation operators, merging functions, connectives, etc.), but keeping as far as possible the standard terminology of mathematics. This is the only way to make the book usable by every researcher or practitioner in every field. As far as possible, every result is given with its proof, unless the proof is long and requires extra material. In this case, a reference to the proof is always given.

The book is intended primarily for researchers and graduate students in applied mathematics and computer sciences, secondarily for practitioners in, for example, decision making, optimization, economics and finance, artificial intelligence, data fusion, computer vision, etc. It could also be used as a textbook for graduate students in applied mathematics and computer sciences. The reader of the book is assumed to have the basic knowledge of a graduate student in algebra and analysis.

The table of contents has been detailed. The main theoretical corpus is given in Chapters 2 to 5. Additional theoretical material is given in Chapters 6 to 9, while Chapters 10 and 11 are more practically oriented. In Chapters 2 to 5, as far as possible, most of the results are given with proof. Due to space limitations and forest saving, it has not been possible to maintain this philosophy in the second part of the book, which has too broad a scope.

– *Chapter 1: Introduction*
  The general idea of an aggregation function is presented, and the scope of the book is defined. After giving some basic examples and definitions, the conventional notation for the whole book is presented.

– *Chapter 2: Properties for aggregation*
  This important chapter defines the basic possible properties for aggregation functions. They are divided into elementary mathematical properties (monotonicity, continuity, symmetry, etc.), grouping properties (associativity, decomposability, etc.), scale invariance (ratio, difference, interval, ordinal scales), and various other properties (neutral and annihilator elements, additivity, etc.).

– *Chapter 3: Conjunctive and disjunctive aggregation functions*
  Conjunctive (respectively, disjunctive) aggregation functions are those functions

acting like a logical "and" (respectively, a logical "or"). In this chapter, full development is given for conjunctive aggregation functions. Disjunctive aggregation functions are merely obtained by duality. A large section is devoted to triangular norms (t-norms for short): different families, continuous Archimedean t-norms, additively generated t-norms, ordinal sums, etc. Another important section is devoted to copulas, well known in probability theory. Two other sections present uninorms and nullnorms (combinations of t-norms and t-conorms).

– *Chapter 4: Means and averages*
This chapter develops perhaps the best known family of aggregation functions, with a long history. The concepts of means and average functions, as well as their relationships, are first presented in full generality. Then main subclasses of means, such as quasi-arithmetic ones, some of their special cases, and some of their generalizations are presented. A section is then devoted to means constructed from the associativity property and another one to those means constructed from a mean value property, such as Cauchy means. A section also concerns some construction methods. Finally, the last section deals with extended means constructed from weight triangles.

– *Chapter 5: Aggregation functions based on nonadditive integrals*
Considering nonadditive integrals (e.g., the Choquet integral) in the discrete finite case defines a new class of aggregation functions, in which interest developed in the 1980s. Nonadditive integrals are defined with respect to capacities (nonadditive monotone measures), and in particular generalize the notion of expected value. A first section defines capacities, their properties and related notions. An important section is devoted to the Choquet integral, since this is the most representative of nonadditive integrals, possessing many appealing properties. Then the case of the Sugeno integral is presented, and finally other families of nonadditive integrals.

– *Chapter 6: Construction methods*
This chapter gives some means to create new aggregation functions from existing ones. The main operations to do this are transformation, composition, introduction of weights on variables, ordinal sums, and various other means (idempotization, etc.). Also optimization tasks yielding aggregation functions are discussed.

– *Chapter 7: Aggregation on specific scale types*
This chapter addresses the important concern of choosing appropriate aggregation functions by taking into account the scale types of the input and output variables. The scale type of a variable is defined by a class of admissible transformations, such as that from grams to pounds or degrees Fahrenheit to degrees centigrade, that change the scale into another acceptable scale. We describe the aggregation functions that are meaningful when considering ratio, difference, interval, and log-ratio scales.

– *Chapter 8: Aggregation on ordinal scales*
On ordinal scales, all usual arithmetic operations become meaningless in the

measurement theoretical point of view, and allowed operations are more or less limited to comparisons and projections. We investigate which aggregation functions are meaningful on ordinal scales.

– *Chapter 9: Aggregation on bipolar scales*
Most aggregation functions are defined on the [0, 1] interval (unipolar scale). This chapter analyzes how to extend them to the interval $[-1, 1]$ (bipolar scale), that is, to perform a kind of symmetrization with respect to 0 while keeping properties of the aggregation function. This nontrivial problem is motivated essentially by decision making, where most often bipolar scales are more suitable than unipolar ones.

– *Chapter 10: Behavioral analysis of aggregation functions*
This chapter gives various ways to understand, analyze and quantify the "behavior" of an aggregation function, that is, how the output of the function behaves with respect to its variables. This is done through various indices and values (like the expected value), which in some sense constitutes the identity card of the aggregation function.

– *Chapter 11: Identification of aggregation functions*
An important topic in practice is how to choose a suitable aggregation function. Chapters 2 to 5 and Chapter 10 provide the keys to selecting the suitable family of aggregation functions and to understanding its behavior, but a precise identification (i.e., what is the value of the parameter(s)?) is not always possible. This chapter gives various ways to identify aggregation functions from data. This often reduces to solving an optimization problem, most of the time a least squares regression problem under constraints.

– *Appendix A: Aggregation of infinitely many arguments*
This appendix explores the rather unexpected consequences of defining an aggregation function with an infinite (either countable or uncountable) number of arguments.

– *Appendix B: Examples and applications*
A short description is given with references to the main fields of application of aggregation functions, namely in decision making, data fusion, and artificial intelligence. A last section details an application to the mixture of uncertainty measures.

The genesis of the book goes back to the summer of 2002, on the shores of Lake Annecy, a charming place in the Alps in the South of France. We were there together for the IPMU Congress, and inspired by the beauty of the landscape, we decided to start the great adventure of writing a book on aggregation functions. During the next six years, we exchanged hundreds of emails, and took advantage as far as possible of many congresses, workshops, and projects to meet, visit each other, discuss the book, and incidentally see many other nice landscapes. We started as colleagues in mathematics and computer science, and finished as close friends, having experienced and learnt a lot, apart from mathematics, about ourselves and each other.

The authors gratefully acknowledge the support of their respective institutions during the long period of writing the manuscript, namely, the *Computer Science Laboratory, University of Paris VI*, the *Center of Economics of the Sorbonne, University of Paris I*, the *Mathematics Research Unit, University of Luxembourg*, the *Department of Mathematics and Descriptive Geometry, Faculty of Civil Engineering, Slovak University of Technology, Bratislava*, the *Department of Mathematics and Informatics, University of Novi Sad*, the *Academy of Sciences and Arts of Vojvodina (Novi Sad)*, and the *European Academy of Sciences (Brussels)*.

During this period, we benefited from the support of various projects which facilitated communication and collaboration among us, in particular the bilateral project between France and Serbia *Pavle Savić* N° 11092SF supported by EGIDE, Paris, and the bilateral project SK-SRB-19 between Slovakia and Serbia, the internal research project *Mathematics Research in Decision Making and Operations Research*, F1R-MTH-PUL-09MRDO, supported by the University of Luxembourg, projects APVV-0375-06, APVV-0012-07, and VEGA 1/4209/07, supported by the Slovak Grant Agency for Sciences, the national grants MNTRS (Serbia, Project 144012), Provincial Secretariat for Science and Technological Development of Vojvodina, and MTA HMTA (Hungary).

Last but not least, the authors are indebted to many colleagues for stimulating discussions, fruitful scientific exchanges, and for having agreed to read parts of the book and thus to correct a number of errors. In particular we would like to thank Jayaram Balasubrahmaniam, Gleb Beliakov, Dieter Denneberg, Jozo Dujmović, János Fodor, Olga Hadžić, Ivan Kojadinovic, Anna Kolesárová, Christophe Labreuche, Gaspar Mayor, Michel Minoux, Branimir Šešelja, and especially Toshiaki Murofushi, whose insightful scrutiny of several chapters permitted us to correct many errors and improve some proofs of theorems. Our warmest thanks are due to Christopher P. Grant from Brigham Young University, for having proofread the entire manuscript, and considerably improved the English. Also, many thanks are due to Professor M. Komorníková, who helped in typing several parts of the manuscript.

The whole manuscript was typeset in LaTeX 2_ε; most of the figures were drawn using Mathematica 5.2 and `pstricks`.

1

Introduction

1.1 Main motivations and scope

The central problem we are investigating in this book is that of aggregation, which refers to the process of combining and merging several (most often numerical) values into a single one. Perhaps the oldest example in this respect is the notion of arithmetic mean or average, which has been used during all the history of physics and all experimental sciences. Any function like the arithmetic mean computing a single output value from an (arbitrarily long) vector of input values is called an aggregation function.

Aggregation functions play an important role in many of the technological tasks scientists are faced with nowadays. They are specifically important in many problems related to the fusion of information. More generally, aggregation functions are widely used in pure mathematics (e.g., functional equations, theory of means and averages, measure and integration theory), applied mathematics (e.g., probability, statistics, decision mathematics), computer and engineering sciences (e.g., artificial intelligence, operations research, information theory, engineering design, pattern recognition and image analysis, data fusion, automated reasoning), economics and finance (e.g., game theory, voting theory, decision making), social sciences (e.g., representational measurement, mathematical psychology) as well as many other applied fields of physics and natural sciences. Thus, a main characteristic of the aggregation functions is that they are used in a large number of areas and disciplines.

The essence of aggregation is that the output value computed by the aggregation function should represent or synthesize "in some sense" all individual inputs, where quotes are put to emphasize the fact that the precise meaning of this expression is highly dependent on the context. In any case, defining or choosing the right class of aggregation functions for a specific problem is a difficult task, considering the huge variety of potential aggregation functions. In this respect, one could ask the following question: Consider a set of n values lying in some real interval $[a, b]$ to be aggregated. Is any function from $[a, b]^n$ to $\mathbb{R}$ a candidate to be an aggregation function? Obviously not. On the other hand, it is not that easy to define the minimal set of properties a function should fulfill to be an aggregation function. A first natural requirement comes from the fact that the output should be a synthetic value. Then, if inputs are supposed

1

to lie in the interval $[a, b]$, the output should also lie in this interval. Moreover, if all input values are identical to the lower bound a, then the output should also be a, and similarly for the case of the upper bound b. This defines a boundary condition. A second natural requirement is nondecreasing monotonicity. It means that if some of the input values increase, the representative output value should reflect this increase, or at worst, stay constant. These two requirements are commonly accepted in the field, and we adopt them as the basic definition of an aggregation function.

Thus defined, the class of aggregation functions is huge, making the problem of choosing the right function (or family) for a given application a difficult one. Besides this practical consideration, the study of the main classes of aggregation functions, their properties and their relationships, is so complex and rich that it becomes a mathematical topic of its own. The content of this book will offer to the reader a solid mathematical analysis of aggregation functions, able to answer to both mathematical and practical concerns. This introductory chapter establishes the basic material to start with, essentially a precise definition of an aggregation function, on the basis of the above discussion, the first elementary and well-known examples of aggregation functions, and the list of all the conventional notation used in the book.

1.2 Basic definitions and examples

First of all, to define a notation for real intervals, we use the international standard ISO 31-11, that is, we use square brackets [and]. For instance, $[a, b]$ is a closed interval while $]a, b[$ is an open interval. Intervals like $[a, b[$ or $]a, b]$ are called half-closed or half-open. Additionally, in the present book, the symbol |, when used in an interval notation, denotes either [or], indifferently. For instance, $|a, b|$ denotes any real interval with a and b as endpoints.

We assume throughout that the variables of any aggregation function have a common domain $\mathbb{I}$ which is a nonempty real interval, bounded or not. In some exceptional cases, $\mathbb{I}$ will represent a nonempty interval of the extended real number system $\overline{\mathbb{R}} := [-\infty, \infty]$. This latter case will always be mentioned explicitly and then we will often observe the convention that $0 \cdot \infty = 0$ and $\infty + (-\infty) = -\infty$. Also, the notation $\text{int}(\mathbb{I})$ denotes the interior of $\mathbb{I}$, that is, the corresponding open interval, and $\overline{\mathbb{I}}$ denotes its (set) closure.

Let n be any nonzero natural integer and set $[n] := \{1, \ldots, n\}$. We will often use bold symbols to denote n-tuples. For instance $(x_1, \ldots, x_n)$ will often be written $\mathbf{x}$.

Let us now introduce the concept of aggregation function in a formal way. We shall make a distinction between *aggregation functions* having a definite number of arguments and *extended aggregation functions* defined for any number of arguments. Let us first examine the simple case $\mathbb{I} = [0, 1]$, which is very often considered in the literature. An aggregation function in $[0, 1]^n$ is merely a function $\mathsf{A}^{(n)} : [0, 1]^n \to [0, 1]$ that is nondecreasing in each variable and that fulfills the boundary conditions

$$\mathsf{A}^{(n)}(0, \ldots, 0) = 0 \quad \text{and} \quad \mathsf{A}^{(n)}(1, \ldots, 1) = 1.$$

In the general case, we have the next definition:

Definition 1.1. An *aggregation function* in $\mathbb{I}^n$ is a function $\mathsf{A}^{(n)} : \mathbb{I}^n \to \mathbb{I}$ that

(i) is nondecreasing (in each variable)
(ii) fulfills the boundary conditions

$$\inf_{\mathbf{x} \in \mathbb{I}^n} \mathsf{A}^{(n)}(\mathbf{x}) = \inf \mathbb{I} \quad \text{and} \quad \sup_{\mathbf{x} \in \mathbb{I}^n} \mathsf{A}^{(n)}(\mathbf{x}) = \sup \mathbb{I}. \tag{1.1}$$

The integer n represents the arity of the aggregation function, that is, the number of its variables. When no confusion can arise, the aggregation functions will simply be written A instead of $\mathsf{A}^{(n)}$.

To give a first instance, the arithmetic mean, defined by

$$\mathsf{AM}^{(n)}(\mathbf{x}) := \frac{1}{n} \sum_{i=1}^{n} x_i, \tag{1.2}$$

is clearly an aggregation function in any domain $\mathbb{I}^n$.

A specific case is the aggregation of a singleton, i.e., the unary function $\mathsf{A}^{(1)} : \mathbb{I} \to \mathbb{I}$. As the aggregation of a singleton is not an actual aggregation, the following convention is often considered:

$$\mathsf{A}^{(1)}(x) = x \tag{1.3}$$

for all $x \in \mathbb{I}$. Unless otherwise specified, we will adopt this convention throughout.

For the sake of clarity, we will often use the letter F (or $\mathsf{G}, \mathsf{H}, \ldots$) to designate an arbitrary function of several variables and the letter A for an aggregation function. The range of any function F will be denoted ran(F).

Remark 1.2. (i) It is easy to see that any function $\mathsf{F} : \mathbb{I}^n \to \overline{\mathbb{R}}$ fulfilling conditions (i) and (ii) of Definition 1.1 is such that ran(F) $\subseteq \overline{\mathbb{I}}$. However, by definition, any aggregation function A in $\mathbb{I}^n$ fulfills ran(A) $\subseteq \mathbb{I}$, which is a much more natural property.

(ii) Note that any n-tuple $\mathbf{x} = (x_1, \ldots, x_n) \in \mathbb{I}^n$, whose coordinates are to be aggregated by an aggregation function A, can itself be considered as a function from $[n]$ to $\mathbb{I}$. In this case the aggregation function A is simply regarded as a *functional* from $\mathbb{I}^{[n]}$ to $\mathbb{I}$. Instances of such functionals are given by integrals constructed from capacities (see Chapter 5).

Definition 1.3. The *diagonal section* of any function $\mathsf{F} : \mathbb{I}^n \to \overline{\mathbb{R}}$ is the unary function $\delta_\mathsf{F} : \mathbb{I} \to \overline{\mathbb{R}}$ defined as $\delta_\mathsf{F}(x) = \mathsf{F}(x, \ldots, x)$ for all $x \in \mathbb{I}$.

The boundary conditions given in Definition 1.1 show that, generally, an aggregation function cannot be defined without specifying its domain. The following proposition shows that, for a nondecreasing function $\mathsf{F} : \mathbb{I}^n \to \overline{\mathbb{R}}$ to be an aggregation function in $\mathbb{I}^n$, the condition $\mathrm{ran}(\mathsf{F}) \subseteq \mathbb{I}$ and the boundary conditions (1.1) are required only for the diagonal section δ_F.

Proposition 1.4. *A nondecreasing function* $\mathsf{F} : \mathbb{I}^n \to \overline{\mathbb{R}}$ *is an aggregation function in* $\mathbb{I}^n$ *if and only if* $\mathrm{ran}(\delta_\mathsf{F}) \subseteq \mathbb{I}$ *holds with*

$$\inf_{x \in \mathbb{I}} \delta_\mathsf{F}(x) = \inf \mathbb{I} \quad \text{and} \quad \sup_{x \in \mathbb{I}} \delta_\mathsf{F}(x) = \sup \mathbb{I}.$$

Proof. Given any nondecreasing function $\mathsf{F} : \mathbb{I}^n \to \overline{\mathbb{R}}$, we have the immediate inequalities

$$\delta_\mathsf{F}(\min(x_1, \ldots, x_n)) \leqslant \mathsf{F}(\mathbf{x}) \leqslant \delta_\mathsf{F}(\max(x_1, \ldots, x_n)) \tag{1.4}$$

for all $\mathbf{x} \in \mathbb{I}^n$, which, in turn, imply

$$\inf_{\mathbf{x} \in \mathbb{I}^n} \mathsf{F}(\mathbf{x}) = \inf_{x \in \mathbb{I}} \delta_\mathsf{F}(x) \quad \text{and} \quad \sup_{\mathbf{x} \in \mathbb{I}^n} \mathsf{F}(\mathbf{x}) = \sup_{x \in \mathbb{I}} \delta_\mathsf{F}(x).$$

The result then follows immediately. $\square$

The following result provides an easy way to determine each subdomain $\mathbb{J}^n$ of $\mathbb{I}^n$, with $\mathbb{J} \subseteq \mathbb{I} \subseteq \mathbb{R}$, in which a given nondecreasing function $\mathsf{F} : \mathbb{I}^n \to \overline{\mathbb{R}}$ is an aggregation function.

Proposition 1.5. *Let* $\mathsf{F} : \mathbb{I}^n \to \overline{\mathbb{R}}$ *be a nondecreasing function and let* $a := \inf \mathbb{I}$ *and* $b := \sup \mathbb{I}$. *Then*

$$\inf_{x \in \mathbb{I}} \delta_\mathsf{F}(x) = a \quad \Leftrightarrow \quad \begin{cases} \delta_\mathsf{F}(a) = a & \text{if } a \in \mathbb{I} \\ \lim_{x \to a^+} \delta_\mathsf{F}(x) = a & \text{if } a \notin \mathbb{I}, \end{cases}$$

and

$$\inf_{x \in \mathbb{I}} \delta_\mathsf{F}(x) = b \quad \Leftrightarrow \quad \begin{cases} \delta_\mathsf{F}(b) = b & \text{if } b \in \mathbb{I} \\ \lim_{x \to b^-} \delta_\mathsf{F}(x) = b & \text{if } b \notin \mathbb{I}. \end{cases}$$

Proof. Let us prove the first part. The second one can be proved similarly.

($\Rightarrow$) Assume

$$\inf_{x \in \mathbb{I}} \delta_\mathsf{F}(x) = a. \tag{1.5}$$

If $a \in \mathbb{I}$ then, due to the monotonicity of δ_F, we have $\delta_\mathsf{F}(a) = \inf_{x \in \mathbb{I}} \delta_\mathsf{F}(x) = a$. Assume now that $a \notin \mathbb{I}$. Two cases are to be considered.

- Suppose $a > -\infty$. Let $\varepsilon > 0$. Then there exists $x^* \in \mathbb{I}$ such that $0 \leqslant \delta_\mathsf{F}(x^*) - a \leqslant \varepsilon$. From the monotonicity of δ_F it follows that, for all $x \in \mathbb{I}$ such that $x \leqslant x^*$, we have $0 \leqslant \delta_\mathsf{F}(x) - a \leqslant \delta_\mathsf{F}(x^*) - a \leqslant \varepsilon$.

- Suppose $a = -\infty$. Let $M < 0$. Then there exists $x^* \in \mathbb{I}$, with $x^* < 0$, such that $\delta_F(x^*) \leqslant M$. From the monotonicity of δ_F it follows that, for all $x \in \mathbb{I}$ such that $x \leqslant x^*$, we have $\delta_F(x) \leqslant \delta_F(x^*) \leqslant M$.

We conclude in both cases that

$$\lim_{x \to a^+} \delta_F(x) = a. \tag{1.6}$$

($\Leftarrow$) If $a \in \mathbb{I}$ and $\delta_F(a) = a$ then (1.5) holds immediately from the monotonicity of δ_F. Assume now that $a \notin \mathbb{I}$ (which implies that $a < b$) and that (1.6) holds. Again, we have two cases to consider.

- Suppose $a > -\infty$. Let $\varepsilon > 0$. Then there is $0 < \eta < b - a$ such that every $x \in \mathbb{I}$ satisfying $x \leqslant a + \eta$ is such that $0 \leqslant \delta_F(x) - a \leqslant \varepsilon$. By choosing $x^* = a + \eta$, we have $x^* \in \mathbb{I}$ and $0 \leqslant \delta_F(x^*) - a \leqslant \varepsilon$.
- Suppose $a = -\infty$. Let $M < 0$. Then there exists $x^* \in \mathbb{I}$, with $x^* < 0$, such that every $x \leqslant x^*$ is such that $\delta_F(x) \leqslant M$. In particular, we have $\delta_F(x^*) \leqslant M$.

In both cases, we conclude that (1.5) holds. $\qquad\square$

Example 1.6. Consider the product function

$$\Pi(\mathbf{x}) := \prod_{i=1}^{n} x_i.$$

Let us restrict this function to $\mathbb{I}^n = [0, \infty]^n$ in which it is continuous and nondecreasing. To ensure the existence of the product, we adopt the convention that $0 \cdot \infty = 0$. If $n > 1$, the solutions of the equation $\delta_\Pi(x) = x$ in $[0, \infty]$ are 0, 1, and ∞. Therefore, according to Propositions 1.4 and 1.5, the product function, when restricted to $[0, \infty]^n$, is an aggregation function in the subdomains $]0, 1]^n$, $]1, \infty]^n$, $]0, \infty]^n$ and only in these.

Example 1.7. Consider the function

$$F(\mathbf{x}) := \frac{\left(\sum_i x_i \right)^2 - \sum_i x_i^2}{\sum_i x_i}.$$

Let us restrict this function to $\mathbb{I}^n =]0, \infty[^n$ in which it is continuous and nondecreasing. If $n > 2$, the equation $\delta_F(x) = x$ has no solution in $]0, \infty[$. Hence, the restriction of F to $]0, \infty[^n$ is an aggregation function but not in a proper subdomain. For $n = 2$, any subdomain can be considered (and then F is the harmonic mean).

We have the immediate corollary:

Corollary 1.8. *Let* $\mathsf{F} : \mathbb{I}^n \to \overline{\mathbb{R}}$ *be nondecreasing. If* F *is idempotent, i.e.,* $\delta_{\mathsf{F}}(x) = x$ *for all* $x \in \mathbb{I}$, *then it is an aggregation function in* $\mathbb{I}^n$ *and even in any subinterval* $\mathbb{J}^n$ *of* $\mathbb{I}^n$, *with* $\mathbb{J} \subseteq \mathbb{I}$.

We now introduce the concept of extended aggregation function. Denote by $\mathbb{N}$ the set of strictly positive integers.

Definition 1.9. An *extended function* in $\cup_{n\in\mathbb{N}}\mathbb{I}^n$ is a mapping

$$\mathsf{F} : \bigcup_{n\in\mathbb{N}} \mathbb{I}^n \to \overline{\mathbb{R}}.$$

An *extended aggregation function* in $\cup_{n\in\mathbb{N}}\mathbb{I}^n$ is an extended function A in $\cup_{n\in\mathbb{N}}\mathbb{I}^n$ whose restriction $\mathsf{A}^{(n)} := \mathsf{A}|_{\mathbb{I}^n}$ to $\mathbb{I}^n$ is an aggregation function in $\mathbb{I}^n$ for any $n \in \mathbb{N}$.

Since an extended function is defined for any number of arguments, it can also be regarded as a sequence $(\mathsf{F}^{(n)})_{n\in\mathbb{N}}$, whose nth element is an n-ary function $\mathsf{F}^{(n)} : \mathbb{I}^n \to \overline{\mathbb{R}}$. When no confusion can arise, an extended function will simply be called a function.

For example, the arithmetic mean as an extended aggregation function is the sequence $(\mathsf{A}^{(n)})_{n\in\mathbb{N}}$, where $\mathsf{A}^{(n)}$ is defined by (1.2) for all $n \in \mathbb{N}$.

Remark 1.10. In an arbitrary extended function, for different n and m the functions $\mathsf{F}^{(n)}$ and $\mathsf{F}^{(m)}$ need not be related to each other. For instance, $\mathsf{F}^{(n)}$ could be the arithmetic mean while $\mathsf{F}^{(m)}$ could be the product. However, as we will see in Chapter 2, they can be related in a relevant way by means of certain grouping properties, such as associativity or decomposability.

For illustration and subsequent use we now give a small list of well-known aggregation functions. Further aggregation functions will be developed in subsequent chapters.

- The *arithmetic mean* function $\mathsf{AM} : \mathbb{I}^n \to \mathbb{I}$ and the *geometric mean* function $\mathsf{GM} : \mathbb{I}^n \to \mathbb{I}$ are respectively defined by

$$\mathsf{AM}(\mathbf{x}) := \frac{1}{n} \sum_{i=1}^{n} x_i, \tag{1.7}$$

$$\mathsf{GM}(\mathbf{x}) := \Big(\prod_{i=1}^{n} x_i \Big)^{1/n}. \tag{1.8}$$

  Note that, when $n > 1$, the geometric mean is not an aggregation function in every domain. We must consider a domain $\mathbb{I}^n$ such that $\mathbb{I} \subseteq [0, \infty]$.
- For any $k \in [n]$, the *projection* function $\mathsf{P}_k : \mathbb{I}^n \to \mathbb{I}$ and the *order statistic* function $\mathsf{OS}_k : \mathbb{I}^n \to \mathbb{I}$ associated with the kth argument, are respectively defined by

$$\mathsf{P}_k(\mathbf{x}) := x_k, \tag{1.9}$$

$$\mathsf{OS}_k(\mathbf{x}) := x_{(k)}, \tag{1.10}$$

where $x_{(k)}$ is the kth lowest coordinate of $\mathbf{x}$, that is,

$$x_{(1)} \leqslant \cdots \leqslant x_{(k)} \leqslant \cdots \leqslant x_{(n)}.$$

The *projections onto the first and the last coordinates* are defined as

$$\mathsf{P}_F(\mathbf{x}) := \mathsf{P}_1(\mathbf{x}) = x_1, \tag{1.11}$$

$$\mathsf{P}_L(\mathbf{x}) := \mathsf{P}_n(\mathbf{x}) = x_n. \tag{1.12}$$

Similarly, the extreme order statistics $x_{(1)}$ and $x_{(n)}$ are respectively the *minimum* and *maximum* functions[1]

$$\mathsf{Min}(\mathbf{x}) := \mathsf{OS}_1(\mathbf{x}) = \min\{x_1, \ldots, x_n\}, \tag{1.13}$$

$$\mathsf{Max}(\mathbf{x}) := \mathsf{OS}_n(\mathbf{x}) = \max\{x_1, \ldots, x_n\}, \tag{1.14}$$

which will sometimes be written by means of the lattice operations $\wedge$ and $\vee$, respectively, that is,

$$\mathsf{Min}(\mathbf{x}) = \bigwedge_{i=1}^{n} x_i \quad \text{and} \quad \mathsf{Max}(\mathbf{x}) = \bigvee_{i=1}^{n} x_i.$$

Note that OS_k can be written in terms of only minima and maxima as follows (see, e.g., Ovchinnikov [337, §7])

$$\mathsf{OS}_k(\mathbf{x}) = \bigwedge_{\substack{K \subseteq [n] \\ |K|=k}} \bigvee_{i \in K} x_i = \bigvee_{\substack{K \subseteq [n] \\ |K|=n-k+1}} \bigwedge_{i \in K} x_i.$$

Also, the *median* of an odd number of values $(x_1, \ldots, x_{2k-1})$ is simply defined by

$$\mathsf{Med}(x_1, \ldots, x_{2k-1}) := x_{(k)},$$

which can be rewritten as

$$\mathsf{Med}(x_1, \ldots, x_{2k-1}) = \bigwedge_{\substack{K \subseteq [2k-1] \\ |K|=k}} \bigvee_{i \in K} x_i = \bigvee_{\substack{K \subseteq [2k-1] \\ |K|=k}} \bigwedge_{i \in K} x_i.$$

For instance, we have

$$\mathsf{Med}(x_1, x_2, x_3) = (x_1 \wedge x_2) \vee (x_1 \wedge x_3) \vee (x_2 \wedge x_3)$$

$$= (x_1 \vee x_2) \wedge (x_1 \vee x_3) \wedge (x_2 \vee x_3).$$

---

[1] We also call them minimum and maximum operators or operations. In the book we will use interchangeably the words "operator" or "operation" for pseudo-additions, pseudo-multiplications, etc. Although the latter would be more correct in an algebraic context, we often use the former (which comes from logic), following the general usage.

For an even number of values $(x_1, \ldots, x_{2k})$, the median is defined by

$$\mathsf{Med}(x_1, \ldots, x_{2k}) := \mathsf{AM}(x_{(k)}, x_{(k+1)}) = \frac{x_{(k)} + x_{(k+1)}}{2}.$$

For any $\alpha \in \mathbb{I}$, we also define the α-median, $\mathsf{Med}_\alpha : \mathbb{I}^n \to \mathbb{I}$, by

$$\mathsf{Med}_\alpha(\mathbf{x}) = \mathsf{Med}(x_1, \ldots, x_n, \underbrace{\alpha, \ldots, \alpha}_{n-1}) = \mathsf{Med}(\mathsf{Min}(\mathbf{x}), \alpha, \mathsf{Max}(\mathbf{x})). \quad (1.15)$$

- For any nonempty subset $K \subseteq [n]$, the *partial minimum* $\mathsf{Min}_K : \mathbb{I}^n \to \mathbb{I}$ and the *partial maximum* $\mathsf{Max}_K : \mathbb{I}^n \to \mathbb{I}$, associated with K, are respectively defined by

$$\mathsf{Min}_K(\mathbf{x}) := \bigwedge_{i \in K} x_i, \quad (1.16)$$

$$\mathsf{Max}_K(\mathbf{x}) := \bigvee_{i \in K} x_i. \quad (1.17)$$

- For any weight vector $\mathbf{w} = (w_1, \ldots, w_n) \in [0,1]^n$ such that $\sum_{i=1}^n w_i = 1$, the *weighted arithmetic mean* function $\mathsf{WAM}_\mathbf{w} : \mathbb{I}^n \to \mathbb{I}$ and the *ordered weighted averaging* function $\mathsf{OWA}_\mathbf{w} : \mathbb{I}^n \to \mathbb{I}$, associated with $\mathbf{w}$, are respectively defined by

$$\mathsf{WAM}_\mathbf{w}(\mathbf{x}) := \sum_{i=1}^n w_i x_i, \quad (1.18)$$

$$\mathsf{OWA}_\mathbf{w}(\mathbf{x}) := \sum_{i=1}^n w_i x_{(i)}. \quad (1.19)$$

- The *sum* $\Sigma : \overline{\mathbb{R}}^n \to \overline{\mathbb{R}}$ and *product* $\Pi : \overline{\mathbb{R}}^n \to \overline{\mathbb{R}}$ functions are respectively defined by

$$\Sigma(\mathbf{x}) := \sum_{i=1}^n x_i, \quad (1.20)$$

$$\Pi(\mathbf{x}) := \prod_{i=1}^n x_i. \quad (1.21)$$

Note that, when $n > 1$, these latter two functions are not aggregation functions in every domain. For the sum, we need to consider the domains $|-\infty, \infty|^n$, $|0, \infty|^n$, $|-\infty, 0|^n$. For the product, when restricted to $[0, \infty]^n$, we have to consider the domains $|0, 1|^n$, $|1, \infty|^n$, $|0, \infty|^n$.

- Assume $\mathbb{I} = [a, b]$ is a closed interval. The *smallest* and the *greatest* aggregation functions in $[a, b]^n$ are respectively defined by

$$A_\perp(\mathbf{x}) := \begin{cases} b & \text{if } x_i = b \text{ for all } i \in [n] \\ a & \text{otherwise.} \end{cases} \quad (1.22)$$

$$\mathsf{A}_\top(\mathbf{x}) := \begin{cases} a & \text{if } x_i = a \text{ for all } i \in [n] \\ b & \text{otherwise.} \end{cases} \tag{1.23}$$

By definition, we have $\mathsf{A}_\perp \leqslant \mathsf{A} \leqslant \mathsf{A}_\top$ for any aggregation function $\mathsf{A} : [a, b]^n \to [a, b]$.

Clearly, the *constant* function $\mathsf{K}_c : \mathbb{I}^n \to \mathbb{I}$, given by

$$\mathsf{K}_c(\mathbf{x}) := c,$$

where $c \in \mathbb{I}$ is a fixed constant, is a trivial example of a function that is not an aggregation function (unless $\mathbb{I} = \{c\}$).

1.3 Conventional notation

The set of strictly positive integers is denoted by $\mathbb{N}$. The set of nonnegative integers is denoted by $\mathbb{N}_0$. The set of integers is denoted by $\mathbb{Z}$ and the set of rational numbers is denoted by $\mathbb{Q}$.

In order to avoid cumbersome notation, we also introduce the following terminology:

- For any subset K of a general set Ω, we let $\mathbf{1}_K : \Omega \to \{0, 1\}$ denote the *characteristic function* of K, defined as $\mathbf{1}_K(\omega) = 1$ if $\omega \in K$, and 0 otherwise. In particular, for any $K \subseteq [n]$, $\mathbf{1}_K$ denotes the *characteristic vector* of K in $\{0, 1\}^n$, that is, the n-tuple whose ith coordinate is 1, if $i \in K$, and 0, otherwise. Also we often write $\mathbf{0}$ and $\mathbf{1}$ instead of $\mathbf{1}_\varnothing$ and $\mathbf{1}_{[n]}$, respectively.
- Ind(*cond*) is the Boolean indicator function that gives 1 if *cond* is true and 0 otherwise.
- The *cardinality* of any set K is denoted $|K|$.
- For any $K \subseteq [n]$ and any $\mathbf{x} \in \mathbb{I}^n$, we denote by $\mathbf{x}|_K$ the restriction of $\mathbf{x}$, when regarded as a function from $[n]$ to $\mathbb{I}$, to the subset K. In other words, $\mathbf{x}|_K$ is the $|K|$-tuple obtained by considering only the coordinates of $\mathbf{x}$ indexed by the elements of K, in the increasing order. For singletons we simply write $\mathbf{x}|_{\{k\}} = x_k$.
- For any $K \subseteq [n]$ and any $\mathbf{x}, \mathbf{y} \in \mathbb{I}^n$, we denote by $\mathbf{x}_K \mathbf{y}$ the n-tuple whose ith coordinate is x_i, if $i \in K$, and y_i, otherwise. We simply write $x_K \mathbf{y}$, $\mathbf{x}_K y$, or $x_K y$, depending on whether $\mathbf{x} = (x, \ldots, x)$, or $\mathbf{y} = (y, \ldots, y)$, or both. For any disjoint $K, L \subseteq [n]$ and any $\mathbf{x}, \mathbf{y}, \mathbf{z} \in \mathbb{I}^n$, we write $\mathbf{x}_K \mathbf{y}_L \mathbf{z}$, etc.
- For $\mathbf{x} \in \mathbb{I}^n$, $\mathbf{y} \in \mathbb{I}^m$, and a function $\mathsf{F} : \mathbb{I}^{n+m} \to \overline{\mathbb{R}}$, the notation $\mathsf{F}(\mathbf{x}, \mathbf{y})$ stands for $\mathsf{F}(x_1, \ldots, x_n, y_1, \ldots, y_m)$, and similarly for more than two vectors. If $\mathbf{x} \in \mathbb{I}^0$ is an empty vector (i.e., with no component), we write for instance $\mathsf{F}(\mathbf{x}, \mathbf{y}) = \mathsf{F}(\mathbf{y})$ and $\mathsf{F}(\mathsf{F}(\mathbf{x}), \mathsf{F}(\mathbf{y})) = \mathsf{F}(\mathsf{F}(\mathbf{y}))$.
- For any $k \in \mathbb{N}$ and any $x \in \mathbb{I}$, we set $k \cdot x := x, \ldots, x$ (k times). For instance,

$$\mathsf{F}(3 \cdot x, 2 \cdot y) = \mathsf{F}(x, x, x, y, y).$$

More generally, if $\mathbf{x} \in \mathbb{I}^n$ then $k \cdot \mathbf{x}$ represents the ordered list of the $(k \times n)$ values obtained by concatenating k copies of $\mathbf{x}$ and then deleting the parentheses.

- The *diagonal section* of any function $\mathsf{F} : \mathbb{I}^n \to \overline{\mathbb{R}}$ is the unary function $\delta_\mathsf{F} : \mathbb{I} \to \overline{\mathbb{R}}$ defined as $\delta_\mathsf{F}(x) := \mathsf{F}(n \cdot x)$. Also, the *diagonal section* of $\mathbb{I}^n$ is denoted by

$$\text{diag}(\mathbb{I}^n) := \{(n \cdot x) : x \in \mathbb{I}\}.$$

- For any n-tuples $\mathbf{x}, \mathbf{x}' \in \mathbb{I}^n$, we denote by $\mathbf{xx}'$ the n-tuple $(x_1 x_1', \ldots, x_n x_n')$ obtained by calculating the product componentwise. Similarly the n-tuples $\mathbf{x} + \mathbf{x}'$, $\mathbf{x}^{\mathbf{x}'}$, $\mathbf{x}/\mathbf{x}'$, $\mathbf{x} \wedge \mathbf{x}'$, and $\mathbf{x} \vee \mathbf{x}'$ are defined componentwise. The inequality $\mathbf{x} \leqslant \mathbf{x}'$ is also understood componentwise. However $\mathbf{x} < \mathbf{x}'$ means $\mathbf{x} \leqslant \mathbf{x}'$ and $\mathbf{x} \neq \mathbf{x}'$. Similarly for functions, $\mathsf{F} < \mathsf{F}'$ means $\mathsf{F} \leqslant \mathsf{F}'$ and $\mathsf{F}(\mathbf{x}) < \mathsf{F}'(\mathbf{x})$ for some $\mathbf{x}$.

- For any n-tuple $\boldsymbol{\varphi} = (\varphi_1, \ldots, \varphi_n)$ of functions $\varphi_i : \mathbb{I} \to \overline{\mathbb{R}}$ $(i = 1, \ldots, n)$ and any $\mathbf{x} \in \mathbb{I}^n$, the symbol $\boldsymbol{\varphi}(\mathbf{x})$ denotes the n-tuple $(\varphi_1(x_1), \ldots, \varphi_n(x_n))$.

- For any function f, $\text{ran}(f)$ denotes its range and $\text{dom}(f)$ denotes its domain of definition.

- For any countable set K, we let $\mathfrak{S}_K$ denote the set of all permutations on K. For any $A \subseteq K$ and any $\sigma \in \mathfrak{S}_K$, we set $\sigma(A) := \{\sigma(a) \mid a \in A\}$.

- For any permutation $\sigma \in \mathfrak{S}_{[n]}$, we set

$$\mathbb{I}^n_\sigma := \{\mathbf{x} \in \mathbb{I}^n \mid x_{\sigma(1)} \leqslant \cdots \leqslant x_{\sigma(n)}\}.$$

- Given an n-tuple $\mathbf{x}$ and a permutation $\sigma \in \mathfrak{S}_{[n]}$, we set

$$[\mathbf{x}]_\sigma := (x_{\sigma(1)}, \ldots, x_{\sigma(n)}).$$

- The identity function $x \mapsto x$ is denoted by id.
- For any number $r \in \overline{\mathbb{R}}$, we set $r^+ := \mathsf{Max}(r, 0) = r \vee 0$, and $r^- := \mathsf{Max}(-r, 0) = (-r) \vee 0$. We then have $r = r^+ - r^-$ and $|r| = r^+ + r^-$, where $|r|$ denotes the *absolute value* of r.
- The *signum* function is defined from $\overline{\mathbb{R}}$ to $\{-1, 0, 1\}$ as

$$\text{sign}\,(x) = \begin{cases} 1 & \text{if } x > 0 \\ 0 & \text{if } x = 0 \\ -1 & \text{if } x < 0. \end{cases}$$

- Concerning the extension of the usual real arithmetical operations of addition and multiplication to the extended real line $\overline{\mathbb{R}} = [-\infty, \infty]$ we adopt the conventions $\infty + (-\infty) = -\infty$ and $0 \cdot \infty = 0$ up to special situations, in which case the convention will always be explicitly stressed. Also, for any closed interval $[a, b] \subseteq \overline{\mathbb{R}}$ we adopt the usual convention that $\sup \varnothing = a$ and $\inf \varnothing = b$.

2

Properties for aggregation

2.1 Introduction

Studies on the aggregation problem have shown that generally the choice of the aggregation function to be used is far from being arbitrary and should be based upon properties dictated by the framework in which the aggregation is performed. For example, in some multicriteria evaluation methods, the aim is to assign an overall score to each alternative, given a set of partial scores with respect to different criteria. Clearly, it would be unnatural to give as an overall score a value that is lower than the lowest partial score, or greater than the highest score, so that only "internal" aggregation functions are allowed. Another example concerns the aggregation of opinions in voting procedures. If, as usual, the voters are anonymous, the aggregation function must be symmetric.

In this chapter we present some properties that are generally considered as relevant for aggregation. Of course, not all these properties are equally important or serve the same purpose. Some of them are imperative conditions whose violation leads to obviously counterintuitive aggregation modes. Others are technical conditions that just facilitate the representation or the calculation of the aggregation function. There are also optional conditions that naturally apply in special circumstances but are not to be universally accepted.

We first introduce some elementary mathematical properties, such as monotonicity and idempotency. Then we present algebraic properties based on grouping procedures, like associativity. We also introduce invariance properties related to the scale types of the variables being aggregated. Finally, we close the chapter with some extra properties, like additivity and such.

Note that many properties defined for n-ary functions can be naturally adapted to extended functions. For instance, with some abuse of language, the extended function $\mathsf{F} : \cup_{n \in \mathbb{N}} \mathbb{I}^n \to \overline{\mathbb{R}}$ is said to be continuous if, for any $n \in \mathbb{N}$, the corresponding n-ary function $\mathsf{F}^{(n)} = \mathsf{F}|_{\mathbb{I}^n}$ is continuous. These adaptations are implicitly assumed throughout.

11

2.2 Elementary mathematical properties

In the present section we introduce basic and standard properties often required for aggregation. For example, increasing monotonicity is an indispensable condition for functions used to aggregate preferences. Idempotency is necessary when the aggregated evaluation represents an average value, etc.

2.2.1 Monotonicity

Let us consider the following monotonicity properties: *nondecreasing monotonicity*, *strict increasing monotonicity*, and *unanimous increasing monotonicity*.

Definition 2.1. The function $\mathsf{F} : \mathbb{I}^n \to \overline{\mathbb{R}}$ is *nondecreasing* (in each argument) if, for any $\mathbf{x}, \mathbf{x}' \in \mathbb{I}^n$,

$$\mathbf{x} \leqslant \mathbf{x}' \quad \Rightarrow \quad \mathsf{F}(\mathbf{x}) \leqslant \mathsf{F}(\mathbf{x}').$$

A nondecreasing function presents a nonnegative response to any increase of the arguments. In other terms, increasing any input value cannot decrease the output value.

Recall that, by definition, nondecreasing monotonicity is a basic property shared by all aggregation functions (cf. Definition 1.1).

Definition 2.2. The function $\mathsf{F} : \mathbb{I}^n \to \overline{\mathbb{R}}$ is *strictly increasing* (in each argument) if, for any $\mathbf{x}, \mathbf{x}' \in \mathbb{I}^n$,

$$\mathbf{x} < \mathbf{x}' \quad \Rightarrow \quad \mathsf{F}(\mathbf{x}) < \mathsf{F}(\mathbf{x}').$$

Thus, a function is strictly increasing if it is nondecreasing and if it presents a positive reaction to any increase of at least one input value.

Note that strict increasing monotonicity trivially implies nondecreasing monotonicity. It also implies *sensitivity* (see for instance Aczél [5]), also called *cancellativity* or *reducibility on each place* (Aczél [3, p. 255]), which is defined as follows:

Definition 2.3. The function $\mathsf{F} : \mathbb{I}^n \to \overline{\mathbb{R}}$ is *sensitive* if, for any index $i \in [n]$, we have $\mathsf{F}(\mathbf{x}) \neq \mathsf{F}(\mathbf{x} + \lambda \mathbf{1}_{\{i\}})$ for all $\mathbf{x} \in \mathbb{I}$ and all $\lambda \neq 0$ such that $\mathbf{x} + \lambda \mathbf{1}_{\{i\}} \in \mathbb{I}$.

From the two definitions above we immediately derive the following result:

Proposition 2.4. *A nondecreasing function* $\mathsf{F} : \mathbb{I}^n \to \overline{\mathbb{R}}$ *is strictly increasing if and only if it is sensitive.*

A *unanimous increasing* function [267, Def. 5.1], also called *jointly strictly monotone* function [49, §2.2], is a nondecreasing function which presents a positive response whenever all the input values strictly increase.

Definition 2.5. The function $\mathsf{F} : \mathbb{I}^n \to \overline{\mathbb{R}}$ is *unanimously increasing* if it is nondecreasing and if, for any $\mathbf{x}, \mathbf{x}' \in \mathbb{I}^n$,

$$x_i < x'_i, \ \forall i \in [n] \quad \Rightarrow \quad \mathsf{F}(\mathbf{x}) < \mathsf{F}(\mathbf{x}').$$

Clearly, strict increasing monotonicity ensures unanimous increasing monotonicity. For example, the arithmetic mean AM is strictly increasing, hence sensitive and unanimously increasing. Functions Min and Max are unanimously increasing but not strictly increasing. The product Π is unanimously increasing on $[0,1]^n$. However, if 0 occurs among inputs, sensitivity of Π is violated. The *bounded sum* $S_L(x) = \text{Min}(\sum_{i=1}^{n} x_i, 1)$ on $[0,1]^n$ (see also (3.33)) is nondecreasing but not unanimously increasing.

Remark 2.6. We observe that nondecreasing monotonicity is needed in Definition 2.5 since it does not follow from the second condition. As an example, consider $F : [0,1]^2 \rightarrow [0,1]$ defined as $F = 0$ on $\{(0,1),(1,0)\}$ and $F = \text{Max}$ elsewhere.

2.2.2 Continuity

We now consider the property of *continuity* as well as some of its strengthenings and weakenings.

Standard continuity

Definition 2.7. $F : \mathbb{I}^n \rightarrow \mathbb{R}$ is a *continuous* function if, for all $x^* \in \mathbb{I}^n$,

$$\lim_{\substack{x \rightarrow x^* \\ x \in \mathbb{I}^n}} F(x) = F(x^*).$$

The continuity property essentially means that any small changes in the arguments (possible minor errors) should not entail a big change in the aggregated value (output error).

For nondecreasing functions, continuity can be characterized differently, as the following result shows; see for instance Klement *et al.* [219, §1.3].

Proposition 2.8. *For a nondecreasing function* $F : \mathbb{I}^n \rightarrow \mathbb{R}$ *the following conditions are equivalent:*

(i) F *is continuous.*
(ii) F *is continuous in each variable, i.e., for any* $x \in \mathbb{I}^n$ *and any* $i \in [n]$, *the unary function*

$$u \mapsto F(x_1, \ldots, x_{i-1}, u, x_{i+1}, \ldots, x_n)$$

is continuous.
(iii) F *has the intermediate value property: For any* $x, y \in \mathbb{I}^n$, *with* $x \leqslant y$, *and any* $c \in [F(x), F(y)]$, *there exists* $z \in \mathbb{I}^n$, *with* $x \leqslant z \leqslant y$, *such that* $F(z) = c$.

Proof. $(i) \Leftrightarrow (ii)$ In Proposition 2.29, we give a proof of this equivalence in the more general cases of left-continuity and right-continuity.

$(i) \Rightarrow (iii)$ It is well known that continuous unary functions have the intermediate value property (independently of whether they are nondecreasing or not). Now, for any $\mathbf{x}, \mathbf{y} \in \mathbb{I}^n$ such that $\mathbf{x} \leqslant \mathbf{y}$ and $\mathbf{x} \neq \mathbf{y}$ (this is the only nontrivial case), we can define a unary function $f : [0, 1] \to \mathbb{R}$ as

$$f(t) := \mathsf{F}((1 - t)\mathbf{x} + t\mathbf{y}).$$

This function is continuous and thus for each $c \in [\mathsf{F}(\mathbf{x}), \mathsf{F}(\mathbf{y})] = [f(0), f(1)]$ there is some $t_0 \in [0, 1]$ such that $f(t_0) = c$. That is, there is $\mathbf{z} = (1 - t_0)\mathbf{x} + t_0\mathbf{y}$ fulfilling $\mathbf{x} \leqslant \mathbf{z} \leqslant \mathbf{y}$ such that $\mathsf{F}(\mathbf{z}) = c$.

(iii) $\Rightarrow$ *(ii)* We observe that the intermediate value property of F when fixing all variables but one means the surjectivity of F as a function of one free variable, taking as the codomain the smallest interval containing all admissible values. This surjectivity is equivalent to the continuity of F in the free variable because of its nondecreasing monotonicity.   □

Continuity is a topological property of real functions. Formally, as already mentioned above, the continuity of a function F prevents it from having big output errors when small input errors (noise) appear. However, in general there is no exact quantification of the relation between input and output errors for continuous functions. To avoid this problem, several stronger forms of continuity have been proposed. First, we consider the well-known uniform continuity. Then we consider absolute continuity, which is closely related to integration and differentiation. Maybe the best known stronger form of continuity is the Lipschitz continuity property (or simply the Lipschitz property) describing explicitly the relation between input and output errors.

Remark 2.9. As will be seen in the sequel, all these properties can be ordered in the following way. Every unary Lipschitzian function is absolutely continuous.[1] Every unary absolutely continuous function is uniformly continuous. Every n-ary uniformly continuous function is continuous. Every n-ary continuous function has the intermediate value property.

A stronger form: uniform continuity

Definition 2.10. Let $\| \cdot \| : \mathbb{R}^n \to [0, \infty[$ be a norm and let $D \subseteq \mathbb{I}^n$. A function $\mathsf{F} : \mathbb{I}^n \to \mathbb{R}$ is *uniformly continuous* in D (with respect to $\| \cdot \|$) if for every $\varepsilon > 0$ there exists $\delta > 0$ such that $|\mathsf{F}(\mathbf{x}) - \mathsf{F}(\mathbf{y})| < \varepsilon$ whenever $\|\mathbf{x} - \mathbf{y}\| < \delta$ and $\mathbf{x}, \mathbf{y} \in D$.

It is immediate and well known that any uniformly continuous function is continuous while the converse is not true (for instance $\mathsf{F}(x) = x^2$ in $\mathbb{R}$). However, both properties coincide for functions on special domains such as closed and bounded intervals.

Proposition 2.11. *A function* $\mathsf{F} : [a, b]^n \to \mathbb{R}$ *is uniformly continuous in* $[a, b]^n$ *if and only if it is continuous in* $[a, b]^n$.

---

[1] Note that this result does not necessarily hold for n-ary functions with $n > 1$ (e.g., Min).

Proof. Suppose F is continuous in $[a,b]^n$ but not uniformly continuous. Then there exists $\varepsilon > 0$ such that for all $k \in \mathbb{N}$ there are $\mathbf{x}^{(k)}, \mathbf{y}^{(k)} \in [a,b]^n$ fulfilling $\|\mathbf{x}^{(k)} - \mathbf{y}^{(k)}\| \leqslant 1/k$ and $|\mathsf{F}(\mathbf{x}^{(k)}) - \mathsf{F}(\mathbf{y}^{(k)})| > \varepsilon$.

From the sequence $\mathbf{x}^{(k)}$, we can extract a subsequence $\mathbf{x}^{(k_m)}$ converging to a limit $\mathbf{x}^* \in [a,b]^n$. Then the subsequence $\mathbf{y}^{(k_m)}$ also converges to $\mathbf{x}^*$ since

$$\|\mathbf{y}^{(k_m)} - \mathbf{x}^*\| \leqslant \|\mathbf{y}^{(k_m)} - \mathbf{x}^{(k_m)}\| + \|\mathbf{x}^{(k_m)} - \mathbf{x}^*\|.$$

Therefore, by continuity $\mathsf{F}(\mathbf{x}^{(k_m)}) - \mathsf{F}(\mathbf{y}^{(k_m)})$ converges to $\mathsf{F}(\mathbf{x}^*) - \mathsf{F}(\mathbf{x}^*) = 0$. This is a contradiction since

$$|\mathsf{F}(\mathbf{x}^{(k_m)}) - \mathsf{F}(\mathbf{y}^{(k_m)})| > \varepsilon. \qquad \square$$

A stronger form: absolute continuity

Before recalling the definition of absolute continuity, we first recall the concept of *variation* of a unary function; see for instance [180, 350, 371].

Definition 2.12. Let $f : \mathbb{I} \to \mathbb{R}$ be a function and let D be a subset of $\mathbb{R}$. The *variation of f on D*, denoted $\mathrm{Var}_D(f)$, is defined as follows: If $D \cap \mathbb{I} = \varnothing$ then $\mathrm{Var}_D(f) = 0$. Otherwise, $\mathrm{Var}_D(f)$ is given by

$$\sup\left\{ \sum_{i=1}^{n} |f(a_i) - f(a_{i-1})| \,\Big|\, a_0, \ldots, a_n \in D \cap \mathbb{I}, \, a_0 \leqslant \cdots \leqslant a_n \right\},$$

where the supremum is over all finite families $\{a_0, \ldots, a_n\}$ for $n \in \mathbb{N}$. If $\mathrm{Var}_D(f)$ is finite, we say that f is *of bounded variation* on D.

Definition 2.13. We say that the unary function $f : [a,b] \to \mathbb{R}$ is *absolutely continuous* if, for every $\varepsilon > 0$, there exists $\delta > 0$ such that for any finite system of pairwise nonintersecting intervals $]a_i, b_i[\subset]a, b[$, $i = 1, \ldots, n$, for which

$$\sum_{i=1}^{n} (b_i - a_i) < \delta$$

the inequality

$$\sum_{i=1}^{n} |f(b_i) - f(a_i)| < \varepsilon$$

holds.

Every absolutely continuous function on a closed interval is continuous on this interval. Indeed, considering only one arbitrary but fixed subinterval $]x, y[$ of $[a,b]$ with $|x - y| < \delta$ as the finite family of intervals from Definition 2.13, we obtain $|f(x) - f(y)| < \varepsilon$.

Proposition 2.14. *An absolutely continuous function* $f : [a, b] \to \mathbb{R}$ *is of bounded variation on* $[a, b]$.

Proof. Let $\varepsilon > 0$ be given. For arbitrary but fixed division $\mathcal{D}$ of the interval $[a, b]$ we can, by possibly adding new division points, group all subintervals of the resulting division $\mathcal{D}'$, going from left to right, such that the complete length of subintervals from the same group is equal to $\delta/2$ from Definition 2.13. The maximal number of such groups of subintervals is

$$C := \left\lfloor \frac{2(b-a)}{\delta} \right\rfloor + 1.$$

Since f is absolutely continuous, we have that $\sum |f(b_i) - f(a_i)| < \varepsilon$ on each subgroup of subintervals, which implies that

$$\sum_{\mathcal{D}'} |f(b_i) - f(a_i)| < C\varepsilon.$$

Therefore, also

$$\sum_{\mathcal{D}} |f(b_i) - f(a_i)| < C\varepsilon. \qquad \square$$

We observe that there are continuous functions of bounded variation which are not absolutely continuous, e.g., the Cantor function[2] (Devil's Staircase); see Hewitt and Stromberg [188].

We now give an example of a continuous function which is not of bounded variation and therefore, by Proposition 2.14, also not absolutely continuous.

Example 2.15. The function

$$f(x) = \begin{cases} x \cos \frac{\pi}{2x} & \text{if } x \in \;]0, 1] \\ 0 & \text{if } x = 0 \end{cases}$$

is continuous on $[0, 1]$ (for a given $\varepsilon > 0$ we have that $0 < |x| < \delta = \varepsilon$ implies $|x \cos \frac{\pi}{2x}| < |x| < \varepsilon$) but for each division $\mathcal{D}_i$ of the interval $[0, 1]$:

$$0 < \frac{1}{2i} < \frac{1}{2i-1} < \cdots < \frac{1}{2} < 1$$

for $i \in \mathbb{N}$ we have

$$\mathrm{Var}_{[0,1]}(f) \geqslant \sum_{\mathcal{D}_i} |f(b_k) - f(a_k)| = \frac{1}{i} + \frac{1}{i-1} + \cdots + \frac{1}{2} + 1.$$

Letting $i \to \infty$ we obtain $\mathrm{Var}_{[0,1]}(f) \to \infty$, i.e., f is not of bounded variation.

---

[2] The Cantor function, defined on the interval $[0, 1]$, can be extended to a function $f : \mathbb{R} \to \mathbb{R}$, with $f(x) = 0$ if $x < 0$ and $f(x) = 1$ if $x > 1$, which is uniformly continuous on $\mathbb{R}$, but not absolutely continuous.

The basic properties of absolutely continuous functions are contained in the following three results. The second one contains the fundamental theorem of calculus. For more details, see for instance [180, 350, 371].

Proposition 2.16. *The following statements hold:*

(i) *An absolutely continuous function on* $[a, b]$ *is uniformly continuous (see Definition 2.10).*

(ii) *If* $f : [a, b] \to \mathbb{R}$ *is absolutely continuous, it is of bounded variation on* $[a, b]$, *so it is differentiable almost everywhere on* $[a, b]$, *and its derivative is integrable over* $[a, b]$.

Theorem 2.17. *Let* $f : [a, b] \to \mathbb{R}$. *Then the following are equivalent:*

(i) *There is an integrable real-valued function* $g : [a, b] \to \mathbb{R}$ *such that*

$$f(x) = f(a) + \int_a^x g(t)\, \mathrm{d}t$$

for every $x \in [a, b]$.

(ii) $\int_a^x f'(t)\, \mathrm{d}t$ *exists and is equal to* $f(x) - f(a)$ *for every* $x \in [a, b]$.

(iii) f *is absolutely continuous.*

Proposition 2.18. *Let* $f : [a, b] \to \mathbb{R}$ *be a continuous function which is differentiable on* $]a, b[$. *If its derivative* f' *is integrable over* $[a, b]$, *then* f *is absolutely continuous, and*

$$f(b) - f(a) = \int_a^b f'(t)\, \mathrm{d}t.$$

We extend the notion of absolute continuity to functions of two variables. We use the approach from Berkson and Gillespie [37], based on Hardy [184] and Krause; see Hobson [189, p. 345]. For that purpose we introduce, for a subrectangle $R = [a', b'] \times [c', d']$ of $[a, b] \times [c, d]$ and a function $\mathsf{F} : [a, b] \times [c, d] \to \mathbb{R}$, the following notation:

$$\Delta_R(\mathsf{F}) = \mathsf{F}(a', c') - \mathsf{F}(b', c') - \mathsf{F}(a', d') + \mathsf{F}(b', d').$$

Definition 2.19. We say that $\mathsf{F} : [a, b] \times [c, d] \to \mathbb{R}$ is *absolutely continuous* if the following two conditions are satisfied:

(i) Given $\varepsilon > 0$, there exists $\delta > 0$ such that

$$\sum_{R \in \mathcal{R}} |\Delta_R(\mathsf{F})| < \varepsilon$$

whenever $\mathcal{R}$ is a finite collection of pairwise nonoverlapping subrectangles $R = [a',b'] \times [c',d']$ of $[a,b] \times [c,d]$ with

$$\sum_{R \in \mathcal{R}} \lambda(R) < \delta,$$

where λ is the Lebesgue measure.

(ii) The marginal functions $\mathsf{F}(\cdot, d)$ and $\mathsf{F}(b, \cdot)$ are absolutely continuous functions of a single variable on $[a, b]$ and $[c, d]$, respectively.

Remark 2.20. Definition 2.19 is equivalent to the condition that there exists absolutely continuous functions g and h on $[a, b]$ and $[c, d]$, respectively, and a function $f \in L_1([a, b] \times [c, d])$ such that

$$\mathsf{F}(x,y) = g(x) + h(y) + \int_a^x \int_c^y f(u, v) \, dv \, du,$$

see Berkson and Gillespie [37].

A stronger form: Lipschitz condition

The continuity property can be strengthened into the well-known Lipschitz condition [247]; see Zygmund [450].

Definition 2.21. Let $\| \cdot \| : \mathbb{R}^n \to [0, \infty[$ be a norm. If a function $\mathsf{F} : \mathbb{I}^n \to \mathbb{R}$ satisfies, for all $\mathbf{x}, \mathbf{y} \in \mathbb{I}^n$, the inequality

$$|\mathsf{F}(\mathbf{x}) - \mathsf{F}(\mathbf{y})| \leqslant c \, \|\mathbf{x} - \mathbf{y}\|, \tag{2.1}$$

for some constant $c \in]0, \infty[$, then we say that F satisfies the *Lipschitz condition* or is *Lipschitzian* (with respect to $\| \cdot \|$). More precisely, any function $\mathsf{F} : \mathbb{I}^n \to \mathbb{R}$ satisfying (2.1) is said to be *c-Lipschitzian*. The greatest lower bound d of constants $c > 0$ in (2.1) is called the *best Lipschitz constant* (which means that F is d-Lipschitzian but, for any $u \in]0, d[$, F is not u-Lipschitzian).

Important examples of norms are given by the Minkowski norm of order $p \in [1, \infty[$, namely

$$\|\mathbf{x}\|_p := \left(\sum_{i=1}^n |x_i|^p \right)^{1/p},$$

also called the L_p-norm, and its limiting case $\|\mathbf{x}\|_\infty := \max_i |x_i|$, which is the Chebyshev norm.

The c-Lipschitz condition has an interesting interpretation when applied in aggregation. It allows us to estimate the relative output error in comparison with input errors

$$|\mathsf{F}(\mathbf{x}) - \mathsf{F}(\mathbf{y})| \leqslant c\varepsilon$$

whenever $\|\mathbf{x} - \mathbf{y}\| \leqslant \varepsilon$ for some $\varepsilon > 0$.

We also have the following result.

Proposition 2.22. *For arbitrary reals $p, q \in [1, \infty]$, a function $\mathsf{F} : \mathbb{I}^n \to \mathbb{R}$ is Lipschitzian with respect to the norm $\|\cdot\|_p$ if and only if it is Lipschitzian with respect to the norm $\|\cdot\|_q$. Moreover, if F is c-Lipschitzian with respect to the norm $\|\cdot\|_p$ then it is also c-Lipschitzian with respect to the norm $\|\cdot\|_q$ for $q \leqslant p$, and for $q > p$ it is nc-Lipschitzian.*

Proof. The result follows from the following inequalities, which are valid for any $\mathbf{x} \in \mathbb{I}^n$ and any reals $q \geqslant p \geqslant 1$:

$$\|\mathbf{x}\|_p \leqslant \|\mathbf{x}\|_1 \leqslant n^{1-\frac{1}{p}} \|\mathbf{x}\|_p, \quad \|\mathbf{x}\|_1 \leqslant n\|\mathbf{x}\|_\infty \leqslant n\|\mathbf{x}\|_p$$

and

$$\|\mathbf{x}\|_q \leqslant \|\mathbf{x}\|_p. \qquad \square$$

From now on, the Lipschitz property of functions is always meant with respect to the L_1-norm, up to the cases when the norm is mentioned explicitly.

The Lipschitz property of functions is defined standardly on domains where the norm cannot achieve ∞. Formally it can be defined also on $\mathbb{I}^n$ for an unbounded interval $\mathbb{I}$. However, if $\mathbb{I}$ contains $-\infty$ or ∞, then the Lipschitz property does not imply continuity, in general. For example, the smallest aggregation function $\mathsf{A}_\perp$ on $[0, \infty]^n$ is Lipschitzian for any norm but it is not continuous.

In all cases when $\mathbb{I} \subseteq \mathbb{R}$, the Lipschitz property for unary functions implies absolute continuity. However, the converse does not hold. For instance, $\sqrt{x}$ on $[0, 1]$ is absolutely continuous but not Lipschitzian.

Example 2.23. (i) The product $\Pi : [0, 1]^2 \to [0, 1]$ is 1-Lipschitzian (with respect to the L_1-norm). Therefore it is absolutely continuous.

(ii) The geometric mean $\mathsf{GM} : [0, 1]^2 \to [0, 1]$ is not Lipschitzian taking into account any norm. However, it is continuous and therefore uniformly continuous by Proposition 2.11.

We also have the following result (see Calvo and Mesiar [51] for the special case $[a, b] = [0, 1]$).

Proposition 2.24. *Let $[a, b]$ be a real interval. The smallest and the greatest aggregation functions defined in $[a, b]^n$ that are 1-Lipschitzian with respect to the norm $\| \cdot \|$ are respectively given by $\mathsf{A}_*^{(n)} : [a, b]^n \to [a, b]$, with*

$$\mathsf{A}_*^{(n)}(\mathbf{x}) := \mathsf{Max}(b - \|n \cdot b - \mathbf{x}\|, a),$$

and $\mathsf{A}^{*(n)} : [a, b]^n \to [a, b]$, with

$$\mathsf{A}^{*(n)}(\mathbf{x}) := \mathsf{Min}(a + \|\mathbf{x} - n \cdot a\|, b).$$

Proof. Let $\mathsf{B} : [a, b]^n \to [a, b]$ be a 1-Lipschitzian (with respect to the norm $\| \cdot \|$) aggregation function. Then for all $\mathbf{x} \in [a, b]^n$ we have

$$|\mathsf{B}(\mathbf{x}) - \mathsf{B}(n \cdot a)| \leqslant \|\mathbf{x} - n \cdot a\|,$$

i.e., $\mathsf{B} \leqslant \mathsf{A}^{*(n)}$. Now, it is routine to show that $\mathsf{A}^{*(n)}$ is an aggregation function. Moreover, $\mathsf{A}^{*(n)}$ is 1-Lipschitzian since

$$\left| \|\mathbf{x} - n \cdot a\| - \|\mathbf{y} - n \cdot a\| \right| \leqslant \|\mathbf{x} - \mathbf{y}\|.$$

Summarizing, $\mathsf{A}^{*(n)}$ is the greatest 1-Lipschitzian n-ary aggregation function on $[a, b]^n$ (with respect to the norm $\| \cdot \|$). The case of the function $\mathsf{A}_*^{(n)}$ can be treated in an analogous way. $\square$

For infinite real intervals $\mathbb{I}$, each Lipschitzian function (with respect to any norm $\| \cdot \|$) is continuous. The converse is false in general.

Example 2.25. The geometric mean GM on the interval $[0, \infty[^n$ is a continuous function which is not Lipschitzian.

As already mentioned for the extended aggregation function $\mathsf{A} : \cup_{n \in \mathbb{N}} \mathbb{I}^n \to \mathbb{R}$, continuity of A means continuity of each $\mathsf{A}^{(n)}$. However, the Lipschitz condition for A is restricted by the existence of a constant $c \in]0, \infty[$ such that each $\mathsf{A}^{(n)}$ is c-Lipschitzian.

Example 2.26. The arithmetic mean $\mathsf{AM} : \cup_{n \in \mathbb{N}} \mathbb{I}^n \to \mathbb{R}$ is 1-Lipschitzian (with respect to the L_1-norm) independently of the interval $\mathbb{I}$. For each $n \in \mathbb{N}$, the best Lipschitz constant for $\mathsf{AM}^{(n)}$ is $1/n$ and $\mathsf{AM}^{(n)}$ is the only n-ary aggregation function having this property. With respect to the L_∞-norm, $\mathsf{AM}^{(n)}$ is 1-Lipschitzian for all n, 1 being the best Lipschitz constant.

The extended aggregation function $\mathsf{Q} : \cup_{n \in \mathbb{N}} [0, 1]^n \to [0, 1]$ given by $\mathsf{Q}(\mathbf{x}) := \prod_i x_i^i$ is not Lipschitzian (with respect to the L_1-norm), though each $\mathsf{Q}^{(n)}$ is Lipschitzian (the best Lipschitz constant for $\mathsf{Q}^{(n)}$ is n).

Weaker forms: left and right continuities

Definition 2.27. A nondecreasing function $F : \mathbb{I}^n \to \mathbb{R}$ is called *lower semi-continuous* or *left-continuous* if, for all $(\mathbf{x}^{(k)})_{k \in \mathbb{N}} \subset (\mathbb{I}^n)^{\mathbb{N}}$ such that $\vee_k \mathbf{x}^{(k)} \in \mathbb{I}^n$,

$$\bigvee_{k \in \mathbb{N}} F(\mathbf{x}^{(k)}) = F\left(\bigvee_{k \in \mathbb{N}} \mathbf{x}^{(k)} \right).$$

Definition 2.28. A nondecreasing function $F : \mathbb{I}^n \to \mathbb{R}$ is called *upper semi-continuous* or *right-continuous* if, for all $(\mathbf{x}^{(k)})_{k \in \mathbb{N}} \subset (\mathbb{I}^n)^{\mathbb{N}}$ such that $\wedge_k \mathbf{x}^{(k)} \in \mathbb{I}^n$,

$$\bigwedge_{k \in \mathbb{N}} F(\mathbf{x}^{(k)}) = F\left(\bigwedge_{k \in \mathbb{N}} \mathbf{x}^{(k)} \right).$$

We have the following important result (see Klement *et al.* [220, Prop. 1.22]).

Proposition 2.29. *A nondecreasing function* $F : \mathbb{I}^n \to \mathbb{R}$ *is lower semi-continuous (respectively, upper semi-continuous) if and only if* F *is lower semi-continuous (respectively, upper semi-continuous) in each variable.*

Proof. We will treat the case of lower semi-continuity only; the case of upper semi-continuity can be shown by similar methods. The necessity is obvious, so we will show the sufficiency only. Suppose that F is lower semi-continuous in each variable and let $(\mathbf{x}^{(k)})_{k \in \mathbb{N}}$ be a nondecreasing sequence of elements of $\mathbb{I}^n$ such that $\mathbf{x} = \vee_k \mathbf{x}^{(k)} \in \mathbb{I}^k$. Then $(x_i^{(k)})_{k \in \mathbb{N}}$ is a nondecreasing sequence of elements of $\mathbb{I}$ such that $\vee_k x_i^{(k)} = x_i$ for all $i \in [n]$. Let $\varepsilon > 0$ be given. The lower semi-continuity and nondecreasing monotonicity of F in the first variable ensure the existence of $j_1 \in \mathbb{N}$ such that

$$F(x_1, x_2, \ldots, x_n) - F(x_1^{(k_1)}, x_2, \ldots, x_n) < \frac{\varepsilon}{n}$$

for each $k_1 \geqslant j_1$. Similarly, because of the lower semi-continuity and nondecreasing monotonicity of F there is $j_2 \in \mathbb{N}$ such that, for each $k_2 \geqslant j_2$,

$$F(x_1^{(j_1)}, x_2, \ldots, x_n) - F(x_1^{(j_1)}, x_2^{(k_2)}, \ldots, x_n) < \frac{\varepsilon}{n},$$

etc. Summing up all n inequalities, defining $j := \max\{j_1, \ldots, j_n\}$ and exploiting the monotonicity of F, we get $F(\mathbf{x}) - F(\mathbf{x}^{(k)}) < \varepsilon$ for each $k \geqslant j$. Due to arbitrariness of $\mathbf{x}$ and ε the above fact implies the lower semi-continuity of F. $\square$

Proposition 2.30. *An aggregation function* $F : \mathbb{I}^n \to \mathbb{R}$ *is continuous if and only if it is both lower and upper semi-continuous.*

Example 2.31. (i) An important example of a left-continuous (lower semi-continuous) but noncontinuous aggregation function is the nilpotent minimum $T^{\mathbf{nM}} : [0, 1]^2 \to [0, 1]$ (see Example 3.28),

$$T^{\mathbf{nM}}(x_1, x_2) := \begin{cases} \mathrm{Min}(x_1, x_2) & \text{if } x_1 + x_2 > 1 \\ 0 & \text{otherwise.} \end{cases}$$

(ii) The drastic product $T_D : [0, 1]^n \to [0, 1]$ (see Proposition 3.19), given by

$$T_D(\mathbf{x}) := \begin{cases} \text{Min}(\mathbf{x}) & \text{if } |\{i \in [n] \mid x_i < 1\}| < 2 \\ 0 & \text{otherwise,} \end{cases}$$

is a noncontinuous but upper semi-continuous aggregation function.

2.2.3 Symmetry

The next property we consider is *symmetry*, also called *commutativity*, *neutrality*, or *anonymity*. The standard commutativity of binary operations $x * y = y * x$, well known in algebra, can be easily generalized to *n*-ary functions, with $n \geqslant 2$, as follows.

Definition 2.32. $F : \mathbb{I}^n \to \overline{\mathbb{R}}$ is a *symmetric* function if

$$F(\mathbf{x}) = F([\mathbf{x}]_\sigma)$$

for all $\mathbf{x} \in \mathbb{I}^n, \sigma \in \mathfrak{S}_{[n]}$.

The symmetry property essentially means that the aggregated value does not depend on the order of the arguments. This is required when combining criteria of equal importance or anonymous experts' opinions.[3]

Many aggregation functions introduced thus far are symmetric. For example, AM, GM, OWA$_w$ are symmetric functions. A prominent example of nonsymmetric aggregation functions is the weighted arithmetic mean WAM$_w$.

The following result, well known in group theory, shows that the symmetry property can be checked with only two equalities; see for instance Rotman [367, Ex. 2.9, p. 24].

Proposition 2.33. $F : \mathbb{I}^n \to \overline{\mathbb{R}}$ *is a symmetric function if and only if, for all* $\mathbf{x} \in \mathbb{I}^n$, *we have*

(i) $F(x_2, x_1, x_3, \ldots, x_n) = F(x_1, x_2, x_3, \ldots, x_n)$,
(ii) $F(x_2, x_3, \ldots, x_n, x_1) = F(x_1, x_2, x_3, \ldots, x_n)$.

This simple test is very efficient, especially when symmetry does not appear immediately, like in the 4-variable expression

$$(x_1 \wedge x_2 \wedge x_3) \vee (x_1 \wedge x_2 \wedge x_4) \vee (x_1 \wedge x_3 \wedge x_4) \vee (x_2 \wedge x_3 \wedge x_4),$$

which is nothing other than the 4-ary order statistic $x_{(2)}$.

Now, an immediate description of the class of symmetric functions is given in the following proposition.

---

[3] Of course, symmetry is more natural in voting procedures than in multicriteria decision making, where criteria usually have different importances.

Proposition 2.34. $F : \mathbb{I}^n \to \overline{\mathbb{R}}$ *is a symmetric function if and only if there exists a function* $G : \mathbb{I}^n \to \overline{\mathbb{R}}$ *such that, for all* $\mathbf{x} \in \mathbb{I}^n$,

$$F(x_1, \ldots, x_n) = G(x_{(1)}, \ldots, x_{(n)}).$$

We note that the symmetric function F considered in Proposition 2.34 may lead to different functions G. For example, when $F = OS_1$ then, for any $K \subseteq [n]$, with $K \ni 1$, we can consider $G = Min_K$.

In situations when judges, criteria, or individual opinions are not equally important, the symmetry property must be omitted. There are some attempts [50,53,205,206,437, 438,442] to incorporate weights into symmetric functions; for instance by repetition of arguments. We will elaborate on this issue in Section 6.4.

Conversely, a nonsymmetric function $F(\mathbf{x})$ can always be symmetrized by replacing it with $F(x_{(1)}, \ldots, x_{(n)})$. Thus, according to this *symmetrization process*, a weighted arithmetic mean $WAM_\mathbf{w}$ gives rise to the corresponding ordered weighted averaging function $OWA_\mathbf{w}$; see also Section 4.6.2.

Going from the symmetric case to the nonsymmetric case

The following technique enables us to describe certain classes of aggregation functions from their subclasses of symmetric functions. We describe it first for two arguments.

Given a function $F : \mathbb{I}^2 \to \overline{\mathbb{R}}$, we define two functions

$$F_1(x_1, x_2) := F(x_{(1)}, x_{(2)}),$$
$$F_2(x_1, x_2) := F(x_{(2)}, x_{(1)}).$$

Then, in addition to the properties these functions might inherit from F (such as continuity, idempotency, etc.), we immediately see that they are symmetric. Moreover,

$$F(x_1, x_2) = \begin{cases} F_1(x_1, x_2) & \text{if } x_1 \leqslant x_2 \\ F_2(x_1, x_2) & \text{if } x_1 \geqslant x_2, \end{cases}$$

that is, F coincides with F_1 above the diagonal of the domain $\mathbb{I}^2$, and with F_2 below this diagonal. This trick has been usefully utilized to describe nonsymmetric associative functions from the symmetric ones; see for instance Fodor [114] and Sander [375].

The above technique easily generalizes to n arguments. Given a function $F : \mathbb{I}^n \to \overline{\mathbb{R}}$, we define the $n!$ symmetric functions

$$F_\sigma(\mathbf{x}) := F(x_{(\sigma(1))}, \ldots, x_{(\sigma(n))})$$

for all $\sigma \in \mathfrak{S}_{[n]}$. Then we have, for all $\mathbf{x} \in \mathbb{I}_\sigma^n$,

$$F(\mathbf{x}) = F_\sigma(\mathbf{x}),$$

which describes F on the whole domain since $\mathbb{I}^n = \cup_{\sigma \in \mathfrak{S}_{[n]}} \mathbb{I}_\sigma^n$.

2.2.4 Idempotency

In algebra, we say that x is an idempotent element with respect to a binary operation $*$ if $x * x = x$. This algebraic property can be extended to n-ary functions, thus defining the *idempotency* property for any n-ary function. Also called *unanimity*, *agreement*, or *reflexivity*, this property means that if all x_i are identical, $F(x_1, \ldots, x_n)$ returns the common value.

Idempotent functions

Definition 2.35. $F : \mathbb{I}^n \to \overline{\mathbb{R}}$ is an *idempotent* function if $\delta_F = \mathrm{id}$, that is,

$$F(n \cdot x) = x$$

for all $x \in \mathbb{I}$.

Idempotency is in some areas supposed to be a natural property of aggregation functions, e.g., in multicriteria decision making (see for instance Fodor and Roubens [119]), where it is commonly accepted that if all criteria are satisfied at the same degree x, implicitly assuming the commensurateness of criteria, then also the overall score should be x.

It is evident that AM, WAM_w, OWA_w, Min, Max, and Med are idempotent functions, while Σ and Π are not. Recall also that any nondecreasing and idempotent function $F : \mathbb{I}^n \to \overline{\mathbb{R}}$ is an aggregation function; see Corollary 1.8.

Idempotent elements

Definition 2.36. An element $x \in \mathbb{I}$ is *idempotent* for $F : \mathbb{I}^n \to \overline{\mathbb{R}}$ if $\delta_F(x) = x$.

In $[0, 1]^n$ the product Π has no idempotent elements other than the extreme elements 0 and 1. As an example of a function in $[0, 1]^n$ which is not idempotent but has a nonextreme idempotent element, take an arbitrarily chosen element $c \in \,]0, 1[$ and define the aggregation function $A_{\{c\}} : [0, 1]^n \to [0, 1]$ as follows:

$$A_{\{c\}}(\mathbf{x}) := \mathrm{Med}\left(0, c + \sum_{i=1}^{n}(x_i - c), 1\right). \tag{2.2}$$

It is easy to see that the only idempotent elements for $A_{\{c\}}$ are 0, 1, and c.

For extended functions we also have the following definition (see also Definition 2.113).

Definition 2.37. An element $x \in \mathbb{I}$ is *asymptotic idempotent* for $\mathsf{F} : \cup_{n \in \mathbb{N}} \mathbb{I}^n \to \overline{\mathbb{R}}$ if

$$\lim_{n \to \infty} \delta_{\mathsf{F}^{(n)}}(x) = x.$$

For example, 0 and 1 are the only asymptotic idempotent elements of the extended product $\Pi : \cup_{n \in \mathbb{N}}[0,1]^n \to [0,1]$. As another example, any $x \in \mathbb{R}$ is an asymptotic idempotent element of the extended function $\mathsf{A} : \cup_{n \in \mathbb{N}} \mathbb{R}^n \to \mathbb{R}$, defined by $\mathsf{A}^{(1)}(x) = x$ and $\mathsf{A}^{(n)}(\mathbf{x}) := \frac{1}{n+1} \sum_{i=1}^{n} x_i$ for all $n > 1$.

Range-idempotent functions

A function $\mathsf{F} : \mathbb{I}^n \to \mathbb{I}$ such that any $x \in \mathrm{ran}(\mathsf{F})$ is idempotent for F is said to be *range-idempotent*. This property will be useful when we introduce the decomposability property (see Section 2.3.2).

Definition 2.38. $\mathsf{F} : \mathbb{I}^n \to \mathbb{I}$ is a *range-idempotent* function if $\delta_{\mathsf{F}} \circ \mathsf{F} = \mathsf{F}$, that is,

$$\mathsf{F}(n \cdot \mathsf{F}(\mathbf{x})) = \mathsf{F}(\mathbf{x})$$

for all $\mathbf{x} \in \mathbb{I}^n$.

Of course, any idempotent function $\mathsf{F} : \mathbb{I}^n \to \mathbb{I}$ is range-idempotent. Conversely, if $\mathsf{F} : \mathbb{I}^n \to \mathbb{I}$ is range-idempotent then F is idempotent if and only if $\mathrm{ran}(\mathsf{F}) = \mathbb{I}$.

Example 2.39. For any numbers $a, b \in \mathbb{I}$, with $a \leqslant b$, and any idempotent function $\mathsf{G} : \mathbb{I}^n \to \mathbb{I}$, the function $\mathsf{F} : \mathbb{I}^n \to [a,b]$ defined as

$$\mathsf{F}(\mathbf{x}) = \mathrm{Med}(a, \mathsf{G}(\mathbf{x}), b)$$

is range-idempotent but not idempotent (unless $\mathbb{I} = [a,b]$). In particular, any constant function is range-idempotent but not idempotent.

By definition, the diagonal section $f = \delta_{\mathsf{F}}$ of any range-idempotent function $\mathsf{F} : \mathbb{I}^n \to \mathbb{I}$ satisfies the functional equation $f \circ f = f$, called the *idempotency equation*; see Kuczma et al. [241, §11.9E]. Instances of such functions are the identity function $f = \mathrm{id}$ and the constant functions $f = c$ ($c \in \mathbb{I}$).

The following result characterizes both the family of solutions of the idempotency equation and the subfamily of continuous and nondecreasing solutions defined on closed intervals; see Schweizer and Sklar [385, §2.1–2.2].

Proposition 2.40. *The function $f : \mathbb{I} \to \overline{\mathbb{R}}$ fulfills the equation $f \circ f = f$ if and only if*

$$f|_{\mathrm{ran}(f)} = \mathrm{id}|_{\mathrm{ran}(f)}.$$

Moreover, if $\mathbb{I}$ *is a closed interval, such a function is continuous and nondecreasing if and only if there are* $a, b \in \mathbb{I}$, *with* $a \leqslant b$, *such that*

$$f(x) = \mathsf{Med}(a, x, b).$$

Proof. Let us prove the first part.

($\Rightarrow$) Assume that $f \circ f = f$, which entails $\mathrm{ran}(f) \subseteq \mathbb{I}$. If $x \in \mathrm{ran}(f)$ then there is $z \in \mathbb{I}$ such that $x = f(z)$ and hence

$$f(x) = f(f(z)) = f(z) = x.$$

($\Leftarrow$) For any $x \in \mathbb{I}, f(x) \in \mathrm{ran}(f)$ and hence $f(f(x)) = f(x)$.

Let us now prove the second part.

($\Rightarrow$) Since f is continuous, $\mathrm{ran}(f)$ is a closed interval $[a, b]$. The result then follows from the first part and the nondecreasing monotonicity of f.

($\Leftarrow$) Trivial. $\square$

Note that the second part of Proposition 2.40 can be extended to any real interval $\mathbb{I}$ by considering $a, b \in \mathbb{I} \cup \{-\infty, \infty\}$, with $a \neq b$ if $a = \pm\infty$ or $b = \pm\infty$.

Remark 2.41. Instances of functions $f : \mathbb{I} \to \mathbb{I}$ fulfilling $f \circ f = f$ that are discontinuous or that fail to be nondecreasing are the signum function $f(x) = \mathrm{sign}(x)$ and the absolute value function $f(x) = |x|$.

Endpoint-preservation

When $\mathbb{I} = [a, b]$ is a bounded closed interval, by definition any aggregation function in $\mathbb{I}^n$ should have the endpoints a and b as idempotent elements. Functions fulfilling this property are said to be *endpoint-preserving*.

Definition 2.42. $\mathsf{F} : [a, b]^n \to \overline{\mathbb{R}}$ is an *endpoint-preserving* function if

$$\mathsf{F}(n \cdot a) = a \quad \text{and} \quad \mathsf{F}(n \cdot b) = b.$$

Strong idempotency

The idempotency property has been generalized to extended functions as follows; see Calvo *et al.* [53].

Definition 2.43. $\mathsf{F} : \cup_{n \in \mathbb{N}} \mathbb{I}^n \to \overline{\mathbb{R}}$ is *strongly idempotent* if, for any $n \in \mathbb{N}$ and for any $\mathbf{x} \in \cup_{m \in \mathbb{N}} \mathbb{I}^m$,

$$\mathsf{F}(n \cdot \mathbf{x}) = \mathsf{F}(\mathbf{x}).$$

For instance, if $\mathsf{F} : \cup_{n \in \mathbb{N}} \mathbb{I}^n \to \overline{\mathbb{R}}$ is strongly idempotent then we have

$$\mathsf{F}(x_1, x_2, x_1, x_2) = \mathsf{F}(x_1, x_2).$$

Proposition 2.44. *Suppose* $\mathsf{F} : \cup_{n\in\mathbb{N}}\mathbb{I}^n \to \overline{\mathbb{R}}$ *is strongly idempotent. Then* F *is idempotent if and only if* $\mathsf{F}(x) = x$ *for all* $x \in \mathbb{I}$.

Proof. If F is strongly idempotent then we have $\mathsf{F}(n \cdot x) = \mathsf{F}(x)$ for all $x \in \mathbb{I}$. Hence the result. □

According to our convention on unary aggregation functions, namely $\mathsf{A}(x) = x$ for all $x \in \mathbb{I}$, it follows immediately from the previous proposition that any strongly idempotent extended aggregation function is idempotent.

Idempotizable functions

We now consider a superset of the class of idempotent functions, called *idempotizable* functions.

Definition 2.45. A function $\mathsf{F} : \mathbb{I}^n \to \overline{\mathbb{R}}$ is *idempotizable* if its diagonal section δ_F is strictly increasing and satisfies $\mathrm{ran}(\delta_\mathsf{F}) = \mathrm{ran}(\mathsf{F})$.

We immediately note that, by (1.4), any nondecreasing and idempotent function $\mathsf{F} : \mathbb{I}^n \to \overline{\mathbb{R}}$ fulfills $\mathrm{ran}(\mathsf{F}) = \mathbb{I}$ and hence is idempotizable.

The following proposition and its corollary yield descriptions of the set of idempotizable functions. The first description is constructive and the second one is not.

Proposition 2.46. *A function* $\mathsf{F} : \mathbb{I}^n \to \overline{\mathbb{R}}$ *is idempotizable if and only if there is a strictly increasing bijection* $f : \mathbb{I} \to \mathrm{ran}(\mathsf{F})$ *and an idempotent function* $\mathsf{G} : \mathbb{I}^n \to \mathbb{I}$ *such that*

$$\mathsf{F} = f \circ \mathsf{G}. \tag{2.3}$$

In this case, $f = \delta_\mathsf{F}$ *is the diagonal section of* F.

Proof. ($\Rightarrow$) Let $\mathsf{F} : \mathbb{I}^n \to \overline{\mathbb{R}}$ be idempotizable. By definition, δ_F is an increasing bijection from $\mathbb{I}$ onto $\mathrm{ran}(\mathsf{F})$. It follows that the function $\mathsf{G} = \delta_\mathsf{F}^{-1} \circ \mathsf{F}$, from $\mathbb{I}^n$ to $\mathbb{I}$, is well defined. Moreover, this function is clearly idempotent and we have $\mathsf{F} = \delta_\mathsf{F} \circ \mathsf{G}$.

($\Leftarrow$) Under the assumptions of the statement, we have $\delta_\mathsf{F} = f \circ \delta_\mathsf{G} = f$ and hence F is idempotizable. □

Corollary 2.47. *A function* $\mathsf{F} : \mathbb{I}^n \to \overline{\mathbb{R}}$ *is idempotizable if and only if* δ_F *is strictly increasing and there is a function* $\mathsf{G} : \mathbb{I}^n \to \mathbb{I}$ *such that* $\mathsf{F} = \delta_\mathsf{F} \circ \mathsf{G}$.

Proof. ($\Rightarrow$) Consider an idempotizable function $\mathsf{F} : \mathbb{I}^n \to \overline{\mathbb{R}}$. By definition, δ_F is strictly increasing and, by Proposition 2.46, there is a function $\mathsf{G} : \mathbb{I}^n \to \mathbb{I}$ such that $\mathsf{F} = \delta_\mathsf{F} \circ \mathsf{G}$.

($\Leftarrow$) We have $\mathrm{ran}(\delta_\mathsf{F}) \subseteq \mathrm{ran}(\mathsf{F}) = \mathrm{ran}(\delta_\mathsf{F} \circ \mathsf{G}) \subseteq \mathrm{ran}(\delta_\mathsf{F})$ and hence F is idempotizable. □

Remark 2.48.   (i) The (idempotent) function G occurring in Proposition 2.46 and
Corollary 2.47 is uniquely determined from F by $G = \delta_F^{-1} \circ F$.

  (ii) Proposition 2.46 makes it possible to generate an idempotent function G from
any idempotizable function F, simply by writing $G := \delta_F^{-1} \circ F$, hence the name
"idempotizable". For instance, from the sum function $F = \Sigma$ we generate the
arithmetic mean $G = AM$. We refer to this generation process as the *idempoti-*
zation process; see for instance Calvo *et al.* [49, §3.1]. We will elaborate on this
process in Section 6.5.1.

 (iii) Proposition 2.46 also permits one to completely describe certain subclasses
of idempotizable functions from descriptions of the corresponding idempotent
functions. Indeed, the function G in (2.3) is idempotent in addition to the properties it might inherit from F (such as symmetry, continuity, etc.) Hence, if such
a function G can be described, so can the function F. This trick has been usefully
utilized, e.g., in Aczél [3, §6.4.3] and Marichal and Mathonet [281, Th. 4.1].

2.2.5 Conjunction, disjunction, and internality

Given two *n*-ary functions $F : \mathbb{I}^n \to \overline{\mathbb{R}}$ and $G : \mathbb{I}^n \to \overline{\mathbb{R}}$, we say that G *dominates*
F if $F \leqslant G$ in $\mathbb{I}^n$. Considering the functions Min and Max as dominating or domi-
nated functions gives rise to three main classes of aggregation functions: *conjunctive*
functions, *disjunctive* functions, and *internal* functions.

Definition 2.49. $F : \mathbb{I}^n \to \overline{\mathbb{R}}$ is *conjunctive* if $\inf \mathbb{I} \leqslant F \leqslant Min$.

Conjunctive functions combine values as if they were related by a logical "and"
operator. That is, the result of combination can be high only if all the values are high.
Thus, a low value can never be compensated by a high value. The most common
conjunctive functions defined on $[0, 1]^n$ are t-norms; see Section 3.3.

Definition 2.50. $F : \mathbb{I}^n \to \overline{\mathbb{R}}$ is *disjunctive* if $Max \leqslant F \leqslant \sup \mathbb{I}$.

Disjunctive functions combine values as an "or" operator, so that the result of combination is high if at least one value is high. Thus, a high value cannot be compensated
by a low value. Such functions are, in this sense, dual of conjunctive functions. The
most common disjunctive functions defined on $[0, 1]^n$ are t-conorms; see Section 3.5.

The following proposition shows that, due to the monotonicity of aggregation
functions, the conjunctiveness (respectively, disjunctiveness) of an aggregation function over the domain $[a, b]^n$ can be checked just on the upper (respectively, lower)
boundary of that domain.

Proposition 2.51. *An aggregation function* $A : [a, b]^n \to \overline{\mathbb{R}}$ *is conjunctive (respec-*
tively, disjunctive) if and only if $A(x_{\{i\}}b) \leqslant x$ *(respectively,* $A(x_{\{i\}}a) \geqslant x$*) for all*
$x \in [a, b]$ *and all* $i \in [n]$.

Proof. We consider only the case of conjunctive functions. The other case is similar.

($\Rightarrow$) Trivial.

($\Leftarrow$) Let $\mathbf{x} \in [a, b]^n$ and choose $i \in [n]$ such that $x_i = \mathsf{Min}(\mathbf{x})$. Then

$$\inf \mathbb{I} \leqslant \mathsf{A}(\mathbf{x}) \leqslant \mathsf{A}(\mathbf{x}_{\{i\}} b) \leqslant x_i = \mathsf{Min}(\mathbf{x}),$$

and A is conjunctive. □

Definition 2.52. A function $\mathsf{F} : \mathbb{I}^n \to \overline{\mathbb{R}}$ is *internal* if $\mathsf{Min} \leqslant \mathsf{F} \leqslant \mathsf{Max}$.

Internality is a property shared by all the means and averaging functions, which are the most often encountered functions in the literature on aggregation. Specifically, Cauchy [56] considered in 1821 the *mean* of n independent variables $x_1, \dots, x_n$ as a function $\mathsf{F}(x_1, \dots, x_n)$ which should be internal to the set of x_i values. Thus, according to Cauchy, a mean is merely an internal function. We will elaborate on this subject in Section 4.1.

Remark 2.53. In multicriteria decision making, these functions are also called *compensative* functions. In fact, for this kind of function, a bad (respectively, good) score on one criterion can generally be compensated by a good (respectively, bad) one on another criterion, so that the result of the aggregation will be medium.

It is clear that the property $\mathrm{ran}(F) \subseteq \mathbb{I}$ holds for any internal function $\mathsf{F} : \mathbb{I}^n \to \overline{\mathbb{R}}$. Moreover, as the following immediate result shows (see for instance de Finetti [79, p. 379]), internality and idempotency are closely related.

Proposition 2.54. *If* $\mathsf{F} : \mathbb{I}^n \to \overline{\mathbb{R}}$ *is internal, then it is idempotent. Conversely, if* $\mathsf{F} : \mathbb{I}^n \to \overline{\mathbb{R}}$ *is nondecreasing and idempotent then it is internal.*

Proof. The first part is immediate. We have

$$\mathrm{id} = \delta_{\mathsf{Min}} \leqslant \delta_{\mathsf{F}} \leqslant \delta_{\mathsf{Max}} = \mathrm{id}.$$

The second part follows immediately from inequalities (1.4). We have

$$\mathsf{Min} = \delta_{\mathsf{F}} \circ \mathsf{Min} \leqslant \mathsf{F} \leqslant \delta_{\mathsf{F}} \circ \mathsf{Max} = \mathsf{Max}. \qquad \square$$

By definition, an internal function is located between Min and Max. Thus, it can be immediately represented as follows.

Proposition 2.55. *Assume that* $\mathbb{I}$ *is a bounded real interval. An idempotent function* $\mathsf{F} : \mathbb{I}^n \to \overline{\mathbb{R}}$ *is internal if and only if there exists a function* $\mathsf{G} : \mathbb{I}^n \setminus \mathrm{diag}(\mathbb{I}^n) \to [0, 1]$ *such that*

$$\mathsf{F}(\mathbf{x}) = \mathsf{Min}(\mathbf{x}) + \mathsf{G}(\mathbf{x})\big(\mathsf{Max}(\mathbf{x}) - \mathsf{Min}(\mathbf{x})\big) \tag{2.4}$$

for any $\mathbf{x} \in \mathbb{I}^n \setminus \mathrm{diag}(\mathbb{I}^n)$.

The function $G : \mathbb{I}^n \setminus \text{diag}(\mathbb{I}^n) \rightarrow [0, 1]$, defined in (2.4) as[4]

$$G(\mathbf{x}) := \frac{F(\mathbf{x}) - \text{Min}(\mathbf{x})}{\text{Max}(\mathbf{x}) - \text{Min}(\mathbf{x})}$$

from an internal function $F : \mathbb{I}^n \rightarrow \overline{\mathbb{R}}$, was introduced by Dujmović [103] (see also [105]) as *the local orness function* associated with F. It was rediscovered independently by Fernández Salido and Murakami [111] as the *orness distribution function* associated with F. We will discuss this concept in Section 10.2.2.

k-conjunctive and k-disjunctive functions

We can refine the definitions of conjunction and disjunction by considering *k-conjunctive* and *k-disjunctive* functions; see Marichal [275].[5]

Definition 2.56. Let $k \in [n]$. A function $F : \mathbb{I}^n \rightarrow \overline{\mathbb{R}}$ is

 (i) *k-conjunctive* if $\inf \mathbb{I} \leqslant F \leqslant OS_k$,
(ii) *k-disjunctive* if $\sup \mathbb{I} \geqslant F \geqslant OS_{n-k+1}$.

According to this definition, it is clear that a function is conjunctive if and only if it is 1-conjunctive. Similarly, it is disjunctive if and only if it is 1-disjunctive. Finally, it is internal if and only if it is n-conjunctive and n-disjunctive.

To give an example, the 3-ary function $F(x_1, x_2, x_3) = \text{Min}(x_1, x_2)$ is 2-conjunctive while not being conjunctive. As another example, consider the ordered weighted averaging function $OWA_{\mathbf{w}} = \sum_{i=1}^{n} w_i \, OS_k$; see (1.19). Then it is clear that $OWA_{\mathbf{w}}$ is k-conjunctive (respectively, k-disjunctive) if and only if $w_i = 0$ for all $i > k$ (respectively, $i < n - k + 1$).

As we will now show, some k-conjunctive functions F are such that $F(\mathbf{x})$ remains unchanged when $x_{(k+1)}, \ldots, x_{(n)}$ are replaced with any other values greater than or equal to $x_{(k)}$. Similarly, some k-disjunctive functions F are such that $F(\mathbf{x})$ remains unchanged when $x_{(1)}, \ldots, x_{(n-k)}$ are replaced with any other values smaller than or equal to $x_{(n-k+1)}$.

More precisely, we have the following definitions.

Definition 2.57. Assume $n \geqslant 2$ and let $k \in [n - 1]$. A function $F : \mathbb{I}^n \rightarrow \overline{\mathbb{R}}$ is *independent of the* $(n - k)$ *highest arguments* if, for any $i \in [n]$ and any $\mathbf{x}, \mathbf{x}' \in \mathbb{I}^n$, with $x_i \geqslant x_{(k+1)}$, we have

$$\left. \begin{array}{l} x'_i \geqslant x_{(k)} \\ x'_j = x_j \ \forall j \neq i \end{array} \right\} \Rightarrow F(\mathbf{x}') = F(\mathbf{x}).$$

---

[4] Note that G can be arbitrarily defined on $\text{diag}(\mathbb{I}^n)$, thus making the relation in (2.4) valid on the whole domain $\mathbb{I}^n$.

[5] Originally, these functions were introduced as k-intolerant and k-tolerant functions.

Definition 2.58. Assume $n \geqslant 2$ and let $k \in [n-1]$. A function $\mathsf{F} : \mathbb{I}^n \to \overline{\mathbb{R}}$ is *independent of the* $(n-k)$ *lowest arguments* if, for any $i \in [n]$ and any $\mathbf{x}, \mathbf{x}' \in \mathbb{I}^n$, with $x_i \leqslant x_{(n-k)}$, we have

$$\left. \begin{array}{l} x'_i \leqslant x_{(n-k+1)} \\ x'_j = x_j \ \forall j \neq i \end{array} \right\} \ \Rightarrow \ \mathsf{F}(\mathbf{x}') = \mathsf{F}(\mathbf{x}).$$

We now have the following result (see Marichal [275, Prop. 3.1]).

Proposition 2.59. *Assume* $n \geqslant 2$ *and let* $k \in [n-1]$. *If* $\mathsf{F} : \mathbb{I}^n \to \overline{\mathbb{R}}$ *is nondecreasing, idempotent, and independent of the* $(n-k)$ *highest (respectively, lowest) arguments, then it is k-conjunctive (respectively, k-disjunctive).*

Proof. We prove the first part only. The other one is similar.

Let $k \in [n-1]$, let $\mathbf{x} \in \mathbb{I}^n$, and choose $K(\mathbf{x}) \subseteq \{i \in [n] \mid x_i \leqslant x_{(k)}\}$ with $|K(\mathbf{x})| = k$. We then have $\inf \mathbb{I} \leqslant \mathsf{F}(\mathbf{x})$ and

$$\mathsf{F}(\mathbf{x}) \leqslant \mathsf{F}\big((x_{(k)})_{K(\mathbf{x})} x_{(n)}\big) \quad \text{(nondecreasing monotonicity)}$$
$$= \mathsf{F}\big((x_{(k)})_{K(\mathbf{x})} x_{(k)}\big) \quad \text{(independence)}$$
$$= x_{(k)} \quad \text{(idempotency).} \qquad \square$$

Example 2.60. As an application, consider students who are evaluated according to n homework assignments and assume that the evaluation procedure states that the two lowest homework scores of each student are dropped, which implies that each student can miss two homework assignments without affecting his/her grade. If the corresponding evaluation function is nondecreasing and idempotent, it must be $(n-2)$-disjunctive.

In descriptive statistics, it is sometimes useful to consider averaging functions that are not sensitive to the extreme values. For example, in Olympics judging, it is common practice to throw out extreme scores when judges may be biased.

The following immediate corollary, which can be seen as a generalization of Proposition 2.54, provides restrictions on the location of such functions.

Corollary 2.61. *Assume* $k \leqslant \frac{n-1}{2}$. *If* $\mathsf{F} : \mathbb{I}^n \to \overline{\mathbb{R}}$ *is nondecreasing, idempotent, and independent of the k lowest and the k highest arguments. Then, for all* $\mathbf{x} \in \mathbb{I}^n$,

$$x_{(k+1)} \leqslant \mathsf{F}(\mathbf{x}) \leqslant x_{(n-k)}.$$

2.3 Grouping-based properties

The properties we will focus on in this section concern the "grouping" character of the aggregation functions. That is to say, we assume that it is possible to partition the set of arguments into disjoint subgroups, build the partial aggregation for each subgroup, and then combine these partial results to get the overall value. Such a condition may take several forms. A strong one we will first present is associativity. Weaker conditions will also be presented, namely decomposability, autodistributivity, and bisymmetry.

2.3.1 Associativity

We consider first the associativity functional equation. Associativity of a binary operation $*$ means that $(x * y) * z = x * (y * z)$, so we can write $x * y * z$ unambiguously. If we write this binary operation as a two-place function $f(a, b) = a * b$, then associativity says that $f(f(a, b), c) = f(a, f(b, c))$. For general f, this is the *associativity functional equation*.

Definition 2.62. $\mathsf{F} : \mathbb{I}^2 \to \mathbb{I}$ is *associative* if, for all $\mathbf{x} \in \mathbb{I}^3$, we have

$$\mathsf{F}(\mathsf{F}(x_1, x_2), x_3) = \mathsf{F}(x_1, \mathsf{F}(x_2, x_3)). \tag{2.5}$$

A large number of papers deal with the associativity functional equation (2.5) even in the field of real numbers. In complete generality, its investigation naturally constitutes a principal subject of algebra. For a list of references see Aczél [3, §6.2] and Alsina *et al.* [15].

Basically, associativity concerns aggregation of only two arguments. However, as stated in the next definition, associativity can be extended to any finite number of arguments.

Recall that, for two vectors $\mathbf{x} = (x_1, \ldots, x_n)$ and $\mathbf{x}' = (x'_1, \ldots, x'_m)$, we use the convenient notation $\mathsf{F}(\mathbf{x}, \mathbf{x}')$ to represent $\mathsf{F}(x_1, \ldots, x_n, x'_1, \ldots, x'_m)$, and similarly for more than two vectors. Also, if $\mathbf{x} \in \mathbb{I}^0$ is an empty vector then it is simply dropped from the function. For instance, $\mathsf{F}(\mathbf{x}, \mathbf{x}') = \mathsf{F}(\mathbf{x}')$ and $\mathsf{F}(\mathsf{F}(\mathbf{x}), \mathsf{F}(\mathbf{x}')) = \mathsf{F}(\mathsf{F}(\mathbf{x}'))$.

Definition 2.63. $\mathsf{F} : \cup_{n \in \mathbb{N}} \mathbb{I}^n \to \mathbb{I}$ is *associative* if $\mathsf{F}(x) = x$ for all $x \in \mathbb{I}$ and if

$$\mathsf{F}(\mathbf{x}, \mathbf{x}') = \mathsf{F}(\mathsf{F}(\mathbf{x}), \mathsf{F}(\mathbf{x}')) \tag{2.6}$$

for all $\mathbf{x}, \mathbf{x}' \in \cup_{n \in \mathbb{N}_0} \mathbb{I}^n$.

As the next proposition shows, associativity means that each subset of consecutive arguments can be replaced with their partial aggregation without changing the overall aggregation.

Proposition 2.64. $\mathsf{F} : \cup_{n \in \mathbb{N}} \mathbb{I}^n \to \mathbb{I}$ *is associative if and only if* $\mathsf{F}(x) = x$ *for all* $x \in \mathbb{I}$ *and*

$$\mathsf{F}(\mathbf{x}, \mathsf{F}(\mathbf{x}'), \mathbf{x}'') = \mathsf{F}(\mathbf{x}, \mathbf{x}', \mathbf{x}'')$$

for all $\mathbf{x}, \mathbf{x}', \mathbf{x}'' \in \cup_{n \in \mathbb{N}_0} \mathbb{I}^n$.

Proof. ($\Rightarrow$) For any $\mathbf{x}, \mathbf{x}', \mathbf{x}'' \in \cup_{n \in \mathbb{N}_0} \mathbb{I}^n$ we have successively

$$
\begin{aligned}
\mathsf{F}(\mathbf{x}, \mathsf{F}(\mathbf{x}'), \mathbf{x}'') &= \mathsf{F}(\mathsf{F}(\mathbf{x}, \mathsf{F}(\mathbf{x}')), \mathsf{F}(\mathbf{x}'')) \\
&= \mathsf{F}(\mathsf{F}(\mathsf{F}(\mathbf{x}), \mathsf{F}(\mathbf{x}')), \mathsf{F}(\mathbf{x}'')) \\
&= \mathsf{F}(\mathsf{F}(\mathbf{x}, \mathbf{x}'), \mathsf{F}(\mathbf{x}'')) \\
&= \mathsf{F}(\mathbf{x}, \mathbf{x}', \mathbf{x}'').
\end{aligned}
$$

($\Leftarrow$) We simply have $\mathsf{F}(\mathbf{x}, \mathbf{x}') = \mathsf{F}(\mathbf{x}, \mathsf{F}(\mathbf{x}')) = \mathsf{F}(\mathsf{F}(\mathbf{x}), \mathsf{F}(\mathbf{x}'))$. $\qquad\square$

Associativity is also a well-known algebraic property which allows one to omit "parentheses" in an aggregation of at least three elements. Implicit in the assumption of associativity is a consistent way of going unambiguously from the aggregation of n elements to $n + 1$ elements, which implies that any associative extended function F is completely determined by its binary function $\mathsf{F}^{(2)}$. Indeed, by associativity, we clearly have

$$
\mathsf{F}(x_1, \ldots, x_{n+1}) = \mathsf{F}(\mathsf{F}(x_1, \ldots, x_n), x_{n+1}).
$$

For practical purposes we can start with the aggregation procedure before knowing all inputs to be aggregated. Additional input data are then simply aggregated with the current aggregated output.

As examples of associative functions, recall Min, Max, Σ, Π, P_F, P_L. Functions like AM and GM are not associative.

One can see that the conjunction of associativity and idempotency immediately cancels the effect of repeating arguments in the aggregation procedure. Indeed, under associativity and idempotency, we clearly have

$$
\mathsf{F}(m \cdot x, n \cdot y) = \mathsf{F}(\mathsf{F}(m \cdot x), \mathsf{F}(n \cdot y)) = \mathsf{F}(x, y)
$$

for all $m, n \in \mathbb{N}$. For instance, we have

$$
\mathsf{F}(x, y, \ldots, y) = \mathsf{F}(x, y),
$$

regardless of the number of arguments y. Thus, it is not possible to simulate the presence of weights in such an aggregation procedure by simply repeating arguments. The reader can find a description of continuous, idempotent, and associative aggregation functions in Section 4.4.

In fact, as we will see in Chapters 3 and 4, associativity is a very strong and rather restrictive property; see also [15, 66, 294, 375].

The following concepts will be used in Chapters 3 and 6.

Definition 2.65. The *backward extension* $F_* : \cup_{n \in \mathbb{N}} \mathbb{I}^n \to \mathbb{I}$ and the *forward extension* $F^* : \cup_{n \in \mathbb{N}} \mathbb{I}^n \to \mathbb{I}$ of a binary function $F : \mathbb{I}^2 \to \mathbb{I}$ are recursively defined by

$$F_*^{(1)} := F^{*(1)} := \mathrm{id},$$
$$F_*^{(2)} := F^{*(2)} := F,$$

and, for $n > 2$,

$$F_*^{(n)}(x_1, \ldots, x_n) := F(x_1, F_*^{(n-1)}(x_2, \ldots, x_n)),$$
$$F^{*(n)}(x_1, \ldots, x_n) := F(F^{*(n-1)}(x_1, \ldots, x_{n-1}), x_n).$$

Remark 2.66. It is a fact that an extended function $F : \cup_{n \in \mathbb{N}} \mathbb{I}^n \to \mathbb{I}$ is associative if and only if the backward and forward extensions of $F^{(2)}$ coincide with F.

2.3.2 Decomposability and strong decomposability

It can be easily verified that the arithmetic mean as an extended function does not fulfill the associativity equation (2.5). So, it seems interesting to know whether there exists a functional equation, similar to associativity, which can be fulfilled by the arithmetic mean, or even by other means such as the geometric mean, the quadratic mean, etc.

On this subject, an acceptable equation, called *associativity of means* [33] or *barycentric associativity* [17, Chap. VI], has been proposed for symmetric extended functions and can be formulated as follows:

$$F(x_1, \ldots, x_k, x_{k+1}, \ldots, x_n) = F\big(k \cdot F(x_1, \ldots, x_k), x_{k+1}, \ldots, x_n\big)$$

for all integers $0 \leqslant k \leqslant n$, with $n \geqslant 1$. Equivalently, we can write

$$F(\mathbf{x}, \mathbf{x}') = F(k \cdot F(\mathbf{x}), \mathbf{x}')$$

for all $k \in \mathbb{N}_0$, all $\mathbf{x} \in \mathbb{I}^k$, and all $\mathbf{x}' \in \cup_{n \in \mathbb{N}_0} \mathbb{I}^n$.

Decomposability

Introduced first in Bemporad [33, p. 87] in a characterization of the arithmetic mean, associativity of means has been used by Kolmogoroff [236] and Nagumo [330] to characterize the so-called mean values. More recently, Marichal and Roubens [289] proposed to call this property "decomposability" in order not to confuse it with classical associativity. Alternative names, such as *associativity with repetitions* or *weighted associativity*, could be naturally considered as well.

When symmetry is not assumed, it is necessary to rewrite this property in such a way that the first variables are not privileged. We then consider the following definition.

Definition 2.67. $F : \cup_{n \in \mathbb{N}} \mathbb{I}^n \to \mathbb{I}$ is *decomposable* if $F(x) = x$ for all $x \in \mathbb{I}$ and if

$$F(\mathbf{x}, \mathbf{x}') = F(k \cdot F(\mathbf{x}), k' \cdot F(\mathbf{x}')) \qquad (2.7)$$

for all $k, k' \in \mathbb{N}_0$, all $\mathbf{x} \in \mathbb{I}^k$, and all $\mathbf{x}' \in \mathbb{I}^{k'}$.

By considering $k = 0$ or $k' = 0$ in (2.7), we see that any decomposable function is range-idempotent. Moreover, as the following proposition shows, decomposability means that each element of any subset of consecutive arguments can be replaced with their partial aggregation without changing the overall aggregation.

Proposition 2.68. $F : \cup_{n \in \mathbb{N}} \mathbb{I}^n \to \mathbb{I}$ *is decomposable if and only if* $F(x) = x$ *for all* $x \in \mathbb{I}$ *and*

$$F(\mathbf{x}, k' \cdot F(\mathbf{x}'), \mathbf{x}'') = F(\mathbf{x}, \mathbf{x}', \mathbf{x}'')$$

for all $k' \in \mathbb{N}_0$, *all* $\mathbf{x}' \in \mathbb{I}^{k'}$, *and all* $\mathbf{x}, \mathbf{x}'' \in \cup_{n \in \mathbb{N}_0} \mathbb{I}^n$.

Proof. The proof can be easily adapted from that of Proposition 2.64.

($\Rightarrow$) For any $k, k', k'' \in \mathbb{N}_0$ and any $\mathbf{x} \in \mathbb{I}^k, \mathbf{x}' \in \mathbb{I}^{k'}, \mathbf{x}'' \in \mathbb{I}^{k''}$, we have successively

$$
\begin{aligned}
F(\mathbf{x}, k' \cdot F(\mathbf{x}'), \mathbf{x}'') &= F((k + k') \cdot F(\mathbf{x}, k' \cdot F(\mathbf{x}')), k'' \cdot F(\mathbf{x}'')) \\
&\overset{(*)}{=} F((k + k') \cdot F(k \cdot F(\mathbf{x}), k' \cdot F(\mathbf{x}')), k'' \cdot F(\mathbf{x}'')) \\
&= F((k + k') \cdot F(\mathbf{x}, \mathbf{x}'), k'' \cdot F(\mathbf{x}'')) \\
&= F(\mathbf{x}, \mathbf{x}', \mathbf{x}''),
\end{aligned}
$$

where, at $(*)$, we have used the fact that F is range-idempotent.

($\Leftarrow$) Trivial. $\qquad\square$

As examples of decomposable functions, we have Min, Max, AM, GM, P_F, P_L. Functions like Σ and Π are not decomposable.

The following result (see Marichal *et al.* [284, §3]) provides a sufficient condition for an associative function to be decomposable.

Proposition 2.69. *If* $F : \cup_{n \in \mathbb{N}} \mathbb{I}^n \to \mathbb{I}$ *is range-idempotent and associative, then it is decomposable.*

Proof. Let $k, k' \in \mathbb{N}_0, \mathbf{x} \in \mathbb{I}^k$, and $\mathbf{x}' \in \mathbb{I}^{k'}$. Then we have

$$
\begin{aligned}
F(k \cdot F(\mathbf{x}), k' \cdot F(\mathbf{x}')) &= F(F(k \cdot F(\mathbf{x})), F(k' \cdot F(\mathbf{x}'))) \quad \text{(associativity)} \\
&= F(F(\mathbf{x}), F(\mathbf{x}')) \quad \text{(range-idempotency)} \\
&= F(\mathbf{x}, \mathbf{x}') \quad \text{(associativity)}.
\end{aligned}
$$

Therefore, F is decomposable. $\qquad\square$

Remark 2.70. Unlike associativity, decomposability does not determine the relationship between the aggregation of n elements and $n+1$ elements. For example, starting from a decomposable function $\mathsf{F} : \cup_{n \in \mathbb{N}} \mathbb{I}^n \to \mathbb{I}$, an integer $q \geqslant 2$, and a constant $c \in \mathbb{R}$, the function $\mathsf{G} : \cup_{n \in \mathbb{N}} \mathbb{I}^n \to \mathbb{I}$ defined as

$$\mathsf{G}^{(n)} := \begin{cases} \mathsf{F}^{(n)} & \text{if } n \leqslant q \\ \mathsf{K}_c^{(n)} & \text{otherwise,} \end{cases}$$

is also decomposable, where $\mathsf{K}_c^{(n)}$ is the n-ary constant function $\mathbf{x} \mapsto c$.

Strong decomposability

Just as for the associativity property, decomposability involves the aggregation of consecutive arguments only. We could as well consider the more general case where *any* subset of arguments is actually aggregated. For example, we might want the following property to hold:

$$\mathsf{F}(x_1, x_2, x_3) = \mathsf{F}\big(\mathsf{F}(x_1, x_3), x_2, \mathsf{F}(x_1, x_3)\big). \tag{2.8}$$

In generality, this stronger version of decomposability has been proposed by Marichal *et al.* [284] and can be formulated as follows.

Definition 2.71. $\mathsf{F} : \cup_{n \in \mathbb{N}} \mathbb{I}^n \to \mathbb{I}$ is *strongly decomposable* if $\mathsf{F}(x) = x$ for all $x \in \mathbb{I}$ and if

$$\mathsf{F}(\mathbf{x}) = \mathsf{F}\Big(\sum_{i \in K} \mathsf{F}(\mathbf{x}|_K) \mathbf{1}_{\{i\}} + \sum_{j \in K^c} \mathsf{F}(\mathbf{x}|_{K^c}) \mathbf{1}_{\{j\}}\Big) \tag{2.9}$$

for all $n \in \mathbb{N}$, all $K \subseteq [n]$, and all $\mathbf{x} \in \mathbb{I}^n$.

By definition, strong decomposability implies decomposability and hence range-idempotency. Furthermore, under symmetry, decomposability and strong decomposability are equivalent.

Just as for decomposability, one can easily show that strong decomposability means that each element of any subset of arguments (which need not be consecutive) from $\mathbf{x} \in \mathbb{I}^n$ can be replaced with the subset's partial aggregation without changing the overall aggregation.

Proposition 2.72. $\mathsf{F} : \cup_{n \in \mathbb{N}} \mathbb{I}^n \to \mathbb{I}$ is strongly decomposable if and only if $\mathsf{F}(x) = x$ for all $x \in \mathbb{I}$ and if

$$\mathsf{F}(\mathbf{x}) = \mathsf{F}\Big(\sum_{i \in K} \mathsf{F}(\mathbf{x}|_K) \mathbf{1}_{\{i\}} + \sum_{j \in K^c} x_j \mathbf{1}_{\{j\}}\Big)$$

for all $n \in \mathbb{N}$, all $K \subseteq [n]$, and all $\mathbf{x} \in \mathbb{I}^n$.

Proof. ($\Rightarrow$) For any $n \in \mathbb{N}$, any $K \subseteq [n]$, and any $\mathbf{x} \in \mathbb{I}^n$, we have successively

$$\mathsf{F}\Big(\sum_{i \in K} \mathsf{F}(\mathbf{x}|_K)\mathbf{1}_{\{i\}} + \sum_{j \in K^c} x_j \mathbf{1}_{\{j\}}\Big) \overset{(*)}{=} \mathsf{F}\Big(\sum_{i \in K} \mathsf{F}(\mathbf{x}|_K)\mathbf{1}_{\{i\}} + \sum_{j \in K^c} \mathsf{F}(\mathbf{x}|_{K^c})\mathbf{1}_{\{j\}}\Big)$$

$$= \mathsf{F}(\mathbf{x}),$$

where, at $(*)$, we have used the fact that F is range-idempotent.

($\Leftarrow$) Trivial. $\qquad\square$

As examples of strongly decomposable functions let us mention Min, Max, AM, GM, P_F, P_L. The following example [284] shows that not all decomposable functions are strongly decomposable.

Example 2.73. The (extended) weighted arithmetic mean defined by

$$\mathsf{A}^{(n)}(x) = \sum_{i=1}^{n} \frac{2^{i-1}}{2^n - 1} x_i$$

is decomposable but not strongly decomposable. Indeed, for any $k, k' \in \mathbb{N}_0$, any $\mathbf{x} \in \mathbb{I}^k$, and any $\mathbf{x}' \in \mathbb{I}^{k'}$, we have

$$\mathsf{A}(k \cdot \mathsf{A}(\mathbf{x}), k' \cdot \mathsf{A}(\mathbf{x}')) = \sum_{i=1}^{k} \frac{2^{i-1}}{2^{k+k'} - 1} \mathsf{A}(\mathbf{x}) + \sum_{i=k+1}^{k+k'} \frac{2^{i-1}}{2^{k+k'} - 1} \mathsf{A}(\mathbf{x}')$$

$$= \frac{2^k - 1}{2^{k+k'} - 1} \mathsf{A}(\mathbf{x}) + \frac{2^k(2^{k'} - 1)}{2^{k+k'} - 1} \mathsf{A}(\mathbf{x}')$$

$$= \sum_{i=1}^{k} \frac{2^{i-1}}{2^{k+k'} - 1} x_i + \sum_{i=1}^{k'} \frac{2^{k+i-1}}{2^{k+k'} - 1} x_i'$$

$$= \mathsf{A}(\mathbf{x}, \mathbf{x}')$$

and A is decomposable. It is not strongly decomposable since

$$\mathsf{A}(x_1, x_2, x_3) = \frac{1}{7} x_1 + \frac{2}{7} x_2 + \frac{4}{7} x_3$$

and

$$\mathsf{A}\big(\mathsf{A}(x_1, x_3), x_2, \mathsf{A}(x_1, x_3)\big) = \frac{5}{21} x_1 + \frac{2}{7} x_2 + \frac{10}{21} x_3,$$

which violates (2.8).

A deep discussion related to decomposable and strongly decomposable functions, together with several historical notes, can be found in [116, 266, 284].

Let us now present a series of results that will be useful as we go on. Most of them are inspired by Nagumo [330, §1].

Lemma 2.74. *If* $\mathsf{F} : \cup_{n \in \mathbb{N}} \mathbb{I}^n \to \mathbb{I}$ *is strongly decomposable and idempotent then, for any* $k, n, p_1, \ldots, p_n \in \mathbb{N}$ *and any* $\mathbf{x}^{(i)} \in \mathbb{I}^{p_i}$, $i = 1, \ldots, n$, *we have*

$$\mathsf{F}(k \cdot \mathbf{x}^{(1)}, \ldots, k \cdot \mathbf{x}^{(n)}) = \mathsf{F}(\mathbf{x}^{(1)}, \ldots, \mathbf{x}^{(n)}).$$

Proof. We simply have

$$\mathsf{F}(k \cdot \mathbf{x}^{(1)}, \ldots, k \cdot \mathbf{x}^{(n)})$$
$$= \mathsf{F}\big((kp_1 + \cdots + kp_n) \cdot \mathsf{F}(\mathbf{x}^{(1)}, \ldots, \mathbf{x}^{(n)})\big) \quad \text{(strong decomposability)}$$
$$= \mathsf{F}(\mathbf{x}^{(1)}, \ldots, \mathbf{x}^{(n)}) \quad \text{(idempotency).} \qquad \square$$

Remark 2.75. Looking at the proof of Lemma 2.74, we can readily see that, in the statement of the lemma, idempotency can be relaxed to the following condition:

$$\mathrm{ran}(\mathsf{F}^{(n)}) \subseteq \mathrm{ran}(\mathsf{F}^{(kn)})$$

for all $k, n \in \mathbb{N}$.

Lemma 2.76. *If* $\mathsf{F} : \cup_{n \in \mathbb{N}} \mathbb{I}^n \to \mathbb{I}$ *is strongly decomposable and idempotent then, for any* $n, p \in \mathbb{N}$ *and any* $\mathbf{x}^{(1)}, \ldots, \mathbf{x}^{(n)} \in \mathbb{I}^p$, *we have*

$$\mathsf{F}(\mathbf{x}^{(1)}, \ldots, \mathbf{x}^{(n)}) = \mathsf{F}\big(\mathsf{F}(\mathbf{x}^{(1)}), \ldots, \mathsf{F}(\mathbf{x}^{(n)})\big).$$

In particular, F *is strongly idempotent.*

Proof. We simply have

$$\mathsf{F}(\mathbf{x}^{(1)}, \ldots, \mathbf{x}^{(n)})$$
$$= \mathsf{F}\big(p \cdot \mathsf{F}(\mathbf{x}^{(1)}), \ldots, p \cdot \mathsf{F}(\mathbf{x}^{(n)})\big) \quad \text{(strong decomposability)}$$
$$= \mathsf{F}\big(\mathsf{F}(\mathbf{x}^{(1)}), \ldots, \mathsf{F}(\mathbf{x}^{(n)})\big) \quad \text{(Lemma 2.74).}$$

The second part is trivial, for we have $\mathsf{F}(n \cdot \mathbf{x}) = \mathsf{F}(n \cdot \mathsf{F}(\mathbf{x})) = \mathsf{F}(\mathbf{x})$. $\qquad \square$

Lemma 2.77. *If* $\mathsf{F} : \cup_{n \in \mathbb{N}} \mathbb{I}^n \to \mathbb{I}$ *is strongly decomposable and idempotent then, for any* $n \in \mathbb{N}$ *and any* $\mathbf{x} \in \mathbb{I}^n$, *we have*

$$\mathsf{F}(x_1, \ldots, x_n) = \mathsf{F}(x'_n, \ldots, x'_1),$$

where $x'_i := \mathsf{F}(x_1, \ldots, x_{i-1}, x_{i+1}, \ldots, x_n)$ *for all* $i = 1, \ldots, n$.

Proof. We simply have

$$\mathsf{F}(x_1, \ldots, x_n) = \mathsf{F}((n-1) \cdot x_1, \ldots, (n-1) \cdot x_n) \quad \text{(Lemma 2.74)}$$
$$= \mathsf{F}\big((n-1) \cdot (x'_n, \ldots, x'_1)\big) \quad \text{(strong decomposability)}$$
$$= \mathsf{F}(x'_n, \ldots, x'_1) \quad \text{(strong idempotency).} \qquad \square$$

Remark 2.78. It is noteworthy that, under idempotency, the definition of strong decomposability can be rewritten by replacing each element x_i with a p-tuple $\mathbf{x}^{(i)} \in \mathbb{I}^p$. For instance, the identity (2.8) can be written with p-tuples $\mathbf{x}^{(1)}, \mathbf{x}^{(2)}, \mathbf{x}^{(3)} \in \mathbb{I}^p$. Indeed, we have

$$
\begin{aligned}
&\mathsf{F}(\mathbf{x}^{(1)}, \mathbf{x}^{(2)}, \mathbf{x}^{(3)}) \\
&= \mathsf{F}\big(p \cdot \mathsf{F}(\mathbf{x}^{(1)}, \mathbf{x}^{(3)}), p \cdot \mathsf{F}(\mathbf{x}^{(2)}), p \cdot \mathsf{F}(\mathbf{x}^{(1)}, \mathbf{x}^{(3)})\big) \quad \text{(strong decomposability)} \\
&= \mathsf{F}\big(\mathsf{F}(\mathbf{x}^{(1)}, \mathbf{x}^{(3)}), \mathsf{F}(\mathbf{x}^{(2)}), \mathsf{F}(\mathbf{x}^{(1)}, \mathbf{x}^{(3)})\big) \quad \text{(Lemma 2.74).}
\end{aligned}
$$

2.3.3 Autodistributivity

We now consider the *autodistributivity* property, also called *self-distributivity*. Defined originally for two arguments, it can be easily extended to n arguments.

Definition 2.79. $\mathsf{F} : \mathbb{I}^2 \to \mathbb{I}$ is *autodistributive* if, for all $\mathbf{x} \in \mathbb{I}^3$, we have

$$
\mathsf{F}\big(x_1, \mathsf{F}(x_2, x_3)\big) = \mathsf{F}\big(\mathsf{F}(x_1, x_2), \mathsf{F}(x_1, x_3)\big), \tag{2.10}
$$

$$
\mathsf{F}\big(\mathsf{F}(x_1, x_2), x_3\big) = \mathsf{F}\big(\mathsf{F}(x_1, x_3), \mathsf{F}(x_2, x_3)\big). \tag{2.11}
$$

The autodistributivity equations (2.10) and (2.11) have been investigated both in general algebraic structures and for real numbers in particular. A list of references can be found in Aczél [3, §6.5]; see also Aczél and Dhombres [9, Chap. 17].

2.3.4 Bisymmetry

Let us consider the *bisymmetry* property, also called *mediality*.

Definition 2.80. $\mathsf{F} : \mathbb{I}^2 \to \mathbb{I}$ is *bisymmetric* if for all $\mathbf{x} \in \mathbb{I}^4$, we have

$$
\mathsf{F}\big(\mathsf{F}(x_1, x_2), \mathsf{F}(x_3, x_4)\big) = \mathsf{F}\big(\mathsf{F}(x_1, x_3), \mathsf{F}(x_2, x_4)\big).
$$

An immediate consequence of this definition is that an idempotent and bisymmetric function $\mathsf{F} : \mathbb{I}^2 \to \mathbb{I}$ is necessarily autodistributive.

The bisymmetry property is very easy to handle and has been investigated from the algebraic point of view by using it mostly in structures without the property of associativity. For a list of references see Aczél [3, §6.4]; see also Aczél and Dhombres [9, Chap. 17], and Soublin [397].

For n arguments, bisymmetry takes the following form (see Aczél [1]).

Definition 2.81. $\mathsf{F} : \mathbb{I}^n \to \mathbb{I}$ is *bisymmetric* if

$$
\begin{aligned}
&\mathsf{F}\big(\mathsf{F}(x_{11}, \ldots, x_{1n}), \ldots, \mathsf{F}(x_{n1}, \ldots, x_{nn})\big) \\
&= \mathsf{F}\big(\mathsf{F}(x_{11}, \ldots, x_{n1}), \ldots, \mathsf{F}(x_{1n}, \ldots, x_{nn})\big)
\end{aligned} \tag{2.12}
$$

for all square matrices

$$\begin{pmatrix} x_{11} & \cdots & x_{1n} \\ \vdots & & \vdots \\ x_{n1} & \cdots & x_{nn} \end{pmatrix} \in \mathbb{I}^{n \times n}.$$

Bisymmetry expresses the condition that aggregation of all the elements of any square matrix can be performed first on the rows, then on the columns, or conversely. However, since only square matrices are involved, this property seems not to have a good interpretation in terms of aggregation. Its usefulness remains theoretical. We then consider it for extended functions as follows; see Marichal *et al.* [284].

Definition 2.82. $\mathsf{F} : \cup_{n \in \mathbb{N}} \mathbb{I}^n \to \mathbb{I}$ is *strongly bisymmetric* if $\mathsf{F}(x) = x$ for all $x \in \mathbb{I}$, and if, for any $n, p \in \mathbb{N}$, we have

$$\mathsf{F}\big(\mathsf{F}(x_{11}, \ldots, x_{1n}), \ldots, \mathsf{F}(x_{p1}, \ldots, x_{pn})\big)$$
$$= \mathsf{F}\big(\mathsf{F}(x_{11}, \ldots, x_{p1}), \ldots, \mathsf{F}(x_{1n}, \ldots, x_{pn})\big)$$

for all matrices

$$\begin{pmatrix} x_{11} & \cdots & x_{1n} \\ \vdots & & \vdots \\ x_{p1} & \cdots & x_{pn} \end{pmatrix} \in \mathbb{I}^{p \times n}.$$

Remark 2.83. Contrary to bisymmetry, the strong bisymmetry property can be justified rather easily. Consider n judges (or criteria, attributes, etc.) giving a numerical score to each of p candidates. These scores, assumed to be defined on the same scale, can be put in a $p \times n$ matrix like

$$\begin{array}{c} \\ C_1 \\ \vdots \\ C_p \end{array} \begin{array}{c} J_1 \quad \cdots \quad J_n \\ \begin{pmatrix} x_{11} & \cdots & x_{1n} \\ \vdots & & \vdots \\ x_{p1} & \cdots & x_{pn} \end{pmatrix} \end{array}$$

Suppose now that we want to aggregate all the entries (scores) of the matrix in order to obtain an overall score of the p candidates. A reasonable way to proceed could be the following. First aggregate the scores of each candidate (aggregation over the rows of the matrix), and then aggregate these overall values. An alternative way to proceed would be to first aggregate the scores given by each judge (aggregation over the columns of the matrix), and then aggregate these values. The strong bisymmetry property means that these two ways to aggregate must lead to the same overall score, which is a natural property. Of course, we could as well consider only one candidate, n judges, and p criteria (assuming commensurateness of the scores along the criteria). In this latter setting, strong bisymmetry seems very natural as well.

Obviously, for any strongly bisymmetric extended function $\mathsf{F} : \cup_{n \in \mathbb{N}} \mathbb{I}^n \to \mathbb{I}$, each n-ary function $\mathsf{F}^{(n)}$ is bisymmetric. Moreover, we have the following result [284].

Proposition 2.84. *If* $F : \cup_{n \in \mathbb{N}} \mathbb{I}^n \to \mathbb{I}$ *is strongly decomposable and idempotent then it is strongly bisymmetric. In particular* $F^{(2)}$ *is bisymmetric.*

Proof. For the sake of understanding, let us first prove that $F^{(2)}$ is bisymmetric. We simply have

$$F\big(F(x_1,x_2), F(x_3,x_4)\big)$$
$$= F(x_1,x_2,x_3,x_4) \quad \text{(Lemma 2.76)}$$
$$= F\big(F(x_1,x_3), F(x_2,x_4), F(x_1,x_3), F(x_2,x_4)\big) \quad \text{(strong decomposability)}$$
$$= F\big(F(x_1,x_3), F(x_2,x_4)\big) \quad \text{(strong idempotency)}.$$

We apply the same reasoning to prove that F is strongly bisymmetric. We have

$$F\big(F(x_{11},\ldots,x_{1n}),\ldots,F(x_{p1},\ldots,x_{pn})\big)$$
$$= F(x_{11},\ldots,x_{1n};\ldots;x_{p1},\ldots,x_{pn}) \quad \text{(Lemma 2.76)}$$
$$= F\big(p \cdot (F(x_{11},\ldots,x_{p1}),\ldots,F(x_{1n},\ldots,x_{pn}))\big) \quad \text{(strong decomposability)}$$
$$= F\big(F(x_{11},\ldots,x_{p1}),\ldots,F(x_{1n},\ldots,x_{pn})\big) \quad \text{(strong idempotency)}. \qquad \square$$

2.4 Invariance properties

One of the main concerns when choosing an appropriate aggregation function is to take into account the scale types of the variables being aggregated. On this issue, Luce [256] observed that the general form of the functional relationship between variables is greatly restricted if we know the scale types of the dependent and independent variables. For instance, if all the variables define a common ordinal scale, it is clear that any relevant aggregation function cannot be constructed from usual arithmetic operations, unless these operations involve only order. Thus, computing the arithmetic mean is forbidden whereas the median or any order statistic is permitted.

Specifically, suppose $x_1,\ldots,x_n,x_{n+1}$ are $n+1$ variables, each x_i having a real interval as a domain, and

$$x_{n+1} = F(x_1,\ldots,x_n)$$

is some unknown (aggregation) function. The problem is to find the general form of the function F knowing the scale types of the input and output variables. The *scale type* of a variable x_i is defined by the class of *admissible transformations*, such as that from grams to pounds or degrees Fahrenheit to degrees centigrade, that change the scale into an alternative acceptable scale.

In the case of a *ratio scale*, for example, an admissible transformation is a similarity of the form $x \mapsto rx$, with some $r > 0$, which changes the unit of the scale. Mass is an example of a ratio scale. The transformation from kilograms into pounds, for example, involves the admissible transformation $\varphi(x) = 2.2\,x$. Length (inches, centimeters) and time intervals (years, seconds) are two other examples of ratio scales.

Similarly, for a *difference scale*, an admissible transformation is a translation of the form $x \mapsto x + s$, with some $s \in \mathbb{R}$, which changes the origin of the scale. More generally, for an *interval scale*, an admissible transformation is a positive affine transformation $x \mapsto rx + s$, with $r > 0$ and $s \in \mathbb{R}$, which modifies both the origin and the unit of the scale. Temperature (except where there is an absolute zero) defines an interval scale. Thus, transformation from centigrade into Fahrenheit involves the admissible transformation $\varphi(x) = (9/5)x + 32$.

For an *ordinal scale*, an admissible transformation is a strictly increasing function $x \mapsto \varphi(x)$, which changes the values of the scale while preserving their order. For example, the scale of air quality being used in a number of cities is an ordinal scale. It assigns a number 1 to unhealthy air, 2 to unsatisfactory air, 3 to acceptable air, 4 to good air, and 5 to excellent air. We could just as well use the numbers 1, 7, 8, 15, 23, or the numbers 1.2, 6.5, 8.7, 205.6, 750, or any numbers that preserve the order.

For more details on the theory of scale types, see Krantz *et al.* [238, 257] and Roberts [364, 365].

Luce's principle, called "principle of theory construction", is based on the requirement that admissible transformations of the input variables must lead to an admissible transformation of the output variable. For example, if the input variables are independent scales, then the function F should satisfy the following condition: For any admissible transformations $\boldsymbol{\varphi} = (\varphi_1, \ldots, \varphi_n)$ of the input variables, there is an admissible transformation $\psi_{\boldsymbol{\varphi}}$ of the output variable so that

$$\mathsf{F}\big(\varphi_1(x_1), \ldots, \varphi_n(x_n)\big) = \psi_{\boldsymbol{\varphi}}(x_{n+1}),$$

or, equivalently,

$$\mathsf{F}\big(\varphi_1(x_1), \ldots, \varphi_n(x_n)\big) = \psi_{\boldsymbol{\varphi}}\big(\mathsf{F}(x_1, \ldots, x_n)\big). \tag{2.13}$$

The solutions of this functional equation constitute the set of the possible functions which are "meaningful", in the sense that they do not depend upon the particular scales of measurement chosen for the variables, but only upon their scale types.

We can also assume that the input variables define the same scale, which implies that the same admissible transformation must be applied to all the input variables. In this case, the condition on F is the following: For any common admissible transformation φ of the input variables, there is an admissible transformation ψ_φ of the output variable so that

$$\mathsf{F}\big(\varphi(x_1), \ldots, \varphi(x_n)\big) = \psi_\varphi\big(\mathsf{F}(x_1, \ldots, x_n)\big). \tag{2.14}$$

Clearly, if a function solves (2.13) then it also solves (2.14).

In the extreme case where all the input and output variables define the same scale, then, for any admissible transformation φ of the input and output variables, we must have

$$F(\varphi(x_1), \ldots, \varphi(x_n)) = \varphi(F(x_1, \ldots, x_n)). \tag{2.15}$$

Equations (2.13)–(2.15) were completely solved in the 1980s for ratio scale variables, interval scale variables, and ordinal scale variables, even under some further assumptions such as symmetry, continuity, and nondecreasing monotonicity. A detailed account of the solutions of those equations is given in Chapters 7 and 8.

Example 2.85. If all the input variables are independent ratio scales and the output variable is also a ratio scale then the meaningful functions $F : [0, \infty[^n \to [0, \infty[$ are exactly the solutions of (2.13), where each admissible transformation is a multiplication by a positive constant. These solutions are given by (see Proposition 7.1)

$$F(x_1, \ldots, x_n) = a \prod_{i=1}^{n} f_i(x_i) \qquad (a > 0),$$

where the functions $f_i : [0, \infty[\to [0, \infty[$ fulfill the equations

$$f_i(x_i y_i) = f_i(x_i) f_i(y_i) \qquad (i = 1, \ldots, n).$$

Under continuity, these solutions are of the form

$$F(x_1, \ldots, x_n) = a \prod_{i=1}^{n} x_i^{c_i} \qquad (a > 0, \ c_1, \ldots, c_n \in \mathbb{R}).$$

In this section we present and rewrite the functional equations above when applied to the following scale types: ratio, difference, interval, log-ratio, and ordinal. The solutions of these equations will be presented and discussed in Chapters 7 and 8. It is noteworthy that these functional equations occur in the so-called *dimensional analysis*, where the general forms of "laws of sciences" are analyzed. The interested reader can find more details in [6, 12, 13].

2.4.1 Ratio, difference, interval, and log-ratio scales

Let us first start with the particular case where all the ratio scales are the same.

Definition 2.86. A function $F : \mathbb{I}^n \to \mathbb{R}$ is *ratio scale invariant* if, for any $r > 0$, we have

$$F(r\mathbf{x}) = r F(\mathbf{x})$$

for all $\mathbf{x} \in \mathbb{I}^n$ such that $r\mathbf{x} \in \mathbb{I}^n$.

Now, consider the same ratio scale for the independent variables and a ratio scale for the dependent variable.

Definition 2.87. A function $F : \mathbb{I}^n \to \mathbb{R}$ is *meaningful on a single ratio scale* if, for any $r > 0$, there exists $R(r) > 0$ such that

$$F(r\mathbf{x}) = R(r)\, F(\mathbf{x})$$

for all $\mathbf{x} \in \mathbb{I}^n$ such that $r\mathbf{x} \in \mathbb{I}^n$.

When the ratio scales are independent, we have the following definition.

Definition 2.88. A function $F : \mathbb{I}^n \to \mathbb{R}$ is *meaningful on independent ratio scales* if, for any $\mathbf{r} \in\,]0, \infty[^n$, there exists $R(\mathbf{r}) > 0$ such that

$$F(\mathbf{r}\mathbf{x}) = R(\mathbf{r})\, F(\mathbf{x})$$

for all $\mathbf{x} \in \mathbb{I}^n$ such that $\mathbf{r}\mathbf{x} \in \mathbb{I}^n$.

The functions that are ratio scale invariant are also called *stable for the same admissible similarity transformations, positively homogeneous,* or *homogeneous of degree one with respect to multiplication.*

Similarly for the difference scales, that is, the scales for which the admissible transformations are translations $\varphi(x) = x + s$, we have the following three definitions.

Definition 2.89. A function $F : \mathbb{I}^n \to \mathbb{R}$ is *difference scale invariant* if, for any $s \in \mathbb{R}$, we have

$$F(\mathbf{x} + s\mathbf{1}) = F(\mathbf{x}) + s$$

for all $\mathbf{x} \in \mathbb{I}^n$ such that $\mathbf{x} + s\mathbf{1} \in \mathbb{I}^n$.

Definition 2.90. A function $F : \mathbb{I}^n \to \mathbb{R}$ is *meaningful on a single difference scale* if, for any $s \in \mathbb{R}$, there exists $S(s) \in \mathbb{R}$ such that

$$F(\mathbf{x} + s\mathbf{1}) = F(\mathbf{x}) + S(s)$$

for all $\mathbf{x} \in \mathbb{I}^n$ such that $\mathbf{x} + s\mathbf{1} \in \mathbb{I}^n$.

Definition 2.91. A function $F : \mathbb{I}^n \to \mathbb{R}$ is *meaningful on independent difference scales* if, for any $\mathbf{s} \in \mathbb{R}^n$, there exists $S(\mathbf{s}) \in \mathbb{R}$ such that

$$F(\mathbf{x} + \mathbf{s}) = F(\mathbf{x}) + S(\mathbf{s})$$

for all $\mathbf{x} \in \mathbb{I}^n$ such that $\mathbf{x} + \mathbf{s} \in \mathbb{I}^n$.

The functions that are difference scale invariant are also called *shift-invariant, stable for the same admissible translations,* or *homogeneous of degree one with respect to addition.*

For the interval scales, we have the following definitions.

Definition 2.92. A function $F : \mathbb{I}^n \to \mathbb{R}$ is *interval scale invariant* if, for any $r > 0$ and any $s \in \mathbb{R}$, we have

$$F(r\mathbf{x} + s\mathbf{1}) = r\,F(\mathbf{x}) + s$$

for all $\mathbf{x} \in \mathbb{I}^n$ such that $r\mathbf{x} + s\mathbf{1} \in \mathbb{I}^n$.

Definition 2.93. A function $F : \mathbb{I}^n \to \mathbb{R}$ is *meaningful on a single interval scale* if, for any $r > 0$ and any $s \in \mathbb{R}$, there exists $R(r,s) > 0$ and $S(r,s) \in \mathbb{R}$ such that

$$F(r\mathbf{x} + s\mathbf{1}) = R(r,s)\,F(\mathbf{x}) + S(r,s)$$

for all $\mathbf{x} \in \mathbb{I}^n$ such that $r\mathbf{x} + s\mathbf{1} \in \mathbb{I}^n$.

Definition 2.94. A function $F : \mathbb{I}^n \to \mathbb{R}$ is *meaningful on independent interval scales* if, for any $\mathbf{r} \in]0, \infty[^n$ and any $\mathbf{s} \in \mathbb{R}^n$, there exists $R(\mathbf{r}, \mathbf{s}) > 0$ and $S(\mathbf{r}, \mathbf{s}) \in \mathbb{R}$ such that

$$F(\mathbf{rx} + \mathbf{s}) = R(\mathbf{r}, \mathbf{s})\,F(\mathbf{x}) + S(\mathbf{r}, \mathbf{s})$$

for all $\mathbf{x} \in \mathbb{I}^n$ such that $\mathbf{rx} + \mathbf{s} \in \mathbb{I}^n$.

The functions that are interval scale invariant are also called *stable for the same admissible positive affine transformations.*

By definition, a function $F : \mathbb{I}^n \to \mathbb{R}$ is interval scale invariant if and only if it is both ratio scale invariant and difference scale invariant. Moreover, we have the following straightforward result; see Marichal *et al.* [284, Prop. 3.2].

Proposition 2.95. *Assume* $0 \in \mathbb{I}$ *and let* $F : \mathbb{I}^n \to \mathbb{R}$ *be any function. If* F *is ratio scale invariant then* $F(\mathbf{0}) = 0$. *If* F *is interval scale invariant then it is idempotent.*

Proof. If F is ratio scale invariant then $F(\mathbf{0}) = F(r\mathbf{0}) = r F(\mathbf{0})$ for every $r > 0$ and hence $F(\mathbf{0}) = 0$. In particular, if F is interval scale invariant then, for any $s \in \mathbb{I}$, we have $F(s\mathbf{1}) = F(\mathbf{0}) + s = s$ and hence F is idempotent. $\qquad\square$

The following definitions concern log-ratio scales, which involve power transformations:

Definition 2.96. Assume $\mathbb{I} \subseteq [0, \infty]$. A function $F : \mathbb{I}^n \to [0, \infty]$ is *log-ratio scale invariant* if, for any $r > 0$, we have

$$F(\mathbf{x}^{r\mathbf{1}}) = F(\mathbf{x})^r$$

for all $\mathbf{x} \in \mathbb{I}^n$ such that $\mathbf{x}^{r\mathbf{1}} \in \mathbb{I}^n$.

Definition 2.97. Assume $\mathbb{I} \subseteq [0, \infty]$. A function $F : \mathbb{I}^n \to [0, \infty]$ is *meaningful on a single log-ratio scale* if, for any $r > 0$, there exists $R(r) > 0$ such that

$$F(\mathbf{x}^{r\mathbf{1}}) = F(\mathbf{x})^{R(r)}$$

for all $\mathbf{x} \in \mathbb{I}^n$ such that $\mathbf{x}^{r\mathbf{1}} \in \mathbb{I}^n$.

Definition 2.98. Assume $\mathbb{I} \subseteq [0, \infty]$. A function $\mathsf{F} : \mathbb{I}^n \to [0, \infty]$ is *meaningful on independent log-ratio scales* if, for any $\mathbf{r} \in]0, \infty[^n$, there exists $R(\mathbf{r}) > 0$ such that

$$\mathsf{F}(\mathbf{x}^{\mathbf{r}}) = \mathsf{F}(\mathbf{x})^{R(\mathbf{r})}$$

for all $\mathbf{x} \in \mathbb{I}^n$ such that $\mathbf{x}^{\mathbf{r}} \in \mathbb{I}^n$.

2.4.2 Ordinal scales

For ordinal scales, the admissible transformations of the independent and dependent variables are strictly increasing functions. However, we assume that the admissible transformations of the input variables are confined to the increasing bijections from $\mathbb{I}$ onto $\mathbb{I}$. This latter assumption, which brings no restriction to the solutions of the functional equations (2.13)–(2.15), enables us to consider closed domains $\mathbb{I}$ whose endpoints remain fixed under any admissible transformation.

Let $\Phi[\mathbb{I}]$ be the set of all increasing bijections of $\mathbb{I}$ onto itself and let $\Phi_n[\mathbb{I}]$ be the diagonal restriction of $\Phi[\mathbb{I}]^n$, that is

$$\Phi_n[\mathbb{I}] := \{(\varphi, \ldots, \varphi) \mid \varphi \in \Phi[\mathbb{I}]\}.$$

We consider the following three definitions.

Definition 2.99. $\mathsf{F} : \mathbb{I}^n \to \mathbb{I}$ is *ordinal scale invariant* if, for any $\varphi \in \Phi[\mathbb{I}]$, we have

$$\mathsf{F}(\varphi(x_1), \ldots, \varphi(x_n)) = \varphi(\mathsf{F}(x_1, \ldots, x_n))$$

for all $\mathbf{x} \in \mathbb{I}^n$.

Definition 2.100. $\mathsf{F} : \mathbb{I}^n \to \mathbb{R}$ is *comparison meaningful on a single ordinal scale* if, for any $\varphi \in \Phi_n[\mathbb{I}]$, there exists a strictly increasing function $\psi_\varphi : \mathrm{ran}(\mathsf{F}) \to \mathrm{ran}(\mathsf{F})$ such that

$$\mathsf{F}(\varphi(\mathbf{x})) = \psi_\varphi(\mathsf{F}(\mathbf{x}))$$

for all $\mathbf{x} \in \mathbb{I}^n$.

Definition 2.101. $\mathsf{F} : \mathbb{I}^n \to \mathbb{R}$ is *comparison meaningful on independent ordinal scales* if, for any $\varphi \in \Phi[\mathbb{I}]^n$, there exists a strictly increasing function $\psi_\varphi : \mathrm{ran}(\mathsf{F}) \to \mathrm{ran}(\mathsf{F})$ such that

$$\mathsf{F}(\varphi(\mathbf{x})) = \psi_\varphi(\mathsf{F}(\mathbf{x}))$$

for all $\mathbf{x} \in \mathbb{I}^n$.

The functions that are ordinal scale invariant are also called *invariant* in the literature [309].

The terminology "comparison meaningful function" is justified by the following results (see Marichal and Mesiar [285]):

Proposition 2.102. $\mathsf{F} : \mathbb{I}^n \to \mathbb{R}$ *is a comparison meaningful function on a single ordinal scale if and only if*

$$\mathsf{F}(\mathbf{x}) \leqslant \mathsf{F}(\mathbf{x}') \quad \Leftrightarrow \quad \mathsf{F}(\boldsymbol{\varphi}(\mathbf{x})) \leqslant \mathsf{F}(\boldsymbol{\varphi}(\mathbf{x}'))$$

for all $\mathbf{x}, \mathbf{x}' \in \mathbb{I}^n$ *and all* $\boldsymbol{\varphi} \in \Phi_n[\mathbb{I}]$.

Proof. $(\Rightarrow)$ Trivial.

$(\Leftarrow)$ Let $\boldsymbol{\varphi} \in \Phi_n[\mathbb{I}]$ and assume that $\mathsf{F} : \mathbb{I}^n \to \mathbb{R}$ is comparison meaningful on a single ordinal scale. For any $u \in \mathrm{ran}(\mathsf{F})$, there exists $\mathbf{x} \in \mathbb{I}^n$ such that $\mathsf{F}(\mathbf{x}) = u$. We then define $\psi_\varphi(u) = \mathsf{F}(\boldsymbol{\varphi}(\mathbf{x}))$. This function is strictly increasing since if $u, u' \in \mathrm{ran}(\mathsf{F})$, there exist $\mathbf{x}, \mathbf{x}' \in \mathbb{I}^n$ such that $u = \mathsf{F}(\mathbf{x})$ and $u' = \mathsf{F}(\mathbf{x}')$, and hence

$$u < u' \Leftrightarrow \mathsf{F}(\mathbf{x}) < \mathsf{F}(\mathbf{x}')$$
$$\Leftrightarrow \mathsf{F}(\boldsymbol{\varphi}(\mathbf{x})) < \mathsf{F}(\boldsymbol{\varphi}(\mathbf{x}'))$$
$$\Leftrightarrow \psi_\varphi(u) < \psi_\varphi(u'),$$

which completes the proof. $\qquad\qquad\qquad\qquad\qquad\qquad\qquad\qquad\qquad\qquad\square$

Proposition 2.103. $\mathsf{F} : \mathbb{I}^n \to \mathbb{R}$ *is a comparison meaningful function on independent ordinal scales if and only if*

$$\mathsf{F}(\mathbf{x}) \leqslant \mathsf{F}(\mathbf{x}') \quad \Leftrightarrow \quad \mathsf{F}(\boldsymbol{\varphi}(\mathbf{x})) \leqslant \mathsf{F}(\boldsymbol{\varphi}(\mathbf{x}'))$$

for all $\mathbf{x}, \mathbf{x}' \in \mathbb{I}^n$ *and all* $\boldsymbol{\varphi} \in \Phi[\mathbb{I}]^n$.

Proof. Similar to that of Proposition 2.102. $\qquad\qquad\qquad\qquad\qquad\qquad\qquad\square$

2.4.3 Inversion of scales

We now consider two stability properties related to the inversion of scales, namely: *self-duality* [391] (see a deeper study of this topic in Sections 6.2.2 and 6.2.3, also [136] for a recent study) and *self-reciprocality* [5, 7].

Definition 2.104. Let $\varphi : \mathbb{I} \to \mathbb{I}$ be a decreasing and involutive (i.e., $\varphi \circ \varphi = \mathrm{id}$) bijection.

- The φ-*dual* of a function $\mathsf{F} : \mathbb{I}^n \to \mathbb{I}$ is the function $\mathsf{F}_\varphi : \mathbb{I}^n \to \mathbb{I}$, defined by

$$\mathsf{F}_\varphi(\mathbf{x}) := \varphi^{-1}\big(\mathsf{F}(\varphi(x_1), \ldots, \varphi(x_n))\big).$$

- A function $\mathsf{F} : \mathbb{I}^n \to \mathbb{I}$ is said to be φ-*self-dual* if $\mathsf{F}_\varphi = \mathsf{F}$.
- A function $\mathsf{F} : \mathbb{I}^n \to \mathbb{I}$ is said to be *weakly self-dual* if it is φ-self-dual for some decreasing and involutive bijection $\varphi : \mathbb{I} \to \mathbb{I}$.

If $\mathbb{I}$ is bounded (which implies that $\mathbb{I}$ is either open or closed), then the only affine decreasing bijection from $\mathbb{I}$ onto itself is given by $\varphi^d(x) := \inf \mathbb{I} + \sup \mathbb{I} - x$, and φ^d-duality is then called *duality*, with notation $\mathsf{F}_{\varphi^d} =: \mathsf{F}^d$. A function $\mathsf{F} : \mathbb{I}^n \to \mathbb{I}$ is said to be *self-dual* if $\mathsf{F}^d = \mathsf{F}$.

In decision making, self-duality means that a reversal of the scale has no effect on the evaluation of alternatives. As observed by Dubois and Koning [91], if we assume that the alternatives are rated in terms of distaste intensities instead of preference intensities, then the overall distaste should be built from individual distastes with the same aggregation function as preferences. Indeed, distaste and preference are just a matter of naming the assessment criterion (choosing the good alternatives or choosing the bad ones) and the aggregation function should not depend on this name.

Remark 2.105. (i) By definition, for any function $\mathsf{F} : \mathbb{I}^n \to \mathbb{I}$ and any decreasing and involutive bijection $\varphi : \mathbb{I} \to \mathbb{I}$, we have $(\mathsf{F}_\varphi)_\varphi = \mathsf{F}$.

(ii) By definition, when $\mathbb{I} = [a, b]$ or $]a, b[$, with $a, b \in \mathbb{R}$, the dual of $\mathsf{F} : \mathbb{I}^n \to \mathbb{I}$ is the function $\mathsf{F}^d : \mathbb{I}^n \to \mathbb{I}$ defined by

$$\mathsf{F}^d(\mathbf{x}) = a + b - \mathsf{F}\big((a+b)\mathbf{1} - \mathbf{x}\big).$$

(iii) For a binary function $\mathsf{F} : [0, 1]^2 \to [0, 1]$, self-duality expresses the stability for the standard negation $x \mapsto 1 - x$ (compare with De Morgan laws in fuzzy set theory; see for instance Fodor and Roubens [119]). This condition can be extended by using any strong negation $f^{-1}(1 - f(x))$ instead of $1 - x$, where $f : [0, 1] \to [0, 1]$ is an increasing bijection; see Proposition 6.8.

Regarding scale invariance, we also have the following result; see Marichal *et al.* [284, Prop. 3.2].

Proposition 2.106. *If* $\mathsf{F} : [0, 1]^n \to \mathbb{R}$ *is ratio scale invariant and self-dual then it is interval scale invariant.*

Proof. Let $\mathbf{x} \in [0, 1]^n$ and $s \in [-1, 1]$ such that $\mathbf{x} + s\mathbf{1} \in [0, 1]^n$. We only need to prove that $\mathsf{F}(\mathbf{x} + s\mathbf{1}) = \mathsf{F}(\mathbf{x}) + s$.

By Proposition 2.95, we have $\mathsf{F}(\mathbf{0}) = 0$ and, by self-duality, we have $\mathsf{F}(\mathbf{1}) = 1 - \mathsf{F}(\mathbf{0}) = 1$. Therefore, we can assume that $s \in]-1, 1[$. Setting $\mathbf{y} = \frac{1}{1-s}\mathbf{x}$, we immediately see that $\mathbf{y} \in [0, 1]^n$ and, using ratio scale invariance and self-duality, we have

$$\mathsf{F}(\mathbf{x}) = (1 - s)\mathsf{F}(\mathbf{y})$$

$$= (1 - s)(1 - \mathsf{F}(\mathbf{1} - \mathbf{y})) = (1 - s) - (1 - s)\mathsf{F}(\mathbf{1} - \mathbf{y})$$

$$= (1 - s) - \mathsf{F}((1 - s)\mathbf{1} - \mathbf{x}) = 1 - s - \mathsf{F}(\mathbf{1} - (\mathbf{x} + s\mathbf{1}))$$

$$= -s + \mathsf{F}(\mathbf{x} + s\mathbf{1}),$$

which was to be proved. $\qquad\square$

Definition 2.107. Assume $\mathbb{I}$ is a real interval which with every element x contains also its reciprocal $1/x$. $\mathsf{F} : \mathbb{I}^n \to \mathbb{I}$ is *self-reciprocal* if

$$\mathsf{F}(1/x_1, \ldots, 1/x_n) = 1/\mathsf{F}(x_1, \ldots, x_n)$$

for all $\mathbf{x} \in \mathbb{I}^n$.

Let a and b be two objects about which the ratio judgements are made (for instance, how much heavier a is than b). If we interchange a and b, then reasonably the judgements change into their reciprocals (if a is judged to be twice as heavy as b, then b should be judged half as heavy as a). Self-reciprocality is that in this case also the aggregated judgement turns into its reciprocal.

2.5 Further properties

Some other specific properties of n-ary functions and extended functions, not mentioned in previous sections, have been investigated in the area of aggregation functions. We briefly recall some of them.

2.5.1 Neutral and annihilator elements

The neutral element is again a well-known notion coming from the area of binary operations. Recall that for a binary operation $*$ defined on a domain X, an element $e \in X$ is called a *neutral element* (of the operation $*$) if

$$x * e = e * x = x$$

for all $x \in X$. Clearly, any binary operation $*$ can have at most one neutral element. From the previous equalities we can see that the action of the neutral element of a binary operation has the same effect as its omission. This idea is the background of the general definition.

Definition 2.108. Let $\mathsf{F} : \cup_{n \in \mathbb{N}} \mathbb{I}^n \to \overline{\mathbb{R}}$ be an extended function. An element $e \in \mathbb{I}$ is called an *extended neutral element* of F if, for any $i \in [n]$ and any $\mathbf{x} \in \mathbb{I}^n$ such that $x_i = e$, then

$$\mathsf{F}(x_1, \ldots, x_n) = \mathsf{F}(x_1, \ldots, x_{i-1}, x_{i+1}, \ldots, x_n). \tag{2.16}$$

So the extended neutral element can be omitted from the input values without influencing the aggregated value. In multicriteria decision making, assigning a score equal to the extended neutral element (if it exists) to some criterion means that only the other criteria fulfillments are decisive for the overall evaluation.

For n-ary functions, there is an alternative approach, given in the following definition:

Definition 2.109. An element $e \in \mathbb{I}$ is called a *neutral element* of a function $\mathsf{F} : \mathbb{I}^n \to \overline{\mathbb{R}}$ if, for any $i \in [n]$ and any $x \in \mathbb{I}$, we have $\mathsf{F}(x_{\{i\}}e) = x$.

Clearly, if $e \in \mathbb{I}$ is an extended neutral element of an extended function F : $\cup_{n \in \mathbb{N}} \mathbb{I}^n \to \mathbb{I}$, with $\mathsf{F}^{(1)}(x) = x$, then e is a neutral element of all $\mathsf{F}^{(n)}$, $n \in \mathbb{N}$. For instance, $e = 0$ is an extended neutral element for the extended sum function Σ. Thus, it is also a neutral element for the n-ary sum function $\Sigma^{(n)}$.

Proposition 2.110. *Consider an aggregation function* $\mathsf{A} : \mathbb{I}^n \to \mathbb{I}$ *with neutral element* $e \in \mathbb{I}$. *Then* A *is conjunctive and* $b := \sup \mathbb{I} \in \mathbb{I}$ *if and only if* $e = b$. *Dually,* A *is disjunctive and* $a := \inf \mathbb{I} \in \mathbb{I}$ *if and only if* $e = a$.

Proof. We consider the case of a conjunctive function. The other case can be dealt with similarly. Assume A is conjunctive and $b := \sup \mathbb{I} \in \mathbb{I}$. Then, for any $i \in [n]$,

$$b = \mathsf{A}(b_{\{i\}}e) \leqslant \mathrm{Min}(b_{\{i\}}e) = e \leqslant b,$$

that is, $e = b$. The converse immediately follows from Proposition 2.51. □

Definition 2.111. An element $a \in \mathbb{I}$ is called an *annihilator element* of a function $\mathsf{F} : \mathbb{I}^n \to \overline{\mathbb{R}}$ if, for any $\mathbf{x} \in \mathbb{I}^n$ such that $a \in \{x_1, \ldots, x_n\}$, we have $\mathsf{F}(\mathbf{x}) = a$.

Proposition 2.112. *Consider an aggregation function* $\mathsf{A} : \mathbb{I}^n \to \mathbb{I}$. *If* A *is conjunctive and* $a := \inf \mathbb{I} \in \mathbb{I}$ *then* a *is an annihilator element. Dually, if* A *is disjunctive and* $b := \sup \mathbb{I} \in \mathbb{I}$ *then* b *is an annihilator element.*

Proof. We consider the case of a conjunctive function. The other case can be dealt with similarly. Let $\mathbf{x} \in \mathbb{I}^n$ such that $a \in \{x_1, \ldots, x_n\}$. Since A is conjunctive, we have

$$a \leqslant \mathsf{A}(\mathbf{x}) \leqslant \mathrm{Min}(\mathbf{x}) = a,$$

which proves the result. □

The converse of Proposition 2.112 is false. For instance, in $[0, 1]^n$, 0 is an annihilator of the geometric mean GM, which is not conjunctive.

Definition 2.113. Let $\mathsf{A} : \cup_{n \in \mathbb{N}} \mathbb{I}^n \to \overline{\mathbb{R}}$ be an extended aggregation function and denote by E_A (respectively, A_A) the set of extended neutral (respectively, annihilator) elements of A.

(i) A *trivial idempotent* element for A is an element of the set $(\{\inf \mathbb{I}, \sup \mathbb{I}\} \cap \mathbb{I}) \cup E_\mathsf{A} \cup A_\mathsf{A}$.

(ii) A is said to be *Archimedean* if, for each $x \in \mathbb{I}$,

$$\lim_{n \to \infty} \delta_{\mathsf{A}^{(n)}}(x) \in \{\inf \mathbb{I}, \sup \mathbb{I}\} \cup E_\mathsf{A} \cup A_\mathsf{A}.$$

Any $x \in \overline{\mathbb{R}}$ is an idempotent element for the arithmetic mean $\mathsf{AM} : \cup_{n \in \mathbb{N}} \overline{\mathbb{R}}^n \to \overline{\mathbb{R}}$. The only trivial idempotent elements are $-\infty$ and ∞.

2.5.2 Additivity and related properties

We now consider functions fulfilling certain functional equations of the form

$$F(x * x') = F(x) * F(x')$$

for all $x, x' \in \mathbb{I}^n$, where $*$ is a given associative operation ($x * x'$ is understood componentwise). We focus on the following special operations : $+, \wedge$, and $\vee$.

Definition 2.114. $F : \mathbb{I}^n \to \overline{\mathbb{R}}$ is *additive* if

$$F(x + x') = F(x) + F(x') \qquad (2.17)$$

for all $x, x' \in \mathbb{I}^n$ such that $x + x' \in \mathbb{I}^n$.

For unary functions, the functional equation (2.17) is known as the *Cauchy equation*. Under continuity or nondecreasing monotonicity, its solutions in $\mathbb{R}$ are exactly the linear functions; see Aczél [3, §2.1] and Thomson [410, §4.2].

Proposition 2.115. *Let $f : \mathbb{R} \to \mathbb{R}$ fulfill the basic Cauchy equation*

$$f(x + x') = f(x) + f(x'). \qquad (2.18)$$

Then either f is of the form $f(x) = cx$ for some $c \in \mathbb{R}$, or the graph of f is everywhere dense in $\mathbb{R}^2$. This latter possibility is excluded as soon as f has a point of continuity or is nondecreasing on some interval.

Proof. From (2.18), it follows by induction that

$$f(x_1 + \cdots + x_n) = f(x_1) + \cdots + f(x_n)$$

and so also that $f(nx) = nf(x)$ for all real x and all natural numbers n. This then extends to $f(\frac{m}{n}x) = \frac{m}{n}f(x)$ for all natural numbers m and n by writing

$$mf(x) = f(mx) = f\left(n\frac{m}{n}x\right) = nf\left(\frac{m}{n}x\right).$$

Thus $f(rx) = rf(x)$ for all positive rational r. For $r = 0$ the same identity holds because, by (2.18), $f(0 + 0) = f(0) + f(0)$ so $f(0) = 0$. Also for r negative we have again the same identity as the computation

$$0 = f(rx - rx) = f(rx) + f(-rx) = f(rx) + (-r)f(x)$$

shows.

Now, if f is not of the form $f(x) = cx$ for some $c \in \mathbb{R}$ then we may select nonzero numbers x_1 and x_2 so that $f(x_1)/x_1 \neq f(x_2)/x_2$. This can be interpreted as asserting that the vectors $(x_1, f(x_1))$ and $(x_2, f(x_2))$ are linearly independent in $\mathbb{R}^2$. Consequently the set of vectors

$$\{r_1(x_1, f(x_1)) + r_2(x_2, f(x_2)) \mid r_1, r_2 \in \mathbb{Q}\}$$

is dense in $\mathbb{R}^2$. But

$$r_1(x_1, f(x_1)) + r_2(x_2, f(x_2)) = (r_1 x_1 + r_2 x_2, f(r_1 x_1 + r_2 x_2))$$

is a point on the graph of f and so the graph must also be dense in $\mathbb{R}^2$, thus proving the first part of the statement.

Finally, it is clear that if f has a point of continuity or is nondecreasing on some interval then it cannot have a dense graph. $\qquad\square$

For n-ary functions, equation (2.17) is called the *generalized Cauchy equation*. Its solutions in $\mathbb{R}^n$ are given in the following proposition (see Aczél [3, §5.1]):

Proposition 2.116. $\mathsf{F} : \mathbb{R}^n \to \mathbb{R}$ *is additive if and only if there exist additive unary functions $f_i : \mathbb{R} \to \mathbb{R}$ $(i = 1, \ldots, n)$ such that, for all $\mathbf{x} \in \mathbb{R}^n$,*

$$\mathsf{F}(\mathbf{x}) = \sum_{i=1}^{n} f_i(x_i).$$

Under continuity (respectively, nondecreasing monotonicity) of each $\mathsf{F}(x1_{\{i\}})$, the function F is of the form

$$\mathsf{F}(\mathbf{x}) = \sum_{i=1}^{n} c_i x_i$$

for all $\mathbf{x} \in \mathbb{R}^n$, where $c_1, \ldots, c_n$ are arbitrary (respectively, nonnegative) real constants.

Proof. Let $\mathbf{x} \in \mathbb{R}^n$. Combining the identity $\mathbf{x} = \sum_{i=1}^{n} x_i 1_{\{i\}}$ with equation (2.17), we immediately obtain

$$\mathsf{F}(\mathbf{x}) = \sum_{i=1}^{n} \mathsf{F}(x1_{\{i\}}) = \sum_{i=1}^{n} f_i(x_i),$$

where each unary function $f_i(x) := \mathsf{F}(x1_{\{i\}})$ is additive. The second part follows from Proposition 2.115. $\qquad\square$

Definition 2.117. $\mathsf{F} : \mathbb{I}^n \to \overline{\mathbb{R}}$ is *minitive* if

$$\mathsf{F}(\mathbf{x} \wedge \mathbf{x}') = \mathsf{F}(\mathbf{x}) \wedge \mathsf{F}(\mathbf{x}')$$

for all $\mathbf{x}, \mathbf{x}' \in \mathbb{I}^n$.

It is noteworthy that nondecreasing unary functions $f : \mathbb{I} \to \overline{\mathbb{R}}$ are exactly the solutions of the functional equation $f(x \wedge x') = f(x) \wedge f(x')$. That is, the class of nondecreasing unary functions is identical to the class of minitive unary functions.

For n-ary functions in bounded closed intervals, we have the following description (see Dubois and Prade [99], and Marichal [267]).

Proposition 2.118. $\mathsf{F} : [a,b]^n \to \overline{\mathbb{R}}$ *is minitive if and only if there exist nondecreasing unary functions* $f_i : [a,b] \to \overline{\mathbb{R}}$ $(i = 1, \ldots, n)$ *such that*

$$\mathsf{F}(\mathbf{x}) = \bigwedge_{i \in [n]} f_i(x_i)$$

for all $\mathbf{x} \in [a,b]^n$.

Proof. ($\Rightarrow$) Let $\mathbf{x} \in [a,b]^n$. By minitivity, we have

$$\mathsf{F}(\mathbf{x}) = \bigwedge_{i \in [n]} \mathsf{F}((x_i)_{\{i\}}b) = \bigwedge_{i \in [n]} f_i(x_i),$$

where $f_i(x) = \mathsf{F}(x_{\{i\}}b)$. Moreover, for each $i \in [n]$, the function f_i is nondecreasing. Indeed, for any $x, x' \in [a,b]$, with $x \leqslant x'$, we have $f_i(x \wedge x') = f_i(x) \wedge f_i(x')$, which means that f_i is nondecreasing.

($\Leftarrow$) Trivial. $\square$

Definition 2.119. $\mathsf{F} : \mathbb{I}^n \to \overline{\mathbb{R}}$ is *maxitive* if

$$\mathsf{F}(\mathbf{x} \vee \mathbf{x}') = \mathsf{F}(\mathbf{x}) \vee \mathsf{F}(\mathbf{x}')$$

for all $\mathbf{x}, \mathbf{x}' \in \mathbb{I}^n$.

We can readily see that the class of nondecreasing unary functions identifies also with the class of maxitive unary functions. For n-ary functions in bounded closed intervals, we have the following description, which can be proved similarly to Proposition 2.118.

Proposition 2.120. $\mathsf{F} : [a,b]^n \to \overline{\mathbb{R}}$ *is maxitive if and only if there exist nondecreasing functions* $f_i : [a,b] \to \overline{\mathbb{R}}$ $(i = 1, \ldots, n)$ *such that*

$$\mathsf{F}(\mathbf{x}) = \bigvee_{i \in [n]} f_i(x_i)$$

for all $\mathbf{x} \in [a,b]^n$.

Weaker versions of minitivity and maxitivity have been introduced by Fodor and Roubens [120] as follows.

Definition 2.121. $\mathsf{F} : \mathbb{I}^n \to \mathbb{I}$ is $\wedge$-*homogeneous* if

$$\mathsf{F}(\mathbf{x} \wedge r\mathbf{1}) = \mathsf{F}(\mathbf{x}) \wedge r$$

for all $\mathbf{x} \in \mathbb{I}^n$ and all $r \in \mathbb{I}$.

Definition 2.122. $F : \mathbb{I}^n \to \mathbb{I}$ is $\vee$-*homogeneous* if

$$F(\mathbf{x} \vee r\mathbf{1}) = F(\mathbf{x}) \vee r$$

for all $\mathbf{x} \in \mathbb{I}^n$ and all $r \in \mathbb{I}$.

We now present the concept of *comonotonicity*, which appeared as early as 1952 in Hardy *et al.* [185]. In the context we are interested in, it is defined as follows:

Definition 2.123. Two vectors $\mathbf{x}, \mathbf{x}' \in \mathbb{I}^n$ are said to be *comonotonic* if there exists a permutation $\sigma \in \mathfrak{S}_{[n]}$ such that

$$x_{\sigma(1)} \leqslant \cdots \leqslant x_{\sigma(n)} \quad \text{and} \quad x'_{\sigma(1)} \leqslant \cdots \leqslant x'_{\sigma(n)}.$$

Thus the permutation σ orders the components of $\mathbf{x}$ and $\mathbf{x}'$ simultaneously. Another way to say that $\mathbf{x}$ and $\mathbf{x}'$ are comonotonic is that $(x_i - x_j)(x'_i - x'_j) \geqslant 0$ for every $i, j \in [n]$. Thus if $x_i < x_j$ for some i, j then $x'_i \leqslant x'_j$.

Definition 2.124. $F : \mathbb{I}^n \to \overline{\mathbb{R}}$ is *comonotonic additive* if

$$F(\mathbf{x} + \mathbf{x}') = F(\mathbf{x}) + F(\mathbf{x}')$$

for all comonotonic vectors $\mathbf{x}, \mathbf{x}' \in \mathbb{I}^n$ such that $\mathbf{x} + \mathbf{x}' \in \mathbb{I}^n$.

Definition 2.125. $F : \mathbb{I}^n \to \overline{\mathbb{R}}$ is *comonotonic minitive* if

$$F(\mathbf{x} \wedge \mathbf{x}') = F(\mathbf{x}) \wedge F(\mathbf{x}')$$

for all comonotonic vectors $\mathbf{x}, \mathbf{x}' \in \mathbb{I}^n$.

Definition 2.126. $F : \mathbb{I}^n \to \overline{\mathbb{R}}$ is *comonotonic maxitive* if

$$F(\mathbf{x} \vee \mathbf{x}') = F(\mathbf{x}) \vee F(\mathbf{x}')$$

for all comonotonic vectors $\mathbf{x}, \mathbf{x}' \in \mathbb{I}^n$.

The concept of comonotonic additivity appeared first in Dellacherie [80] and more recently in Schmeidler [380]. Comonotonic minitivity and maxitivity were introduced for the first time (in the context of fuzzy integrals) in de Campos *et al.* [78]. Note that a justification of these two latter properties has been given by Ralescu and Ralescu [360] in the framework of aggregation of fuzzy subsets.

A description of comonotonic maxitive functions in bounded closed intervals is given in the next proposition:

Proposition 2.127. *A function* $F : [a, b]^n \to [a, b]$ *is comonotonic maxitive if and only if there is a system* $M = (\xi_t)_{t \in [a,b]}$ *of nondecreasing set functions* $\xi_t : 2^{[n]} \to$

$[a, b]$ *such that* $\xi_t(\varnothing) = a$ *for all* $t \in [a, b]$, $\xi_a(K) = a$ *for all* $K \subseteq [n]$, *and* $\xi_b([n]) = b$, *satisfying*

$$F(\mathbf{x}) = \sup_{t \in [a,b]} \xi_t(\{i \in [n] \mid x_i \geqslant t\}).$$

Proof. ($\Leftarrow$) Follows from the fact that for any comonotonic vectors $\mathbf{x}$ and $\mathbf{y}$, we have

$$\xi_t(\{i \in [n] \mid x_i \vee y_i \geqslant t\}) = \xi_t(\{i \in [n] \mid x_i \geqslant t\}) \vee \xi_t(\{i \in [n] \mid y_i \geqslant t\}).$$

($\Rightarrow$) We observe that we can suppose with no loss of generality that $[a, b] = [0, 1]$. Then each vector $\mathbf{x} \in [0, 1]^n$ has comonotonic maxitive representation

$$\mathbf{x} = \bigvee_{j=1}^{n} x_j \mathbf{1}_{\{i \in [n] \mid x_i \geqslant x_j\}},$$

and thus for a comonotonic maxitive function F it follows that

$$F(\mathbf{x}) = \bigvee_{j=1}^{n} F(x_j \mathbf{1}_{\{i \in [n] \mid x_i \geqslant x_j\}}).$$

Now it is enough to set $\xi_t(K) = F(t\mathbf{1}_K) = F(t_K 0)$. $\qquad\square$

For comonotonic minitivity of F we can use similar arguments. The only difference is that the comonotonic minitive representation of $\mathbf{x}$ is now

$$\mathbf{x} = \bigwedge_{j=1}^{n} \left(x_j \mathbf{1} + (1 - x_j) \mathbf{1}_{\{i \in [n] \mid x_i > x_j\}} \right)$$

and we put $\xi_t(K) = F(t\mathbf{1} + (1 - t)\mathbf{1}_K) = F((1 - t)_K 1)$. Then (already on general $[a, b]$),

$$F(\mathbf{x}) = \inf_{t \in [a,b]} \xi_t(\{i \in [n] \mid x_i > t\}),$$

where ξ_t is a nondecreasing set function, $\xi_a(\varnothing) = a$, $\xi_t([n]) = b$ for all $t \in [a, b]$, and $\xi_b(K) = b$ for all $K \subseteq [n]$.

3

Conjunctive and disjunctive aggregation functions

In this chapter we discuss first a general approach to conjunctive and disjunctive aggregation functions, and then several important special classes of such functions. We work in this chapter on the unit interval, i.e., $\mathbb{I} = [0, 1]$ (when $[a, b]$ or some other interval is taken into account, it is always clearly stated). The main representative of conjunctive and disjunctive aggregation functions is undoubtedly the class of triangular norms and their dual operations, triangular conorms. We pay special attention to the class of copulas, especially 2-copulas, which are generally neither associative nor commutative, but if they are associative they are triangular norms. Finally, hybrid aggregation functions, which combine conjunctive and disjunctive aggregation functions, are discussed, especially uninorms and nullnorms.

More details on this area can be found in the books [15, 216, 220, 385].

3.1 Preliminaries and general notes

By Definition 2.49 (respectively, Definition 2.50) an aggregation function A is called conjunctive (respectively, disjunctive) whenever $0 \leqslant \mathsf{A} \leqslant \mathsf{Min}$ (respectively, $\mathsf{Max} \leqslant \mathsf{A} \leqslant 1$). Obviously, the smallest aggregation function $\mathsf{A}_\perp$, given by

$$\mathsf{A}_\perp(\mathbf{x}) := \begin{cases} 1 & \text{if } x_i = 1 \text{ for all } i \in [n] \\ 0 & \text{otherwise,} \end{cases}$$

is also the smallest conjunctive aggregation function, while Min is the greatest conjunctive aggregation function. Min is the only idempotent conjunctive aggregation function, since idempotency implies internality (Proposition 2.54). We summarize.

Proposition 3.1. *The smallest aggregation function $\mathsf{A}_\perp$ and Min are conjunctive aggregation functions. For any conjunctive aggregation function A,*

(i) $\mathsf{A}_\perp \leqslant \mathsf{A} \leqslant \mathsf{Min}$;
(ii) A is idempotent if and only if $\mathsf{A} = \mathsf{Min}$.

Though more explanation will be given in subsequent sections, we list here some distinguished classes of conjunctive aggregation functions.

56

Definition 3.2. Let $A : [0,1]^2 \to [0,1]$ be an aggregation function.

(i) A is a *boundary weak triangular norm* (*bwt-norm* for short) if it is an associative symmetric conjunctive aggregation function.

(ii) If A has a neutral element $e = 1$, then A is called a *conjunctor*.

(iii) A is a *triangular norm* (*t-norm* in short) if it is a bwt-norm and a conjunctor.

(iv) A is a *quasi-copula* if it is a conjunctive aggregation function and satisfies the Lipschitz condition with constant 1, i.e., such that for all $x, y, u, v, \in [0,1]$ we have

$$|A(x,y) - A(u,v)| \leqslant |x - u| + |y - v|.$$

(v) A is a *copula* if it is a conjunctor and fulfills the *moderate growth property*, i.e., such that for all $x, y, u, v \in [0,1]$, with $x \leqslant u$, $y \leqslant v$, we have

$$A(x,y) + A(u,v) \geqslant A(x,v) + A(u,y).$$

Remark 3.3. We have the following comments related to Definition 3.2 with the same numberings as in Definition 3.2.

(i) Bwt-norms were considered in [414, 415].

(ii) Conjunctors are known under several different names, e.g., semicopulas [108], weak t-norms [401], etc. We call these aggregation functions conjunctors following [303]. Conjunctors are conjunctive aggregation functions; see Proposition 2.110.

(iii) For more details see Section 3.3.

(iv) Quasi-copulas are special conjunctors, and they were considered in [138]; see also Section 3.4.4.

(v) For more details see Section 3.4. The class of copulas is a subclass of quasi-copulas.

Bwt-norms and t-norms are associative and thus their extension to extended aggregation functions is trivial, hence we keep the same name and notation for the binary and the extended bwt-norms and t-norms. An extended conjunctor is an extended aggregation function on $[0,1]$ with extended neutral element $e = 1$. Similarly, a 1-Lipschitzian conjunctive extended aggregation function is called a (extended) quasi-copula. Extended copulas are discussed in Section 3.4.

Remark 3.4. Each t-norm (quasi-copula) is a conjunctor. Moreover, each copula is 1-Lipschitzian and thus a quasi-copula; see Proposition 3.67(ii). Associative quasi-copulas are necessarily also copulas, and they are a special subclass of continuous t-norms (Proposition 3.83).

The relations between the preceding classes (and t-subnorms, which will be introduced later, and which are not aggregation functions, in general) of conjunctive binary aggregation functions are given in Figure 3.1.

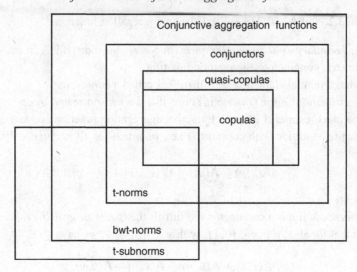

Figure 3.1 Relations between various particular binary conjunctive aggregation functions

Remark 3.5. Conjunctive aggregation functions on the interval $[a, b]$ necessarily have a as annihilator, and if they have neutral element e, then $e = b$. However, if $\mathbb{I} =]a, b[$, then a conjunctive aggregation function A can possess neither annihilator nor neutral element; see Propositions 2.110 and 2.112.

In the class of conjunctive aggregation functions, several construction methods discussed in Chapter 6 can be applied. For example, for any idempotent extended aggregation function A we have the following important result.

Proposition 3.6. *Let* A *be an idempotent extended aggregation function, and let for* $m \in \mathbb{N}, A_1, \ldots, A_m$ *be conjunctive extended aggregation functions. Then the composed extended aggregation function* $B : \cup_{n \in \mathbb{N}}[0, 1]^n \to [0, 1]$ *given by*

$$B(\mathbf{x}) = A(A_1(\mathbf{x}), \ldots, A_m(\mathbf{x}))$$

is a conjunctive extended aggregation function.

Proof. Based on Proposition 6.21, it is immediate that B is an extended aggregation function. To see its conjunctiveness, it is enough to apply Proposition 2.51. □

Remark 3.7. (i) Proposition 3.6 remains true also if we restrict the functions $A_1, \ldots, A_m$ to be conjunctors (and then also B is a conjunctor),

(ii) Proposition 3.6 does not hold for bwt-norms, t-norms, quasi-copulas nor copulas. However, it can be modified for quasi-copulas (see Section 3.4) by requiring A to have Chebyshev norm equal to 1, i.e., for all $n \in \mathbb{N}, \mathbf{x}, \mathbf{y} \in [0, 1]^n$,

$$|A(\mathbf{x}) - A(\mathbf{y})| \leqslant \|\mathbf{x} - \mathbf{y}\|_\infty.$$

Then B is a quasi-copula whenever all $A_1, \ldots, A_m$ are quasi-copulas. This holds also for copulas (supposing A to be a weighted arithmetic mean).

Another constructive result is based on the (isomorphic) transformation of aggregation functions.

Proposition 3.8. *Let φ be an increasing bijection from $[0, 1]$ onto $[0, 1]$ and let A be a conjunctive extended aggregation function. Then $A_\varphi : \cup_{n \in \mathbb{N}}[0, 1]^n \to [0, 1]$ given by*

$$A_\varphi(\mathbf{x}) = \varphi^{-1}(A(\varphi(x_1), \ldots, \varphi(x_n)))$$

(see Section 6.2) is a conjunctive extended aggregation function.

Proof. Similarly as in the proof of the previous proposition, from Proposition 6.1 we see that A_φ is an extended aggregation function, and Proposition 2.51 ensures its conjunctiveness.   □

For the sake of simplicity, we call the functions A and A_φ isomorphic (borrowing the algebraic terminology), and then φ is called the isomorphism between A and A_φ.

Remark 3.9.   (i) Proposition 3.8 remains true if we replace the conjunctive extended aggregation function by bwt-norms, t-norms or conjunctors. However, it fails for quasi-copulas and copulas, in general.

(ii) As another distinguished construction method preserving conjunctive aggregation functions we mention the conjunctive ordinal sum discussed in Section 6.7. Conjunctive ordinal sums (Section 6.7) preserve the class of all conjunctive aggregation functions, but also of all other mentioned distinguished subclasses.

(iii) For each binary conjunctive aggregation function $A^{(2)}$, its backward or forward extension to an aggregation function A (see Definition 2.65) is a conjunctive aggregation function. This is, e.g., the case of associative conjunctive aggregation functions, namely of bwt-norms and t-norms, but this claim is also true for functions like the binary aggregation function $A : [0, 1]^2 \to [0, 1]$ given by $A(x, y) = x^3 y$; then its ternary backward extension $A_* : [0, 1]^3 \to [0, 1]$ is given by $A_*(x, y, z) = A(x, A(y, z)) = x^3 y^3 z$, while its forward extension $A^* : [0, 1]^3 \to [0, 1]$ is given by $A^*(x, y, z) = x^9 y^3 z$.

(iv) Any nondecreasing function $F : [0, 1]^n \to [0, 1]$, bounded from above by Min, i.e., $F \leqslant$ Min, can be redefined to a conjunctive aggregation function $F^\sim$, simply by putting $F^\sim(\mathbf{1}) = 1$ and $F^\sim(\mathbf{x}) = F(\mathbf{x})$ in all other cases (so, for example, if F is identically zero, $F^\sim$ is just the smallest aggregation function, $F^\sim = A_\perp$). This redefinition preserves the symmetry, but it may violate the associativity of binary or extended F, in general.

3.2 Generated conjunctive aggregation functions

Several distinguished conjunctive (disjunctive) aggregation functions can be represented/constructed by means of additive/multiplicative generators; see Section 6.2

and [237]. Because of the equivalence of both types of generators, we discuss in this section additive generators only.

Formally, a generated aggregation function A can be defined as suggested in [237].

Definition 3.10. Let $\mathbb{I}$ be a given real interval and let a family

$$\mathfrak{F} = \left\{ (g_n, f_{1,n}, \ldots, f_{n,n}) \mid n \in \mathbb{N} \right\}$$

be given so that $f_{i,n} : \mathbb{I} \to [-\infty, \infty], i = 1, \ldots, n$, are nondecreasing (respectively, nonincreasing) functions,

$$g_n : \left\{ \sum_{i=1}^{n} u_i \mid u_i \in \mathrm{ran}\,(f_{i,n}) \right\} \to \mathbb{I}$$

are nondecreasing (respectively, nonincreasing) surjective functions, for all $n \in \mathbb{N}$, and $g_1 = f_{1,1}^{-1}$ (i.e., $f_{1,1}$ is strictly monotone). Then $\mathfrak{F}$ is called an *extended generating family* (EGS for short) on $\mathbb{I}$, and the extended function $A : \cup_{n \in \mathbb{N}} \mathbb{I}^n \to \mathbb{I}$ given by

$$A(\mathbf{x}) = g_n \left(\sum_{i=1}^{n} f_{i,n}(x_i) \right)$$

is called a *generated extended aggregation function*. All involved one-place functions are called *additive generators* of A.

The monotonicity of a generated extended aggregation function A follows from the same type of monotonicity of all involved additive generators, and this fact together with the surjectivity of the additive generators g_n, $n \in \mathbb{N}$, guarantees that the boundary conditions for an extended aggregation function are satisfied.

Lemma 3.11. *A generated extended aggregation function* $A : \cup_{n \in \mathbb{N}} [0, 1]^n \to [0, 1]$ *is conjunctive if and only if for all $n > 1, i \in [n]$ and $x \in [0, 1[$,*

$$g_n \left(\sum_{\substack{j=1 \\ j \neq i}}^{n} f_{j,n}(1) + f_{i,n}(x) \right) \leqslant x. \tag{3.1}$$

The above result is a direct consequence of Proposition 2.51.

Recall the convention for a closed subinterval $[a, b]$ of the extended interval $[-\infty, \infty]$, that sup $\varnothing = a$ and inf $\varnothing = b$. We shall need the following generalization of the notion of the inverse of a monotone function.

Definition 3.12. Let $[a, b]$ and $[c, d]$ be two closed subintervals of the extended interval $[-\infty, \infty]$, and let $f : [a, b] \to [c, d]$ be a monotone and nonconstant function.

Then the *pseudo-inverse* $f^{(-1)} : [c,d] \to [a,b]$ is defined by

$$f^{(-1)}(y) := \sup\{x \in [a,b] \mid (f(x) - y)(f(b) - f(a)) < 0\} \tag{3.2}$$

for all $y \in [c,d]$.

Remark 3.13. Under the suppositions of Definition 3.12 we have the following properties of pseudo-inverses of monotone functions.

(i) For a nondecreasing and nonconstant function $f : [a,b] \to [c,d], f(a) < f(b)$, and we have a simpler form for (3.2) given by

$$f^{(-1)}(y) = \sup\{x \in [a,b] \mid f(x) < y\}$$

for all $y \in [c,d]$. Moreover, $\left(f^{(-1)}\right)^{(-1)} = f$ if and only if f is left-continuous and $f(a) = c$.

(ii) Analogously, if $f : [a,b] \to [c,d]$ is a nonincreasing and nonconstant function, then $f(a) > f(b)$, and we have

$$f^{(-1)}(y) = \sup\{x \in [a,b] \mid f(x) > y\}$$

for all $y \in [c,d]$. Moreover, $\left(f^{(-1)}\right)^{(-1)} = f$ if and only if f is right-continuous and $f(b) = c$.

(iii) If f is a bijection, then its pseudo-inverse $f^{(-1)}$ coincides with its inverse function f^{-1}. This also holds in the opposite direction; if $f^{(-1)} = f^{-1}$, then f is a bijection.

(iv) The pseudo-inverse of f is continuous if and only if f is strictly monotone on the set $f^{(-1)}([c,d])$.

(v) If f is surjective then we have $f \circ f^{(-1)} = \mathrm{id}_{[c,d]}$.

We can describe the *geometrical construction* of the graph of the pseudo-inverse $f^{(-1)}$ of a nonconstant monotone function $f : [a,b] \to [c,d]$ in three steps:

(i) Complete the graph of f to be a continuous curve by drawing vertical line segments at discontinuities of f (Figure 3.2 (right)).

(ii) Reflect the resulting curve with respect to the line $y = x$ (Figure 3.3 (left)).

(iii) Delete any vertical line segment from the reflected graph except for its lower point (Figure 3.3 (right)).

For more details on pseudo-inverses (and even more general quasi-inverses) see [218, 220, 384, 389].

Going back to Definition 3.10 with the additional supposition that $\mathbb{I} = [0,1]$, suppose that there exists a decreasing function f such that $f(1) = 0$, and such that for all i, n we have $f_{i,n} = f$, and that there exists a decreasing nonnegative function g such that $g_n = g|_{\mathrm{ran}(g_n)}$ for all n. Then the greatest additively generated conjunctive

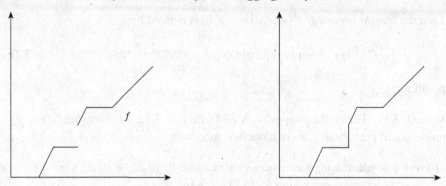

Figure 3.2 The function f (left), and the step (i) of the continuation (right)

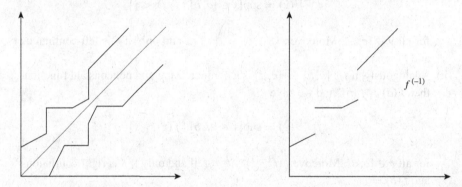

Figure 3.3 The step (ii) (left), and the step (iii) and the pseudo-inverse $f^{(-1)}$ (right)

aggregation function A related to f corresponds to the pseudo-inverse $g = f^{(-1)}$: $[0, \infty] \to [0, 1]$ (see [218]) given by

$$g(y) = \sup\{x \in [0, 1] \mid f(x) > y\}.$$

In such a case the conjunctive extended aggregation function A_f is given by

$$A_f(\mathbf{x}) = f^{(-1)}\Big(\sum_{i=1}^{n} f(x_i)\Big),\tag{3.3}$$

and it is called a generated conjunctor in [303]. Each generated conjunctor is symmetric and has a neutral element $e = 1$ (i.e., it is a symmetric conjunctor); however, A_f need not be associative, in general. One sufficient condition to ensure associativity of A is the relative closedness of $\text{ran}(f)$ under addition, i.e., for all $x, y \in [0, 1]$ we have $f(x) + f(y) \in \text{ran}(f)$ or $f(x) + f(y) > f(0+)$; see [220]. Some sufficient conditions to ensure associativity of A_f (which then necessarily becomes a t-norm) will be given in the next section. Associativity of A_f may be violated in two different ways: either $A_f^{(2)}$ is not associative, or $A_f^{(2)}$ is associative but A_f itself is not the genuine (the backward and forward extensions coincide in this associative case) extension of the corresponding binary function.

Example 3.14. (i) Let $f : [0, 1] \to [0, \infty]$ be given by

$$f(x) = \begin{cases} \dfrac{1}{x} & \text{if } x \leqslant 0.5 \\ 1 - x & \text{otherwise,} \end{cases}$$

then

$$f^{(-1)}(x) = \begin{cases} 1 - x & \text{if } x \leqslant 0.5 \\ 0.5 & \text{for } x \in [0.5, 2] \\ \dfrac{1}{x} & \text{otherwise,} \end{cases}$$

however, in this case $A_f^{(2)}$ is not associative. To see this, observe that $A_f(0.7, A_f(0.7, 0.9)) = 0.5$, while $A_f(A_f(0.7, 0.7), 0.9) = \frac{10}{21}$.

(ii) Following [420], let $f : [0, 1] \to [0, 2]$ be given by

$$f(x) = \begin{cases} 2 - x & \text{if } x < 0.5 \\ 1 - x & \text{otherwise.} \end{cases}$$

In this case $A_f^{(2)}$ is a t-norm, i.e., it is an associative binary conjunctive aggregation function, and 0.5 is its nontrivial idempotent element. Still $A_f^{(3)}$ is its genuine extension, but already $A_f^{(4)}$ is not. So, for example

$$A_f^{(4)}(0.5, 0.5, 0.5, 0.5) = f^{(-1)}(4f(0.5)) = f^{(-1)}(2) = 0,$$

while $A_f^{(2)}(A_f^{(3)}(0.5, 0.5, 0.5), 0.5) = 0.5$.

As already observed in Remark 3.9(iv), each nondecreasing function $A : [0, 1]^n \to [0, 1]$ bounded from above by Min, can be redefined to become a conjunctive aggregation function. This observation allows us to relax requirements on additively generated aggregation functions to become conjunctive aggregation functions.

Lemma 3.15. *For $n \in \mathbb{N}$, let $f_i : [0, 1] \to [-\infty, \infty], i = 1, \dots, n$, and*

$$g : \left\{ \sum_{i=1}^{n} u_i \,\middle|\, u_i \in \mathrm{ran}(f_i) \right\} \to [0, 1]$$

be nonincreasing functions such that (3.1) is fulfilled. Then the function $F : [0, 1]^n \to [0, 1]$ given by

$$F(\mathbf{x}) := \begin{cases} 1 & \text{if } \mathbf{x} = 1 \\ g\left(\displaystyle\sum_{i=1}^{n} f_i(x_i) \right) & \text{otherwise} \end{cases}$$

is a conjunctive aggregation function.

Proof. The nondecreasing monotonicity of F follows from the nondecreasing monotonicity of all involved functions $g, f_1, \ldots, f_n$. Due to Proposition 2.51 and Remark 3.9(iv), the function F is bounded by Min, i.e., $F(\mathbf{x}) \leqslant \text{Min}(\mathbf{x})$ for all $\mathbf{x} \in [0, 1]^n$, and it is an aggregation function.   □

Example 3.16. Let $n = 2$, $f_1 = f_2 = \text{id}_{[0,1]}$, and $g : [0, 2] \to [0, 1]$ be given by

$$g(x) := \begin{cases} 1 & \text{for } x = 2 \\ 0 & \text{otherwise.} \end{cases}$$

The function g is not a surjection, and thus does not fulfill the requirements of Lemma 3.11. However, we can apply Lemma 3.15 and the function F obtains the following form:

$$F(x, y) = g(f_1(x) + f_2(x)) = \begin{cases} 1 & \text{for } x = y = 1 \\ 0 & \text{otherwise,} \end{cases}$$

i.e., $F = A_\perp$.

We can replace the nondecreasing monotonicity in Lemma 3.15 by the nonincreasing monotonicity of all involved one-place functions, however, then the convention $\infty + (-\infty) = \infty$ should be applied.

3.3 Triangular norms and related conjunctive aggregation functions

The most important class of conjunctive aggregation functions are triangular norms (t-norms for short), i.e., conjunctors which are also bwt-norms. T-norms (in a more general form) were originally introduced by Menger as operators for the fusion of distribution functions needed by the triangle inequality generalization of a metric on statistical metric spaces. The present axioms of t-norms are due to Schweizer and Sklar [381–384], requiring associativity and neutral element $e = 1$. Associativity allows us to extend the triangle inequality to the polygonal inequality, using the fact that t-norms can be applied to any finite number of inputs. T-norms have become especially popular as models for fuzzy sets intersection; see [220, 255, 334]. They are applied also in probabilistic metric spaces, many-valued logic, nonadditive measures and integrals, etc. For more details on t-norms (and t-conorms) we recommend monographs [15, 220, 384, 385] and an edited volume [216]. Though the t-norms are the most typical (and most applied) class of conjunctive aggregation functions, we first discuss two more general classes of conjunctive aggregation functions, intersection of which is just the class of all t-norms.

Semicopulas were introduced in a binary form in [108]; however, while in binary form the class of semicopulas includes copulas and quasi-copulas, this is no longer true for $n > 2$, and thus we avoid the name semicopula for extended aggregation functions (see [401], where these operations were called weak t-norms; however, in current terminology in many-valued logics, weak t-norms are not symmetric). Thus to avoid confusion we use the name conjunctor from Definition 3.2(ii).

3.3.1 Conjunctors and bwt-norms

Definition 3.17. An extended aggregation function A is a *conjunctor* if it has an extended neutral element $e = 1$.

Any symmetric conjunctive aggregation function A can be redefined to be a symmetric conjunctor just by forcing 1 to be a neutral element; see [197, 220].

Lemma 3.18. *Let* A *be a symmetric conjunctive extended aggregation function. Then the function* $A^\#$ *given by*

$$A^\#(\mathbf{x}) := A(\mathbf{y})$$

is a conjunctor, where with the convention $A(\varnothing) = 1$, $\mathbf{y}$ *is obtained from* $\mathbf{x}$ *by deleting coordinates with value 1.*

If the conjunctive aggregation function is associative, so is the conjunctor $A^\#$. However, the continuity of A need not be preserved by redefining to $A^\#$.

Proposition 3.19. *The smallest conjunctor is the drastic product* T_D *(also the notation* Z *is commonly used) which is associative, symmetric (and thus a t-norm), and which is given by (see Figure 3.4 (left))*

$$T_D(\mathbf{x}) := \begin{cases} \text{Min}(\mathbf{x}) & \text{if } |\{i \in [n] \mid x_i < 1\}| < 2 \\ 0 & \text{otherwise.} \end{cases}$$

The greatest conjunctor is Min *(see Figure 3.4 (right)), i.e., for any conjunctor* A,

$$T_D \leqslant A \leqslant \text{Min}.$$

Moreover, a binary aggregation function A *is a conjunctor if and only if* $T_D \leqslant A \leqslant$ Min.

Proof. Both T_D and Min are conjunctors. Moreover, two conjunctors may differ on the set $\bigcup_{n \in \mathbb{N} \setminus \{1\}} [0, 1]^n$ only, and there its smallest possible value is 0, corresponding to T_D aggregation. Thus T_D is the smallest conjunctor. Now assuming $x \leqslant y$, we have

$$A(x, y) \leqslant A(x, 1) = x = \text{Min}(x, y)$$

(and similarly for the general case).

On the other hand, if for an aggregation function $A : [0, 1]^2 \to [0, 1]$ it is the case that $T_D \leqslant A \leqslant$ Min, then necessarily

$$T_D(x, 1) = x \leqslant A(x, 1) \leqslant \text{Min}(x, 1) = x,$$

i.e., $A(x, 1) = x$ for all $x \in [0, 1]$. Similarly, $A(1, x) = x$ for all $x \in [0, 1]$, i.e., A is a conjunctor. $\qquad \square$

A conjunctor need not be symmetric, in general.

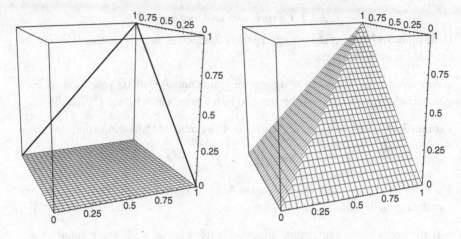

Figure 3.4 Two basic t-norms $\mathsf{T_D}$ (left) and Min (right)

Example 3.20. Let an extended aggregation function A in $\cup_{n \in \mathbb{N}}[0, 1]^n$ be given by

$$\mathsf{A}(\mathbf{x}) := \left(\prod_{i=1}^{n} x_i\right)\left(1 + \prod_{i=1}^{n}\left((x_i)^i(1 - x_i)\right)\right).$$

Then A is a continuous conjunctor which is not symmetric (A is a copula, see Definition 3.59, and thus 1-Lipschitzian).

Another special class of conjunctive aggregation functions is formed by bwt-norms, introduced in [414]; see Definition 3.2(i). As observed in [414], for any bwt-norm A, the function $v : [0, 1] \to [0, 1]$ given by $v(x) = \mathsf{A}(x, 1)$ (also $v(x) = \mathsf{A}(x, 1, \ldots, 1) = \mathsf{A}(1, \ldots, 1, x)$) is idempotent in the sense that $v(v(x)) = v(x)$ (and obviously $v(1) = 1$ and v is nondecreasing). Thus two typical types of bwt-norms are introduced from functions v with the just-mentioned properties:

(i) $\mathsf{A}(\mathbf{x}) = \mathsf{Min}(v(x_1), \ldots, v(x_n))$;
(ii) $\mathsf{A}(\mathbf{x}) = \mathsf{T_D}(v(x_1), \ldots, v(x_n))$.

Proposition 3.21. *The smallest bwt-norm is the smallest aggregation function* $\mathsf{A}_\perp$, *while the greatest bwt-norm is* Min, *i.e., for any bwt-norm* A,

$$\mathsf{A}_\perp \leqslant \mathsf{A} \leqslant \mathsf{Min}.$$

Proof. This follows from the symmetry and associativity of $\mathsf{A}_\perp$ and Min.   □

Bwt-norms as extended aggregation functions have a special type of monotonicity.

Proposition 3.22. *Let* A *be a (extended) bwt-norm. Then for all* $n \in \mathbb{N}, \mathbf{x} \in [0, 1]^n$ *and* $x_{n+1} \in [0, 1]$ *it follows that*

$$\mathsf{A}(\mathbf{x}) \geqslant \mathsf{A}(x_1, \ldots, x_n, x_{n+1}). \tag{3.4}$$

Proof. From the associativity of A we have

$$A(x_1, \ldots, x_n, x_{n+1}) = A(A(\mathbf{x}), x_{n+1}).$$

Then the conjunctiveness of A leads to

$$A(x_1, \ldots, x_n, x_{n+1}) \leqslant \text{Min}(A(\mathbf{x}), x_{n+1}) \leqslant A(\mathbf{x}). \qquad \square$$

Property (3.4) is called *downwards attitude* of A.

3.3.2 Basic t-norms

Definition 3.2(iii) gives us the binary t-norm $T^{(2)} : [0,1]^2 \to [0,1]$. Associativity of t-norms $T^{(2)} : [0,1]^2 \to [0,1]$ allows us to consider their extensions to n-ary functions $T^{(n)} : [0,1]^n \to [0,1]$ in the following way

$$T^{(n)}(\mathbf{x}) := T^{(2)}(T^{(n-1)}(x_1, \ldots, x_{n-1}), x_n).$$

So we can give the definition of a t-norm in extended form.

Definition 3.23. *An extended t-norm* $T : \bigcup_{n \in \mathbb{N}} [0,1]^n \to [0,1]$ *is an associative symmetric extended aggregation function with extended neutral element 1.*

Proposition 3.24. *(i) Each t-norm* T *is an aggregation function with annihilator 0, i.e.,* $T(\mathbf{x}) = 0$ *for all* $\mathbf{x} \in [0,1]^n$ *such that* $0 \in \{x_1, \ldots, x_n\}$.
(ii) The smallest t-norm is the drastic product T_D. *The greatest (and the only idempotent) t-norm is the standard* Min, *i.e., for any t-norm* T,

$$T_D \leqslant T \leqslant \text{Min}$$

(see Figure 3.4 for $n = 2$*).*

Proof. (i) Follows from the fact that each t-norm T is a conjunctive aggregation function, and Proposition 2.51.
(ii) It follows from monotonicity of t-norms that for any $(x, y) \in [0,1]^2$

$$T^{(2)}(x, y) \leqslant T^{(2)}(x, 1) = x \text{ and } T^{(2)}(x, y) \leqslant T^{(2)}(1, y) = y.$$

Hence $T \leqslant \text{Min}$. Trivially for any $(x, y) \in]0, 1[^2$ we have

$$T^{(2)}(x, y) \geqslant 0 = T_D^{(2)}(x, y).$$

Now, it is enough to apply Proposition 3.19 and take into account the associativity and symmetry of T_D and Min, i.e., that both T_D and Min are t-norms.

By Proposition 3.1 Min is the only idempotent conjunctive aggregation function, and therefore it is the only idempotent t-norm.

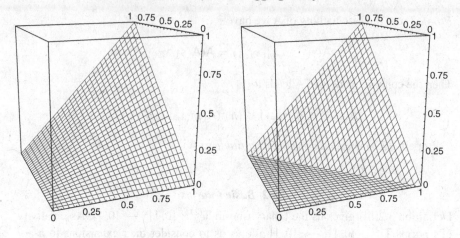

Figure 3.5 Two basic t-norms Π (left) and T_L (right)

$\Box$

Example 3.25. (i) The third basic t-norm is the product

$$\Pi(\mathbf{x}) = \prod_{i=1}^{n} x_i,$$

see Figure 3.5 (left) for $n = 2$.

(ii) The fourth basic t-norm is the *Łukasiewicz t-norm* T_L given by

$$T_L(\mathbf{x}) := \mathsf{Max}\left(0, \sum_{i=1}^{n} x_i - (n-1)\right), \tag{3.5}$$

see Figure 3.5 (right) for $n = 2$.

Definition 3.26. Let T be a t-norm.

(i) T has a *zero divisor* if there is an element $x \in \,]0, 1[$ such that for some $y \in \,]0, 1[$ we have $T(x, y) = 0$. Then both x, y are called zero divisors.

(ii) T is *strictly monotone* if for every $x \in \,]0, 1]$ and every $y, z \in [0, 1]$ such that $y < z$ we have $T(x, y) < T(x, z)$ (i.e., T is strictly increasing on $]0, 1]^2$).

(iii) T is *cancellative* if $T(x, y) = T(x, z)$ implies $x = 0$ or $y = z$.

It is easy to see that a t-norm is cancellative if and only if it is strictly monotone, and that a strictly monotone t-norm is always without zero divisors.

3.3.3 Families of t-norms

We list some important families of t-norms.

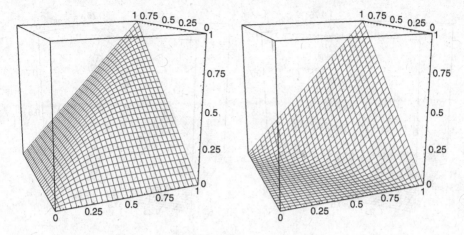

Figure 3.6 Elements of the family T_λ^F for $\lambda = 0.0001$ (left) and $\lambda = 10^6$ (right)

Example 3.27. (i) The family $(T_\lambda^F)_{\lambda \in [0,\infty]}$ of *Frank t-norms* [122] is given by (see Figure 3.6)

$$T_\lambda^F(x,y) = \begin{cases} \text{Min}(x,y) & \text{if } \lambda = 0 \\ \Pi(x,y) & \text{if } \lambda = 1 \\ T_L(x,y) & \text{if } \lambda = \infty \\ \log_\lambda\left(1 + \dfrac{(\lambda^x - 1)(\lambda^y - 1)}{\lambda - 1}\right) & \text{otherwise.} \end{cases}$$

(ii) The family $(T_\lambda^Y)_{\lambda \in [0,\infty]}$ of *Yager t-norms* [434] is given by (see Figure 3.7)

$$T_\lambda^Y(x,y) = \begin{cases} T_D(x,y) & \text{if } \lambda = 0 \\ \text{Min}(x,y) & \text{if } \lambda = \infty \\ \text{Max}\left(0, 1 - ((1-x)^\lambda + (1-y)^\lambda)^{\frac{1}{\lambda}}\right) & \text{otherwise.} \end{cases} \quad (3.6)$$

(iii) The family $(T_\lambda^{SW})_{\lambda \in [-1,\infty]}$ of *Sugeno–Weber t-norms* [404,428] is given by (see Figure 3.8)

$$T_\lambda^{SW}(x,y) = \begin{cases} T_D(x,y) & \text{if } \lambda = -1 \\ \Pi(x,y) & \text{if } \lambda = \infty \\ \text{Max}\left(0, \dfrac{x+y-1+\lambda xy}{1+\lambda}\right) & \text{otherwise.} \end{cases} \quad (3.7)$$

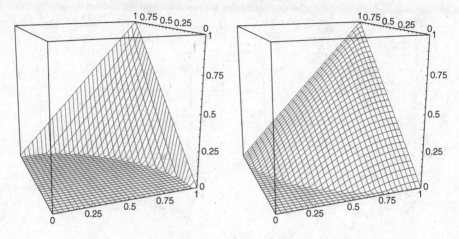

Figure 3.7 Elements of the family T_λ^Y for $\lambda = 0.6$ (left) and $\lambda = 2$ (right)

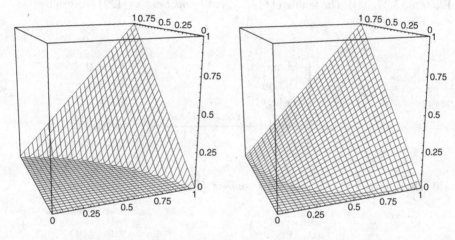

Figure 3.8 Elements of the family T_λ^{SW} for $\lambda = 0.6$ (left) and $\lambda = 2$ (right)

(iv) The family $(T_\lambda^H)_{\lambda \in [0,\infty]}$ of *Hamacher t-norms* [181] is given by (see Figure 3.9)

$$T_\lambda^H(x,y) = \begin{cases} T_D(x,y) & \text{if } \lambda = \infty \\ 0 & \text{if } \lambda = x = y = 0 \\ \dfrac{xy}{\lambda + (1-\lambda)(x+y-xy)} & \text{if } \lambda \in [0,\infty[\text{ and } (\lambda,x,y) \neq (0,0,0). \end{cases}$$

$$(3.8)$$

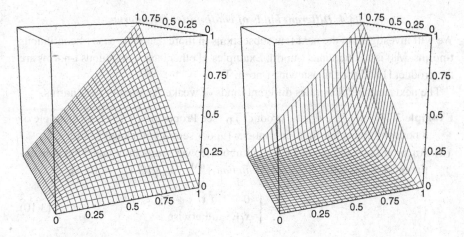

Figure 3.9 Elements of the family T_λ^H for $\lambda = 0.6$ (left) and $\lambda = 20$ (right)

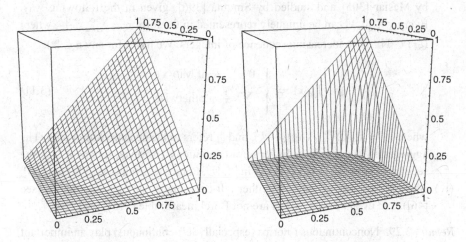

Figure 3.10 Elements of the family T_λ^{SS} for $\lambda = 0.6$ (left) and $\lambda = 4$ (right)

(v) The family $(T_\lambda^{SS})_{\lambda \in [-\infty, \infty]}$ of *Schweizer–Sklar t-norms* [382, 383] is given by (see Figure 3.10)

$$T_\lambda^{SS}(x, y) = \begin{cases} \text{Min}(x, y) & \text{if } \lambda = -\infty \\ \Pi(x, y) & \text{if } \lambda = 0 \\ T_D(x, y) & \text{if } \lambda = \infty \\ \left(\text{Max}\left(0, (x^\lambda + y^\lambda - 1)\right)\right)^{\frac{1}{\lambda}} & \text{if } \lambda \in]-\infty, 0[\cup]0, \infty[. \end{cases} \qquad (3.9)$$

3.3.4 Different kinds of continuities for t-norms

We will investigate in the next few subsections in more detail the case of continuous t-norms. Min is a continuous t-norm. Examples of other basic continuous t-norms are the product Π and the Łukasiewicz t-norm T_L.

The next example illustrates different kinds of weaker continuity for t-norms.

Example 3.28. (i) The drastic product T_D (see Proposition 3.19) is an example of a noncontinuous but right-continuous (upper semi-continuous) t-norm.

(ii) An important example of a left-continuous (lower semi-continuous) but noncontinuous t-norm is the *nilpotent minimum* $T^{nM} : \cup_{n \in \mathbb{N}}[0, 1]^n \to [0, 1]$,

$$T^{nM}(\mathbf{x}) := \begin{cases} 0 & \text{if } x_{(1)} + x_{(2)} \leqslant 1 \\ x_{(1)} & \text{otherwise,} \end{cases} \tag{3.10}$$

where $(x_{(1)}, \ldots, x_{(n)})$ is a nondecreasing permutation of $(x_1, \ldots, x_n)$.

(iii) An example of a peculiar noncontinuous t-norm is the function $T_\diamond : \cup_{n \in \mathbb{N}}[0, 1]^n \to [0, 1]$, initiated by Budinčević and Kurilić [46], introduced by Mesiar [305] and studied by Smutná [396], given in the following way. Every $x \in]0, 1]$ can be uniquely represented in the form $x = \sum_{k=1}^{\infty} \frac{1}{2^{\xi_k}}$, where $(\xi_k) \subset \mathbb{N}^{\mathbb{N}}$ is an increasing sequence of integers. We have (for any $n \in \mathbb{N}$):

$$T_\diamond(\mathbf{x}) := \begin{cases} 0 & \text{if Min}(\mathbf{x}) = 0 \\ \displaystyle\sum_{k=1}^{\infty} \frac{1}{2^{u_k}} & \text{otherwise,} \end{cases} \tag{3.11}$$

where $u_k = k + \sum_{i=1}^{n} ((\xi_i)_k - k)$, and ξ_i refers to the decomposition of x_i. The aggregation function $T_\diamond$ is lower semi-continuous. However, for any $n \geqslant 2$, the set of discontinuity points is dense in $[0, 1]^n$. For more details see [396] or [220].

(iv) There are t-norms which are neither left-continuous nor right-continuous (see [46]), and even t-norms which are not Borel measurable [213]; see [220].

Remark 3.29. Noncontinuous t-norms (especially left-continuous) play an important role in several applications. For example, the key role of left-continuous t-norms is in the theory of probabilistic metric spaces [176,384], in many-valued logic based on residuated lattices [178,220], the general theory of nonadditive measures [348,349], and in preference modeling [119].

3.3.5 Continuous Archimedean t-norms

An important subclass of continuous t-norms is the class of Archimedean t-norms, which have a powerful representation given in Theorem 3.36.

For $x_i = x$ for all $i \in [n]$ we shall use the following notation $x_T^{(n)} := T^{(n)}(n \cdot x)$. We take, by convention, for any $x \in [0, 1]$

$$x_T^{(0)} = 1 \quad \text{and} \quad x_T^{(1)} = x.$$

If a general t-norm T (even noncontinuous) is an Archimedean aggregation function, by Definition 2.113 we have $\lim_{n\to\infty} x_{\mathsf{T}}^{(n)} \in \{0, 1\}$, implying $\lim_{n\to\infty} x_{\mathsf{T}}^{(n)} = 0$, whenever $x < 1$. Thus it possesses only trivial idempotent elements 0 and 1. As a consequence, the Archimedean property of t-norms can be equivalently introduced in the following way.

Proposition 3.30. *For a t-norm T the following are equivalent:*

(i) For each $x, y \in]0, 1[$ there is an $n \in \mathbb{N}$ such that

$$x_{\mathsf{T}}^{(n)} < y. \tag{3.12}$$

(ii) T is Archimedean, i.e., for every $x \in]0, 1[$

$$\lim_{n\to\infty} x_{\mathsf{T}}^{(n)} = 0. \tag{3.13}$$

Proof. If T satisfies (i) then for every $x \in]0, 1[$ and every $\varepsilon > 0$ we have $0 \leqslant x_{\mathsf{T}}^{(n_0)} < \varepsilon$ for some $n_0 \in \mathbb{N}$. Therefore by Proposition 3.22 we obtain $0 \leqslant x_{\mathsf{T}}^{(n)} < \varepsilon$ for every $n \geqslant n_0$, which implies (3.13), i.e., (ii).

Suppose now that the t-norm T satisfies (ii), i.e., for every $x \in]0, 1[$ we have $\lim_{n\to\infty} x_{\mathsf{T}}^{(n)} = 0$. Then for every $y \in]0, 1[$ there exists a natural number n such that $x_{\mathsf{T}}^{(n)} < y$, which gives (i). $\qquad\square$

Remark 3.31. If a t-norm T has only trivial idempotent elements and it is right-continuous, then it is Archimedean; see [220].

Example 3.32. (i) The t-norms $\sqcap$ and $\mathsf{T_L}$ are Archimedean, but Min is not.
(ii) The t-norm $\mathsf{T_D}$ is Archimedean (since $x_{\mathsf{T_D}}^{(2)} = \mathsf{T_D}(x, x) = 0$ for all $x \in [0, 1[)$, although it is not continuous.
(iii) The t-norms $\mathsf{T^{nM}}$ and $\mathsf{T_\diamond}$ given in Example 3.28 are not Archimedean.

By Remark 3.31, for continuous t-norms, the fact that T has only trivial idempotent elements is also sufficient to ensure that T is Archimedean. Therefore, for continuous t-norms, Definition 2.113 can be relaxed in the following sense.

Proposition 3.33. *If a t-norm T is continuous, then it is Archimedean if and only if we have*

$$\mathsf{T}(x, x) < x \qquad \text{for each } x \in]0, 1[. \tag{3.14}$$

Proof. Suppose that T is a continuous Archimedean t-norm. If we had $\mathsf{T}(x, x) = x$ for some $x \in]0, 1[$, then it would be $x_{\mathsf{T}}^{(n)} = x$ for each $n \in \mathbb{N}$, which contradicts the fact that T is Archimedean.

Suppose that T satisfies (3.14) for each $x \in]0, 1[$. By monotonicity of T we have that for any $u \in]0, 1[$ the sequence $\left(u_{\mathsf{T}}^{(2^k)}\right)_{k\in\mathbb{N}}$ is nonincreasing, and therefore it converges to some $u_0 \leqslant u < 1$. It follows by continuity of T that

$$T(u_0, u_0) = \lim_{k \to \infty} T\left(u_T^{(2^k)}, u_T^{(2^k)}\right) = \lim_{k \to \infty} \left(u_T^{(2^k)}\right)_T^{(2)} = \lim_{k \to \infty} u_T^{(2^{k+1})} = u_0.$$

Hence by (3.14) $u_0 = 0$. Therefore by Proposition 3.30, the t-norm T is Archimedean. □

We show that continuous t-norms have nice representations. We start with the subclass of continuous Archimedean t-norms. For this representation of continuous t-norms T we extend powers $x_T^{(n)}$ to rational exponents.

Definition 3.34. For a continuous t-norm T the pseudo-inverse $f^{(-1)} : [0, 1] \to [0, 1]$ of the power function $f_n : [0, 1] \to [0, 1]$ given by $f_n(x) := x_T^{(n)}$ is the *nth root* with respect to T, denoted by $f_n^{(-1)}(x) =: x_T^{(\frac{1}{n})}$.

Proposition 3.35. *Let T be a continuous t-norm. Then the nth root functions have the following properties.*

(i) *Let $n \in \mathbb{N}$ and $x \in [0, 1]$. The nth root function is given by the following formula*

$$x_T^{(\frac{1}{n})} = \sup\{z \in [0, 1] \mid z_T^{(n)} < x\}.$$

(ii) *We have $\left(x_T^{(\frac{1}{n})}\right)_T^{(n)} = x$ for each $x \in [0, 1]$.*

(iii) *If we define*

$$x_T^{(\frac{m}{n})} := \left(x_T^{(\frac{1}{n})}\right)_T^{(m)},$$

then we have for $x \in [0, 1]$ and $m, n \in \mathbb{N}$ that $x_T^{(\frac{m}{n})} = x_T^{(\frac{km}{kn})}$ for every $k \in \mathbb{N}$, and for all $r, s \in \mathbb{Q} \cap]0, \infty[$ we have

$$x_T^{(r+s)} = T(x_T^{(r)}, x_T^{(s)}).$$

(iv) *If T is an Archimedean t-norm, then for all $x \in]0, 1]$, it follows that*

$$\lim_{n \to \infty} x_T^{(\frac{1}{n})} = 1.$$

Proof. (i) follows from the facts that the power function $f_n(x) = x_T^{(n)}$ is nondecreasing, $f_n(0) = 0$ and $f_n(1) = 1$.

(ii) follows from the fact that f_n is surjective and by Remark 3.13(v).

(iii) $x_T^{(\frac{m}{n})}$ is well defined since it is easy to check that

$$x_T^{(\frac{m}{n})} = \sup\{y_T^{(m)} \mid y \in [0,1], y_T^{(n)} < x\}$$
$$= \sup\{z_T^{(km)} \mid z \in [0,1], z_T^{(kn)} < x\}$$
$$= x_T^{(\frac{km}{kn})}$$

for every $k \in \mathbb{N}$.

We have for every $x \in [0,1]$ and $m, n, p, q \in \mathbb{N}$ that

$$x_T^{(\frac{m}{n} + \frac{p}{q})} = x_T^{(\frac{mq+np}{nq})}$$
$$= \left(x_T^{(\frac{1}{nq})}\right)_T^{(mq+np)}$$
$$= T\left(\left(x_T^{(\frac{1}{nq})}\right)_T^{(mq)}, \left(x_T^{(\frac{1}{nq})}\right)_T^{(np)}\right)$$
$$= T\left(x_T^{(\frac{m}{n})}, x_T^{(\frac{p}{q})}\right).$$

(iv) For the sequence $(f_n)_{n \in \mathbb{N}}$, where $f_n(x) := x_T^{(n)}$, the corresponding sequence of the pseudo-inverses $(f_n^{(-1)})_{n \in \mathbb{N}}$ is increasing. Hence for each $x \in [0,1]$, there exists the limit $\lim_{n \to \infty} x_T^{(\frac{1}{n})} = x_0$. If $x > 0$, then also $x_0 > 0$. Moreover, using arguments similar to those in the proof of Proposition 3.33, one can show that x_0 is an idempotent element of T. Since T is Archimedean, we obtain $x_0 = 1$. □

In Section 6.2 a construction by additive generators is given. We are using them for the following representation. Namely, continuous Archimedean t-norms can be characterized (and constructed) by means of the next representation theorem of Ling [246]; see [320].

Theorem 3.36. *An aggregation function* $T : \bigcup_{n \in \mathbb{N}}[0,1]^n \to [0,1]$ *is a continuous Archimedean t-norm if and only if there exists a continuous decreasing mapping* $t : [0,1] \to [0,\infty]$, $t(1) = 0$, *which is uniquely determined up to a positive multiplicative constant, such that*

$$T(\mathbf{x}) = t^{(-1)}\left(\sum_{i=1}^{n} t(x_i)\right). \tag{3.15}$$

Proof. Let $t : [0,1] \to [0,\infty]$ be a continuous decreasing function such that $t(1) = 0$, and let T be given by (3.15). Symmetry and monotonicity of T are obvious. Since 0 is a neutral element of the usual addition of reals, and $t(1) = 0$, from (3.15) we conclude that 1 is a neutral element of T.

Since for all $x, y, z \in [0, 1]$ we have

$$
\begin{aligned}
\mathsf{T}(\mathsf{T}(x,y),z) &= t^{-1}(\mathrm{Min}(t(\mathsf{T}(x,y)) + t(z), t(0))) \\
&= t^{-1}(\mathrm{Min}(\mathrm{Min}(t(x) + t(y), t(0)) + t(z), t(0))) \\
&= t^{-1}(\mathrm{Min}(t(x) + t(y) + t(z), t(0)) \\
&= t^{-1}(\mathrm{Min}(t(x) + \mathrm{Min}(t(y) + t(z), t(0)), t(0))) \\
&= t^{-1}(\mathrm{Min}(t(x) + t(\mathsf{T}(y,z)), t(0))) \\
&= \mathsf{T}(x, \mathsf{T}(y,z)),
\end{aligned}
$$

we conclude that $\mathsf{T}^{(2)}$ is an associative binary function, and therefore a t-norm. Moreover, the ternary extension of $\mathsf{T}^{(2)}$ is given, for $x, y, z \in [0, 1]$, by

$$
\begin{aligned}
\mathsf{T}^{(2)}(\mathsf{T}^{(2)}(x,y),z) &= t^{-1}(\mathrm{Min}(t \circ t^{-1}(\mathrm{Min}(t(x) + t(y), t(0)) + t(z), t(0)) \\
&= t^{-1}(\mathrm{Min}(t(x) + t(y), t(0)) + t(z), t(0))) \\
&= t^{-1}(t(x) + t(y) + t(z), t(0)) \\
&= \mathsf{T}^{(3)}(x,y,z).
\end{aligned}
$$

By induction it can be shown that the extended aggregation function related to the associative binary function $\mathsf{T}^{(2)}$ is exactly T, hence T is an extended t-norm.

To prove the converse, we suppose that T is a continuous Archimedean t-norm. We remark that if for some $x \in [0, 1]$ and some $n \in \mathbb{N}_0$, $x_{\mathsf{T}}^{(n)} = x_{\mathsf{T}}^{(n+1)}$ holds, then by induction we obtain

$$
x_{\mathsf{T}}^{(n)} = x_{\mathsf{T}}^{(2n)} = \left(x_{\mathsf{T}}^{(n)}\right)_{\mathsf{T}}^{(2)},
$$

and since T is a continuous Archimedean t-norm we have $x_{\mathsf{T}}^{(n)} \in \{0, 1\}$. Therefore we have always $x_{\mathsf{T}}^{(n)} > x_{\mathsf{T}}^{(n+1)}$ for $x_{\mathsf{T}}^{(n)} \in]0, 1[$.

Let $c \in]0, 1[$ be arbitrary but fixed. We denote $\mathbb{Q}^+ := \mathbb{Q} \cap [0, \infty[$. We define a function $h : \mathbb{Q}^+ \to [0, 1]$ with $h(r) = c_{\mathsf{T}}^{(r)}$. Since T is continuous and by Proposition 3.35(iv), we have that for every $r \in \mathbb{Q}^+$ the function h is continuous. On the other hand, since we have

$$
h(r + s) = c_{\mathsf{T}}^{(r+s)} = \mathsf{T}(c_{\mathsf{T}}^{(r)}, c_{\mathsf{T}}^{(s)}) \leqslant c_{\mathsf{T}}^{(r)} = h(r),
$$

we obtain that h is a nonincreasing function. It is decreasing on the interval $h^{-1}(]0, 1])$, since for every $\frac{m}{n}, \frac{p}{q} \in \mathbb{Q}^+$ such that $h(\frac{m}{n}) > 0$ we have

$$
h\left(\frac{m}{n} + \frac{p}{q}\right) \leqslant h\left(\frac{mq + 1}{nq}\right) = \left(c^{\left(\frac{1}{nq}\right)}\right)^{(mq+1)} < \left(c^{\left(\frac{1}{nq}\right)}\right)^{(mq)} = h\left(\frac{m}{n}\right).
$$

Using the monotonicity and continuity of the function h on $\mathbb{Q}^+$ we can uniquely extend it with the function $\overline{h} : [0, \infty] \to [0, 1]$ given by

$$\overline{h}(x) = \inf \left\{ h(r) \mid r \in \mathbb{Q}^+, r \leqslant x \right\}.$$

It is easy to check that $\overline{h}$ is a continuous and nonincreasing function and that

$$\overline{h}(x + y) = T(\overline{h}(x), \overline{h}(y)). \tag{3.16}$$

The function $\overline{h}$ is decreasing on the interval $\overline{h}^{-1}(]0, 1])$. We introduce the following function $t : [0, 1] \to [0, \infty]$ defined by

$$t(x) = \sup \left\{ y \in [0, \infty] \mid \overline{h}(y) > x \right\},$$

where $\sup \varnothing = 0$. By the definition it follows that t is a continuous, decreasing function such that $t(1) = 0$. We remark that $\overline{h}(x) = 0$ if and only if $x \geqslant t(0)$, and that for every $x \in [0, \infty]$ such that $\overline{h}(x) > 0$ we have $\overline{h}(x) = t^{-1}(x)$ (since the function $\overline{h}$ is decreasing on the interval $\overline{h}^{-1}(]0, 1])$). Therefore, for every $(x, y) \in [0, 1]^2$ we have by (3.16)

$$\begin{aligned}
T(x, y) &= T(\overline{h}(t(x)), \overline{h}(t(y))) \\
&= \overline{h}(t(x) + t(y)) \\
&= t^{-1}(\text{Min}(t(x) + t(y), t(0))).
\end{aligned}$$

Therefore (3.15) holds for every $x, y \in [0, 1]$.

We prove that two functions t_1 and t_2 which satisfy (3.15) differ only by a positive multiplicative constant. Let $t_1, t_2 : [0, 1] \to [0, \infty]$ be two continuous, decreasing functions with $t_1(1) = t_2(1) = 0$ and such that for every $x, y \in [0, 1]$,

$$t_1^{-1}(\text{Min}(t_1(x) + t_1(y), t_1(0))) = t_2^{-1}(\text{Min}(t_2(x) + t_2(y), t_2(0))).$$

Taking $u = t_2(x)$ and $v = t_2(y)$ we obtain that for every $u, v \in [0, t_2(0)]$,

$$t_2 \circ t_1^{-1}(\text{Min}(t_1 \circ t_2^{-1}(u) + t_1 \circ t_2^{-1}(v), t_1(0))) = \text{Min}(u + v, t_2(0)).$$

Introducing a continuous and increasing function $f : [0, t_2(0)] \to [0, \infty]$ by $f = t_1 \circ t_2^{-1}$, we obtain by the previous equality that for every $u, v \in [0, t_2(0)]$,

$$\text{Min}(f(u) + f(v), t_1(0)) = f(\text{Min}(u + v, t_2(0))).$$

Therefore by the continuity of the function f for every $u, v \in [0, t_2(0)]$ such that $u + v \in [0, t_2(0)]$ we have

$$f(u) + f(v) = f(u + v).$$

As is well known this is the Cauchy functional equation, whose only continuous and increasing solutions are of the form $f(u) = cu$ for every $u \in [0, t_2(0)]$ and some positive constant $c \in \mathbb{R}$. Therefore $t_1 = ct_2$. □

3.3.6 Additive generators of t-norms

The function t from Theorem 3.36 is called an *additive generator* of T, and it is unique up to a positive multiplicative constant (compare with the general Definition 3.10 of additive generator for an aggregation function).

Example 3.37. The product Π has additive generator $t_\Pi : [0, 1] \to [0, \infty]$, $t_\Pi(u) = -\log u$, while the Łukasiewicz t-norm T_L has additive generator $t_L : [0, 1] \to [0, 1]$, $t_L(u) = 1 - u$. The t-norm Min is continuous but not Archimedean, and it has no additive generator, see [18].

Definition 3.38. A continuous Archimedean t-norm with unbounded additive generator is called a *strict t-norm*. Nonstrict continuous Archimedean t-norms are called *nilpotent*.

Theorem 3.39. *The following holds.*

(i) *A strict t-norm is strictly monotone on $\bigcup_{n \in \mathbb{N}}]0, 1]^n$. All strict t-norms are mutually isomorphic, i.e., if T_1, T_2 are strict t-norms, then there exists a bijection $\varphi :$ $[0, 1] \to [0, 1]$ such that*

$$\varphi^{-1}(T_1(\varphi(x), \varphi(y))) = T_2(x, y).$$

A function $T : [0, 1]^2 \to [0, 1]$ is a strict t-norm if and only if it is isomorphic to the product Π.

(ii) *All nilpotent t-norms are mutually isomorphic, i.e., if T_1, T_2 are nilpotent t-norms, then there exists a bijection $\varphi : [0, 1] \to [0, 1]$ such that*

$$\varphi^{-1}(T_1(\varphi(x), \varphi(y))) = T_2(x, y).$$

A function $T : [0, 1]^2 \to [0, 1]$ is a nilpotent t-norm if and only if it is isomorphic to the Łukasiewicz t-norm T_L.

Proof. The first statement in (i) is a consequence of the strict monotonicity of the usual addition on $[0, \infty[$.

We prove now statements on isomorphisms in (i) and (ii). Let T_1 and T_2 be two strict or two nilpotent t-norms with continuous additive generators t_1 and t_2, respectively (with the property $t_1(0) = t_2(0)$). Then the function $\varphi : [0, 1] \to [0, 1]$ defined by $\varphi = t_1^{(-1)} \circ t_2$ is an isomorphism between T_1 and T_2.

The last statements in (i) and (ii) follow from the corresponding second statements and the fact that if t is a continuous additive generator of a t-norm T, then for any

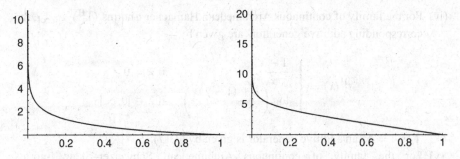

Figure 3.11 Additive generators of the family T_λ^F for $\lambda = 0.5$ (left) and $\lambda = 100$ (right)

increasing bijection $\varphi : [0, 1] \to [0, 1]$, the function $t_\varphi = t \circ \varphi$ is an additive generator of some continuous Archimedean t-norm, which is isomorphic to T. $\qquad\square$

The corresponding additive generators for the Archimedean members of families of t-norms from Example 3.27 are given in the following example.

Example 3.40. (i) A family of additive generators $(t_\lambda^F : [0, 1] \to [0, \infty])_{\lambda \in]0,\infty]}$ for the family $(T_\lambda^F)_{\lambda \in]0,\infty]}$ of Archimedean Frank t-norms is given by (see Figure 3.11)

$$t_\lambda^F(x) = \begin{cases} -\log x & \text{if } \lambda = 1 \\ 1 - x & \text{if } \lambda = \infty \\ -\log \dfrac{\lambda^x - 1}{\lambda - 1} & \text{otherwise.} \end{cases}$$

(ii) A family of additive generators $(t_\lambda^Y : [0, 1] \to [0, 1])_{\lambda \in]0,\infty[}$ for the family $(T_\lambda^Y)_{\lambda \in]0,\infty[}$ of continuous Archimedean Yager t-norms is given by

$$t_\lambda^Y(x) = (1 - x)^\lambda.$$

For $\lambda = 0$, an additive generator $t_0^Y : [0, 1] \to [0, 2]$ for the Archimedean (noncontinuous) t-norm $T_0^Y = T_D$ is given by (see [220])

$$t_D(x) = \begin{cases} 2 - x & \text{if } x \in [0, 1[\\ 0 & \text{if } x = 1. \end{cases} \tag{3.17}$$

(iii) For the family of continuous Archimedean Sugeno–Weber t-norms $(T_\lambda^{SW})_{\lambda \in]-1,\infty]}$, the corresponding additive generators are given by

$$t_\lambda^{SW}(x) = \begin{cases} 1 - x & \text{if } \lambda = 0 \\ -\log x & \text{if } \lambda = \infty \\ 1 - \dfrac{\log(1 + \lambda x)}{\log(1 + \lambda)} & \text{if } \lambda \in]-1, \infty[\setminus \{0\}. \end{cases}$$

For $\lambda = -1$ an additive generator is given by (3.17).

(iv) For the family of continuous Archimedean Hamacher t-norms $(T_\lambda^H)_{\lambda \in [0,\infty[}$, the corresponding additive generators are given by

$$t_\lambda^H(x) = \begin{cases} \dfrac{1-x}{x} & \text{if } \lambda = 0 \\ \log\left(\dfrac{\lambda + (1-\lambda)x}{x}\right) & \text{if } \lambda \in]0, \infty[. \end{cases}$$

For $\lambda = \infty$ an additive generator is given by (3.17).

(v) For the family of continuous Archimedean Schweizer–Sklar t-norms $(T_\lambda^{SS})_{\lambda \in]-\infty,\infty[}$, the corresponding additive generators $(t_\lambda^{SS} : [0,1] \to [0,\infty])_{\lambda \in]-\infty,\infty[}$ are given by

$$t_\lambda^{SS}(x) = \begin{cases} -\log x & \text{if } \lambda = 0 \\ \dfrac{1-x^\lambda}{\lambda} & \text{if } \lambda \in]-\infty, \infty[\setminus \{0\}. \end{cases}$$

For $\lambda = \infty$ an additive generator is given by (3.17).

Remark 3.41. (i) Noncontinuous or non-Archimedean t-norms may be generated by (necessarily) noncontinuous additive generators; see Example 3.14(ii) and (3.17).

(ii) Continuous Archimedean t-norms are related to the quasi-arithmetic means; see Section 4.2. Indeed, quasi-arithmetic means transform the arithmetic mean by a (additive) generator, while t-norms (continuous Archimedean) transform the addition (truncated addition); see (3.15). Therefore, several properties of quasi-arithmetic means are similar to the relevant properties of continuous Archimedean t-norms. For example, for two continuous Archimedean t-norms T_1 and T_2 with additive generators t_1 and t_2, respectively, we have $T_1 \leqslant T_2$ if and only if the composite function $h = t_1 \circ t_2^{-1} : [0, t_2(0)] \to [0, t_1(0)]$ is subadditive, that is,

$$h(u+v) \leqslant h(u) + h(v) \quad \text{for all } u, v, u+v \in [0, t_2(0)].$$

Put

$$h = t_L \circ t_\Pi^{-1} : [0, \infty] \to [0,1], \qquad h(u) = 1 - \exp(-u).$$

For all $u, v \in [0, \infty]$ we have

$$h(u+v) = 1 - \exp(-u-v) = 1 - \exp(-u)\exp(-v)$$
$$\leqslant 1 - \exp(-u) + 1 - \exp(-v) = h(u) + h(v),$$

that is, $T_L \leqslant \Pi$. Each continuous Archimedean t-norm T with an additive generator t can be idempotized by a method proposed by Calvo and Mesiar in [52], yielding a quasi-arithmetic mean M_t generated by t; see Section 4.2. Then

$M_{t_1} \leqslant M_{t_2}$ if and only if the composite function $h = t_1 \circ t_2^{-1} : [0, t_2(0)] \to [0, t_1(0)]$ is convex, compare also with Proposition 4.6. Observe that $h = t_L \circ t_\Pi^{-1}$ is concave, and its inverse $h^{-1} = t_\Pi \circ t_L^{-1}$ is convex, and thus

$$M_{t_\Pi} = GM \leqslant AM = M_{t_L}.$$

For practical use, often a parameterized family of t-norms is needed. Then the next result is of importance.

Proposition 3.42. *Let* $t : [0,1] \to [0, \infty]$ *be an additive generator of some continuous Archimedean t-norm* T. *Then for all* $\lambda \in]0, \infty[$, t^λ *also generates a continuous Archimedean t-norm* $T_{(\lambda)}$. *The family* $(T_{(\lambda)})_{\lambda \in]0, \infty[}$ *is increasing and*

$$\lim_{\lambda \to \infty} T_{(\lambda)} = T_{(\infty)} = \text{Min}$$

uniformly,

$$\lim_{\lambda \to 0^+} T_{(\lambda)} = T_{(0)} = T_D$$

pointwisely.

As we can see, the limit members $T_{(\infty)}$ and $T_{(0)}$ of the family $(T_{(\lambda)})_{\lambda \in]0, \infty[}$ are independent of the original additive generator t, or, equivalently, of $T = T_{(1)}$. Several well-known families are constructed by means of Proposition 3.42.

Example 3.43. (i) The Yager family $(T_\lambda^Y)_{\lambda \in]0, \infty[}$ is related to the Łukasiewicz t-norm $T_L = T_1^Y$, and $t_\lambda^Y(x) = (1-x)^\lambda = (t_L(x))^\lambda$.

(ii) Starting from the product Π, we obtain the Aczél–Alsina family $(T_\lambda^{AA})_{\lambda \in]0, \infty[}$, with additive generators $t_\lambda^{AA}(x) = (t_\Pi(x))^\lambda = (-\log x)^\lambda$.

Remark 3.44. Let $t : [0,1] \to [0, \infty]$ be an additive generator of the t-norm T. Then the function $\theta : [0,1] \to [0,1]$ defined by $\theta(x) := e^{-t(x)}$ is the *multiplicative generator* of T since it satisfies for all $x, y \in [0,1]$ the following equality:

$$T(x,y) = \theta^{(-1)}(\theta(x)\theta(y)).$$

3.3.7 Ordinal sums of t-norms and representation of continuous t-norms

The following construction (see Section 6.7) of a t-norm by a family of general t-norms comes from algebra; see [63, 64, 126, 220].

Definition 3.45. Let $(T_k)_{k \in K}$ be a family of t-norms and $(]a_k, b_k[)_{k \in K}$ be a family of nonempty, pairwise disjoint open subintervals of $[0,1]$. The extended function

$\mathsf{T}: \cup_{n \in \mathbb{N}}[0,1]^n \to [0,1]$ defined by

$$\mathsf{T}(\mathbf{x}) := \begin{cases} a_k + (b_k - a_k)\mathsf{T}_k \left(\dfrac{\mathrm{Min}(x_1, b_k) - a_k}{b_k - a_k}, \ldots, \dfrac{\mathrm{Min}(x_n, b_k) - a_k}{b_k - a_k} \right) \\ \qquad\qquad\qquad\qquad\qquad\qquad\qquad \text{if } \mathrm{Min}(\mathbf{x}) \in \,]a_k, b_k[\\[2ex] \mathrm{Min}(\mathbf{x}) \qquad\qquad\qquad\qquad\qquad\qquad\qquad\quad \text{otherwise} \end{cases}$$

(3.18)

is called the *(t-norm) ordinal sum* of summands $< a_k, b_k, \mathsf{T}_k >, k \in K$, and we denote it by

$$\mathsf{T} = (< a_k, b_k, \mathsf{T}_k >)_{k \in K}.$$

Theorem 3.46. *The (t-norm) ordinal sum* $(< a_k, b_k, \mathsf{T}_k >)_{k \in K}$ *from Definition 3.45 given by (3.18) is a t-norm.*

Proof. We prove that the function $\mathsf{T}^{(2)}$ defined by (3.18) is a t-norm (with no confusion we use the notation T instead of $\mathsf{T}^{(2)}$). It is obvious that T defined by (3.18) is symmetric and has 1 as a neutral element. We prove the monotonicity of T. For that, it is enough to prove the monotonicity of the function $\mathsf{T}(x, \cdot) : [0,1] \to [0,1]$ for every $x \in [0,1]$.

If $x \notin \cup_{\alpha \in K} \,]a_k, b_k[$, then for every $y \in [0,1]$ it follows $\mathsf{T}(x, y) = \mathrm{Min}(x, y)$, which implies that $\mathsf{T}(x, \cdot)$ is monotone. If $x \in \,]a_{k_0}, b_{k_0}[$ for some $k_0 \in K$ then we have (φ_k is the affine increasing bijection of the interval $[a_k, b_k]$ on the interval $[0,1]$, defined by $\varphi_k(u) := \frac{u - a_k}{b_k - a_k}$)

$$\mathsf{T}(x, y) = \begin{cases} y & \text{for } y \in [0, a_{k_0}] \\ \varphi_{k_0}^{-1}(\mathsf{T}_{k_0}(\varphi_{k_0}(x), \varphi_{k_0}(y))) & \text{for } y \in \,]a_{k_0}, b_{k_0}[\\ x & \text{for } y \in [b_{k_0}, 1]. \end{cases}$$

Since we have for every $y \in \,]a_{k_0}, b_{k_0}[$

$$a_{k_0} = \varphi_{k_0}^{-1}(0) \leqslant \mathsf{T}(x, y) \leqslant \varphi_{k_0}^{-1}(\mathrm{Min}(\varphi_{k_0}(x), \varphi_{k_0}(y))) \leqslant x,$$

then the monotonicity of T_{k_0} implies the monotonicity of $\mathsf{T}(x, \cdot)$.

By the boundary condition for T_k it follows that $\mathsf{T}(x, y) = \varphi_k^{-1}(\mathsf{T}_k(\varphi_k(x), \varphi_k(y)))$ for every $(x, y) \in [a_k, b_k]^2$.

To prove the associativity of T, we have to consider four cases for $x, y, z \in [0,1]$.

(i) Let $x, y, z \in [a_{k_0}, b_{k_0}]$ for some $k_0 \in K$. Then by the associativity of T_{k_0} it follows that

$$\mathsf{T}(x, \mathsf{T}(y, z)) = \varphi_{k_0}^{-1}\left(\mathsf{T}_{k_0}(\varphi_{k_0}(x), \mathsf{T}_{k_0}(\varphi_{k_0}(y), \varphi_{k_0}(z))) \right)$$

$$= \varphi_{k_0}^{-1}\left(\mathsf{T}_{k_0}(\mathsf{T}_{k_0}(\varphi_{k_0}(x), \varphi_{k_0}(y)), \varphi_{k_0}(z)) \right)$$

$$= \mathsf{T}(\mathsf{T}(x, y), z).$$

(ii) Let $x, z \in [a_{k_0}, b_{k_0}]$ and $y \notin [a_{k_0}, b_{k_0}]$ for some $k_0 \in K$. Then we have

$$
\begin{aligned}
\mathsf{T}(x, \mathsf{T}(y, z)) &= \mathsf{T}(x, \mathrm{Min}(y, z)) \\
&= \mathrm{Min}(\mathsf{T}(x, y), \mathsf{T}(x, z)) \\
&= \mathrm{Min}(\mathrm{Min}(x, y), \mathsf{T}(x, z)) \\
&= \mathrm{Min}(y, \mathsf{T}(x, z)) \\
&= \mathrm{Min}(\mathrm{Min}(y, z), \mathsf{T}(x, z)) \\
&= \mathrm{Min}(\mathsf{T}(y, z), \mathsf{T}(x, z)) \\
&= \mathsf{T}(\mathrm{Min}(x, y), z) \\
&= \mathsf{T}(\mathsf{T}(x, y), z),
\end{aligned}
$$

by monotonicity of T, and the fact that for $y < a_{k_0}$ we have $\mathrm{Min}(x, y) = y$ and for $y > b_{k_0}$ we have $\mathrm{Min}(y, \mathsf{T}(x, z)) = \mathsf{T}(x, z)$.

(iii) Let $(x, y \in [a_{k_0}, b_{k_0}]$ and $z \notin [a_{k_0}, b_{k_0}])$ or $(y, z \in [a_{k_0}, b_{k_0}]$ and $x \notin [a_{k_0}, b_{k_0}])$ for some $k_0 \in K$. Analogously to (ii) we obtain

$$
\mathsf{T}(x, \mathsf{T}(y, z)) = \mathsf{T}(\mathsf{T}(x, y), z).
$$

(iv) For all other cases we have

$$
\mathsf{T}(x, \mathsf{T}(y, z)) = \mathrm{Min}(x, y, z) = \mathsf{T}(\mathsf{T}(x, y), z).
$$

Therefore it follows that T as a binary function is a t-norm. We have to show that the extended aggregation function $\mathsf{T} : \cup_{n \in \mathbb{N}} [0, 1]^n \to [0, 1]$ is the genuine extension of its binary associative form $\mathsf{T}^{(2)}$. Suppose that $\mathsf{T}^{(n)}$ given by (3.18) is the n-ary extension of $\mathsf{T}^{(2)}$. Then the $(n+1)$-ary extension of $\mathsf{T}^{(2)}$ applied to $(x_1, \ldots, x_n, x_{n+1}) \in [0, 1]^{n+1}$ is given by $\mathsf{T}^{(2)}(\mathsf{T}^{(n)}(x_1, \ldots, x_n), x_{n+1})$. If there is $k \in K$ such that both $\mathrm{Min}(x_1, \ldots, x_n), \mathrm{Min}(x_1, \ldots, x_{n+1}) \in \,]a_k, b_k[$, then we have

$$
\begin{aligned}
&\mathsf{T}^{(2)}(\mathsf{T}^{(n)}(x_1, \ldots, x_n), x_{n+1}) \\
&= a_k + (b_k - a_k)\mathsf{T}_k\left(\frac{\mathrm{Min}(x_1, b_k) - a_k}{b_k - a_k}, \ldots, \frac{\mathrm{Min}(x_{n+1}, b_k) - a_k}{b_k - a_k}\right) \\
&= \mathsf{T}^{(n+1)}(x_1, \ldots, x_{n+1}).
\end{aligned}
$$

If $\mathrm{Min}(x_1, \ldots, x_{n+1}) \in \,]a_k, b_k[$, but $\mathrm{Min}(x_1, \ldots, x_n) \notin \,]a_k, b_k[$, then due to (3.18) we have $\mathsf{T}^{(n)}(x_1, \ldots, x_n) \geqslant b_k$ and $x_1, \ldots, x_n > b_k$, and then

$$
\mathsf{T}^{(2)}(\mathsf{T}^{(n)}(x_1, \ldots, x_n), x_{n+1}) = x_{n+1} = \mathsf{T}^{(n+1)}(x_1, \ldots, x_{n+1}).
$$

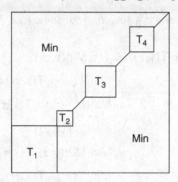

Figure 3.12 The representation of a binary form of an ordinal sum
t-norm with four summands

Similarly, if $\mathsf{Min}(x_1,\ldots,x_{n+1}) \notin \cup_{k \in K}\,]a_k,b_k[$ one can show that

$$\mathsf{T}^{(2)}(\mathsf{T}^{(n)}(x_1,\ldots,x_n),x_{n+1}) = \mathsf{Min}(x_1,\ldots,x_{n+1}) = \mathsf{T}^{(n+1)}(x_1,\ldots,x_{n+1}).$$

By induction, the proof is complete. □

An illustration of a t-norm which is an ordinal sum with four summands is given in Figure 3.12.

Example 3.47. We consider the following ordinal sum

$$(< 1/30, 11/30, \mathsf{T_L} >, < 13/30, 28/30, \mathsf{T_L} >)$$

of two summands; see Figure 3.13.

Corollary 3.48. *Let us consider a (t-norm) ordinal sum $(< a_k,b_k,\mathsf{T}_k >)_{k \in K}$ from Definition 3.45, and suppose that each t-norm $\mathsf{T}_k, k \in K$, has a continuous additive generator $t_k : [0,1] \to [0,\infty]$. Then we have*

$$\mathsf{T}(\mathbf{x}) = \begin{cases} f_k^{-1}\left(\mathsf{Min}(f_k(a_k), \sum_{i=1}^{n} f_k(\mathsf{Min}(x_i,b_k)))\right) & \text{if } \mathsf{Min}(\mathbf{x}) \in \,]a_k,b_k[\\ \mathsf{Min}(\mathbf{x}) & \text{otherwise,} \end{cases} \quad (3.19)$$

where $f_k : [a_k,b_k] \to [0,\infty]$ is given by $f_k(x) := t_k\left(\frac{x-a_k}{b_k-a_k}\right)$.

Based on the statements above, we have the next important representation theorem for a general continuous t-norm T; see [220].

Theorem 3.49. *A function $\mathsf{T} : \cup_{n \in \mathbb{N}}[0,1]^n \to [0,1]$ is a continuous t-norm if and only if it is an ordinal sum of continuous Archimedean t-norms, i.e., there exists a*

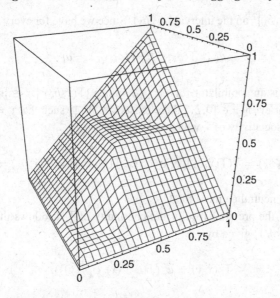

Figure 3.13 Ordinal sum of t-norms from Example 3.47

family $(T_k)_{k \in K}$ *of continuous Archimedean t-norms and of pairwise disjoint nonempty intervals* $]a_k, b_k[, k \in K$, *such that*

$$T = (< a_k, b_k, T_k >)_{k \in K}.$$

Proof. ($\Leftarrow$) If $(T_k)_{k \in K}$ is a family of continuous Archimedean t-norms, then by Theorem 3.46, $T = (< a_k, b_k, T_k >)_{k \in K}$ is a t-norm (obviously continuous).

($\Rightarrow$) Suppose that T is a continuous t-norm. We prove that the set I_T of all idempotent elements of T is a closed subset of the interval $[0, 1]$. If $(x_n)_{n \in \mathbb{N}}$ is a sequence of idempotent elements of T which converges to $x \in [0, 1]$, then by the continuity of T we have $x = \lim_{n \to \infty} x_n = \lim_{n \to \infty} T(x_n, x_n) = T(x, x)$, implying that x is also an idempotent element of T, and therefore I_T is a closed set.

If $I_T = [0, 1]$ then $T = \text{Min}$, i.e., $K = \varnothing$. If I_T is a proper subset of the interval $[0, 1]$, then there exists an at most countable nonempty set of indices K and a family of disjoint open subintervals $\{]a_k, b_k[\}_{k \in K}$ of $[0, 1]$ such that

$$[0, 1] \setminus I_T = \bigcup_{\alpha \in K}]a_k, b_k[.$$

For arbitrary but fixed $k \in K$ both endpoints a_k and b_k are idempotent elements of T, and no element from the open interval $]a_k, b_k[$ is an idempotent element for T. By the monotonicity of T we obtain for every $(x, y) \in [a_k, b_k]^2$

$$a_k = T(a_k, a_k) \leqslant T(x, y) \leqslant T(b_k, b_k) = b_k,$$

i.e., T maps $[a_k, b_k]^2$ on the interval $[a_k, b_k]$. Since we have for every $x \in [a_k, 1]$ that

$$a_k \geqslant T(a_k, x) \geqslant T(a_k, a_k) = a_k,$$

the element a_k is an annihilator for $T|_{[a_k, 1]^2}$. Since $\{T(x, b_k) \mid x \in [0, 1]\} = [0, b_k]$ we have that for every $y \in [0, b_k]$ there exists $x \in [0, 1]$ such that $y = T(x, b_k)$, and therefore by associativity of T we have

$$T(y, b_k) = T(T(x, b_k), b_k) = T(x, T(b_k, b_k)) = T(x, b_k) = y.$$

Hence b_k is the neutral element for $T|_{[0, b_k]^2}$.

Therefore by the previous results and continuity of T it follows that the function $T_k : [0, 1]^2 \to [0, 1]$ given by

$$T_k(x, y) = \varphi_k(T(\varphi_k^{-1}(x), \varphi_k^{-1}(y))),$$

where $\varphi_k : [a_k, b_k] \to [0, 1]$ is an increasing bijection given by $\varphi_k(u) = \frac{u - a_k}{b_k - a_k}$, is a continuous t-norm. Since T has no idempotent elements in the interval $]a_k, b_k[$ we have that $T_k(x, x) < x$ for every $x \in \,]0, 1[$, and therefore T_k is a continuous Archimedean t-norm.

For $(x, y) \in \,]a_k, b_k[^2$ we have $T(x, y) = \varphi_k^{-1}(T_k(\varphi_k(x), \varphi_k(y)))$. For $(x, y) \notin \,]a_k, b_k[^2$ for every $k \in K$ and $x \leqslant y$, there always exists an idempotent element $c \in I_T$ such that $x \leqslant c \leqslant y$. This c is the neutral element for $T|_{[0, c]^2}$ and annihilator for $T|_{[c, 1]^2}$ (for $c \leqslant x$ we have $c = T(c, c) \leqslant T(c, x) \leqslant T(c, 1) = c$). Therefore

$$T(x, y) = T(T(x, c), y) = T(x, T(c, y)) = T(x, c) = x = \text{Min}(x, y).$$

Finally using Theorem 3.36 we obtain the representation (3.19), see also Corollary 3.48. □

Remark 3.50. The mapping $t_{(k)} : [0, 1] \to [0, \infty]$ given by

$$t_k(u) = f_k(a_k + (b_k - a_k)u)$$

is an additive generator of a continuous Archimedean t-norm T_k, $k \in K$ from the previous proof of Theorem 3.49.

Remark 3.51. The function T from (3.18) is also an ordinal sum of aggregation functions; see Section 6.7. Namely, it is a lower idempotent ordinal sum of aggregation functions A_k defined on $[a_k, b_k]$, $k \in K$, where each A_k is additively generated by t_k (and it is simply a linear transformation of the corresponding continuous Archimedean t-norm T_k).

3.3.8 T-subnorms

Typical examples of nondecreasing functions bounded by Min but not necessarily being conjunctive aggregation functions are triangular subnorms introduced by Jenei [198]; see [220, 316, 317].

Definition 3.52. A symmetric, nondecreasing, associative function $R : [0, 1]^2 \to [0, 1]$ such that $R \leqslant Min$ is called a *triangular subnorm, t-subnorm* in short.

The smallest t-subnorm is the constant 0 two-place function, while the greatest t-subnorm is Min.

T-subnorms which are also aggregation functions are bwt-norms. This fact is depicted in Figure 3.1, where also some other relationships of conjunctive binary aggregation functions are given.

Though t-subnorms are not aggregation functions in general, as we have already seen there is a close relationship with conjunctive aggregation functions and t-norms. Indeed, each t-subnorm R can be redefined as shown in Remark 3.9(iv) to a conjunctive aggregation function $R^\sim$ (however, associativity of $R^\sim$ cannot be guaranteed anymore). If we redefine a t-subnorm R to a conjunctor $R^\#$ (see Lemma 3.18), we end up with a t-norm. On the other hand, for any t-norm T, its contraction $T^{[a]}$, given by

$$T^{[a]}(x, y) := \frac{T(ax, ay)}{a},$$

is a t-subnorm. T-subnorms play a crucial role in the characterization of the structure of t-norms; see [221, 224].

For each nondecreasing continuous function $f : [0, 1] \to [0, 1]$ and each continuous t-norm $T : [0, 1]^2 \to [0, 1]$, the function $T_{(f)} : [0, 1]^2 \to [0, 1]$ given by

$$T_{(f)}(x, y) := f^{(-1)}(T(f(x), f(y)))$$

is a t-subnorm.

Example 3.53. Let $f : [0, 1] \to [0, 1]$ be given by $f(x) = Min(2x, 1)$. Then its pseudo-inverse $f^{(-1)} : [0, 1] \to [0, 1]$ is given by $f^{(-1)}(t) = \frac{t}{2}$, and for the greatest t-norm Min we can introduce the t-subnorm $Min_{(f)}$ given by

$$Min_{(f)}(x, y) = Min\left(x, y, \frac{1}{2}\right).$$

We mention the result of Mesiarová on generated t-subnorms [316].

Lemma 3.54. *Let* $f : [0, 1] \to [0, \infty]$ *be a nonincreasing continuous function. Then the extended function* $F : \cup_{n \in \mathbb{N}}[0, 1]^n \to [0, 1]$ *given by (for $n > 1$)*

$$F(\mathbf{x}) = \begin{cases} 1 & \text{if } \mathbf{x} = 1 \\ f^{(-1)}\left(\sum_{i=1}^{n} f(x_i)\right) & \text{otherwise} \end{cases}$$

is a symmetric conjunctive extended aggregation function. It is associative only if $f^{(-1)}(t) < 1$ *for all* $t > 0$. *It is left-continuous possibly up to the point* $(1, \ldots, 1)$.

The proof follows directly from Proposition 2.51.

3.3.9 Convergence of t-norms

T-norms have the advantage with respect to general real functions that the pointwise convergence of a sequence of t-norms (which may include as members also discontinuous t-norms) to a continuous t-norm is equivalent to the uniform convergence of this sequence [199].

We present in this section two convergence theorems for t-norms, without proofs (since they are long and technical, and they all can be found in [220, Chap. 8]). The first result says that each continuous t-norm can be approximated uniformly by a strict t-norm (as well as by a nilpotent t-norm) [196, 199]; see [220, Th. 8.12, Cor. 8.13]. First, we make precise the kind of approximation.

Definition 3.55. For an arbitrary but fixed $\varepsilon > 0$ we say that two t-norms T_1 and T_2 are ε-*close* if
$$|\mathsf{T}_1(x,y) - \mathsf{T}_2(x,y)| < \varepsilon \quad \text{for all } x, y \in [0,1].$$

Theorem 3.56. *Let* T *be a continuous t-norm. For an arbitrary but fixed* $\varepsilon > 0$ *there exists a strict (or nilpotent) t-norm* T_ε *such that* T *and* T_ε *are* ε-*close.*

We have seen that, for continuous Archimedean t-norms, by Theorem 3.36, all information on them is related to their additive generators. Therefore it is natural to expect a connection between continuous Archimedean t-norms and additive generators also with respect to convergence [196]; see [220, Cor. 8.21].

Theorem 3.57. *Let* $(\mathsf{T}_n)_{n \in \mathbb{N}}$ *be a sequence of continuous Archimedean t-norms with the corresponding sequence of additive generators* $(t_n)_{n \in \mathbb{N}}$, *and let* T *be a continuous Archimedean t-norm with additive generator* t. *Then the following are equivalent:*

(i) $\lim_{n \to \infty} \mathsf{T}_n = \mathsf{T}$.
(ii) For each $x \in \,]0, 1]$ *we have* $\displaystyle \lim_{n \to \infty} \frac{t_n(x)}{t_n(0.5)} = \frac{t(x)}{t(0.5)}$.

Remark 3.58. We mention also the following result from [417]: for each pointwisely convergent sequence $(\mathsf{T}_n)_{n \in \mathbb{N}}$ of continuous t-norms, the corresponding limit T is a t-norm (not necessarily continuous).

3.4 Copulas and quasi-copulas

3.4.1 General copulas

Copulas were introduced in the multivariate statistical framework (Sklar [394]) to build a joint distribution function from the marginal distributions; see Theorem 3.65.

In this context, n-ary copulas are characterized by the nonnegative probability of an n-dimensional box $[x_1, y_1] \times [x_2, y_2] \times \cdots \times [x_n, y_n]$, which we shall denote by $[\mathbf{x}, \mathbf{y}]$. For $\mathbf{x}, \mathbf{y} \in [0, 1]^n$ such that $\mathbf{x} \leqslant \mathbf{y}$, let $[\mathbf{x}, \mathbf{y}]$ be the corresponding n-box, and let $\mathbf{z} = (z_1, \ldots, z_n)$ be a vertex of $[\mathbf{x}, \mathbf{y}]$. Then we define $\mathrm{sign}_{[\mathbf{x}, \mathbf{y}]}(\mathbf{z})$ in the following way:

$$\mathrm{sign}_{[\mathbf{x}, \mathbf{y}]}(\mathbf{z}) := \begin{cases} 1 & \text{if } z_m = x_m \text{ for an even number of } m\text{'s} \\ -1 & \text{if } z_m = x_m \text{ for an odd number of } m\text{'s}. \end{cases}$$

If the vertices of the n-box $[\mathbf{x}, \mathbf{y}]$ are not all distinct, then $\mathrm{sign}_{[\mathbf{x}, \mathbf{y}]}(\mathbf{z}) = 0$.

Definition 3.59. For a fixed $n \geqslant 2$, let $\mathsf{C} : [0, 1]^n \to [0, 1]$ be an n-ary aggregation function with a neutral element $e = 1$, such that for all $\mathbf{x}, \mathbf{y} \in [0, 1]^n, \mathbf{x} \leqslant \mathbf{y}$, the following inequality (called n-increasing monotonicity or moderate growth) is fulfilled:

$$\sum \mathrm{sign}_{[\mathbf{x}, \mathbf{y}]}(\mathbf{z}) \mathsf{C}(\mathbf{z}) \geqslant 0, \tag{3.20}$$

where the sum is taken over all vertices $\mathbf{z}$ of $[\mathbf{x}, \mathbf{y}]$. Then C is called an n-copula.

An extended aggregation function $\mathsf{C} : \cup_{n \in \mathbb{N}} [0, 1]^n \to [0, 1]$ such that for each $n \geqslant 2$ the corresponding n-ary aggregation function $\mathsf{C}^{(n)}$ is an n-copula is called a general copula.

Remark 3.60. (i) The condition of n-increasing monotonicity can also be written in the following form:

$$\sum_{\mathbf{d}} (\prod_{i=1}^n d_i) \mathsf{C}(u_1^{(d_1)}, \ldots, u_n^{(d_n)}) \geqslant 0, \tag{3.21}$$

where the sum is taken over all n-tuples $\mathbf{d} = (d_1, \ldots, d_n) \in \{-1, 1\}^n$ and where $u_i^{(-1)} := x_i, u_i^{(1)} := y_i$.

(ii) In the case of 2-copulas $\mathsf{C} : [0, 1]^2 \to [0, 1]$, introduced in Definition 3.2(v) (sometimes 2-copulas are simply called copulas), the moderate growth, or 2-increasing monotonicity (3.20), for the 2-box $[(x_1, x_2), (y_1, y_2)]$, reads

$$\mathsf{C}(y_1, y_2) + \mathsf{C}(x_1, x_2) \geqslant \mathsf{C}(x_1, y_2) + \mathsf{C}(x_2, y_1). \tag{3.22}$$

(iii) For 3-copulas $\mathsf{C} : [0, 1]^3 \to [0, 1]$, (3.20) can be rewritten into

$$\mathsf{C}(y_1, y_2, y_3) + \mathsf{C}(y_1, x_1, x_2) + \mathsf{C}(x_1, y_2, x_3) + \mathsf{C}(x_1, x_2, y_3)$$

$$-\mathsf{C}(x_1, x_2, x_3) - \mathsf{C}(x_1, y_2, y_3) - \mathsf{C}(y_1, x_2, y_3) - \mathsf{C}(y_1, y_2, x_3) \geqslant 0.$$

Example 3.61. (i) The product Π is a general copula. Namely, the condition (3.20) for $\Pi^{(n)}$ reduces to

$$\prod_{i=1}^n (y_i - x_i) \geqslant 0.$$

The product generates the joint distribution in the case of independent marginal random variables; see also Remark 3.66(ii).

(ii) Min as an extended aggregation function is a general copula. Specially, for any $n \in \mathbb{N}$, $\text{Min}^{(n)}$ is an n-copula, since the condition (3.20) for $\text{Min}^{(n)}$ reduces to

$$\text{Max}\left(\text{Min}(\mathbf{y}) - \text{Max}(\mathbf{x}), 0\right) \geqslant 0.$$

(iii) $\text{T}_{\text{L}}^{(n)}$ is an n-copula only for $n = 2$. In particular, for $n > 2$ we have that for $\text{T}_{\text{L}}^{(n)}$ on the n-box $[\frac{1}{2}, 1]^n$ the left side in (3.20) gives $1 - \frac{n}{2} < 0$.

Proposition 3.62. *Let* $\text{C} : [0, 1]^n \to [0, 1]$ *be an n-copula. Then for any $n \in \mathbb{N}$ we have* $\text{C} \leqslant \text{Min}$, *i.e.,* C *is a conjunctive aggregation function, and* $\text{T}_{\text{L}} < \text{C}$ *for $n > 2$* $(\text{T}_{\text{L}} \leqslant \text{C}$ *for $n = 2$).*

Proof. The fact that each n-copula has neutral element 1 ensures by Proposition 2.110 that n-copulas are conjunctive aggregation functions, i.e., $\text{C} \leqslant \text{Min}$. Due to Proposition 3.67, the m-copula C is 1-Lipschitz. Since T_{L} is the smallest 1-Lipschitzian aggregation function we have $\text{T}_{\text{L}} < \text{C}$. □

Remark 3.63. The bounds from Proposition 3.62 are the best possible; see [332]. T_{L}, as lower bound for copulas, is also called the *lower Frechet–Hoeffding bound,* while Min is called the *upper Frechet–Hoeffding bound.* For $n > 2$, there is no smallest n-copula (refer to Example 3.61(iii)), while Min is the greatest n-copula for all $n \geqslant 2$.

n-copulas can be defined in an alternative way, replacing the monotonicity by the requirement that 0 is an annihilator (this was the original approach of Sklar in [394]).

Proposition 3.64. *For a fixed $n \geqslant 1$, an n-ary function* $\text{C} : [0, 1]^n \to [0, 1]$ *is an n-copula if and only if it is n-increasing, it has annihilator 0 and a neutral element $e = 1$.*

Proof. ($\Rightarrow$) If $\text{C} : [0, 1]^n \to [0, 1]$ is an n-copula then the result follows by Definition 3.59 and the fact that C is a conjunctive aggregation function.

($\Leftarrow$) In the other direction, suppose that $\text{C} : [0, 1]^n \to [0, 1]$ is an n-ary function with a neutral element $e = 1$ which is n-increasing, and has 0 as annihilator. Then it suffices to prove that C is nondecreasing coordinatewise. For an arbitrary $\mathbf{x} \in [0, 1]^n$ take for $x < y$ the n-tuples $(x_1, \ldots, x_{i-1}, x, x_{i+1}, \ldots, x_n)$ and $(x_1, \ldots, x_{i-1}, y, x_{i+1}, \ldots, x_n)$. Applying on the n-box

$$[(\underbrace{0, \ldots, 0}_{i-1}, x, \underbrace{0, \ldots, 0}_{n-i}), (x_1, \ldots, x_{i-1}, y, x_{i+1}, \ldots, x_n)]$$

the inequality (3.20) and keeping in mind that 0 is an annihilator of C, the inequality (3.20) reduces to the inequality

$$\text{C}(x_1, \ldots, x_{i-1}, y, x_{i+1}, \ldots, x_n) - \text{C}(x_1, \ldots, x_{i-1}, x, x_{i+1}, \ldots, x_n) \geqslant 0,$$

which gives the nondecreasing monotonicity of C. □

To better understand the statistical background of copulas we recall here the Sklar theorem introduced in [394].

Theorem 3.65. *(i) If* $H : [-\infty, \infty]^n \to [0, 1]$ *is an n-dimensional (cumulative) distribution function with one-dimensional marginal (cumulative) distribution functions* $F_1, \ldots, F_n : [-\infty, \infty] \to [0, 1]$, *then there exists an n-copula* C *such that*

$$H(\mathbf{x}) = C(F_1(x_1), \ldots, F_n(x_n)) \tag{3.23}$$

for all $\mathbf{x} \in \mathbb{R}^n$. *If* $F_1, \ldots, F_n$ *are continuous, then* C *is unique; otherwise* C *is uniquely determined on* $\mathrm{ran}(F_1) \times \cdots \times \mathrm{ran}(F_n)$.

(ii) For any one-dimensional distribution functions $F_1, \ldots, F_n$, *and any n-copula* C, *the function* H *given by (3.23) is an n-dimensional distribution function with one-dimensional marginals* $F_1, \ldots, F_n$.

Remark 3.66. (i) Each *n*-copula can be seen as (a restriction on $[0, 1]^n$ of) an *n*-dimensional distribution function with marginals which have uniform distribution on $[0, 1]$.

(ii) A nice probabilistic characterization of the three basic continuous t-norms (T_L, Π, and Min), which are also copulas, is the next one: For events $E_1, \ldots, E_n$ of the form $E_i := \{X_i \leqslant x\}$, let $P(E_1), \ldots, P(E_n)$ be their respective probabilities. What can we say about the probability of the intersection $\overset{n}{\underset{i=1}{\bigcap}} E_i$?

The probability $P(E_1 \cap \cdots \cap E_n)$ can be computed using Theorem 3.65 by means of a (in most cases unknown) copula C,

$$P(E_1 \cap \cdots \cap E_n) = C(P(E_1), \ldots, P(E_n)).$$

Due to the fact that $T_L < C \leqslant \text{Min}$ for any copula C we have the (best) estimation

$$T_L(P(E_1), \ldots, P(E_n)) < P(E_1 \cap \cdots \cap E_n) \leqslant \text{Min}(P(E_1), \ldots, P(E_n)).$$

If the events $E_1, \ldots, E_n$ are jointly independent, then $C = \Pi$ and

$$P(E_1 \cap \cdots \cap E_n) = \Pi(P(E_1), \ldots, P(E_n)).$$

(iii) In the case described in Theorem 3.65 (ii), the left-hand side of the inequality (3.20) is exactly the probability of the *n*-dimensional box $[\mathbf{x}, \mathbf{y}]$ (which is clearly nonnegative).

We have the following basic properties of *n*-copulas [384].

Proposition 3.67. *Let* $C : [0, 1]^n \to [0, 1]$ *be an n-copula. Then the following holds.*

(i) Let $i \in [n]$. *Then for all* $x, y \in [0, 1]$ *and all* $\mathbf{x} \in [0, 1]^n$,

$$|C(x_1, \ldots, x_{i-1}, x, x_{i+1}, \ldots, x_n) - C(x_1, \ldots, x_{i-1}, y, x_{i+1}, \ldots, x_n)| \leqslant |x - y|. \tag{3.24}$$

(ii) For any $\mathbf{x}, \mathbf{y} \in [0,1]^n$ we have

$$|C(\mathbf{x}) - C(\mathbf{y})| \leqslant \sum_{i=1}^{n} |x_i - y_i|, \qquad (3.25)$$

i.e., C *is* 1-*Lipchitzian and therefore a continuous aggregation function.*

Proof. (i) Suppose that $x \leqslant y$. For $n = 2$, we obtain by (3.22)

$$C(y, 1) - C(x, 1) - C(y, x_2) + C(x, x_2) \geqslant 0$$

and

$$C(1, y) - C(1, x) - C(x_1, y) + C(x_1, x) \geqslant 0,$$

which imply (3.24).

For $n \geqslant 3$, we suppose $x \leqslant y$ and we consider the n-boxes $B_1, \ldots, B_{n-1}$ defined in the following way. We denote $B_j = [\mathbf{x}_j, \mathbf{y}_j]$ for $j = 1, 2, \ldots, n-1$, and for the ith coordinate we require that $(\mathbf{x}_j)_i = x$ and $(\mathbf{y}_j)_i = y$. Also, for $j < i$, we set $(\mathbf{x}_j)_k = 0$ if $k \notin \{i, j\}$ and $(\mathbf{x}_j)_j = x_j$, and $(\mathbf{y}_j)_k = 1$ for $k \leqslant j$ and $(\mathbf{y}_j)_k = x_k$ if $k > j, k \neq i$. For $j > i$, we set $(\mathbf{x}_j)_{j+1} = x_{j+1}$ and $(\mathbf{x}_j)_k = 0$ if $k \notin \{i, j+1\}$, and $(\mathbf{y}_j)_k = 1$ for $k \leqslant j, k \neq i$, and $(\mathbf{y}_j)_k = x_k$ if $k > j$. So we obtain

$$B_1 = \big[(\underbrace{x_1, 0, \ldots, 0, x}_{i}, 0, \ldots, 0), (1, x_2, \ldots, x_{i-1}, y, x_{i+1}, \ldots, x_n) \big],$$

$$B_2 = \big[(\underbrace{0, x_2, 0, \ldots, 0, x}_{i}, 0, \ldots, 0), (1, 1, x_3, \ldots, x_{i-1}, y, x_{i+1}, \ldots, x_n) \big],$$

$$\vdots$$

$$B_{n-1} = \big[(\underbrace{0, 0, \ldots, 0, x}_{i}, 0, \ldots, 0, x_n), (1, 1, \ldots, 1, y, 1, \ldots, 1) \big].$$

Applying C on the n-box $B_k, k = 1, \ldots, n-1$, gives us by (3.20)

$$C(\underbrace{1, \ldots, 1}_{k}, \ldots, y, \ldots, x_n) - C(\underbrace{1, \ldots, 1}_{k}, \ldots, x, \ldots, x_n)$$

$$-C(1, \ldots, x_k, \ldots, y, \ldots, x_n) + C(1, \ldots, x_k, \ldots, x, \ldots, x_n) \geqslant 0,$$

for $k = 1, \ldots, n-1$. Summing up these $n-1$ inequalities we obtain

$$C(\underbrace{1, \ldots, 1, y}_{i}, 1 \ldots, 1) - C(\underbrace{1, \ldots, 1, x}_{i}, 1, \ldots, 1)$$

$$-C(x_1, \ldots, x_{i-1}, y, x_{i+1}, \ldots, x_n) + C(x_1, \ldots, x_{i-1}, x, x_{i+1}, \ldots, x_n) \geqslant 0,$$

which implies

$$C(x_1,\ldots,x_{i-1},y,x_{i+1},\ldots,x_n) - C(x_1,\ldots,x_{i-1},x,x_{i+1},\ldots,x_n) \leqslant y - x.$$

Hence by coordinatewise nondecreasing monotonicity of C we obtain (3.24).

(ii) Using (3.24) n times, we obtain (3.25). □

Remark 3.68. Using the Sklar Theorem 3.65 we can give a probabilistic proof of Proposition 3.67(ii). For the proof, it is enough to show the 1-Lipschitz property of C in each coordinate. With no loss of generality we show it in the first coordinate. Let $C : [0,1]^n \to [0,1]$ be an n-copula which links random variables $(X_1,\ldots,X_n)$ such that each $X_i, i \in [n]$, is uniformly distributed over $[0,1]$; see Theorem 3.65(ii). Then for all $\mathbf{x} \in [0,1]^n$ and $\varepsilon \in [0,1-x_1]$ we have

$$C(x_1 + \varepsilon, x_2,\ldots,x_n) - C(x_1,\ldots,x_n)$$

$$= P(X_1 < x_1 + \varepsilon,\ldots,X_n < x_n) - P(X_1 < x_1,\ldots,X_n < x_n)$$

$$= P(X_1 \in [x_1,x_1+\varepsilon[,X_2 < x_2,\ldots,X_n < x_n) \leqslant P(X_1 \in [x_1,x_1+\varepsilon[) = \varepsilon,$$

thus showing the 1-Lipschitz property of C in the first coordinate.

It is straightforward to check that the class of all n-copulas is a convex compact subclass of the class of all n-ary aggregation functions (and the class of general copulas is a convex compact subclass of the class of all extended aggregation functions). Note that these classes are not closed under Min or Max aggregation of its members, nor under the geometric mean aggregation [332].

Remark 3.69. We introduce some examples of copulas based on statistical properties of random variables.

(i) As we have already noticed, the independence of random variables is expressed by the product copula Π, i.e., any n-tuple $(X_1,\ldots,X_n)$ of n independent random variables has joint distribution

$$F_{X_1,\ldots,X_n}(\mathbf{x}) = \prod_{i=1}^{n} F_{X_i}(x_i).$$

(ii) As already mentioned above, another general copula is Min. Min relates random variables which are totally positively dependent in the sense that in the random vector $(X_1,\ldots,X_n)$, each X_i can be expressed in the form $X_i = f_i(X_1)$, where f_i is a real function increasing on the range of X_1. Then

$$F_{X_1,\ldots,X_n}(\mathbf{x}) = \text{Min}(F_{X_1}(x_1),\ldots,F_{X_n}(x_n)).$$

(iii) In the case of 2-copulas, the smallest 2-copula T_L relates two negatively dependent random variables X_1 and X_2, $X_2 = f(X_1)$, where f is a real function decreasing on the range of X_1.

3.4.2 Representation of copulas and Archimedean copulas

For 2-copulas, we have a representation similar to the representation of continuous t-norms given in Theorem 3.49.

Proposition 3.70. *Let* $C : [0,1]^2 \to [0,1]$ *be a binary aggregation function, and let* I_C *be the set of its idempotent elements. Then* C *is a 2-copula if and only if* I_C *is the complement of the (possibly empty) union* $\cup_{k \in K}]a_k, b_k[$ *of disjoint open nonempty subintervals* $]a_k, b_k[$ *of* $[0,1]$, *and*

$$C(x,y) = \begin{cases} a_k + (b_k - a_k)C_k \left(\dfrac{x - a_k}{b_k - a_k}, \dfrac{y - a_k}{b_k - a_k} \right) & \text{if } (x,y) \in]a_k, b_k[^2 \\ \text{Min}(x,y) & \text{otherwise,} \end{cases}$$

(3.26)

where each $C_k : [0,1]^2 \to [0,1]$ *is a 2-copula with no nontrivial idempotent element, i.e.,* C *is an ordinal sum of copulas* C_k.

Proof. Let C be a 2-copula. From its continuity it follows that I_C is a closed subset of $[0,1]$, and thus its complement $[0,1] \setminus I_C$ is the union of nonempty open subintervals $]a_k, b_k[, k \in K$. For each $k \in K$, define a mapping $C_k : [0,1]^2 \to \mathbb{R}$ given by

$$C_k(x,y) = \frac{C(a_k + (b_k - a_k)x, a_k + (b_k - a_k)y) - a_k}{b_k - a_k}.$$

The idempotency of b_k, i.e., the fact that $C(b_k, b_k) = b_k$, the conjunctivity of C ensuring $C(0, b_k) = C(b_k, 0) = 0$, and the 1-Lipschitz property of C ensure $C(u, b_k) = C(b_k, u) = u$ for all $u \in [0, b_k]$, and thus 1 is a neutral element of C_k. Obviously, C_k is nondecreasing and $C_k(0,0) = 0$, i.e., C_k is a conjunctive aggregation function with neutral element 1. The 2-increasing monotonicity of C_k is inherited from the 2-increasing monotonicity of C, thus proving that C_k is a 2-copula. To see the opposite implication, note that each ordinal sum of conjunctive aggregation functions is a conjunctive aggregation function (see Chapter 6), hence the function C given by (3.26) is a conjunctive aggregation function. The neutral element of C is 1. The 2-increasing monotonicity of C follows from the fact that each 2-box $[\mathbf{x}, \mathbf{y}] = [x_1, y_1] \times [x_2, y_2]$ can be decomposed as a union of nonoverlapping rectangles which are subsets either of some of the squares $[a_k, b_k]^2$ (and there the 2-increasing monotonicity of C follows from the 2-increasing monotonicity of C_k), or of the set $[0,1]^2 \setminus]a_k, b_k[^2$ (and there the 2-increasing monotonicity follows from the 2-increasing monotonicity of the greatest 2-copula Min). □

Remark 3.71. (i) Proposition 3.70 allows us to study the associativity of 2-copulas having trivial idempotent elements only.

(ii) In [310], Proposition 3.70 is shown to be true also for n-ary copulas with $n > 2$.

Definition 3.72. A mapping $C : [0,1]^2 \to [0,1]$ which is an associative 2-copula with only trivial idempotent element is called an *Archimedean copula*. It is called a *strict copula* if $C(x, x) < x$ for all $x \,]0, 1[$ and it is called a *nonstrict Archimedean copula* otherwise.

The next representation theorem is due to Moynihan [321].

Proposition 3.73. *A mapping* $C : [0, 1]^2 \to [0, 1]$ *is an Archimedean copula if and only if there is a convex decreasing continuous function* $t : [0, 1] \to [0, \infty]$ *with* $t(1) = 0$ *such that*

$$C(x, y) = t^{-1}(\mathrm{Min}(t(x) + t(y), t(0))). \qquad (3.27)$$

C *is a strict copula if and only if* $t(0) = \infty$.

For the proof, see [321, 384].

Summarizing the above two propositions, we see that each associative 2-copula with only trivial idempotent elements is a 1-Lipschitzian t-norm (and therefore symmetric). This also holds vice-versa, i.e., associative 2-copulas are exactly 1-Lipschitzian (binary) t-norms; see [321]. Though the associativity of these 2-copulas allows their extension to *n*-ary 1-Lipschitzian t-norms for any $n > 2$ (respectively, to extended 1-Lipschitzian t-norms), these extensions need not be *n*-copulas (respectively, general copulas). For example, the ternary 1-Lipschitzian t-norm $T_L : [0, 1]^3 \to [0, 1]$ is not a 3-copula (Example 3.61(iii)).

There are continuous Archimedean t-norms (even strict) greater than T_L which are not copulas; see [15].

Example 3.74. The strict t-norm T generated by

$$t(x) := \begin{cases} \dfrac{3}{2x} - 1 & \text{for } x \in \left[0, \frac{1}{2}\right] \\[2mm] \dfrac{2}{x} - 2 & \text{for } x \in \left[\frac{1}{2}, 1\right] \end{cases}$$

is a t-norm greater than T_L which is not a copula.

The next result is due to Kimberling [210]. For a continuous Archimedean t-norm T with an additive generator t, the analytical properties of the pseudo-inverse $t^{(-1)}$ are strongly connected with the *n*-monotonicity of T.

Proposition 3.75. *Let* T *be a continuous Archimedean t-norm with an additive generator* t *with its pseudo-inverse* $t^{(-1)} : [0, \infty] \to [0, 1]$ *given by*

$$t^{(-1)}(u) = t^{-1}(\mathrm{Min}(u, t(0))).$$

Then $t^{(-1)}$ *is a completely monotone function on* $]0, \infty[$, *(i.e., it has all derivatives on* $]0, \infty[$, *and these derivatives alter their signs in the sense that* $(-1)^n \dfrac{\mathrm{d}^n t^{(-1)}(x)}{\mathrm{d}x^n} \geqslant 0, n \in \mathbb{N})$ *if and only if* T *is a general copula, i.e., for each* $n > 1$, *it is an n-copula.*

Example 3.76. (i) A typical example of a general Archimedean copula is the product Π with additive generator $t : [0, 1] \to [0, \infty]$ given by $t(x) = -\log x$.

(ii) *Hamacher product* [181] (or *Ali–Mikhail–Haq copula* with parameter 0 (see [332])): C_H is a general Archimedean copula generated by an additive generator $t : [0, 1] \rightarrow [0, \infty]$, given by $t(x) = \frac{1-x}{x}$.

(iii) Families of t-norms from Example 3.27 are copulas for given values of parameter λ: $(T_\lambda^F)_{\lambda \in [0, \infty]}$, $(T_\lambda^Y)_{\lambda \in [1, \infty]}$, $(T_\lambda^{SW})_{\lambda \in [0, \infty]}$, $(T_\lambda^H)_{\lambda \in [0, 2]}$, $(T_\lambda^{SS})_{\lambda \in [-\infty, 1]}$.

3.4.3 *Some additional results on copulas*

Copulas are neither symmetric nor associative, in general.

Example 3.77. (i) The *Farlie–Gumbel–Morgenstern family* of copulas (symmetric but nonassociative for $\lambda \neq 0$) is given by

$$C_\lambda^{FGM}(x, y) := xy + \lambda xy(1 - x)(1 - y), \text{ for } \lambda \in [-1, 1].$$

(ii) The family of *cubic 2-copulas* (nonassociative and asymmetric) is given by

$$C_{\alpha, \beta, \gamma, \delta}(x, y) := xy + xy(1-x)(1-y)(\alpha xy + \beta x(1-y) + \gamma y(1-x) + \delta(1-x)(1-y)),$$

where $\alpha, \beta, \gamma, \delta \in [0, 1]$ are given parameters.

(iii) A linear combination $C = p\Pi + (1 - p)\text{Min}$ is an example of a general nonassociative symmetric copula (whenever $p \in \,]0, 1[$). In its binary form C is given by (see Figure 3.14)

$$C(x, y) = pxy + (1 - p)\text{Min}(x, y) = x'(1 - p(1 - y')), \qquad (3.28)$$

where $x' = \text{Min}(x, y)$ and $y' = \text{Max}(x, y)$.

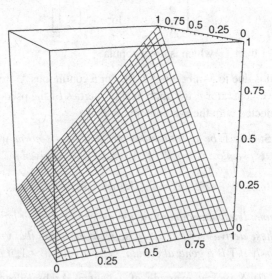

Figure 3.14 Nonassociative copula from Example 3.77(iii) for $p = 0.7$

In the following proposition we introduce an important subclass of 2-copulas, namely the Archimax copulas [67].

Proposition 3.78. *Let* $t : [0, 1] \rightarrow [0, \infty]$ *be a convex decreasing function such that* $t(1) = 0$ *(i.e.,* t *is an additive generator of some 2-copula* C_t*), and let* $D :$ $[0, 1] \rightarrow [0, 1]$ *be a convex function bounded from below by* $\mathsf{Max}(x, 1 - x)$*. (D is a so-called dependence function.) Then the mapping* $C_{t,D} : [0, 1]^2 \rightarrow [0, 1]$ *given by (for* $(x, y) \in]0, 1[^2)$

$$C_{t,D}(x,y) = t^{-1}\left(\mathsf{Min}\left(t(0), (t(x) + t(y))D\left(\frac{t(x)}{t(x) + t(y)}\right)\right)\right)$$

is a 2-copula. This copula is called an Archimax copula.

The smallest Archimax copula with fixed t corresponds to the constant dependence function $D = 1$, and then $C_{t,1} = C_t$ is an Archimedean copula generated by t. On the other hand, for the lower dependence function $D_*(x) := \mathsf{Max}(x, 1 - x)$, we have $C_{t,D_*} = \mathsf{Min}^{(2)}$, independently of t. More details about Archimax copulas can be found also in [223, 225]. In the special case $t(x) = -\log x$ (i.e., when $C_t = \Pi$), the corresponding Archimax copulas $C_{t,D}$ are known in statistics as Max-attractor copulas, or extreme values copulas [55, 135, 409] and they are characterized by log-ratio scale stability (also called power stability), i.e.,

$$C_{t,D}(x^p, y^p) = (C_{t,D}(x,y))^p$$

for all $p \in]0, \infty[$; see also Proposition 7.41.

Max-attractors are closed under Max-composition and under weighted geometric mean composition.

For a given 2-copula $C : [0, 1]^2 \rightarrow [0, 1]$, a dual 2-copula $\tilde{C} : [0, 1]^2 \rightarrow [0, 1]$ is given by $\tilde{C}(x, y) := x + y - C(x, y)$. Dual 2-copulas are not necessarily dual aggregation functions to 2-copulas. Dual 2-copulas are 1-Lipschitzian aggregation functions with neutral element $e = 0$, and if they are associative, then they are continuous t-conorms (related to convex additive generators). An interesting problem is when a dual associative 2-copula $\tilde{C}$ coincides with the dual (in the sense of Definition 2.104) aggregation function C^d, that is,

$$x + y - C(x, y) = 1 - C(1 - x, 1 - y) \qquad (3.29)$$

for all $x, y \in [0, 1]$. Frank has shown in [122] that for Archimedean associative 2-copulas, the only solutions of (3.29) are the members of the Frank family $(\mathsf{T}^{\mathsf{F}}_\lambda)_{\lambda \in]0, \infty]}$, that is $\mathsf{T}^{\mathsf{F}}_1 = \Pi$, $\mathsf{T}^F_\infty = \mathsf{T_L}$, and for $\lambda \in]0, 1[\cup]1, \infty[$,

$$\mathsf{T}^{\mathsf{F}}_\lambda(x, y) = \log\left(1 + \frac{(\lambda^x - 1)(\lambda^y - 1)}{\lambda - 1}\right). \qquad (3.30)$$

We have that

$$\lim_{\lambda \to 0^+} \mathsf{T}^{\mathsf{F}}_\lambda = \mathsf{T}^{\mathsf{F}}_0 = \mathsf{Min}$$

is also an associative solution of (3.29), as well as any appropriate t-norm ordinal sum related to the Frank family $\left(T_\lambda^F\right)_{\lambda \in]0,\infty]}$.

Remark 3.79. We mention here one more place where copulas play an important role. Let $\star$ be the binary operation defined on the set of 2-copulas by

$$(C_1 \star C_2)(x,y) := \int_0^1 \frac{\partial C_1(x,t)}{\partial t} \frac{\partial C_2(t,y)}{\partial t} \, dt,$$

where C_1, C_2 are 2-copulas (these partial derivatives exist almost everywhere); see [71]. Then $C_1 \star C_2$ is a 2-copula, and the set of 2-copulas is a noncommutative semigroup under the operation $\star$. The strong interpretation in the context of Markov processes is the following: If $(X_t)_{t \in I}$ is a real stochastic process with parameter set I and if C_{st} is the copula of X_s and X_t, then the transition probabilities of the process satisfy the Kolmogoroff–Chapman equation if and only if $C_{st} = C_{su} \star C_{ut}$, for all $s, t, u \in I$ with $s < u < t$; see [71].

3.4.4 Quasi-copulas

In order to generalize the notion of n-copulas, quasi-copulas of dimension n were introduced in Alsina *et al.* [16] as special n-ary functions Q defined on $[0,1]^n$, such that for any continuous random variables $X_1, \ldots, X_n$ with support on $[0,1]$, there is a copula C such that

$$Q(F_{X_1}(t), \ldots, F_{X_n}(t)) = C(F_{X_1}(t), \ldots, F_{X_n}(t))$$

for all $t \in [0,1]$. In particular, if the random variables $X_1, \ldots, X_n$ have the same distribution function, we obtain that for each quasi-copula Q there is a copula C (with the same diagonal section), i.e., $Q(u, \ldots, u) = C(u, \ldots, u)$ for all $u \in [0,1]$.

Some of the properties of copulas (1 is a neutral element and they are nondecreasing 1-Lipschitzian functions) are inherited by quasi-copulas, but for example not the n-increasing monotonicity (3.20). The following result was shown in [138] for $n = 2$, and in [67] for $n > 2$. It is now used to define quasi-copulas more transparently than in the original paper [16]; see also Definition 3.2(iv).

Theorem 3.80. *A function* $Q : [0,1]^n \to [0,1]$, $n \geqslant 2$, *is a quasi-copula if and only if it is a* 1-*Lipschitzian conjunctive aggregation function.*

A *general quasi-copula* is an extended aggregation function such that each of its n-ary restrictions is an n-dimensional quasi-copula. Though each of these n-ary quasi-copulas possesses 1 as neutral element, the general quasi-copula need not have an extended neutral element.

Example 3.81. Let $Q : \cup_{n \in \mathbb{N}} [0,1]^n \to [0,1]$ be given by

$$Q(\mathbf{x}) := x_1 \operatorname{Min}(x_2, \ldots, x_n).$$

Then Q is a nonsymmetric (and thus nonassociative) quasi-copula (it is even a copula; see Definition 3.59) which is not a conjunctor. Indeed, $Q(0.5, 1, 0.5) = 0.25$ while $Q(1, 0.5, 0.5) = 0.5$, i.e., 1 is not a neutral element of Q.

The class of all n-dimensional quasi-copulas is a convex compact subclass of the set of all n-ary aggregation functions, with smallest element $T_L^{(n)}$ and greatest element $Min^{(n)}$. Moreover, the class of all n-ary quasi-copulas is closed not only under Min- and Max-composition and even under uncountable sup- and inf-composition, but also under any aggregation function with Chebyshev norm 1; see [234].

Proposition 3.82. *Let for $m \geqslant 2$, A $: [0, 1]^m \to [0, 1]$ be an aggregation function with Chebyshev norm 1, i.e.,*

$$|A(\mathbf{u}) - A(\mathbf{v})| \leqslant \|\mathbf{u} - \mathbf{v}\|_\infty.$$

Then for any $n \geqslant 2$, and any quasi-copulas $Q_i : [0, 1]^n \to [0, 1]$, $i = 1, \ldots, m$, the composed function $Q : [0, 1]^n \to [0, 1]$ given by

$$Q(\mathbf{x}) := A(Q_1(\mathbf{x}), \ldots, Q_m(\mathbf{x}))$$

is also an n-ary quasi-copula.

An interesting example of a symmetric binary quasi-copula which is not a copula (such quasi-copulas are called proper quasi-copulas) is given by $Q = Med(a, T_L, \Pi)$, $a \in]0, 1[$. As already mentioned, each associative 1-Lipschitzian binary t-norm is a 2-copula, but not necessarily an n-copula for $n > 2$. For $n = 2$ it is then evident that each associative quasi-copula is also a copula. Contrary to the case of copulas, each n-ary extension of an associative quasi-copula is an n-ary quasi-copula, and thus associative quasi-copulas can be extended to general quasi-copulas.

Proposition 3.83. *An associative extended aggregation function $Q : \cup_{n \in \mathbb{N}}[0, 1]^n \to [0, 1]$ is a general quasi-copula if and only if there is a disjoint family $\{]a_k, b_k[\}_{k \in K}$ of nonempty open subintervals of $[0, 1]$, and a family $t_k : [a_k, b_k] \to [0, \infty]$ of convex continuous decreasing functions with $t_k(b_k) = 0$, $k \in K$, so that for all $n \in \mathbb{N}$ and $\mathbf{x} \in [0, 1]^n$,*

$$Q(\mathbf{x}) = \begin{cases} t_k^{-1}\left(Min\left(t_k(a_k), \sum_{i=1}^{n} t_k\left(Min(x_i, b_k)\right)\right)\right) \\ \qquad\qquad \text{if } Min(\mathbf{x}) \in]a_k, b_k[\\ Min(\mathbf{x}) \qquad\qquad \text{otherwise.} \end{cases}$$

Proof. The proof follows from Propositions 3.70 and 3.73, and the fact that the 1-Lipschitz property of a binary associative function is inherited also by the corresponding n-ary extensions. □

In spite of Proposition 3.75, we can conclude that the extended aggregation functions related to the binary nonstrict Archimedean copulas are general quasi-copulas but never general copulas. As a typical example, recall again that T_L is a copula for $n = 2$ only, however, it is a general quasi-copula.

In general, any family $(Q_n)_{n \in \mathbb{N}}$ of binary quasi-copulas can be used to construct a general quasi-copula Q. (Recall the forward extension of binary aggregation function to an extended aggregation function; see Definition 2.65.)

Proposition 3.84. *Let* $(Q_n)_{n \in \mathbb{N}}$ *be a family of binary quasi-copulas. Then the extended function* $Q : \cup_{n \in \mathbb{N}}[0, 1]^n \to [0, 1]$ *given by induction by*

$$Q(x_1, x_2) = Q_1(x_1, x_2),$$

and for $n > 2$

$$Q(\mathbf{x}) = Q_{n-1}(Q(x_1, \ldots, x_{n-1}), x_n),$$

is a general quasi-copula.

Proof. It is obvious that $Q^{(2)} = Q_1$ is a binary quasi-copula. Suppose that $Q^{(n-1)}$ is an $(n-1)$-quasi-copula. Then

$$Q^{(n)}(1, \ldots, 1, x_n) = Q_{n-1}(Q^{(n-1)}(1, \ldots, 1), x_n)$$
$$= Q_{n-1}(1, x_n) = x_n.$$

If $x_i < 1$ for some $i \in [n-1]$ and $x_j = 1$ for all $j \neq i$, then

$$Q^{(n)}(x_1, \ldots, 1, x_n) = Q_{n-1}(x_i, 1) = x_i.$$

Finally, the 1-Lipschitz property of $Q^{(n)}$ follows from the 1-Lipschitz property of $Q^{(n-1)}$ and Q_{n-1}. $\qquad \square$

Remark 3.85. The associative general quasi-copula Q discussed in Proposition 3.83 is related to the family $(Q_n)_{n \in \mathbb{N}}$, where for each $n \in \mathbb{N}$, $Q_n = Q^{(2)}$ is a given associative 2-copula.

3.5 Disjunctive aggregation functions

Functions which are dual (see Definition 2.104) to conjunctive aggregation functions are called *disjunctive aggregation functions*. Disjunctive aggregation functions are those which are greater than Max (i.e., than the greatest idempotent aggregation function). Though disjunctive aggregation functions can be discussed on an arbitrary real interval $\mathbb{I}$, we will restrict our considerations to the case $\mathbb{I} = [0, 1]$, as in the case of conjunctive aggregation functions. There is a genuine connection between these two classes of aggregation functions.

Lemma 3.86. *Let* $\varphi : [0, 1] \to [0, 1]$ *be a decreasing bijection. Then the (extended) aggregation function* A *is disjunctive if and only if its transform* A_φ *given by*

$$\mathsf{A}_\varphi(\mathbf{x}) := \varphi^{-1}(\mathsf{A}(\varphi(x_1), \ldots, \varphi(x_n)))$$

(see (6.3)) is conjunctive.

Proof. An aggregation function A is disjunctive if and only if for any $\mathbf{x}$ from its domain it holds that

$$\mathsf{A}(\mathbf{x}) \geqslant \mathsf{Max}(\mathbf{x}).$$

Therefore also

$$\mathsf{A}(\varphi(x_1), \ldots, \varphi(x_n)) \geqslant \mathsf{Max}(\varphi(x_1), \ldots, \varphi(x_n)),$$

and due to the decreasing monotonicity of φ^{-1} we obtain

$$\mathsf{A}_\varphi(\mathbf{x}) = \varphi^{-1}(\mathsf{A}(\varphi(x_1), \ldots, \varphi(x_n)) \leqslant \varphi^{-1}(\mathsf{Max}(\varphi(x_1), \ldots, \varphi(x_n)) = \mathsf{Min}(\mathbf{x}). \qquad \square$$

Remark 3.87. (i) In fuzzy logic (see [178, 220]), an involutive decreasing bijection $\varphi : [0, 1] \to [0, 1]$ (i.e., $\varphi(\varphi(x)) = x$ for all $x \in [0, 1]$) plays the role of negation. For any aggregation function A we have $(\mathsf{A}_\varphi)_\varphi = \mathsf{A}$, i.e., φ-transformation brings a kind of duality into the class of aggregation functions; see also Definition 6.7. Due to Lemma 3.86, this duality also connects the class of disjunctive aggregation functions and the class of conjunctive aggregation functions. Moreover, if a t-norm T models the conjunction in fuzzy logic and φ models the negation, then the triplet $(\mathsf{T}, \mathsf{T}_\varphi, \varphi)$ is called a *de Morgan triplet*.

(ii) For $N : [0, 1] \to [0, 1]$ given by $N(x) = 1 - x$, the dual aggregation function A^d (see Definition 2.104) can be introduced as $\mathsf{A}^d = \mathsf{A}_N$. Thus disjunctive aggregation functions are just dual functions to conjunctive aggregation functions, and therefore we can derive all their properties from the corresponding properties of conjunctive aggregation functions. So, for example, the smallest and the only idempotent disjunctive aggregation function is Max. In fuzzy logic N is called the standard negation.

Modifying Proposition 3.1, we have the next result.

Proposition 3.88. *The greatest extended aggregation function* $\mathsf{A}^\top$ *and* Max *are disjunctive extended aggregation functions. For any disjunctive extended aggregation function* A,

(i) $\mathsf{A}^\top \geqslant \mathsf{A} \geqslant \mathsf{Max}$;
(ii) A *is idempotent if and only if* $\mathsf{A} = \mathsf{Max}$.

Remark 3.89.   (i) Each disjunctive aggregation function has 1 as its annihilator, and
if a disjunctive aggregation function has a neutral element e, then necessarily
$e = 0$.

(ii) Since disjunctive and conjunctive aggregation functions are dual of each other,
this allows us to introduce several classes of disjunctive aggregation functions in
analogy to the corresponding classes of conjunctive aggregation functions. For
example, disjunctors are aggregation functions on $[0, 1]$ with neutral element 0.

Additively generated disjunctors are defined by means of increasing functions
$g : [0, 1] \to [0, \infty]$, $g(0) = 0$ as follows:

$$A_g(\mathbf{x}) = g^{(-1)}\left(\sum_{i=1}^{n} g(x_i)\right),$$

where the pseudo-inverse $g^{(-1)} : [0, \infty] \to [0, 1]$ is defined in (3.2).

Definition 3.90. The dual aggregation function to a t-norm $\mathsf{T} : \cup_{n\in\mathbb{N}}[0, 1]^n \to [0, 1]$,
i.e., an associative symmetric aggregation function $\mathsf{S} : \cup_{n\in\mathbb{N}}[0, 1]^n \to [0, 1]$ with
extended neutral element 0 is called a *triangular conorm* or a *t-conorm* for short.

By duality, t-conorms have annihilator $a = 1$. For each t-conorm S, we have (see
Figure 3.15) $\mathsf{Max} \leqslant \mathsf{S} \leqslant \mathsf{S_D}$, where

$$\mathsf{S_D}(\mathbf{x}) := \begin{cases} \mathsf{Max}(\mathbf{x}) & \text{if } |\{i \mid x_i > 0\}| < 2 \\ 1 & \text{otherwise.} \end{cases} \tag{3.31}$$

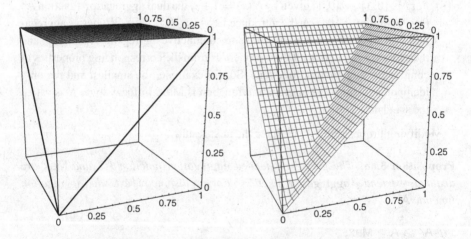

Figure 3.15 Two basic t-conorms $\mathsf{S_D}$ (left) and Max (right)

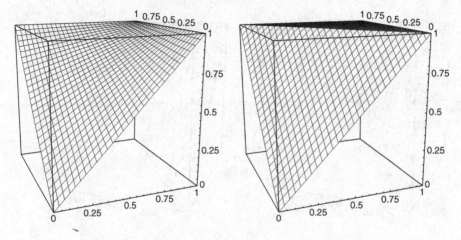

Figure 3.16 Two basic t-conorms S_P (left) and S_L (right)

The dual function to the product Π is called the *probabilistic sum* and it is denoted by S_P (see Figure 3.16),

$$S_P(\mathbf{x}) := 1 - \prod_{i=1}^{n}(1 - x_i). \tag{3.32}$$

The Łukasiewicz t-conorm S_L is often called the *bounded sum* because of

$$S_L(\mathbf{x}) := \text{Min}\left(1, \sum_{i=1}^{n} x_i\right). \tag{3.33}$$

We give some important families of t-conorms dual to families of t-norms given in Example 3.27 (with the exception of the Sugeno–Weber family).

Example 3.91. (i) The family $(S_\lambda^F)_{\lambda \in [0,\infty]}$ of *Frank t-conorms* is given by (see Figure 3.17)

$$S_\lambda^F(x,y) = \begin{cases} \text{Max}(x,y) & \text{if } \lambda = 0 \\ S_P(x,y) & \text{if } \lambda = 1 \\ S_L(x,y) & \text{if } \lambda = \infty \\ 1 - \log_\lambda\left(1 + \dfrac{(\lambda^{1-x} - 1)(\lambda^{1-y} - 1)}{\lambda - 1}\right) & \text{otherwise.} \end{cases} \tag{3.34}$$

(ii) The family $(S_\lambda^Y)_{\lambda \in [0,\infty]}$ of *Yager t-conorms* is given by

$$S_\lambda^Y(x,y) = \begin{cases} S_D(x,y) & \text{if } \lambda = 0 \\ \text{Max}(x,y) & \text{if } \lambda = \infty \\ \text{Min}\left(1, (x^\lambda + y^\lambda)^{\frac{1}{\lambda}}\right) & \text{otherwise.} \end{cases} \tag{3.35}$$

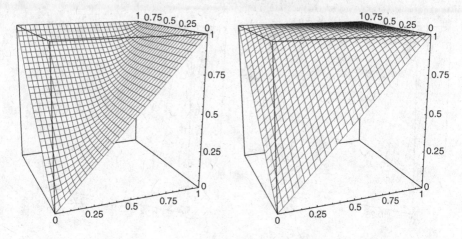

Figure 3.17 Figures of elements of the family S_λ^F for $\lambda = 0.000001$ (left) and $\lambda = 10^5$ (right)

(iii) The family $(S_\lambda^{SW})_{\lambda \in [-1,\infty]}$ of *Sugeno–Weber t-conorms* is given by

$$S_\lambda^{SW}(x,y) = \begin{cases} S_P(x,y) & \text{if } \lambda = -1 \\ S_D & \text{if } \lambda = \infty \\ \text{Min}\,(1, x+y+\lambda xy) & \text{otherwise.} \end{cases} \quad (3.36)$$

Note that the t-conorm $S_\lambda^{SW}, \lambda \in \,]-1, \infty[$, is dual to the t-norm T_μ^{SW}, where $\mu = -\frac{\lambda}{1+\lambda}$.

(iv) The family $(S_\lambda^H)_{\lambda \in [0,\infty]}$ of *Hamacher t-conorms* is given by

$$S_\lambda^H(x,y) = \begin{cases} S_D(x,y) & \text{if } \lambda = \infty \\ 1 & \text{if } \lambda = 0 \text{ and } x = y = 1 \\ \dfrac{x+y+(\lambda-2)xy}{1+(\lambda-1)xy} & \text{if } \lambda \in \,]0,\infty[\text{ and } (\lambda, x, y) \neq (0,1,1). \end{cases}$$

$$(3.37)$$

(v) The family $(S_\lambda^{SS})_{\lambda \in [-\infty,\infty]}$ of *Schweizer–Sklar t-conorms* is given by (see Figure 3.18)

$$S_\lambda^{SS}(x,y) = \begin{cases} \text{Max}(x,y) & \text{if } \lambda = -\infty \\ S_P(x,y) & \text{if } \lambda = 0 \\ S_D(x,y) & \text{if } \lambda = \infty \\ 1 - \left(\text{Max}\left(0, (1-x)^\lambda + (1-y)^\lambda - 1\right)\right)^{1/\lambda} & \text{if } \lambda \in \,]-\infty, \infty[\setminus \{0\}. \end{cases}$$

$$(3.38)$$

Remark 3.92. (i) A continuous Archimedean t-conorm S is characterized by the diagonal inequality $S(x,x) > x$ for all $x \in \,]0, 1[$.

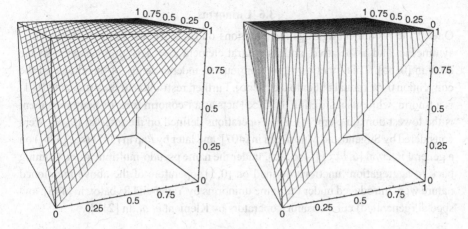

Figure 3.18 Elements of the family S_λ^{SS} for $\lambda = 0.6$ (left) and $\lambda = 4$ (right)

(ii) A continuous Archimedean t-conorm S is always related to some continuous increasing *additive generator* $s : [0, 1] \to [0, \infty], s(0) = 0$, by

$$S(\mathbf{x}) = s^{-1}\left(\mathrm{Min}\left(s(1), \sum_{i=1}^{n} s(x_i)\right)\right). \tag{3.39}$$

(iii) The t-conorms which are dual to strict t-norms are called *strict t-conorms*. They have unbounded additive generators, and they are isomorphic to S_P. Similarly *nilpotent t-conorms* are dual to nilpotent t-norms (with bounded additive generators, isomorphic to S_L). The duality of continuous Archimedean t-norms and t-conorms is reflected by the duality $s = t \circ N$ (where N is the standard negation, $N(x) = 1 - x$) of the corresponding additive generators, i.e., $s(u) = t(1 - u)$, $u \in [0, 1]$. Consequently, $s_P(u) = -\log(1 - u)$ generates the probabilistic sum S_P, while $s_L(u) = u$ generates the bounded sum S_L.

(iv) The representation of continuous t-norms (3.19) is reflected by the dual representation of continuous t-conorms,

$$S(\mathbf{x}) = \begin{cases} s_k^{-1}\left(\mathrm{Min}\left(s_k(b_k), \sum_{i=1}^{n} s_k(\mathrm{Max}(x_i, a_k))\right)\right) & \text{if } \mathrm{Max}(\mathbf{x}) \in \,]a_k, b_k[\\ \mathrm{Max}(\mathbf{x}) & \text{otherwise,} \end{cases}$$

where $(]a_k, b_k[)_{k \in K}$ is a family of pairwise disjoint subintervals of $[0, 1]$, and $s_k : [a_k, b_k] \to [0, \infty]$, $s_k(a_k) = 0$, is a corresponding family of continuous increasing mappings. A continuous t-conorm S is, in general, an upper idempotent ordinal sum of aggregation functions defined on $[a_k, b_k]$, $k \in K$. This type of ordinal sum is called a t-conorm ordinal sum and it results in a t-conorm.

3.6 Uninorms

One of the prominent aggregation functions on $[0, \infty]$ is the product Π, which is symmetric, and associative, and its neutral element $e = 1$ is an inner point of the domain $[0, \infty]$. This function is not continuous, independently of the choice of the convention $0 \cdot \infty$ (equal either to 0 or to ∞). Further, restriction of the product to $[0, 1]$ is a t-norm, while its restriction to $[1, \infty]$ acts as a t-conorm (i.e., its neutral element is the lowest domain element). Such operations defined on the interval $[0, \infty]$ were considered by Sugeno and Murofushi in [407], and later by Pap in [347] (see [349]) on a general interval $[a, b] \subset [-\infty, \infty]$, under the name pseudo-multiplication. Coming back to aggregation functions defined on $[0, 1]$, operators of the above-mentioned nature were introduced under the name uninorms by Yager and Rybalov in [445], and special (generated) compensatory operators by Klement *et al.* in [217].

3.6.1 Basic properties

Definition 3.93. An aggregation function $U : \cup_{n \in \mathbb{N}}[0, 1]^n \to [0, 1]$ which is symmetric, associative, and possesses an extended neutral element $e \in]0, 1[$ is called a *uninorm*.

Proposition 3.94. *Let* $U : \cup_{n \in \mathbb{N}}[0, 1]^n \to [0, 1]$ *be a uninorm with extended neutral element* $e \in]0, 1[$. *Put* $a_U := U(0, 1)$. *Then the following holds:*

(i) a_U *is an annihilator of* U.
(ii) $a_U \in \{0, 1\}$.
(iii) U *is not continuous.*

Proof. (i) From the associativity of U it follows that

$$U(0, a_U) = U(0, U(0, 1)) = U(U(0, 0), 1) = U(0, 1) = a_U.$$

Similarly, $U(a_U, 1) = a_U$.
    The symmetry and monotonicity of U ensures

$$a_U = U(0, a_U) \leqslant U(x, a_U) \leqslant U(1, a_U) = a_U$$

for all $x \in [0, 1]$, i.e., a_U is an annihilator of $U^{(2)}$. The result follows from the associativity of U.
    (ii) The neutral element e of U should differ from the annihilator a_U. Suppose that $a_U < e$. Then by monotonicity of U we get

$$a_U = U(0, a_U) \leqslant U(0, e) = 0,$$

i.e., $a_U = 0$. Similarly, if $a_U > e$ then $a_U = 1$.

(iii) Suppose that $a_\mathsf{U} = 0$ and that U is continuous. Then for $x \in [0, 1]$ there exists $y \in [0, 1]$ such that $x = \mathsf{U}(y, 1)$. However, then

$$\mathsf{U}(x, 1) = \mathsf{U}(\mathsf{U}(y, 1), 1) = \mathsf{U}(y, \mathsf{U}(1, 1)) = \mathsf{U}(y, 1) = x,$$

i.e., 1 is a neutral element of U different from e, a contradiction. Similarly, U cannot be continuous if $a_\mathsf{U} = 1$. □

The uninorms with $a_\mathsf{U} = 0$ are called *conjunctive uninorms*, the remaining uninorms with $a_\mathsf{U} = 1$ are called *disjunctive uninorms*.

3.6.2 Characterization of uninorms

The structure of uninorms is strongly connected with t-norms and t-conorms. For a given uninorm U with a neutral element e, we introduce the related t-norm T_U : $[0, e]^2 \to [0, e]$ and the t-conorm $\mathsf{S}_\mathsf{U} : [e, 1]^2 \to [e, 1]$, given by

$$\mathsf{T}_\mathsf{U}(x, y) := \frac{\mathsf{U}(ex, ey)}{e} \tag{3.40}$$

and

$$\mathsf{S}_\mathsf{U}(x, y) := \frac{\mathsf{U}(e + (1 - e)x, e + (1 - e)y) - e}{1 - e}. \tag{3.41}$$

We characterize the binary form of a uninorm U, which due to the associativity of U, gives complete information about U.

Proposition 3.95. *Let* $\mathsf{U} : [0, 1]^2 \to [0, 1]$ *be a (binary) uninorm with neutral element* $e \in {]}0, 1{[}$. *Then there are three binary aggregation functions* $\mathsf{T}, \mathsf{S}, \mathsf{H} : [0, 1]^2 \to [0, 1]$ *such that* T *is a t-norm,* S *a t-conorm, and* H *is a symmetric mean aggregation function (see Chapter 4, Definition 4.1), and for any* $\mathbf{x} \in [0, 1]^2$ *we have (see Figure 3.19)*

$$\mathsf{U}(\mathbf{x}) = \begin{cases} \mathsf{T}(\mathbf{x}) & \text{if } \mathbf{x} \in [0, e]^2 \\ \mathsf{S}(\mathbf{x}) & \text{if } \mathbf{x} \in [e, 1]^2 \\ \mathsf{H}(\mathbf{x}) & \text{otherwise.} \end{cases} \tag{3.42}$$

Proof. It is enough to put

$$\mathsf{T}(x, y) = \begin{cases} \mathsf{U}(x, y) & \text{if } (x, y) \in [0, e]^2 \\ \mathrm{Min}(x, y) & \text{otherwise,} \end{cases}$$

$$\mathsf{S}(x, y) = \begin{cases} \mathsf{U}(x, y) & \text{if } (x, y) \in [e, 1]^2 \\ \mathrm{Max}(x, y) & \text{otherwise,} \end{cases}$$

and

$$\mathsf{H}(x, y) = \begin{cases} \mathrm{Min}(x, y) & \text{if } (x, y) \in [0, e]^2 \\ \mathrm{Max}(x, y) & \text{if } (x, y) \in [e, 1]^2 \\ \mathsf{U}(x, y) & \text{otherwise.} \end{cases}$$

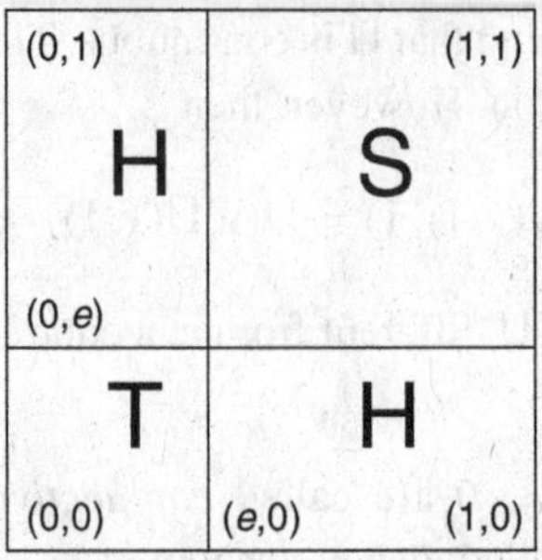

Figure 3.19 The representation of a uninorm from Proposition 3.95

From the fact that e is a neutral element of U it follows that $T = (< 0, e, T_U >)$ is an ordinal sum of t-norms and $S = (< e, 1, S_U >)$ is an ordinal sum of t-conorms. Moreover, $H(x, x) = x$ for all $x \in [0, 1]$. To see the monotonicity of H, due to its symmetry, it is enough to deal with the monotonicity in the first coordinate. Then if $y \in [0, e]$ is arbitrary but fixed, the function $H_y : [0, 1] \to [0, 1]$ given by

$$H_y(x) := \begin{cases} \text{Min}(x, y) & \text{if } x \in [0, e] \\ U(x, y) & \text{otherwise} \end{cases}$$

is nondecreasing due to the fact that $\text{Min}(e, y) = y = U(e, y)$, and the nondecreasing monotonicity of the aggregation functions Min and U. Similarly, for $y \in [e, 1]$ arbitrary but fixed

$$H_y(x) = \begin{cases} U(x, y) & \text{if } x \in [0, y] \\ \text{Max}(x, y) & \text{otherwise,} \end{cases}$$

and the nondecreasing monotonicity of H_y then follows from the equality

$$U(e, y) = y = \text{Max}(e, y). \qquad \square$$

Proposition 3.95 gives the necessary but not sufficient representation of (binary) uninorms by means of t-norms, t-conorms, and symmetric mean functions. For a given t-norm T_U, t-conorm S_U, and neutral element $e \in]0, 1[$, to find an appropriate uninorm U means to find a symmetric mean aggregation function H so that (3.42) holds, where $T = (< 0, e, T_U >)$ and $S = (< e, 1, S_U >)$. The main problem is to ensure the associativity of the function U constructed in such a way.

Proposition 3.96. *Let $e \in]0, 1[$ be a given constant, and let $T = (< 0, e, T_U >)$ and $S = (< e, 1, S_U >)$ be an ordinal sum of t-norms and an ordinal sum of t-conorms, respectively. Then the following holds.*

(i) For any uninorm U characterized by e, T_U, and S_U, we have

$$T < U_{e,T,S} \leqslant U \leqslant U_{T,S,e} < S, \tag{3.43}$$

where

$$U_{e,\mathsf{T},\mathsf{S}}(x,y) := \begin{cases} e\mathsf{T}\left(\frac{x}{e},\frac{y}{e}\right) & \text{if } (x,y) \in [0,e]^2 \\ e + (1-e)\mathsf{S}\left(\frac{x-e}{1-e},\frac{y-e}{1-e}\right) & \text{if } (x,y) \in [e,1]^2 \\ \mathsf{Min}(x,y) & \text{otherwise,} \end{cases} \quad (3.44)$$

and

$$U_{\mathsf{T},\mathsf{S},e}(x,y) := \begin{cases} e\mathsf{T}\left(\frac{x}{e},\frac{y}{e}\right) & \text{if } (x,y) \in [0,e]^2 \\ e + (1-e)\mathsf{S}\left(\frac{x-e}{1-e},\frac{y-e}{1-e}\right) & \text{if } (x,y) \in [e,1]^2 \\ \mathsf{Max}(x,y) & \text{otherwise.} \end{cases} \quad (3.45)$$

(ii) $U_{e,\mathsf{T},\mathsf{S}}$ *and* $U_{\mathsf{T},\mathsf{S},e}$ *are uninorms.*

Proof. Part (i) follows from the representation (3.42), taking into account that for any (symmetric) mean aggregation function H we have $\mathsf{Min} \leqslant H \leqslant \mathsf{Max}$, and that $\mathsf{T} \leqslant \mathsf{Min} < \mathsf{Max} \leqslant \mathsf{S}$ holds for any t-norm and any t-conorm S.

To prove (ii), we remark that the symmetry of both $U_{e,\mathsf{T},\mathsf{S}}$ and $U_{\mathsf{T},\mathsf{S},e}$ is obvious. Similarly, we easily see that e is a neutral element of both $U_{e,\mathsf{T},\mathsf{S}}$ and $U_{\mathsf{T},\mathsf{S},e}$. To prove the monotonicity of $U_{e,\mathsf{T},\mathsf{S}}$, observe that

$$U_{e,\mathsf{T},\mathsf{S}}(x,e) = e\mathsf{T}\left(\frac{x}{e},1\right) = x = \mathsf{Min}(x,e)$$

for all $x \in [0,e]$, and then the monotonicity of T and of Min ensures the monotonicity of $U_{e,\mathsf{T},\mathsf{S}}(x,\cdot)$ for $x \in [0,e]$.

For $x \in\ ]e,1]$,

$$\mathsf{Min}(x,e) = e < x = e + (1-e)\mathsf{S}\left(\frac{x-e}{1-e};0\right) = U_{e,\mathsf{T},\mathsf{S}}(x,e),$$

again ensuring the monotonicity of $U_{e,\mathsf{T},\mathsf{S}}(x,\cdot)$ for $x \in [e,1]$. Due to symmetry of $U_{e,\mathsf{T},\mathsf{S}}$, its monotonicity follows. Similarly one can show the monotonicity of $U_{\mathsf{T},\mathsf{S},e}$. Finally, to prove the associativity of both introduced functions, note that they both can be understood as operations in ordinal sums of semigroups $([0,e],\mathsf{T}|_{[0,e]})$ and $([e,1],\mathsf{S}|_{[e,1]})$ (concerning $U_{e,\mathsf{T},\mathsf{S}}$), and of semigroups $([e,1],\mathsf{S}|_{[e,1]})$ and $([0,e],\mathsf{T}|_{[0,e]})$. Concerning $U_{\mathsf{T},\mathsf{S},e}$, note that in ordinal sums of semigroups, their ordering is crucial for the final result. Due to [63,64] both $U_{e,\mathsf{T},\mathsf{S}}$ and $U_{\mathsf{T},\mathsf{S},e}$ are associative. $\square$

Remark 3.97. (i) The original purpose of the introduction of uninorms by Yager and Rybalov [445], and Klement *et al.* [217], was a need for the so-called compensatory operators improving the lack of upwards (respectively, downwards) compensation by t-norms (respectively, t-conorms), observed already by Zimmermann and Zysno in the 1980s [448,449]; see Definition 3.115. This desirable effect of compensation in both directions (present, e.g., in quasi-arithmetic means) appears in the class of uninorms continuous on $]0, 1[^2$ up to some points with contradictory inputs, investigated by Klement *et al.* [217]; see Theorem 3.100.

(ii) For any T, S, e, the function $U_{e,T,S}$ given by (3.44) is a conjunctive uninorm, while the function $U_{T,S,e}$ given by (3.45) is a disjunctive uninorm.

(iii) Proposition 3.96 allows us to introduce the smallest and the greatest uninorm with a given neutral element e. As T_D is the smallest t-norm and Max is the smallest t-conorm, the *smallest uninorm* U_e with neutral element $e \in]0, 1[$ is given (in binary form) by

$$U_e(x, y) := \begin{cases} 0 & \text{if } (x, y) \in [0, e[^2 \\ \text{Max}(x, y) & \text{if } (x, y) \in [e, 1]^2 \\ \text{Min}(x, y) & \text{otherwise.} \end{cases}$$

Similarly, the *greatest uninorm* U^e with neutral element $e \in]0, 1[$ is related to Min and S_D, and it is given (in binary form) by

$$U^e(x, y) := \begin{cases} \text{Min}(x, y) & \text{if } (x, y) \in [0, e]^2 \\ 1 & \text{if } (x, y) \in]e, 1]^2 \\ \text{Max}(x, y) & \text{otherwise.} \end{cases}$$

(iv) The class of all uninorms is closed under duality, that is, the dual U^d of a uninorm U is again a uninorm. If U is a conjunctive (respectively, disjunctive) uninorm with neutral element e, its dual U^d is a disjunctive (respectively, conjunctive) uninorm with neutral element $1 - e$. Consequently, no uninorm is self-dual (see Definition 2.104; also called symmetric sum; see Section 6.2.3). As an example observe that the uninorm dual to the smallest uninorm U_e with neutral element e (which is conjunctive) is the disjunctive uninorm U^{1-e}, i.e., the greatest uninorm possessing the neutral element $1 - e$.

3.6.3 Idempotent uninorms

The intersection of the class of uninorms and the class of means, i.e., *idempotent uninorms*, was investigated, e.g., in [74]. In spite of Proposition 3.95, idempotent uninorms are related to the unique idempotent t-norm Min and the unique idempotent t-conorm Max. The symmetric case of Theorem 4.47 corresponds to idempotent uninorms.

Two typical idempotent uninorms related to a given neutral element $e \in]0, 1[$ are given by

$$U_{e,\text{Min},\text{Max}}(\mathbf{x}) = \begin{cases} \text{Max}(\mathbf{x}) & \text{if } \text{Min}(\mathbf{x}) \geqslant e \\ \text{Min}(\mathbf{x}) & \text{otherwise,} \end{cases} \tag{3.46}$$

and

$$U_{\mathsf{Min},\mathsf{Max},e}(\mathbf{x}) = \begin{cases} \mathsf{Min}(\mathbf{x}) & \text{if } \mathsf{Max}(\mathbf{x}) \leqslant e \\ \mathsf{Max}(\mathbf{x}) & \text{otherwise.} \end{cases} \tag{3.47}$$

Though there is a unique idempotent t-norm (Min) and a unique idempotent t-conorm (Max), the class of idempotent uninorms is rather rich.

Example 3.98. Let $\varphi : [0, 1] \to [0, 1]$ be an increasing bijection and define $U^{(\varphi)}$: $[0, 1]^2 \to [0, 1]$ by

$$U^{(\varphi)}(x, y) := \begin{cases} \mathsf{Min}(x, y) & \text{if } \varphi(x) + \varphi(y) \leqslant 1 \\ \mathsf{Max}(x, y) & \text{otherwise.} \end{cases}$$

Then $U^{(\varphi)}$ is a (left-continuous, conjunctive) uninorm with neutral element $e = \varphi^{-1}(0.5)$.

3.6.4 Generated uninorms

Next, we consider an important class of uninorms.

Definition 3.99. A uninorm $U : \cup_{n \in \mathbb{N}}[0, 1]^n \to [0, 1]$ is *cancellative* on $\cup_{n \in \mathbb{N}}]0, 1[^n$ if for all $\mathbf{x}, \mathbf{y}, \mathbf{z} \in \cup_{n \in \mathbb{N}}]0, 1[^n$ we have that $U(\mathbf{x}, \mathbf{y}) = U(\mathbf{x}, \mathbf{z})$ implies $U(\mathbf{y}) = U(\mathbf{z})$.

Theorem 3.100. *A function* $U : \cup_{n \in \mathbb{N}}[0, 1]^n \to [0, 1]$ *is a uninorm continuous and cancellative on* $\cup_{n \in \mathbb{N}}]0, 1[^n$ *if and only if there exists a monotone bijection* $u : [0, 1] \to [-\infty, \infty]$ *such that*

$$U(\mathbf{x}) = u^{-1}\left(\sum_{i=1}^{n} u(x_i)\right), \tag{3.48}$$

with convention $\infty + (-\infty) = -\infty$. *The uninorm* U *is then called a generated uninorm with additive generator* u.

Proof. For the binary function $F = U|_{]0,1[^2}$, by the Aczél representation theorem [2] there is an increasing bijection $g :]0, 1[\to]-\infty, \infty[$ such that

$$F(x, y) = g^{-1}(g(x) + g(y)) \text{ for all } (x, y) \in [0, 1]^2.$$

If U is conjunctive, due to the monotonicity of U and its associativity, the representation (3.48) holds with $u : [0, 1] \to [-\infty, \infty]$ given by

$$u(x) := \begin{cases} -\infty & \text{if } x = 0 \\ \infty & \text{if } x = 1 \\ g(x) & \text{otherwise.} \end{cases}$$

Similarly, if U is disjunctive, it is enough to put

$$u(x) := \begin{cases} \infty & \text{if } x = 0 \\ -\infty & \text{if } x = 1 \\ -g(x) & \text{otherwise.} \end{cases}$$

The opposite implication is trivial.   □

Remark 3.101. (i) The requirements of Theorem 3.100 can be relaxed, omitting the cancellativity of U; see [121]. Moreover, each generated uninorm is continuous in all points of the domain $\cup_{n \in \mathbb{N}}[0, 1]^n$ up to points **x** such that $x_i = 0$ and $x_j = 1$ for some $i, j \in [n]$.

(ii) Archimedeanity of a uninorm U is the corresponding property of the related t-norm T_U and t-conorm S_U, in fact. For example, any generated uninorm U is Archimedean, but not the uninorms $U^{(\varphi)}$ introduced in Example 3.98.

Generated uninorms transform the standard summation function defined on $[-\infty, \infty]$ to the unit interval $[0, 1]$. The neutral element e of a generated uninorm U is given by $e = u^{-1}(0)$. The increasing monotonicity of an additive generator u of a generated uninorm U is equivalent to its conjunctive form (i.e., disjunctive generated uninorms are related to the decreasing additive generators).

Example 3.102. A typical example of a conjunctive generated uninorm is the 3-П-operator E given by (see Figure 3.20)

$$E(\mathbf{x}) = \frac{\prod\limits_{i=1}^{n} x_i}{\prod\limits_{i=1}^{n} x_i + \prod\limits_{i=1}^{n}(1 - x_i)}, \quad \text{with the convention } \frac{0}{0} = 0.$$

Its additive generator $u : [0, 1] \to [-\infty, \infty]$ (necessarily unique up to a positive multiplicative constant) is given by $u(x) = \log \frac{x}{1-x}$.

Generated uninorms are always related to strict t-norms and strict t-conorms (in the sense of Proposition 3.95 and formulas (3.40), (3.41). For corresponding additive generators u, t, s of U, T_U, S_U we have the next relationships

$$u(x) = \begin{cases} -t\left(\frac{x}{e}\right) & \text{if } x \in [0, e] \\ s\left(\frac{x-e}{1-e}\right) & \text{if } x \in]e, 1], \end{cases} \tag{3.49}$$

$$t(x) = -u(ex), \quad x \in [0, 1], \tag{3.50}$$

$$s(x) = u(e + (1 - e)x), \quad x \in [0, 1]. \tag{3.51}$$

Here e is the neutral element of the discussed generated uninorm U.

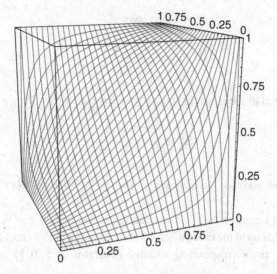

Figure 3.20 The uninorm 3-Π

The freedom in the choice of an additive generator of a given strict t-norm T_U and a given strict t-conorm S_U allows us to construct a parameterized class of (conjunctive) generated uninorms related to T_U and S_U as in Proposition 3.100.

Let $t : [0, 1] \rightarrow [0, \infty]$ be a (unique) additive generator of a given strict t-norm T such that $t(0.5) = 1$, and similarly, let $s : [0, 1] \rightarrow [0, \infty]$, $s(0.5) = 1$, be an additive generator of a given strict t-conorm S. For a given parameter $p \in \,]0, \infty[$, define an additive generator $u_p : [0, 1] \rightarrow [-\infty, \infty]$ related to a generated uninorm U_p,

$$u_p(x) = \begin{cases} -t\left(\frac{x}{e}\right) & \text{if } x \in [0, e] \\ ps\left(\frac{x-e}{1-e}\right) & \text{if } x \in \,]e, 1]. \end{cases}$$

For each $p \in \,]0, \infty[$, U_p is related to T and S as stated in Proposition 3.95, as well as to T_U (see (3.40)), and to S_U (see (3.41)). Further, the family $(U_p)_{p \in]0, \infty[}$ is nondecreasing and its limit member is

$$U_0 := \lim_{p \to 0^+} U_p = U_{e,T,S}.$$

The other limit member

$$U_\infty := \lim_{p \to \infty} U_p$$

coincides with $U_{T,S,e}$ on $\cup_{n \in \mathbb{N}}]0, 1]^n$.

Example 3.103. The 3-Π-operator E (see Example 3.102) is related to the Hamacher t-norm $T_2^H = T_E$ (see (3.8)), generated by an additive generator $t : [0, 1] \rightarrow$

$[0, \infty]$, $t(x) = \log_3 \frac{2-x}{x}$, $t(0.5) = 1$. We have

$$T_2^H(x,y) = \frac{xy}{2 - x - y + xy}.$$

Next, S_E is related to the Einstein sum (Hamacher t-conorm) S_2^H, given by

$$S_2^H(x,y) = \frac{x+y}{1+xy},$$

generated by the additive generator $s : [0,1] \rightarrow [0,\infty]$, $s(x) = \log_3 \frac{1+x}{1-x}$, $s(0.5) = 1$.

S_2^H is the dual t-conorm to T_2^H. The neutral element of E is $e = 0.5$, and $E^d = E$ (self-duality) holds up to the cases when inputs containing both 0 and 1 are aggregated. For $p \in \ ]0, \infty[$, the corresponding additive generator $u_p : [0,1] \rightarrow [-\infty, \infty]$ is given by

$$u_p(x) = \begin{cases} \log_3 \frac{x}{1-x} & \text{if } x \in [0, 0.5] \\ p \log_3 \frac{x}{1-x} & \text{if } x \in \ ]0.5, 1]. \end{cases}$$

Aggregating, e.g., $x = 0.1$ and $y = 0.9$, we obtain

$$U_p(0.1, 0.9) = h_p^{-1} \left(\log_3 \frac{1}{9} + p \log_3 9 \right) = h_p^{-1}(2p - 2),$$

that is,

for $p \in \ ]0, 1[$, $\quad U_p(0.1, 0.9) = \dfrac{9^p}{9 + 9^p} \quad$ (tending to 0.1, when $p \rightarrow 0^+$),

for $p = 1$, $\quad U_p(0.1, 0.9) = 0.5$,

for $p \in]1, \infty[$, $\quad U_p(0.1, 0.9) = \dfrac{9}{9 + 9^{\frac{1}{p}}} \quad$ (tending to 0.9, when $p \rightarrow \infty$).

Remark 3.104. (i) Limit properties of generated uninorms with respect to the powers of additive generators are discussed by Mesiar and Komorníková [307]. The limit functions are specific aggregation functions depending on the original additive generator. Compare with Proposition 3.42, from which we know that in the case of generated t-norms the limit functions do not depend on starting additive generators; the same holds, by duality, for generated t-conorms. These limit functions are related to the symmetric maximum on $[-1, 1]$; see Chapter 9.

(ii) The associativity of uninorms, t-norms, and t-conorms allows us to derive for each uninorm U the n-ary function $U^{(n)}$ from the binary function $U^{(2)}$. Let T and S be a t-norm and a t-conorm, respectively, which are related to U as given in

Proposition 3.95. Then

$$U^{(n)}(\mathbf{x}) =$$
$$U^{(2)}\left(T\left(Min(x_1,e),\ldots,Min(x_n,e)\right), S\left(Max(x_1,e),\ldots,Max(x_n,e)\right)\right). \quad (3.52)$$

Equality (3.52) allows us to introduce for uninorms several notions known for t-norms and t-conorms, such as the weighted uninorms; see Chapter 6.

3.7 Nullnorms

Uninorms are aggregation functions related to ordinal sums of a t-norm defined on $[0, e]$ and a t-conorm defined on $[e, 1]$. Among several possible extensions of such functions, the minimal one is the conjunctive uninorm $U_{e,T,S}$, and the maximal one is the disjunctive uninorm $U_{T,S,e}$. However, if we discuss the possible extensions of a t-conorm defined on an interval $[0, a]$, $a \in]0, 1[$ and a t-norm defined on $[a, 1]$, in spite of Proposition 6.55, there is a unique such extension, that is, the lower ordinal sum and the upper ordinal sum coincide and a is the annihilator of the resulting aggregation function. This class of functions are called nullnorms. Nullnorms are associative and symmetric. Due to their associativity, it is enough to define (axiomatically) the relevant binary function (with the same notation).

Definition 3.105. A symmetric associative aggregation function $V : [0, 1]^2 \to [0, 1]$ is called a nullnorm if there is an element $a \in]0, 1[$ such that

$$V(x, 0) = x \quad \text{for all} \quad x \leqslant a, \quad V(x, 1) = x \quad \text{for all} \quad x \geqslant a. \quad (3.53)$$

As $V(0, a) = V(1, a) = V(a, 0) = V(a, 1) = a$, the monotonicity of V ensures that a is the annihilator of V. Furthermore, on $\cup_{n \in \mathbb{N}}[0, a]^n$, 0 acts as an extended neutral element of V (and a is annihilator), that is, V acts on $[0, a]$ as a t-conorm. Indeed, define a binary function $S_V : [0, 1]^2 \to [0, 1]$ by

$$S_V(x, y) := \frac{V(ax, ay)}{a}. \quad (3.54)$$

Then S_V is a t-conorm, and

$$V|_{[0,a]^2} = (< 0, a, S_V >)|_{[0,a]^2}.$$

Similarly, V acts on $[a, 1]$ as a t-norm,

$$V|_{[a,1]^2} = (< a, 1, T_V >)|_{[a,1]^2},$$

where
$$T_V(x, y) := \frac{V(a + (1 - a)x, a + (1 - a)y) - a}{1 - a} \quad (3.55)$$

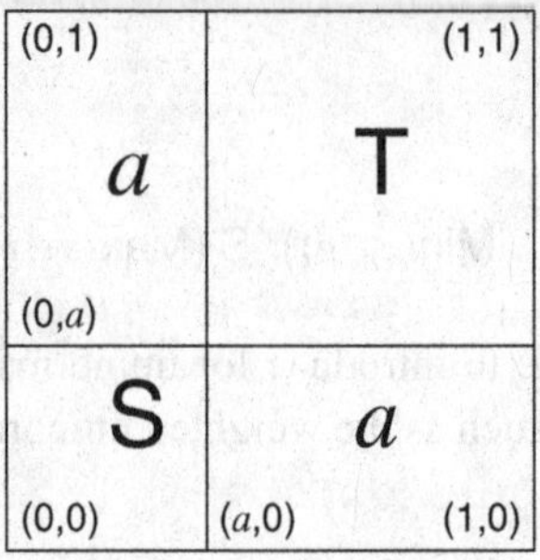

Figure 3.21 The representation of a nullnorm

for all $(x,y) \in [0,1]^2$. Fixing T_V, S_V and $a \in]0, 1[$, we have the unique nullnorm V satisfying (3.54) and (3.55), since by monotonicity of V

$$V(x,y) = a \quad \text{whenever } (x,y) \in [0,1]^2 \setminus \left([0,a]^2 \cup [a,1]^2 \right)$$

(see Figure 3.21).

Due to the associativity of V, we can extend these results to an arbitrary number of inputs, i.e.,

$$V(\mathbf{x}) = \begin{cases} aS_V \left(\frac{x_1}{a}, \ldots, \frac{x_n}{a} \right) & \text{if } \text{Max}(\mathbf{x}) \leqslant a \\ a + (1-a)T_V \left(\frac{x_1 - a}{1-a}, \ldots, \frac{x_n - a}{1-a} \right) & \text{if } \text{Min}(\mathbf{x}) \geqslant a \\ a & \text{otherwise.} \end{cases} \quad (3.56)$$

Example 3.106. We define the nullnorm $V : [0,1]^2 \rightarrow [0,1]$ in the following way (see Figure 3.22):

$$V(x,y) = \begin{cases} \text{Max}(x,y) & \text{if } (x,y) \in [0,1/3]^2 \\ \dfrac{3xy - x - y + 1}{2} & \text{if } (x,y) \in [1/3,1]^2 \\ 1/3 & \text{otherwise.} \end{cases}$$

Here $a = \frac{1}{3}$, $S_V = \text{Max}$ and $T_V = \Pi$.

For a given annihilator $a \in]0, 1[$, there is a unique idempotent nullnorm (related to $S = \text{Max}$ and $T = \text{Min}$), namely Med_a (a-median), introduced in Section 1.2,

$$\text{Med}_a(x,y) = \text{Med}(x,y,a).$$

These important functions were introduced by Fung and Fu [131] and further studied by Fodor [114]. The next result clarifying the structure of nullnorms is based on a-medians.

Proposition 3.107. *An aggregation function* $V : \cup_{n \in \mathbb{N}}[0,1]^n \rightarrow [0,1]$ *is a nullnorm if and only if there exist a t-norm* T, *a t-conorm* S, *and an element* $a \in]0, 1[$ *such*

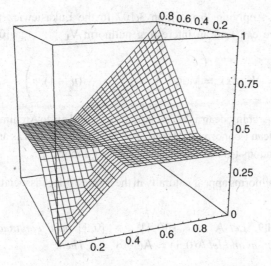

Figure 3.22 The nullnorm from Example 3.106

that V *is a composed aggregation function (see Proposition 6.16),* $V = \text{Med}_a(T, S)$, *that is,*

$$V(\mathbf{x}) = \text{Med}\left(T(\mathbf{x}), S(\mathbf{x}), a\right). \tag{3.57}$$

Proof. For a given nullnorm V with an annihilator a, the representation (3.57) holds with $T = (< a, 1, T_V >)$ and $S = (< 0, a, S_V >)$.

To prove the opposite implication, let T be any given t-norm, S any given t-conorm and $a \in \,]0, 1[$. Then the function given by (3.57) is a symmetric aggregation function. If $a \in \{x_1, \ldots, x_n\}$, then $T(\mathbf{x}) \leqslant a \leqslant S(\mathbf{x})$, and thus $V(\mathbf{x}) = a$, i.e., a is an annihilator of V. For arbitrary elements $\mathbf{x}, \mathbf{y} \in \cup_{n \in \mathbb{N}}[0, 1]^n$, if $T(\mathbf{x}, \mathbf{y}) \leqslant a \leqslant S(\mathbf{x}, \mathbf{y})$, then we have $V(\mathbf{x}, \mathbf{y}) = a$. Moreover, if $a \in \{V(\mathbf{x}), V(\mathbf{y})\}$, then also $V(\mathbf{x}, \mathbf{y}) = a$. If both $V(\mathbf{x}) = T(\mathbf{x}) \geqslant a$ and $V(\mathbf{y}) = T(\mathbf{y}) \geqslant a$, necessarily $S(V(\mathbf{x}), V(\mathbf{y})) \geqslant a$ and $T(V(\mathbf{x}), V(\mathbf{y})) \leqslant a$, again ensuring $V(\mathbf{x}, \mathbf{y}) = a$. Similar is the case $V(\mathbf{x}) = S(\mathbf{x}) \leqslant a$ and $V(\mathbf{y}) = S(\mathbf{y}) \geqslant a$. Finally, if $V(\mathbf{x}) = T(\mathbf{x}) \geqslant a$ and $V(\mathbf{x}) = S(\mathbf{x}) \leqslant a$, then obviously $V(V(\mathbf{x}), V(\mathbf{y})) = a$ (similarly if $V(\mathbf{x}) = S(\mathbf{x}) \leqslant a$ and $V(\mathbf{y}) = T(\mathbf{x}) \geqslant a$). Summarizing,

$$V(\mathbf{x}, \mathbf{y}) = a = V(V(\mathbf{x}), V(\mathbf{y})).$$

If $S(\mathbf{x}, \mathbf{y}) < a$, then both $S(\mathbf{x}) < a$ and $S(\mathbf{y}) < a$, and thus

$$V(\mathbf{x}, \mathbf{y}) = S(\mathbf{x}, \mathbf{y}) = S(S(\mathbf{x}), S(\mathbf{y})) = V(V(\mathbf{x}), V(\mathbf{y})),$$

due to the associativity of S. Similarly, if $T(\mathbf{x}, \mathbf{y}) > a$, we have

$$V(\mathbf{x}, \mathbf{y}) = T(\mathbf{x}, \mathbf{y}) = T(T(\mathbf{x}), T(\mathbf{y})) = V(V(\mathbf{x}), V(\mathbf{y})).$$

Summarizing, V is associative and thus a nullnorm. □

Example 3.108. Applying Proposition 3.107 to the Łukasiewicz t-norm $\mathsf{T_L}$ and t-conorm $\mathsf{S_L}$, we can find an interesting nullnorm $\mathsf{V_{L,a}} : \cup_{n\in\mathbb{N}}[0,1]^n \to [0,1]$ given by

$$\mathsf{V_{L,a}}(\mathbf{x}) := \mathrm{Med}\left(\sum_{i=1}^{n} x_i, \sum_{i=1}^{n} x_i - (n-1), a\right). \qquad (3.58)$$

This nullnorm is Archimedean as are all nullnorms based on an Archimedean t-norm T and an Archimedean t-conorm S. Moreover, it is also continuous as are all nullnorms based on a continuous t-norm T and a continuous t-conorm S.

Continuous nullnorms appear naturally in the framework of associative aggregation functions.

Proposition 3.109. *Let* $\mathsf{A} : \cup_{n\in\mathbb{N}}[0,1]^n \to [0,1]$ *be a continuous associative aggregation function and let* $\mathsf{A}(0,1) = \mathsf{A}(1,0) = a$. *Then:*

(i) if $a = 0$, A *is a t-norm;*
(ii) if $a = 1$, A *is a t-conorm;*

(iii) if $a \in\,]0, 1[$, A *is a nullnorm with annihilator* a.

Proof. Cases (i) and (ii) are special cases of the representation of topological semigroups of Mostert and Shields [320]; see [220, Th. 2.43].

Suppose that $a \in\,]0, 1[$. Then $\mathsf{A}(a, 1) = \mathsf{A}(\mathsf{A}(0, 1), 1) = \mathsf{A}(0, \mathsf{A}(1, 1)) = a$, and similarly $\mathsf{A}(1, a) = \mathsf{A}(0, a) = \mathsf{A}(a, 0) = a$.

From the monotonicity of A, the element a is an annihilator of $\mathsf{A}^{(2)}$ and thus, due to the associativity, also A. Moreover, for any $x \in [a, 1]$ the continuity of A ensures that $x = \mathsf{A}(y, 1)$ for some y. However, then $\mathsf{A}(x, 1) = \mathsf{A}(\mathsf{A}(y, 1), 1) = \mathsf{A}(y, \mathsf{A}(1, 1)) = x$. Similarly, $\mathsf{A}(1, x) = x$ for all $x \in [a, 1]$ and $\mathsf{A}(0, x) = \mathsf{A}(x, 0) = x$ for all $x \in [0, a]$. We have that $([a, 1], \mathsf{A}|_{[a,1]^2})$ is a topological semigroup with annihilator a and due to [320] it is Abelian. Similarly, $\mathsf{A}|_{[0,a]^2}$ is symmetric and thus $\mathsf{A}^{(2)}$ is symmetric. Due to Definition 3.105, V is a nullnorm. $\qquad\square$

Remark 3.110. Following Mayor and Torrens [300], we can relax the continuity requirement in Proposition 3.109 to the continuity of the partial functions $\mathsf{A}(0, \cdot)$ and $\mathsf{A}(1, \cdot)$. However, then the symmetry of A should be required.

Nullnorms satisfy a counterpart of Proposition 3.36 and Theorem 3.100 concerning additive generators.

Definition 3.111. A nullnorm $\mathsf{V} : \cup_{n\in\mathbb{N}}[0,1]^n \to [0,1]$ is *nilpotent* whenever, for any $x \in [0, 1]$, there exists $k \in \mathbb{N}$ such that $\mathsf{V}^{(k)}(n \cdot x) \in \{0, a, 1\}$.

Proposition 3.112. *A function* $\mathsf{V} : \cup_{n\in\mathbb{N}}[0,1]^n \to [0,1]$ *is a continuous nilpotent nullnorm with annihilator* $a \in\,]0, 1[$ *if and only if there exists an increasing bijection* $q : [0,1] \to [0,1]$ *such that*

$$V(\mathbf{x}) = q^{-1} \left(\text{Med} \left(\sum_{i=1}^{n} q(x_i), \sum_{i=1}^{n} q(x_i) - (n-1), q(\bar{a}) \right) \right). \tag{3.59}$$

Proof. Each nilpotent nullnorm is related to a nilpotent t-conorm S_V given by (3.54) (with normed additive generator $s : [0, 1] \to [0, \infty]$, $s(1) = 1$) and a nilpotent t-norm T_V given by (3.55) (with normed additive generator $t : [0, 1] \to [0, \infty]$, $t(0) = 1$), and then

$$q(x) = \begin{cases} as\left(\frac{x}{a}\right) & \text{if } x \in [0, a] \\ 1 - (1-a)t\left(\frac{x-a}{1-a}\right) & \text{if } x \in \,]a, 1]. \end{cases}$$

To prove the opposite implication, observe that V introduced in (3.59) is, in fact, a transformation by q of $V_{L,a}$, i.e., $V = (V_{L,q(a)})_q$; see Proposition 6.1. $\qquad\square$

Example 3.113. (i) The function $V_{L,a}$ introduced in (3.58) related to S_L and T_L has an additive generator $q : [0, 1] \to [0, 1]$, $q(x) = x$ (independently of a).

(ii) Archimedean continuous nullnorms related to a strict t-conorm S and/or to a strict t-norm T cannot be represented by means of additive generators as in (3.59). However, then some multiplicative version of (3.59) is of use.

Remark 3.114. (i) A dual aggregation function to a nullnorm V represented by T, S and a in (3.57) is a nullnorm V^d represented by dual functions S^d, T^d and $1 - a$. Thus V is self-dual (also called a symmetric sum; see Section 6.2.3) if and only if it has representation (3.57) by means of $T, S = T^d$ and $a = 0.5$, where T is an arbitrary t-norm.

(ii) Nullnorms are special (symmetric) associative aggregation functions with an annihilator $a \in \,]0, 1[$. One can investigate the class of general (symmetric) associative aggregation functions with such an annihilator, however, this investigation turns then to the study of (symmetric) aggregation functions with annihilator $a = 0$ (the case of $a = 1$ follows by duality). Such functions include t-norms and conjunctive uninorms (t-conorms and disjunctive uninorms), among others. For more details see [295].

3.8 More aggregation functions related to t-norms

Several other aggregation functions, besides uninorms and nullnorms, are related to t-norms and t-conorms. For ease of reference, we use here their original names from the literature [443, 448]. As already observed when discussing uninorms (see Remark 3.97(i)), t-conorms lack upwards compensation (see definition below) while t-norms lack downwards compensation, both properties being naturally present in human decision making. Therefore, in the 1980s, several alternative attempts were made to overcome these undesirable properties, while still staying close to t-norms/t-conorms, especially because of the acceptable computational complexity.

Definition 3.115. An extended aggregation function $A : \cup_{n\in\mathbb{N}}[0,1]^n \to [0,1]$ possesses the *downward* (respectively, *upward*) compensation property whenever for any $n \in \mathbb{N}$, $\mathbf{x} \in [0,1]^n$, such that $A(\mathbf{x}) > 0$ (respectively, $A(\mathbf{x}) < 1$) it is also the case that $A(\mathbf{x}) > A(x_1,\ldots,x_n,0)$ (respectively, $A(\mathbf{x}) < A(x_1,\ldots,x_n,1)$).

(i) Gamma operators The gamma operators $\Gamma_\gamma : \cup_{n\in\mathbb{N}}[0,1]^n \to [0,1]$ were introduced by Zimmermann and Zysno [448] and applied to car control. For a parameter $\gamma \in [0,1]$, the *gamma operator* Γ_γ is given by $\Gamma_\gamma := \Pi^{1-\gamma}S_\mathbf{P}^\gamma$, that is,

$$\Gamma_\gamma(\mathbf{x}) := \left(\prod_{i=1}^n x_i\right)^{1-\gamma} \left(1 - \prod_{i=1}^n(1-x_i)\right)^\gamma. \tag{3.60}$$

Gamma operators are composed operators related to the weighted geometric mean (as the outer function) and to the product Π and probabilistic sum $S_\mathbf{P}$ (as the inner operators). The parameter γ can be viewed as a degree of upwards compensation. Indeed, if $\gamma = 1$ then $\Gamma_1 = S_\mathbf{P}$ (total upwards compensation) while if $\gamma = 0$ then $\Gamma = \Pi$ (absolute lack of upwards compensation). For all $\gamma \in [0,1[$, $a = 0$ is the annihilator of Γ_γ. All gamma operators are symmetric continuous and Archimedean aggregation functions, which neither are associative nor possess a neutral element (up to the boundary cases $\gamma \in \{0,1\}$).

(ii) Exponential convex T–S-operators Gamma operators are a special subclass of the so-called *exponential convex T–S-operators* [258], that is, of weighted geometric means of a t-norm T, and a t-conorm S (not necessarily a dual pair), $E_{\mathsf{T},\mathsf{S},\gamma} : \cup_{n\in\mathbb{N}}[0,1]^n \to [0,1]$,

$$E_{\mathsf{T},\mathsf{S},\gamma}(\mathbf{x}) := \left(\mathsf{T}(\mathbf{x})\right)^{1-\gamma}\left(\mathsf{S}(\mathbf{x})\right)^\gamma. \tag{3.61}$$

We have that $E_{\mathsf{T},\mathsf{S},0} = \mathsf{T}$ and $E_{\mathsf{T},\mathsf{S},1} = \mathsf{S}$. Any exponential convex T–S-operator is symmetric, and for $\gamma < 1$, $a = 0$ is its annihilator. The continuity of $E_{\mathsf{T},\mathsf{S},\gamma}$, $\gamma \in\ ]0,1[$, is equivalent to the continuity of T and S, while its Archimedeanity is equivalent to the Archimedeanity of T. The only idempotent exponential convex T–S-operators are related to $\mathsf{T} = \mathsf{Min}$ and $\mathsf{S} = \mathsf{Max}$, in which case we obtain a special ordered weighted geometric mean,

$$E_{\mathsf{Min},\mathsf{Max},\gamma}(\mathbf{x}) = \left(x_{\sigma(1)}\right)^{1-\gamma}\left(x_{\sigma(n)}\right)^\gamma, \tag{3.62}$$

$(x_{\sigma(1)},\ldots,x_{\sigma(n)})$ being as usual, a nondecreasing permutation of $(x_1,\ldots,x_n)$. For a fixed $n \in \mathbb{N}$, some other exponential convex T–S-operators can also be idempotent. For example, let T be the Hamacher product, $\mathsf{T}_0^\mathbf{H}(x,y) = \frac{xy}{x+y-xy}$ (with convention $\frac{0}{0} = 0$), and let $\mathsf{S} = \mathsf{S}_\mathbf{P}$, $\gamma = 0.5$. Then

$$\left(E_{\mathsf{T}_0^\mathbf{H},\mathsf{S},0.5}\right)^{(2)}(x,y) = \sqrt{xy} = \mathsf{G}^{(2)}(x,y).$$

However, the corresponding ternary function is not idempotent,

$$\left(\mathsf{E}_{\mathsf{T}_0^{\mathsf{H}},\mathsf{S},0.5}\right)^{(3)}(x,x,x) = x\sqrt{\frac{3-3x+x^2}{3-2x}}$$

for all $x \in [0,1]$.

(iii) Linear convex T–S-operators Another composed aggregation approach based on t-norms and t-conorms is related to the weighted arithmetic mean (as the outer function) [258]. A linear convex T–S-operator $\mathsf{L}_{\mathsf{T},\mathsf{S},\gamma} : \cup_{n\in\mathbb{N}}[0,1]^n \to [0,1]$ is given by

$$\mathsf{L}_{\mathsf{T},\mathsf{S},\gamma}(\mathbf{x}) := (1-\gamma)\mathsf{T}(\mathbf{x}) + \gamma\mathsf{S}(\mathbf{x}). \tag{3.63}$$

These operators were successfully applied in fuzzy linear programming. Linear convex T–S-operators are symmetric, continuous whenever T and S are continuous, neither with annihilator nor with neutral element whenever $\gamma \in \,]0,1[$.

Example 3.116. Consider the following linear convex operator:

$$L_{\mathsf{T}_{\mathsf{L}},\mathsf{Max},0.3}(x,y) = 0.7 \cdot \mathsf{T}_{\mathsf{L}}(x,y) + 0.3 \cdot \mathsf{Max}(x,y)$$

(see Figure 3.23).

If T and S are Archimedean, then for all $x \in \,]0,1[$, $\lim_{n\to\infty}\left(\mathsf{L}_{\mathsf{T},\mathsf{S},\gamma}\right)^{(n)}(n \cdot x) = \gamma$. Moreover, the only idempotent linear convex T–S-operators are special ordered weighted averaging functions

$$\mathsf{L}_{\mathsf{Min},\mathsf{Max},\gamma}(\mathbf{x}) = (1-\gamma)x_1' + \gamma x_n', \tag{3.64}$$

where $x_1' = \mathsf{Min}(\mathbf{x})$, $x_n' = \mathsf{Max}(\mathbf{x})$.

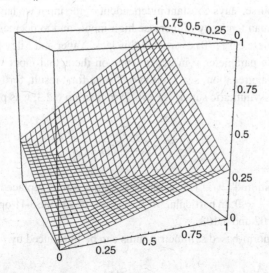

Figure 3.23 Linear convex $L_{\mathsf{T}_{\mathsf{L}},\mathsf{Max},0.3}$-operator from Example 3.116

Some specific n-ary linear convex T–S-operators can be idempotent and different from (3.64). Namely, for any Frank t-norm $\mathsf{T}^{\mathsf{F}}_\lambda$, $\lambda \in]0, \infty]$ given in (3.30), and its dual t-conorm $\mathsf{S}^{\mathsf{F}}_\lambda$, $\left(\mathsf{L}_{\mathsf{T}^{\mathsf{F}}_\lambda, \mathsf{S}^{\mathsf{F}}_\lambda, 0.5}\right)^{(2)}$ is exactly the arithmetic mean $\mathsf{AM}^{(2)}$. For example, for $\lambda = 1$ we have $\mathsf{T}^{\mathsf{F}}_1 = \Pi$, and then

$$\mathsf{L}_{\Pi, \mathsf{S}_{\mathbf{P}}, 0.5}(x, y) = 0.5xy + 0.5(x + y - xy) = \frac{x + y}{2},$$

while

$$\mathsf{L}_{\Pi, \mathsf{S}_{\mathbf{P}}, 0.5}(x, x, x) = x^3 + \frac{3}{2}(x - x^2).$$

Similarly, for $\lambda = \infty$ we have $\mathsf{T}^{\mathsf{F}}_\infty = \mathsf{T}_{\mathbf{L}}$ and then

$$\mathsf{L}_{\mathsf{T}_{\mathbf{L}}, \mathsf{S}_{\mathbf{L}}, 0.5}(x, y) = 0.5\,\mathsf{Max}(0, x + y - 1) + 0.5\,\mathsf{Min}(1, x + y) = \frac{x + y}{2},$$

while

$$\mathsf{L}_{\mathsf{T}_{\mathbf{L}}, \mathsf{S}_{\mathbf{L}}, 0.5}(x, x, x) = \begin{cases} \dfrac{3x}{2} & \text{if} \quad x \in \left[0, \frac{1}{3}\right[\\[2mm] \dfrac{1}{2} & \text{if} \quad x \in \left[\frac{1}{3}, \frac{2}{3}\right] \\[2mm] \dfrac{3x - 1}{2} & \text{if} \quad x \in \left]\frac{2}{3}, 1\right[. \end{cases}$$

(iv) Symmetric sums related to t-norms and t-conorms The parameter $\gamma \in [0, 1]$ in previous items (i)–(iii) can be viewed as a kind of orness parameter. Then if we fix γ, it, of course, stays constant independent of the input we have to aggregate. However, the human tendency to increase high inputs and to decrease low inputs is not reflected in these cases. To overcome this lack, Yager and Filev [443] proposed to choose first the parameter γ in dependence on the actual input values and then provide the final aggregation; see Section 6.5. As a final result, for t-norms with no zero divisors, the symmetric sum $\mathsf{T}^\sharp$, see (6.7) in Section 6.2.3, was proposed,

$$\mathsf{T}^\sharp(\mathbf{x}) := \frac{\mathsf{T}(\mathbf{x})}{\mathsf{T}(\mathbf{x}) + \mathsf{T}(1 - \mathbf{x})}, \tag{3.65}$$

where the convention $\frac{0}{0} = \frac{1}{2}$ (for symmetric sums) can be replaced by some other convention, e.g., $\frac{0}{0} = 0$. In particular, if $\mathsf{T} = \Pi$, we obtain the 3-Π-operator $\mathsf{E} = \Pi^\sharp$, see Examples 3.102 and 3.103.

Similarly, t-conorm-based symmetric sums can be introduced by

$$\mathsf{S}^\sharp(\mathbf{x}) := \frac{\mathsf{S}(\mathbf{x})}{\mathsf{S}(\mathbf{x}) + \mathsf{S}(1 - \mathbf{x})}. \tag{3.66}$$

As a special idempotent symmetric self-dual continuous aggregation function we can introduce $\mathsf{Min}^\sharp$ and $\mathsf{Max}^\sharp$ given by

$$\mathsf{Min}^\sharp(\mathbf{x}) := \frac{x_{\sigma(1)}}{x_{\sigma(1)} + 1 - x_{\sigma(n)}} \qquad (3.67)$$

and

$$\mathsf{Max}^\sharp(\mathbf{x}) := \frac{x_{\sigma(n)}}{x_{\sigma(n)} + 1 - x_{\sigma(1)}}, \qquad (3.68)$$

where $(x_{\sigma(1)}, \ldots, x_{\sigma(n)})$ is a nondecreasing permutation of $(x_1, \ldots, x_n)$. Motivated by (3.67) and (3.68), for any fixed $n \in \mathbb{N}$, $i,j \in [n]$, we can introduce the function $\mathsf{A}_{i,j} : [0,1]^n \to [0,1]$ given by the formula

$$\mathsf{A}_{i,j}(\mathbf{x}) := \frac{x_{\sigma(i)}}{x_{\sigma(i)} + 1 - x_{\sigma(j)}}. \qquad (3.69)$$

This $\mathsf{A}_{i,j}$-function generalizes the order statistics $\mathsf{P}'_i = \mathsf{A}_{i,i}$. Moreover, any $\mathsf{A}_{i,j}$-function is idempotent, symmetric, continuous, and self-dual whenever $i + j = n + 1$.

3.9 Restricted distributivity

In this section we present a relation between a pair consisting of a uninorm (or t-norm) and a t-conorm under the name restricted distributivity; see [219, 220]. Such pairs of operations play a crucial role in the generalization of utility theory [92] (see [351]), presented in Appendix B, as well as in integration theory [219]; see Section 5.6. Further investigations on the distributivity condition can be found in [4, 376].

As is well known (and can easily be proved), the following connection holds.

Proposition 3.117. *A t-conorm* T *is distributive over a t-norm* S, *i.e., for all* $x, y, z \in [0,1]$

$$T(x, S(y,z)) = S(T(x,y), T(x,z)),$$

if and only if $\mathsf{S} = \mathsf{Max}$.

Proof. Put $y = z = 1$. Then $x = \mathsf{S}(x,x)$ for all $x \in [0,1]$, therefore $\mathsf{S} = \mathsf{Max}$ by Proposition 3.88(ii). □

Relaxing only weakly the domain of distributivity, the class of pairs of t-norms and t-conorms for which the so-called restricted distributivity holds is much bigger. We start from a pair consisting of a uninorm and a t-conorm.

Let U be a left-continuous uninorm or t-norm, and S a continuous t-conorm.

Definition 3.118. U *is restrictedly distributive* (RD for short) *over* S *if they satisfy*

$$U(x, S(y,z)) = S(U(x,y), U(x,z)) \qquad (3.70)$$

for all $x, y, z \in [0,1]$ *such that* $\mathsf{S}(y,z) < 1$.

In this way $([0, 1], \mathsf{S}, \mathsf{U})$ is a restrictedly distributive semiring.

First we consider a special important case when U is a t-norm. This case has important applications in utility theory; see Appendix B.

The next result shows that the continuity of T and S implies that distributivity can be extended to a wider domain.

Proposition 3.119. *Let* T *be a continuous t-norm restrictedly distributive over a continuous t-conorm* S. *Let* $y, z \in [0, 1]$ *such that* $\mathsf{S}(y, z) = 1$, *and for every* $b < y$ *we have* $\mathsf{S}(b, z) < 1$, *or for every* $c < z$ *we have* $\mathsf{S}(y, c) < 1$. *Then the distributivity* $\mathsf{T}(x, \mathsf{S}(y, z)) = \mathsf{S}(\mathsf{T}(x, y), \mathsf{T}(x, z))$ *holds.*

The following theorem from [220, Th. 5.21] gives the complete characterization of the family of continuous pairs (S, T) which satisfy the condition (RD) (originally denoted by (CD) and called conditional distributivity).

Theorem 3.120. *A continuous t-norm* T *is restrictedly distributive over a continuous t-conorm* S *if and only if either* $\mathsf{S} = \mathsf{Max}$ *(and* T *is arbitrary), or there exists a value* $a \in [0, 1]$, *a strict t-norm* T^*, *and a nilpotent t-conorm* S^*, *such that the additive generator* s^* *of* S^* *satisfying* $s^*(1) = 1$ *is also a multiplicative generator of* T^*, *and*

$$\mathsf{T} = (< 0, a, \mathsf{T}_1 >, < a, 1, \mathsf{T}^* >)$$

where T_1 *is an arbitrary continuous t-norm, and* $\mathsf{S} = (< a, 1, \mathsf{S}^* >)$.

Proof. ($\Rightarrow$) Suppose that a continuous t-norm T is restrictedly distributive over a continuous t-conorm S. If $b \in [0, 1[$ is an idempotent element of S, then, for each $x \in [0, 1]$, $\mathsf{T}(x, b)$ is an idempotent element of S. Therefore by the continuity of T each element in $[0, b]$ is an idempotent element of S. Hence, either all elements in $[0, 1]$ are idempotent elements of S, and thus $\mathsf{S} = \mathsf{Max}$ by Proposition 3.88(ii), or there is an element $a \in [0, 1[$ such that the set of all idempotent elements of S is $[0, a] \cup \{1\}$. (Take for a the largest b, which exists by the representation theorem for continuous t-conorms in Remark 3.92(iv).) By Remark 3.31, it follows that S is Archimedean on $[a, 1]$, therefore $\mathsf{S} = (\langle a, 1, \mathsf{S}^* \rangle)$, where S^* is a continuous Archimedean t-conorm.

For this last case, we shall prove that a is also an idempotent element of T. For every $x \in]a, 1]$ with $\mathsf{S}(x, x) < 1$ we obtain by (3.70) and $\mathsf{T}(a, x) \in [0, a]$

$$\mathsf{T}(a, \mathsf{S}(x, x)) = \mathsf{S}(\mathsf{T}(a, x), \mathsf{T}(a, x)) = \mathsf{T}(a, x),$$

which can be rewritten as $\mathsf{T}(a, x_\mathsf{S}^{(2)}) = \mathsf{T}(a, x)$. Since $x_\mathsf{S}^{(\frac{1}{2})} \in]a, 1]$, this relation holds for $x_\mathsf{S}^{(\frac{1}{2})}$ too, hence by the dual of Proposition 3.35(ii) for t-conorms, we get

$$\mathsf{T}(a, x_\mathsf{S}^{(\frac{1}{2})}) = \mathsf{T}(a, x) = \mathsf{T}(a, x_\mathsf{S}^{(2)}).$$

We distinguish two cases, when S^* is nilpotent and strict. For the case when S^* is a nilpotent t-conorm we take $c = \inf\{x \mid x_\mathsf{S}^{(2)} = 1, x \in [0, 1]\}$. Then for every $x \in [0, c[$

we have $T(a,x) = T(a,x_S^{(2)})$. Consequently, by continuity of T and S, we obtain

$$T(a,c) = T(a,c_S^{(2)}) = T(a,1) = a.$$

Proceeding as above, by induction we obtain $T(a,c) = T(a,c_S^{(2^{-n})})$ for every $n \in \mathbb{N}$. Since $\lim_{n\to\infty} c_S^{(2^{-n})} = a$ we obtain $T(a,a) = a$. Similarly, for the case when S^* is a strict t-conorm, taking now $c = \frac{a+1}{2}$, and using that $\lim_{n\to\infty} c_S^{(2^n)} = 1$, we obtain that a is an idempotent element of T. Therefore, T can be written as an ordinal sum (see Theorem 3.49), one of its summands being $\langle a, 1, T^* \rangle$, where T^* is some continuous t-norm. Since T is restrictedly distributive over S, T^* must be restrictedly distributive over the Archimedean t-conorm S^*.

We show that T^* is also Archimedean. The existence of a nontrivial idempotent element c of T^* would imply the existence of $x \in [0,1]$ with $x < c < S^*(x,x) < 1$, leading to the contradiction

$$c = T^*(c, S^*(x,x)) = S^*(T^*(c,x), T^*(c,x)) = S^*(x,x).$$

Moreover, T^* cannot be nilpotent: if

$$0 < d = \sup\{x \in [0,1] \mid T(x,x) = 0\},$$

then there exists $y \in [0,1]$ with $y < d < S^*(y,y) < 1$, leading to the contradiction

$$0 < T^*(d, S^*(y,y)) = S^*(T^*(d,y), T^*(d,y)) = 0.$$

Let θ be an arbitrary but fixed multiplicative generator of the strict t-norm T^* and s an additive generator of the continuous Archimedean t-conorm S^*. Note that we have $S(y,z) = s^{-1}(s(y) + s(z))$ for all $(y,z) \in [0,1]^2$ with $S(y,z) < 1$. We define the continuous, increasing function $f : [0,s(1)] \to [0,1]$ by $f = \theta \circ s^{-1}$ and note that $f(s(1)) = 1$. Taking $u = s(x)$, $v = s(y)$ and $w = s(z)$, the restricted distributivity of T^* over S^* can be rewritten as

$$f(u)f(v+w) = f(f^{-1}(f(u)f(v)) + f^{-1}(f(u)f(w))) \tag{3.71}$$

for all $u,v,w \in [0,s(1)]$ and $v + w < s(1)$. For a fixed $u \in {]}0,s(1)]$, we define the continuous, increasing function $g_u : [0,s(1)] \to [0,s(1)]$ by $g_u(x) = f^{-1}(f(u)f(x))$ and observe that $g_u(0) = 0$ and $g_u(s(1)) = u$. Then (3.71) transforms into the Cauchy equation

$$g_u(v+w) = g_u(v) + g_u(w)$$

for all $v,w \in [0,s(1)]$ and $v + w \leqslant s(1)$, where the case $v + w = s(1)$ follows from the continuity of g_u. If $s(1) = \infty$ then this equation has no solution, so S^* must be a nilpotent t-conorm. From Proposition 2.115, it follows that $g_u(x) = \frac{u}{s(1)}x$, i.e.,

$$f\left(\frac{u}{s(1)}x\right) = f(u)f(x)$$

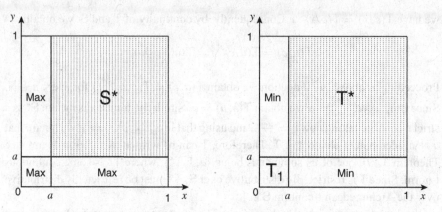

Figure 3.24 Representation of the restricted distributive pair (S, T) for $a \in \,]0, 1[$

for all $x, u \in [0, s(1)]$. The case $u = 0$ follows from $f(0) = 0$. The only solutions of this modified Cauchy equation are given by $f(x) = \left(\frac{x}{s(1)}\right)^c$, where $c \in \,]0, \infty[$. Since $s(1)$ can be chosen arbitrarily in $]0, \infty[$ we may take $s(1) = 1$, leading to $f(x) = x^c$ and, consequently, we have $\theta = s^c$, i.e., s is a multiplicative generator of T^*.

($\Leftarrow$) Conversely, assume that a continuous t-norm T and a continuous t-conorm S have the forms given in the theorem; then T is restrictedly distributive over S. $\square$

The restricted distributive pair of continuous t-conorm $\mathsf{S} = (< a, 1, \mathsf{S}^* >)$ and t-norm $\mathsf{T} = (< 0, a, \mathsf{T}_1 >, < a, 1, \mathsf{T}^* >)$ from Theorem 3.120 is represented in Figure 3.24.

The following example, containing three cases, taking into account the representation of Archimedean continuous t-norms and t-conorms, gives us the canonical representations of (RD) pairs.

Example 3.121.   (i) The extreme case $a = 0$ reduces to the pair $\mathsf{S}_{\mathbf{L}}$ and Π.
 (ii) The other extreme case $a = 1$ reduces to the pair Max and an arbitrary continuous t-norm T_1.
(iii) For $0 < a < 1$ the pair consisting of the continuous t-conorm $\mathsf{S} = (< a, 1, \mathsf{S}_{\mathbf{L}} >)$ and t-norm $\mathsf{T} = (< 0, a, \mathsf{T}_1 >, < a, 1, \Pi >)$ gives us the hybrid idempotent-probabilistic case.

We give a characterization of all pairs (U, S) satisfying (RD) where U is a left-continuous uninorm with neutral element $e \in \,]0, 1[$ and S is a continuous *t*-conorm, based on [201]. This case has important applications in integration theory; see [219]. We distinguish two cases. The first case is when the neutral element e of the uninorm U is an idempotent element of the t-conorm S. The second case is when the neutral element e of the uninorm U is not an idempotent element of the t-conorm S.

The first case is completely characterized by the following theorem.

Theorem 3.122. *A left-continuous uninorm* U *with a neutral element* $e \in]0,1[$ *and a continuous t-conorm* S *for which* e *is an idempotent element satisfy the condition (RD) if and only if* S = Max.

Proof. Each uninorm U is distributive over Max because of the monotonicity of U. Conversely, if U is restrictedly distributive over S and the neutral element e of uninorm U is an idempotent element for S, then for all $x \in [0,1]$ the following equality holds:

$$x = U(x,e) = U(x, S(e,e)) = S(U(x,e), U(x,e)) = S(x,x).$$

Therefore each element from $[0,1]$ is idempotent for S, and S = Max. $\square$

In order to characterize the second case, which is more complicated, we shall prove a lemma where the ordinal sum structure for the corresponding t-conorm S is considerably simplified.

Lemma 3.123. *Let* U *be a left-continuous uninorm with neutral element* $e \in]0,1[$, *and let* S *be a continuous t-conorm for which* e *is not an idempotent element. If the pair* (U, S) *satisfies the condition (RD), then the following hold:*

  (i) The ordinal sum for S *consists of one summand* S^*, *i.e.,* $S = (< a, b, S^* >)$.
  (ii) $U(x,y) \in [a,b]$ *for all* $x, y \in [a,b]$, *where* a, b *are from (i).*

Proof. (i) Since the neutral element e is not an idempotent element of S then $e \in]a_\alpha, e_\alpha[$ for some $\alpha \in A$. We shall prove that each $x \geqslant e_\alpha$ and each $x \leqslant a_\alpha$ are idempotent elements of S. We know that $S(a_\alpha, a_\alpha) = a_\alpha$ and $S(e_\alpha, e_\alpha) = e_\alpha$. The case when $e_\alpha = 1$ is obvious. Assume that $e_\alpha < 1$. Since (RD) holds we have for all $x \in [0,1]$ the following equality:

$$U(x, e_\alpha) = U(x, S(e_\alpha, e_\alpha)) = S(U(x, e_\alpha), U(x, e_\alpha)).$$

Therefore for each $x \in [0,1]$, $U(x, e_\alpha)$ is an idempotent element for S. The function $U(x, e_\alpha)$ for $x \geqslant e$ is a continuous increasing function on $[e, 1]$ with values in $[e_\alpha, 1]$. Thus each element from $[e_\alpha, 1]$ is an idempotent element for S.

Using similar arguments we shall show that each element $x \leqslant a_\alpha$ is an idempotent element of S. Assume that $a_\alpha > 0$ (the case when $a_\alpha = 0$ is trivial). We have because of (RD) that for all $x \in [0,1]$ the following equality holds:

$$U(x, a_\alpha) = U(x, S(a_\alpha, a_\alpha)) = S(U(x, a_\alpha), U(x, a_\alpha)).$$

Therefore for all $x \in [0,1]$ we have that $U(x, a_\alpha)$ is an idempotent element of S. The continuous function $U(x, a_\alpha)$ for $x \leqslant e$ is a continuous increasing function from $[0, e]$ to $[0, a_\alpha]$. Thus each element in $[0, a_\alpha]$ is an idempotent element for S. From the previous considerations we conclude that $|A| = 1$, i.e., $S = (< a, b, S^* >)$ where S^* is a continuous Archimedean t-conorm.

(ii) We shall prove that a, b are also idempotent elements for the uninorm U. From the representation of continuous t-conorms we know that S^* is a continuous Archimedean t-conorm which is either strict or nilpotent. First, we consider the case when S^* is strict.

(a) If S^* is strict then $S(e, e) < 1$ because $e < 1$. Let us take the points b and e and apply (RD), whence we obtain the following:

$$U(b, S(e, e)) = S(U(b, e), U(b, e)) = U(b, e) = b.$$

By induction we get for all $n \in \mathbb{N}$

$$b = U(b, e) = U\left(b, e_S^{(2^n)}\right).$$

Since $\lim_{n \to \infty} e_S^{(2^n)} = b$ this together with the continuity of U on $[e, 1]^2$ implies $b = U(b, b)$.

Let us prove now that $U(a, a) = a$. Similarly to the previous case we shall take the points a and e and again apply (RD), whence we obtain the following:

$$U(a, S(e, e)) = S(U(a, e), U(a, e)) = U(a, e) = a$$

and consequently we obtain $U\left(a, e_S^{(\frac{1}{2})}\right) = U(a, e) = a$ (see Remark 3.5 in [220]). By induction we get for all $n \in \mathbb{N}$

$$U\left(a, e_S^{(2^{-n})}\right) = U(a, e) = a.$$

Since $\lim_{n \to \infty} e_S^{(2^{-n})} = a$, this together with the continuity of S and U on $[0, e]^2$ implies $U(a, a) = U(a, e) = a$.

(b) Let S^* be a nilpotent t-conorm and fix

$$c = \inf\{x \in [0, 1] \mid S(x, x) = 1\} < 1.$$

Then immediately we get $S(b, b) = b$. Therefore it only remains to show $U(a, a) = a$.

If $e < c$ then $S(e, e) < 1$ and in the same manner as in the strict case we get $U(a, a) = a$.

If $c \leqslant e$ then for $x < c$, $S(x, x) < 1$ holds, and applying (RD) on the points a and x we have the following:

$$U(a, S(x, x)) = S(U(a, x), U(a, x)) = U(a, x).$$

When $x \to c$, because of the continuity of S and U on $[0, e]^2$, we obtain

$$U(a, S(c, c)) = U(a, 1) = U(a, c).$$

By induction we get $U(a, c_S^{(2^n)}) = U(a, c)$ for all $n \in \mathbb{N}$, implying $U(a, a) = U(a, 1) \geqslant a$. The opposite inequality is trivial because $U(a, a) \leqslant U(a, e) = a$. Therefore $U(a, a) = a$ in this case too. $\qquad\qquad\square$

Summarizing, we have seen that when (RD) is satisfied, the ordinal sum representation for t-conorm S is simplified because we have only one summand $< a, b, S^* >$. Also we have shown that $U(x, y) \in [a, b]$ when $x, y \in [a, b]$, i.e., the uninorm U is compatible with the structure of t-conorm S.

Applying a result from [219], we have for the second case the following characterization.

Theorem 3.124. *A left-continuous uninorm U with a neutral element $e \in]0, 1]$, and a continuous t-conorm S for which e is not an idempotent element satisfy the condition (RD) if and only if the ordinal sum for S consists of one summand S^*, i.e., $< a, b, S^* >$, and*

  (i) *If S^* is a strict t-conorm with additive generator $s : [0, 1] \to [0, \infty]$, then U is generated by cs for some constant $c \in]0, \infty[$ and hence has the neutral element $s^{-1}(\frac{1}{2})$.*
  (ii) *If S^* is a nilpotent t-conorm with additive generator s which can be seen as an increasing bijection $s : [0, 1] \to [0, 1]$, then $b = 1$ and U is a t-norm of the form*

$$U = (< 0, a, T_1 >, < a, 1, T^* >)$$

  where T_1 is an arbitrary continuous t-norm, and T^* is a strict t-norm with multiplicative generator s.

4

Means and averages

4.1 Introduction and definitions

It would be very unnatural to propose a book on aggregation functions without dealing somehow with *means* and *averaging functions*. Already discovered and studied by the ancient Greeks,[1] the concept of mean has given rise today to a very wide field of investigation with a huge variety of applications. Actually, a tremendous amount of literature on the properties of several means (such as the arithmetic mean, the geometric mean, etc.) has already been produced, especially since the nineteenth century, and is still developing today. For a good overview, see the expository paper by Frosini [124] and the remarkable monograph by Bullen [47].

The first modern definition of mean was probably due to Cauchy [56], who considered in 1821 a *mean* as an internal (see Definition 2.52) function. We adopt this approach and assume further that a mean should be a nondecreasing function.

As usual, $\mathbb{I}$ represents a nonempty real interval, bounded or not. The more general cases where $\mathbb{I}$ includes $-\infty$ and/or ∞ will always be mentioned explicitly.

Definition 4.1. An *n*-ary *mean* in $\mathbb{I}^n$ is an internal aggregation function $\mathsf{M} : \mathbb{I}^n \to \mathbb{I}$. An *extended mean* in $\cup_{n \in \mathbb{N}} \mathbb{I}^n$ is an extended function $\mathsf{M} : \cup_{n \in \mathbb{N}} \mathbb{I}^n \to \mathbb{I}$ whose restriction to each $\mathbb{I}^n$ is a mean.

It follows immediately from Proposition 2.54 that a mean is nothing other than an idempotent aggregation function. Moreover, by Corollary 1.8, if $\mathsf{M} : \mathbb{I}^n \to \mathbb{I}$ is a mean in $\mathbb{I}^n$, then it is also a mean in $\mathbb{J}^n$, for any subinterval $\mathbb{J} \subseteq \mathbb{I}$.

The concept of mean as an *average* or *numerical equalizer* is usually ascribed to Chisini [60, p. 108], who gave in 1929 the following definition:

Let $y = \mathsf{F}(x_1, \ldots, x_n)$ be a function of n independent variables $x_1, \ldots, x_n$. A mean of $x_1, \ldots, x_n$ with respect to the function F is a number M such that, if each of $x_1, \ldots, x_n$ is replaced by M, the function value is unchanged, that is,

$$\mathsf{F}(M, \ldots, M) = \mathsf{F}(x_1, \ldots, x_n).$$

---

[1] See Antoine [17, Chap. 3] for a historical discussion of the various Greek notions of "mean".

When F is considered as the sum, the product, the sum of squares, the sum of inverses, or the sum of exponentials, the solution of Chisini's equation corresponds respectively to the arithmetic mean, the geometric mean, the quadratic mean, the harmonic mean, and the exponential mean.

Unfortunately, as noted by de Finetti [79, p. 378] in 1931, Chisini's definition is so general that it does not even imply that the "mean" (provided there exists a real and unique solution to Chisini's equation) fulfills Cauchy's internality property.

To ensure existence, uniqueness, and internality of the solution of Chisini's equation, we assume that F is nondecreasing and idempotizable; see Definition 2.45. Therefore we propose the following definition:

Definition 4.2. A function $M : \mathbb{I}^n \to \mathbb{I}$ is an *average* in $\mathbb{I}^n$ if there exists a nondecreasing and idempotizable function $F : \mathbb{I}^n \to \mathbb{R}$ such that $F = \delta_F \circ M$. In this case, we say that M is an *average associated with F in* $\mathbb{I}^n$.

Averages are also known as *Chisini means* or *level surface means*. The average associated with F is also called the F-*level mean*; see Bullen [47, §VI.4.1]. The following result shows that, thus defined, the concepts of mean and average coincide.

Proposition 4.3. *The following assertions hold:*

(i) *Any average is a mean.*
(ii) *Any mean is the average associated with itself.*
(iii) *Let M be the average associated with a function* $F : \mathbb{I}^n \to \mathbb{R}$*. Then M is the average associated with a function* $G : \mathbb{I}^n \to \mathbb{R}$ *if and only if there exists an increasing bijection* $\varphi : \operatorname{ran}(F) \to \operatorname{ran}(G)$ *such that* $G = \varphi \circ F$.

Proof. (i) If $M : \mathbb{I}^n \to \mathbb{I}$ is the average associated with a function $F : \mathbb{I}^n \to \mathbb{R}$ then, by Proposition 2.46, $M = \delta_F^{-1} \circ F$ is nondecreasing and idempotent and hence it is a mean.

(ii) If $M : \mathbb{I}^n \to \mathbb{I}$ is a mean then M is idempotizable and $M = \delta_M \circ M$.

(iii) ($\Rightarrow$) If M is the average associated with both F and G, then clearly $G = \varphi \circ F$, where $\varphi := \delta_G \circ \delta_F^{-1}$ is an increasing bijection from $\operatorname{ran}(F)$ to $\operatorname{ran}(G)$.

($\Leftarrow$) Assume M is the average associated with F and let $G = \varphi \circ F$, where $\varphi : \operatorname{ran}(F) \to \mathbb{R}$ is a strictly increasing function. Then $\delta_G = \varphi \circ \delta_F$ and hence G is idempotizable. Moreover, $G = \varphi \circ F = \varphi \circ \delta_F \circ M = \delta_G \circ M$ and hence M is the average associated with G. □

Proposition 4.3 shows that, thus defined, the concepts of mean and average are identical and, in a sense, rather general. Note that some authors (see for instance Bullen [47, p. xxvi], Sahoo and Riedel [374, §7.2], and Bhatia [42, Chap. 4]) define the concept of mean by adding conditions such as continuity, symmetry, and homogeneity, which is $M(r\,\mathbf{x}) = r\,M(\mathbf{x})$ for all admissible $r \in \mathbb{R}$.

The purpose of this chapter is not to present a state-of-the-art of all the known results in this vast realm of means. Instead, we just skim the surface of the subject by pointing out characterization results for the best known and most often used families of means.

In the next section we deal with the class of quasi-arithmetic means and some of their special cases. Section 4.3 is devoted to some generalizations of quasi-arithmetic means such as nonstrict quasi-arithmetic means. Section 4.4 deals with means defined from the associativity property. Section 4.5 presents some further definitions of means mainly defined from a mean value property such as Lagrangian means. In Section 4.6 we briefly discuss three construction methods for means, namely idempotization, symmetrization, and minimization. Finally, in Section 4.7 we define extended weighted arithmetic means and extended ordered weighted averaging functions constructed from weight triangles.

Many other means, such as those aggregation functions constructed from nonadditive integrals (Choquet and Sugeno integrals), will be presented in Chapter 5. Also, the study of medians and order statistics, which are particular means designed to aggregate ordinal scales, will be postponed to Chapter 8.

4.2 Quasi-arithmetic means

A well-studied class of means is the class of *quasi-arithmetic means* (see for instance Bullen [47, Chap. IV]), introduced as extended aggregation functions as early as 1930 by Kolmogoroff [236], Nagumo [330], and then as n-ary functions in 1948 by Aczél [1]. In this section we introduce the quasi-arithmetic means and describe some of their properties and axiomatizations.

Definition 4.4. Let $f : \mathbb{I} \to \mathbb{R}$ be a continuous and strictly monotonic function. The n-ary *quasi-arithmetic mean generated by f* is the function $\mathsf{M}_f : \mathbb{I}^n \to \mathbb{I}$ defined as

$$\mathsf{M}_f(\mathbf{x}) := f^{-1}\Big(\frac{1}{n}\sum_{i=1}^n f(x_i)\Big). \tag{4.1}$$

The *extended quasi-arithmetic mean generated by f* is the function $\mathsf{M}_f : \cup_{n \in \mathbb{N}} \mathbb{I}^n \to \mathbb{I}$ whose restriction to $\mathbb{I}^n$ is the n-ary quasi-arithmetic mean generated by f.

Remark 4.5. (i) Each quasi-arithmetic mean M_f is a mean in the sense of Definition 4.1. It is also the average associated with $n(f \circ \mathsf{M}_f)$. For instance, the arithmetic mean $\mathsf{M}_f = \mathsf{AM}$ (with $f = \mathrm{id}$) is the average associated with the sum Σ.

(ii) In certain applications it may be convenient to extend the range of f to the extended real line $\overline{\mathbb{R}} = [-\infty, \infty]$. Evidently, in this case it is necessary to define the expression $\infty - \infty$, which will often be considered as $-\infty$.

The class of quasi-arithmetic means comprises most of the algebraic means of common use, such as the arithmetic mean and the geometric mean. Table 4.1 provides some well-known instances of quasi-arithmetic means.

Table 4.1. *Examples of quasi-arithmetic means*

$f(x)$	$M_f(\mathbf{x})$	Name	Notation
x	$\frac{1}{n}\sum\limits_{i=1}^{n} x_i$	arithmetic mean	AM
x^2	$\left(\frac{1}{n}\sum\limits_{i=1}^{n} x_i^2\right)^{1/2}$	quadratic mean	QM
$\log x$	$\left(\prod\limits_{i=1}^{n} x_i\right)^{1/n}$	geometric mean	GM
x^{-1}	$\dfrac{1}{\frac{1}{n}\sum\limits_{i=1}^{n}\frac{1}{x_i}}$	harmonic mean	HM
$x^{\alpha}\ (\alpha \in \mathbb{R}\setminus\{0\})$	$\left(\frac{1}{n}\sum\limits_{i=1}^{n} x_i^{\alpha}\right)^{1/\alpha}$	root-mean-power	$M_{id^{\alpha}}$
$e^{\alpha x}\ (\alpha \in \mathbb{R}\setminus\{0\})$	$\frac{1}{\alpha}\ln\left(\frac{1}{n}\sum\limits_{i=1}^{n} e^{\alpha x_i}\right)$	exponential mean	EM_{α}

The function f occurring in (4.1) is called a *generator* of M_f. Aczél [1] showed that f is determined up to a linear transformation. More generally, we have the following result (see Bullen *et al.* [48, p. 226]):

Proposition 4.6. *Let $f,g : \mathbb{I} \to \mathbb{R}$ be continuous and strictly monotonic functions. Assume also that g is increasing (respectively, decreasing). Then*

(i) $M_f \leqslant M_g$ if and only if $g \circ f^{-1}$ is convex (respectively, concave);
(ii) $M_f = M_g$ if and only if $g \circ f^{-1}$ is linear, that is,

$$g(x) = rf(x) + s$$

for all $r, s \in \mathbb{R}$, $r \neq 0$.

Proof. Assume without loss of generality that g is increasing. Setting $u_i = f(x_i)$ $(i \in [n])$, we have

$$M_f \leqslant M_g \Leftrightarrow f^{-1}\left(\frac{1}{n}\sum_{i=1}^{n} f(x_i)\right) \leqslant g^{-1}\left(\frac{1}{n}\sum_{i=1}^{n} g(x_i)\right)$$

$$\Leftrightarrow (g \circ f^{-1})\left(\frac{1}{n}\sum_{i=1}^{n} u_i\right) \leqslant \frac{1}{n}\sum_{i=1}^{n}(g \circ f^{-1})(u_i).$$

This is Jensen's inequality for the function $g \circ f^{-1}$, satisfied only if this function is convex, which proves (i).

Let us now prove (ii). Suppose first that both f and g are increasing. According to (i), we have $M_f = M_g$ if and only if both functions $g \circ f^{-1}$ and $f \circ g^{-1} = (g \circ f^{-1})^{-1}$ are convex. This amounts to saying that $g \circ f^{-1}$ is both convex and concave, that is, linear. Suppose now that f is decreasing and g is increasing. According to (i), $g \circ f^{-1}$ is convex while $f \circ g^{-1}$ is concave. However, then $g \circ f^{-1} = (f \circ g^{-1})^{-1}$ is concave and therefore linear. The other two cases are similar. $\square$

Example 4.7 (Kolesárová [229]). Assume $\mathbb{I} =]0,1[$ and consider the function $M : \mathbb{I}^n \to \mathbb{I}$ defined as

$$M(\mathbf{x}) := \frac{GM(\mathbf{x})}{GM(\mathbf{x}) + GM(1 - \mathbf{x})},$$

where GM is the geometric mean. It is easy to see that the function M is a quasi-arithmetic mean generated by the increasing function $g(x) = \log \frac{x}{1-x}$, whose inverse function is given by $g^{-1}(x) = \frac{e^x}{1+e^x}$.

Let us compare M with the geometric mean GM, which is generated by $f(x) = \log x$. Since $(g \circ f^{-1})(x) = \log \frac{e^x}{1-e^x}$ is convex, by Proposition 4.6 we have $GM \leqslant M$.

Proposition 4.6 makes it possible to compare quasi-arithmetic means. For example, denoting by M_{id^α} the quasi-arithmetic mean generated by $f(x) = x^\alpha$ (root-mean-power), we retrieve the well-known equality (see for instance Beckenbach and Bellman [28, §16] and Steele [398, Chap. 8])

$$\alpha_1 < \alpha_2 \quad \Rightarrow \quad M_{id^{\alpha_1}}(\mathbf{x}) \leqslant M_{id^{\alpha_2}}(\mathbf{x})$$

for all $\mathbf{x} \in]0,\infty[^n$, with equality if and only if all x_i are equal.

Remark 4.8. As already discussed in Remark 3.41(ii), it is important to mention also the relationship between quasi-arithmetic means and continuous Archimedean t-norms, continuous Archimedean t-conorms, and representable uninorms (as defined in Section 3.6) when defined by the same generator function; see, e.g., Gehrke *et al.* [137]. Procedures to find the corresponding quasi-arithmetic mean from those functions can be found in Calvo *et al.* [49].

4.2.1 Axiomatization of quasi-arithmetic means

We now present an axiomatization of the class of quasi-arithmetic means as extended aggregation functions, originally called *mean values*. This axiomatization was obtained independently by Kolmogoroff [236] and Nagumo [330] in 1930. We follow Kolmogoroff's approach as it contains the following useful lemma.

Lemma 4.9. *If* $F : \cup_{n \in \mathbb{N}} \mathbb{I}^n \to \mathbb{R}$ *is symmetric, idempotent, and decomposable, then, for any bounded interval* $[a,b] \subseteq \mathbb{I}$, *there exists a function* $\psi : [0,1] \cap \mathbb{Q} \to \mathbb{R}$, *with*

$\psi(0) = a$ and $\psi(1) = b$, such that, for all $\mathbf{z} \in \cup_{n \in \mathbb{N}}([0, 1]^n \cap \mathbb{Q}^n)$,

$$F(\psi(z_1), \ldots, \psi(z_n)) = \psi\left(\frac{1}{n} \sum_{i=1}^{n} z_i\right).$$

Moreover, if F *is nondecreasing (or strictly increasing), then so is* ψ.

Proof. First note that F is strongly decomposable, being symmetric and decomposable.

Consider an arbitrary bounded interval $[a, b] \subseteq \mathbb{I}$ and define $\psi : [0, 1] \cap \mathbb{Q} \to \mathbb{R}$ as follows. For any rational $z = \frac{p}{q} \in [0, 1] \cap \mathbb{Q}$ $(p \in \mathbb{N}_0, q \in \mathbb{N}, p \leqslant q)$, we set

$$\psi(z) := F(p \cdot b, (q - p) \cdot a).$$

The function ψ is well defined. Indeed, if $\frac{p}{q} = \frac{p'}{q'}$ are two representations of the same rational, then, using Lemma 2.74, we have

$$\begin{aligned}
F(p \cdot b, (q - p) \cdot a) &= F(p'p \cdot b, p'(q - p) \cdot a) \\
&= F(pp' \cdot b, p(q' - p') \cdot a) \\
&= F(p' \cdot b, (q' - p') \cdot a).
\end{aligned}$$

By idempotency, we immediately have $\psi(0) = a$ and $\psi(1) = b$.

Now, given $\mathbf{z} \in [0, 1]^n \cap \mathbb{Q}^n$, we can always write $z_i = \frac{p_i}{q}$ $(i = 1, \ldots, n)$, with a common denominator q. Then, using Lemma 2.76 and symmetry, we have

$$\begin{aligned}
F(\psi(z_1), \ldots, \psi(z_n)) &= F((\textstyle\sum_i p_i) \cdot b, (nq - \sum_i p_i) \cdot a) \\
&= \psi\left(\tfrac{1}{nq} \textstyle\sum_i p_i\right) \\
&= \psi\left(\tfrac{1}{n} \textstyle\sum_i z_i\right).
\end{aligned}$$

Finally, assuming that F is nondecreasing, for $z = \frac{p}{q}$ and $z' = \frac{p'}{q}$, with $p \leqslant p'$, we have

$$\psi(z) = F(p \cdot b, (q - p) \cdot a) \leqslant F(p' \cdot b, (q - p') \cdot a) = \psi(z'),$$

where the inequalities are strict in case F is strictly increasing. $\qquad\square$

Theorem 4.10. $F : \cup_{n \in \mathbb{N}} \mathbb{I}^n \to \mathbb{R}$ *is symmetric, continuous, strictly increasing, idempotent, and decomposable if and only if there is a continuous and strictly monotonic function* $f : \mathbb{I} \to \mathbb{R}$ *such that* $F = M_f$ *is the extended quasi-arithmetic mean generated by* f.

Proof. ($\Leftarrow$) Easy.

($\Rightarrow$) We first assume that $\mathbb{I}$ is a closed interval $[a, b]$. By Lemma 4.9 there exists a strictly increasing function $\psi : [0, 1] \cap \mathbb{Q} \to \mathbb{R}$, with $\psi(0) = a$ and $\psi(1) = b$, such that

$$\mathsf{F}\big(\psi(z_1), \ldots, \psi(z_n)\big) = \psi\Big(\frac{1}{n} \sum_{i=1}^n z_i\Big) \tag{4.2}$$

for any $\mathbf{z} \in \cup_{n \in \mathbb{N}}([0, 1]^n \cap \mathbb{Q}^n)$.

Let us show that the function ψ can be extended continuously in $[0, 1]$. Suppose on the contrary that there is $x \in {]0, 1[}$ such that

$$\psi(x - 0) = u, \quad \psi(x + 0) = v, \quad u < v.$$

Let $(z_m)_{m \in \mathbb{N}}$ and $(z'_m)_{m \in \mathbb{N}}$ be sequences in $[0, 1] \cap \mathbb{Q}$ converging to x such that $z_m < x < z'_m$ and $\frac{1}{2}(z_m + z'_m) < x$. Then, using (4.2), we obtain

$$u = \lim_{m \to \infty} \psi\Big(\frac{z_m + z'_m}{2}\Big) = \lim_{m \to \infty} \mathsf{F}(\psi(z_m), \psi(z'_m)) = \mathsf{F}(u, v) > \mathsf{F}(u, u) = u,$$

a contradiction. The same conclusion holds for $x = 0$ or $x = 1$.

We thus see that the set $\{\psi(z) : z \in [0, 1] \cap \mathbb{Q}\}$ is dense everywhere in $[a, b] = [\psi(0), \psi(1)]$. Therefore, by continuity, we can extend the function ψ to all points in $[0, 1]$ and define its inverse in $[a, b]$, which proves the result when $\mathbb{I} = [a, b]$.

Let us now prove the result for a general interval $\mathbb{I}$, possibly unbounded (see Aczél [3, §6.4] for a discussion on the technique used here). Consider the intervals $[a_m, b_m]$, where $(a_m)_{m \in \mathbb{N}}$ (respectively, $(b_m)_{m \in \mathbb{N}}$) is an arbitrary monotonic decreasing (respectively, increasing) sequence of $\mathbb{I}$ converging to $a := \inf \mathbb{I}$ (respectively, $b := \sup \mathbb{I}$). Then, according to what has been already proved, we have $\mathsf{F} = \mathsf{M}_{f_m}$ in $[a_m, b_m]^n$, where f_m is a generator of F in $[a_m, b_m]$. Similarly, we have $\mathsf{F} = \mathsf{M}_{f_{m+1}}$ in $[a_{m+1}, b_{m+1}]^n$, where f_{m+1} is a generator of F in $[a_{m+1}, b_{m+1}]$. Since $\mathsf{M}_{f_m} = \mathsf{M}_{f_{m+1}}$ in $[a_m, b_m]^n$, by Proposition 4.6 we can choose $f_{m+1} = f_m$ in $[a_m, b_m]$. Finally, define, for all $x \in {]a, b[}$,

$$f(x) := \lim_{m \to \infty} f_m(x),$$

and, if $a \in \mathbb{I}$ (respectively, $b \in \mathbb{I}$), $f(a) := \inf_{m \in \mathbb{N}} f_m(a_m)$ (respectively, $f(b) := \sup_{m \in \mathbb{N}} f_m(b_m)$). Then $\mathsf{F} = \mathsf{M}_f$ in $\mathbb{I}^n$, where $f : \mathbb{I} \to \mathbb{R}$ is continuous and strictly monotonic. $\square$

The following alternative axiomatization shows that, replacing decomposability with strong decomposability in Theorem 4.10, the symmetry condition becomes redundant. For a proof, see Marichal [266].

Corollary 4.11. $\mathsf{F} : \cup_{n \in \mathbb{N}} \mathbb{I}^n \to \mathbb{R}$ *is continuous, strictly increasing, idempotent, and strongly decomposable if and only if there is a continuous and strictly monotonic function $f : \mathbb{I} \to \mathbb{R}$ such that $\mathsf{F} = \mathsf{M}_f$ is the extended quasi-arithmetic mean generated by f.*

Remark 4.12. In looking at the previous corollary, one could think that strong decomposability alone naturally implies symmetry. However, it is immediate to see that, for instance, the projections onto the first and the last coordinates, denoted P_F and P_L as defined in (1.11) and (1.12), are strongly decomposable but not symmetric.

We now present an axiomatization of n-ary quasi-arithmetic means, which is due to Aczél [1]; see also Aczél [3, §6.4], Aczél and Dhombres [9, Chap. 17].

Theorem 4.13. *The function* $F : \mathbb{I}^n \to \mathbb{R}$ *is symmetric, continuous, strictly increasing, idempotent, and bisymmetric if and only if there is a continuous and strictly monotonic function* $f : \mathbb{I} \to \mathbb{R}$ *such that* $F = M_f$ *is the quasi-arithmetic mean generated by* f.

Proof. ($\Leftarrow$) Easy.

($\Rightarrow$) We prove the theorem only for binary functions. The proof we present here uses a nice argument proposed by Horváth [190]. The general case is discussed in Aczél [1].

Call a *dyadic extended function* any function $G : \cup_{n \in \mathbb{N}} \mathbb{I}^{2^n} \to \mathbb{R}$ and call *dyadic decomposability* the decomposability property restricted to such functions, that is,

$$G(x_1, \ldots, x_{2^k}, x_{2^k+1}, \ldots, x_{2^n}) = G(2^k \cdot G(x_1, \ldots, x_{2^k}), x_{2^k+1}, \ldots, x_{2^n}).$$

Let $F : \mathbb{I}^2 \to \mathbb{R}$ be symmetric, continuous, strictly increasing, idempotent, and bisymmetric. Define a dyadic extended function $G : \cup_{n \in \mathbb{N}} \mathbb{I}^{2^n} \to \mathbb{R}$ as $G^{(2)} = F$ and, for all $n \in \mathbb{N}$ and all $\mathbf{x}_1, \mathbf{x}_2 \in \mathbb{I}^{2^n}$,

$$G^{(2^{n+1})}(\mathbf{x}_1, \mathbf{x}_2) = G^{(2)}\big(G^{(2^n)}(\mathbf{x}_1), G^{(2^n)}(\mathbf{x}_2)\big).$$

It is then easy to see that G is symmetric, continuous, strictly increasing, idempotent, and dyadically decomposable. As Theorem 4.10 can be easily adapted to the dyadic extended functions, replacing decomposability with dyadic decomposability, we can see that there is a continuous and strictly monotonic function $f : \mathbb{I} \to \mathbb{R}$ such that

$$G^{(2^n)} = M_f^{(2^n)}.$$

If follows that $F = G^{(2)} = M_f^{(2)}$. $\qquad\qquad\qquad\qquad\qquad\qquad\qquad\square$

It is worth mentioning that further axiomatizations of n-ary quasi-arithmetic means can be found in Aczél and Alsina [7]; see also Aczél [5].

Remark 4.14. Note that the results given in Theorem 4.10, Corollary 4.11, and Theorem 4.13 can be extended to subintervals $\mathbb{I}$ of the extended real line containing ∞ or $-\infty$ with a slight modification of the requirements. Namely, the codomain of F should be $[-\infty, \infty]$, and the strict monotonicity and continuity are required for bounded input vectors only. Observe also that if $\mathbb{I} = [-\infty, \infty]$ then the corresponding quasi-arithmetic means are no longer continuous due to the noncontinuity of the standard summation on $[-\infty, \infty]$.

4.2.2 Subclasses of quasi-arithmetic means

Nagumo [330] investigated some subfamilies of the class of quasi-arithmetic means. He proved the following result; see also Aczél and Alsina [7, §4], Aczél and Dhombres [9, Chap. 15].

Theorem 4.15. *(i) The quasi-arithmetic mean* $\mathsf{M} : \mathbb{I}^n \to \mathbb{I}$ *is difference scale invariant if and only if either* M *is the arithmetic mean* AM *or* M *is the exponential mean, i.e., there exists* $\alpha \in \mathbb{R} \setminus \{0\}$ *such that*

$$\mathsf{M}(\mathbf{x}) = \frac{1}{\alpha} \ln\Big(\frac{1}{n} \sum_{i=1}^{n} e^{\alpha x_i}\Big).$$

(ii) Assume $\mathbb{I} \subseteq]0, \infty[$. *The quasi-arithmetic mean* $\mathsf{M} : \mathbb{I}^n \to \mathbb{I}$ *is ratio scale invariant if and only if either* M *is the geometric mean* GM *or* M *is the root-mean-power, i.e., there exists* $\alpha \in \mathbb{R} \setminus \{0\}$ *such that*

$$\mathsf{M}(\mathbf{x}) = \Big(\frac{1}{n} \sum_{i=1}^{n} x_i^{\alpha}\Big)^{\frac{1}{\alpha}}.$$

Proof. We first prove (i).

($\Leftarrow$) Trivial.

($\Rightarrow$) Putting equation (4.1) into the assumption

$$\mathsf{M}_f(\mathbf{x} + s\mathbf{1}_{[n]}) = \mathsf{M}_f(\mathbf{x}) + s$$

and introducing $g_s(t) := f(t + s)$, we immediately get $\mathsf{M}_{g_s} = \mathsf{M}_f$, that is, by Proposition 4.6, $g_s(t) = a(s)f(t) + b(s)$, with $a(s) \neq 0$. It follows that f satisfies the functional equation

$$f(t + s) = a(s)f(t) + b(s)$$

with $a(s) \neq 0$, from which we immediately see that $b(0) = 0$ and hence $f(0) = 0$.

Setting $t = 0$ immediately leads to $f(s) = b(s)$ and hence the functional equation becomes

$$f(t + s) = a(s)f(t) + f(s) \tag{4.3}$$

or, setting $t = \Delta x$,

$$\frac{f(s + \Delta x) - f(s)}{\Delta x} = a(s)\frac{f(\Delta x) - f(0)}{\Delta x}. \tag{4.4}$$

As $f(s)$ is strictly monotonic, it is differentiable almost everywhere. Assuming $f(s)$ is differentiable at $s = s_1$, from (4.4) $f(s)$ is differentiable at $s = 0$, and then at any s. From (4.3) it follows that

$$a(s) = \frac{f(s + 1) - f(s)}{f(1)},$$

which shows that $a(s)$ is differentiable and hence continuous at s. From (4.4) we see that $f(s)$ is continuously differentiable, and then so is $a(s)$.

Differentiating both sides of (4.3) with respect to s and then setting $s = 0$ leads to the linear differential equation

$$f'(t) = \alpha f(t) + \beta,$$

where $\alpha = a'(0)$ and $\beta = f'(0)$. Since $f(0) = 0$, the solutions of this equation are simply given by $f(t) = \frac{\beta}{\alpha}(e^{\alpha t} - 1)$, if $\alpha \neq 0$, and $f(t) = \beta t$, if $\alpha = 0$.

We now prove (ii).

($\Leftarrow$) Trivial.

($\Rightarrow$) We observe that M_f is ratio scale invariant if and only if $\mathsf{M}_{f \circ \exp}$ is difference scale invariant. We then conclude by using (i). $\qquad\square$

The following corollary immediately follows from Theorem 4.15. It was already reached in 1926 by Bemporad [33, p. 87].

Corollary 4.16. *Assume* $\mathbb{I} \subseteq]0, \infty[$. *The quasi-arithmetic mean* $\mathsf{M} : \mathbb{I}^n \to \mathbb{I}$ *is interval scale invariant if and only if* $\mathsf{M} = \mathsf{AM}$ *(the arithmetic mean).*

4.3 Generalizations of quasi-arithmetic means

Many authors have attempted to generalize the concept of quasi-arithmetic means either by directly defining wider classes of means containing the quasi-arithmetic ones, or by relaxing some conditions that characterize the quasi-arithmetic means such as symmetry or strict increasing monotonicity (while keeping nondecreasing monotonicity). In some cases, even the idempotency property has been dropped, thus considering other functions than means and averages.

4.3.1 Quasi-linear means and quasi-linear functions

The first generalization of quasi-arithmetic means we discuss here consists of the concept of *weighted quasi-arithmetic means*,[2] also called *quasi-linear means*. Aczél [1] (see also Aczél [3, §6.4], Aczél and Dhombres [9, Chap. 17]) investigated those quasi-linear means, simply by dropping the symmetry property from the axiomatization of quasi-arithmetic means based on the bisymmetry property; see Theorem 4.13. Then he continued by dropping both the symmetry and the idempotency properties, thus introducing the so-called *quasi-linear functions*.

He established the next two theorems:

Theorem 4.17. *The function* $\mathsf{F} : \mathbb{I}^n \to \mathbb{R}$ *is continuous, strictly increasing, idempotent, and bisymmetric if and only if there exists a continuous and strictly monotonic*

---

[2] Weighted quasi-arithmetic means will also be discussed in Section 6.4; see Example 6.29.

*function $f : \mathbb{I} \to \mathbb{R}$ and real numbers $w_1, \ldots, w_n > 0$ satisfying $\sum_i w_i = 1$
such that*

$$F(\mathbf{x}) = f^{-1}\left(\sum_{i=1}^n w_i f(x_i) \right) \tag{4.5}$$

for all $\mathbf{x} \in \mathbb{I}^n$.

Proof. ($\Leftarrow$) Easy.

($\Rightarrow$) Without any loss of generality (see Aczél [1]) we confine ourselves to binary functions $F : \mathbb{I}^2 \to \mathbb{R}$. Recall that since F is idempotent and bisymmetric it is also autodistributive.

Take $a \in \mathbb{I}$ arbitrarily. The function $H : \mathbb{I}^2 \to \mathbb{R}$ defined by $H(x,y) := F(F(a,x), F(y,a))$ is continuous and strictly increasing, hence it is idempotizable (that is, δ_H is strictly increasing and $\mathrm{ran}(\delta_H) = \mathrm{ran}(H)$). It follows that the function $G := \delta_H^{-1} \circ H$ is well defined on $\mathbb{I}^2$. Moreover, it is continuous, strictly increasing, idempotent, and even symmetric (since F is bisymmetric).

Let us now prove that G is also bisymmetric. To this end, we first prove that

$$F(G(x,y), G(u,v)) = G(F(x,u), F(y,v)) \tag{4.6}$$

for all $x, y, u, v \in \mathbb{I}$. We have

$(\delta_H \circ F)(G(x,y), G(u,v))$

$= F(F(a, F(G(x,y), G(u,v))), F(F(G(x,y), G(u,v)), a))$

$= F(F(F(a, G(x,y)), F(a, G(u,v))), F(F(G(x,y), a), F(G(u,v), a)))$
(autodistributivity)

$= F(F(F(a, G(x,y)), F(G(x,y), a)), F(F(a, G(u,v)), F(G(u,v), a)))$
(bisymmetry)

$= F((\delta_H \circ G)(x,y), (\delta_H \circ G)(u,v)) = F(H(x,y), H(u,v))$

$= F(F(F(a,x), F(y,a)), F(F(a,u), F(v,a)))$

$= F(F(F(a,x), F(a,u)), F(F(y,a), F(v,a)))$ (bisymmetry)

$= F(F(a, F(x,u)), F(F(y,v), a))$ (autodistributivity)

$= H(F(x,u), F(y,v))$

$= (\delta_H \circ G)(F(x,u), F(y,v))$

and (4.6) is proved.

Then, we have

$(\delta_H \circ G)(G(x,y), G(u,v))$

$= H(G(x,y), G(u,v)) = F(F(a, G(x,y)), F(G(u,v), a))$

$$= \mathsf{F}(\mathsf{F}(\mathsf{G}(a,a),\mathsf{G}(y,x)),\mathsf{F}(\mathsf{G}(u,v),\mathsf{G}(a,a)))$$
(idempotency and symmetry of G)

$$= \mathsf{F}(\mathsf{G}(\mathsf{F}(a,y),\mathsf{F}(a,x)),\mathsf{G}(\mathsf{F}(u,a),\mathsf{F}(v,a))) \quad \text{(by (4.6))}$$
$$= \mathsf{G}(\mathsf{F}(\mathsf{F}(a,y),\mathsf{F}(u,a)),\mathsf{F}(\mathsf{F}(a,x),\mathsf{F}(v,a))) \quad \text{(by (4.6))}.$$

By bisymmetry of F, however, y and u may be interchanged on the far right of this series of equalities, so also on the far left. This yields the bisymmetry of G. Thus, by Theorem 4.13, there exists a continuous and strictly monotonic function $k : \mathbb{I} \to \mathbb{R}$ such that

$$\mathsf{G}(x,y) = k^{-1}\left(\frac{k(x)+k(y)}{2}\right)$$

for all $x,y \in \mathbb{I}$. Substitute this into (4.6) with

$$X := k(x), \quad Y := k(y), \quad U := k(u), \quad V := k(v),$$
$$\mathsf{F}_k(X,U) := k(\mathsf{F}(k^{-1}(X),k^{-1}(U))),$$

and get the Jensen equation for F_k

$$\mathsf{F}_k\left(\frac{X+Y}{2},\frac{U+V}{2}\right) = \frac{\mathsf{F}_k(X,U)+\mathsf{F}_k(Y,V)}{2}.$$

By the continuity of F and k, the new variables X, Y, U, V range over an interval $\mathbb{J} = k(\mathbb{I})$ and F_k is continuous on $\mathbb{J}^2$. As continuous solutions of the Jensen equation are of the form (see for instance Aczél [3, §5.1.1])

$$\mathsf{F}_k(X,U) = pX + qU + r,$$

with constants p, q, r, we get

$$\mathsf{F}(x,u) = k^{-1}(pk(x) + qk(u) + r).$$

Now, idempotency of F yields $p + q = 1$ and $r = 0$, and the strict monotonicity of F excludes $p = 0$ or $q = 0$. $\qquad\square$

Theorem 4.18. *The function* $\mathsf{F} : \mathbb{I}^n \to \mathbb{R}$ *is continuous, strictly increasing, and bisymmetric if and only if there is a continuous and strictly monotonic function* $f : \mathbb{I} \to \mathbb{R}$ *and real numbers* $p_1, \ldots, p_n > 0$, *and* $q \in \mathbb{R}$, *such that*

$$\mathsf{F}(\mathbf{x}) = f^{-1}\left(\sum_{i=1}^n p_i f(x_i) + q\right) \tag{4.7}$$

for all $\mathbf{x} \in \mathbb{I}^n$.

Proof. ($\Leftarrow$) Easy.

($\Rightarrow$) As in the proof of Theorem 4.17, we confine ourselves to binary functions $\mathsf{F} : \mathbb{I}^2 \to \mathbb{R}$.

Since F is continuous and strictly increasing, it is idempotizable (that is, δ_F is strictly increasing and $\mathrm{ran}(\delta_\mathsf{F}) = \mathrm{ran}(\mathsf{F})$). It follows that the function $\mathsf{G} := \delta_\mathsf{F}^{-1} \circ \mathsf{F}$ is well defined on $\mathbb{I}^2$. Moreover, it is continuous, strictly increasing, and idempotent. It is also bisymmetric since the expression

$$
\begin{aligned}
&(\delta_\mathsf{F} \circ \delta_\mathsf{F} \circ \mathsf{G})(\mathsf{G}(x,y), \mathsf{G}(u,v)) \\
&= (\delta_\mathsf{F} \circ \mathsf{F})(\mathsf{G}(x,y), \mathsf{G}(u,v)) \\
&= \mathsf{F}(\mathsf{F}(\mathsf{G}(x,y), \mathsf{G}(u,v)), \mathsf{F}(\mathsf{G}(x,y), \mathsf{G}(u,v))) \\
&= \mathsf{F}(\mathsf{F}(\mathsf{G}(x,y), \mathsf{G}(x,y)), \mathsf{F}(\mathsf{G}(u,v), \mathsf{G}(u,v))) \quad \text{(bisymmetry of } \mathsf{F}) \\
&= \mathsf{F}((\delta_\mathsf{F} \circ \mathsf{G})(x,y), (\delta_\mathsf{F} \circ \mathsf{G})(u,v)) \\
&= \mathsf{F}(\mathsf{F}(x,y), \mathsf{F}(u,v))
\end{aligned}
$$

is symmetric in y and u. By Theorem 4.17, there is a continuous and strictly monotonic function $f : \mathbb{I} \to \mathbb{R}$ and a real number $p > 0$ such that

$$\mathsf{G}(x,y) = f^{-1}(pf(x) + (1-p)f(y)). \tag{4.8}$$

On the other hand, bisymmetry of F implies

$$(\delta_\mathsf{F} \circ \mathsf{F})(x,y) = \mathsf{F}(\delta_\mathsf{F}(x), \delta_\mathsf{F}(y)),$$

which can be rewritten as

$$(\delta_\mathsf{F} \circ \mathsf{G})(x,y) = \mathsf{G}(\delta_\mathsf{F}(x), \delta_\mathsf{F}(y))$$

or, using (4.8),

$$(\delta_\mathsf{F} \circ f^{-1})(pf(x) + (1-p)f(y)) = f^{-1}(p(f \circ \delta_\mathsf{F})(x) + (1-p)(f \circ \delta_\mathsf{F})(y)).$$

With $u := f(x)$, $v := f(y)$, and $\psi := f \circ \delta_\mathsf{F} \circ f^{-1}$, we obtain the equation

$$\psi(pu + (1-p)v) = p\,\psi(u) + (1-p)\psi(v)$$

whose continuous solutions are of the form (see for instance Aczél [3, §2.2.6])

$$\psi(u) = au + q,$$

with constants a and q, that is,

$$\delta_\mathsf{F}(x) = f^{-1}(af(x) + q).$$

Table 4.2. *Examples of quasi-linear means*

$f(x)$	$M(\mathbf{x})$	Name	Notation
x	$\sum_{i=1}^{n} w_i x_i$	weighted arithmetic mean	$\mathsf{WAM_w}$
x^2	$\left(\sum_{i=1}^{n} w_i x_i^2\right)^{1/2}$	weighted quadratic mean	$\mathsf{WQM_w}$
$\log x$	$\prod_{i=1}^{n} x_i^{w_i}$	weighted geometric mean	$\mathsf{WGM_w}$
$x^\alpha \ (\alpha \in \mathbb{R} \setminus \{0\})$	$\left(\sum_{i=1}^{n} w_i x_i^\alpha\right)^{1/\alpha}$	weighted root-mean-power	$\mathsf{WM}_{\mathrm{id}^\alpha,\mathbf{w}}$

Finally, we obtain

$$\mathsf{F}(x,y) = (\delta_{\mathsf{F}} \circ \mathsf{G})(x,y) = f^{-1}(apf(x) + a(1-p)f(y) + q)$$
$$= f^{-1}(p_1 f(x) + p_2 f(y) + q),$$

with $p_1 > 0$ and $p_2 > 0$ since F is strictly increasing. □

The *quasi-linear means* (4.5) and the *quasi-linear functions* (4.7) are weighted aggregation functions. Notice, however, that in the set of properties given for axiomatizing these functions, the weights are not given beforehand.

The question of uniqueness with respect to f is dealt with in detail in Aczél [3, §6.4]. More generally, the extension of Proposition 4.6 to quasi-linear means is discussed in Berrone [38, Th. 1].

Table 4.2 provides some particular cases of quasi-linear means.

Remark 4.19. As Fuchs [125] showed, the results and proofs of Theorems 4.13, 4.17, and 4.18 can be applied *mutatis mutandis* to arbitrary completely ordered sets. In order to avoid arguments concerning metric, the continuity property has been replaced by a property of pure algebraic character, called "Archimedean axiom".

Based on a prior result [372], Aczél [3, §6.5] (see also [9, Chap. 17]) showed that the binary quasi-linear means are also the general continuous strictly increasing solutions of the autodistributivity equations (cf. Definition 2.79).

Theorem 4.20. *The function* $\mathsf{F} : \mathbb{I}^2 \to \mathbb{I}$ *is continuous, strictly increasing, and autodistributive if and only if there exists a continuous strictly monotonic function* $f : \mathbb{I} \to \mathbb{R}$ *and an arbitrary constant* $w \in \,]0, 1[$ *such that*

$$\mathsf{F}(x,y) = f^{-1}((1-w)f(x) + wf(y))$$

for all $(x,y) \in \mathbb{I}^2$.

Of course, by adding the symmetry property to the previous theorem, we obtain the binary quasi-arithmetic means, which indicates the equivalence between bisymmetry and autodistributivity for strictly increasing means.

The classical *weighted arithmetic mean* $\mathsf{WAM_w}$, as already defined in (1.18), is simply a quasi-linear mean for which the generator f is the identity function.

The family of weighted arithmetic means on $\mathbb{R}^n$ can be easily characterized using the additivity property; see Definition 2.114.

Proposition 4.21. $\mathsf{F} : \mathbb{R}^n \to \mathbb{R}$ *is additive, nondecreasing, and idempotent if and only if there exists a weight vector* $\mathbf{w} \in [0,1]^n$ *satisfying* $\sum_i w_i = 1$ *such that* $\mathsf{F} = \mathsf{WAM_w}$.

Proof. ($\Leftarrow$) Trivial.

($\Rightarrow$) By Proposition 2.116, F is of the form $\mathsf{F}(\mathbf{x}) = \sum_i w_i x_i$ with arbitrary constants $w_1, \ldots, w_n \geqslant 0$. By idempotency of F, these constants sum up to one. $\square$

Corollary 4.22. $\mathsf{F} : \mathbb{R}^n \to \mathbb{R}$ *is additive, nondecreasing, symmetric, and idempotent if and only if* $\mathsf{F} = \mathsf{AM}$ *is the arithmetic mean.*

Remark 4.23. As will be discussed in Chapter 5, the weighted arithmetic means $\mathsf{WAM_w}$ are exactly the Choquet integrals with respect to additive normalized capacities; see Proposition 5.50(v). If we further assume the symmetry property, we obtain the arithmetic mean AM.

The following two results provide axiomatizations of certain supersets of the family of weighted arithmetic means. Recall that, for any subset $K \subseteq [n]$, Min_K and Max_K denote respectively the partial minimum and partial maximum functions associated with K; see (1.16) and (1.17).

Theorem 4.24 (Marichal *et al.* [284]). *Assume* $\mathbb{I} \supseteq [0,1]$. *The function* $\mathsf{F} : \mathbb{I}^n \to \mathbb{R}$ *is nondecreasing, bisymmetric, and interval scale invariant if and only if*

$$\mathsf{F} \in \{\mathsf{Min}_K, \mathsf{Max}_K \mid K \subseteq [n]\} \cup \{\mathsf{WAM_w} \mid \mathbf{w} \in [0,1]^n, \textstyle\sum_i w_i = 1\}.$$

Theorem 4.25 (Marichal *et al.* [284]). *Assume* $\mathbb{I} \supseteq [0,1]$. *The function* $\mathsf{F} : \cup_{n \in \mathbb{N}} \mathbb{I}^n \to \mathbb{R}$ *is nondecreasing, strongly bisymmetric, and interval scale invariant if and only if*

(i) *either, for any* $n \in \mathbb{N}$, *there is* $K_n \subseteq [n]$ *such that* $\mathsf{F}^{(n)} = \mathsf{Min}_{K_n}$,

(ii) *or, for any* $n \in \mathbb{N}$, *there is* $K_n \subseteq [n]$ *such that* $\mathsf{F}^{(n)} = \mathsf{Max}_{K_n}$,

(iii) *or, for any* $n \in \mathbb{N}$, *there is* $\mathbf{w}_n \in [0,1]^n$ *with* $\sum_i w_{n,i} = 1$ *such that* $\mathsf{F}^{(n)} = \mathsf{WAM}_{\mathbf{w}_n}$.

We also observe that further axiomatizations of special n-ary quasi-linear means, such as self-reciprocal (cf. Definition 2.107) quasi-linear means, ratio scale invariant quasi-linear means, log-ratio scale invariant quasi-linear means, can be found in Aczél [5]; see also Aczél and Alsina [7].

4.3.2 *Quasi-arithmetic means with weight function*

A natural way to generalize the quasi-arithmetic mean consists in incorporating weights as in the quasi-linear mean (4.5). To generalize a step further, we could assume that the weights are not constant. On this issue, Losonczi [249, 250] considered and investigated in 1971 nonsymmetric functions of the form

$$M(\mathbf{x}) = f^{-1}\left(\frac{\sum_{i=1}^{n} p_i(x_i) f(x_i)}{\sum_{i=1}^{n} p_i(x_i)}\right),$$

where $f : \mathbb{I} \to \mathbb{R}$ is a continuous and strictly monotonic function and $p_1, \ldots, p_n :$ $\mathbb{I} \to \,]0, \infty[$ are positive-valued functions. The special case where $p_1 = \cdots = p_n$ was previously introduced in 1958 by Bajraktarević [23], who defined the concept of *quasi-arithmetic mean with weight function* as follows; see also Páles [346].[3]

Definition 4.26. Let $f : \mathbb{I} \to \mathbb{R}$ be a continuous and strictly monotonic function and let $p : \mathbb{I} \to \,]0, \infty[$ be a positive-valued function. The n-ary *quasi-arithmetic mean generated by f with weight function p* is the function $\mathsf{M}_{f,p} : \mathbb{I}^n \to \mathbb{I}$ defined as

$$\mathsf{M}_{f,p}(\mathbf{x}) = f^{-1}\left(\frac{\sum_{i=1}^{n} p(x_i) f(x_i)}{\sum_{i=1}^{n} p(x_i)}\right). \tag{4.9}$$

The *extended quasi-arithmetic mean generated by f with weight function p* is the function $\mathsf{M}_{f,p} : \cup_{n \in \mathbb{N}} \mathbb{I}^n \to \mathbb{I}$ whose restriction to $\mathbb{I}^n$ is the n-ary quasi-arithmetic mean generated by f with weight function p.

It is very important to note that, even though quasi-arithmetic means with weight function are (clearly) idempotent, they need not be nondecreasing, which implies that they need not be means or even aggregation functions. To give an example, consider the case where $n = 2, f(x) = x$, and $p(x) = 2x + 1$, that is,

$$\mathsf{M}_{f,p}(x_1, x_2) = \frac{2x_1^2 + 2x_2^2 + x_1 + x_2}{2x_1 + 2x_2 + 2}.$$

We can readily see that the section $x \mapsto \mathsf{M}_{f,p}(x, 1)$ of this binary function is not nondecreasing.

Assuming that the weight function p is nondecreasing and differentiable, Marques Pereira and Ribeiro [293] and Mesiar and Špirková [311] found sufficient conditions on p to ensure nondecreasing monotonicity of $\mathsf{M}_{\mathrm{id},p}$. Here we assume $\mathbb{I} = [0,1]$ as in [311], but the conditions easily extend to arbitrary intervals. For extended arithmetic means $\mathsf{M}_{\mathrm{id},p}$ with weight function p, the simplest sufficient condition to ensure nondecreasing monotonicity is $p(x) \geqslant p'(x) \geqslant 0$. A more general one is

$$p(x) \geqslant (1 - x)p'(x) \geqslant 0, \qquad \forall x \in [0, 1].$$

---

[3] The subcase where $f = \mathrm{id}$, called *Beckenbach–Gini means* or *mixture operators*, has been investigated by Marques Pereira and Ribeiro [293], Matkowski [298], and Yager [441].

Remark 4.27. For extended quasi-arithmetic means $M_{f,p}$ with weight function p, assuming that both f and p are increasing and differentiable and that $\text{ran}(f) = [0, 1]$, the above sufficient condition generalizes into

$$f'(x)p(x) \geqslant (1 - f(x))p'(x) \geqslant 0, \qquad \forall x \in [0, 1].$$

For n-ary arithmetic means $M_{\text{id},p}$ with weight function p, we also have the sufficient condition

$$\frac{p^2(x)}{(n-1)p(1)} + p(x) \geqslant (1 - x)p'(x), \qquad \forall x \in [0, 1].$$

Remark 4.28. It is worth mentioning that $M_{f,p}$ can also be obtained by the minimization problem

$$M_{f,p}(\mathbf{x}) = \arg\min_{r \in \mathbb{R}} \sum_{i=1}^{n} p(x_i) \left(f(x_i) - f(r) \right)^2.$$

Evidently, in the same way, classical quasi-arithmetic means (p is constant) and weighted quasi-arithmetic means (replace $p(x_i)$ with w_i) are obtained. For more details, see Calvo *et al.* [53] and Mesiar and Špirková [312].

Páles [346] established the following axiomatization of the class of extended quasi-arithmetic means with weight function, thus generalizing the Kolmogoroff–Nagumo characterization of extended quasi-arithmetic means (cf. Theorem 4.10). The detailed proof is rather lengthy so we omit it.

Theorem 4.29. *Assume* $\mathbb{I}$ *is open. The function* $\mathsf{F} : \cup_{n \in \mathbb{N}} \mathbb{I}^n \to \mathbb{R}$ *is an extended quasi-arithmetic mean with weight function if and only if the following properties are satisfied:*

(i) $\mathsf{F}(x) = x$ *for all* $x \in \mathbb{I}$.

(ii) F *is symmetric.*

(iii) *For any* $x < u < v < y$ *in* $\mathbb{I}$, *there can be found natural numbers* n, m *such that*

$$u < \mathsf{F}(n \cdot x, m \cdot y) < v.$$

(iv) *For any* $n, m \in \mathbb{N}$ *and any* $\mathbf{x} \in \mathbb{I}^n$ *and* $\mathbf{y} \in \mathbb{I}^m$,

$$\lim_{k \to \infty} \mathsf{F}(k \cdot x_1, \ldots, k \cdot x_n, \mathbf{y}) = \mathsf{F}(\mathbf{x}).$$

(v) *For any* $n, m \in \mathbb{N}$, *any* $k, l \in \mathbb{N}_0$, *and any* $\mathbf{x} \in \mathbb{I}^n$, $\mathbf{y} \in \mathbb{I}^m$, $\mathbf{u} \in \mathbb{I}^k$, $\mathbf{v} \in \mathbb{I}^l$, *the inequalities*

$$\mathsf{F}(\mathbf{x}, \mathbf{u}) \leqslant \mathsf{F}(\mathbf{x}, \mathbf{v}) \quad \text{and} \quad \mathsf{F}(\mathbf{y}, \mathbf{u}) \leqslant \mathsf{F}(\mathbf{y}, \mathbf{v})$$

imply

$$\mathsf{F}(\mathbf{x}, \mathbf{u}, \mathbf{y}, \mathbf{u}) \leqslant \mathsf{F}(\mathbf{x}, \mathbf{v}, \mathbf{y}, \mathbf{v}).$$

Starting from a prior result from Aczél and Daróczy [8], Páles [346] also described the class of extended quasi-arithmetic means with weight function that are ratio scale invariant, thus generalizing Theorem 4.15. Note that, here again, increasing monotonicity is not guaranteed.

Theorem 4.30. *The quasi-arithmetic mean* M : $]0, \infty[^n \to \mathbb{I}$ *with weight function is ratio scale invariant if and only if there exist* m : $]0, \infty[\to]0, \infty[$, *with* $m(xy) = m(x)m(y)$, *and* $\alpha \in \mathbb{R}$ *such that*

$$
M(x) = \begin{cases} \left(\dfrac{\sum_i m(x_i) x_i^\alpha}{\sum_i m(x_i)} \right)^{\frac{1}{\alpha}} & \text{if } \alpha \neq 0 \\[4mm] \exp\left(\dfrac{\sum_i m(x_i) \ln x_i}{\sum_i m(x_i)} \right) & \text{if } \alpha = 0. \end{cases}
$$

If m is bounded (or continuous or monotone) then $m(x) = x^c$ *for some* $c \in \mathbb{R}$.

4.3.3 Nonstrict quasi-arithmetic means

Yet another generalization of the class of quasi-arithmetic means consists in replacing, in their axiomatizations, the strict increasing monotonicity property with the nondecreasing monotonicity property. This generalization was investigated by Fodor and Marichal [116, 117], who succeeded in generalizing both Kolmogoroff–Nagumo's axiomatization (cf. Theorem 4.10) and Aczél's axiomatization (cf. Theorem 4.13), in the case where $\mathbb{I}$ is a closed interval, by relaxing the condition that the means be strictly increasing, requiring only that they be nondecreasing. The family obtained, which has a rather intricate structure, is very similar to that of *ordinal sums* well known in the theory of semigroups; see Section 3.3.7. This family naturally includes nonstrict means such as Min and Max.

We first present the result in the case of binary means. The whole description is stated in Theorems 4.32, 4.34, and 4.35.

We start with the following lemma:

Lemma 4.31. *If* M : $[a, b]^2 \to [a, b]$ *is symmetric, continuous, nondecreasing, idempotent, and bisymmetric then the following statements are equivalent:*

(i) $M(a, x) < x < M(x, b)$, *for all* $x \in]a, b[$,
(ii) $x < M(x, y) < y$, *for all* $x, y \in]a, b[$, $x < y$,
(iii) M *is strictly increasing on* $]a, b[$.

Proof. (*ii*) $\Rightarrow$ (*i*). For all $x \in]a, b[$, there exist $u, v \in]a, b[$ such that $a < u < x < v < b$. From (*ii*) we have $M(a, x) \leqslant M(u, x) < x < M(x, v) \leqslant M(x, b)$.

(*i*) $\Rightarrow$ (*ii*). Assume first that there exist $x_0, y_0 \in]a, b[$, $x_0 < y_0$ such that $M(x_0, y_0) = y_0$. Define

$$X := \{x \in [a, b] \mid x \leqslant y_0 \text{ and } M(x, y_0) = y_0\}.$$

On the one hand, it is clear that $X \neq \varnothing$ since $x_0 \in X$. On the other hand, by continuity, X is closed. Introducing $x^* := \inf X$, we have $a < x^* \leqslant x_0 < y_0$ since, from (*i*), we have $a \notin X$. Moreover, by nondecreasing monotonicity, we have $[x^*, y_0] \subseteq X$. We should have $x^* > M(a, y_0)$. Indeed, if $x^* \leqslant M(a, y_0)$, then, since $M(a, y_0) < y_0$ by hypothesis, we have $M(a, y_0) \in X$, that is $M(M(a, y_0), y_0) = y_0$ and, by idempotency and bisymmetry,

$$M(M(a, x^*), y_0) = M(M(a, x^*), M(y_0, y_0)) = M(M(a, y_0), M(x^*, y_0))$$
$$= M(M(a, y_0), y_0) = y_0.$$

Since $M(a, x^*) \leqslant x^* < y_0$, we have $M(a, x^*) \in X$ and, by the definition of x^*, we have $M(a, x^*) = x^*$, which contradicts (*i*).

It follows that $M(a, y_0) < x^* < y_0 = M(x^*, y_0)$ and, by continuity, there exists $z \in]a, x^*[$ such that $x^* = M(z, y_0)$. Consequently, we have, using idempotency and bisymmetry,

$$M(M(z, x^*), y_0) = M(M(z, x^*), M(y_0, y_0)) = M(M(z, y_0), M(x^*, y_0))$$
$$= M(x^*, y_0) = y_0.$$

Since $M(z, x^*) \leqslant x^* < y_0$, we have $M(z, x^*) \in X$ and, by the definition of x^*, we have $M(z, x^*) = x^*$. Finally, we have, using idempotency and bisymmetry,

$$x^* = M(x^*, x^*) = M(x^*, M(z, y_0)) = M(M(x^*, x^*), M(z, y_0))$$
$$= M(M(x^*, z), M(x^*, y_0)) = M(x^*, y_0) = y_0,$$

a contradiction. Consequently, we have $M(x, y) < y$ for all $x, y \in]a, b[$, $x < y$. One can prove in a similar way that $x < M(x, y)$.

(*ii*) $\Leftrightarrow$ (*iii*). By Theorem 4.13, condition (*ii*) is equivalent to

$$M(x, y) = f^{-1}\left(\frac{f(x) + f(y)}{2}\right)$$

for all $x, y \in]a, b[$, where f is any continuous strictly monotonic function on $]a, b[$, which is sufficient. $\qquad\square$

For any $\theta \in [a, b]$, we define $\mathcal{B}_{a,b,\theta}$ as the set of binary functions $M : [a, b]^2 \to [a, b]$ that are symmetric, continuous, nondecreasing, idempotent, bisymmetric, and such that $M(a, b) = \theta$. The extreme cases $\mathcal{B}_{a,b,a}$ and $\mathcal{B}_{a,b,b}$ play an important role in the description of the means. For example, we have Min $\in \mathcal{B}_{a,b,a}$ and Max $\in \mathcal{B}_{a,b,b}$.

Theorem 4.32. $M : [a,b]^2 \to [a,b]$ *is symmetric, continuous, nondecreasing, idempotent, and bisymmetric if and only if there exist two numbers α and β fulfilling $a \leqslant \alpha \leqslant \beta \leqslant b$, two functions $M_{a,\alpha,\alpha} \in \mathcal{B}_{a,\alpha,\alpha}$ and $M_{\beta,b,\beta} \in \mathcal{B}_{\beta,b,\beta}$, and a continuous and strictly monotonic function $f : [\alpha,\beta] \to \mathbb{R}$ such that, for all $x,y \in [a,b]$,*

$$M(x,y) = \begin{cases} M_{a,\alpha,\alpha}(x,y) & \text{if } x,y \in [a,\alpha] \\ M_{\beta,b,\beta}(x,y) & \text{if } x,y \in [\beta,b] \\ f^{-1}\left(\dfrac{f(\operatorname{Med}(\alpha,x,\beta)) + f(\operatorname{Med}(\alpha,y,\beta))}{2}\right) & \text{otherwise.} \end{cases}$$

Proof. ($\Leftarrow$). Straightforward.

($\Rightarrow$) Assume that $M : [a,b]^2 \to [a,b]$ is symmetric, continuous, nondecreasing, idempotent, and bisymmetric. Define

$$X_a := \{x \in [a,b] \mid M(a,x) = x\} \quad \text{and} \quad X_b := \{x \in [a,b] \mid M(x,b) = x\}.$$

On the one hand, it is clear that $X_a \neq \varnothing$ and $X_b \neq \varnothing$ since $a \in X_a$ and $b \in X_b$. On the other hand, by continuity, X_a and X_b are closed. Introducing $\alpha := \sup X_a$ and $\beta := \inf X_b$, we have $\alpha \leqslant \beta$, otherwise we would have

$$M(a,b) \geqslant M(a,\alpha) = \alpha > \beta = M(\beta,b) \geqslant M(a,b),$$

a contradiction.

Let $x,y \in [a,b]$. If $x,y \in [a,\alpha]$, then we have $M(x,y) = M_{a,\alpha,\alpha}(x,y)$, where $M_{a,\alpha,\alpha} \in \mathcal{B}_{a,\alpha,\alpha}$. Likewise, if $x,y \in [\beta,b]$, then we have $M(x,y) = M_{\beta,b,\beta}(x,y)$, where $M_{\beta,b,\beta} \in \mathcal{B}_{\beta,b,\beta}$. Otherwise, we have two mutually exclusive cases:

(i) If $\alpha = \beta$, then we have

$$\alpha = M(a,\alpha) \leqslant M(x,y) \leqslant M(\alpha,b) = \alpha,$$

that is $M(x,y) = \alpha$.

(ii) If $\alpha < \beta$, then we have

$$M(a,y) = M(\alpha,y), \quad \forall y \in [\alpha, M(\alpha,b)], \tag{4.10}$$

$$M(x,b) = M(x,\beta), \quad \forall x \in [M(a,\beta), \beta]. \tag{4.11}$$

Indeed, if $y \in [\alpha, M(\alpha,b)]$ then, by continuity, there exists $z \in {]\alpha, b[}$ such that $y = M(\alpha,z)$. So, we have

$$M(a,y) = M(M(a,a), M(\alpha,z)) = M(M(a,\alpha), M(a,z))$$

$$= M(M(\alpha,\alpha), M(a,z)) = M(M(\alpha,a), M(\alpha,z))$$

$$= M(\alpha,y),$$

which proves (4.10). We can show that (4.11) is true by using the same argument.

Moreover, we have

$$M(\alpha, \beta) = M(\alpha, b) = M(a, \beta) = M(a, b). \tag{4.12}$$

Indeed, setting $\theta := M(a, b)$, we have

$$\alpha = M(a, \alpha) \leqslant M(a, \beta) \leqslant \theta \leqslant M(\alpha, b) \leqslant M(\beta, b) = \beta$$

and we can apply (4.10) and (4.11) to $y = \theta$. Therefore, we have

$$\theta = M(M(a, b), \theta) = M(M(a, \theta), M(\theta, b)) = M(M(\alpha, \theta), M(\theta, \beta))$$
$$= M(M(\alpha, \beta), \theta) = M(M(a, \alpha), M(\beta, b)) = M(\alpha, \beta),$$

and

$$M(\alpha, b) = M(M(a, \alpha), b) = M(M(\alpha, b), \theta) = M(M(\alpha, b), M(\alpha, \beta)) = M(\alpha, \beta),$$

and

$$M(a, \beta) = M(a, M(\beta, b)) = M(\theta, M(a, \beta)) = M(M(\alpha, \beta), M(a, \beta)) = M(\alpha, \beta),$$

which proves (4.12).

We also have

$$M(a, x) = M(\alpha, x), \qquad \forall x \in [\alpha, \beta], \tag{4.13}$$
$$M(x, b) = M(x, \beta), \qquad \forall x \in [\alpha, \beta]. \tag{4.14}$$

By (4.10)–(4.12), it suffices to prove that $M(a, x) = M(\alpha, x)$ for all $x \in [\theta, \beta]$, and $M(x, b) = M(x, \beta)$ for all $x \in [\alpha, \theta]$.

M is continuous, thus for any $x \in [\theta, \beta]$ there exists $z \in [a, b]$ such that $x = M(\beta, z)$. Thus we have

$$M(a, x) = M(a, M(\beta, z)) = M(M(a, \beta), M(a, z))$$
$$= M(M(\alpha, \beta), M(a, z)) = M(M(\beta, z), \alpha)$$
$$= M(\alpha, x),$$

which proves (4.13). We can prove (4.14) similarly.

For any $x \leqslant \alpha$, $y \geqslant \beta$ we do have $M(x, y) = \theta$. Indeed, from (4.12), we have $\theta = M(a, \beta) \leqslant M(x, y) \leqslant M(\alpha, b) = \theta$.

Finally, by Theorem 4.13 and Lemma 4.31, it suffices to show that $M(\alpha, x) < x < M(x, \beta)$ for all $x \in {]}\alpha, \beta{[}$. Suppose the first inequality is not true. Then, from (4.13), there exists $x \in {]}\alpha, \beta{[}$ such that $M(a, x) = M(\alpha, x) = x$, which contradicts the definition of α. We can prove the second inequality in a similar way. $\square$

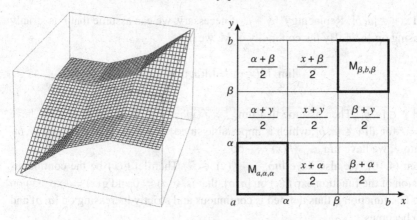

Figure 4.1 Example of nonstrict arithmetic mean from Theorem 4.32 with $f = \text{id}$

As we can see in the description of Theorem 4.32, the definition set $[a, b]^2$ is partitioned into at most nine cells. In each of these cells, the function M takes a specific form. Figure 4.1 presents graphics showing the special case $f(x) = x$ (nonstrict arithmetic mean). Out of the two extreme cells, which correspond to the families $\mathcal{B}_{a,\alpha,\alpha}$ and $\mathcal{B}_{\beta,b,\beta}$, we find the arithmetic mean with arguments depending on each cell itself. This comes from the presence of the median function in the expression for M. For example, if $x \in [\beta, b]$ and $y \in [\alpha, \beta]$ then we get the arithmetic mean for the arguments β and y. In order to obtain a clear and readable three-dimensional representation, we have chosen the Min and Max functions in the extreme cells.

We now present a description of the two families $\mathcal{B}_{a,\alpha,\alpha}$ and $\mathcal{B}_{\beta,b,\beta}$. By internality (due to idempotency), they can be assimilated with $\mathcal{B}_{a,b,b}$ and $\mathcal{B}_{a,b,a}$ respectively, simply by the help of a redefinition of the bounds of the intervals $[a, \alpha]$ and $[\beta, b]$.

Before going on, we consider a lemma.

Lemma 4.33. $M \in \mathcal{B}_{a,b,a}$ *(respectively, $\mathcal{B}_{a,b,b}$) is strictly increasing on $]a, b[^2$ if and only if there exists a continuous strictly increasing (respectively, decreasing) function $g : [a, b] \to \mathbb{R}$, with $g(a) = 0$ (respectively, $g(b) = 0$), such that*

$$M(x, y) = g^{-1}\left(\sqrt{g(x)\, g(y)}\right) \tag{4.15}$$

for all $x, y \in [a, b]$.

Proof. Let us consider the case $\mathcal{B}_{a,b,a}$; the other one is symmetric.

($\Leftarrow$) Easy.

($\Rightarrow$) Let $M \in \mathcal{B}_{a,b,a}$ be strictly increasing on $]a, b[^2$. From Theorem 4.13, there exists a function f which is continuous and strictly monotonic on $]a, b[$, such that

$$2f(M(x, y)) = f(x) + f(y) \tag{4.16}$$

for all $x, y \in]a, b[$. Replacing f by $-f$, if necessary, we can assume that f is strictly increasing on $]a, b[$. By the continuity of M, we have

$$\lim_{x \to a^+} M(x, y) = M(a, y) = a$$

for all $y \in]a, b[$. Then assume that $\lim_{x \to a^+} f(x) = r \in \mathbb{R}$. From (4.16), we have $f(y) = r$ for all $y \in]a, b[$, which is impossible since f is strictly increasing on $]a, b[$. Therefore, we have $\lim_{x \to a^+} f(x) = -\infty$.

From (4.16), we also have $\lim_{y \to b^-} f(y) \in \mathbb{R}$. Then let $g(x)$ be the continuous extension of the function $\exp f(x)$ on $[a, b]$, that is, $g(a) = 0$ and $g(x) = \exp f(x)$ on $]a, b]$. The function g thus defined is continuous and strictly increasing on $[a, b]$ and (4.16) becomes

$$\log g[M(x, y)] = \frac{\log g(x) + \log g(y)}{2}$$

for all $x, y \in]a, b]$, and so we have

$$M(x, y) = g^{-1}\left(\sqrt{g(x)\, g(y)}\right)$$

on $]a, b]^2$ and even on $[a, b]^2$ since M is continuous.   □

Theorem 4.34. *We have* $M \in \mathcal{B}_{a,b,a}$ *if and only if*

(i) *either* $M = \mathrm{Min}$,

(ii) *or there exists a continuous strictly increasing function* $g : [a, b] \to \mathbb{R}$, *with* $g(a) = 0$, *such that, for all* $x, y \in [a, b]$,

$$M(x, y) = g^{-1}\left(\sqrt{g(x)\, g(y)}\right),$$

(iii) *or there exist a countable index set* $K \subseteq \mathbb{N}$, *a family of disjoint open subintervals* $\{]a_k, b_k[\mid k \in K\}$ *of* $[a, b]$ *and a family* $\{g_k \mid k \in K\}$ *of continuous and strictly increasing functions* $g_k : [a_k, b_k] \to \mathbb{R}$, *with* $g_k(a_k) = 0$, *such that, for all* $x, y \in [a, b]$,

$$M(x, y) = \begin{cases} g_k^{-1}\left(\sqrt{g_k(\mathrm{Min}(x, b_k))\, g_k(\mathrm{Min}(y, b_k))}\right) & \text{if } \mathrm{Min}(x, y) \in]a_k, b_k[\\ & \text{for some } k \in K \\ \mathrm{Min}(x, y) & \text{otherwise.} \end{cases}$$

Proof. ($\Leftarrow$) Straightforward.

($\Rightarrow$) Let $x, y \in [a, b]$ and $M \in \mathcal{B}_{a,b,a}$. Define a set $X \subseteq [a, b]$ by

$$X := \{x \in [a, b] \mid M(x, b) = x\}.$$

It is clear that X is closed and nonempty. Thus $Y := [a,b] \setminus X$ is open and bounded. In fact $Y = \varnothing$ if and only if $\mathsf{M}(x,b) = x$ for all $x \in [a,b]$, that is

$$\mathsf{M}(x,y) = \mathsf{Min}(x,y)$$

since assuming $x \leqslant y$, with $x,y \in [a,b]$, we have

$$\mathsf{M}(x,y) \leqslant \mathsf{M}(x,b) = x = \mathsf{M}(x,x) \leqslant \mathsf{M}(x,y)$$

and hence $\mathsf{M}(x,y) = x$.

In the other extreme case we have $Y =]a,b[$, that is $X = \{a,b\}$, if and only if $x < \mathsf{M}(x,b)$ for all $x \in]a,b[$. However, $\mathsf{M}(a,a) = a$ and $\mathsf{M}(a,b) = a$ imply $\mathsf{M}(a,x) = a < x$ for all $x \in]a,b[$. It follows, from Lemma 4.31, that $\mathsf{M}(x,y)$ is strictly increasing on $]a,b[^2$, and from Lemma 4.33 that

$$\mathsf{M}(x,y) = g^{-1}\left(\sqrt{g(x)\,g(y)}\right),$$

where g is any continuous strictly increasing function on $[a,b]$, with $g(a) = 0$.

Consider the remaining case, that is $\varnothing \subsetneq Y \subsetneq]a,b[$. Then there exists a countable index set $K \subseteq \mathbb{N}$ and a class of pairwise disjoint open intervals $\{]a_k, b_k[\mid k \in K\}$ of $[a,b]$ such that

$$Y = \bigcup_{k \in K}]a_k, b_k[.$$

For all $k \in K$, we obviously have $\mathsf{M}(a_k, b) = a_k$ and $\mathsf{M}(b_k, b) = b_k$ since $a_k, b_k \in X$, but also

$$\mathsf{M}(x,b) > x \quad \forall x \in]a_k, b_k[, \tag{4.17}$$

$$\mathsf{M}(a_k, x) = a_k \quad \forall x \in [a_k, b], \tag{4.18}$$

$$\mathsf{M}(b_k, x) = b_k \quad \forall x \in [b_k, b]. \tag{4.19}$$

To establish (4.17), we can notice that $x \in]a_k, b_k[$ implies $x \notin X$. For (4.18) and (4.19), we obviously have

$$a_k = \mathsf{M}(a_k, a_k) \leqslant \mathsf{M}(a_k, x) \leqslant \mathsf{M}(a_k, b) = a_k, \quad \forall x \in [a_k, b],$$
$$b_k = \mathsf{M}(b_k, b_k) \leqslant \mathsf{M}(b_k, x) \leqslant \mathsf{M}(b_k, b) = b_k, \quad \forall x \in [b_k, b].$$

Then we can see that, if $\mathsf{Min}(x,y) \in X$, then

$$\mathsf{M}(x,y) = \mathsf{Min}(x,y).$$

If $\mathsf{Min}(x,y) \in Y$, that is $\mathsf{Min}(x,y) \in]a_k, b_k[$ for some $k \in K$, then, assuming that $x \in]a_k, b_k[$ and $y \in [b_k, b]$, we have

$$\mathsf{M}(x,y) = \mathsf{M}(x, b_k). \tag{4.20}$$

Indeed, since from (4.18) we have $M(a_k, b_k) = a_k$ and since $M(b_k, b_k) = b_k$, then, by continuity of M, there exists $z \in]a_k, b_k[$ such that $x = M(z, b_k)$. Then, from (4.19) we have

$$M(x,y) = M(M(z,b_k), M(y,y)) = M(M(z,y), M(b_k,y)) = M(M(z,y), b_k)$$
$$= M(M(z,y), M(b_k, b_k)) = M(M(z,b_k), M(y,b_k)) = M(x, b_k).$$

Now, we can show that if $x, y \in]a_k, b_k[$, then

$$M(x,y) = g_k^{-1}\left(\sqrt{g_k(x)\, g_k(y)}\right)$$

where g_k is any continuous strictly increasing function on $[a_k, b_k]$, with $g_k(a_k) = 0$. It is sufficient, from Lemmas 4.31 and 4.33, to show that

$$M(a_k, x) < x < M(x, b_k)$$

for all $x \in]a_k, b_k[$. The first inequality comes from (4.18). For the second one, we notice that if $x = M(x, b_k)$ for one $x \in]a_k, b_k[$ then, from (4.20), we would have $x = M(x, b_k) = M(x, b)$, which contradicts (4.17).   □

We can note that, in the previous result, the third case includes the first two. Indeed, we get the first case if no subinterval $]a_k, b_k[$ is considered, and we get the second case if only one subinterval is considered and if it coincides with $]a, b[$. Consequently, it would have sufficed to state only the third case, the first two cases being merely degenerate cases of the third one.

Figure 4.2 represents an example from the third case. As we can see, there exists a partition of $[a, b]$ into disjoint open subintervals $]a_k, b_k[$, which divide the definition set $[a, b]^2$ into several pieces. If, given $(x, y) \in [a, b]^2$, there exists an index $k \in K$ for which $Min(x, y)$ lies in $]a_k, b_k[$ then (x, y) is in one of the unshaded regions.

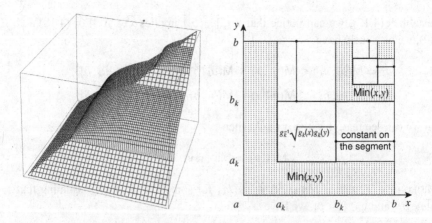

Figure 4.2 Example of mean from $\mathcal{B}_{a,b,a}$

A quasi-geometric mean $g_k^{-1}(\sqrt{g_k(x)g_k(y)})$ is defined in the central square of this region. Moreover, due to the presence of the Min function in the expression of M, there are constant values on each horizontal or vertical segment going from the edge of the square to the extremity of the definition set. Finally, the Min function is defined in all the shaded regions.

Theorem 4.35. *We have* M $\in \mathcal{B}_{a,b,b}$ *if and only if*

(i) either M = Max,

(ii) or there exists a continuous strictly decreasing function $g : [a,b] \to \mathbb{R}$, *with* $g(b) = 0$, *such that, for all* $x,y \in [a,b]$,

$$M(x,y) = g^{-1}\left(\sqrt{g(x)\,g(y)}\right),$$

(iii) or there exist a countable index set $K \subseteq \mathbb{N}$, *a family of disjoint open subintervals* $\{]a_k,b_k[\mid k \in K\}$ *of* $[a,b]$ *and a family* $\{g_k \mid k \in K\}$ *of continuous and strictly increasing functions* $g_k : [a_k,b_k] \to \mathbb{R}$, *with* $g_k(b_k) = 0$, *such that, for all* $x,y \in [a,b]$,

$$M(x,y) = \begin{cases} g_k^{-1}\!\left(\sqrt{g_k(\mathsf{Max}(a_k,x))\,g_k(\mathsf{Max}(a_k,y))}\right) & \text{if } \mathsf{Max}(x,y) \in\,]a_k,b_k[\\ & \text{for some } k \in K \\ \mathsf{Max}(x,y) & \text{otherwise.} \end{cases}$$

Proof. Similar to the proof of Theorem 4.34. □

Figure 4.3 represents an example from the third case. We do not elaborate on this representation, which is very similar to that of Figure 4.2.

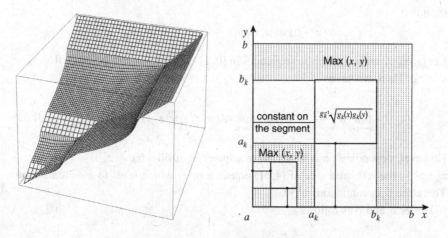

Figure 4.3 Example of mean from $\mathcal{B}_{a,b,b}$

We now discuss the case of extended means. The whole description is stated in Theorems 4.36, 4.40, and 4.41.

For any $\theta \in [a, b]$, we define $\mathcal{D}_{a,b,\theta}$ as the set of extended functions M : $\cup_{n\in\mathbb{N}}[a, b]^n \to [a, b]$ that are symmetric, continuous, nondecreasing, idempotent, decomposable, and such that $\mathsf{M}(a, b) = \theta$. Here also, the extreme cases $\mathcal{D}_{a,b,a}$ and $\mathcal{D}_{a,b,b}$ play an important role.

Theorem 4.36. *The function* M : $\cup_{n\in\mathbb{N}}[a, b]^n \to [a, b]$ *is symmetric, continuous, nondecreasing, idempotent, and decomposable if and only if there exist two numbers α and β fulfilling $a \leqslant \alpha \leqslant \beta \leqslant b$, two functions $\mathsf{M}_{a,\alpha,\alpha} \in \mathcal{D}_{a,\alpha,\alpha}$ and $\mathsf{M}_{\beta,b,\beta} \in \mathcal{D}_{\beta,b,\beta}$, and a continuous and strictly monotonic function $f : [\alpha, \beta] \to \mathbb{R}$ such that, for all $n \in \mathbb{N}$ and all $\mathbf{x} \in [a, b]^n$,*

$$
\mathsf{M}(\mathbf{x}) = \begin{cases}
\mathsf{M}_{a,\alpha,\alpha}(\mathbf{x}) & \text{if } \mathrm{Max}(\mathbf{x}) \in [a, \alpha] \\
\mathsf{M}_{\beta,b,\beta}(\mathbf{x}) & \text{if } \mathrm{Min}(\mathbf{x}) \in [\beta, b] \\
f^{-1}\Big(\dfrac{1}{n}\sum_{i=1}^{n} f(\mathrm{Med}(\alpha, x_i, \beta))\Big) & \text{otherwise.}
\end{cases}
$$

Proof. ($\Leftarrow$) We can easily show that M satisfies the stated properties.

($\Rightarrow$) By Lemma 4.9 there exists a strictly increasing function $\psi : [0, 1] \cap \mathbb{Q} \to [a, b]$, with $\psi(0) = a$ and $\psi(1) = b$, such that

$$
\mathsf{M}\big(\psi(z_1), \ldots, \psi(z_n)\big) = \psi\Big(\frac{1}{n}\sum_{i=1}^{n} z_i\Big)
$$

for any $\mathbf{z} \in \cup_{n\in\mathbb{N}}([0, 1]^n \cap \mathbb{Q}^n)$.

Let us show that the function ψ can be extended continuously in $]0, 1[$. The proof is similar to that of Theorem 4.10. Suppose on the contrary that there is $x \in \,]0, 1[$ such that

$$
\psi(x - 0) = u, \quad \psi(x + 0) = v, \quad u < v.
$$

Let $(z_m)_{m\in\mathbb{N}}$ and $(z'_m)_{m\in\mathbb{N}}$ be sequences in $[0, 1] \cap \mathbb{Q}$ converging to x such that $z_m < x < z'_m$. Then, we have

$$
\lim_{m\to\infty} \psi\Big(\frac{z_m + z'_m}{2}\Big) = \lim_{m\to\infty} \mathsf{M}(\psi(z_m), \psi(z'_m)) = \mathsf{M}(u, v). \tag{4.21}
$$

However, depending on whether these sequences fulfill $\frac{1}{2}(z_m + z'_m) < x$ or $\frac{1}{2}(z_m + z'_m) > x$, the left-hand side of (4.21) equals u or v, which leads to a contradiction. Therefore ψ is continuous in $]0, 1[$.

Define α and β as follows:

$$
a \leqslant \alpha = \lim_{t\to 0^+} \psi(t) \leqslant \lim_{t\to 1^-} \psi(t) = \beta \leqslant b.
$$

Then, for any $k \in \mathbb{N}$, we have

$$M(k \cdot a, \alpha) = \alpha, \tag{4.22}$$

$$M(\beta, k \cdot b) = \beta. \tag{4.23}$$

Indeed, by continuity, we have

$$M(k \cdot a, \alpha) = \lim_{t \to 0^+} M(k \cdot \psi(0), \psi(t)) = \lim_{t \to 0^+} \psi\left(\frac{t}{k+1}\right) = \alpha$$

and

$$M(\beta, k \cdot b) = \lim_{t \to 1^-} M(\psi(t), k \cdot \psi(1)) = \lim_{t \to 1^-} \psi\left(\frac{k+t}{k+1}\right) = \beta.$$

Then let $n \in \mathbb{N}$ and $\mathbf{x} \in [a, b]^n$. If $\mathsf{Max}(\mathbf{x}) \in [a, \alpha]$ then, from (4.22), we have $M(\mathbf{x}) = M_{a,\alpha,\alpha}(\mathbf{x})$, where $M_{a,\alpha,\alpha} \in \mathcal{D}_{a,\alpha,\alpha}$. Similarly, if $\mathsf{Min}(\mathbf{x}) \in [\beta, b]$ then, from (4.23), we have $M(\mathbf{x}) = M_{\beta,b,\beta}(\mathbf{x})$, where $M_{\beta,b,\beta} \in \mathcal{D}_{\beta,b,\beta}$. Otherwise, we have two mutually exclusive cases:

 (i) If $\alpha = \beta$ then, from (4.22) and (4.23), we have

$$\alpha = M((n-1) \cdot a, \alpha) \leqslant M(\mathbf{x}) \leqslant M(\alpha, (n-1) \cdot b) = \alpha,$$

 that is $M(\mathbf{x}) = \alpha$.
(ii) If $\alpha < \beta$ then ψ is strictly increasing on $[0, 1]$. Indeed, suppose there exist $t_1, t_2 \in\,]0, 1[,\, t_1 < t_2$, such that $\psi(t_1) = \psi(t_2)$. Then, for any $p, q \in \mathbb{N}_0, p \leqslant q$, $q \neq 0$, we obtain

$$M(p \cdot \psi(t_1), (q - p) \cdot \psi(0)) = M(p \cdot \psi(t_2), (q - p) \cdot \psi(0)),$$

 that is,

$$\psi\left(\frac{p}{q} t_1\right) = \psi\left(\frac{p}{q} t_2\right).$$

Therefore, for any $r \in [0, 1] \cap \mathbb{Q}$, we have $\psi(r\, t_1) = \psi(r\, t_2)$, which still holds, by continuity of ψ, for all $r \in [0, 1]$. Choosing $r = t_1/t_2 \in\,]0, 1[$, the previous equality becomes

$$\psi(r\, t_1) = \psi(t_1) = \psi(t_2).$$

By iteration, we get, for all $m \in \mathbb{N}$,

$$\psi(r^m\, t_1) = \psi(t_2),$$

and by continuity of ψ,

$$\alpha = \lim_{m \to \infty} \psi(r^m\, t_1) = \psi(t_2).$$

One can show, in a similar way, that $\psi(t_1) = \beta$. Indeed, for all $p, q \in \mathbb{N}_0, p \leqslant q$, $q \neq 0$, we obtain

$$\mathsf{M}(p \cdot \psi(t_1), (q - p) \cdot \psi(1)) = \mathsf{M}(p \cdot \psi(t_2), (q - p) \cdot \psi(1)),$$

that is, $\psi(1 - r(1 - t_1)) = \psi(1 - r(1 - t_2))$ for all $r \in [0, 1]$. Choosing $r = (1 - t_2)/(1 - t_1) \in]0, 1[$, the previous equality implies

$$\psi(1 - (1 - t_1)) = \psi(t_1) = \psi(t_2) = \psi(1 - r(1 - t_1)).$$

By iteration and then by continuity of ψ, we get

$$\psi(t_1) = \lim_{m \to \infty} \psi(1 - r^m(1 - t_1)) = \beta.$$

Finally, we obtain $\alpha = \beta$, a contradiction. Consequently, ψ is strictly increasing in $]0, 1[$ and hence in $[0, 1]$. Since ψ is continuous in $]0, 1[$, its inverse ψ^{-1} is defined on $]\alpha, \beta[\cup \{a, b\}$ and is continuous on $]\alpha, \beta[$.

Set $n_1, n_2, n_3 \in \mathbb{N}$ such that $n_1, n_3 < n$ and $n_1 + n_2 + n_3 = n$ and let $\mathbf{x} \in [a, \alpha]^{n_1}$, $\mathbf{y} \in]\alpha, \beta[^{n_2}$ and $\mathbf{z} \in [\beta, b]^{n_3}$. By continuity, we obtain

$$\mathsf{M}(n_1 \cdot a, \mathbf{y}, n_3 \cdot \beta)$$
$$= \lim_{t \to 1^-} \mathsf{M}\left(n_1 \cdot \psi(0), (\psi \circ \psi^{-1})(y_1), \ldots, (\psi \circ \psi^{-1})(y_{n_2}), n_3 \cdot \psi(t)\right)$$
$$= \lim_{t \to 1^-} \psi\left(\frac{n_1}{n} 0 + \frac{1}{n} \sum_{i=1}^{n_2} \psi^{-1}(y_i) + \frac{n_3}{n} t\right)$$
$$= \psi\left(\frac{n_1}{n} 0 + \frac{1}{n} \sum_{i=1}^{n_2} \psi^{-1}(y_i) + \frac{n_3}{n} 1\right).$$

Since $n_1 < n$, this latter expression is also equal to $\mathsf{M}(n_1 \cdot \alpha, \mathbf{y}, n_3 \cdot b)$ and even to $\mathsf{M}(\mathbf{x}, \mathbf{y}, \mathbf{z})$ since, by nondecreasing monotonicity, we have

$$\mathsf{M}(n_1 \cdot a, \mathbf{y}, n_3 \cdot \beta) \leqslant \mathsf{M}(\mathbf{x}, \mathbf{y}, \mathbf{z}) \leqslant \mathsf{M}(n_1 \cdot \alpha, \mathbf{y}, n_3 \cdot b).$$

Then, let $f(x)$ be the continuous extension on $[\alpha, \beta]$ of the function $\psi^{-1}(x)$, that is, $f(\alpha) = 0, f(\beta) = 1$ and $f(x) = \psi^{-1}(x)$ on $]\alpha, \beta[$. Thus the function f is continuous and strictly monotonic on $[\alpha, \beta]$ and we have

$$\mathsf{M}(\mathbf{x}, \mathbf{y}, \mathbf{z}) = f^{-1}\left(\frac{n_1}{n} f(\alpha) + \frac{1}{n} \sum_{i=1}^{n_2} f(y_i) + \frac{n_3}{n} f(\beta)\right).$$

The proof is now complete.   □

We now present a description of the two families $\mathcal{D}_{a,\alpha,\alpha}$ and $\mathcal{D}_{\beta,b,\beta}$. Here also, they can be assimilated with $\mathcal{D}_{a,b,b}$ and $\mathcal{D}_{a,b,a}$ respectively, simply with the help of a redefinition of the bounds of the intervals $[a, \alpha]$ and $[\beta, b]$.

We first consider three lemmas.

Lemma 4.37. *Let* $\mathsf{F} : \cup_{n \in \mathbb{N}} \mathbb{I}^n \to \mathbb{I}$ *be decomposable. If* $\mathsf{F}^{(2)}$ *is symmetric then so is* F.

Proof. Let us proceed by induction on n. Assume $\mathsf{F}^{(n)}$ is symmetric for some $n \geqslant 2$. Then, for any $\mathbf{x} \in \mathbb{I}^{n+1}$, by decomposability, we have

$$\mathsf{F}(\mathbf{x}) = \mathsf{F}(x_1, n \cdot \mathsf{F}(x_2, \dots, x_{n+1})) = \mathsf{F}(n \cdot \mathsf{F}(x_1, \dots, x_n), x_{n+1}). \tag{4.24}$$

On the other hand, since $\mathsf{F}^{(n)}$ is symmetric, we have

$$\mathsf{F}(x_2, x_1, x_3, \dots, x_{n+1}) = \mathsf{F}(\mathbf{x}) = \mathsf{F}(x_2, x_3, \dots, x_{n+1}, x_1),$$

which, in view of (4.24), shows that $\mathsf{F}^{(n+1)}$ is symmetric (cf. Proposition 2.33). □

Lemma 4.38. *Let* $\mathsf{F} : \cup_{n \in \mathbb{N}} \mathbb{I}^n \to \mathbb{I}$ *be idempotent and decomposable. If* $\mathsf{F}^{(2)} = \mathsf{Min}$ *(respectively,* Max*) then* $\mathsf{F} = \mathsf{Min}$ *(respectively,* Max*).*

Proof. Let us proceed by induction on n. Suppose that $\mathsf{F}^{(n)} = \mathsf{Min}$ for a fixed $n \geqslant 2$. By Lemma 4.37, F is symmetric and hence strongly decomposable. Let $\mathbf{x} \in \mathbb{I}^{n+1}$ with $x_1 \leqslant \cdots \leqslant x_{n+1}$. Using Lemma 2.77 twice, we obtain

$$\mathsf{F}^{(n+1)}(\mathbf{x}) = \mathsf{F}^{(n+1)}(x_1, \dots, x_1, x_2) = \mathsf{F}^{(n+1)}(x_1, \dots, x_1) = x_1 = \mathsf{Min}(\mathbf{x}).$$

The same can be done for Max. □

Lemma 4.39. *Let* $\mathsf{F} : \cup_{n \in \mathbb{N}} \mathbb{I}^n \to \mathbb{I}$ *be continuous, idempotent, and decomposable and let* $f : \mathbb{I} \to \mathbb{R}$ *be a continuous and strictly monotonic function. If* $\mathsf{F}^{(2)} = \mathsf{M}_f^{(2)}$ *is the binary quasi-arithmetic mean generated by* f, *then* F *is the extended quasi-arithmetic mean generated by* f.

Proof sketch. By Lemma 4.37, F is symmetric. On the other hand, define $\Omega := f(\mathbb{I}) = \{f(x) \mid x \in \mathbb{I}\}$. The extended function $\mathsf{G} : \cup_{n \in \mathbb{N}} \Omega^n \to \Omega$ defined as

$$\mathsf{G}(\mathbf{z}) := f\big(\mathsf{F}(f^{-1}(z_1), \dots, f^{-1}(z_n))\big)$$

for all $\mathbf{z} \in \cup_{n \in \mathbb{N}} \Omega^n$, is symmetric, continuous, idempotent, and decomposable and we have $\mathsf{G}^{(2)} = \mathsf{AM}^{(2)}$. By using Lemma 2.77, we can show by induction that $\mathsf{G} = \mathsf{AM}$ (see Nagumo [330, §4]), which completes the proof. □

Theorem 4.40. *We have* $\mathsf{M} \in \mathcal{D}_{a,b,a}$ *if and only if*

(i) *either* $\mathsf{M} = \mathsf{Min}$,

(ii) *or there exists a continuous and strictly increasing function* $g : [a, b] \to \mathbb{R}$, *with* $g(a) = 0$, *such that, for all* $n \in \mathbb{N}$ *and all* $\mathbf{x} \in [a, b]^n$,

$$M(\mathbf{x}) = g^{-1}\left(\sqrt[n]{\prod_{i=1}^{n} g(x_i)}\right),$$

(iii) *or there exist a countable index set* $K \subseteq \mathbb{N}$, *a family of disjoint open subintervals* $\{]a_k, b_k[\mid k \in K\}$ *of* $[a, b]$ *and a family* $\{g_k \mid k \in K\}$ *of continuous and strictly increasing functions* $g_k : [a_k, b_k] \to \mathbb{R}$, *with* $g_k(a_k) = 0$, *such that, for all* $n \in \mathbb{N}$ *and all* $\mathbf{x} \in [a, b]^n$,

$$M(\mathbf{x}) = \begin{cases} g_k^{-1}\left(\sqrt[n]{\prod_{i=1}^{n} g_k(\mathrm{Min}(x_i, b_k))}\right) & \text{if } \mathrm{Min}(\mathbf{x}) \in]a_k, b_k[\\ & \text{for some } k \in K \\ \mathrm{Min}(\mathbf{x}) & \text{otherwise.} \end{cases}$$

Proof. ($\Leftarrow$) Straightforward.

($\Rightarrow$) Since M is symmetric and decomposable, it is strongly decomposable and, by Proposition 2.84, $M^{(2)}$ is bisymmetric. Therefore $M^{(2)} \in \mathcal{B}_{a,b,a}$ and we can use Theorem 4.34. Let $n \in \mathbb{N}$ and $x \in [a, b]^n$. We have three mutually exclusive cases:

(i) $M^{(2)} = \mathrm{Min}^{(2)}$, and so, by Lemma 4.38, $M = \mathrm{Min}$.

(ii) There exists a continuous strictly increasing function $g : [a, b] \to \mathbb{R}$, with $g(a) = 0$, such that $M(x, y) = g^{-1}\left(\sqrt{g(x)g(y)}\right)$ for all $x, y \in [a, b]$. In that case, defining $f(x) := \log g(x)$ on $]a, b]$, we have, by Lemma 4.39,

$$M(\mathbf{x}) = g^{-1}\left(\sqrt[n]{\prod_{i=1}^{n} g(x_i)}\right)$$

for all $x \in]a, b]^n$ and even for all $x \in [a, b]^n$ since M is continuous.

(iii) There exist a countable index set $K \subseteq \mathbb{N}$, a family of disjoint subintervals $\{]a_k, b_k[\mid k \in K\}$ of $[a, b]$ and a family $\{g_k \mid k \in K\}$ of continuous strictly increasing functions $g_k : [a, b] \to \mathbb{R}$, with $g_k(a_k) = 0$, such that, for all $x, y \in [a, b]$,

$$M(x, y) = \begin{cases} g_k^{-1}\left(\sqrt{g_k(\mathrm{Min}(x, b_k))\, g_k(\mathrm{Min}(y, b_k))}\right) & \text{if } \exists k \in K \text{ such that} \\ & \mathrm{Min}(x, y) \in]a_k, b_k[\\ \mathrm{Min}(x, y) & \text{otherwise.} \end{cases}$$

Suppose that there exists $k \in K$ such that $\mathrm{Min}(\mathbf{x}) \in]a_k, b_k[$. Then for all $j \in [n]$, we have

$$M^{(n)}(x_1, \ldots, x_j, x_{j+1}, \ldots, x_n) = M^{(n)}(x_1, \ldots, x_j, b_k, \ldots, b_k)$$

whenever $x_1, \ldots, x_j \in]a_k, b_k[$ and $x_{j+1}, \ldots, x_n \in [b_k, b]$. Indeed, if $n = 2$ then if $x \in]a_k, b_k[$ and $y \in [b_k, b]$, we have $\mathsf{M}(x, y) = \mathsf{M}(x, b_k)$. Suppose the result is true for n ($n \geqslant 2$) and also $x_1, \ldots, x_j \in]a_k, b_k[$ and $x_{j+1}, \ldots, x_{n+1} \in [b_k, b]$, $j \in [n + 1]$. So, using Lemma 2.77 twice, we have

$$\mathsf{M}^{(n+1)}(x_1, \ldots, x_j, x_{j+1}, \ldots, x_{n+1})$$
$$= \mathsf{M}^{(n+1)}(\mathsf{M}^{(n)}(x_1, \ldots, x_j, b_k, \ldots, b_k), \ldots, \mathsf{M}^{(n)}(x_2, \ldots, x_j, b_k, \ldots, b_k))$$
$$= \mathsf{M}^{(n+1)}(x_1, \ldots, x_j, b_k, \ldots, b_k).$$

Thus, the result is still true for $n + 1$.

To end, we can use Lemma 4.39 to show that if $x \in]a_k, b_k[$ then

$$\mathsf{M}(\mathbf{x}) = g^{-1}\left(\sqrt[n]{\prod_{i=1}^{n} g(x_i)}\right).$$ $\square$

Theorem 4.41. *We have $\mathsf{M} \in \mathcal{D}_{a,b,b}$ if and only if*

(i) either $\mathsf{M} = \mathsf{Max}$,

(ii) or there exists a continuous and strictly decreasing function $g : [a, b] \to \mathbb{R}$, with $g(b) = 0$, such that, for all $n \in \mathbb{N}$ and all $\mathbf{x} \in [a, b]^n$,

$$\mathsf{M}(\mathbf{x}) = g^{-1}\left(\sqrt[n]{\prod_{i=1}^{n} g(x_i)}\right),$$

(iii) or there exist a countable index set $K \subseteq \mathbb{N}$, a family of disjoint open subintervals $\{]a_k, b_k[\mid k \in K\}$ of $[a, b]$ and a family $\{g_k \mid k \in K\}$ of continuous and strictly decreasing functions $g_k : [a_k, b_k] \to \mathbb{R}$, with $g_k(b_k) = 0$, such that, for all $n \in \mathbb{N}$ and all $\mathbf{x} \in [a, b]^n$,

$$\mathsf{M}(\mathbf{x}) = \begin{cases} g_k^{-1}\left(\sqrt[n]{\prod_{i=1}^{n} g_k(\mathsf{Max}(a_k, x_i))}\right) & \text{if } \mathsf{Max}(\mathbf{x}) \in]a_k, b_k[\\ & \text{for some } k \in K \\ \mathsf{Max}(\mathbf{x}) & \text{otherwise.} \end{cases}$$

Proof. The proof is similar to that of Theorem 4.40. $\square$

4.4 Associative means

In this section we discuss means and extended means fulfilling the associativity property (2.5) and (2.6). As already observed in Section 2.3.1, the conjunction of associativity and idempotency cancels the effect of repeating arguments in the aggregation procedure. As a result, associative means are usually not appropriate for a weighted aggregation.

The class of continuous, nondecreasing, idempotent, and associative binary functions is described in the next theorem. The result is due to Fodor [114] who obtained this description in a more general framework, where the domain of variables is any connected order topological space. Alternative proofs were obtained independently in Marichal [267, §3.4] and [268, §5].

Theorem 4.42. $\mathsf{M} : \mathbb{I}^2 \to \mathbb{I}$ *is continuous, nondecreasing, idempotent, and associative if and only if there exist* $\alpha, \beta \in \mathbb{I}$ *such that*

$$\mathsf{M}(x, y) = (\alpha \wedge x) \vee (\beta \wedge y) \vee (x \wedge y). \tag{4.25}$$

Notice that, by distributivity of $\wedge$ and $\vee$, M can be written also in the equivalent form

$$\mathsf{M}(x, y) = (\beta \vee x) \wedge (\alpha \vee y) \wedge (x \vee y).$$

The graphical representation of M is given in Figure 4.4.

Theorem 4.42 can be generalized straightforwardly to extended means as follows.

Theorem 4.43. $\mathsf{M} : \cup_{n \in \mathbb{N}} \mathbb{I}^n \to \mathbb{I}$ *is continuous, nondecreasing, idempotent, and associative if and only if there exist* $\alpha, \beta \in \mathbb{I}$ *such that, for any* $n \in \mathbb{N}$,

$$\mathsf{M}^{(n)}(\mathbf{x}) = (\alpha \wedge x_1) \vee \left(\bigvee_{i=2}^{n-1} (\alpha \wedge \beta \wedge x_i) \right) \vee (\beta \wedge x_n) \vee \left(\bigwedge_{i=1}^{n} x_i \right). \tag{4.26}$$

Remark 4.44. Means described in Theorem 4.42 are nothing other than idempotent binary lattice polynomial functions, that is, binary Sugeno integrals; see Section 5.5.

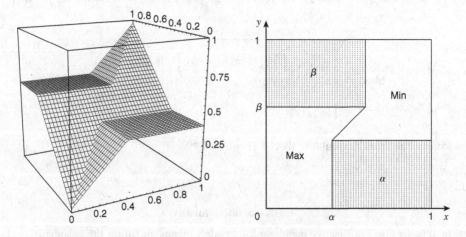

Figure 4.4 Representation on $[0, 1]^2$ of function (4.25) when $\alpha \leqslant \beta$

We also observe that the *n*-ary lattice polynomial function given in (4.26) is an *n*-ary Sugeno integral defined from a particular normalized capacity.

The special case of symmetric associative means was already discussed by Fung and Fu [131] and revisited in Dubois and Prade [95]. It turns out that these functions are the α-medians (1.15). The description is the following.

Theorem 4.45. $M : \mathbb{I}^2 \to \mathbb{I}$ *is symmetric, continuous, nondecreasing, idempotent, and associative if and only if there exist* $\alpha \in \mathbb{I}$ *such that* $M = \text{Med}_\alpha$. *Similarly,* $M :$ $\cup_{n \in \mathbb{N}} \mathbb{I}^n \to \mathbb{I}$ *is symmetric, continuous, nondecreasing, idempotent, and associative if and only if there exist* $\alpha \in \mathbb{I}$ *such that, for any* $n \in \mathbb{N}$, $M^{(n)} = \text{Med}_\alpha^{(n)}$.

Remark 4.46. Since the conjunction of symmetry and associativity implies bisymmetry, we immediately see that the α-medians Med_α are particular nonstrict arithmetic means; see Theorem 4.32.

Czogała and Drewniak [70] have examined the case when M has a neutral element $e \in \mathbb{I}$. They obtained the following result.

Theorem 4.47. *If* $M : \mathbb{I}^2 \to \mathbb{I}$ *is nondecreasing, idempotent, associative, and has a neutral element* $e \in \mathbb{I}$, *then there is a nonincreasing function* $g : \mathbb{I} \to \mathbb{I}$ *with* $g(e) = e$ *such that, for all* $x, y \in \mathbb{I}$,

$$M(x, y) = \begin{cases} x \wedge y & \text{if } y < g(x) \\ x \vee y & \text{if } y > g(x) \\ x \wedge y \text{ or } x \vee y & \text{if } y = g(x). \end{cases}$$

Furthermore, if M *is continuous, then* M = Min *or* M = Max.

Remark 4.48. (i) Fodor [114] showed that Theorem 4.47 still holds in the more general framework of connected order topological spaces.
(ii) The restriction of Theorem 4.47 to symmetric functions corresponds to idempotent uninorms, already discussed in Section 3.6.

4.5 Means constructed from a mean value property

We now consider binary means stemming from functional equations associated with a mean value property. For an account of such binary means, see for instance Sahoo and Riedel [374].

4.5.1 Lagrangian means

Let us consider the intermediate point $M_{x,y}$ in the classical mean value formula

$$F(y) - F(x) = F'(M_{x,y})(y - x), \qquad \forall x, y \in \mathbb{I},$$

as a function of the variables x, y, with the convention $M_{x,x} = x$, where $F : \mathbb{I} \to \mathbb{R}$ is a given continuously differentiable and strictly convex or strictly concave function. Reformulating this definition in terms of integrals instead of derivatives leads to the concept of *Lagrangian mean*; see Berrone and Moro [39] and Bullen *et al.* [48, p. 343].

Definition 4.49. Let $f : \mathbb{I} \to \mathbb{R}$ be a continuous and strictly monotonic function. The *Lagrangian mean* $M_{[f]} : \mathbb{I}^2 \to \mathbb{I}$ associated with f is a mean defined as

$$M_{[f]}(x, y) := \begin{cases} f^{-1}\left(\dfrac{1}{y - x} \displaystyle\int_x^y f(t)\, dt \right) & \text{if } x \neq y \\ x & \text{if } x = y. \end{cases} \tag{4.27}$$

The uniqueness of the generator is the same as for quasi-arithmetic means: Let f and g be two generators of the same Lagrangian mean. Then, there exist $r, s \in \mathbb{R}$, $r \neq 0$ such that $g(x) = rf(x) + s$; see [39, Cor. 7], [48, p. 344], and [297, Th. 1].

Many classical means are Lagrangian. The arithmetic mean, the geometric mean, and the so-called *Stolarsky means* [399], defined by

$$M_S(x, y) := \begin{cases} \left(\dfrac{x^r - y^r}{r(x - y)} \right)^{\frac{1}{r-1}} & \text{if } x \neq y \\ x & \text{if } x = y, \end{cases}$$

correspond to taking $f(x) = x, f(x) = 1/x^2$, and $f(x) = x^{r-1}$, respectively, in (4.27). The harmonic mean, however, is not Lagrangian.

In general, some of the most common means are both quasi-arithmetic and Lagrangian, but there are quasi-arithmetic means, like the harmonic one, which are not Lagrangian. Conversely, the *logarithmic mean*

$$M(x, y) := \begin{cases} \dfrac{x - y}{\log x - \log y} & \text{for } x, y > 0,\, x \neq y \\ x & \text{for } x = y > 0, \end{cases}$$

is an example of a Lagrangian mean (actually a Stolarsky mean, $f(x) = 1/x$), that is not quasi-arithmetic. A characterization of the class of Lagrangian means and a study of its connections with the class of quasi-arithmetic means can be found in Berrone and Moro [39]. Further properties of Lagrangian means and other extensions are investigated for instance in Aczél and Kuczma [11], Berrone [38], Głazowska and Matkowski [139], Horwitz [191, 192], Kuczma [240], Sándor [379], and Wimp [432].

4.5.2 Cauchy means

Let us now consider the Cauchy mean value theorem, which asserts that, for any functions F and g, continuous on an interval $[x, y]$ and differentiable on $]x, y[$, there exists an intermediate point $M_{x,y}$ such that

$$\frac{F(y) - F(x)}{g(y) - g(x)} = \frac{F'(M_{x,y})}{g'(M_{x,y})}.$$

If the functions g and $f := F'/g'$ are strictly monotonic on $]x,y[$, the mean value $M_{x,y}$ is unique and leads to the concept of *Cauchy mean*; see [40].

Definition 4.50. Let $f,g : \mathbb{I} \to \mathbb{R}$ be continuous and strictly monotonic functions. The *Cauchy mean* $\mathsf{M}_{[f,g]} : \mathbb{I}^2 \to \mathbb{I}$ associated with the pair (f,g) is a mean defined as

$$\mathsf{M}_{[f,g]}(x,y) := \begin{cases} f^{-1}\left(\dfrac{1}{g(y) - g(x)} \displaystyle\int_x^y f(t)\,\mathrm{d}g(t) \right) & \text{if } x \neq y \\ x & \text{if } x = y. \end{cases}$$

We note that any Cauchy mean is continuous, idempotent, symmetric, and strictly increasing.

When $g = f$ (respectively, g is the identity function), we retrieve the quasi-arithmetic (respectively, the Lagrangian) mean generated by f. The *anti-Lagrangian mean* [40] is obtained when f is the identity function. For example, the harmonic mean is an anti-Lagrangian mean generated by the function $g = 1/x^2$. We also note that the generator of an anti-Lagrangian mean is defined up to a nonzero affine transformation.

Further studies on Cauchy means can be found for instance in Berrone [38], Lorenzen [248], and Losonczi [251, 252]. Extensions of Lagrangian and Cauchy means, called *generalized weighted mean values*, including discussions on their monotonicity properties, can be found in Chen and Qi [58, 59], Qi *et al.* [356–358], and Witkowski [433].

4.5.3 A more general definition

We observe that Losonczi and Páles [253] generalized the previous definitions by considering two variable means $\mathsf{M}_{f,g,\mu} : \mathbb{I}^2 \to \mathbb{I}$ (where $\mathbb{I}$ is open) of the form

$$\mathsf{M}_{f,g;\mu}(x,y) := \left(\frac{f}{g}\right)^{-1}\left(\frac{\int_0^1 f(tx + (1-t)y)\,\mathrm{d}\mu(t)}{\int_0^1 g(tx + (1-t)y)\,\mathrm{d}\mu(t)} \right),$$

where $f,g : \mathbb{I} \to \mathbb{R}$ are continuous functions such that g is positive and f/g is strictly monotone, and μ is a probability measure on the Borel subsets of $[0,1]$.

If $\mu = \frac{\delta_0 + \delta_1}{2}$ (where δ_s denotes the Dirac measure concentrated at $s \in [0,1]$), $\varphi : \mathbb{I} \to \mathbb{R}$ is continuous strictly monotone, and $p : \mathbb{I} \to \mathbb{R}$ is continuous and positive, then

$$\mathsf{M}_{p\varphi,p;\mu}(x,y) = \varphi^{-1}\left(\frac{p(x)\varphi(x) + p(y)\varphi(y)}{p(x) + p(y)} \right)$$

is exactly the binary quasi-arithmetic mean generated by φ with weight function p; see Definition 4.26. In the particular case $p = 1$, we retrieve the classical binary quasi-arithmetic mean.

If μ is the Lebesgue measure on $[0, 1]$ and $\varphi, \psi : \mathbb{I} \to \mathbb{R}$ are continuously differentiable functions, with ψ' positive and φ'/ψ' strictly monotone, then we retrieve the Cauchy mean

$$M_{\varphi,\psi;\mu}(x,y) = \begin{cases} \left(\dfrac{\varphi'}{\psi'}\right)^{-1}\left(\dfrac{\varphi(y) - \varphi(x)}{\psi(y) - \psi(x)}\right) & \text{if } x \neq y \\ x & \text{if } x = y. \end{cases}$$

When $\psi(x) = x$, this mean reduces to the Lagrangian mean

$$M_{\varphi',1;\mu}(x,y) = \begin{cases} (\varphi')^{-1}\left(\dfrac{\varphi(y) - \varphi(x)}{y - x}\right) & \text{if } x \neq y \\ x & \text{if } x = y. \end{cases}$$

For more details on those generalized means and for a discussion on the general comparison problem

$$M_{f,g;\mu}(x,y) \leqslant M_{h,k;\nu}(x,y), \qquad \forall x, y \in \mathbb{I},$$

see the paper by Losonczi and Páles [253].

4.6 Constructing means

Means can also be defined by certain construction methods, some of which will be discussed thoroughly in Chapter 6. In this small section, we simply intend to mention three of them: *idempotization*, *symmetrization*, and *minimization*.

4.6.1 Idempotization

We have seen in Section 2.2.4 that we can generate an idempotent function G from any idempotizable function F, simply by writing $G = \delta_F^{-1} \circ F$, where δ_F, from $\mathbb{I}$ *onto* ran(F), is the diagonal section of F. Of course, if F is nondecreasing then so is G and hence G is a mean. Thus, it is very easy to generate means from idempotizable functions.

For instance, from the nondecreasing polynomial $F(x_1, x_2) = x_1 + x_2^2$ in $[0, 1]^2$ we immediately generate the mean

$$G(x_1, x_2) = \frac{-1 + \sqrt{4x_1 + 4x_2^2 + 1}}{2}.$$

This *idempotization process* will be further discussed in Section 6.5.1.

It is noteworthy that Dodd [87, §5] proposed an alternative way to generate means from idempotizable functions. He observed that, given any nondecreasing and idempotizable function $F : \mathbb{I}^n \to \mathbb{R}$, the function $M : \mathrm{ran}(F)^n \to \mathrm{ran}(F)$ defined as

$$M(\mathbf{y}) := F\big(\delta_F^{-1}(y_1), \ldots, \delta_F^{-1}(y_n)\big)$$

is a mean. Indeed M is nondecreasing and, for any $y \in \mathrm{ran}(F)$, we have

$$M(n \cdot y) = F(n \cdot \delta_F^{-1}(y)) = (\delta_F \circ \delta_F^{-1})(y) = y.$$

For instance, using again the polynomial $F(x_1, x_2) = x_1 + x_2^2$ in $[0,1]^2$ we generate the mean

$$M(y_1, y_2) = y_2 + \frac{\sqrt{4y_1 + 1} - \sqrt{4y_2 + 1}}{2}.$$

4.6.2 Symmetrization

We have seen in Section 2.2.3 that any nonsymmetric function $F(\mathbf{x})$ can be symmetrized by replacing its variables $x_1, \ldots, x_n$ with the corresponding order statistic functions $x_{(1)}, \ldots, x_{(n)}$, that is, by replacing the function itself with $F(x_{(1)}, \ldots, x_{(n)})$. This process is called the *symmetrization process*.

One of the simplest examples is given by the *ordered weighted averaging function*

$$\mathrm{OWA}_{\mathbf{w}}(\mathbf{x}) = \sum_{i=1}^{n} w_i x_{(i)},$$

as already defined in (1.19), which merely results from the symmetrization of the corresponding weighted arithmetic mean $\mathrm{WAM}_{\mathbf{w}}$.

Remark 4.51. The concept of ordered weighted averaging function was introduced by Yager[4] in 1988; see Yager [435], and also the book [444] edited by Yager and Kacprzyk. Since then, the family of these functions has been axiomatized in various ways; see for instance Fodor *et al.* [118] and Marichal and Mathonet [280]. Also, as will be discussed in Chapter 5, these functions are exactly the Choquet integrals with respect to symmetric normalized capacities; see Proposition 5.50(vi).

The symmetrization process can naturally be applied to the quasi-linear mean (i.e., to the weighted quasi-arithmetic mean) (4.5) to produce the *quasi-ordered weighted averaging function* $\mathrm{OWA}_{\mathbf{w},f} : \mathbb{I}^n \to \mathbb{R}$, which is defined as

$$\mathrm{OWA}_{\mathbf{w},f}(\mathbf{x}) := f^{-1}\Big(\sum_{i=1}^{n} w_i f(x_{(i)})\Big),$$

---

[4] Note, however, that linear (not necessarily convex) combinations of ordered statistics were already studied previously in statistics; see for instance Weisberg [430] (and David and Nagaraja [72, §6.5] for a more recent overview).

where the generator $f : \mathbb{I} \to \mathbb{R}$ is a continuous and strictly monotonic function; see Fodor *et al.* [118]. Surprisingly, it seems that no axiomatization of this latter family is known in the literature.

4.6.3 *Minimization*

Means can also be constructed by minimization of functions. This construction method will be thoroughly discussed in Section 6.6.

To give here a simple example, consider weights $w_1, w_2 \in \,]0, \infty[$ and minimize (in r) the expression

$$f(r) = w_1|x_1 - r| + w_2(x_2 - r)^2.$$

This minimization problem leads to the unique solution

$$r = \mathsf{M}(x_1, x_2) = \mathsf{Med}\big(x_1, x_2 - \frac{w_1}{2w_2}, x_2 + \frac{w_1}{2w_2}\big),$$

which defines a mean $\mathsf{M} : \mathbb{R}^2 \to \mathbb{R}$; see also Example 6.51(iii).

4.7 **Further extended means**

In the previous sections we have discussed either symmetric extended means, such as the arithmetic mean or the quasi-arithmetic means, or means with a fixed arity n, such as weighted arithmetic means (see (1.18)), and ordered weighted averaging functions (see (1.19)). For a fixed arity n, both the weighted arithmetic mean $\mathsf{WAM}_\mathbf{w}$ (weighted quasi-arithmetic mean) and the ordered weighted averaging function $\mathsf{OWA}_\mathbf{w}$ are characterized by a normalized weight vector $\mathbf{w} = (w_1, \ldots, w_n) \in [0, 1]^n$, that is, such that $\sum_i w_i = 1$. To define an extended weighted arithmetic mean (an extended weighted quasi-arithmetic mean) or an extended ordered weighted averaging function we need to introduce a system of weight vectors, one for each arity; see Calvo *et al.* [49, §4].

Definition 4.52. A system $\triangle = (\mathbf{w}_n : n \in \mathbb{N}) = (w_{i,n} : n \in \mathbb{N}, i \in [n])$ of normalized weight vectors is called a *weight triangle*. The *extended weighted arithmetic mean* $\mathsf{WAM}_\triangle : \cup_{n \in \mathbb{N}} \mathbb{R}^n \to \mathbb{R}$ and the *extended ordered weighted averaging function* $\mathsf{OWA}_\triangle : \cup_{n \in \mathbb{N}} \mathbb{R}^n \to \mathbb{R}$ *associated with the weight triangle* $\triangle$ are respectively defined by

$$\mathsf{WAM}_\triangle(\mathbf{x}) := \sum_{i=1}^{n} w_{i,n} x_i,$$

$$\mathsf{OWA}_\triangle(\mathbf{x}) := \sum_{i=1}^{n} w_{i,n} x_{(i)}.$$

Though in general the weight vectors of different arities in a given weight triangle $\triangle$ need not be related to each other, in several applications one expects some dependence among the different weight vectors. This dependence is expressed by means of the way in which the weight triangle is constructed.

Example 4.53. As an example of a weight triangle we mention the normalized Pascal triangle $\triangle_P$ given by $w_{i,n} := \frac{1}{2^{n-1}}\binom{n-1}{i-1}$. As another example, we can consider the triangle given by $w_{i,n} = \frac{2^{i-1}}{2^n-1}$, already considered in Example 2.73.

4.7.1 Sierpiński carpet

The idea of the Sierpiński carpet (see Calvo *et al.* [49, §4] and references therein) comes from multicriteria decision making, when alternatives described by n criteria are evaluated by means of an n-ary weighted arithmetic mean. When adding a new, $(n + 1)$th criterion, in the new evaluation by means of an $(n + 1)$-ary weighted arithmetic mean one expects that the ratios between the weights of the first n criteria are preserved, and thus only the weight of the $(n+1)$th criterion should be determined. Denoting this weight as a_{n+1}, and the original n-ary weight vector being $(w_1, \ldots, w_n)$, evidently the new $(n + 1)$-dimensional weight vector should be

$$\big((1 - a_{n+1})w_1, \ldots, (1 - a_{n+1})w_n, a_{n+1}\big).$$

To describe a Sierpiński carpet $\triangle_S$ one needs to state the weights a_{n+1} for $n \in \mathbb{N}$, $a_1 = 1$ by convention. Then $\triangle_S = (w_{i,n} : n \in \mathbb{N}, i \in [n])$ is given by $w_{n,n} = a_n$ and

$$w_{i,n} = a_i \prod_{j=i+1}^{n} (1 - a_j), \qquad 1 \leqslant i < n.$$

Note that the extended weighted arithmetic mean $\mathsf{WAM}_{\triangle_S}$ can be obtained also by means of consecutive composition described in Corollary 6.18, where the system $\mathfrak{A} := (A_n)_{n \in \mathbb{N}}$ consists of binary weighted arithmetic means linked to weight vectors $\mathbf{w}_n = (1 - a_{n+1}, a_{n+1})$.

Example 4.54. Fixing $a_n = p \in [0, 1]$ for all $n \geqslant 2$, the corresponding Sierpiński carpet is given by $w_{1,n} = (1 - p)^{n-1}$ and $w_{i,n} = p(1 - p)^{n-i}$ for $i = 2, \ldots, n$.

4.7.2 Generated weight triangles

Another important method of constructing weight triangles is based on the idea of increments (differences) of a weight-generating function. The idea of generated weight triangle $\triangle_q$, constructed from a nondecreasing function $q : [0, 1] \rightarrow [0, 1]$ satisfying $q(0) = 0$ and $q(1) = 1$, comes from the Yager and Filev monograph [443].

The corresponding weights are given by

$$w_{i,n} = q\left(\frac{i}{n}\right) - q\left(\frac{i-1}{n}\right).$$

Example 4.55. Let $q : [0, 1] \to [0, 1]$ be given by $q(x) = x^2$. Then the corresponding generated weight triangle $\triangle_q$ is given by $w_{i,n} = \left(\frac{i}{n}\right)^2 - \left(\frac{i-1}{n}\right)^2 = \frac{2i-1}{n^2}$.

Note that some of the properties of the generating function q are related to some of the properties of the induced extended means. For example, $\mathsf{OWA}_{\triangle_q}$ is related to a system of symmetric 2-additive capacities $M = (m_n)_{n \in \mathbb{N}}$ (see Section 5.3) if and only if q is a polynomial of the second degree (quadratic function); compare also with Proposition 5.18. Moreover, the convexity of q is equivalent to the *supermodularity* of $\mathsf{OWA}_{\triangle_q}$ (supermodularity means that, for any $n \in \mathbb{N}$ and any $\mathbf{x}, \mathbf{y} \in \mathbb{R}^n$, we have $\mathsf{A}(\mathbf{x} \vee \mathbf{y}) + \mathsf{A}(\mathbf{x} \wedge \mathbf{y}) \geqslant \mathsf{A}(\mathbf{x}) + \mathsf{A}(\mathbf{y})$).

Evidently, each n-ary weighted arithmetic mean $\mathsf{WAM}_{\mathbf{w}}$ is self-dual. However, $\mathsf{OWA}_{\mathbf{w}}$ is self-dual only if the weight vector $\mathbf{w}$ is symmetric, i.e., if $w_i = w_{n-i+1}$ for all $i \in [n]$. Then the extended function $\mathsf{OWA}_{\triangle_q}$ is self-dual if and only if $q(x) + q(1-x) = 1$ for all $x \in [0, 1]$, that is, if the graph of q is symmetric with respect to the point $(\frac{1}{2}, \frac{1}{2})$.

5

Aggregation functions based on
nonadditive integrals

5.1 Introduction

The primitive idea behind integration is the summation of an infinite number of infinitely small quantities, the symbol $\int$ being nothing other than the letter "S", standing for summation. Restricted to a finite universe, integration thus amounts to computing a finite sum, which can be viewed as a particular aggregation function, one of the simplest one can imagine. The reader may wonder then why such a chapter is needed. The above view of integration is in fact the limited perspective offered by the Riemann integral, but if we turn to the viewpoint of Lebesgue, that is, an integration with respect to a measure, the situation becomes much more interesting, and a new realm is offered to us. The main reason is that the notion of measure permits the introduction of "weights" on subsets of the universe. If a classical (additive) measure is used, the Lebesgue integral on a finite universe amounts to computing a weighted sum, but if a nonadditive measure (otherwise called fuzzy measure, or capacity) is used – in this case we speak of the Choquet integral – the result is a nonlinear continuous aggregation function, which is in some sense a concatenation of several different weighted sums.

Other definitions of integration with respect to a measure exist, such as the Sugeno integral where the basic operation is the supremum rather than the sum, or more complex ones, where more general definitions of sums are used, e.g., t-conorms. Just as the Choquet integral generalizes the weighted sum, the Sugeno integral generalizes the weighted maximum, and integrals based on t-conorms generalize t-conorms, in the sense that they produce a kind of mosaic of weighted maxima or t-conorms, while preserving continuity.

This chapter gives a thorough study of aggregation functions produced by integrals defined with respect to a nonadditive measure, with an emphasis on the Choquet integral and the Sugeno integral. Section 5.2 introduces nonadditive measures (called capacities throughout the chapter), viewed as particular set functions, while Section 5.3 introduces useful linear transformations on set functions. Sections 5.4 and 5.5 are devoted to the Choquet and Sugeno integrals, respectively, and Section 5.6 concludes the chapter by introducing more general classes of integrals.

171

Since we deal with aggregation, our framework will be finite, most of the time. For more general studies on nonadditive integrals and measures, we refer the reader to the monographs of Denneberg [82], Grabisch *et al.* [169], Pap [349], Wang and Klir [425], and to the *Handbook of Measure Theory*, edited by Pap [350].

Throughout the chapter we assume $n > 1$. Also, to avoid cumbersome notation, we often omit braces for singletons, writing, e.g., $A \cup i$, $K \setminus i$, etc., and we often denote by corresponding small letters the cardinality of sets, i.e., $k := |K|$, $a := |A|$, etc.

5.2 Set functions, capacities, and games

5.2.1 Starting from weight vectors

Let us consider without loss of generality $\mathbb{I} := [0, 1]$, and suppose we use as an aggregation function the weighted arithmetic mean $\mathsf{WAM_w}$ with respect to some weight vector $\mathbf{w} \in [0, 1]^n$. It is easy to relate $\mathbf{w}$ to the values taken on by $\mathsf{WAM_w}$, using particular vectors in $[0, 1]^n$, namely $\mathbf{1}_{\{i\}}\mathbf{0}$ (more simply the characteristic function $\mathbf{1}_{\{i\}}$):

$$\mathsf{WAM_w}(\mathbf{1}_{\{i\}}) = w_i$$

for all $i \in [n]$. This means that the value of the function $\mathsf{WAM_w}$ on $[0, 1]^n$ is solely determined by its values at the endpoints of the n dimensions, which represent the weights of each dimension. In fact, the exact way $\mathsf{WAM_w}(\mathbf{x})$, $\mathbf{x} \in [0, 1]^n$, is determined from $\mathsf{WAM_w}(\mathbf{1}_{\{i\}})$, $i = 1, \ldots, n$, is linear interpolation.

One may construct more complicated aggregation functions A by using more points in $[0, 1]^n$ to determine A. A natural yet simple choice would be to take all vertices of $[0, 1]^n$, namely $\{\mathbf{1}_A\}_{A \subseteq [n]}$. These include the previous endpoints of dimensions. Doing so, we have defined a set of weights $\{w_A\}_{A \subseteq [n]}$, by

$$\mathsf{A_w}(\mathbf{1}_A) = w_A$$

for all $A \subseteq [n]$. It remains to construct $\mathsf{A_w}$ on $[0, 1]^n$ by some means (e.g., linear interpolation), using these points. This will be done in Section 5.4.2. By analogy with the previous case, w_A is the weight of the subset A of dimensions.

In the case of $\mathsf{WAM_w}$, the weight vector has no peculiar property, besides non-negativeness and normalization $\sum_i w_i = 1$. If weights are assigned to subsets of dimensions, then some properties are natural, especially if dimensions represent criteria or attributes, or individuals (voters, experts). In this framework, $\mathbf{x} \in [0, 1]^n$ is a vector of scores, and $\mathsf{A_w}(\mathbf{x})$ is the aggregated overall score, synthesizing the scores along criteria or individuals. Hence, $\mathsf{A_w}(\mathbf{1}_A)$ is the overall score of an object having the maximal score for all criteria (individuals) in A and the minimal score otherwise, so that the following properties are natural:

(i) $w_\varnothing = 0$, since the object $\mathbf{1}_\varnothing = \mathbf{0}$ is the worst possible;
(ii) $w_{[n]} = 1$, since the object $\mathbf{1}_{[n]} = \mathbf{1}$ is the best possible;

(iii) $w_A \leqslant w_B$ whenever $A \subseteq B$, since object $\mathbf{1}_B$ is at least as good as $\mathbf{1}_A$ on each coordinate.

Considering $\mathbf{w}$ as a set function on $[n]$, what we have defined above is nothing other than a *capacity*.

5.2.2 Capacities and related set functions

Definition 5.1.   (i) A *set function* ξ on $[n]$ is a function from $2^{[n]}$ to $\mathbb{R}$.

(ii) A *game* $v : 2^{[n]} \to \mathbb{R}$ on $[n]$ is a set function on $[n]$ satisfying $v(\varnothing) = 0$.

(iii) A *capacity* $\mu : 2^{[n]} \to [0, \infty[$ on $[n]$ is a game on $[n]$ such that $\mu(A) \leqslant \mu(B)$ whenever $A \subseteq B$ (*monotonicity*). A capacity is *normalized* if $\mu([n]) = 1$. The set of capacities over $[n]$ is denoted by $\mathcal{F}(n)$, while $\mathcal{F}^*(n)$ is the subset of normalized capacities.

Throughout the chapter, unless otherwise specified, ξ (respectively, v, μ) always denotes a set function (respectively, a game, a capacity).

We have already noted above the bijection between vertices of $[0, 1]^n$ and subsets of $[n]$. Hence a subset $A \subseteq [n]$ is equivalently denoted by $\mathbf{1}_A 0 \in [0, 1]^n$ or by its characteristic function $\mathbf{1}_A$ defined over $[n]$.

Using the above equivalence, to any set function ξ on $[n]$ bijectively corresponds a *pseudo-Boolean function* $f_\xi : \{0, 1\}^n \to \mathbb{R}$ given by

$$f_\xi(\mathbf{x}) := \xi(A_\mathbf{x})$$

for all $\mathbf{x} \in \{0, 1\}^n$, where $A_\mathbf{x} := \{i \in [n] \mid x_i = 1\}$. Conversely, to any pseudo-Boolean function f corresponds a unique set function ξ_f such that $\xi_f(A) := f(\mathbf{1}_A)$. Pseudo-Boolean functions are widely used in operations research; see [183].

The *conjugate* or *dual* of a set function ξ is defined by

$$\bar{\xi}(A) := \xi([n]) - \xi(A^c) \tag{5.1}$$

for all $A \in 2^{[n]}$, with $A^c := [n] \setminus A$. A set function is *self-conjugate* if $\bar{\xi} = \xi$.

When the range of μ is $\{0, 1\}$, we say that μ is a *0–1 capacity* (and similarly for games and set functions). The set of 0–1 capacities is denoted by $\mathcal{F}_{0-1}(n)$.

Remark 5.2.   (i) Games come from cooperative game theory (see, e.g., [68,88,345, 354]), where their exact name is *transferable utility games in characteristic form*. In this book, we call them *games* for simplicity. In the context of game theory, the set $[n]$ is the set of players, and 0–1 games are called *simple games*.

(ii) The term "capacity" was introduced by Choquet in 1953 [62]. Capacities were rediscovered by Sugeno in 1974 under the name *fuzzy measure* [404] (see also [328] for a connection with the work of Choquet); other common names are *nonadditive measure*, *monotone measure* [82], *monotone set function* [349], or *pre-measure* [393].

(iii) As noted in [292], the use of integrals with respect to nonadditive set functions can be traced back as far as 1925, in an article by Vitali [422]. Vitali's integral for inner and outer Lebesgue measures is exactly the Choquet integral for these measures, and his formula coincides with Definition 5.21.

Some particular cases are of interest.

Definition 5.3. Let μ be a capacity on $[n]$. We say that μ is:

 (i) *additive* if for any disjoint subsets $A, B \subseteq [n]$, $\mu(A \cup B) = \mu(A) + \mu(B)$;
 (ii) *symmetric* if for any $A, B \subseteq [n]$, $|A| = |B|$ implies $\mu(A) = \mu(B)$;
 (iii) *maxitive* if for any subsets $A, B \subseteq [n]$, $\mu(A \cup B) = \mu(A) \vee \mu(B)$;
 (iv) *minitive* if for any subsets $A, B \subseteq [n]$, $\mu(A \cap B) = \mu(A) \wedge \mu(B)$.

Note that the above definitions apply to any game. We introduce some examples.

Example 5.4. (i) The smallest normalized capacity is $\mu_{\min}(A) := 0, \forall A \subsetneq [n]$.
(ii) The greatest normalized capacity is $\mu_{\max}(A) := 1, \forall A \subseteq [n], A \neq \varnothing$.
(iii) For any $i \in [n]$, the *Dirac measure centered on i* is defined by, for any $A \subseteq [n]$

$$\delta_i(A) = \begin{cases} 1 & \text{if } i \in A \\ 0 & \text{otherwise.} \end{cases}$$

(iv) For any integer k, $1 \leqslant k \leqslant n$, the *threshold measure τ_k* is defined by

$$\tau_k(A) := \begin{cases} 1 & \text{if } |A| \geqslant k \\ 0 & \text{otherwise.} \end{cases}$$

(v) For any $A \subseteq [n]$, the *unanimity game u_A* on $[n]$ is defined by

$$u_A(B) := \begin{cases} 1 & \text{if } B \supseteq A \\ 0 & \text{otherwise.} \end{cases}$$

We can introduce also a slight variation defined by

$$\hat{u}_A(B) := \begin{cases} 1 & \text{if } B \supset A \\ 0 & \text{otherwise.} \end{cases}$$

(vi) The *uniform capacity μ_{unif}* is defined by

$$\mu_{\text{unif}}(A) = \frac{|A|}{n}$$

for all $A \subseteq [n]$.

Remark 5.5. (i) $\mu_{\min} = u_{[n]}$ (respectively, $\mu_{\max} = \hat{u}_\varnothing$) is minitive (respectively, maxitive). Both are symmetric but not additive. Dirac measures are unanimity

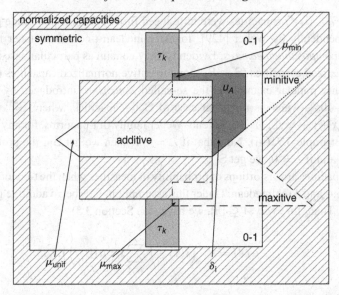

Figure 5.1 Relations between various families of normalized capacities

games u_i, $i \in [n]$; they are the only additive 0–1 capacities. Threshold measures are the only symmetric 0–1 capacities. The uniform capacity is the probability measure induced by the uniform distribution on $[n]$. It is the unique additive symmetric normalized capacity.

(ii) Additive capacities are self-conjugate.

(iii) Maxitive (respectively, minitive) capacities are usually called *possibility measures* (respectively, *necessity measures*). Possibility measures were originally introduced by Zadeh [447], and developed as a whole theory by Dubois and Prade [98]. They appear also as a fundamental tool in the theory of idempotent analysis of Maslov and Samborskiĭ [296], and in pseudo-analysis [349,350].

(iv) Any unanimity game is a minitive 0–1 capacity, except $u_\varnothing$, which is even not a game since $u_\varnothing(\varnothing) = 1$. In fact, $u_\varnothing$ is usually discarded from the set of unanimity games, but this is unimportant here.

Figure 5.1 shows the above relationships between normalized capacities introduced so far.

We introduce another important class of capacities.

Definition 5.6. Let S be a t-conorm. A normalized capacity μ is called an S-*capacity* if for every $A, B \subseteq [n]$ such that $A \cap B = \varnothing$, we have

$$\mu(A \cup B) = \mathsf{S}(\mu(A), \mu(B)).$$

Note that nondecreasing monotonicity of t-conorms ensures the monotonicity of S-capacities.

Remark 5.7.　(i) S-capacities were introduced first by Dubois and Prade [94], and independently by Weber [429], for Archimedean t-conorms, under the name of *decomposable measures*. Evidently, they contain as particular cases additive normalized capacities ($S = S_L$), and maxitive normalized capacities ($S = \vee$). Another popular example is the so-called λ-*measure* introduced by Sugeno [403, 405], which is a special case of S_{SW}-capacities, where $S_\lambda^{SW}(x,y) :=$ Min$(x+y+\lambda xy, 1)$ is the Sugeno–Weber family of t-conorms, for any $\lambda \geqslant -1$; see Example 3.91(iii). Note that if $\lambda = -1$, then we get S_P, the probabilistic sum, and if $\lambda = 0$, we get S_L.

(ii) S-capacities are distortions of probability or measures when the t-conorm is continuous and Archimedean. Under this assumption, let s be an additive generator of S. Then, for every $A \subseteq [n]$, we have (see Section 3.5)

$$\mu(A) = s^{-1}\Big(s(1) \wedge \Big(\sum_{i\in A} s \circ \mu(\{i\})\Big)\Big).$$

We can view $s \circ \mu$ as a (truncated) measure on $[n]$, defined by

$$s \circ \mu(A) := s(1) \wedge \sum_{i\in A} s \circ \mu(\{i\}).$$

If S is strict, then $s(1) = \infty$. Since $\mu([n]) = 1$, we get $s \circ \mu([n]) = \infty$, i.e., it is an infinite measure. If S is nilpotent, then $s(1)$ is finite, and $s \circ \mu$ is a finite measure if $\sum_{i\in[n]} s \circ \mu(\{i\}) = s(1)$ (otherwise additivity is lost, and μ is not normalized). If in addition $s \circ \mu([n]) = 1$, then it is a probability measure.

The above-mentioned λ-measures are distorted measures. The case $\lambda = -1$ leads to an infinite measure since S_P is strict. Otherwise, for $\lambda > -1$ and $\lambda \neq 0$, an additive generator is $s_\lambda(x) = \log_{(1+\lambda)}(1 + \lambda x)$, which gives $s_\lambda(1) = 1$, hence the nilpotent case. Then, from the above, a λ-measure is a distorted probability if and only if

$$\sum_{i\in[n]} \log_{(1+\lambda)}(1 + \lambda\mu(\{i\})) = 1,$$

which is equivalent to the well-known condition

$$1 + \lambda = \prod_{i\in[n]}(1 + \lambda\mu(\{i\})).$$

(iii) It is possible to replace the t-conorm in Definition 5.6 by similar operators, gathered under the general name of *pseudo-addition* (see some definitions in Section 5.6, and in Section 9.2.1), thus getting *pseudo-additive capacities*.

5.3 Some linear transformations of set functions

Definition 5.8. Let ξ be a set function on $[n]$, i.e., an element of $\mathbb{R}^{2^{[n]}}$. A *transformation of set functions* is any mapping $T : \mathbb{R}^{2^{[n]}} \to \mathbb{R}^{2^{[n]}}$. The set function $T(\xi)$ is called the *transform* of ξ by T.

The transformation is *linear* if for any ξ_1, ξ_2 in $\mathbb{R}^{2^{[n]}}$ and any $\lambda_1, \lambda_2 \in \mathbb{R}$ we have $T(\lambda_1 \xi_1 + \lambda_2 \xi_2) = \lambda_1 T(\xi_1) + \lambda_2 T(\xi_2)$, and it is *invertible* if T^{-1} exists.

There are several useful invertible linear transformations of set functions. The best known one is undoubtedly the *Möbius transformation*, and is part of a general theory of *Möbius functions* due to Rota [366]; see also [36] for a comprehensive presentation. We give here only a short explanation and focus on the case of set functions. Let f, g be real-valued functions on some partially ordered set (poset for short) $(X, \leqslant)$, being finite and having a least element 0, and consider the equation

$$f(x) = \sum_{y \leqslant x} g(y) \tag{5.2}$$

for all $x \in X$. Knowing f, the problem is to solve Equation (5.2), that is, to express g in terms of f. The function g is called the *Möbius inverse* of f, and its general expression is given by

$$g(x) = \sum_{y \leqslant x} \mu(y, x) f(y) \tag{5.3}$$

where μ is defined inductively by

$$\mu(x, y) := \begin{cases} 1 & \text{if } x = y \\ -\sum_{x \leqslant t < y} \mu(x, t) & \text{if } x < y \\ 0 & \text{otherwise.} \end{cases} \tag{5.4}$$

μ is called the *Möbius function*, and depends solely on the structure of $(X, \leqslant)$.

If we take as a poset $(2^{[n]}, \subseteq)$, the function f being any set function denoted by ξ, we obtain the following definition.

Definition 5.9. Let ξ be a set function on $[n]$. The *Möbius transform* (or *Möbius inverse*) of ξ is the set function m that is the solution of the equation

$$\xi(A) = \sum_{B \subseteq A} m(B) \tag{5.5}$$

for all $A \subseteq [n]$. Its explicit expression is (using (5.3) and (5.4))

$$m(A) = \sum_{B \subseteq A} (-1)^{|A \setminus B|} \xi(B). \tag{5.6}$$

We denote the Möbius transform preferably by m^ξ to see it as a transform. Clearly, it is a linear transformation, and it is invertible. The inverse transform is called the *Zeta transform* [366]. Note that $m^\xi(\varnothing) = \xi(\varnothing)$.

Remark 5.10. Interestingly enough, the Möbius transformation has been rediscovered many times. In the field of pseudo-Boolean functions, it appears as real coefficients (denoted by m_B below) in the multilinear polynomial form of any pseudo-Boolean function f, see [183]:

$$f(\mathbf{x}) = \sum_{B \subseteq [n]} \left(m_B \prod_{i \in B} x_i \right) \tag{5.7}$$

for all $\mathbf{x} \in \{0, 1\}^n$. In the field of cooperative game theory, the Möbius transform is known as the *dividends* of a game [186], while (5.7) was found by Shapley [388] in the form

$$v(A) = \sum_{B \subseteq [n]} m_B u_B(A) \tag{5.8}$$

for all $A \subseteq [n]$. Note that (5.7) and (5.8) are equivalent to (5.5), with $m_B = m(B)$, $B \subseteq [n]$. Equation (5.8) shows that any game (in fact, any set function) can be expressed in a unique way by unanimity games, hence the latter form a 2^n-dimensional basis of the vector space of set functions.

Definition 5.11. [168] The *co-Möbius transformation* $\check{m}$ is a linear invertible transformation, defined for any set function ξ by

$$\check{m}^\xi(A) := \sum_{B \supseteq [n] \setminus A} (-1)^{n - |B|} \xi(B) = \sum_{B \subseteq A} (-1)^{|B|} \xi([n] \setminus B) \tag{5.9}$$

for all $A \subseteq [n]$.

The inverse transformation is given by

$$\xi(A) = \sum_{B \subseteq [n] \setminus A} (-1)^{|B|} \check{m}^\xi(B). \tag{5.10}$$

Möbius and co-Möbius transforms are related by

$$\check{m}^\xi(A) = \sum_{B \supseteq A} m^\xi(B).$$

Remark 5.12. The co-Möbius transformation takes its name from the fact that it is closely related to the Möbius transformation of the conjugate set function:

$$\check{m}^{\bar{\xi}}(A) = (-1)^{|A| + 1} m^\xi(A) \tag{5.11}$$

for all $A \subseteq [n]$, $A \neq \varnothing$. It is known in Dempster–Shafer theory under the name of "commonality function" [387], and in possibility theory under the name of "guaranteed possibility measure"; see e.g. [101].

Definition 5.13. [148] The *interaction transformation* I is a linear invertible transformation, defined for any set function ξ by

$$I^\xi(A) := \sum_{B \subseteq [n] \setminus A} \frac{(n-b-a)!b!}{(n-a+1)!} \sum_{K \subseteq A} (-1)^{a-k} \xi(K \cup B) \qquad (5.12)$$

for all $A \subseteq [n]$, where a, b, k are cardinalities of subsets A, B, K, respectively.

The inverse transformation is given by

$$\xi(A) = \sum_{K \subseteq [n]} \beta^{|K|}_{|A \cap K|} I^\xi(K)$$

for all $A \subseteq [n]$, with β^l_k defined by

$$\beta^l_k := \sum_{j=0}^{k} \binom{k}{j} B_{l-j}, \quad k, l = 0, 1, 2, \ldots \qquad (5.13)$$

where B_k are the Bernoulli numbers, defined by the recurrence relation

$$B_k := -\sum_{l=0}^{k-1} \frac{B_l}{k-l+1} \binom{k}{l}, \quad k > 0, \qquad (5.14)$$

and $B_0 = 1$. ($B_1 = -1/2$, $B_2 = 1/6$, $B_3 = 0$, $B_4 = -1/30$, $B_5 = 0$, etc.)

The expression of I^ξ in terms of the Möbius transform is very simple:

$$I^\xi(A) = \sum_{K \supseteq A} \frac{1}{k-a+1} m^\xi(K) \qquad (5.15)$$

for all $A \subseteq [n]$. Conversely,

$$m^\xi(A) = \sum_{K \supseteq A} B_{k-a} I^\xi(K). \qquad (5.16)$$

Lastly, the relation between I^ξ and the co-Möbius transform is given by

$$\check{m}^\xi(A) = \sum_{K \supseteq A} (-1)^{k-a} B_{k-a} I^\xi(K). \qquad (5.17)$$

Remark 5.14. The interpretation of the interaction transform will be given in Section 10.4. At this stage, we mention that I^ξ generalizes the Shapley value $\phi^\xi \in \mathbb{R}^n$ [388], and the interaction index I^ξ_{ij} proposed by Murofushi and Soneda [325] (in fact already introduced by Owen in 1972 [343], under the name of *co-value* of i and j), in the following sense:

$$\phi^\xi_i := I^\xi(\{i\}), \quad \forall i \in [n], \qquad I^\xi_{ij} := I^\xi(\{i,j\}), \quad \forall i, j \in [n]. \qquad (5.18)$$

All technical details about I^ξ can be found in [83, 168].

Since the case of capacities will be important in the sequel, it is necessary to know whether a given set function could be the inverse Möbius or interaction transform of some capacity. The following result provides an answer to this question.

Proposition 5.15. *Let ξ be a set function on $[n]$, and m, I its Möbius and interaction transforms. The following propositions are equivalent:*

(i) *ξ is a normalized capacity.*

(ii) *m satisfies*

  (a) *$m(\varnothing) = 0$,*

  (b) *$\sum_{K \subseteq [n]} m(K) = 1$,*

  (c) *$\sum_{i \in L \subseteq K} m(L) \geqslant 0$, for all $K \subseteq [n]$, for all $i \in K$.*

(iii) *I satisfies*

  (a) $\displaystyle\sum_{K \subseteq [n]} B_k I(K) = 0$,

  (b) $\displaystyle\sum_{i \in [n]} I(\{i\}) = 1$,

  (c) $\displaystyle\sum_{K \subseteq [n] \setminus \{i\}} \beta_{|K \cap L|}^{|K|} I(K \cup \{i\}) \geqslant 0$, *for all $i \in [n]$, for all $L \subseteq [n] \setminus \{i\}$.*

The equivalence between (i) and (ii) is easy to establish (see Chateauneuf and Jaffray [57]), while the equivalence between (i) and (iii) was proved by Grabisch [148]. If the condition "normalized" is dropped in (i), then (b) has to be dropped in (ii) and (iii).

An important notion in applications, based on the Möbius and interaction transforms, is the notion of *k-additive capacity*[1] [148].

Definition 5.16. A capacity μ is said to be *k-additive* for some integer $k \in [n]$ if $m^\mu(A) = 0$ whenever $|A| > k$, and there exists some A such that $|A| = k$, and $m^\mu(A) \neq 0$.

In terms of pseudo-Boolean functions, this says that f is k-additive if and only if its multilinear polynomial form (5.7) has degree k [182]. Using the relation between m^μ and I^μ (Equation (5.15)), it is easy to see that m^μ can be replaced by I^μ in the above definition without changing the meaning.

Remark 5.17. (i) Since a k-additive capacity has its Möbius transform vanishing for subsets of more than k elements, it requires substantially fewer coefficients to be defined (precisely $\binom{n}{1} + \cdots + \binom{n}{k} - 1$, if normalized), hence its interest in applications.

(ii) If $k = 1$, we recover additive capacities, since, as is easy to check, additive capacities are such that $m(\{i\}) = \mu(\{i\})$, $i \in [n]$ and $m(A) = 0$ otherwise. A less obvious result is given in the next proposition.

---

[1] The definition can be extended to any set function as well.

The following result is due to Gajdos [134].

Proposition 5.18. *Consider a symmetric capacity μ on $[n]$. Then μ is k-additive if and only if there exists a unique polynomial $f : [0, 1] \to [0, 1]$ of degree k such that $\mu(L) = f\left(\frac{|L|}{n}\right)$, for all $L \subseteq N$.*

5.4 The Choquet integral

Capacities, viewed as nonadditive measures, can serve to define new integrals. The so-called Choquet integral [62] is the exact counterpart of the Lebesgue integral when the measure is nonadditive.

5.4.1 Definitions

We consider the Choquet integral as an aggregation function over $\mathbb{I}^n$, and hence we abandon the usual integral notation with the $\int$ sign. First, we consider nonnegative vectors.

Definition 5.19. Let μ be a capacity on $[n]$, and $\mathbf{x} \in [0, \infty[^n$. The *Choquet integral* of $\mathbf{x}$ with respect to μ is defined by

$$\mathcal{C}_\mu(\mathbf{x}) := \sum_{i=1}^n (x_{\sigma(i)} - x_{\sigma(i-1)})\mu(A_{\sigma(i)})$$

with σ a permutation on $[n]$ such that $x_{\sigma(1)} \leqslant x_{\sigma(2)} \leqslant \cdots \leqslant x_{\sigma(n)}$, with the convention $x_{\sigma(0)} := 0$, and $A_{\sigma(i)} := \{\sigma(i), \ldots, \sigma(n)\}$.

It is straightforward to see that an equivalent formula is

$$\mathcal{C}_\mu(\mathbf{x}) = \sum_{i=1}^n x_{\sigma(i)}\big(\mu(A_{\sigma(i)}) - \mu(A_{\sigma(i+1)})\big), \tag{5.19}$$

with $A_{\sigma(n+1)} := \varnothing$.

We mention at this stage that we will sometimes use the more compact notation $x_{(i)}$ instead of $x_{\sigma(i)}$, which is introduced in Section 1.2 (OS_k aggregation function; see (1.10)).

Remark 5.20. It is important to note that μ need not be monotone in order for the Choquet integral to be well defined, so that we could take as well a game instead of a capacity. As will be shown in Proposition 5.38(ii), monotonicity of μ is equivalent to monotonicity of the integral. Due to our definition of aggregation functions, we restrict to the case of capacities. The same remark applies to subsequent definitions as well. Similarly, if $\mathbb{I}$ is bounded, only normalized capacities ensure that bounds of $\mathbb{I}$ are preserved, so that a Choquet integral is an aggregation function if and only if

μ is a normalized capacity. If $\mathbb{I} := [0, \infty[$, this condition is no longer necessary. For the sake of generality, we will drop the normalization condition as far as possible.

It is instructive to give the original definition, applicable to continuous spaces [62].

Definition 5.21. Let $\Omega := [n], f : \Omega \to [0, \infty[$, and let μ be a capacity on Ω. The *Choquet integral* of f with respect to μ is defined by

$$(C) \int f \, d\mu := \int_0^\infty \mu(\{\omega \in \Omega \mid f(\omega) > \alpha\}) \, d\alpha.$$

It can be proved that the strict inequality can be replaced by a weak one in the above equation [328]. The equivalence of Definitions 5.19 and 5.21 is straightforward to check.

Remark 5.22. This definition applies to arbitrary spaces provided μ is defined on a family of subsets containing $\{\omega \in \Omega \mid f(\omega) \geqslant \alpha\}$ for all $\alpha \geqslant 0$ (measurability of f; see Denneberg [82], Pap [349] for full details). The function $\mu(\{\omega \mid f(\omega) > \alpha\})$ is the *decumulative function* of μ, nonincreasing by monotonicity of μ, denoted by $G_\mu(\alpha)$. Hence, the Choquet integral is the area under the decumulative function. This simple definition permits us to understand many properties.

The case of real integrands leads to several definitions.

Definition 5.23. Let $\mathbf{x} \in \mathbb{R}^n$, μ be a capacity on $[n]$, and denote by $\mathbf{x}^+, \mathbf{x}^-$ the absolute values of the positive and negative parts of $\mathbf{x}$, i.e., $\mathbf{x}^+ := \mathbf{x} \vee \mathbf{0}$ and $\mathbf{x}^- := (-\mathbf{x})^+$, where $\mathbf{0}$ stands for the 0 vector in $\mathbb{R}^n$.

(i) The *symmetric Choquet integral* of $\mathbf{x}$ with respect to μ is defined by

$$\check{\mathcal{C}}_\mu(\mathbf{x}) := \mathcal{C}_\mu(\mathbf{x}^+) - \mathcal{C}_\mu(\mathbf{x}^-).$$

(ii) The *asymmetric Choquet integral* of $\mathbf{x}$ with respect to μ is defined by[2]

$$\mathcal{C}_\mu(\mathbf{x}) := \mathcal{C}_\mu(\mathbf{x}^+) - \mathcal{C}_{\overline{\mu}}(\mathbf{x}^-).$$

Remark 5.24. (i) The asymmetric integral is taken as the classical definition of the Choquet integral for real-valued functions [82], hence no special symbol is needed to denote it. Indeed, it can be checked that if $\mathbf{x}$ is allowed to be in $\mathbb{R}^n$ in Definition 5.19, we get the asymmetric integral (no change in the formula). This is not the

---

[2] This definition is not to be confused with a Choquet integral fulfilling the symmetry property.

case for the continuous formula of Definition 5.21, which becomes (see, e.g., [82])

$$(C) \int f \, d\mu = \int_{-\infty}^{0} \left(\mu(\{\omega \in \Omega \mid f(\omega) > \alpha\}) - \mu(\Omega) \right) d\alpha$$

$$+ \int_{0}^{\infty} \mu(\{\omega \in \Omega \mid f(\omega) > \alpha\}) \, d\alpha. \tag{5.20}$$

(ii) The symmetric integral has been introduced by Šipoš [393]. Although apparently more natural, it leads to more complicated formulas. Its explicit expression in the finite case is

$$\check{\mathcal{C}}_\mu(\mathbf{x}) = \sum_{i=1}^{p-1} (x_{\sigma(i)} - x_{\sigma(i+1)}) \mu(\{\sigma(1), \ldots, \sigma(i)\}) + x_{\sigma(p)} \mu(\{\sigma(1), \ldots, \sigma(p)\})$$

$$+ x_{\sigma(p+1)} \mu(\{\sigma(p+1), \ldots, \sigma(n)\})$$

$$+ \sum_{i=p+2}^{n} (x_{\sigma(i)} - x_{\sigma(i-1)}) \mu(\{\sigma(i), \ldots, \sigma(n)\}), \tag{5.21}$$

where σ is a permutation on $[n]$ so that $x_{\sigma(1)} \leqslant x_{\sigma(2)} \leqslant \cdots \leqslant x_{\sigma(p)} < 0 \leqslant x_{\sigma(p+1)} \leqslant \cdots \leqslant x_{\sigma(n)}$.

These two integrals take their names from the following property. For any $\mathbf{x} \in \mathbb{R}^n$,

$$\mathcal{C}_\mu(-\mathbf{x}) = -\mathcal{C}_{\overline{\mu}}(\mathbf{x}), \tag{5.22}$$

$$\check{\mathcal{C}}_\mu(-\mathbf{x}) = -\check{\mathcal{C}}_\mu(\mathbf{x}). \tag{5.23}$$

The case of real vectors will be studied further in Chapter 9.

5.4.2 Relation to interpolation and lattice polynomial functions

In this section, we show two ways of introducing the Choquet integral very naturally, in the context of aggregation. We begin by interpolation.

Let us start again from the weighted arithmetic mean (WAM), as in the beginning of Section 5.2. It was shown that $\mathsf{WAM}_\mathbf{w}(\mathbf{x})$ with respect to some weight vector $\mathbf{w} \in [0, 1]^n$, for any $\mathbf{x} \in [0, 1]^n$, could be obtained as a linear interpolation between all $\mathsf{WAM}_\mathbf{w}(\mathbf{1}_{\{i\}})$'s, $i = 1, \ldots, n$, recalling that $\mathsf{WAM}_\mathbf{w}(\mathbf{1}_{\{i\}}) = w_i$.

In Section 5.2.1, we suggested using more interpolation points to get more complex aggregation functions $\mathsf{A}_\mathbf{w}$, and we proposed using the vertices of $[0, 1]^n$, denoted by $\mathbf{1}_A$ or $\mathbf{1}_A \mathbf{0}$, $A \subseteq [n]$, as these points, and to consider $\mathsf{A}_\mathbf{w}(\mathbf{1}_A) =: w_A$. We discovered that w_A, as a function of $A \subseteq [n]$, is a capacity, usually denoted $\mu(A)$, but we did not construct $\mathsf{A}_\mathbf{w}$ at this stage. Let us now construct it by interpolation, and denote it by A_μ. We assume in the rest of the section that μ is normalized, which entails $\mathsf{A}_\mu(\mathbf{1}_{[n]}) = 1$.

As many types of interpolation exist, we are looking here for a linear interpolation using the fewest possible points (parsimonious interpolation), which are here vertices of $[0, 1]^n$. For a given $\mathbf{x} \in [0, 1]^n$, let us denote by $\mathcal{V}(\mathbf{x})$ the set of vertices used for the linear interpolation, which gives

$$A_\mu(\mathbf{x}) = \sum_{A \subseteq [n] | 1_A \in \mathcal{V}(\mathbf{x})} \left(\alpha_0^{\mathbf{x}}(A) + \sum_{i=1}^n \alpha_i^{\mathbf{x}}(A) x_i \right) A_\mu(1_A), \tag{5.24}$$

where $\alpha_i^{\mathbf{x}}(A) \in \mathbb{R}$, $i = 0, \ldots, n$, $\forall A \subseteq [n]$. Note that these constants depend on $\mathbf{x}$, in fact only on $\mathcal{V}(\mathbf{x})$. To keep the meaning of interpolation, we require that the convex hull $\mathrm{conv}(\mathcal{V}(\mathbf{x}))$ contains $\mathbf{x}$, and any $\mathbf{x} \in [0, 1]^n$ should belong to a unique polyhedron $\mathrm{conv}(\mathcal{V}(\mathbf{x}))$ (except for common facets), and continuity should be ensured. Hence, the hypercube is partitioned into q polyhedra defined by their sets of vertices $\mathcal{V}_1, \ldots, \mathcal{V}_q$, all vertices being vertices of $[0, 1]^n$. Such an operation is called a *triangulation*. Note that the least possible number of vertices is $n + 1$, otherwise the polyhedra would not be n-dimensional. Such polyhedra are called *simplices*.

Many different triangulations are possible, but there is one which is of particular interest, since it leads to an interpolation where all constant terms $\alpha_0^{\mathbf{x}}(A)$ are null. This triangulation uses the $n!$ *canonical simplices* of $[0, 1]^n$:

$$\mathrm{conv}(\mathcal{V}_\sigma) = [0, 1]_\sigma^n := \{\mathbf{x} \in [0, 1]^n \mid x_{\sigma(1)} \leqslant \cdots \leqslant x_{\sigma(n)}\}, \text{ for some permutation}$$

$$\sigma \text{ on } [n].$$

Proposition 5.25. *The linear interpolation* (5.24) *using the canonical simplices gives*

$$A_\mu(\mathbf{x}) = \sum_{i=1}^n (x_{\sigma(i)} - x_{\sigma(i-1)}) \mu(\{\sigma(i), \ldots, \sigma(n)\}) \tag{5.25}$$

for all $\mathbf{x} \in \mathrm{conv}(\mathcal{V}_\sigma)$. *Moreover,* A_μ *is continuous on* $[0, 1]^n$.

Proof. Let $\mathbf{x} \in [0, 1]^n$, and choose a permutation σ on $[n]$ such that $x_{\sigma(1)} \leqslant \cdots \leqslant x_{\sigma(n)}$. Let us take $\mathcal{V}(\mathbf{x}) = \mathcal{V}_\sigma = \{1_{A_{\sigma(1)}}, \ldots, 1_{A_{\sigma(n)}}, 1_\varnothing\}$, with $A_{\sigma(i)} := \{\sigma(i), \sigma(i + 1), \ldots, \sigma(n)\}$. We require that A_μ must coincide on all vertices of $\mathcal{V}(\mathbf{x})$ with the fixed values $A_\mu(1_A)$, $A \in \mathcal{V}(\mathbf{x})$. A first fact to notice is that all constant terms $\alpha_0^{\mathbf{x}}(A)$ are null since the vertex $1_\varnothing = \mathbf{0}$ belongs to $\mathcal{V}_\sigma$, and $A_\mu(\mathbf{0}) = 0$. This leads to the following n systems of n linear equations, by equating coefficients in Equation (5.24):

$$\sum_{i \in A_{\sigma(j)}} \alpha_i^{\mathbf{x}}(A_{\sigma(j)}) = 1,$$

$$\sum_{i \in A_{\sigma(j)}} \alpha_i^{\mathbf{x}}(A_{\sigma(k)}) = 0, \quad k = 1, \ldots, n, k \neq j,$$

for any $j = 1, \ldots, n$. Regrouping all equations pertaining to the same vector $\alpha(A_{\sigma(j)})$ leads to the n linear systems of n equations with n unknowns

$$\sum_{i \in A_{\sigma(j)}} \alpha_i^{\mathbf{x}}(A_{\sigma(j)}) = 1,$$

$$\sum_{i \in A_{\sigma(k)}} \alpha_i^{\mathbf{x}}(A_{\sigma(j)}) = 0, \quad k = 1, \ldots, n, k \neq j,$$

for any $j = 1, \ldots, n$. These are triangular systems whose solutions are easy to find:

$$\alpha_{\sigma(1)}^{\mathbf{x}}(A_{\sigma(j)}) = \alpha_{\sigma(2)}^{\mathbf{x}}(A_{\sigma(j)}) = \cdots = \alpha_{\sigma(j-2)}^{\mathbf{x}}(A_{\sigma(j)}) = 0,$$

$$\alpha_{\sigma(j-1)}^{\mathbf{x}} = -1,$$

$$\alpha_{\sigma(j)}^{\mathbf{x}} = 1,$$

$$\alpha_{\sigma(j+1)}^{\mathbf{x}}(A_{\sigma(j)}) = \alpha_{\sigma(j+2)}^{\mathbf{x}}(A_{\sigma(j)}) = \cdots = \alpha_{\sigma(n)}^{\mathbf{x}}(A_{\sigma(j)}) = 0,$$

for all $j = 1, \ldots, n$. Hence, we get

$$\mathbf{A}_\mu(\mathbf{x}) = \sum_{j=1}^{n} (x_{\sigma(j)} - x_{\sigma(j-1)}) \mathbf{A}(\mathbf{1}_{A_{\sigma(j)}}),$$

which is the desired result. Continuity is ensured since for any $\mathbf{x}$ belonging to a common facet (intersection of several $\mathrm{conv}(\mathcal{V}_\sigma)$ with different σ's), i.e., if $x_{\sigma(j)} = x_{\sigma(j-1)}$ for some j, $\mathbf{A}_\mu(\mathbf{x})$ is obtained by the interpolation using only the vertices of this facet. □

We recognize in (5.25) the Choquet integral for finite spaces.

Remark 5.26. Lovász [254] discovered this formula while considering the problem of extending the domain of pseudo-Boolean functions (hence capacities, games: see Section 5.2.2) to $\mathbb{R}^n$. Later, Singer [392] proved the above result (uniqueness of the interpolation). The fact that the so-called *Lovász extension* is the Choquet integral was remarked by Marichal [262, 270].

Continuing with Lovász extension naturally leads to lattice polynomial functions. Basically, an n-place *lattice polynomial function* $p : [0, 1]^n \to [0, 1]$ is a function defined from any well-formed expression involving n real variables $x_1, \ldots, x_n$ linked by $\vee, \wedge$ in an arbitrary combination of parentheses; see Section 5.5.1 for a complete exposition of this topic. For example, $p(x_1, x_2, x_3) = (x_1 \wedge x_2) \vee x_3$ is a 3-place lattice polynomial function.

Given a pseudo-Boolean function $f : \{0, 1\}^n \to \mathbb{R}$, its *Lovász extension* $\hat{f} : [0, 1]^n \to \mathbb{R}$ is the unique continuous function, affine in each canonical simplex, and coinciding with f on $\{0, 1\}^n$. Proposition 5.25 above proves that such an extension always exists, and gives its expression, which we rewrite below in the notation of pseudo-Boolean functions:

$$\hat{f}(\mathbf{x}) = \sum_{i=1}^{n} (x_{\sigma(i)} - x_{\sigma(i-1)}) f(\mathbf{1}_{\{\sigma(i),\dots,\sigma(n)\}})$$

for all $\mathbf{x} \in [0,1]^n$. The following result shows the relationship between lattice polynomial functions and Lovász extensions (hence Choquet integrals).

Proposition 5.27. *The class of Lovász extensions coincides with the class of affine combinations of lattice polynomial functions.*

Proof. Consider any affine combination of lattice polynomial functions

$$h(\mathbf{x}) := \alpha_0 + \sum_{i=1}^{m} \alpha_i p_i(\mathbf{x}),$$

$\alpha_i \in \mathbb{R}$, $i = 0, \dots, m$. Clearly, this is a continuous function whose restriction to any canonical simplex is an affine function. Hence, h is the Lovász extension of its restriction on vertices of $[0,1]^n$, i.e., $h = \widehat{h|_{\{0,1\}^n}}$.

Conversely, any continuous function $h : [0,1]^n \to \mathbb{R}$ that reduces to an affine function on each canonical simplex is an affine combination of lattice polynomial functions:

$$h(\mathbf{x}) = \sum_{A \subseteq [n], A \neq \varnothing} m^h(A) \bigwedge_{i \in A} x_i + m^h(\varnothing) \qquad (5.26)$$

for all $\mathbf{x} \in [0,1]^n$, where m^h is the Möbius transform of $\xi_{h|_{\{0,1\}^n}}$, the set function corresponding to the pseudo-Boolean function $h|_{\{0,1\}^n}$; see Section 5.2.2. Indeed, this expression is affine in each canonical simplex, and coincides with h for each $\mathbf{1}_B$, $B \subseteq [n]$ due to (5.5). $\square$

Remark 5.28. (i) This result was shown by Marichal and Kojadinovic [278]. For the class of Choquet integrals, it can be rephrased as follows, since monotonicity of the capacity is equivalent to nondecreasing monotonicity of the Choquet integral (see Propositions 5.36(i) and 5.38(ii)): the class of Choquet integrals with respect to a capacity coincides with the class of convex combinations of lattice polynomial functions; see Radojević [359].

(ii) Equation (5.26) is the Lovász extension of the pseudo-Boolean function $h|_{\{0,1\}^n}$. Comparing with (5.7), it simply amounts to using the minimum operator instead of the product (which both coincide on $\{0,1\}^n$). Keeping the product in the above equation leads to the so-called *multilinear extension*, originally introduced by Owen [344]; see (5.30).

5.4.3 Expressions of the Choquet integral

We give the expression of the Choquet integral in terms of various transformations of a set function.

Proposition 5.29. *Let μ be a capacity, m its Möbius transform, and $\mathbf{x} \in \mathbb{R}^n$. Then we have*

$$\mathcal{C}_\mu(\mathbf{x}) = \sum_{A \subseteq [n]} m(A) \bigwedge_{i \in A} x_i, \tag{5.27}$$

$$\check{\mathcal{C}}_\mu(\mathbf{x}) = \sum_{A \subseteq [n]} m(A) \left(\bigwedge_{i \in A} x_i^+ - \bigwedge_{i \in A} x_i^- \right) \tag{5.28}$$

$$= \sum_{A \subseteq [n]^+} m(A) \bigwedge_{i \in A} x_i + \sum_{A \subseteq [n]^-} m(A) \bigvee_{i \in A} x_i, \tag{5.29}$$

where $[n]^+ := \{i \in [n] \mid x_i \geqslant 0\}$ and $[n]^- := [n] \setminus [n]^+$.

Proof. Take the unanimity game u_A for any $A \subseteq [n]$. Let us show that $\mathcal{C}_{u_A}(\mathbf{x}) = \wedge_{i \in A} x_i$. Indeed, using (5.19), let us denote by j the leftmost index in the ordered sequence $\{\sigma(i), i \in A\}$. Then $\mathcal{C}_{u_A}(\mathbf{x}) = x_j = \wedge_{i \in A} x_i$. Now, using (5.8) and the linearity of the integral with respect to capacities (see Proposition 5.36(ii)), (5.27) follows directly.

To prove (5.28), write $\mathbf{x} = \mathbf{x}^+ + (-\mathbf{x}^-)$ and remark that $\mathbf{x}^+$ and $-\mathbf{x}^-$ are comonotonic; see Definition 5.35. Applying comonotonic additivity of the Choquet integral (see Proposition 5.36(iii)) and (5.27) twice gives the desired result. Lastly, (5.29) easily follows from (5.28). □

Equation (5.27) was first proved by Chateauneuf and Jaffray [57] (also by Walley [424]), extending a result of Dempster [81]. We recognize here the Lovász extension (5.26).

As stated above, the *multilinear extension* (Owen [344]) amounts to replacing the minimum operator with a product:

$$\mathsf{MLE}_\mu(\mathbf{x}) := \sum_{A \subseteq [n]} m(A) \prod_{i \in A} x_i, \quad \forall \mathbf{x} \in \mathbb{R}^n. \tag{5.30}$$

Remark 5.30. (i) It was proved by Owen that MLE_μ is the only multilinear function (i.e., linear in each of the variables x_i) on $\mathbb{R}^n$ that coincides with μ on $\{0, 1\}^n$. More precisely, MLE_μ corresponds to the classical linear interpolation (with respect to each of the n variables) of μ.

(ii) The multilinear extension is used in utility theory under the name *multilinear utility function* [207]. Note that in this field, the constants $m(A)$, $A \subseteq [n]$, have no particular meaning, and are determined experimentally.

(iii) The symmetric version of MLE_μ could be considered as well; see [167] for details. It is easy to get its expression directly in terms of μ.

(iv) Still other generalizations of (5.27) can be thought of, replacing the minimum operator by some other aggregation function, especially a copula (see Section 3.4), and can be found in [231].

Proposition 5.31. *Let μ be a capacity, and $\mathbb{I} := \mathbb{R}$. The multilinear extension MLE_μ on $\mathbb{I}^n$ can be expressed as*

$$\mathsf{MLE}_\mu(\mathbf{x}) = \sum_{A \subseteq [n]} \mu(A) \prod_{i \in A} x_i \prod_{i \notin A} (1 - x_i). \tag{5.31}$$

Proof. As (5.31) is a multilinear polynomial, it has the form

$$\mathsf{MLE}_\mu(\mathbf{x}) = \sum_{A \subseteq [n]} c(A) \prod_{i \in A} x_i.$$

Considering $\mathbf{x} = \mathbf{1}_B$ and substituting it into the above and in (5.31) leads to $\sum_{A \subseteq B} c(A) = \mu(B)$, which proves that c is the Möbius transform of μ, hence we retrieve (5.30). $\square$

This result was shown by Owen [344]. It is valid for any set function ξ as well.

Proposition 5.32. *Let μ be a capacity, $\check{m}^\mu$ its co-Möbius transform, and $\mathbf{x} \in \mathbb{R}^n$.*

$$\mathcal{C}_\mu(\mathbf{x}) = \sum_{A \subseteq [n], A \neq \varnothing} (-1)^{|A|+1} \check{m}^\mu(A) \bigvee_{i \in A} x_i = \sum_{A \subseteq [n]} m^{\overline{\mu}}(A) \bigvee_{i \in A} x_i, \tag{5.32}$$

$$\check{\mathcal{C}}_\mu(\mathbf{x}) = \sum_{A \cap [n]^+ \neq \varnothing} (-1)^{|A|+1} \check{m}^\mu(A) \bigvee_{i \in A} x_i + \sum_{A \cap [n]^- \neq \varnothing} (-1)^{|A|+1} \check{m}^\mu(A) \bigwedge_{i \in A} x_i, \tag{5.33}$$

$$\check{\mathcal{C}}_\mu(\mathbf{x}) = \sum_{A \subseteq [n]^+} (-1)^{|A|+1} m^{\overline{\mu}}(A) \bigwedge_{i \in A} x_i + \sum_{A \subseteq [n]^-} (-1)^{|A|+1} \check{m}^{\overline{\mu}}(A) \bigvee_{i \in A} x_i, \tag{5.34}$$

where $[n]^+ := \{i \in [n] \mid x_i \geqslant 0\}$, and $[n]^- := [n] \setminus [n]^+$.

Proof. Let $\mathbf{x} \in \mathbb{R}^n$. We know from (5.22) that $\mathcal{C}_\mu(\mathbf{x}) = -\mathcal{C}_{\overline{\mu}}(-\mathbf{x})$. Applying (5.27) and (5.11), and remarking that $m^{\overline{\mu}}(\varnothing) = 0$, we get

$$-\mathcal{C}_{\overline{\mu}}(-\mathbf{x}) = -\sum_{A \subseteq [n], A \neq \varnothing} m^{\overline{\mu}}(A) \bigwedge_{i \in A} (-x_i)$$

$$= \sum_{A \subseteq [n], A \neq \varnothing} (-1)^{|A|+1} \check{m}^\mu(A) \bigvee_{i \in A} x_i.$$

We turn now to the symmetric integral. By definition, $\check{\mathcal{C}}_v(\mathbf{x}) = \mathcal{C}_\mu(\mathbf{x}^+) - \mathcal{C}_\mu(\mathbf{x}^-)$, with $\mathbf{x}^+, \mathbf{x}^-$ defined as before. Applying (5.32), we get

$$\check{\mathcal{C}}_\mu(\mathbf{x}) = \sum_{A \cap [n]^+ \neq \varnothing} (-1)^{|A|+1} \check{m}^\mu(A) \bigvee_{i \in A} x_i^+ - \sum_{A \cap [n]^- \neq \varnothing} (-1)^{|A|+1} \check{m}^\mu(A) \bigvee_{i \in A} x_i^-$$

$$= \sum_{A \cap [n]^+ \neq \varnothing} (-1)^{|A|+1} \check{m}^\mu(A) \bigvee_{i \in A} x_i + \sum_{A \cap [n]^- \neq \varnothing} (-1)^{|A|+1} \check{m}^\mu(A) \bigwedge_{i \in A} x_i.$$

For the second expression, we start from (5.29), and applying (5.11) again, we get the desired result. $\qquad\square$

Proposition 5.33. *Let μ be a capacity, I its interaction transform, and $\mathbf{x} \in \mathbb{R}^n$.*

$$\mathcal{C}_\mu(\mathbf{x}) = \sum_{A \subseteq [n]} \left(\sum_{K \subseteq [n] \setminus A} B_{|K|} I^+(A \cup K) \right) \bigwedge_{i \in A} x_i$$

$$+ \sum_{A \subseteq [n], A \neq \varnothing} (-1)^{|A|+1} \left(\sum_{K \subseteq [n] \setminus A} \beta_{|K|}^{|K|} I^-(A \cup K) \right) \bigvee_{i \in A} x_i, \qquad (5.35)$$

$$\check{\mathcal{C}}_\mu(\mathbf{x}) = \sum_{A \subseteq [n]^+} \left(\sum_{K \subseteq [n] \setminus A} B_{|K|} I^+(A \cup K) \right) \bigwedge_{i \in A} x_i$$

$$+ \sum_{A \subseteq [n]^-} \left(\sum_{K \subseteq [n] \setminus A} B_{|K|} I^+(A \cup K) \right) \bigvee_{i \in A} x_i$$

$$+ \sum_{A \cap [n]^+ \neq \varnothing} (-1)^{|A|+1} \left(\sum_{K \subseteq [n] \setminus A} \beta_{|K|}^{|K|} I^-(A \cup K) \right) \bigvee_{i \in A} x_i$$

$$+ \sum_{A \cap [n]^- \neq \varnothing} (-1)^{|A|+1} \left(\sum_{K \subseteq [n] \setminus A} \beta_{|K|}^{|K|} I^-(A \cup K) \right) \bigwedge_{i \in A} x_i, \qquad (5.36)$$

where $I^+(A) = I(A)$ if $I(A) > 0$ and 0 otherwise, and $I^-(A) = I(A)$ if $I(A) < 0$ and 0 otherwise.

Proof. Let $\mathbf{x} \in \mathbb{R}^n$, and let μ be fixed, with interaction index $I(A)$. We define the set functions μ^+, μ^- by their interaction indices

$$I^{\mu^+}(A) = \begin{cases} I(A) & \text{if } I(A) > 0 \\ 0 & \text{otherwise} \end{cases}, \quad I^{\mu^-}(A) = \begin{cases} I(A) & \text{if } I(A) < 0 \\ 0 & \text{otherwise} \end{cases}$$

so that, by linearity of I with respect to μ, we have $\mu = \mu^+ + \mu^-$. We start with the asymmetric Choquet integral. By linearity of the integral with respect to the capacity,

$\mathcal{C}_\mu(\mathbf{x}) = \mathcal{C}_{\mu^+}(\mathbf{x}) + \mathcal{C}_{\mu^-}(\mathbf{x})$. Using (5.27) and (5.32), we have for all $\mathbf{x} \in \mathbb{R}^n$

$$\mathcal{C}_{\mu^+}(\mathbf{x}) = \sum_{A \subseteq [n]} m^{\mu^+}(A) \bigwedge_{i \in A} x_i,$$

$$\mathcal{C}_{\mu^-}(\mathbf{x}) = \sum_{A \subseteq [n], A \neq \varnothing} (-1)^{|A|+1} \check{m}^{\mu^-}(A) \bigvee_{i \in A} x_i.$$

Using (5.16), (5.17), and (5.13) leads directly to the desired result.

The case of the symmetric integral proceeds similarly: it suffices to write $\check{\mathcal{C}}_\mu(\mathbf{x}) = \check{\mathcal{C}}_{\mu^+}(\mathbf{x}) + \check{\mathcal{C}}_{\mu^-}(\mathbf{x})$, to express $\check{\mathcal{C}}_{\mu^+}$ and $\check{\mathcal{C}}_{\mu^-}$ by (5.29) and (5.33), and then to use (5.16), (5.17), and (5.13) again. $\square$

The two propositions above were proved by Grabisch and Labreuche [162].

The case of 2-additive capacities leads to formulas with particularly interesting interpretations. This will be detailed in Chapter 10.

Proposition 5.34. *Let* $\mathbf{x} \in \mathbb{R}^n$, *and* μ *be a 2-additive capacity, with* ϕ_i, I_{ij} *its Shapley value and interaction index (see (5.18)).*

$$\mathcal{C}_\mu(\mathbf{x}) = \sum_{I_{ij}>0} (x_i \wedge x_j) I_{ij} + \sum_{I_{ij}<0} (x_i \vee x_j)|I_{ij}| + \sum_{i=1}^n x_i \left(\phi_i - \frac{1}{2} \sum_{j \neq i} |I_{ij}| \right) \quad (5.37)$$

$$= \sum_{i=1}^n \phi_i x_i - \frac{1}{2} \sum_{\{i,j\} \subseteq [n]} I_{ij}|x_i - x_j|, \quad (5.38)$$

$$\check{\mathcal{C}}_\mu(\mathbf{x}) = \sum_{i,j \in [n]^+, I_{ij}>0} (x_i \wedge x_j) I_{ij} + \sum_{i,j \in [n]^-, I_{ij}>0} (x_i \vee x_j) I_{ij} \quad (5.39)$$

$$+ \sum_{i,j \in [n]^+, I_{ij}<0} (x_i \vee x_j)|I_{ij}| + \sum_{i,j \in [n]^-, I_{ij}<0} (x_i \wedge x_j)|I_{ij}|$$

$$+ \sum_{i \in [n]^+} x_i \left(\sum_{j \in [n]^-, I_{ij}<0} |I_{ij}| \right) + \sum_{i \in [n]^-} x_i \left(\sum_{j \in [n]^+, I_{ij}<0} |I_{ij}| \right)$$

$$+ \sum_{i=1}^n x_i \left(\phi_i - \frac{1}{2} \sum_{j \neq i} |I_{ij}| \right),$$

with $[n]^+ := \{i \in [n] \mid x_i \geqslant 0\}$, *and* $[n]^- := [n] \setminus [n]^+$.

Proof. Equation (5.37) comes from (5.35) after some rearrangement, using the fact that the interaction index I vanishes for subsets of more than two elements. Equation (5.38) comes after rearrangement of (5.37).

We prove (5.39) in the same way. Since $m(\varnothing) = 0$ and due to (5.16), we can replace in (5.36) the summations $A \subseteq [n]^+$ and $A \subseteq [n]^-$ by $A \subseteq [n]^+, A \neq \varnothing$ and

$A \subseteq [n]^-, A \neq \emptyset$. Specifically

$$\check{C}_\mu(\mathbf{x}) = \sum_{\substack{i \in [n]^+}} x_i \left(\phi_i - \frac{1}{2} \sum_{\substack{j \neq i \\ I_{ij} > 0}} I_{ij} \right) + \sum_{\substack{i,j \in [n]^+ \\ I_{ij} > 0}} (x_i \wedge x_j) I_{ij}$$

$$+ \sum_{\substack{i \in [n]^-}} x_i \left(\phi_i - \frac{1}{2} \sum_{\substack{j \neq i \\ I_{ij} > 0}} I_{ij} \right) + \sum_{\substack{i,j \in [n]^- \\ I_{ij} > 0}} (x_i \vee x_j) I_{ij}$$

$$+ \sum_{\substack{i \in [n]^+}} x_i \left(\frac{1}{2} \sum_{\substack{j \neq i \\ I_{ij} < 0}} I_{ij} \right) + \sum_{\substack{i,j \in [n]^+ \\ I_{ij} < 0}} (x_i \vee x_j)|I_{ij}| + \sum_{\substack{i \in [n]^+ \\ j \in [n]^- \\ I_{ij} < 0}} (x_i \vee x_j)|I_{ij}|$$

$$+ \sum_{\substack{i \in [n]^-}} x_i \left(\frac{1}{2} \sum_{\substack{j \neq i \\ I_{ij} < 0}} I_{ij} \right) + \sum_{\substack{i,j \in [n]^- \\ I_{ij} < 0}} (x_i \wedge x_j)|I_{ij}| + \sum_{\substack{i \in [n]^- \\ j \in [n]^+ \\ I_{ij} < 0}} (x_i \wedge x_j)|I_{ij}|.$$

Noting that

$$\sum_{\substack{i \in [n]^+ \\ j \in [n]^- \\ I_{ij} < 0}} (x_i \vee x_j)|I_{ij}| = \sum_{\substack{i \in [n]^+}} x_i \sum_{\substack{j \in [n]^-, I_{ij} < 0}} |I_{ij}|,$$

$$\sum_{\substack{i \in [n]^- \\ j \in [n]^+ \\ I_{ij} < 0}} (x_i \wedge x_j)|I_{ij}| = \sum_{\substack{i \in [n]^-}} x_i \sum_{\substack{j \in [n]^+, I_{ij} < 0}} |I_{ij}|$$

and regrouping terms, we get the desired result.   □

Equation (5.37) was introduced in [147], and (5.38) in [270].

5.4.4 Properties of the Choquet integral

We give some specific properties of the Choquet integral, then properties related to aggregation. We recall from Chapter 2 the following definition (Definition 2.123).

Definition 5.35. Let $\mathbf{x}, \mathbf{x}' \in \mathbb{R}^n$. We say that $\mathbf{x}, \mathbf{x}'$ are *comonotonic* if there exists a permutation σ on $[n]$ such that $x_{\sigma(1)} \leqslant x_{\sigma(2)} \leqslant \cdots \leqslant x_{\sigma(n)}$ and $x'_{\sigma(1)} \leqslant x'_{\sigma(2)} \leqslant \cdots \leqslant x'_{\sigma(n)}$ (equivalently if there is no $i, j \in [n]$ such that $x_i > x_j$ and $x'_i < x'_j$).

Proposition 5.36. *The Choquet integral satisfies the following properties:*

(i) *For any $A \subseteq [n]$ and any game v on $[n]$, we have $C_v(\mathbf{1}_A) = v(A)$.*

(ii) *The Choquet integral is linear with respect to the game: for any games v_1, v_2 on $[n]$, any $\lambda_1, \lambda_2 \in \mathbb{R}$,*

$$C_{\lambda_1 v_1 + \lambda_2 v_2} = \lambda_1 C_{v_1} + \lambda_2 C_{v_2}.$$

For capacities, the property holds for $\lambda_1, \lambda_2 \in [0, \infty[$ (positive cone), and for normalized capacities, we have in addition $\lambda_1 + \lambda_2 = 1$ (convex combination).

(iii) *The Choquet integral satisfies* comonotonic additivity *(Definition 2.124): for any comonotonic vectors $\mathbf{x}, \mathbf{x}' \in \mathbb{R}$, and any game v,*

$$C_v(\mathbf{x} + \mathbf{x}') = C_v(\mathbf{x}) + C_v(\mathbf{x}').$$

(iv) *Let v, v' be two games on $[n]$. Then $v \leqslant v'$ if and only if $C_v \leqslant C_{v'}$.*

(v) *If μ is a 0–1 capacity, then, for all $\mathbf{x} \in \mathbb{R}^n$,*

$$C_\mu(\mathbf{x}) = \bigvee_{\substack{A \subseteq [n] \\ \mu(A) = 1}} \bigwedge_{i \in A} x_i.$$

Proof. Property (i) is obvious by the construction of the Choquet integral as an interpolator. Properties (ii), (iii), and (iv) are clear from Definition 5.19 and (i).

(v) Let $a := \bigvee_{K \subseteq [n], \mu(K) = 1} \bigwedge_{i \in K} x_i$. Using Definition 5.21, it suffices to prove that

$$\mu(\{i \in [n] \mid x_i > \alpha\}) = \begin{cases} 1 & \text{if } \alpha < a \\ 0 & \text{if } \alpha > a. \end{cases}$$

Assume $\alpha < a$. Then there exists $A \subseteq [n]$ such that $\mu(A) = 1$ and $\alpha < \bigwedge_{i \in A} x_i$. This inequality implies that $A \subseteq \{i \mid x_i > \alpha\}$, and hence that $\mu(\{i \mid x_i > \alpha\}) = 1$. Now assume $\alpha > a$. If $\mu(\{i \mid x_i > \alpha\}) = 1$, then it follows that $\alpha > a \geqslant \bigwedge_{i \mid x_i > \alpha} x_i \geqslant \alpha$, a contradiction. Therefore, $\mu(\{i \mid x_i > \alpha\}) = 0$. $\square$

Remark 5.37.   (i) Assertion (v) was proved by Murofushi and Sugeno [329].

(ii) The symmetric integral satisfies (i) and (ii), but does not satisfy comonotonic additivity, as shown in the following example: Fix $1 < i < j < n$, consider $A := \{i, i+1, \ldots, n\}$, $B := \{1, \ldots, j\}$, and $\mathbf{x} := \mathbf{1}_A$, $\mathbf{x}' := -\mathbf{1}_B$. Then $\mathbf{x}, \mathbf{x}'$ are comonotonic, and we have

$$\check{C}_v(\mathbf{x} + \mathbf{x}') = C_v(\mathbf{1}_{\{j+1,\ldots,n\}}) - C_v(\mathbf{1}_{\{1,\ldots,i-1\}})$$

$$= v(\{j+1, \ldots, n\}) - v(\{1, \ldots, i-1\}),$$

$$\check{C}_v(\mathbf{x}) + \check{C}_v(\mathbf{x}') = C_v(\mathbf{1}_{\{i,\ldots,n\}}) - C_v(\mathbf{1}_{\{1,\ldots,j\}})$$

$$= v(\{i, \ldots, n\}) - v(\{1, \ldots, j\}),$$

which are different in general.

(iii) The symmetric integral does not satisfy (iv). To see this, it suffices to take $\mathbf{x} \leq \mathbf{0}$. Then $\check{C}_v(\mathbf{x}) = -C_v(|\mathbf{x}|) \geqslant -C_{v'}(|\mathbf{x}|) = \check{C}_{v'}(\mathbf{x})$.

(iv) The multilinear extension MLE_μ satisfies (i) since it is an extension, and (ii) as is clear from (5.31).

Proposition 5.38. *Let v be a game on $[n]$, and $\mathbb{I} := \mathbb{R}$. The Choquet integral C_v and symmetric Choquet integral $\check{C}_v$ satisfy the following properties (see Chapter 2 for definitions):*

  (i) Continuity.
 (ii) Nondecreasing monotonicity if and only if v is a capacity.
(iii) Strict increasing monotonicity if and only if v is a strictly monotone capacity, i.e., $A \subsetneq B$ implies $v(A) < v(B)$.
 (iv) Idempotency if $v([n]) = 1$.
 (v) Internality if v is a normalized capacity.

Proof. Property (i) is shown in Proposition 5.25. To prove, (ii), (iii), and (iv), it suffices to show them on $\mathbb{I} := [0, \infty[$. Extension to the real line for both integrals follows from their definition (Definition 5.23). Property (ii) is obvious from (5.19). Using (5.19) again, we see that strict increasing monotonicity holds if and only if $v(A_{\sigma(i)}) - v(A_{\sigma(i+1)}) > 0$ for any $i \in [n]$ and any permutation σ, which is equivalent to strict monotonicity of v. Idempotency is obvious from Proposition 5.36(i). Lastly, (v) follows from (ii) and (iv). □

The case of the multilinear extension will not be treated in detail hereafter, since as the following proposition shows, its properties are weaker.

Proposition 5.39. *Let μ be a capacity on $[n]$, m its Möbius transform, and $\mathbb{I} = [0, 1]$. The multilinear extension MLE_μ satisfies the following properties:*

  (i) Continuity.
 (ii) Nondecreasing monotonicity.
(iii) Strict increasing monotonicity if and only if μ is strictly monotone, i.e., $A \subsetneq B$ implies $\mu(A) < \mu(B)$.

Proof. Let us recall Equation (5.31):

$$\mathsf{MLE}_\mu(\mathbf{x}) = \sum_{A \subseteq [n]} \mu(A) \prod_{i \in A} x_i \prod_{i \notin A} (1 - x_i).$$

(i) clearly holds from the above equation. To prove (ii) and (iii), we have, for any $\mathbf{x} \in [0,1]^n$ and any $k \in [n]$

$$\frac{\partial \text{MLE}_\mu(\mathbf{x})}{\partial x_k} = \sum_{A \subseteq [n] \setminus k} \mu(A \cup k) \prod_{i \in A} x_i \prod_{i \notin A, i \neq k} (1 - x_i)$$

$$- \sum_{A \subseteq [n] \setminus k} \mu(A) \prod_{i \in A} x_i \prod_{i \notin A, i \neq k} (1 - x_i)$$

$$= \sum_{A \subseteq [n] \setminus k} (\mu(A \cup k) - \mu(A)) \prod_{i \in A} x_i \prod_{i \notin A, i \neq k} (1 - x_i).$$

Clearly, this expression is nonnegative (respectively, positive) for any $k \in [n]$ if and only if μ is monotonic (respectively, strictly monotonic). $\qquad\square$

Remark 5.40. (ii) and (iii) were proved by Grabisch *et al.* [167]. MLE_μ does not fulfill idempotency, and hence not internality, as shown in the example below. Moreover, if $\mathbf{x} \notin [0,1]^n$, it may violate nondecreasing monotonicity: Let us take $n = 2$, with $\mu(\{1\}) = \mu(\{2\}) = 0.9$, we have

$$\text{MLE}_\mu\left(\frac{1}{2}, \frac{1}{2}\right) = \frac{1}{4} 0.9 + \frac{1}{4} 0.9 + \frac{1}{4} = 0.7,$$

$$\text{MLE}_\mu(3, 3) = (-6)0.9 + (-6)0.9 + 9 = -1.8 < \text{MLE}_\mu\left(\frac{1}{2}, \frac{1}{2}\right).$$

Proposition 5.41. *Let* $\mathbb{I} := \mathbb{R}$. *The Choquet integral* $\mathcal{C}_\mu$ *and symmetric Choquet integral* $\check{\mathcal{C}}_\mu$ *satisfy the following properties (see Chapter 2 for definitions):*

 (i) Symmetry (or neutrality, commutativity) if and only if μ is symmetric.
(ii) Additivity if and only if μ is additive.

Let $\mathbb{I} := [0, \infty[$. *The Choquet integral* $\mathcal{C}_\mu$ *satisfies*

(iii) Maxitivity if and only if μ is a 0–1 maxitive capacity.
(iv) Minitivity if and only if μ is a 0–1 minitive capacity.
 (v) k-disjunctiveness if and only if $\mu(A) = 1$, $\forall A \subseteq [n]$ such that $|A| \geq k$.
(vi) k-conjunctiveness if and only if $\mu(A) = 0$, $\forall A \subseteq [n]$ such that $|A| \leq n - k$.

Proof. (i) It suffices to prove the property for nonnegative vectors, and to apply Definition 5.23. For an arbitrary $\mathbf{x} \in [0, \infty[^n$, we have

$$\mathcal{C}_\mu(\mathbf{x}) = \sum_{i=1}^n (x_{\sigma(i)} - x_{\sigma(i-1)})\mu(A_{\sigma(i)}).$$

A permutation τ of the terms leads to

$$\mathcal{C}_\mu(x_{\tau(1)}, \ldots, x_{\tau(n)}) = \sum_{i=1}^n (x_{\sigma(i)} - x_{\sigma(i-1)})\mu(A_{\sigma \circ \tau^{-1}(i)}).$$

If we impose commutativity, then we must have $\mu(A_{\sigma(i)}) = \mu(A_{\sigma \circ \tau^{-1}(i)})$, for all $i \in [n]$ and all permutations τ on $[n]$. Clearly, this is possible if and only if $\mu(A)$ depends only on the cardinality of A.

(ii) Suppose $\mathcal{C}_\mu$ is additive. In particular, taking $A, B \subsetneq [n]$ such that $A \cap B = \varnothing$, we have by Proposition 5.36(i) $\mathcal{C}_\mu(\mathbf{1}_A + \mathbf{1}_B) = \mathcal{C}_\mu(\mathbf{1}_{A \cup B}) = \mu(A \cup B)$. Since $\mathcal{C}_\mu$ is additive, we get $\mathcal{C}_\mu(\mathbf{1}_A + \mathbf{1}_B) = \mathcal{C}_\mu(\mathbf{1}_A) + \mathcal{C}_\mu(\mathbf{1}_B) = \mu(A) + \mu(B)$, which proves additivity of μ.

It suffices to prove the converse for the Choquet integral, since μ being additive, is also self-conjugate (see Remark 5.5(i)) so that both integrals coincide. Now, the result is obvious since the Choquet integral reduces to a weighted arithmetic mean with $w_i = \mu(\{i\})$ for all i (use (5.19) and Remark 5.24(i)).

(iii) ($\Rightarrow$) Suppose μ is not a 0–1 capacity. Then there exists $\varnothing \neq A \subsetneq [n]$ such that $0 < \mu(A) < 1$, and every $A' \supset A$ is such that $\mu(A') = 1$. Take $0 < \alpha < \mu(A)$. Then, for any $A' \supset A$

$$\mathcal{C}_\mu(\mathbf{1}_A \vee \alpha \mathbf{1}_{A'}) = \alpha \mu(A') + (1 - \alpha)\mu(A)$$

$$= \alpha + (1 - \alpha)\mu(A) > \mu(A),$$

$$\mathcal{C}_\mu(\mathbf{1}_A) \vee \mathcal{C}_\mu(\alpha \mathbf{1}_{A'}) = \mu(A) \vee \alpha = \mu(A).$$

Hence, equality cannot occur. Suppose now that μ is not maxitive. Then $\mathcal{C}_\mu$ is not maxitive since its restriction to binary vectors $\mathbf{1}_A$, $A \subseteq [n]$, coincides with μ.

($\Leftarrow$) Follows directly from Proposition 5.36(v) and mutual distributivity of $\vee, \wedge$.

(iv) is similar to (iii).

(v) Suppose $\mathcal{C}_\mu(\mathbf{x}) \geqslant \mathsf{OS}_{n-k+1}$. In particular for $\mathbf{x} := \mathbf{1}_B$, $B \subseteq [n]$, we get $\mu(B) = \mathcal{C}_\mu(\mathbf{1}_B)$. If $|B| \geqslant k$, we deduce that $\mu(B) = 1$.

Conversely, take the threshold measure τ_k; see Example 5.4(iv). Then τ_k is a 0–1 capacity, and using Proposition 5.36(v), we get

$$\mathcal{C}_{\tau_k}(\mathbf{x}) = \bigvee_{\substack{A \subseteq [n] \\ |A| \geqslant k}} \bigwedge_{i \in A} x_i = \bigvee_{\substack{A \subseteq [n] \\ |A| = k}} \bigwedge_{i \in A} x_i = x_{(n-k+1)}.$$

Since any capacity μ such that $\mu(A) = 1$ if $|A| \geqslant 1$ satisfies $\mu \geqslant \tau_k$, we get the result by monotonicity of the integral; see Proposition 5.36(iv).

(vi) is similar to (v). $\qquad\square$

As seen in Section 2.3, grouping-based properties, such as associativity, decomposability, bisymmetry, etc., are not very compatible with weighted aggregation functions, *a fortiori* they are not compatible with the Choquet integral. However, the Choquet integral possesses some invariance properties.

Proposition 5.42. *Let* $\mathbb{I} := \mathbb{R}$, *and* μ *be a normalized capacity. The following properties hold (see Chapter 2 for definitions):*

(i) The Choquet integral is interval scale invariant.

(ii) The symmetric Choquet integral is homogeneous of degree one, i.e.,

$$\check{C}_\mu(\alpha\mathbf{x}) = \alpha\check{C}_\mu(\mathbf{x}), \quad \forall \mathbf{x} \in \mathbb{I}^n, \forall \alpha \in \mathbb{R}.$$

Proof. (i) Let $\mathbf{x} \in \mathbb{I}^n, \alpha > 0$ and $\beta \in \mathbb{I}$. If σ is a permutation reordering the components of $\mathbf{x}$ in increasing order, then σ rearranges $\alpha\mathbf{x} + \beta\mathbf{1}$ (componentwise) in increasing order as well. Hence

$$C_\mu(\alpha\mathbf{x} + \beta\mathbf{1}) = (\alpha x_{\sigma(1)} + \beta)\mu([n]) + \sum_{i=2}^{n}(\alpha x_{\sigma(i)} + \beta - \alpha x_{\sigma(i-1)} - \beta)\mu(A_{\sigma(i)})$$

$$= \alpha x_{\sigma(1)} + \beta + \sum_{i=2}^{n}\alpha(x_{\sigma(i)} - x_{\sigma(i-1)})\mu(A_{\sigma(i)})$$

$$= \alpha C_\mu(\mathbf{x}) + \beta.$$

(ii) Let us take $\alpha > 0$ and consider first $\mathbf{x} \in [0, \infty[^n$. Using (i) with $\beta = 0$, we get $C_\mu(\alpha\mathbf{x}) = \alpha C_\mu(\mathbf{x})$.

Let $\mathbf{x} \in \mathbb{I}^n$ and $\alpha > 0$. Using the above, we have

$$\check{C}_\mu(\alpha\mathbf{x}) = C_\mu(\alpha\mathbf{x}^+) - C_\mu(\alpha\mathbf{x}^-)$$

$$= \alpha(C_\mu(\mathbf{x}^+) - C_\mu(\mathbf{x}^-))$$

$$= \alpha\check{C}_\mu(\mathbf{x}).$$

For $\alpha < 0$, by (5.23), $\check{C}_\mu(\alpha\mathbf{x}) = -\check{C}_\mu(|\alpha|\mathbf{x}) = \alpha\check{C}_\mu(\mathbf{x}).$ □

The above result shows that for the Choquet integral, the components of the input vector $\mathbf{x}$ should be defined on a common interval scale, while for the symmetric Choquet integral, they should be defined on a common ratio scale. More general properties with independent input scales do not hold since $C_\mu(\mathbf{x})$ depends on the permutation reordering the components of $\mathbf{x}$ in increasing order.

Remark 5.43. As the following example shows, MLE_μ does not fulfill either of these properties since positive homogeneity (ratio scale invariance) does not hold: Taking $n = 2$ and any $\alpha > 0$

$$\mathsf{MLE}_\mu(\alpha\mathbf{x}) = m(\{1\})\alpha x_1 + m(\{2\})\alpha x_2 + m(\{1,2\})\alpha^2 x_1 x_2$$

$$\neq \alpha\mathsf{MLE}_\mu(x_1, x_2).$$

Proposition 5.44. *Let $\mathbb{I} = \mathbb{R}$ or $\mathbb{I} = [0, 1]$, and μ be a normalized capacity on $[n]$. The Choquet integral satisfies*

$$C_\mu(\mathbf{1} - \mathbf{x}) = 1 - C_{\overline{\mu}}(\mathbf{x})$$

for all $\mathbf{x} \in \mathbb{I}^n$.

Proof. Since **1** is comonotonic with any **x**, we have by comonotonic additivity (Proposition 5.36(iii))

$$C_\mu(\mathbf{1} - \mathbf{x}) = C_\mu(\mathbf{1}) + C_\mu(-\mathbf{x})$$
$$= 1 + C_\mu(-\mathbf{x})$$
$$= 1 - C_{\overline{\mu}}(\mathbf{x}). \qquad \square$$

Remark 5.45.   (i) This shows that C_μ defined on $[0, 1]^n$ is self-dual (see Definition 2.104) if and only if μ is self-conjugate.

(ii) If μ is not normalized, the above result generalizes to

$$C_\mu(\mu([n])\mathbf{1} - \mathbf{x}) = \mu^2([n]) - C_{\overline{\mu}}(\mathbf{x})$$

for all $\mathbf{x} \in \mathbb{I}^n$, with $\mathbb{I} := [0, \mu([n])]$.

(iii) The property does not hold for the symmetric integral. For example, taking $\mathbb{I} = \mathbb{R}$, $n = 2$, and $\mathbf{x} := (-1, 1)$, we get:

$$\check{C}_\mu(\mathbf{1} - \mathbf{x}) = C_\mu(2, 0) = 2\mu(\{1\}),$$

$$1 - \check{C}_{\overline{\mu}}(-1, 1) = 1 - C_{\overline{\mu}}(0, 1) + C_{\overline{\mu}}(1, 0) = 1 + \mu(\{1\}) - \mu(\{2\}).$$

5.4.5 *Characterization of the Choquet integral*

Theorem 5.46. *Let* $\mathbb{I} := \mathbb{R}$ *and a function* $\mathsf{F} : \mathbb{I}^n \to \mathbb{I}$. *Then there exists a unique normalized capacity* μ *such that* $\mathsf{F} = C_\mu$ *if and only if* F *fulfills the following properties:*

(i) Comonotonic additivity.
(ii) Nondecreasing monotonicity.
(iii) $\mathsf{F}(\mathbf{1}_{[n]}) = 1$, $\mathsf{F}(\mathbf{0}) = 0$.

Moreover, μ *is defined by* $\mu(A) := \mathsf{F}(\mathbf{1}_A)$.

Proof. ($\Rightarrow$) Obvious from previous propositions.

($\Leftarrow$) A first remark is that positive homogeneity can be deduced from (i) and (ii). Indeed, (i) implies that $\mathsf{F}(n\mathbf{x}) = n\mathsf{F}(\mathbf{x})$ for any positive integer n and any $\mathbf{x} \in \mathbb{I}$. For two positive integers n, m we have

$$\frac{m}{n}\mathsf{F}(\mathbf{x}) = \frac{m}{n}\mathsf{F}\left(n\frac{\mathbf{x}}{n}\right) = m\mathsf{F}\left(\frac{\mathbf{x}}{n}\right) = \mathsf{F}\left(\frac{m}{n}\mathbf{x}\right),$$

hence positive homogeneity is true for rationals. Lastly, for any positive real number r, take any increasing sequence of positive rationals r_i converging to r, and any decreasing sequence of positive rationals s_i converging to r. Then $r_i\mathsf{F}(\mathbf{x}) = \mathsf{F}(r_i\mathbf{x}) \leqslant$

$F(r\mathbf{x}) \leqslant F(s_i\mathbf{x}) = s_i F(\mathbf{x})$ implies $rF(\mathbf{x}) \leqslant F(r\mathbf{x}) \leqslant rF(\mathbf{x})$. Hence, we have proved that, considering that $F(\mathbf{0}) = 0$,

$$F(r\mathbf{x}) = rF(\mathbf{x}), \quad \forall r \geqslant 0. \tag{5.40}$$

Moreover, $F(-\mathbf{1}_{[n]}) = -1$ since by comonotonic additivity we have

$$0 = F(\mathbf{0}) = F(\mathbf{1}_{[n]} + (-\mathbf{1}_{[n]})) = F(\mathbf{1}_{[n]}) + F(-\mathbf{1}_{[n]}) = 1 + F(-\mathbf{1}_{[n]}).$$

Hence, we deduce that

$$F(r\mathbf{1}_{[n]}) = r, \quad \forall r \in \mathbb{R}. \tag{5.41}$$

Consider without loss of generality $\mathbf{x} \in \mathbb{R}^n$ such that $x_1 \leqslant x_2 \leqslant \cdots \leqslant x_n$ (if not, apply some permutation on $[n]$). It is easy to check that

$$\mathbf{x} = \sum_{i=1}^{n}(x_i - x_{i-1})\mathbf{1}_{A_i},$$

with $A_i := \{i, i+1, \ldots, n\}$, and $x_0 := 0$. Define $\boldsymbol{\xi}^i \in \mathbb{R}^n$ by $\boldsymbol{\xi}^i := (x_i - x_{i-1})\mathbf{1}_{A_i}$, $i \in [n]$. Then $\boldsymbol{\xi}^i$ and $\sum_{j=i+1}^{n} \boldsymbol{\xi}^j$ are comonotonic vectors for $i = 1, \ldots, n-1$. Using (i), we get

$$F(\mathbf{x}) = F\left(\boldsymbol{\xi}^1 + \sum_{j=2}^{n}\boldsymbol{\xi}^j\right) = F(\boldsymbol{\xi}^1) + F\left(\sum_{j=2}^{n}\boldsymbol{\xi}^j\right).$$

Iterating this we finally get $F(\mathbf{x}) = \sum_{i=1}^{n} F(\boldsymbol{\xi}^i)$. Observe that $(x_i - x_{i-1})$ are nonnegative for $i \geqslant 2$, and that $\mathbf{1}_{A_1} = \mathbf{1}_{[n]}$. Then by (5.40) and (5.41), we obtain that

$$F(\mathbf{x}) = \sum_{i=1}^{n}(x_i - x_{i-1})F(\mathbf{1}_{A_i}).$$

Putting $\mu(A) := F(\mathbf{1}_A)$, by Remark 5.24(i), we deduce that $F(\mathbf{x}) = \mathcal{C}_\mu(\mathbf{x})$. $\qquad\square$

Remark 5.47. The above result limited to nonnegative vectors was shown by de Campos and Bolaños [77], assuming in addition positive homogeneity, which can in fact be deduced from (i) and (ii). The proof in the continuous case is due to Schmeidler [380].

We present another type of characterization, where the aggregation function is supposed beforehand to depend on a capacity, hence we denote it by F_μ, $\mu \in \mathcal{F}^*(n)$. We recall that $\mathcal{F}^*(n)$ is the set of normalized capacities on $[n]$.

Theorem 5.48. *Let us consider* $\mathbb{I} := \mathbb{R}$, *and a family of functions* $\{F_\mu : \mathbb{I}^n \to \mathbb{I} \mid \mu \in \mathcal{F}^*(n)\}$. *Then* $F_\mu = \mathcal{C}_\mu$ *for all* $\mu \in \mathcal{F}^*(n)$, *if and only if the family satisfies the following properties:*

(i) Each function F_μ is a linear expression of μ, i.e., there exist 2^n functions G_L : $\mathbb{I}^n \to \mathbb{I}$, $L \subseteq [n]$, such that $F_\mu = \sum_{L \subseteq [n]} \mu(L)G_L$ for all $\mu \in \mathcal{F}^*(n)$.

(ii) For any $\mu \in \mathcal{F}^*(n)$, F_μ is nondecreasing.

(iii) For any $\mu \in \mathcal{F}^*(n)$, F_μ is interval scale invariant.

(iv) For any $\mu \in \mathcal{F}^*(n)$, F_μ is an extension of μ: $F_\mu(1_A) = \mu(A)$, for all $A \subseteq [n]$.

This result is due to Marichal [262, Th. 6.1.1], [263].

Proof. ($\Rightarrow$) Immediate from previous propositions.

($\Leftarrow$) Let us take some F_μ in the family. By linearity (i), and using the decomposition of μ into unanimity games (5.8), we get

$$F_\mu = \sum_{L \subseteq [n]} m(L)F_{u_L}. \tag{5.42}$$

By (iv), we deduce that

$$F_{u_L}(1_A) = u_L(A) \in \{0, 1\}, \quad \forall A \subseteq [n]. \tag{5.43}$$

Let us now show that $F_{u_L}(\mathbf{x}) = \wedge_{i \in L} x_i$. Let $\mathbf{x} \in [0, 1]^n$. On the one hand, for all $K \subseteq [n]$, by (ii), (iii), and (5.43) we have

$$F_{u_L}(\mathbf{x}) \geqslant F_{u_L}\left(\left(\bigwedge_{i \in K} x_i\right) 1_K\right) = u_L(K) \bigwedge_{i \in K} x_i.$$

Hence,

$$F_{u_L}(\mathbf{x}) \geqslant \bigvee_{K \subseteq [n]} \left(u_L(K) \bigwedge_{i \in K} x_i\right).$$

On the other hand, let $K^* \subseteq [n]$ such that

$$u_L(K^*) \bigwedge_{i \in K^*} x_i = \bigvee_{K \subseteq [n]} \left(u_L(K) \bigwedge_{i \in K} x_i\right),$$

and define $J := \{j \in [n] \mid x_j \leqslant u_L(K^*) \bigwedge_{i \in K^*} x_i\}$. J is not empty, otherwise we would have $x_j > u_L(K^*) \bigwedge_{i \in K^*} x_i$ for all $j \in [n]$, which entails, since $u_L([n]) = 1$, $u_L([n]) \bigwedge_{i \in [n]} x_i > u_L(K^*) \bigwedge_{i \in K^*} x_i$, which contradicts the definition of K^*. Moreover, $u_L([n] \setminus J) = 0$ since otherwise we would have (assuming $[n] \setminus J \neq \varnothing$)

$$u_L([n] \setminus J) \bigwedge_{i \in [n] \setminus J} x_i = \bigwedge_{i \in [n] \setminus J} x_i > u_L(K^*) \bigwedge_{i \in K^*} x_i,$$

a contradiction. Finally, by (ii), (iii), and (5.43) we have

$$\mathsf{F}_{u_L}(\mathbf{x}) \leqslant \mathsf{F}_{u_L}\left(\left(u_L(K^*) \bigwedge_{i \in K^*} x_i\right) \mathbf{1}_J + \mathbf{1}_{[n]\setminus J}\right)$$

$$= u_L(K^*) \bigwedge_{i \in K^*} x_i + \left(1 - u_L(K^*) \bigwedge_{i \in K^*} x_i\right) u_L([n] \setminus J)$$

$$= u_L(K^*) \bigwedge_{i \in K^*} x_i = \bigvee_{K \subseteq [n]} \left(u_L(K) \bigwedge_{i \in K} x_i\right).$$

So, finally, for any $\mathbf{x} \in [0,1]^n$

$$\mathsf{F}_{u_L}(\mathbf{x}) = \bigvee_{K \subseteq [n]} \left(u_L(K) \bigwedge_{i \in K} x_i\right) = \bigvee_{\substack{K \subseteq [n] \\ u_L(K)=1}} \bigwedge_{i \in K} x_i.$$

By Proposition 5.36 (v), we get $\mathsf{F}_{u_L}(\mathbf{x}) = \mathcal{C}_{u_L}(\mathbf{x})$ for any $\mathbf{x} \in [0,1]^n$. By (iii), $\mathsf{F}_{u_L} = \mathcal{C}_{u_L}$ on $\mathbb{R}^n$. Using Proposition 5.36(v) again, for any $x \in \mathbb{R}^n$

$$\mathsf{F}_{u_L}(\mathbf{x}) = \mathcal{C}_{u_L}(\mathbf{x}) = \bigvee_{\substack{A \subseteq [n] \\ u_L(A)=1}} \bigwedge_{i \in A} x_i$$

$$= \bigvee_{A \supseteq L} \bigwedge_{i \in A} x_i = \bigwedge_{i \in L} x_i.$$

Using the above in (5.42) and comparing with (5.27) concludes the proof.   □

Proposition 5.49. *Let us consider* $\mathbb{I} := \mathbb{R}$, *and a family of functions* $\{\mathsf{F}_\mu : \mathbb{I}^n \to \mathbb{I} \mid \mu \in \mathcal{F}^*(n)\}$. *Then* $\mathsf{F}_\mu = \check{\mathcal{C}}_\mu$ *for all* $\mu \in \mathcal{F}^*(n)$, *if and only if the family satisfies the following properties:*

(i) *Each function* F_μ *is a linear expression of* μ, *i.e., there exist* 2^n *functions* $\mathsf{G}_L : \mathbb{R}^n \to \mathbb{R}$, $L \subseteq [n]$, *such that* $\mathsf{F}_\mu = \sum_{L \subseteq [n]} \mu(L) \mathsf{G}_L$ *for all* $\mu \in \mathcal{F}^*(n)$.

(ii) *For any* $\mu \in \mathcal{F}^*(n)$, F_μ *is nondecreasing in each place.*

(iii) *For any* $\mu \in \mathcal{F}^*(n)$, F_μ *is homogeneous of degree one, i.e., for all* $\alpha \in \mathbb{R}$,

$$\mathsf{F}_\mu(\alpha \mathbf{x}) = \alpha \mathsf{F}_\mu(\mathbf{x}).$$

(iv) *For any* $\mu \in \mathcal{F}^*(n)$, F_μ *is invariant to nonnegative shifts, i.e.,* $\forall \mathbf{x} \in [0, \infty[^n$, $\forall \alpha \geqslant 0$, $\mathsf{F}_\mu(\mathbf{x} + \alpha \mathbf{1}) = \mathsf{F}_\mu(\mathbf{x}) + \alpha$.

(v) *For any* $\mu \in \mathcal{F}^*(n)$, F_μ *satisfies independence between positive and negative parts, i.e., for any* $\mathbf{x}, \mathbf{y}, \mathbf{z}, \mathbf{w} \in \mathbb{I}^n$, $\mathbf{x} \geqslant \mathbf{0}, \mathbf{y} \geqslant \mathbf{0}, \mathbf{z} \leqslant \mathbf{0}, \mathbf{w} \leqslant \mathbf{0}$, $\forall A \subseteq [n]$, *we have*

$$\mathsf{F}_\mu(\mathbf{x}_A \mathbf{z}) - \mathsf{F}_\mu(\mathbf{x}_A \mathbf{w}) = \mathsf{F}_\mu(\mathbf{y}_A \mathbf{z}) - \mathsf{F}_\mu(\mathbf{y}_A \mathbf{w}).$$

(vi) For any $\mu \in \mathcal{F}^*(n)$, F_μ is an extension of μ, i.e., $F_\mu(1_A) = \mu(A)$, $\forall A \subseteq [n]$.

This result is due to Grabisch and Labreuche [162].

Proof. ($\Rightarrow$) Obvious.

($\Leftarrow$) Let $\mathbf{x} \in \mathbb{R}^n$, with $\mathbf{x}^+, \mathbf{x}^-$ defined as before. We apply (v) to $\mathbf{x} = \mathbf{x}^+, \mathbf{y} = \mathbf{0}, \mathbf{z} = -\mathbf{x}^-, \mathbf{w} = \mathbf{0}$, and $A = \{i \in [n] \mid x_i \geqslant 0\}$. Then, for any $\mu \in \mathcal{F}(n)$

$$F_\mu(\mathbf{x}_A^+(-\mathbf{x}^-)) - F_\mu(\mathbf{x}_A^+ \mathbf{0}) = F_\mu(\mathbf{0}_A(-\mathbf{x}^-)) - F_\mu(\mathbf{0})$$

which leads to, using (iii),

$$F_\mu(\mathbf{x}) = F_\mu(\mathbf{x}^+) - F_\mu(\mathbf{x}^-). \tag{5.44}$$

Let us now restrict to $\mathbf{x} \in [0, \infty[^n$. Combining axioms (iii) and (iv) implies the invariance to positive affine transformations. This property combined with (i), (ii), and (vi) leads to the fact that F_μ restricted to $[0, \infty[^n$ is a Choquet integral $\mathcal{C}_\mu$. Due to (5.44), we finally have for any $\mathbf{x} \in \mathbb{I}^n$

$$F_\mu(\mathbf{x}) = \mathcal{C}_\mu(\mathbf{x}^+) - \mathcal{C}_\mu(\mathbf{x}^-) = \check{\mathcal{C}}_\mu(\mathbf{x}). \qquad \square$$

5.4.6 Particular Choquet integrals

In this section, we show the relation of the Choquet integral with other aggregation functions.

Proposition 5.50. *Let μ be a normalized capacity, and $\mathbb{I} = \mathbb{R}$. The following holds (see definitions in Example 5.4, and (1.19) for $\mathsf{OWA_w}$).*

(i) $\mathcal{C}_\mu = \mathsf{Min}$ if and only if $\mu = \mu_{\min}$.

(ii) $\mathcal{C}_\mu = \mathsf{Max}$ if and only if $\mu = \mu_{\max}$.

(iii) $\mathcal{C}_\mu = \mathsf{OS}_k$ if and only if μ is the threshold measure τ_{n-k+1}.

(iv) $\mathcal{C}_\mu = \mathsf{P}_k = \check{\mathcal{C}}_\mu$ if and only if μ is the Dirac measure δ_k.

(v) $\mathcal{C}_\mu = \mathsf{WAM_w} = \check{\mathcal{C}}_\mu$ if and only if μ is additive, with $\mu(\{i\}) = w_i$, $\forall i \in [n]$.

(vi) $\mathcal{C}_\mu = \mathsf{OWA_w}$ if and only if μ is symmetric, with $w_i = \mu(A_{n-i+1}) - \mu(A_{n-i})$, $i = 2, \ldots, n$, and $w_1 = 1 - \sum_{i=2}^n w_i$, where A_i is any subset of X with $|A_i| = i$ (equivalently, $\mu(A) = \sum_{j=0}^{i-1} w_{n-j}$, $\forall A, |A| = i$).

(vii) $\mathcal{C}_\mu$ is a lattice polynomial function if and only if μ is a 0–1 capacity. Moreover, any lattice polynomial function on $\mathbb{R}$ is a Choquet integral with respect to a 0–1 capacity.

Proof. Results (i), (ii), and (iii) are particular cases of (vi). Result (iv) is a particular case of (v).

(v) Let **w** be a weight vector. By using (5.19), it is straightforward to verify that taking μ additive with $\mu(\{i\}) := w_i$, for all $i \in [n]$, we get $\mathsf{WAM_w} = \mathcal{C}_\mu$. Conversely, since $\mathsf{WAM_w}$ is additive, we know by Proposition 5.41(ii) that μ is necessarily additive in $\mathcal{C}_\mu$, and equal to $\check{\mathcal{C}}_\mu$ since $\mu = \overline{\mu}$.

(vi) As above, it suffices to use (5.19) and to check that the above μ leads to $\mathsf{OWA_w}$. Conversely, since any $\mathsf{OWA_w}$ is symmetric, we know that μ is necessarily symmetric by Proposition 5.41(i).

(vii) If μ is a 0–1 capacity, then by Proposition 5.36(v), $\mathcal{C}_\mu$ is a lattice polynomial function. The converse is obvious. Finally, by Proposition 5.55, any lattice polynomial function has the form $\bigvee_{\substack{A \subseteq [n] \\ \alpha(A)=1}} \bigwedge_{i \in A} x_i$, with α a set function such that $\alpha(\varnothing) = 0$, which can be chosen as monotone with respect to inclusion; see Remark 5.56. $\square$

Most of these properties were shown by Murofushi and Sugeno [329], and (vi) was also shown by Fodor *et al.* [112]; see also [144].

Figure 5.2 shows the relation between various particular Choquet integrals, summarizing results proved so far. Observe that this figure comes from Figure 5.1, taking only relevant parts of it.

For the case $n = 2$, it is possible to have a graphical representation of the Choquet integral, the weighted arithmetic mean, and the ordered weighted averaging (OWA) function, which clearly shows their relationship [150]. For this purpose, we consider the expression of the Choquet integral with respect to the interaction transform, and since $n = 2$, all capacities are 2-additive, so that Equation (5.37) can be used.

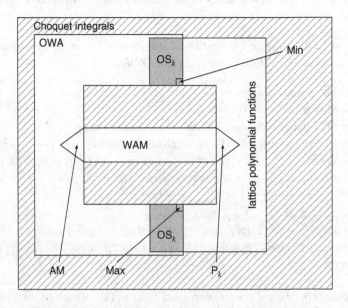

Figure 5.2 Relations between various particular Choquet integrals

Rewriting it for $n = 2$ leads to

$$C_\mu(x) = \begin{cases} (x_1 \wedge x_2)I_{12} + x_1(\phi_1 - \frac{1}{2}I_{12}) + x_2(\phi_2 - \frac{1}{2}I_{12}) & \text{if } I_{12} \geqslant 0 \\ (x_1 \vee x_2)I_{12} + x_1(\phi_1 + \frac{1}{2}I_{12}) + x_2(\phi_2 + \frac{1}{2}I_{12}) & \text{if } I_{12} \leqslant 0. \end{cases} \quad (5.45)$$

For a given $x \in \mathbb{R}^2$, all possible values of $C_\mu(x)$ are obtained when ϕ_1, ϕ_2, and I_{12} vary on their domain, which is given by Proposition 5.15(iii). Rewriting these conditions for $n = 2$ leads to

$$\phi_1 - \frac{1}{2}I_{12} \geqslant 0,$$

$$\phi_2 - \frac{1}{2}I_{12} \geqslant 0,$$

$$\phi_1 + \frac{1}{2}I_{12} \geqslant 0,$$

$$\phi_2 + \frac{1}{2}I_{12} \geqslant 0,$$

$$\phi_1 + \phi_2 = 1.$$

Due to the last equation, this domain can be represented with the (ϕ_1, I_{12}) coordinates only, and is the shaded area on Figure 5.3. In other words, the Choquet integral is the convex hull of the four vertices of Figure 5.3. Let us interpret the vertices and the two axes of the diamond. Consider first the horizontal axis, where $I_{12} = 0$. In the case $n = 2$, this is equivalent to saying that the capacity is additive, and thus the Choquet integral is a weighted arithmetic mean (see Proposition 5.50(v)), with weights $\mu(\{1\})$ and $\mu(\{2\})$, coinciding with ϕ_1 and ϕ_2. In conclusion, the horizontal axis represents the set of all possible weighted arithmetic means, with left extremity corresponding to $C_\mu = P_2$, and right extremity to P_1.

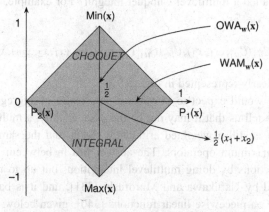

Figure 5.3 Interpretation in terms of interaction index

Let us examine the vertical axis, where $\phi_1 = \phi_2 = \frac{1}{2}$. Assuming $I_{12} > 0$ (the converse case leads to the same result), formula (5.45) becomes

$$\mathcal{C}_\mu(\mathbf{x}) = (x_1 \wedge x_2)I_{12} + \frac{1}{2}(x_1 + x_2)(1 - I_{12})$$

$$= x_{(1)}I_{12} + \frac{1}{2}(x_{(1)} + x_{(2)})(1 - I_{12})$$

$$= \frac{1}{2}x_{(1)}(1 + I_{12}) + \frac{1}{2}x_{(2)}(1 - I_{12}). \tag{5.46}$$

We recognize here an ordered weighted averaging (OWA) function, with weights $\frac{1}{2}(1+I_{12})$ and $\frac{1}{2}(1-I_{12})$. Moreover, since any OWA function is such that $\phi_1 = \phi_2 = \frac{1}{2}$ when $n = 2$, the vertical axis is the locus of all possible OWA functions. The upper vertex ($I_{12} = 1$) corresponds to the minimum operator and the lower vertex to the maximum operator, as can be seen from (5.46).

All these results are indicated in Figure 5.3. It clearly shows that, when $n = 2$, any Choquet integral can be written as a convex combination of a minimum, a maximum, and two projections, i.e., for any capacity μ, there exist nonnegative numbers $\alpha, \beta, \gamma, \delta$ such that $\alpha + \beta + \gamma + \delta = 1$, and

$$\mathcal{C}_\mu(\mathbf{x}) = \alpha(x_1 \wedge x_2) + \beta(x_1 \vee x_2) + \gamma x_1 + \delta x_2.$$

The converse holds also: any convex combination of a minimum, a maximum, and two projections is a Choquet integral. The n-ary case was already discussed in Remark 5.28(i).

5.4.7 *Multilevel Choquet integral*

Since the Choquet integral covers a wide range of aggregation functions, a natural question is: Can we cover more by combining different Choquet integrals, defining what could be called a multilevel Choquet integral? For example, on $\mathbb{R}^3$ one may consider, for any $\mathbf{x} \in \mathbb{R}^3$,

$$\mathbf{A}(\mathbf{x}) := \mathcal{C}_{\mu_3}(\mathcal{C}_{\mu_{11}}(x_1, x_2), \mathcal{C}_{\mu_2}(\mathcal{C}_{\mu_{11}}(x_1, x_2), \mathcal{C}_{\mu_{12}}(x_1, x_2, x_3)), x_3), \tag{5.47}$$

which is more clearly represented in Figure 5.4.

Although one would expect to discover a new realm of aggregation functions, simple examples tell us that it may not be the case. Clearly, a multilevel weighted arithmetic mean is still a weighted arithmetic mean, and the same holds for the minimum and maximum operators. The answer lies in between: we do get new aggregation functions by doing multilevel integration, but up to two levels only. This was proved by Narukawa and Murofushi [331], and it is based on a result by Ovchinnikov on piecewise linear functions [340], given below. We borrow the following development from Murofushi [324].

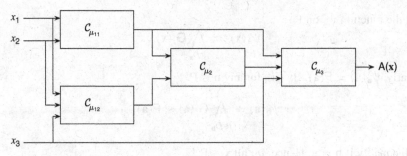

Figure 5.4 Example of multilevel Choquet integral

A real-valued function F on a convex closed subset $\Gamma \subseteq \mathbb{R}^n$ is *piecewise linear* if Γ can be written as a union of closed subspaces $\Gamma_1, \ldots, \Gamma_q$ of the same dimension as Γ, such that $F|_{\Gamma_i}$ is linear, $i = 1, \ldots, q$. A linear function G on $\mathbb{R}^n$ which coincides with F on some Γ_i is a *component* of F.

Clearly, any piecewise linear function on Γ is continuous.

Proposition 5.51. [340] *Let F be a piecewise linear function on $\Gamma \subseteq \mathbb{R}^n$, and $G_1, \ldots, G_q$ be its distinct components. Then there exists a family $\{D_j\}_{j \in J}$ of incomparable (with respect to inclusion) subsets of $\{1, \ldots, q\}$ such that*

$$F(\mathbf{x}) = \bigvee_{j \in J} \bigwedge_{i \in D_j} G_i(\mathbf{x})$$

for all $\mathbf{x} \in \Gamma$.

Proof. The proof goes in three steps.

(i) Take any F piecewise linear on $[a, b] \subseteq \mathbb{R}$, and $G_1, \ldots, G_q$ the set of its components, corresponding to line segments $\ell_1, \ldots, \ell_q$, enumerated in the direction from a to b. Then there exists k such that $G_k(a) \leqslant F(a)$ and $G_k(b) \geqslant F(b)$. Indeed, let α be the slope of the segment $[(a, F(a)), (b, F(b))]$ in $\mathbb{R}^2$. If the slope of G_1 (respectively, G_q) is greater than or equal to α, then G_1 (respectively, G_q) satisfies the conditions. If not, the slopes of G_1, G_q are both smaller than α, and by continuity some ℓ_k with slope greater than α intersects the segment $[(a, F(a)), (b, F(b))]$, hence G_k satisfies the conditions.

(ii) Consider now F being piecewise linear on Γ, and $G_1, \ldots, G_q$ its components. For any points $\mathbf{a}, \mathbf{b} \in \Gamma$, there exists k such that $G_k(\mathbf{a}) \leqslant F(\mathbf{a})$ and $G_k(\mathbf{b}) \geqslant F(\mathbf{b})$. Indeed, it suffices to consider the restriction of F to the segment $[\mathbf{a}, \mathbf{b}]$ and to apply (i).

(iii) For any $\mathbf{a} \in \Gamma$, we define

$$D_{\mathbf{a}} := \{i \in \{1, \ldots, q\} \mid G_i(\mathbf{a}) \geqslant F(\mathbf{a})\}$$

and the function $\psi_{\mathbf{a}}$ on Γ

$$\psi_{\mathbf{a}}(\mathbf{x}) := \bigwedge_{i \in D_{\mathbf{a}}} G_i(\mathbf{x}).$$

Clearly, $\psi_{\mathbf{a}}(\mathbf{a}) = F(\mathbf{a})$. By (ii), for any $\mathbf{b} \in \Gamma$

$$\psi_{\mathbf{b}}(\mathbf{a}) = \bigwedge_{i \in D_{\mathbf{b}}} G_i(\mathbf{a}) \leqslant F(\mathbf{a}),$$

with equality if $\mathbf{b} = \mathbf{a}$. Hence, for all $\mathbf{x} \in \Gamma$,

$$F(\mathbf{x}) = \bigvee_{\mathbf{a} \in \Gamma} \bigwedge_{i \in D_{\mathbf{a}}} G_i(\mathbf{x}).$$

Defining $\{D_j\}_{j \in J}$ the family of distinct minimal (with respect to inclusion) elements in the family $\{D_{\mathbf{a}}\}_{\mathbf{a} \in \Gamma}$, we get the desired result. $\square$

Let us give a formal definition of a multilevel Choquet integral.

Definition 5.52. Let $\Gamma \subseteq \mathbb{R}^n$. For any $i \in [n]$, the projection P_i is a *0-level Choquet integral*. Let us consider $F_i : \Gamma \to \mathbb{R}$, $i \in M := \{1, \ldots, m\}$, being k_i-level Choquet integrals, and a capacity μ on M. Then

$$F(\mathbf{x}) := \mathcal{C}_\mu(F_1(\mathbf{x}), \ldots, F_m(\mathbf{x}))$$

is a *k-level Choquet integral*, with $k := \mathsf{Max}(k_1, \ldots, k_m) + 1$. A *multilevel Choquet integral* is a function that is a k-level Choquet integral for some integer $k > 1$.

Theorem 5.53. *Let $\Gamma \subseteq \mathbb{R}$ be a convex closed n-dimensional set, and $F : \Gamma \to \mathbb{R}$. The following are equivalent.*

(i) F is a multilevel Choquet integral.
(ii) F is a 2-level Choquet integral, with all capacities of the first level being additive, and the capacity of the second level being 0–1 valued.
(iii) F is nondecreasing and positively homogeneous piecewise linear.

Proof. (i) $\Rightarrow$ (iii) Clear from the fact that the Choquet integral and projection functions are nondecreasing, positively homogeneous and continuous piecewise linear functions (see Propositions 5.38 and 5.42), and from Definition 5.52.

(iii) $\Rightarrow$ (ii) Since F is continuous piecewise linear, by Proposition 5.51, we can write $F = \bigvee_{j=1}^k \bigwedge_{i \in K_j} F_i$, with each F_i being linear. Since F is positively homogeneous and nondecreasing, there is no constant term in each F_i, and all coefficients in each F_i are nonnegative. Hence each F_i is a Choquet integral with respect to an additive (nonnormalized) capacity. Lastly, we know from Proposition 5.36(v) that the max–min expression is a Choquet integral with respect to a 0–1 capacity.

(ii) $\Rightarrow$ (i) Clear. $\square$

5.5 The Sugeno integral

The Sugeno integral was introduced by Sugeno in 1972 [402], as a way to compute the expected value of a function with respect to a nonadditive probability (called by Sugeno a "fuzzy measure", with the intention to give a subjective flavor to probability). As we will see in the next section, it is formally very similar to the Choquet integral, although the works of Choquet were not known by Sugeno at the time, and present many similar properties. In fact, as remarked by Denneberg, the Sugeno integral was already introduced by Ky Fan in 1944 [110], as a particular distance $\|f - 0\|_0$ of a function f to the null function.

Although mathematically very similar since, roughly speaking, they differ only by their mathematical operations (sum and product being replaced by maximum and minimum respectively), it is more difficult to introduce the Sugeno integral in a natural way; it has fewer properties than the Choquet integral, and uniqueness is often lost. An example of this is the following: we introduced the Choquet integral as the unique parsimonious linear interpolator; trying to do the same with the Sugeno integral leads to infinitely many solutions, the least one being precisely the Sugeno integral [155].

Following Marichal [261], a convenient way to introduce the Sugeno integral is to use weighted lattice polynomial functions, which are arbitrary combinations of minimum and maximum expressions involving variables and constants, e.g., $(c \vee x_1) \wedge x_2$. It turns out that they contain the Sugeno integral as a particular case.

5.5.1 Weighted lattice polynomial functions

We limit our exposition to the case where the underlying lattice is the interval $\mathbb{I}$. Then we naturally consider $\wedge = \min$ and $\vee = \max$.

Definition 5.54. [174, §I.4] The class of *lattice polynomial functions* from $\mathbb{I}^n$ to $\mathbb{I}$ is defined as follows:

(i) For any $k \in [n]$, the projection P_k is a lattice polynomial function from $\mathbb{I}^n$ to $\mathbb{I}$.
(ii) If p, q are lattice polynomial functions from $\mathbb{I}^n$ to $\mathbb{I}$, then $p \vee q$ and $p \wedge q$ are lattice polynomial functions from $\mathbb{I}^n$ to $\mathbb{I}$.
(iii) Every lattice polynomial function from $\mathbb{I}^n$ to $\mathbb{I}$ is formed by finitely many applications of rules (i) and (ii).

A lattice polynomial function can have several equivalent representations (lattice polynomials). For instance, $x_1 \vee (x_1 \wedge x_2)$ and x_1 are equivalent.

Note that lattice polynomial functions are nondecreasing in each variable. Moreover, it is easy to see that any lattice polynomial function is unanimously increasing.

Lattice polynomial functions can be written in disjunctive and conjunctive normal forms.

Proposition 5.55. [44, §II.5] *Let $p : \mathbb{I}^n \to \mathbb{I}$ be any lattice polynomial function. Then there exist integers $k, l \geqslant 1$ and families $\{A_j\}_{j=1}^k$ and $\{B_j\}_{j=1}^l$ of nonempty subsets of*

[n] *such that*

$$p(\mathbf{x}) = \bigvee_{j=1}^{k} \bigwedge_{i \in A_j} x_i = \bigwedge_{j=1}^{l} \bigvee_{i \in B_j} x_i.$$

Equivalently, there exist nonconstant set functions $\alpha : 2^{[n]} \to \{0,1\}$ *and* $\beta : 2^{[n]} \to \{0,1\}$, *with* $\alpha(\varnothing) = 0$ *and* $\beta(\varnothing) = 1$, *such that*

$$p(\mathbf{x}) = \bigvee_{\substack{A \subseteq [n] \\ \alpha(A)=1}} \bigwedge_{i \in A} x_i = \bigwedge_{\substack{A \subseteq [n] \\ \beta(A)=0}} \bigvee_{i \in A} x_i.$$

Remark 5.56. Set functions α, β above are not unique: for instance, $x_1 \vee (x_1 \wedge x_2)$ and x_1 are equivalent. One can always choose α (respectively, β) to be monotone nondecreasing (respectively, nonincreasing) with respect to inclusion, and in this case it is the greatest (respectively, the smallest) one; see Proposition 5.58.

The concept of a lattice polynomial function can be generalized by fixing some variables as constants.

Definition 5.57. [261] The class of *weighted lattice polynomial functions* from $\mathbb{I}^n$ to $\mathbb{I}$ is defined as follows:

(i) For any $k \in [n]$ and any $c \in \mathbb{I}$, the projection P_k and the constant function K_c are weighted lattice polynomial functions from $\mathbb{I}^n$ to $\mathbb{I}$.

(ii) If p, q are weighted lattice polynomial functions from $\mathbb{I}^n$ to $\mathbb{I}$, then $p \vee q$ and $p \wedge q$ are weighted lattice polynomial functions from $\mathbb{I}^n$ to $\mathbb{I}$.

(iii) Every weighted lattice polynomial function from $\mathbb{I}^n$ to $\mathbb{I}$ is formed by finitely many applications of rules (i) and (ii).

Let us express them in conjunctive and disjunctive normal forms, using Proposition 5.55. We obtain, regrouping constants,

$$p(\mathbf{x}) = \bigvee_{j=1}^{k} \left(a_j \wedge \bigwedge_{i \in A_j} x_i \right) = \bigwedge_{j=1}^{l} \left(b_j \vee \bigvee_{i \in B_j} x_i \right)$$

for all $x \in \mathbb{I}^n$. Equivalently, there exist set functions $\alpha, \beta : 2^{[n]} \to \mathbb{I}$ such that

$$p(\mathbf{x}) = \bigvee_{A \subseteq [n]} \left(\alpha(A) \wedge \bigwedge_{i \in A} x_i \right) = \bigwedge_{A \subseteq [n]} \left(\beta(A) \vee \bigvee_{i \in A} x_i \right). \qquad (5.48)$$

It follows from (5.48) that any n-ary weighted lattice polynomial function is completely determined by 2^n parameters at most. As above, the set functions α and β are not necessarily unique. The next proposition establishes all possible solutions for these set functions. For any set functions α, β, we denote by $p_\alpha^\vee$ and $p_\beta^\wedge$ the respective weighted lattice polynomial functions generated by (5.48).

Proposition 5.58. [261] *Let p be an n-ary weighted lattice polynomial function, and consider two set functions α, β on $[n]$.*

(i) $p = p_\alpha^\vee$ *if and only if* $\alpha_* \leqslant \alpha \leqslant \alpha^*$, *where for any* $A \subseteq [n]$

$$\alpha_*(A) := \begin{cases} p(1_A) & \text{if } p(1_A) > p(1_{A \setminus i}), \forall i \in A \\ 0 & \text{otherwise.} \end{cases}$$

$$\alpha^*(A) := p(1_A).$$

(ii) $p = p_\beta^\wedge$ *if and only if* $\beta_* \leqslant \beta \leqslant \beta^*$, *where for any* $A \subseteq [n]$

$$\beta^*(A) := \begin{cases} p(1_{[n]\setminus A}) & \text{if } p(1_{[n]\setminus A}) < p(1_{([n]\setminus A)\cup i}), \forall i \in A \\ 1 & \text{otherwise.} \end{cases}$$

$$\beta_*(A) := p(1_{[n]\setminus A}).$$

Proof. Let us prove (i). Assertion (ii) can be proved similarly.

($\Leftarrow$) We show first that $p = p_{\alpha^*}^\vee$. We know by (5.48) that there exists a set function α such that $p = p_\alpha^\vee$. It follows that

$$\alpha^*(B) = \bigvee_{A \subseteq B} \alpha(A)$$

for all $B \subseteq [n]$. Therefore we have, for any $\mathbf{x} \in \mathbb{I}^n$

$$p_{\alpha^*}^\vee(\mathbf{x}) = \bigvee_{B \subseteq [n]} \left(\alpha^*(B) \wedge \bigwedge_{i \in B} x_i \right) = \bigvee_{B \subseteq [n]} \left(\bigvee_{A \subseteq B} \alpha(A) \wedge \bigwedge_{i \in B} x_i \right)$$

$$= \bigvee_{B \subseteq [n]} \bigvee_{A \subseteq B} \left(\alpha(A) \wedge \bigwedge_{i \in B} x_i \right) = \bigvee_{A \subseteq [n]} \bigvee_{B \supseteq A} \left(\alpha(A) \wedge \bigwedge_{i \in B} x_i \right)$$

$$= \bigvee_{A \subseteq [n]} \left(\alpha(A) \wedge \bigvee_{B \supseteq A} \bigwedge_{i \in B} x_i \right) = \bigvee_{A \subseteq [n]} \left(\alpha(A) \wedge \bigwedge_{i \in A} x_i \right)$$

$$= p(\mathbf{x}).$$

Take $A \subseteq [n]$ and assume there exists $i \in A$ such that $\alpha^*(A) \leqslant \alpha^*(A \setminus i)$. Then

$$\left(\alpha^*(A \setminus i) \wedge \bigwedge_{j \in A \setminus i} x_j \right) \vee \left(\alpha^*(A) \wedge \bigwedge_{j \in A} x_j \right) = \left(\alpha^*(A \setminus i) \wedge \bigwedge_{j \in A \setminus i} x_j \right)$$

and thus $\alpha^*(A)$ can be replaced by any lower value without altering $p_{\alpha^*}^\vee$, hence the result.

($\Rightarrow$) Assume $p_\alpha^\vee = p$ and take $A \subseteq [n]$. On the one hand, we have

$$0 \leqslant \alpha(A) \leqslant \bigvee_{K \subseteq A} \alpha(K) = \alpha^*(A).$$

On the other hand, if $\alpha^*(A) > \alpha^*(A \setminus i)$ for all $i \in A$, we get $\alpha(A) = \alpha^*(A)$, which proves the results since α is nonnegative. Indeed, otherwise, there would exist $K^* \subsetneq A$ such that

$$\alpha^*(A) = \bigvee_{K \subseteq A} \alpha(K) = \alpha(K^*) \leqslant \alpha^*(K^*) < \alpha^*(A)$$

since α^* is a monotone set function by construction.   □

In particular, the proposition shows that any weighted lattice polynomial is completely determined by its restriction to $\{0, 1\}^n$. More material on lattice polynomial functions can be found in Section 8.3.3.

5.5.2 Definition and expressions of the Sugeno integral

As for the Choquet integral, we consider from now on the Sugeno integral as an aggregation function over $\mathbb{I}^n$, and hence adopt the notation $\mathcal{S}_\mu(\mathbf{x})$ instead of the usual one $(S) \int f \, d\mu$. Also, we restrict our attention to the case of capacities, although the definition works for nonnegative games as well, but as for the Choquet integral, monotonicity of the set function is necessary in order to get a nondecreasing aggregation function.

First, we consider nonnegative vectors.

Definition 5.59. Let μ be a capacity on $[n]$, and $\mathbf{x} \in [0, \mu([n])]^n$. The *Sugeno integral* of $\mathbf{x}$ with respect to μ is defined by

$$\mathcal{S}_\mu(\mathbf{x}) := \bigvee_{i=1}^{n} \left(x_{\sigma(i)} \wedge \mu(A_{\sigma(i)}) \right)$$

with σ a permutation on $[n]$ such that $x_{\sigma(1)} \leqslant x_{\sigma(2)} \leqslant \cdots \leqslant x_{\sigma(n)}$, with $A_{\sigma(i)} := \{\sigma(i), \ldots, \sigma(n)\}$.

Remark 5.60.   (i) The similarity with the Choquet integral is striking, although apparently expressions are not exactly identical up to a change of operations (sum and product replaced by maximum and minimum respectively). We will however show in Section 5.6 that put in a more general framework, they do coincide up to a change of operations.

 (ii) The above definition requires only comparison operations, no arithmetic ones. Hence, the definition works on any totally ordered set $\mathbb{I}$, without additional structure.

(iii) Since order statistics can be expressed as a combination of minima and maxima, the Sugeno integral is an n-ary weighted lattice polynomial function. We will show in Theorem 5.64 their exact relationship.

(iv) The vector $\mathbf{x}$ should have components not greater than $\mu([n])$, otherwise they are "cut" by $\mu([n])$. This is again due to the essence of the Sugeno integral, which is only based on comparisons. Hence, input vectors and capacities should have the same range.

We give the original definition, applicable to continuous spaces [110, 404].

Definition 5.61. Let μ be a capacity on $\Omega := [n]$, and $f : \Omega \to [0, \mu(\Omega)]$. The *Sugeno integral* of f with respect to μ is defined by

$$(S) \int f \, d\mu := \sup_{\alpha \in [0, \mu(\Omega)]} (\alpha \wedge \mu(\{\omega \mid f(\omega) > \alpha\})) \tag{5.49}$$

$$= \inf_{\alpha \in [0, \mu(\Omega)]} (\alpha \vee \mu(\{\omega \mid f(\omega) > \alpha\})). \tag{5.50}$$

Remark 5.62. As for the Choquet integral, the same remark on arbitrary Ω and measurability applies (see Remark 5.22), and it can be shown that $>$ can be replaced by $\geqslant$; see [404] for a proof using continuity of the capacity, but this condition is not necessary. It can be checked that we recover Definition 5.59 with a discrete space. The equivalence between (5.49) and (5.50) is immediate from a figure, since in both formulas, the value of the Sugeno integral is obtained by the intersection point of the decumulative function and the diagonal.

Since the Sugeno integral is a particular weighted lattice polynomial function, we can use Proposition 5.58. We obtain the following.

Proposition 5.63. *For any* $\mathbf{x} \in [0, \mu([n])]^n$ *and any capacity* μ *on* $[n]$, *the Sugeno integral of* $\mathbf{x}$ *with respect to* μ *can be written as*

$$\mathcal{S}_\mu(\mathbf{x}) = \bigvee_{A \subseteq [n]} \left(\bigwedge_{i \in A} x_i \wedge m(A) \right), \tag{5.51}$$

$$\mathcal{S}_\mu(\mathbf{x}) = \bigwedge_{A \subseteq [n]} \left(\bigvee_{i \in A} x_i \vee \overline{m}(A) \right) \tag{5.52}$$

where m is any set function such that $m_* \leqslant m \leqslant m^*$, with $m^* := \mu$ and

$$m_*(A) := \begin{cases} \mu(A) & \text{if } \mu(A) > \mu(A \setminus i), \quad \forall i \in A \\ 0 & \text{otherwise,} \end{cases} \tag{5.53}$$

for any $A \subseteq [n]$, and $\overline{m}$ is any set function such that $\overline{m}_* \leqslant \overline{m} \leqslant \overline{m}^*$, with $\overline{m}_*(A) := \mu([n] \setminus A)$, $A \subseteq [n]$, and

$$\overline{m}^*(A) := \begin{cases} \mu([n] \setminus A) & \text{if } \mu([n] \setminus A) < \mu(([n] \setminus A) \cup i), \quad \forall i \in A \\ 1 & \text{otherwise,} \end{cases} \tag{5.54}$$

for any $A \subseteq [n]$.

Proof. Since the Sugeno integral is a weighted lattice polynomial function, there exists a set function m on $[n]$ such that $\mathcal{S}_\mu = p_m^\vee$ for all $m_* \leqslant m \leqslant m^*$, with m_*, m^* corresponding to α_*, α^* in Proposition 5.58. Since $\mathcal{S}_\mu(1_A) = \mu(A)$, for all $A \subseteq [n]$ (see Proposition 5.73(i)), this proves the first equation. The second one can be proved similarly. $\qquad\square$

The result with m^* is already in the original work of Sugeno [404]. We will comment further on these formulas at the end of this section.

The following result gives the exact relation between weighted lattice polynomial functions and the Sugeno integral.

Theorem 5.64. *Let* $\mathbb{I} := [0, 1]$ *and* $\mathsf{F} : \mathbb{I}^n \to \mathbb{I}$ *be a function. The following assertions are equivalent.*

(i) *There exists a unique normalized capacity* μ *such that* $\mathsf{F} = \mathcal{S}_\mu$.
(ii) F *is an idempotent weighted lattice polynomial function.*
(iii) F *is an endpoint-preserving weighted lattice polynomial function.*

Proof. (i)$\Rightarrow$(ii)$\Rightarrow$(iii) Trivial. To show (iii)$\Rightarrow$(i), we show that for any weighted lattice polynomial function p, there exists a normalized capacity μ such that for any $\mathbf{x} \in [0, 1]^n$

$$p(\mathbf{x}) = \mathsf{Med}(p(\mathbf{0}), \mathcal{S}_\mu(\mathbf{x}), p(\mathbf{1})),$$

which proves the result. Let us take $\mu(A) := p(1_A) = \alpha^*(A)$ for all $A \subsetneq [n], A \neq \varnothing$. Then, using (5.51) and since $p(\mathbf{0}) = \alpha^*(\varnothing) \leqslant \alpha^*([n]) = p(\mathbf{1})$,

$$\mathsf{Med}(p(\mathbf{0}), \mathcal{S}_\mu(\mathbf{x}), p(\mathbf{1}))$$

$$= \left(\alpha^*(\varnothing) \vee \bigvee_{\varnothing \neq A \subsetneq [n]} \left(\mu(A) \wedge \bigwedge_{i \in A} x_i \right) \vee \left(\bigwedge_{i \in [n]} x_i \right) \right) \wedge \alpha^*([n])$$

$$= \left(\alpha^*(\varnothing) \vee \bigvee_{\varnothing \neq A \subsetneq [n]} \left(\alpha^*(A) \wedge \bigwedge_{i \in A} x_i \right) \vee \left(\bigwedge_{i \in [n]} x_i \right) \right) \wedge \alpha^*([n])$$

$$= \bigvee_{A \subseteq [n]} \left(\alpha^*(A) \wedge \bigwedge_{i \in A} x_i \right)$$

$$= p(\mathbf{x}). \qquad\square$$

This result is due to Marichal [261, 269], and shows that the Sugeno integral is a rather unavoidable concept if one restricts to ordinal operations.

Several equivalent expressions of the Sugeno integral exist in the discrete case.

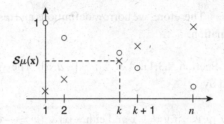

Figure 5.5 Value of $\mathcal{S}_\mu(\mathbf{x})$. $\times$: $x_{(i)}$, $\circ$: $\mu_{(i)}$

Proposition 5.65. *Let μ be a capacity. The following are equivalent formulas for the Sugeno integral $\mathcal{S}_\mu$.*

$$\mathcal{S}_\mu(\mathbf{x}) = \bigwedge_{i=1}^{n} \left(x_{\sigma(i)} \vee \mu(A_{\sigma(i+1)}) \right) \tag{5.55}$$

$$= \bigvee_{i=1}^{n} \left(x_i \wedge \mu(\{ j \mid x_j \geqslant x_i \}) \right) \tag{5.56}$$

$$= \mathrm{Med}(x_1, \ldots, x_n, \mu(A_{\sigma(2)}), \ldots, \mu(A_{\sigma(n)})), \tag{5.57}$$

with $A_{\sigma(n+1)} := \varnothing$.

Proof. Formula (5.55) can be obtained directly from (5.50) in the same way $\mathcal{S}_\mu$ in Definition 5.59 can be recovered from (5.49). Formula (5.56) is merely a translation in the discrete case of (5.49).

Let us prove (5.57) (see Figure 5.5). To avoid cumbersome notation, we use $x_{(i)}$ and introduce $\mu_{(i)} := \mu(A_{(i)})$. Note that $\mathcal{S}_\mu(\mathbf{x})$ is either equal to $x_{(k)}$ or to $\mu_{(k)}$ for some $k \in [n]$, and that we have $x_{(1)} \leqslant \cdots \leqslant x_{(n)}$, and $1 = \mu_{(1)} \geqslant \cdots \geqslant \mu_{(n)}$. By using Definition 5.59, index k corresponds to the place where the $x_{(i)}$'s and the $\mu_{(i)}$'s cross over. Let us suppose that $\mathcal{S}_\mu(\mathbf{x}) = x_{(k)}$. Then $x_{(k)} \leqslant \mu_{(k)}$, and $x_{(1)}, \ldots, x_{(k-1)}, \mu_{(k+1)}, \ldots, \mu_{(n)}$ are smaller than or equal to $\mathcal{S}_\mu$ (hence $n-1$ values). Similarly, $x_{(k+1)}, \ldots, x_{(n)}, \mu_{(2)}, \ldots, \mu_{(k)}$ are greater than or equal to $\mathcal{S}_\mu$ (again $n-1$ values). Consequently, $\mathcal{S}_\mu$ is the median of the values $x_{(1)}, \ldots, x_{(n)}, \mu_{(2)}, \ldots, \mu_{(n)}$. When $\mathcal{S}_\mu(\mathbf{x}) = \mu_{(k)}$, the proof is much the same. □

Remark 5.66. A direct proof of (5.55) from Definition 5.59 is tedious. It has been shown for possibility and necessity measures only by Inuiguchi *et al.* [195], while a general proof has been given by Grabisch and Sugeno [173]. Another proof using weighted lattice polynomial functions has been done by Marichal [267]. Formula (5.57) was shown by Kandel and Byatt [204]; see also Marichal [267].

We turn now to the case of real-valued vectors. The detailed study of the case where the input vector may contain negative values is postponed to Chapter 9, since due to the ordinal nature of the Sugeno integral, the computation with negative values causes many difficulties. Therefore, we borrow definitions and results from Chapter 9, without further explanation.

Definition 5.67 (see Section 9.3.1). Let $\mathbb{I} := [-a, a]$. The *symmetric maximum* $\varovee : \mathbb{I}^2 \to \mathbb{I}$ is defined by

$$
x \varovee y := \begin{cases} -(|x| \vee |y|) & \text{if } y \neq -x \text{ and either } |x| \vee |y| = -x \text{ or } = -y \\ 0 & \text{if } y = -x \\ |x| \vee |y| & \text{otherwise.} \end{cases} \tag{5.58}
$$

Observe that, except for the case $y = -x$, $x \varovee y$ equals the absolutely larger one of the two values x and y. It is easy to see that $\varovee$ is nondecreasing, and noncontinuous on the antidiagonal. As shown in Proposition 9.18, the symmetric maximum is associative if in the sequence of terms involved, say $x_1, \ldots, x_p$, $\bigvee_{i=1}^{p} x_i \neq - \bigwedge_{i=1}^{p} x_i$. In particular, $\varovee$ is associative for expressions involving only terms of the same sign.

Definition 5.68 (see Section 9.3.2). Let $\mathbb{I} := [-a, a]$. The *symmetric minimum* $\varowedge$: $\mathbb{I}^2 \to \mathbb{I}$ is defined by

$$
x \varowedge y := \begin{cases} -(|x| \wedge |y|) & \text{if sign}(x) \neq \text{sign}(y) \\ |x| \wedge |y| & \text{otherwise.} \end{cases} \tag{5.59}
$$

The absolute value of $x \varowedge y$ equals $|x| \wedge |y|$, and $x \varowedge y < 0$ if and only if the two elements x and y have opposite signs. The symmetric minimum is associative, but distributivity with the symmetric maximum holds only for expressions involving terms of the same sign; see Proposition 9.18.

Definition 5.69. Let μ be a capacity on $[n]$, $\mathbf{x} \in [-\mu([n]), \mu([n])]^n$, and denote by $\mathbf{x}^+, \mathbf{x}^-$ the absolute values of positive and negative parts of $\mathbf{x}$, i.e., $\mathbf{x}^+ := \mathbf{x} \vee \mathbf{0}$ and $\mathbf{x}^- := (-\mathbf{x})^+$. The *symmetric Sugeno integral* is defined by

$$
\check{\mathcal{S}}_\mu(\mathbf{x}) := \mathcal{S}_\mu(\mathbf{x}^+) \varovee (-\mathcal{S}_\mu(\mathbf{x}^-)). \tag{5.60}
$$

From the definition, it is immediate that

$$
\check{\mathcal{S}}_\mu(-\mathbf{x}) = -\check{\mathcal{S}}_\mu(\mathbf{x}) \tag{5.61}
$$

which justifies the name "symmetric".

Remark 5.70. Definition 5.69 is the exact counterpart of the symmetric Choquet integral. The symmetric maximum and the symmetric Sugeno integral were introduced by Grabisch [151, 154]. A study of the symmetric integral in the general case (continuous spaces, mixed discrete–continuous spaces) can be found in [84].

It is easy to check that the explicit expression of the symmetric Sugeno integral is

$$\check{S}_\mu(\mathbf{x}) = \left(\overset{p}{\underset{i=1}{\varovee}} \left(x_{\sigma(i)} \varoast \mu(\{\sigma(1),\ldots,\sigma(i)\}) \right) \right) \varovee$$
$$\left(\overset{n}{\underset{i=p+1}{\varovee}} \left(x_{\sigma(i)} \varoast \mu(\{\sigma(i),\ldots,\sigma(n)\}) \right) \right), \tag{5.62}$$

where σ is a permutation on $[n]$ such that $-\mu([n]) \leqslant x_{\sigma(1)} \leqslant \cdots \leqslant x_{\sigma(p)} < 0$, and $0 \leqslant x_{\sigma(p+1)} \leqslant \cdots \leqslant x_{\sigma(n)} \leqslant \mu([n])$. Note that the above formula is well defined with respect to associativity.

What about an *asymmetric Sugeno integral*, as for the Choquet integral? As studied in [151], it seems that there is no suitable definition for such a notion. The most natural way would be to keep the original definition (formula in Definition 5.59), simply replacing $\vee, \wedge$ by $\varovee, \varoast$, and separating positive and negative terms to avoid associativity problems, specifically, for any $\mathbf{x} \in [-\mu([n]), \mu([n])]^n$

$$S_\mu(\mathbf{x}) := \left(\overset{p}{\underset{i=1}{\varovee}} \left(x_{\sigma(i)} \varoast \mu(A_{\sigma(i)}) \right) \right) \varovee \left(\overset{n}{\underset{i=p+1}{\varovee}} \left(x_{\sigma(i)} \varoast \mu(A_{\sigma(i)}) \right) \right)$$

with the same notation as above. It is not difficult, however, to see that the negative terms always reduce to

$$(x_{\sigma(1)} \varoast \mu([n])) \varovee \overset{p}{\underset{i=2}{\varovee}} \left(x_{\sigma(i)} \varoast \mu(\{(i),\ldots,(n)\}) \right) = x_{\sigma(1)}.$$

Consequently, the only solution seems to be to keep the original definition of the Sugeno integral, without considering negative numbers. This is consistent with the fact that for the asymmetric Choquet integral, the position of the zero is arbitrary, and hence, can be moved to the lower bound. Hence, in the sequel, we deal with the Sugeno integral on $\mathbb{I} := [0, \mu([n])]$, and the symmetric Sugeno integral on $\mathbb{I}' := [-\mu([n]), \mu([n])]$.

We end this section by coming back to formulas in Proposition 5.63, in particular the first one:

$$S_\mu(\mathbf{x}) = \bigvee_{A \subseteq [n]} \left(\bigwedge_{i \in A} x_i \wedge m(A) \right).$$

Note the analogy with the expression of the Choquet integral using the Möbius transform; see (5.27). Interestingly enough, any set function m satisfying $m_* \leqslant m \leqslant m^*$ can indeed be called an *ordinal Möbius transform* of μ, as the following development shows.

Proposition 5.71. *Let L be a totally ordered set, with least element 0, $(X, \geqslant)$ a (finite) partially ordered set with a least element, and $f, g : X \rightarrow L$, with g being isotone.*

The solution of the equation

$$g(x) = \bigvee_{y \leqslant x} f(y),$$ (5.63)

which we call the ordinal Möbius transform of g, *is given by the interval* $[f_*, f^*]$, *with, for all* $x \in X$

$$f^*(x) = g(x),$$

$$f_*(x) = \begin{cases} g(x) & \text{if } g(x) > g(y), \forall y \prec x \\ 0 & \text{otherwise,} \end{cases}$$

with $y \prec x$ *if and only if* $y < x$ *and there is no* $z \in X$ *such that* $y < z < x$.

Remark 5.72. Equation (5.63) is the ordinal counterpart of (5.2), hence the terminology. Applied to the case of capacities, with $X = 2^{[n]}$, we obtain that the ordinal Möbius transform of a capacity μ is the interval $[m_*, m^*]$, with m^*, m_* as defined in Proposition 5.63. Since the upper bound is trivial, the *canonical (ordinal) Möbius transform* is taken as m_*. Formula (5.53) was first proposed as the (ordinal) Möbius transform of a capacity by Marichal *et al.* [283], and Mesiar [302] independently. A theory of the Möbius transform on symmetric ordered structures using operators $\oslash, \ominus$, leading in particular to Proposition 5.71, was developed by Grabisch [156].

Although many properties of the classical Möbius transform are preserved for the canonical Möbius transform, some of them are lost, in particular m_* is not maxitive as expected: $m_*^{\mu \vee \mu'} \neq m_*^{\mu} \vee m_*^{\mu'}$. Also, m_* is always nonnegative; see [154, 156] for details.

5.5.3 *Properties of the Sugeno integral*

We begin with specific properties of the Sugeno integral.

Proposition 5.73. *Let* $\mathbb{I} = [0, \mu([n])]$. *The Sugeno integral satisfies the following properties:*

(i) *For any* $A \subseteq [n]$, *any game* v *on* $[n]$, $\mathcal{S}_v(1_A) = v(A)$.
(ii) *The Sugeno integral commutes with max–min combinations of nonnegative games: for any nonnegative games* v_1, v_2 *on* $[n]$, *any* $\lambda_1, \lambda_2 \in [0, \infty[$,

$$\mathcal{S}_{(\lambda_1 \wedge v_1) \vee (\lambda_2 \wedge v_2)} = (\lambda_1 \wedge \mathcal{S}_{v_1}) \vee (\lambda_2 \wedge \mathcal{S}_{v_2}),$$ (5.64)

$$\mathcal{S}_{(\lambda_1 \vee v_1) \wedge (\lambda_2 \vee v_2)} = (\lambda_1 \vee \mathcal{S}_{v_1}) \wedge (\lambda_2 \vee \mathcal{S}_{v_2}),$$ (5.65)

with the convention $((\lambda_1 \vee v_1) \wedge (\lambda_2 \vee v_2))(\varnothing) := 0$.

(iii) *The Sugeno integral satisfies comonotonic maxitivity and comonotonic minitiv-ity: for any comonotonic vectors* $\mathbf{x}, \mathbf{x}' \in \mathbb{I}^n$, *and any nonnegative game* v,

$$\mathcal{S}_v(\mathbf{x} \vee \mathbf{x}') = \mathcal{S}_v(\mathbf{x}) \vee \mathcal{S}_v(\mathbf{x}'), \tag{5.66}$$

$$\mathcal{S}_v(\mathbf{x} \wedge \mathbf{x}') = \mathcal{S}_v(\mathbf{x}) \wedge \mathcal{S}_v(\mathbf{x}'). \tag{5.67}$$

(iv) *Let* v, v' *be two nonnegative games on* $[n]$. *Then* $v \leqslant v'$ *if and only if* $\mathcal{S}_v \leqslant \mathcal{S}_{v'}$.
(v) $\mathcal{C}_\mu = \mathcal{S}_\mu$ *if and only if* μ *is a 0–1 capacity.*
(vi) *For any normalized capacity* μ *and any* $\mathbf{x} \in \mathbb{I}^n$, $|\mathcal{C}_\mu(\mathbf{x}) - \mathcal{S}_\mu(\mathbf{x})| \leqslant \frac{1}{4}$.

Proof. Properties (i), (ii) and (iv) are clear from Definition 5.59 and the proper-ties of $\vee, \wedge$ (mutual distributivity, nondecreasing monotonicity). For (5.65), use Equation (5.55).

(iii) For two comonotonic vectors, there exists a common permutation reordering them. Hence the same coefficients $\mu(A_{(i)})$ are used, and the result holds by mutual distributivity of $\vee, \wedge$. For (5.67), start from Equation (5.55).

(v) Suppose the capacity is 0–1-valued. Then the decumulative function $\mu(\omega \mid f(\omega) > \alpha)$ is a rectangle of height 1 and width a, $0 < a \leqslant 1$. Hence, the area under the decumulative function is a, and the intersection of the diagonal with the decumulative function has coordinate (a, a), which proves the equality of the integrals.

Conversely, take μ such that $0 < \mu(A) < 1$ for some $A \subset [n]$, and $0 < \alpha < 1$. Then

$$\mathcal{C}_\mu(\alpha \mathbf{1}_A) = \alpha\mu(A) < \alpha \wedge \mu(A) = \mathcal{S}_\mu(\alpha \mathbf{1}_A).$$

(vi) We prove this result using the definitions in the continuous case; see Figure 5.6. Let us fix $\alpha \in [0, 1]$, and consider some $\mathbf{x}$ such that $\mathcal{S}_\mu(\mathbf{x}) = \alpha$. This means that the decumulative function intersects the diagonal exactly at α. The smallest possible Choquet integral is obtained for $\mathbf{x}$ giving the decumulative function given by the dashed line, whose area below is α^2. Similarly the largest one is obtained by the decumulative function given by the thick line, with area equal to $1 - (1 - \alpha)^2$. The difference between the Choquet integral and the Sugeno integral is in both cases

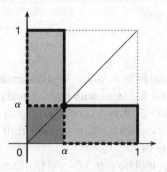

Figure 5.6 Proof of Proposition 5.73(vi)

$\alpha - \alpha^2$. This function attains its maximum value for $\alpha = \frac{1}{2}$, and then the difference is equal to $\frac{1}{4}$. □

Remark 5.74.   (i) Assertion (vi) was shown by Murofushi and Sugeno [326]. The idea of the proof used here is due to Denneberg.
(ii) The symmetric Sugeno integral satisfies none of the above properties, even with $\vee, \wedge$ replaced by $\oslash, \oslash$, except (i) of course. Property (ii), whose counterpart (linearity) holds for the Choquet integral, fails to hold due essentially to the nonassociativity of $\oslash$. This can be easily seen, taking normalized capacities $\mu_1, \mu_2, \lambda_1 = \lambda_2 = 1$, and a vector $\mathbf{x}$ such that $\mathcal{S}_{\mu_1}(\mathbf{x}^+) = \mathcal{S}_{\mu_1}(\mathbf{x}^-)$, and $\mathcal{S}_{\mu_1}(\mathbf{x}^+) > \mathcal{S}_{\mu_2}(\mathbf{x}^+) > \mathcal{S}_{\mu_2}(\mathbf{x}^-) > 0$. Then, applying (ii) above,

$$\check{\mathcal{S}}_{\mu_1 \vee \mu_2}(\mathbf{x}) = \left(\mathcal{S}_{\mu_1}(\mathbf{x}^+) \vee \mathcal{S}_{\mu_2}(\mathbf{x}^+)\right) \oslash \left(-\left(\mathcal{S}_{\mu_1}(\mathbf{x}^-) \vee \mathcal{S}_{\mu_2}(\mathbf{x}^-)\right)\right)$$
$$= \mathcal{S}_{\mu_1}(\mathbf{x}^+) \oslash \left(-\mathcal{S}_{\mu_1}(\mathbf{x}^-)\right) = 0,$$

$$\check{\mathcal{S}}_{\mu_1}(\mathbf{x}) \oslash \check{\mathcal{S}}_{\mu_2}(\mathbf{x}) = \left(\mathcal{S}_{\mu_1}(\mathbf{x}^+) \oslash (-\mathcal{S}_{\mu_1}(\mathbf{x}^-))\right) \oslash \left(\mathcal{S}_{\mu_2}(\mathbf{x}^+) \oslash (-\mathcal{S}_{\mu_2}(\mathbf{x}^-))\right)$$
$$= 0 \oslash \mathcal{S}_{\mu_2}(\mathbf{x}^+) = \mathcal{S}_{\mu_2}(\mathbf{x}^+).$$

To see that (iii) does not hold, proceed as for the symmetric Choquet integral (see Remark 5.37(ii)), and for (iv), the reasoning is also the same as with the symmetric Choquet integral. Property (v) obviously does not hold.

Proposition 5.75. *Let μ be a capacity on $[n]$, and $\mathbb{I} := [0, \mu([n])]$ for the Sugeno integral, and $\mathbb{I} := [-\mu([n]), \mu([n])]$ for the symmetric Sugeno integral. The Sugeno integral $\mathcal{S}_\mu$ and symmetric Sugeno integral $\check{\mathcal{S}}_\mu$ satisfy the following properties:*

(i) Continuity everywhere for the Sugeno integral, continuity on $[0, \mu([n])]^n$ and $[-\mu([n]), 0]^n$ for the symmetric Sugeno integral.
(ii) Nondecreasing monotonicity.
(iii) Unanimous increasing monotonicity if and only if μ is a 0–1 capacity (not valid for the symmetric integral).
(iv) Idempotency.
(v) Internality.

Proof. (i) Clear by continuity of $\vee, \wedge$. Since $\oslash$ is discontinuous on the antidiagonal, discontinuities may occur for functions with positive and negative parts.

(ii) Clear from Definition 5.59 and nondecreasing monotonicity of $\vee, \wedge$ when $\mathbb{I} = [0, \mu([n])]$. For the symmetric integral, the result holds too by (5.60) and nondecreasing monotonicity of $\oslash$.

(iii) If μ is a 0–1 capacity, by Theorem 5.64 and (5.48), we know that $\mathcal{S}_\mu$ is a lattice polynomial function which is unanimously increasing.

Conversely, assume that μ is not a 0–1 capacity, i.e., there exists $A \subsetneq [n], A \neq \emptyset$ such that $0 < \mu(A) < 1$. Let us define $\mathbf{x}, \mathbf{x}' \in [0, \mu([n])]^n$ by

$$x_i := \begin{cases} \mu(A) & \text{if } i \in A \\ 0 & \text{otherwise,} \end{cases} \qquad x_i' := \begin{cases} 1 & \text{if } i \in A \\ \mu(A) & \text{otherwise.} \end{cases}$$

Then $x_i < x_i'$ for all $i \in [n]$, and

$$S_\mu(\mathbf{x}) = 0 \vee (\mu(A) \wedge \mu(A)) = \mu(A) = \mu(A) \vee (1 \wedge \mu(A)) = S_\mu(\mathbf{x}').$$

(iv) Clear from Definition 5.59 and (5.60).

(v) Clear by (ii) and (iv).   □

Remark 5.76. Note that, contrary to the Choquet integral, these properties hold even if μ is not a normalized capacity (compare with Proposition 5.38). Increasing monotonicity properties of the Sugeno integral have been studied by Murofushi [323]; see also Marichal [267]. The Sugeno integral is never strictly increasing: take any nonempty proper subset A of $[n]$ and consider $\mathbf{x}, \mathbf{x}'$ as defined in the proof of (iii) above. Then $\mathbf{x} \leqslant \mathbf{x}'$ and $\mathbf{x} \neq \mathbf{x}'$, but $S_\mu(\mathbf{x}) = S_\mu(\mathbf{x}')$, whatever the capacity μ is.

Proposition 5.77. *Given a capacity μ, let $\mathbb{I} := [0, \mu([n])]$. The Sugeno integral S_μ satisfies the following properties:*

(i) *Symmetry (or neutrality, commutativity) if and only if μ is symmetric.*

(ii) *Additivity if and only if μ is a 0–1 additive capacity (Dirac measure).*

(iii) *Maxitivity if and only if μ is a maxitive capacity (possibility measure).*

(iv) *Minitivity if and only if μ is a minitive capacity (necessity measure).*

Proof. (i) Similar to the proof of Proposition 5.41(i).

(ii) If μ is a 0–1 capacity then $S_\mu = C_\mu$ by Proposition 5.73(v). If moreover μ is additive, then C_μ is additive by Proposition 5.41(ii), hence S_μ too.

Conversely, if S_μ is additive, then it is comonotone additive. Then by Proposition 5.73(i), Proposition 5.75(ii), and Theorem 5.46, it coincides with the (additive) Choquet integral C_μ, hence μ is additive too by Proposition 5.41(ii), and a 0–1 capacity by Proposition 5.73(v).

(iii) If the integral is maxitive, then μ is maxitive too by Proposition 5.73(i). Conversely, let μ be maxitive. Applying Proposition 5.86(v) and mutual distributivity of $\vee, \wedge$, we get

$$S_\mu(\mathbf{x} \vee \mathbf{x}') = \bigvee_{i \in [n]} ((x_i \vee x_i') \wedge \mu(\{i\}))$$

$$= \bigvee_{i \in [n]} (x_i \wedge \mu(\{i\})) \vee \bigvee_{i \in [n]} (x_i' \wedge \mu(\{i\})) = S_\mu(\mathbf{x}) \vee S_\mu(\mathbf{x}').$$

(iv) Works as (iii) applying Proposition 5.86(vi).   □

Remark 5.78. Only (i) holds for the symmetric Sugeno integral. Property (ii) obviously does not hold. To see that (iii) does not hold, take μ maxitive and $A, B \subseteq [n]$ such that $\mu(A \cap B) = 1$, $\mu(A \setminus B) = 0.5$, and $\mu(B \setminus A) = 0$. Then we have, by (5.60),

$$\check{\mathcal{S}}_\mu(\mathbf{1}_A \otimes (-\mathbf{1}_B)) = \mathcal{S}_\mu(\mathbf{1}_{A \setminus B}) \otimes (-\mathcal{S}_\mu(\mathbf{1}_{B \setminus A})) = 0.5 \otimes (-0) = 0.5,$$

$$\check{\mathcal{S}}_\mu(\mathbf{1}_A) \otimes \check{\mathcal{S}}_\mu(-\mathbf{1}_B) = \mu(A) \otimes (-\mu(B)) = 1 \otimes (-1) = 0.$$

(Property (iv) fails similarly.)

The Sugeno integral does not satisfy any of the scale invariance properties listed in Chapter 2. Despite its ordinal nature, it fails to be ordinal scale invariant. The reason is fairly obvious if we consider the expression of the Sugeno integral as a median; see (5.57). Changing only $\mathbf{x}$ by some automorphism φ on $\mathbb{I}$ without changing μ as well perturbs the result, which cannot be recovered by φ^{-1}. But if both are changed, then a property of ordinal scale invariance appears.

Let $\Phi[\mathbb{I}]$ be the set of all automorphisms (increasing bijections) of $\mathbb{I}$ onto itself, and let $\Phi_n[\mathbb{I}] := \{(\underbrace{\varphi, \dots, \varphi}_{n}) \mid \varphi \in \Phi[\mathbb{I}]\}$.

Proposition 5.79. *Let μ be a capacity and $\mathbb{I} := [0, \mu([n])]$ for the Sugeno integral, and $\mathbb{I} := [-\mu([n]), \mu([n])]$ for the symmetric Sugeno integral. The following holds.*

(i) *For any $\boldsymbol{\varphi} \in \Phi_n[\mathbb{I}]$ and any $\mathbf{x} \in \mathbb{I}^n$, we have*

$$\mathcal{S}_{\varphi \circ \mu}(\boldsymbol{\varphi}(\mathbf{x})) = \varphi(\mathcal{S}_\mu(\mathbf{x})).$$

(ii) *For any $\boldsymbol{\varphi} \in \Phi_n[\mathbb{I}]$ such that $\varphi(-\alpha) = -\varphi(\alpha)$, any $\alpha \in \mathbb{I}$ and any $\mathbf{x} \in \mathbb{I}^n$, we have*

$$\check{\mathcal{S}}_{\varphi \circ \mu}(\boldsymbol{\varphi}(\mathbf{x})) = \varphi(\check{\mathcal{S}}_\mu(\mathbf{x})).$$

(iii) *The Sugeno integral satisfies $\vee$-homogeneity and $\wedge$-homogeneity, i.e., for any $\alpha > 0$ and any $\mathbf{x} \in \mathbb{I}^n$,*

$$\mathcal{S}_\mu(\alpha \mathbf{1} \vee \mathbf{x}) = \alpha \vee \mathcal{S}_\mu(\mathbf{x}), \quad \mathcal{S}_\mu(\alpha \mathbf{1} \wedge \mathbf{x}) = \alpha \wedge \mathcal{S}_\mu(\mathbf{x}).$$

Proof. (i) Using (5.57), we get

$$\mathcal{S}_{\varphi \circ \mu}(\boldsymbol{\varphi}(\mathbf{x})) = \mathsf{Med}(\varphi(x_1), \dots, \varphi(x_n), \varphi(\mu(A_{\sigma(2)})), \dots, \varphi(\mu(A_{\sigma(n)})))$$

$$= \varphi(\mathsf{Med}(x_1, \dots, x_n, \mu(A_{\sigma(2)}), \dots, \mu(A_{\sigma(n)}))) = \varphi(\mathcal{S}_\mu(\mathbf{x})).$$

(ii) Since $\varphi(0) = 0$, we have

$$\check{S}_{\varphi \circ \mu}(\varphi(\mathbf{x})) = S_{\varphi \circ \mu}(\varphi(\mathbf{x}^+)) \ominus (-S_{\varphi \circ \mu}(\varphi(\mathbf{x}^-)))$$

$$= \varphi(S_\mu(\mathbf{x}^+)) \ominus \varphi(-S_\mu(\mathbf{x}^-))$$

$$= \varphi\Big(S_\mu(\mathbf{x}^+) \ominus (-S_\mu(\mathbf{x}^-))\Big) = \varphi(\check{S}_\mu(\mathbf{x})),$$

the next-to-last equality coming from the symmetry of φ.

(iii) Clear from Definition 5.59, (5.55), and mutual distributivity of $\vee, \wedge$. □

The symmetric Sugeno integral does not satisfy (iii).

Proposition 5.80. *Let μ be a capacity on $[n]$, and $\mathbb{I} := [0, \mu([n])]$. The Sugeno integral satisfies*

$$S_\mu(\mu([n])\mathbf{1} - \mathbf{x}) = \mu([n]) - S_{\overline{\mu}}(\mathbf{x})$$

for all $\mathbf{x} \in \mathbb{I}^n$.

Proof. We prove it in the general case (arbitrary space Ω, assuming measurability of f and $\mu([n]) - f$). We use the fact that for any numbers $x_i \in [0, a]$, $i \in J$, we have $\vee_{i \in J}(a - x_i) = a - \wedge_{i \in J} x_i$, and $\wedge_{i \in J}(a - x_i) = a - \vee_{i \in J} x_i$. We expand the right side:

$$\mu([n]) - (S)\int f \, d\overline{\mu} = \mu([n]) - \sup_{\beta \in \mathbb{I}} \big(\beta \wedge \overline{\mu}(\{\omega \mid f(\omega) > \beta\})\big)$$

$$= \mu([n]) - \sup_{\beta \in \mathbb{I}} \big(\beta \wedge (\mu([n]) - \mu(\{\omega \mid f(\omega) \leqslant \beta\}))\big)$$

$$= \inf_{\beta \in \mathbb{I}} \big(\mu([n]) - (\beta \wedge (\mu([n]) - \mu(\{\omega \mid f(\omega) \leqslant \beta\})))\big)$$

$$= \inf_{\beta \in \mathbb{I}} \big((\mu([n]) - \beta) \vee \mu(\{\omega \mid f(\omega) \leqslant \beta\})\big)$$

$$= \inf_{\alpha \in \mathbb{I}} \big(\alpha \vee \mu(\{\omega \mid \mu([n]) - f(\omega) \geqslant \alpha\})\big) \text{ with } \alpha := \mu([n]) - \beta$$

$$= (S)\int (\mu([n]) - f) \, d\mu.$$

The last equality follows from Definition 5.61 and Remark 5.62. □

This result proves that the Sugeno integral is self-dual if and only if μ is a normalized self-conjugate capacity.

5.5.4 *Characterization of the Sugeno integral*

Theorem 5.81. *Let $\mathbb{I} := [0, 1]$ and $F : \mathbb{I}^n \to \mathbb{I}$. Then there exists a unique normalized capacity μ, such that $F = S_\mu$ if and only if the following properties hold:*

(i) Comonotonic maxitivity.

(ii) $F(1_{[n]}) = 1$.
(iii) $\wedge$-*homogeneity.*

Moreover, μ is defined by $\mu(A) := F(1_A)$.

Proof. ($\Rightarrow$) Obvious from previous propositions.

($\Leftarrow$) Consider without loss of generality $\mathbf{x} \in \mathbb{I}^n$ such that $x_1 \leqslant x_2 \leqslant \cdots \leqslant x_n$ (if not, apply some permutation on $[n]$). It is easy to check that

$$\mathbf{x} = \bigvee_{i=1}^{n} \left(x_i \wedge 1_{A_i} \right),$$

with $A_i := \{i, i+1, \ldots, n\}$. Define $\boldsymbol{\xi}^i \in \mathbb{I}^n$ with $\boldsymbol{\xi}^i := x_i \wedge 1_{A_i}$, $i \in [n]$. Then $\boldsymbol{\xi}^i$ and $\vee_{j=i+1}^n \boldsymbol{\xi}^j$ are comonotonic vectors for $i = 1, \ldots, n-1$. Using (i), we get

$$F(\mathbf{x}) = F\left(\boldsymbol{\xi}^1 \vee \bigvee_{j=2}^{n} \boldsymbol{\xi}^j \right) = F(\boldsymbol{\xi}^1) \vee F\left(\bigvee_{j=2}^{n} \boldsymbol{\xi}^j \right).$$

Iterating this we finally get $F(\mathbf{x}) = \bigvee_{i=1}^{n} F(\boldsymbol{\xi}^i)$, and by (iii), we obtain that

$$F(\mathbf{x}) = \bigvee_{i=1}^{n} \left(x_i \wedge F(1_{A_i}) \right).$$

Let $\mu(A) := F(1_A)$, then clearly $F(\mathbf{x}) = \mathcal{S}_\mu(\mathbf{x})$. It remains to show that μ is a normalized capacity. We have immediately $\mu([n]) = 1$ by (ii). Let $\alpha \in]0, 1]$. Then applying (iii) and (ii), we have $F(\alpha 1_{[n]}) = F(\alpha \wedge 1_{[n]}) = \alpha \wedge F(1_{[n]}) = \alpha \wedge 1 = \alpha$. Now, using (i) we get $\alpha = F(\alpha 1_{[n]}) = F(\alpha 1_{[n]} \vee 1_\varnothing) = F(\alpha 1_{[n]}) \vee F(1_\varnothing) = \alpha \vee F(1_\varnothing)$. Hence $F(1_\varnothing) \leqslant \alpha$ for any $\alpha \in]0, 1]$, so that $F(1_\varnothing) = \mu(\varnothing) = 0$ since F is nonnegative. Finally, let $A \subseteq B \subseteq [n]$. Then $1_A \leqslant 1_B$ and $1_A, 1_B$ are comonotonic. By (i), we obtain that $F(1_B) = F(1_A \vee 1_B) = F(1_A) \vee F(1_B)$, which entails $F(1_A) \leqslant F(1_B)$. Hence, μ is monotone. $\square$

Remark 5.82. The nondecreasing monotonicity property is not needed. This was remarked by Rico [361], simplifying the result established by de Campos and Bolaños [77].

The next characterization is due to Marichal [267]. Still others can be found in this reference.

Theorem 5.83. *Let $\mathbb{I} := [0, 1]$, and $F : \mathbb{I}^n \to \mathbb{I}$. Then there exists a capacity μ on $[n]$ such that $F = \mathcal{S}_\mu$ if and only if F satisfies (i) nondecreasingness, (ii) $\vee$-homogeneity, and (iii) $\wedge$-homogeneity.*

Proof. ($\Rightarrow$) Obvious from previous propositions.

($\Leftarrow$) F being given, let us define a set function $\mu : 2^{[n]} \to [0,1]$ by $\mu(A) := \mathsf{F}(1_A)$. Properties (ii) and (iii) imply that $\mathsf{F}(0) = 0$ and $\mathsf{F}(1) = 1$, and since μ is monotone by (i), we deduce that μ is a capacity.

Consider $\mathbf{x} \in \mathbb{I}^n$. For any $B \subseteq [n]$, we have by (i) and (iii)

$$\mathsf{F}(\mathbf{x}) \geqslant \mathsf{F}\Big(\big(\bigwedge_{i \in B} x_i\big) 1_B\Big) = \mu(B) \wedge \big(\bigwedge_{i \in B} x_i\big).$$

This implies that

$$\mathsf{F}(\mathbf{x}) \geqslant \bigvee_{B \subseteq [n]} \Big(\mu(B) \wedge \big(\bigwedge_{i \in B} x_i\big)\Big).$$

Consider $B^* \subseteq [n]$ such that $\mu(B^*) \wedge \big(\bigwedge_{i \in B^*} x_i\big)$ is maximum, and define

$$A := \Big\{ j \in [n] \mid x_j \leqslant \mu(B^*) \wedge \big(\bigwedge_{i \in B^*} x_i\big)\Big\}.$$

We have $A \neq \varnothing$, for otherwise $x_j > \mu(B^*) \wedge \big(\bigwedge_{i \in B^*} x_i\big)$ for all $j \in [n]$, and since $\mu([n]) = 1$, we would have

$$\mu([n]) \wedge \big(\bigwedge_{i \in [n]} x_i\big) > \mu(B^*) \wedge \big(\bigwedge_{i \in B^*} x_i\big),$$

which contradicts the definition of B^*. Also, we have $\mu([n] \setminus A) \leqslant \mu(B^*) \wedge \big(\bigwedge_{i \in B^*} x_i\big)$, for otherwise we would have, by definition of A,

$$\mu([n] \setminus A) \wedge \big(\bigwedge_{i \in [n] \setminus A} x_i\big) > \Big(\mu(B^*) \wedge \big(\bigwedge_{i \in B^*} x_i\big)\Big) \wedge \Big(\mu(B^*) \wedge \big(\bigwedge_{i \in B^*} x_i\big)\Big)$$

$$= \mu(B^*) \wedge \big(\bigwedge_{i \in B^*} x_i\big),$$

which again contradicts the definition of B^*. Then we have, by (i) and (ii)

$$\mathsf{F}(\mathbf{x}) \leqslant \mathsf{F}\Big(\big(\mu(B^*) \wedge \big(\bigwedge_{i \in B^*} x_i\big)\big) 1_A + 1_{[n] \setminus A}\Big)$$

$$= \Big(\mu(B^*) \wedge \big(\bigwedge_{i \in B^*} x_i\big)\Big) \vee \mu([n] \setminus A)$$

$$= \mu(B^*) \wedge \big(\bigwedge_{i \in B^*} x_i\big) = \bigvee_{B \subseteq [n]} \Big(\mu(B) \wedge \big(\bigwedge_{i \in B} x_i\big)\Big).$$

Hence, by Proposition 5.63, F is the Sugeno integral. $\qquad\square$

5.5.5 *Particular Sugeno integrals*

We show in this section the relation of the Sugeno integral with other aggregation functions.

We begin by introducing several aggregation functions.

Definition 5.84. Let $\mathbf{w} \in [0,1]^n$ satisfying $\bigvee_{i=1}^n w_i = 1$, and consider $\mathbb{I} = [0,1]$. Then, for any $\mathbf{x} \in \mathbb{I}^n$:

(i) The *weighted maximum* with respect to $\mathbf{w}$ is the aggregation function defined by

$$\mathsf{WMax}_{\mathbf{w}}(\mathbf{x}) := \bigvee_{i=1}^n (w_i \wedge x_i).$$

(ii) The *weighted minimum* with respect to $\mathbf{w}$ is the aggregation function defined by

$$\mathsf{WMin}_{\mathbf{w}}(\mathbf{x}) := \bigwedge_{i=1}^n ((1 - w_i) \vee x_i).$$

(iii) The *ordered weighted maximum* with respect to $\mathbf{w}$ is the aggregation function defined by

$$\mathsf{OWMax}_{\mathbf{w}}(\mathbf{x}) := \bigvee_{i=1}^n (w_i \wedge x_{(i)}),$$

with $x_{(1)} \leqslant \cdots \leqslant x_{(n)}$, and $w_1 \geqslant w_2 \geqslant \cdots \geqslant w_n$.

(iv) The *ordered weighted minimum* with respect to $\mathbf{w}$ is the aggregation function defined by

$$\mathsf{OWMin}_{\mathbf{w}}(\mathbf{x}) := \bigwedge_{i=1}^n ((1 - w_i) \vee x_{(i)}),$$

with $x_{(1)} \leqslant \cdots \leqslant x_{(n)}$, and $w_1 \leqslant w_2 \leqslant \cdots \leqslant w_n$.

Clearly, $\mathsf{WMax}_{\mathbf{w}}$ and $\mathsf{WMin}_{\mathbf{w}}$ are respectively maxitive and minitive.

Remark 5.85. (i) The usual minimum and maximum are recovered from their weighted versions and weighted ordered versions when $\mathbf{w} = \mathbf{1}$. The weighted minimum and weighted maximum were proposed by Dubois and Prade [97], and their ordered versions were introduced in [102] by Dubois *et al.*

(ii) In the case of the ordered weighted maximum, since

$$\bigvee_{i=1}^n (w_i \wedge x_{(i)}) = \bigvee_{i=1}^n \left(\left(\bigvee_{k=i}^n w_k \right) \wedge x_{(i)} \right)$$

the assumption $w_1 \geqslant w_2 \geqslant \cdots \geqslant w_n$ is not necessary; however, it is useful in the next proposition. The same remark applies to the ordered weighted minimum.

Proposition 5.86. *Let μ be a capacity, and $\mathbb{I} = [0, \mu([n])]$. The following holds.*

(i) $S_\mu = \text{Min}$ *if and only if* $\mu = \mu_{\min}$.

(ii) $S_\mu = \text{Max}$ *if and only if* $\mu = \mu_{\max}$.

(iii) $S_\mu = \text{OS}_k$ *if and only if* μ *is the threshold capacity* τ_{n-k+1}.

(iv) $S_\mu = \text{P}_k$ *if and only if* μ *is the Dirac measure* δ_k.

(v) $S_\mu = \text{WMax}_\mathbf{w}$ *if and only if* μ *is a normalized maxitive capacity, with* $\mu(\{i\}) = w_i$, *for all* $i \in [n]$.

(vi) $S_\mu = \text{WMin}_\mathbf{w}$ *if and only if* μ *is a normalized minitive capacity, with* $\mu([n] \setminus \{i\}) = \mu([n]) - w_i$, *for all* $i \in [n]$.

(vii) $S_\mu = \text{OWMax}_\mathbf{w}$ *if and only if* μ *is a normalized symmetric capacity such that* $\mu(A) = w_{n-|A|+1}$, *for any* $A \subseteq [n]$, $A \neq \varnothing$.

(viii) $S_\mu = \text{OWMin}_\mathbf{w}$ *if and only if* μ *is a normalized symmetric capacity such that* $\mu(A) = 1 - w_{n-|A|}$, *for any* $A \subsetneq [n]$.

(ix) *The set of Sugeno integrals with respect to 0–1 capacities coincides with the set of lattice polynomial functions.*

Proof. Results (i), (ii), (iii), and (iv) hold by Proposition 5.50(i), (ii), (iii), and (iv) respectively, since the corresponding capacities are 0–1, hence, by Proposition 5.73, Choquet and Sugeno integrals coincide. They are also particular cases of subsequent propositions.

(v) Suppose μ is normalized maxitive, and define $w_i := \mu(\{i\})$ for each $i \in [n]$. This defines a weight vector $\mathbf{w}$ satisfying $\vee_i w_i = 1$. Consider the last k in the sequence $1, \ldots, n$ such that $S_\mu(\mathbf{x}) = x_{(k)} \wedge \mu(\{(k), \ldots, (n)\})$, and note that $\mu(\{(k), \ldots, (n)\}) = w_{(k)} \vee \cdots \vee w_{(n)}$.

First, we show that if $k < n$, then $w_{(k)} > w_{(i)}$ for $k < i \leq n$. Indeed, if there exists k_0 such that $k < k_0 \leq n$ and $w_{(k_0)} \geq w_{(i)}$, $i = k, \ldots, n$ we would have

$$S_\mu(\mathbf{x}) = x_{(k_0)} \wedge (w_{(k_0)} \vee \cdots \vee w_{(n)})$$

since $x_{(k_0)} \geq x_{(k)}$, and this contradicts the definition of k.

Assume that $S_\mu(\mathbf{x}) = x_{(k)} \leq \mu(\{(k), \ldots, (n)\}) = w_{(k)} \vee \cdots \vee w_{(n)}$. We have $x_{(k)} \wedge w_{(k)} = x_{(k)} \geq x_{(i)} \wedge w_{(i)}$ for $1 \leq i \leq k$. Also, $x_{(k)} \wedge w_{(k)} > x_{(i)} \wedge w_{(i)}$, $k < i \leq n$. Indeed, assume that there exists $k < k_0 \leq n$ such that $x_{(k)} \wedge w_{(k)} \leq x_{(k_0)} \wedge w_{(k_0)}$. Then

$$S_\mu(\mathbf{x}) = x_{(k)} \wedge w_{(k)} \leq x_{(k_0)} \wedge w_{(k_0)} \leq x_{(k_0)} \wedge \underbrace{(w_{(k_0)} \vee \cdots \vee w_{(n)})}_{\mu(\{(k_0), \ldots, (n)\})},$$

which contradicts the definition of the Sugeno integral or the definition of k. In summary,

$$S_\mu(\mathbf{x}) = \bigvee_{i=1}^{n} (x_{(i)} \wedge w_{(i)}) = \bigvee_{i=1}^{n} (x_i \wedge w_i) = \text{WMax}_\mathbf{w}(\mathbf{x}). \tag{5.68}$$

Assume on the contrary that $S_\mu(\mathbf{x}) = \mu(\{(k), \ldots, (n)\}) = w_{(k)} \vee \cdots \vee w_{(n)} \leqslant x_{(k)}$. We have $x_{(k)} \wedge w_{(k)} = w_{(k)} > x_{(i)} \wedge w_{(i)}$ for $k < i \leqslant n$ because $x_{(i)} \geqslant x_{(k)} \geqslant w_{(k)} > w_{(i)}$. Also, $x_{(k)} \wedge w_{(k)} > x_{(i)} \wedge w_{(i)}$ for $1 \leqslant i < k$. Indeed, suppose there exists $1 \leqslant k_0 < k$ such that $x_{(k)} \wedge w_{(k)} < x_{(k_0)} \wedge w_{(k_0)}$. Then

$$S_\mu(\mathbf{x}) = x_{(k)} \wedge w_{(k)} < x_{(k_0)} \wedge w_{(k_0)} \leqslant x_{(k_0)} \wedge \underbrace{\left(w_{(k_0)} \vee \cdots \vee w_{(n)}\right)}_{\mu(\{(k_0), \ldots, (n)\})},$$

which contradicts the definition of the Sugeno integral. Hence, again (5.68) holds.

Conversely, since WMax is maxitive, we know by Proposition 5.73(i) that necessarily μ is maxitive too, and $\mathsf{WMax}_\mathbf{w}(\mathbf{1}_i) = w_i = \mu(\{i\})$.

Result (vi) holds by (v) and duality (Proposition 5.80).

(vii) Take any weight vector $\mathbf{w}$ such that $\bigvee_i w_i = 1$ and $w_1 \geqslant \cdots \geqslant w_n$, and define a symmetric capacity by $\mu(A) = w_{n-|A|+1}$, for all $A \subseteq [n]$, $A \neq \varnothing$. Then, by Definition 5.59, we get

$$S_\mu(\mathbf{x}) = \bigvee_{i=1}^n \left(x_{(i)} \wedge \mu(A_{(i)})\right)$$

$$= \bigvee_{i=1}^n \left(x_{(i)} \wedge w_i\right) = \mathsf{OWMax}_\mathbf{w}(\mathbf{x}).$$

The converse is immediate since by Proposition 5.77(i), a Sugeno integral is symmetric if and only if μ is symmetric, and $\mathsf{OWMax}_\mathbf{w}(\mathbf{1}_A) = w_{n-|A|+1} = \mu(A)$ by Proposition 5.73(i).

Result (viii) holds by (vii) and duality (Proposition 5.80).

Result (ix) follows directly from Proposition 5.55 and the fact that the set function α can be chosen to be monotone; see Remark 5.56. $\qquad\qquad\square$

Results (vii) and (viii) clearly show that the class of $\mathsf{OWMin}_\mathbf{w}$ and $\mathsf{OWMax}_\mathbf{w}$ coincide.

Figure 5.7 shows the relation between various particular Sugeno integrals, summarizing results of Proposition 5.86. Observe that, as for the Choquet integral (Figure 5.2), this figure comes from Figure 5.1, taking only relevant parts of it. Comparing Figures 5.2 and 5.7 clearly shows the common parts between the two integrals, specifically the case of 0–1 capacities, which gives the lattice polynomial functions. Thus, we recover (v) of Proposition 5.73.

To end this section, let us remark that a multilevel Sugeno integral (defined by analogy with multilevel Choquet integral, see Section 5.4.7) is nothing but a Sugeno integral. This is due to Theorem 5.64, since combining idempotent weighted lattice polynomial functions always produces an idempotent weighted lattice polynomial function.

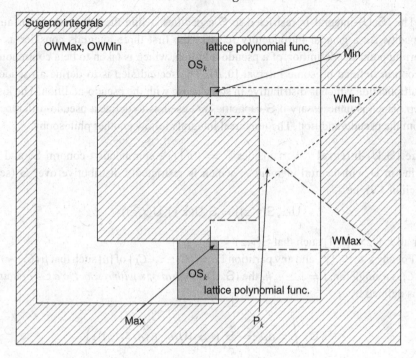

Figure 5.7 Relations between various particular Sugeno integrals

5.6 Other integrals

It is possible to define other integrals, by replacing the operations used in the definitions of Choquet and Sugeno integrals (Definitions 5.19 and 5.59) by more general ones, say pseudo-additions and pseudo-multiplications. Many studies have been done in this direction, starting from Weber [429], Kruse [239], and more recently by Sander and Siedekum [376–378]. The complexity of the topic, and the fact that such studies are done in a measure-theoretic framework and not from the viewpoint of aggregation functions, oblige us to keep to a minimum level of detail, and to restrict ourselves to the main ideas. The interested reader can consult the references we cite, and in particular the impressive analysis done by Sander and Siedekum [376–378].

We focus in the sequel on four approaches: the (S, U)-integral of Klement *et al.* [219, 220], the fuzzy t-conorm integral of Murofushi and Sugeno [327] (which will be called the *Murofushi integral*), the integral proposed by Benvenuti *et al.* [35] (which will be called the *Benvenuti integral*), which is a continuation of the work initiated by Sugeno and Murofushi [407], and finally a geometric approach to integration by Klement *et al.* [222], coinciding with the universal integrals of Struk [400]. Up to some minor details, these approaches include all previous efforts by Weber, Kruse, Imaoka and others.

The (S, U)-integral is restricted to S-capacities, while the others work for any capacity. As a general introductory remark, the first three integrals consider as a starting point the definition of a pseudo-addition, which is taken to be a continuous t-conorm defined on some interval $[0, B]$. The second step is to define a pseudo-multiplication which is distributive in some sense with the pseudo-addition. The last step, which is unnecessary if S-capacities are used, is to define a pseudo-difference from the pseudo-addition. The universal integrals follow another philosophy.

The (S, U)-integral We consider $\mathbb{I} := [0, 1]$, a continuous t-conorm S, and a uninorm U with neutral element e, which is restrictedly distributive over S (see Section 3.9), i.e.,

$$U(x, S(y, z)) = S(U(x, y), U(x, z))$$

for all $x, y, z \in [0, 1]$ such that $S(y, z) < 1$.

For any $\mathbf{x} \in [0, 1]^n$, and any partition $\Pi := \{C_1, \ldots, C_k\}$ of $[n]$ such that $\mu(C_i) < 1$ or C_i is a singleton, $i = 1, \ldots, k$, the (S, U)-*integral of* $\mathbf{x}$ *with respect to a* S-*capacity* μ is defined by

$$(S, U) \int \mathbf{x} \; d\mu := \mathop{S}_{j=1}^{k} \left(\mathop{S}_{i=1}^{m} \left(U(a_i, \mu(A_i \cap C_j)) \right) \right)$$

where $a_1, \ldots, a_m$ are all the values taken on by $x_1, \ldots, x_n$, and $A_i \subseteq [n]$ is the set of indices j such that $x_j = a_i$. This expression comes from the general definition in the infinite case, and it is proved that it does not depend on the particular partition chosen. Taking as partition the finest one, we immediately get the following, by definition of S-capacities:

$$(S, U) \int \mathbf{x} \; d\mu = \mathop{S}_{i=1}^{n} \left(U(x_i, \mu(\{i\})) \right).$$

The (S, U)-integral satisfies the following specific properties:

(i) If $U(S(x_i, y_i), a) = S(U(x_i, a), U(y_i, a))$ for all $i \in [n]$ and all $a \in [0, 1]$, we have

$$(S, U) \int S(\mathbf{x}, \mathbf{y}) \; d\mu = S\left((S, U) \int \mathbf{x} \; d\mu, (S, U) \int \mathbf{y} \; d\mu \right).$$

(ii) For every $a \in [0, 1]$

$$(S, U) \int U(\mathbf{x}, a) \; d\mu = U\left(a, (S, U) \int \mathbf{x} \; d\mu \right).$$

It can be shown that the pseudo-additive integral proposed by Sugeno and Murofushi in [407] (which differs from the Murofushi integral presented next) can be recovered from the (S, U)-integral if the pseudo-multiplication is associative and symmetric.

The Murofushi integral Since any continuous t-conorm is an ordinal sum of Archimedean continuous t-conorms (see Remark 3.92(iv)), Murofushi and Sugeno restricted their study to the case where the pseudo-addition is either the maximum operator or a continuous Archimedean t-conorm on the interval $[0, 1]$. The original feature of their approach is that they distinguish three spaces: the spaces of values for the integrand, for the measure, and for the integral, hence the following definition.

Definition 5.87. A *t-conorm system for integration* is a quadruple $(F, M, I, \odot)$ consisting of $F = ([0, 1], S_1)$, $M = ([0, 1], S_2)$, $I = ([0, 1], S_3)$, where S_1, S_2, S_3 are continuous t-conorms which are either the maximum operator or Archimedean, and $\odot : F \times M \to I$ is a pseudo-multiplication, i.e., an operator satisfying:

(M1) $\odot$ is nondecreasing in each place
(M2) $\odot$ is continuous on $]0, 1]^2$
(M3) $a \odot x = 0 \Leftrightarrow a = 0$ or $x = 0$
(M4) $S_1(a, b) < 1$ implies $(S_1(a, b)) \odot x = S_3((a \odot x), (b \odot x))$
(M5) $S_2(x, y) < 1$ implies $a \odot (S_2(x, y)) = S_3((a \odot x), (a \odot y))$.

(M4) and (M5) are similar to restricted distributivity of $\odot$ over S_1 and S_2. The additive generators of S_1, S_2, S_3 are denoted by k, g, h respectively, when they exist, and for convenience the t-conorm system is denoted by $(S_1, S_2, S_3, \odot)$.

There are two interesting types of such t-conorm systems. The first one is $(\vee, \vee, \vee, \odot)$, where $\odot$ can be, for example, any strict t-norm. The second type is when all three t-conorms are Archimedean. Then it can be proved that $\odot$ is either identically 1 on $]0, 1]^2$, or given by

$$a \odot x = h^{(-1)}(k(a)g(x))$$

for all $a, x \in [0, 1]$, where $h^{(-1)}(x) := h^{-1}(x \wedge h(1))$ is the pseudo-inverse of h; see Definition 3.12, and (3.39).

Definition 5.88 (Definition 9.1). For any t-conorm S, its associated S-*difference* $\overset{S}{-}$ is defined by

$$a \overset{S}{-} b := \inf\{c \mid S(b, c) \geqslant a\}$$

for any (a, b) in $[0, 1]^2$.

The two noteworthy cases are when $S = \vee$ and S is continuous Archimedean with additive generator k:

$$a \overset{\vee}{-} b = \begin{cases} a & \text{if } a > b \\ 0 & \text{otherwise,} \end{cases}$$

$$a \overset{S}{-} b = k^{-1}(0 \vee (k(a) - k(b))).$$

(See Section 9.1 for more details.)

Definition 5.89. Let $\mathcal{S} := (\mathsf{S}_1, \mathsf{S}_2, \mathsf{S}_3, \odot)$ be a t-conorm system for integration, μ be a capacity on $[n]$, and $\mathbf{x} \in [0,1]^n$. The *Murofushi integral* of $\mathbf{x}$ with respect to μ is defined by

$$\mathcal{M}_\mu^{\mathcal{S}}(\mathbf{x}) := \mathop{\mathsf{S}_3}_{i=1}^{n} (x_{\sigma(i)} \overset{\mathsf{S}_1}{-} x_{\sigma(i-1)}) \odot \mu(A_{\sigma(i)})$$

with the same notation as in Definition 5.19.

It is not difficult to see that the Choquet and Sugeno integrals correspond to the t-conorm systems $(\mathsf{S}_\mathsf{L}, \mathsf{S}_\mathsf{L}, \mathsf{S}_\mathsf{L}, \mathsf{T}_\mathsf{P})$ (i.e., the bounded sum and the product), and $(\vee, \vee, \vee, \wedge)$ respectively. More generally, the system $(\vee, \vee, \vee, \odot)$ leads to an integral which can be written in the general case as

$$(\vee, \vee, \vee, \odot) \int f \, d\mu = \sup_{\alpha \in [0,1]} \left(\alpha \odot \mu(\{\omega \mid f(\omega) > \alpha\}) \right)$$

borrowing notation from Definition 5.61. If the t-conorm system is Archimedean, then we obtain, again in the general case,

$$(\mathsf{S}_1, \mathsf{S}_2, \mathsf{S}_3, \odot) \int f \, d\mu = h^{(-1)} \left((C) \int k \circ f \, d(g \circ \mu) \right).$$

Remark 5.90. Let us consider the case where $\mathsf{S}_1 = \mathsf{S}_2 = \mathsf{S}_3 =: \mathsf{S}$, and $\odot$ is a t-norm T. Since restricted distributivity is required, by Theorem 3.120, we know that T and S necessarily have the form

$$\mathsf{T} = (< 0, a, \mathsf{T}_1 >, < a, 1, \mathsf{T}^* >),$$
$$\mathsf{S} = (< a, 1, \mathsf{S}^* >),$$

where $a \in [0,1]$, T_1 is a strict t-norm, and S^* is a nilpotent t-conorm such that its additive generator s^* satisfying $s^*(1) = 1$ is a multiplicative generator of T^*. Two particular cases arise: if $a = 0$, S is any nilpotent t-conorm (e.g., the bounded sum), and $\odot$ the corresponding t-norm (e.g., the product), while if $a = 1$, $\mathsf{S} = \mathsf{Max}$ and $\odot$ is any strict t-norm.

The Benvenuti integral   We consider an interval $[0, B]$ and a pseudo-addition $\oplus : [0, B]^2 \to [0, B]$ defined as an operator that is associative, nondecreasing and continuous in each place, with neutral element 0. Hence, $\oplus$ is isomorphic to some continuous t-conorm on $[0, 1]$, which can be written as an ordinal sum of Archimedean continuous t-conorms. Here we use the $\oplus$-difference defined similarly to the S-difference used for the Murofushi integral, and we denote it by $\ominus$.

A *pseudo-multiplication fitting with* $\oplus$ is an operator $\odot : [0, B] \times [0, M] \to [0, B]$ satisfying:

(B1) $\odot$ is nondecreasing in each place
(B2) $(\sup_n a_n) \odot (\sup_m b_m) = \sup_{n,m} a_n \odot b_m$ (continuity from below)
(B3) $a \odot 0 = 0 \odot a = 0$

(B4) $(a \oplus b) \odot y = (a \odot y) \oplus (b \odot y)$ (right distributivity).

Note that (B2) and (B3) are weaker than (M2) and (M3). On the other hand, the right distributivity is required on the whole domain, contrarily to (M4). To find all possible pseudo-multiplications fitting with a given $\oplus$ amounts to solving the following Cauchy functional equation for all y:

$$f_y(a \oplus b) = f_y(a) \oplus f_y(b)$$

with $f_y(a) := a \odot y$.

Definition 5.91. Let $\oplus, \ominus, \odot$ be respectively a pseudo-addition, its corresponding $\oplus$-difference, and a fitting pseudo-multiplication, μ be a capacity on $[n]$, and $\mathbf{x} \in [0, B]^n$. The *Benvenuti integral* of $\mathbf{x}$ with respect to μ is defined by

$$\mathcal{B}_\mu^{\oplus,\odot}(\mathbf{x}) := \bigoplus_{i=1}^n \left((x_{\sigma(i)} \ominus x_{\sigma(i-1)}) \odot \mu(A_{\sigma(i)}) \right)$$

with the same notation as in Definition 5.19.

Note that the expression of the integral is formally the same as the Murofushi integral, only the definitions of the operators change. The following theorem is an important characterization result of the integral in the general continuous case (see [35]), which contains previous characterizations of the Choquet and Sugeno integrals.

Theorem 5.92. *Let $(\Omega, \mathcal{A}, \mu)$ be a measurable space with μ a capacity that is continuous from below. Let $I : \mathcal{F} \to [0, B]$ be a functional, where $\mathcal{F}$ is the set of $\mathcal{A}$-measurable functions. Then I is a Benvenuti integral with respect to μ and $\oplus, \ominus, \odot$ defined as above if and only if*

(i) $I(a1_A) = a \odot I(1_A)$, $\forall A \in \mathcal{A}, \forall a \in [0, B]$.
(ii) $f = (f \wedge a) \oplus (f \ominus a)$ implies $I(f) = I(f \wedge a) \oplus I(f \ominus a)$, $\forall a \in [0, B]$.
(iii) I is continuous from below.

Property (ii) is a weaker condition than *comonotonic pseudo-additivity*, i.e., f, g comonotone implies $I(f \oplus g) = I(f) \oplus I(g)$, since $f \wedge a$ and $f \ominus a$ are comonotonic functions. It can be proved that the Benvenuti integral is monotone with respect to the integrand and comonotonic pseudo-additive.

The universal integral [226] There exist still more general notions of nonadditive integrals than those presented above. Let us consider $\mathbb{I} := [0, 1]$. According to Struk [400], a nonadditive integral (called *fuzzy integral* by this author) is a function I assigning a value $I(\mathbf{x}, \mu)$ in $\mathbb{I}$ to any $\mathbf{x} \in \mathbb{I}^n$ and any capacity μ, such that I is nondecreasing with respect to $\mathbf{x}$ and μ, $I(n \cdot x, \mu) = x$ for every $x \in \mathbb{I}$, and I is an extension of μ, that is, $I(1_A, \mu) = \mu(A)$ for every $A \subseteq [n]$.

This somewhat loose definition can be strengthened by considering those integrals satisfying $I(\mathbf{x}, \mu) = I(\mathbf{y}, \mu)$ whenever $\mathbf{x}, \mathbf{y}$ induce the same decumulative function (see Definition 5.21), i.e.,

$$\mu(\{i \in [n] \mid x_i \geqslant t\}) = \mu(\{i \in [n] \mid y_i \geqslant t\}), \quad \forall t \in \mathbb{I}.$$

We call these integrals *universal* (they are called "regular" in [400]). The fundamental point is that each universal integral I can be represented as a (possibly) nonadditive measure V on the Borel subsets of $]0, 1[^2$:

$$I(\mathbf{x}, \mu) = V(\{(\alpha, \beta) \in]0, 1[^2 \mid \beta < \mu(\{i \in [n] \mid x_i \geqslant \alpha\}),$$

with V satisfying

$$V(]0, t[\times]0, 1[) = V(]0, 1[\times]0, t[) = t, \quad \forall t \in [0, 1].$$

This geometric view of integration was first proposed by Klement *et al.* [222]. Roughly speaking, a universal integral computes a kind of area under the decumulative function. This general form allows the recovery of many known nonadditive integrals:

(i) If V is a σ-additive measure (i.e., a probability measure on the Borel subsets of $]0, 1[^2$), then V is in one-to-one correspondence with a 2-copula C; see Section 3.4. More precisely, V is a probability measure on Borel subsets of $]0, 1[^2$ with uniform marginal probabilities such that

$$V(]0, u[\times]0, t[) = \mathsf{C}(u, t),$$

i.e., any such V is represented by a joint distribution function whose restriction to $[0, 1]^2$ is just the copula C. Using the notation of Definition 5.19, we have two equivalent formulas for the integral I:

$$I(\mathbf{x}, \mu) = \sum_{i=1}^{n} \left(\mathsf{C}(x_{\sigma(i)}, \mu(A_{\sigma(i)})) - \mathsf{C}(x_{\sigma(i-1)}, \mu(A_{\sigma(i)})) \right)$$

$$= \sum_{i=1}^{n} \left(\mathsf{C}(x_{\sigma(i)}, \mu(A_{\sigma(i)})) - \mathsf{C}(x_{\sigma(i)}, \mu(A_{\sigma(i+1)})) \right),$$

with the convention $A_{\sigma(n+1)} = \varnothing$, and $x_{\sigma(0)} = 0$.

(ii) In the above σ-additive case, when C is a Frank t-norm, then the Imaoka integral is recovered [193, 194].

(iii) In particular, if C is the product, then V is the standard Lebesgue measure on $]0, 1[^2$, and I is the Choquet integral.

(iv) If $\mathsf{C} = \mathsf{Min}$ (greatest copula), V is uniformly distributed over the main diagonal, and I is the Sugeno integral.

(v) If $C = T_L$ (smallest copula), then V is uniformly distributed on the opposite diagonal, and I is the so-called opposite Sugeno integral; see Imaoka [193,194].

(vi) The Shilkret integral [390] can be recovered by taking

$$V(E) := \sup\{\mathsf{Min}(u, v) \mid (u, v) \in E\}.$$

This is an example which cannot be obtained by a copula (i.e., V is not σ-additive).

Final remarks

Remark 5.93. (i) Sander and Siedekum [376–378] have done a thorough analysis of integrals defined with respect to pseudo-addition and pseudo-multiplication, trying to keep the minimal set of conditions imposed on these operators. In particular, a key notion is the definition of distributivity on restricted domains, like in the work of Murofushi and Sugeno. The reader can find there an exhaustive study of properties of systems of operators with various conditions imposed on them.

(ii) Even if we restrict to S-capacities, the Murofushi integral covers the (S, U)-integral when U is a conjunctive uninorm. Indeed, $\odot$ is more general than a uninorm since it need not be symmetric nor associative, nor have a neutral element. On the other hand, condition (M2) is satisfied only by conjunctive uninorms.

(iii) None of the previous works address the problem of defining an integral for real-valued functions, that is, to define asymmetric and symmetric integrals. The underlying problem is to define suitable extensions of $\oplus, \odot$ on negative values. This problem is addressed in Chapter 9 of this book.

6

Construction methods

6.1 Introduction

There is a well-known demand for an ample variety of aggregation functions having predictable and tailored properties to be used in modeling processes. Several construction methods have been introduced and developed for extending the known classes of aggregation functions (defined either on $[0, 1]$ or, possibly, on some other domains). Obviously, new construction methods should be a central issue in the rapidly developing field of aggregation functions. In this chapter we present some well-established construction methods as well as some new ones.

The first group of construction methods can be characterized "from simple to complex". They are based on standard arithmetical operations on the real line and fixed real functions. The second group of construction methods starts from given aggregation functions to construct new ones. Here we can start either from aggregation functions with a fixed number of inputs (e.g., from binary functions only) or from extended aggregation functions. Observe that some methods presented are applicable to all aggregation functions (for example, transformation), while some of them can be applied only to specific cases. Finally, there are construction methods allowing us to find aggregation functions when only some partial knowledge about them is available. These extension methods are discussed in the last two sections of this chapter.

6.2 Transformed aggregation functions

The idea of transformation of aggregation functions can be clearly illustrated on the well-known relation of the two basic arithmetic operations of addition and multiplication. Indeed, addition Σ on $]-\infty, \infty[$ (respectively, on $[0, \infty|, | - \infty, 0], [-\infty, \infty])$ and multiplication Π on $]0, \infty[$ (respectively, on $]0, 1], [1, \infty|, [0, \infty])$ are related by the logarithmic transformation

$$\sum_{i=1}^{n} (-\log x_i) = -\log \prod_{i=1}^{n} x_i. \tag{6.1}$$

Formally, (6.1) can be rewritten as

$$\prod_{i=1}^{n} x_i = \varphi^{-1}\left(\sum_{i=1}^{n} \varphi(x_i)\right), \tag{6.2}$$

where $\varphi :]0, \infty[\rightarrow]-\infty, \infty[$ is given by $\varphi(x) = -\log x$. The relation (6.2) between Π and Σ can be generalized to construct new aggregation functions from a given one.

We present the following transformation construction method for n-ary aggregation functions only, though the extension to the construction of extended aggregation functions is obvious.

Proposition 6.1. *Let* $\mathbb{I}, \mathbb{J}$ *be real intervals and let* $\varphi : \mathbb{J} \rightarrow \mathbb{I}$ *be a monotone bijection. For* $n \in \mathbb{N}$, *let* $\mathsf{A} : \mathbb{I}^n \rightarrow \mathbb{I}$ *be an* n-*ary aggregation function. Then the function* $\mathsf{A}_\varphi : \mathbb{J}^n \rightarrow \mathbb{J}$ *given by*

$$\mathsf{A}_\varphi(x_1, \ldots, x_n) := \varphi^{-1}(\mathsf{A}(\varphi(x_1), \ldots, \varphi(x_n))) \tag{6.3}$$

is an n-*ary aggregation function on* $\mathbb{J}^n$. A_φ *is called the* φ-*transform of* A (φ-*conjugate in* [39, 40]).

Proof. The nondecreasing monotonicity of A on $\mathbb{I}^n$ as well as the same type of monotonicity of the bijections φ and φ^{-1} results in the nondecreasing monotonicity of A_φ on $\mathbb{J}^n$. Moreover, the surjectivity of φ and φ^{-1} with these bijections having the same type of monotonicity ensures that the boundary conditions are fulfilled by A_φ on $\mathbb{J}^n$ once they are fulfilled by A on $\mathbb{I}^n$. $\qquad\square$

Remark 6.2. (i) The transformed aggregation functions A_φ inherit the algebraic and topological properties of the original aggregation function A (and then φ is an isomorphism between $(\mathbb{I}, \mathsf{A})$ and $(\mathbb{J}, \mathsf{A}_\varphi)$), for example the associativity, symmetry, bisymmetry, existence of the neutral element and/or annihilator, continuity, strict monotonicity, etc. On the other hand, analytical properties of A need not be inherited by the transform A_φ, in general. This is, for example, the case of the Lipschitz property, difference scale invariance, homogeneity, additivity, linearity, etc.

(ii) Transformations can be applied consecutively, i.e., if $\mathsf{A} : \mathbb{I}^n \rightarrow \mathbb{I}$ is a given aggregation function, and $\varphi : \mathbb{J} \rightarrow \mathbb{I}$ and $\psi : \mathbb{L} \rightarrow \mathbb{J}$ are given monotone bijections, then A_φ is an aggregation function on $\mathbb{I}$ and hence $(\mathsf{A}_\varphi)_\psi$ is an aggregation function on $\mathbb{L}$. We have

$$(\mathsf{A}_\varphi)_\psi = \mathsf{A}_{\varphi \circ \psi}. \tag{6.4}$$

(iii) There are many examples of aggregation functions among those already introduced in the previous chapters, which can be seen as transformations of some other aggregation functions. For example, the geometric mean GM defined on

[0, 1] is the transformation of the arithmetic mean AM defined on $[0, \infty]$. Indeed, take $\varphi : [0, 1] \to [0, \infty]$, $\varphi(x) = -\log x$. Then

$$AM_\varphi(\mathbf{x}) = \exp\left(-AM(-\log x_1, \ldots, -\log x_n)\right)$$

$$= \exp\left(\frac{1}{n}\sum_{i=1}^{n}\log x_i\right) = \left(\prod_{i=1}^{n}x_i\right)^{\frac{1}{n}}$$

for all n-tuples $\mathbf{x} \in [0, 1]^n$, $n \in \mathbb{N}$. Here $-\log 0 = \infty$ gives the standard extension of the real-valued function log to an extended real-valued function. GM has annihilator $a = 0$ which corresponds to the annihilator $\varphi(a) = -\log 0 = \infty$ of AM on $[0, \infty]$.

6.2.1 φ-invariant aggregation functions

From Remark 6.2(ii), if $\mathbb{I} = \mathbb{J}$ and $\varphi : \mathbb{I} \to \mathbb{I}$ is a monotone bijection, starting from any (n-ary) aggregation function A on $\mathbb{I}$, A_φ and $A_{\varphi \circ \varphi}$ are also (n-ary) aggregation functions on $\mathbb{I}$. The bijection φ can be understood as a transformation of the scale $\mathbb{I}$, and then it is of interest when the corresponding transformation A_φ of A yields the same aggregation function as the original A, i.e., when $A_\varphi = A$.

Definition 6.3. Let $\varphi : \mathbb{I} \to \mathbb{I}$ be a monotone bijection, and let A be an n-ary (extended) aggregation function on $\mathbb{I}$ such that $A_\varphi = A$. Then A is called φ-*invariant*.

The next result is of interest with respect to the characterization of φ-invariance of an aggregation function; see Section 8.4.3.

Theorem 6.4. *For* $n \geqslant 2$, *let* $A : [0, 1]^n \to [0, 1]$ *be a continuous n-ary aggregation function. Then we have the following.*

(i) A *is* φ-*invariant for each increasing bijection* $\varphi : [0, 1] \to [0, 1]$ *if and only if* A *is a lattice polynomial function; see Section 5.5.1.*

(ii) A *is* φ-*invariant for each monotone bijection* $\varphi : [0, 1] \to [0, 1]$ *if and only if* A *is a lattice polynomial function with exchangeable conjunctive and disjunctive form, i.e., there is a system* $\mathcal{B}$ *of subsets of* $[n]$ *such that*

$$A(\mathbf{x}) = \bigvee_{B \in \mathcal{B}} \bigwedge_{i \in B} x_i = \bigwedge_{B \in \mathcal{B}} \bigvee_{i \in B} x_i.$$

Proof. For more details and proof of (i) we recommend [270]. Concerning (ii), it is enough to examine solutions of (i) which are self-dual, i.e., those lattice polynomial functions A for which $A = A^d$. $\quad\square$

Remark 6.5. (i) Part (i) of Theorem 6.4 was first shown by Ovchinnikov and Dukhovny [341], where they have shown that continuous aggregation functions on [0, 1] which are invariant with respect to all increasing bijections are characterized by the Choquet integral with respect to 0–1 capacities; see Section 5.2.2. However, this is only another form of the result of Marichal [270]. In part (ii) of Theorem 6.4, one can relate each n-ary continuous aggregation function on $[0, 1]$ invariant with respect to any monotone bijection of $[0, 1]$ to a self-dual 0–1 capacity μ on $[n]$ (i.e., $\mu(B) + \mu(B^c) = 1$ for any subset B of $[n]$).

(ii) Continuity requirement cannot be omitted in Theorem 6.4. For example, the binary aggregation function $A : [0, 1]^2 \to [0, 1]$ given by

$$A(x, y) = \begin{cases} y & \text{if } y \in [0, 1[\\ x & \text{otherwise} \end{cases}$$

is not a lattice polynomial function, though it is φ-invariant for each monotone bijection $\varphi : [0, 1] \to [0, 1]$. For more details we recommend [309].

(iii) Typical examples of aggregation functions on $[0, 1]$ invariant with respect to any monotone bijection of $[0, 1]$ are medians with an odd number of arguments, including all projections $P_i, i \in [n]$. Moreover, such aggregation functions are closed under composition of aggregation functions discussed in Section 6.3. So, for example, for $n = 4$, $A : [0, 1]^4 \to [0, 1]$ given by

$$A(\mathbf{x}) = \text{Med}(\text{Med}(x_1, x_2, x_3), x_2, x_4)$$

is an aggregation function on $[0, 1]$ invariant with respect to any monotone bijection of $[0, 1]$.

(iv) When dropping the continuity of A in Theorem 6.4, part (i), the class of all aggregation functions which are φ-invariant for any increasing bijection φ contains also the extremal aggregation functions $A_\perp$ and $A^\top$, extremal t-norm T_D and extremal t-conorm S_D, among others. A complete description of all such aggregation functions can be found in [309]. In particular, if $n = 2$ and $\mathbb{I} = [a, b] \subseteq \mathbb{R}$, then there are two aggregation functions φ-invariant for each (monotone) bijection $\varphi : [0, 1] \to [0, 1]$ (namely P_F and P_L). Moreover, there are exactly 68 aggregation functions which are φ-invariant for any increasing bijection φ, among which four of them are continuous ($P_F, P_L, \text{Min}, \text{and Max}$).

6.2.2 φ-duality

We are seeking the monotone bijections φ for which the equality $A = (A_\varphi)_\varphi$ holds for any aggregation function A. Of course, the identity function is a solution to this functional equation, as well as any involutive bijection, i.e., satisfying $\varphi \circ \varphi = \text{id}$; see Remark 6.2(ii). The following lemma shows that there is no solution other than involutions.

Lemma 6.6. *Let $n \geqslant 2$ be fixed, and let $\varphi : [0, 1] \to [0, 1]$ be a monotone bijection. Then for all n-ary aggregation functions A, we have $A = A_{\varphi \circ \varphi}$ if and only if φ is involutive.*

Proof. We only have to prove the necessity. Let $A : [0,1]^n \to [0,1]$ be given by $A(\mathbf{x}) := x_1 x_2$. Denote $\varphi \circ \varphi = \psi$. Then ψ is a monotone bijection on $[0,1]$ and $A = A_\psi$ means that $\psi(x_1 x_2) = \psi(x_1)\psi(x_2)$ for all $x_1, x_2 \in [0,1]$, which is the Cauchy functional equation. Due to [4], ψ is given by $\psi(x) = x^p$ for some positive constant p. However, then $AM_\psi = AM$ only if $p = 1$, i.e., $\psi = \varphi \circ \varphi = \mathrm{id}$, proving the result. $\square$

Assuming that φ is an involutive monotone bijection on $[0,1]$ different from the identity, it is easy to see that φ must be decreasing. Indeed, if φ were increasing this would mean that for some $x \in\,]0,1[$, either $\varphi(x) > x$ or $\varphi(x) < x$, and thus $x = \varphi(\varphi(x)) > \varphi(x) > x$ (or $\varphi(\varphi(x)) < \varphi(x) < x$). Therefore φ is necessarily decreasing. This leads us to the following definition; see Definition 2.104 for general domains.

Definition 6.7. Let $\varphi : [0,1] \to [0,1]$ be a decreasing involutive bijection. Then the mapping $\Phi : A \mapsto A_\varphi$ is called φ-*duality*. The function A_φ itself is called the φ-*dual* of A.

The next proposition gives a characterization of all monotone involutive bijections φ on $[0,1]$ different from the identity, and is due to Trillas [412]. As we have shown, these transformations are necessarily decreasing involutive bijections on $[0,1]$ and play the role of negations in fuzzy logic; see [143, 178].

Proposition 6.8. *A function* $\varphi : [0,1] \to [0,1]$ *is a monotone involutive bijection different from the identity if and only if there is an increasing bijection* $f : [0,1] \to [0,1]$ *such that*

$$\varphi(x) = f^{-1}(1 - f(x)). \tag{6.5}$$

The function f *generating* φ *is unique up to the transform* $\frac{1}{2} + \eta\left(f(x) - \frac{1}{2}\right)$, *where* η *is an odd automorphism of the interval* $[-1/2, 1/2]$ *(i.e.,* $\eta(-x) = -\eta(x)$*), i.e.,* φ *is generated by an increasing bijection* $f_1 : [0,1] \to [0,1]$ *if and only if*

$$f_1(x) = \frac{1}{2} + \eta\left(f(x) - \frac{1}{2}\right).$$

Proof. ($\Leftarrow$) Evidently φ given by (6.5) is a decreasing bijection on $[0,1]$. Moreover, for each $x \in [0,1]$,

$$\varphi(\varphi(x)) = f^{-1}(1 - f(f^{-1}(1 - f(x)))) = f^{-1}(f(x)) = x.$$

($\Rightarrow$) We already know from previous development that φ is necessarily decreasing. Define a function $f : [0,1] \to [0,1]$ by

$$f(x) := \frac{1 + x - \varphi(x)}{2}.$$

It is easy to see that f is an increasing bijection and satisfies $f(\varphi(x)) = 1 - f(x)$ and hence (6.5).

For the last part, see [119, p. 5]. $\qquad\qquad\qquad\qquad\qquad\qquad\qquad\qquad\qquad\square$

Example 6.9. (i) The most prominent involutive decreasing bijection N (we borrow this notation from fuzzy logic, where it is called the standard negation) on $[0, 1]$ corresponds to $f = \mathrm{id}$ in (6.5), and it is given by $N(x) = 1 - x$. The N-duality of aggregation functions on $[0, 1]$ is called for simplicity *duality* with notation $A_N =: A^d$ (this is Definition 2.104 with $[a, b] = [0, 1]$), i.e.,

$$A^d(\mathbf{x}) = 1 - A(1 - \mathbf{x}). \qquad (6.6)$$

(ii) Taking $\varphi(x) := \frac{1-x}{1+\lambda x}$ the *Sugeno negation*, with $\lambda > -1$, we can consider, e.g.,

$$f(x) = \frac{(\lambda x + \lambda + 2)x}{2\lambda x + 2} \quad \text{or} \quad f_1(x) = \frac{x}{\left(1 - \frac{1}{\sqrt{1+\lambda}}\right)x + \frac{1}{\sqrt{1+\lambda}}}.$$

Couples of dual aggregation functions are, for example, Min and Max, $A_\perp$ and $A^\top$, Med_a and Med_{1-a} for $a \in [0, 1]$, etc.

Remark 6.10. (i) Some aggregation functions are *self-dual*, i.e., with the property $A^d = A$. This holds, e.g., for the arithmetic mean AM, $\mathrm{Med}_{0.5}$, Med and all weighted arithmetic means WAM which are discussed in detail in Chapter 4. Several aspects of self-duality are discussed also in [136]; see also Definition 2.104 and Section 6.2.3 below.

(ii) Duality is especially important in Chapter 3, where t-norms and t-conorms are discussed, which are just dual functions to each other, while the classes of uninorms and nullnorms are closed under duality.

(iii) As already observed for φ-transforms, the dual aggregation function A^d inherits the algebraic and topological properties of A, with modifications in some cases. For example, if A has a neutral element e (respectively, an annihilator a), then A^d has a neutral element $1 - e$ (respectively, an annihilator $1 - a$); if A is left- (right-) continuous then A^d is right- (left-) continuous; if A is conjunctive then A^d is disjunctive (compare with Section 3.5).

(iv) Though the φ-duality can be simply called involutive φ-transform, to stress the connection of some distinguished classes of aggregation functions by means of these transforms, we prefer to keep the name "duality". We remark that on an unbounded interval $\mathbb{I}$ there exists a counterpart of the standard negation N (defined on $[0, 1]$) only if $\mathbb{I} = \mathbb{R}$ or $\mathbb{I} = [-\infty, \infty]$, in which case one can introduce $N(x) = -x$. For bounded open $]a, b[$ or closed $[a, b]$ intervals, one can introduce N as $N(x) = a + b - x$, see Definition 2.104, and in such cases only φ-duality can be applied.

6.2.3 Self-dual aggregation functions

Self-dual aggregation functions are also called *symmetric sums* by Silvert; see [391] or [96]. These functions are characterized by the equality

$$A(x) + A(1 - x) = 1,$$

which is fulfilled by all *n*-tuples $x \in [0, 1]^n$, $n \in \mathbb{N}$.

Modifying Silvert's result from [391], we obtain the following characterization; see [260].

Proposition 6.11. *An aggregation function* $A : [0, 1]^n \to [0, 1]$ *is self-dual if and only if there is an aggregation function* $B : [0, 1]^n \to [0, 1]$ *such that* $A = B^\sharp$ *where*

$$B^\sharp(x) := \frac{B(x)}{B(x) + B(1 - x)}, \tag{6.7}$$

with convention $\frac{0}{0} = 0.5$.

Proof. The necessity easily follows putting $B = A$. To see the sufficiency, observe that for any aggregation function B,

$$B^\sharp(0) = 0 \text{ and } B^\sharp(1) = 1.$$

Moreover, from the monotonicity of B, for any $x, y \in [0, 1]^n$ such that $x \leqslant y$ we have

$$B(y) = B(x) + \varepsilon$$

for some $\varepsilon \geqslant 0$, and similarly

$$B(1 - y) = B(1 - x) - \delta$$

for some $\delta \geqslant 0$. Thus

$$B^\sharp(y) = \frac{B(y)}{B(y) + B(1 - y)} = \frac{B(x) + \varepsilon}{B(x) + B(1 - x) + \varepsilon - \delta}$$
$$\geqslant \frac{B(x)}{B(x) + B(1 - x)} = B^\sharp(x);$$

and hence $B^\sharp$ is an aggregation function. Moreover, $B^\sharp(1 - x) = 1 - B^\sharp(x)$, and hence $B^\sharp$ is self-dual. $\square$

Some other methods of constructing symmetric sums are described in [260].

Example 6.12. (i) For the product Π, the corresponding symmetric sum $\Pi^\sharp$ is given by

$$\Pi^\sharp(\mathbf{x}) = \frac{\prod\limits_{i=1}^{n} x_i}{\prod\limits_{i=1}^{n} x_i + \prod\limits_{i=1}^{n}(1 - x_i)},$$

with the convention $0/0 = 0.5$, i.e., up to the cases when this convention should be applied, $\Pi^\sharp$ coincides with the uninorm E (3-Π-operator) introduced and discussed in Section 3.6.

(ii) Let $\mathsf{A} : [0,1]^n \to [0,1]$ be given by

$$\mathsf{A}(\mathbf{x}) = \begin{cases} \mathsf{AM}(\mathbf{x})/2 & \text{if } \mathsf{AM}(\mathbf{x}) < 1 \\ 1 & \text{otherwise.} \end{cases}$$

Then A is not continuous. However, $\mathsf{A}^\sharp = \mathsf{AM}$ is continuous.

(iii) It is obvious that any weighted arithmetic mean is also a symmetric sum. However, weighted arithmetic means different from the standard arithmetic mean are not symmetric aggregation functions.

6.2.4 More general transformations

Among several previously discussed aggregation functions recall the strict t-norms and the strict t-conorms. These aggregation functions are transforms of the standard addition on $[0,\infty]$ (see Theorem 3.36), and the relevant monotone bijection is then called an additive generator (due to Remark 6.2 and relation (6.2) the concept of multiplicative generators can also be introduced). A similar relation exists between the (weighted) quasi-arithmetic means and the (weighted) arithmetic mean, as already exemplified in the case of the geometric mean. The concept of additive (multiplicative) generators can be quite significantly generalized as given in Definition 3.10. Several special cases of this generalization are discussed in Section 3.2, see, e.g., Example 3.14(ii). The idea of additively generated aggregation functions can be exploited to generalize the method of transformation of aggregation functions. We formulate it for a fixed $n \geqslant 2$ and closed intervals only.

Proposition 6.13. *Let* $\mathsf{A} : [c,d]^n \to [c,d]$ *be an aggregation function and let* $f_1,\ldots,f_n : [a,b] \to [c,d]$ *be nondecreasing (respectively, nonincreasing) functions such that*

$$\mathsf{A}(f_1(a),\ldots,f_n(a)) = u < v = \mathsf{A}(f_1(b),\ldots,f_n(b)),$$

and for the nonincreasing case

$$\mathsf{A}(f_1(b),\ldots,f_n(b)) = u < v = \mathsf{A}(f_1(a),\ldots,f_n(a)).$$

Let $g : [u, v] \to [a, b]$ be a nondecreasing (respectively, nonincreasing) function such that $g(u) = a$ and $g(v) = b$ (respectively, $g(u) = b$ and $g(v) = a$). Then the function $A_{f_1, \ldots, f_n, g} : [a, b]^n \to [a, b]$ given by

$$A_{f_1, \ldots, f_n, g}(\mathbf{x}) := g(A(f_1(x_1), \ldots, f_n(x_n))) \tag{6.8}$$

is an aggregation function on $[a, b]$.

Proof. The nondecreasing monotonicity of A and the same type of monotonicity of functions $f_1, \ldots, f_n$ and g ensures the nondecreasing monotonicity of $A_{f_1, \ldots, f_n, g}$. Moreover, if all functions $f_1, \ldots, f_n, g$ are nondecreasing then

$$A_{f_1, \ldots, f_n, g}(a, \ldots, a) = g(u) = a$$

while

$$A_{f_1, \ldots, f_n, g}(b, \ldots, b) = g(v) = b.$$

A similar result is obtained in the nonincreasing case. □

Remark 6.14. For a monotone bijection $\varphi : [a, b] \to [c, d]$, put $f_1 = \ldots = f_n = \varphi$ and $g = \varphi^{-1}$. Let A be an arbitrary n-ary aggregation function on $[c, d]$. Then all requirements of Proposition 6.13 are satisfied and $A_{\varphi, \ldots, \varphi, \varphi^{-1}} = A_\varphi$. Thus (6.8) generalizes (6.3).

Example 6.15. For $i \in \mathbb{N}$, let $f_i : [0, 1] \to [0, 1]$ be given by $f_i(x) = x^i$. Moreover, let g be the identity on $[0, 1]$. Then for any aggregation function $A : [0, 1]^n \to [0, 1]$ the function $B = A_{f_1, \ldots, f_n, g} : [0, 1]^n \to [0, 1]$ given by

$$B(\mathbf{x}) = A(x_1, x_2^2, \ldots, x_n^n)$$

is also an aggregation function on $[0, 1]$.

6.3 Composed aggregation

The idea of composed aggregation has two different roots leading to two different composition construction methods.

6.3.1 Composition based on associativity

The algebraic origin of the first one is closely related to the notion of associativity, which requires the equality of the two possible ternary extensions of a given binary operation $*$, namely $(a*b)*c = a*(b*c)$. In the language of (aggregation) functions, the associativity (in the binary case), discussed in Section 2.3.1, is characterized by the equality

$$A(A(x, y), z) = A(x, A(y, z)),$$

which is then supposed to define also the ternary aggregation $A(x, y, z)$. Recall that in general form the associativity of an extended aggregation function $A : \cup_{n \in \mathbb{N}} \mathbb{I}^n \to \mathbb{I}$ is characterized by Definition 2.63, i.e., for any $n, m \in \mathbb{N}$, any $\mathbf{x} \in \mathbb{I}^n$ and $\mathbf{y} \in \mathbb{I}^m$ the following equality holds:

$$A(A(\mathbf{x}), A(\mathbf{y})) = A(\mathbf{x}, \mathbf{y}). \tag{6.9}$$

In general, the aggregation functions in (6.9) may differ on different positions, yet yield a (new) aggregation function.

Proposition 6.16. *Let $\mathbb{I}$ be a real interval, $n, m \in \mathbb{N}$, and let $A : \mathbb{I}^2 \to \mathbb{I}, B : \mathbb{I}^n \to \mathbb{I}$ and $C : \mathbb{I}^m \to \mathbb{I}$ be aggregation functions on $\mathbb{I}$. Then the composite function $D_{A;B,C} : \mathbb{I}^{n+m} \to \mathbb{I}$ given by*

$$D_{A;B,C}(x_1, \ldots, x_{n+m}) := A(B(x_1, \ldots, x_n), C(x_{n+1}, \ldots, x_{n+m})) \tag{6.10}$$

is an $(n+m)$-ary aggregation function on $\mathbb{I}$.

Proof. The nondecreasing monotonicity of the function $D_{A;B,C}$ follows from the non-decreasing monotonicity of the functions A, B and C. Moreover, if $\sup \mathbb{I} = u \in \mathbb{I}$, then

$$D_{A;B,C}((n+m) \cdot u) = A(B(n \cdot u), C(m \cdot u)) = A(u, u) = u.$$

If $u \notin \mathbb{I}$, then due to the boundary conditions fulfilled by A, for any $\varepsilon > 0$ there exists $(x_0, y_0) \in \mathbb{I}^2$ such that $A(x_0, y_0) > u - \varepsilon$. Similarly there exists $\mathbf{x} \in \mathbb{I}^n$ and $\mathbf{y} \in \mathbb{I}^m$ such that $B(\mathbf{x}) > x_0$ and $C(\mathbf{y}) > y_0$. The nondecreasing monotonicity of A ensures now

$$D_{A;B,C}(\mathbf{x}, \mathbf{y}) = A(B(\mathbf{x}), C(\mathbf{y})) \geqslant A(x_0, y_0) > u - \varepsilon,$$

i.e.,

$$\sup \operatorname{ran}(D_{A;B,C}) = u.$$

Similarly, the boundary condition concerning $\inf \mathbb{I} = v$ is satisfied by $D_{A;B,C}$, and thus it is an aggregation function on $\mathbb{I}$. □

Remark 6.17. (i) The construction (6.10) can be generalized by induction to the case of a k-ary outer aggregation function A and k inner aggregation functions $B_1, \ldots, B_k$ defined on n_1-,$\ldots, n_k$-dimensional input vectors, i.e., for $n = \sum_{i=1}^{k} n_i$ we obtain an aggregation function $D_{A;B_1,\ldots,B_k} : \mathbb{I}^n \to \mathbb{I}$ given by

$$D_{A;B_1,\ldots,B_k}(x_1, \ldots, x_k) := A(B_1(\mathbf{x}_1), \ldots, B_k(\mathbf{x}_k)),$$

where $\mathbf{x}_i \in \mathbb{I}^{n_i}, i = 1, \ldots, k$.

(ii) The construction (6.10) is also known as *double aggregation*, and it was investigated deeply in [54].

The construction (6.10) can be applied consecutively to construct an *n*-ary ($n \geqslant 3$), or an extended aggregation function from a given binary aggregation function; see Section 2.3.1.·

Corollary 6.18. *Let* $\mathbb{I}$ *be a real interval and let* $\mathfrak{A} = (A_n)_{n \in \mathbb{N}}$ *be a family of binary aggregation functions on* $\mathbb{I}$, $A_n : \mathbb{I}^2 \to \mathbb{I}, n \in \mathbb{N}$. *Define two mappings* $\mathfrak{A}^*, \mathfrak{A}_* : \cup_{n \in \mathbb{N}} \mathbb{I}^n \to \mathbb{I}$ *by*

$$\mathfrak{A}^{*(1)}(x) := \mathfrak{A}_*^{(1)}(x) := x,$$

$$\mathfrak{A}^{*(2)} := \mathfrak{A}_*^{(2)} := A_1,$$

and for $n > 2$,

$$\mathfrak{A}^{*(n)}(x_1, \ldots, x_n) := A_{n-1}(\mathfrak{A}^{*(n-1)}(x_1, \ldots, x_{n-1}), x_n)$$

and

$$\mathfrak{A}_*^{(n)}(x_1, \ldots, x_n) := A_{n-1}(x_1, \mathfrak{A}_*^{(n-1)}(x_2, \ldots, x_n)).$$

Then both $\mathfrak{A}^*$ *and* $\mathfrak{A}_*$ *are extended aggregation functions.*

Note that if $A_n = A$ for all $n \in \mathbb{N}$, we recover the backward and forward extensions; see Definition 2.65.

Remark 6.19. Extended aggregation functions constructed by means of Corollary 6.18 were introduced and discussed in [69].

Example 6.20. (i) For the binary aggregation functions GM and AM on [0, 1], the quaternary aggregation function $D_{GM;AM,AM} : [0, 1]^4 \to [0, 1]$ is given by

$$D_{GM;AM,AM}(x_1, x_2, x_3, x_4) = \frac{\sqrt{(x_1 + x_2)(x_3 + x_4)}}{2}.$$

(ii) For the binary arithmetic mean AM on any real interval $\mathbb{I}$, its forward extension $AM^* : \cup_{n \in \mathbb{N}} \mathbb{I}^n \to \mathbb{I}$ is given by

$$AM^*(\mathbf{x}) = \frac{(x_1 + x_2)}{2^{n-1}} + \frac{x_3}{2^{n-2}} + \cdots + \frac{x_n}{2},$$

i.e., AM^* is an extended weighted arithmetic mean on $\mathbb{I}$ given by weights

$$w_{1,n} = w_{2,n} = 2^{1-n} \text{ and } w_{i,n} = 2^{i-1-n} \text{ for } i = 3, \ldots, n.$$

Similarly, the backward extension AM_* is an extended weighted arithmetic mean on $\mathbb{I}$ with weights

$$w_{i,n} = 2^{-i}, i = 1, \ldots, n - 2 \text{ and } w_{n-1,n} = w_{n,n} = 2^{1-n}.$$

(iii) For a real interval $\mathbb{I}$ and for $n \in \mathbb{N}$, let $A_n : \mathbb{I}^2 \to \mathbb{I}$ be given by

$$A_n(x, y) = \frac{nx + y}{n + 1}.$$

For the family $\mathfrak{A} = (A_n)_{n\in\mathbb{N}}$, the mapping $\mathfrak{A}^* : \cup_{n\in\mathbb{N}}\mathbb{I}^n \to \mathbb{I}$ introduced in Corollary 6.18 is just the extended arithmetic mean on $\mathbb{I}$, $\mathfrak{A}^* = \mathsf{AM}$. On the other hand, $\mathfrak{A}_* : \cup_{n\in\mathbb{N}}\mathbb{I}^n \to \mathbb{I}$ is an extended weighted mean on $\mathbb{I}$ with weights

$$w_{i,n} = \frac{(n-i)(n-i)!}{n!}$$

for $i \in [n-1]$, and $w_{n,n} = 1/n!$.

6.3.2 Composition of functions

The second root of composition-based constructions of aggregation functions comes from the standard composition of real functions.

Proposition 6.21. *Let $\mathbb{I}$ be a real interval and let $k, n \in \mathbb{N} \setminus \{1\}$. Let $\mathsf{A} : \mathbb{I}^k \to \mathbb{I}$ and $\mathsf{B}_1, \ldots, \mathsf{B}_k : \mathbb{I}^n \to \mathbb{I}$ be aggregation functions. Then the function $\mathsf{C} = \mathsf{A}(\mathsf{B}_1, \ldots, \mathsf{B}_k) : \mathbb{I}^n \to \mathbb{I}$ given by*

$$\mathsf{C}(\mathbf{x}) := \mathsf{A}(\mathsf{B}_1(\mathbf{x}), \ldots, \mathsf{B}_k(\mathbf{x})) \tag{6.11}$$

is an n-ary aggregation function on $\mathbb{I}$.

The proof is similar to the proof of Proposition 6.16, and is therefore omitted.

Example 6.22. (i) Let A in (6.11) be a weighted arithmetic mean with weights $w_1, \ldots, w_k$. Then the function C given by (6.11) is the well-known convex combination (convex sum) of aggregation functions $\mathsf{B}_1, \ldots, \mathsf{B}_k$,

$$\mathsf{C} = \sum_{i=1}^{k} w_i \mathsf{B}_i.$$

(ii) The class of nullnorms discussed in Section 3.7 is obtained by the construction (6.11). Indeed, due to Proposition 3.107, V is a nullnorm with an annihilator a in $]0, 1[$ if and only if $\mathsf{V}(\mathbf{x}) = \mathsf{A}(\mathsf{B}_1(\mathbf{x}), \mathsf{B}_2(\mathbf{x}))$, where $\mathsf{A} : [0, 1]^2 \to [0, 1]$ is the a-median,

$$\mathsf{A}(x, y) = \mathsf{Med}_a(x, y) := \mathsf{Med}(x, y, a),$$

and B_1 and B_2 are a t-norm and a t-conorm, respectively.

An essential difference between composition-based constructions (6.10) and (6.11) is in the formal occurrence of single inputs x_i in the composed aggregation. Indeed, in (6.10) each input x_i is aggregated by exactly one inner function B or C (in the extended version described in Remark 6.17(i) by exactly one B_j). On the other hand, in the case (6.11), each input x_i is aggregated by any of the involved inner aggregation functions $\mathsf{B}_1, \ldots, \mathsf{B}_k$. Several intermediate approaches can be introduced, too. For example, the n-ary lattice polynomial functions [270] (see also Theorem 6.4) can be characterized in the disjunctive form as composite functions $L : [0, 1]^n \to [0, 1]$,

$$L(\mathbf{x}) = \text{Max}(\text{Min}(\mathbf{z}_1), \ldots, \text{Min}(\mathbf{z}_k)), \tag{6.12}$$

where $k \in \mathbb{N}$ and the vectors $\mathbf{z}_i$ are obtained as projections of the input vector $\mathbf{x}$ to index subsets $K_1, \ldots, K_k \subseteq [n]$. For $n = 3$, let $K_1 = \{1, 2\}, K_2 = \{2, 3\}$, and $K_3 = \{1, 3\}$. Applying (6.12), we have

$$A(x_1, x_2, x_3) = \text{Max}(\text{Min}(x_1, x_2), \text{Min}(x_2, x_3), \text{Min}(x_1, x_3))$$
$$= \text{Med}(x_1, x_2, x_3).$$

Related generalized composition methods are the 2-level Choquet integral (see Definition 5.52) and its generalizations discussed in [130, 315].

Finally, we recall a rather peculiar composition-based method proposed in [318].

Definition 6.23. Let $A, B : \cup_{n \in \mathbb{N}}[0, 1]^n \to [0, 1]$ be two idempotent aggregation functions, and assume that A is symmetric. For any $k \in \mathbb{N}$, the aggregation function $A_k^B : \cup_{n \in \mathbb{N}}[0, 1]^n \to [0, 1]$ given by

$$A_k^B(\mathbf{x}) :=$$
$$A^{(n^k)}\left(B^{(k)}(x_1, \ldots, x_1), B^{(k)}(x_1, \ldots, x_1, x_2), \ldots, B^{(k)}(x_n, \ldots, x_n)\right) \tag{6.13}$$

is called a *k-Cartesian A–B product.*

The right-hand side in (6.13) runs over all points $(x_{\alpha_1}, \ldots, x_{\alpha_k})$, where α is an element of the Cartesian product $[n]^k$.

Remark 6.24. Observe that while in the composition of aggregation functions given in (6.11) the number of inner aggregation functions $B_1, \ldots, B_k$ is fixed, in (6.13) we apply B n^k-times. Note that $\text{Max}_k^B = \text{Max}$ and $\text{Min}_k^B = \text{Min}$ for any idempotent aggregation function B and $k \in \mathbb{N}$. Moreover, for any symmetric idempotent aggregation function A, we have $A_1^B = A$, independently of B.

Example 6.25. (i) Put $A = AM$ and $B = \text{Max}$. Then $AM_k^{\text{Max}} =: C_k$ is an ordered weighted averaging function which is generated by a nondecreasing quantifier $q(x) = x^k$, where

$$C_k(\mathbf{x}) := \sum_{i=1}^n \left| \left(\frac{i}{n}\right)^k - \left(\frac{i-1}{n}\right)^k \right| x_{(i)}, \tag{6.14}$$

where $(x_{(1)}, \ldots, x_{(n)})$ is a nondecreasing permutation of $(x_1, \ldots, x_n)$.

(ii) Similarly to (i), $D_k := AM_k^{Min}$ is an ordered weighted averaging function related to a decreasing quantifier $q(x) = (1-x)^k$, where

$$D_k(\mathbf{x}) := \sum_{i=1}^{n} \left| \left(1 - \frac{i}{n}\right)^k - \left(1 - \frac{i-1}{n}\right)^k \right| x_{(i)}. \tag{6.15}$$

(iii) Denote $AM_{1/k} := AM_k^{GM}$. Then

$$AM_{1/k}(\mathbf{x}) = \left(\frac{1}{n}\sum_{i=1}^{n} x_i^{\frac{1}{k}}\right)^k, \tag{6.16}$$

i.e., $AM_{1/k}$ is a root-mean-power function (special quasi-arithmetic mean).

(iv) The function GM_k^{AM}, $k > 1$, is a new function not belonging to any of the classes discussed in the previous and next sections. For example, for $k = 2$ we obtain

$$GM_2^{AM}(x,y) = \left(xy \left(\frac{x+y}{2}\right)^2\right)^{1/4},$$

while

$$GM_3^{AM}(x,y) = \left(xy \left(\frac{2x+y}{3}\right)^3 \left(\frac{x+2y}{3}\right)^3\right)^{1/8}.$$

In general,

$$GM_k^{AM}(x,y) = \left(\prod_{i=0}^{k} \left(\frac{(k-i)x+iy}{k}\right)^{\binom{k}{i}}\right)^{1/2^k}.$$

6.4 Weighted aggregation functions

In several applications some weights (importances) are assigned to single inputs. This is for example the case in multiperson decision making when aggregating scores given by some experienced and some unexperienced jurymen.

6.4.1 Integer weights

One possible approach to how to incorporate (integer) weights into a symmetric aggregation is based on the following idea, which is given for a fixed number n of inputs to be aggregated. Let $m_1, \ldots, m_n \in \mathbb{N}_0$ be given integer weights and let $\mathbf{m} := (m_1, \ldots, m_n)$ be the corresponding nonzero weight vector. For a given symmetric aggregation function $A : \cup_{n \in \mathbb{N}} \mathbb{I}^n \to \mathbb{I}$, we can incorporate weights m_i as follows:

$$A_{\mathbf{m}}(\mathbf{x}) := A(m_1 \cdot x_1, m_2 \cdot x_2, \ldots, m_n \cdot x_n). \tag{6.17}$$

It is easy to check that A_m acts as an n-ary aggregation function on $\mathbb{I}$. Moreover, if $m_i = 0$ for some $i \in [n]$, then the value x_i has no influence on the global weighted evaluation output. Applying (6.17) to the arithmetic mean AM, we obtain the class of weighted means (with rational weights $m_i / \sum_{j=1}^{n} m_j$). Similarly, (6.17) applied to GM leads to the weighted geometric mean. However, applying (6.17) to the Max function, we get the function

$$Max_m(x) = \max\{x_i \mid i \in [n], m_i > 0\}.$$

Hence, if all weights m_i are positive, $Max_m = Max$.

The above cardinality-based approach of introducing weights into symmetric extended aggregation functions can be straightforwardly extended to rational weights in the case when the original extended aggregation function is not only symmetric but also strongly idempotent; see Definition 2.43. We follow the approach introduced for decomposable aggregation functions in [119] and for strongly idempotent aggregation functions in [53].

Proposition 6.26. *Let* $A : \cup_{n \in \mathbb{N}} \mathbb{I}^n \to \mathbb{I}$ *be a symmetric strongly idempotent aggregation function, and let* $v := (v_1, \ldots, v_n)$ *be an n-dimensional nonzero weight vector with nonnegative rational coordinates. Then the function* $A_v : \mathbb{I}^n \to \mathbb{I}$ *defined by*

$$A_v(x) := A_m(x),$$

where A_m *is given by (6.17) and* $m := kv, k \in \mathbb{N}$, *such that* m *is an integer weight vector, is a well-defined idempotent n-ary aggregation function on* $\mathbb{I}$. A_v *is called a* (*v*-)*weighted aggregation function* A, *and* $A_v = A_w$, *where*

$$w := \frac{v}{\sum_{i=1}^{n} v_i},$$

i.e., w *is a normalized weight vector related to* v *with sum of weights equal to 1.*

Proof. To see that A_v is well defined, let $m^{(1)} := k_1 v$ and $m^{(2)} := k_2 v, k_1, k_2 \in \mathbb{N}$, be two integer weight vectors. Then also $m := k_1 k_2 v$ is an integer weight vector. Due to the strong idempotency and symmetry of A, we have $A_m = A_{m^{(1)}}$ as well as $A_m = A_{m^{(2)}}$, i.e., $A_{m^{(1)}} = A_{m^{(2)}}$. Moreover, this argument proves also that $A_v = A_{rv}$ for any positive rational constant r. Putting $r = 1/(\sum_{i=1}^{n} v_i)$ one gets $A_v = A_w$. The nondecreasing monotonicity of A_v (for a fixed weight vector v) follows from the nondecreasing monotonicity of A, and similarly the boundary conditions for A_v are forced by the corresponding conditions (and nondecreasing monotonicity) satisfied by A. Finally, the strong idempotency of A ensures its idempotency and consequently also the idempotency of A_v. $\qquad\square$

6.4.2 Nonnegative real weights

The problem how to extend the last proposition for arbitrary (nonzero and nonnegative) weight vectors has several possible solutions, in general. Obviously, any weight vector $\mathbf{v}$ can be approached as a limit of rational weight vectors $\mathbf{v}^{(k)}, k \in \mathbb{N}$, i.e., $\mathbf{v} = \lim_{k \to \infty} \mathbf{v}^{(k)}$. However, the limit $A_{\mathbf{v}^{(k)}}$ of related weighted aggregation functions need not exist, in general, as shown in [53]. One of the possible ways to overcome this possible failure is by replacing the (possibly nonexisting) limit $\lim_{k \to \infty} A_{\mathbf{v}^{(k)}}$ by the (always existing) $\liminf_{k \to \infty} A_{\mathbf{v}^{(k)}}$.

Proposition 6.27. *Let* $A : \cup_{n \in \mathbb{N}} \mathbb{I}^n \to \mathbb{I}$ *be a symmetric strongly idempotent extended aggregation function, and let* $\mathbf{v} \in [0, \infty[^n$ *be an n-dimensional weight vector. For* $k \in \mathbb{N}$, *define* $\mathbf{w}^{(k)} = (w_1^{(k)}, \ldots, w_n^{(k)})$ *by*

$$v_i^{(k)} := \inf \left\{ \frac{m}{k} \,\middle|\, m \in \mathbb{N}_0, \frac{m}{k} \geq v_i \right\}, \quad \mathbf{w}^{(k)} := \frac{\mathbf{v}^{(k)}}{\sum_{i=1}^n v_i^{(k)}}. \tag{6.18}$$

Then $\mathbf{w}^{(k)}$ *is a normalized rational weight vector for all* $k \in \mathbb{N}$. *Define a function* $A_{\mathbf{v}} : \mathbb{I}^n \to \mathbb{I}$ *by*

$$A_{\mathbf{v}}(\mathbf{x}) := \liminf_{k \to \infty} A_{\mathbf{w}^{(k)}}(\mathbf{x}).$$

Then $A_{\mathbf{v}}$ *is an idempotent n-ary aggregation function on* $\mathbb{I}$, *which is called a (v-) weighted aggregation function* A.

Proof. The rationality of all weights $v_i^{(k)}$ introduced in (6.18) is evident, and thus the vectors $\mathbf{w}^{(k)}$ are normalized rational weight vectors. Moreover, for each $k \in \mathbb{N}$ and $i \in [n]$, we have

$$w_i + 1/k > v_i^{(k)} \geq w_i,$$

ensuring that each vector $\mathbf{v}^{(k)}$ is nonzero and that $\lim_{k \to \infty} \mathbf{v}^{(k)} = \mathbf{w}$. Consequently, also $\lim_{k \to \infty} \mathbf{w}^{(k)} = \mathbf{w}$. The result follows from the fact that for any sequence A_k of (*n*-ary idempotent) aggregation functions on $\mathbb{I}$ the function $A = \liminf A_k$ is an (*n*-ary idempotent) aggregation function on $\mathbb{I}$. □

Remark 6.28. When applying Proposition 6.27, the equality $A_{\mathbf{v}} = A_{c\mathbf{v}}$, where c is a positive real constant, holds by the construction of $A_{\mathbf{v}}$. Moreover, we can start the construction of weighted aggregation functions *a priori* based on normalized weight vectors.

Example 6.29. (i) Let $A : \cup_{n \in \mathbb{N}} \mathbb{I}^n \to \mathbb{I}$ be a quasi-arithmetic mean (see Section 4.2), i.e., there is a continuous strictly monotone function $f : \mathbb{I} \to [-\infty, \infty]$ such that

$$A(\mathbf{x}) = f^{-1} \left(\sum_{i=1}^n \frac{f(x_i)}{n} \right).$$

Applying Proposition 6.27, for any weight vector $\mathbf{v}$ we have

$$\mathsf{A}_{\mathbf{v}}(\mathbf{x}) = f^{-1}\left(\frac{\sum_{i=1}^{n} v_i f(x_i)}{\sum_{i=1}^{n} v_i}\right) = f^{-1}\left(\sum_{i=1}^{n} w_i f(x_i)\right) = \mathsf{A}_{\mathbf{w}}(\mathbf{x}),$$

where

$$\mathbf{w} = \frac{\mathbf{v}}{\sum_{i=1}^{n} v_i}.$$

Hence $\mathsf{A}_{\mathbf{v}} = \mathsf{A}_{\mathbf{w}}$ is a ($\mathbf{w}$-)weighted quasi-arithmetic mean.

(ii) Let $q : [0,1] \to [0,1]$ be a nondecreasing continuous function satisfying $q(0) = 0$ and $q(1) = 1$. For an arbitrary real interval $\mathbb{I}$, the mapping $\mathsf{OWA}_q : \cup_{n \in \mathbb{N}} \mathbb{I}^n \to \mathbb{I}$ given by

$$\mathsf{OWA}_q(\mathbf{x}) := \sum_{i=1}^{n} \left(q\left(\frac{i}{n}\right) - q\left(\frac{i-1}{n}\right)\right) x_{(i)}, \qquad (6.19)$$

where $(x_{(1)}, \ldots, x_{(n)})$ is a nondecreasing permutation of $(x_1, \ldots, x_n)$, is an extended ordered weighted averaging function; see (1.19). Though OWA_q is not decomposable, in general, it is symmetric and strongly idempotent, and thus we can apply Proposition 6.27. For any normalized weight vector $\mathbf{w} \in [0,1]^n$, we then have

$$\mathsf{OWA}_{q,\mathbf{w}}(\mathbf{x}) = \sum_{i=1}^{n} \left(q(c_i) - q(c_{i-1})\right) x_{(i)},$$

where $c_i := \sum_{j=1}^{i} w_j$.

6.4.3 Qualitative approach

The approach to weighted aggregation as introduced in Proposition 6.27 can be understood as a quantitative approach (weights include the number of repetitions of inputs to be aggregated). A related approach for aggregation functions constructed by means of some optimization task will be introduced in Section 6.6. In the case of an extended aggregation function A with an extended neutral element e, we can apply another approach which can be called qualitative (weights include how the data should be transformed before aggregation). Its idea is based on transformation of an input x_i and the weight u_i into a new quantity $y_i = h(u_i, x_i)$ and then to aggregate these new quantities y_i by means of A. For deeper motivation, applications and some details on this approach (on the unit interval only) we recommend [259, 373, 436]. In this qualitative approach we deal with weight vectors $\mathbf{u} \in [0,1]^n$ such that $\mathsf{Max}(\mathbf{u}) = 1$.

Definition 6.30. Let $\mathbb{I}$ be a real interval and $e \in \mathbb{I}$ a fixed constant. Let a function $h : [0,1] \times \mathbb{I} \to \mathbb{I}$ satisfy the following conditions:

(i) $h(0,x) = e$ and $h(1,x) = x$;
(ii) h is nondecreasing in the second coordinate;

(iii) $h(\cdot, x)$ is nondecreasing for all $x \geqslant e$ and nonincreasing for all $x \leqslant e$.

Then h is called an *e-weighting transformation function*.

Proposition 6.31. *Let* $A : \cup_{n \in \mathbb{N}} \mathbb{I}^n \to \mathbb{I}$ *be an extended aggregation function with an extended neutral element* e. *Let* $h : [0, 1] \times \mathbb{I} \to \mathbb{I}$ *be an e-weighting transformation function, and let* $\mathbf{u} \in [0, 1]^n$ *be a weight vector such that* $\mathsf{Max}(\mathbf{u}) = 1$. *Then the function* $A_{h,\mathbf{u}} : \cup_{n \in \mathbb{N}} \mathbb{I}^n \to \mathbb{I}$ *given by*

$$A_{h,\mathbf{u}}(\mathbf{x}) := A(h(u_1, x_1), \dots, h(u_n, x_n)) \tag{6.20}$$

is an extended aggregation function on $\mathbb{I}$.

Proof. The nondecreasing monotonicity of $A_{h,\mathbf{u}}$ follows from the nondecreasing monotonicity of A and from nondecreasing monotonicity of h in the second coordinate. For any $x \geqslant e$, due to the property $\mathsf{Max}(\mathbf{u}) = 1$ of $\mathbf{u}$ and the fact that e is an extended neutral element of a nondecreasing function A, it follows that

$$A_{h,\mathbf{u}}(n \cdot x) \geqslant x.$$

Similarly, for each $x \leqslant e$ we have

$$A_{h,\mathbf{u}}(n \cdot x) \leqslant x.$$

The last two claims ensure that $A_{h,\mathbf{u}}$ satisfies the boundary conditions for an n-ary aggregation function on $\mathbb{I}$. $\qquad\square$

Example 6.32. (i) Each (binary) t-norm T (see Section 3.3) is a 0-weighting transformation function on the unit interval $[0, 1]$. Recall that each t-conorm S (see Section 3.5) is an extended aggregation function with extended neutral element 0. Then for each n-dimensional $\mathbf{u}$ such that $\mathsf{Max}(\mathbf{u}) = 1$, the corresponding function $\mathsf{S}_{\mathsf{T},\mathbf{u}} : [0, 1]^n \to [0, 1]$ is given by

$$\mathsf{S}_{\mathsf{T},\mathbf{u}}(\mathbf{x}) = \mathsf{S}(\mathsf{T}(u_1, x_1), \dots, \mathsf{T}(u_n, x_n)).$$

In the special case $\mathsf{T} = \mathsf{Min}$ and $\mathsf{S} = \mathsf{Max}$ we obtain the well-known weighted maximum (see Definition 5.84(i)), given by

$$\mathsf{Max}_{\mathsf{Min},\mathbf{u}}(\mathbf{x}) = \mathsf{Max}(\mathsf{Min}(u_1, x_1), \dots, \mathsf{Min}(u_n, x_n)).$$

(ii) For an arbitrary real interval $\mathbb{I}$ with a fixed element $e \in \mathbb{I}$, the function $h :$ $[0, 1] \times \mathbb{I} \to \mathbb{I}$ given by

$$h(u, x) = ux + (1 - u)e$$

is an e-weighting transformation function on $\mathbb{I}$. For $\mathbb{I} = [-1, 1]$, define an extended function $\mathsf{A} : \cup_{n \in \mathbb{N}} [-1, 1]^n \to [-1, 1]$ by

$$\mathsf{A}(\mathbf{x}) := \frac{\Pi_{i=1}^n (1 + x_i) - \Pi_{i=1}^n (1 - x_i)}{\Pi_{i=1}^n (1 + x_i) + \Pi_{i=1}^n (1 - x_i)},$$

with convention $0/0 = -1$. Then A is an associative extended aggregation function with extended neutral element 0 (in fact, a linear transform of the 3-Π-operator (see (6.3) and Example 3.102) from the unit interval $[0, 1]$ into interval $[-1, 1]$). For the 0-weighted transformation function h on $[-1, 1]$ given by $h(u, x) = ux$ and an n-dimensional weight vector $\mathbf{u}$ such that $\mathsf{Max}(\mathbf{u}) = 1$, the corresponding weighted aggregation function is given by

$$\mathsf{A}_{h, \mathbf{u}}(\mathbf{x}) = \frac{\Pi_{i=1}^n (1 + u_i x_i) - \Pi_{i=1}^n (1 - u_i x_i)}{\Pi_{i=1}^n (1 + u_i x_i) + \Pi_{i=1}^n (1 - u_i x_i)}.$$

(iii) On $[0, 1]$, take the aggregation function $\mathsf{A}_{\{c\}}$ (see (2.2)) with neutral element $e = c$ given by

$$\mathsf{A}_{\{c\}}(\mathbf{x}) := \mathsf{Med}\left(0, c + \sum_{i=1}^n (x_i - c), 1\right).$$

As an appropriate mapping h we can choose the mapping $h(u, x) = ux + (1 - u)c$. Then

$$\mathsf{A}_{\{c\}, h, \mathbf{u}}(\mathbf{x}) = \mathsf{Med}\left(0, c + \sum_{i=1}^n u_i(x_i - c), 1\right).$$

6.5 Some other aggregation-based construction methods

There are several construction methods for some special classes of aggregation functions. For example, the widely used additive continuous generators in the field of t-norms and t-conorms can be generalized to special noncontinuous generators. Then several surprising results, never appearing in the continuous case, may emerge, e.g., the existence of nontrivial idempotent elements. For interested readers we recommend the works of Viceník [418, 419, 421]. Similarly, transformations discussed in Section 6.2 can be further generalized applying noncontinuous or nonstrictly monotone functions, compare also with Proposition 6.13. However, to preserve some algebraic properties of the original aggregation functions, instead of standard inverse functions, so-called quasi-inverses and pseudo-inverses should be applied; see, e.g., [220, 384].

In this section we summarize some other construction methods yielding a new aggregation function from some given aggregation functions. The lack of some property for an aggregation function A can be compensated by forcing that property by some relevant construction method modifying A (see, e.g., idempotization described in Proposition 2.46), and symmetrization; see Section 2.2.3. We recall here four construction methods.

6.5.1 Idempotization

Recall that the basic (standard, classical) aggregation functions defined on some specific subsets of the real line are functions related to addition, multiplication, minimization, and maximization. All these functions are continuous, symmetric, associative and unanimously increasing; see Definition 2.5. These functions are the background for many other (continuous, symmetric) aggregation functions. For example, the arithmetic mean AM and the geometric mean GM are results of idempotization of the sum and product, respectively.

We summarize Proposition 2.46 and Corollary 2.47.

Proposition 6.33. *A function* $\mathsf{F} : \mathbb{I}^n \to \overline{\mathbb{R}}$ *is idempotizable if and only if* δ_F *is strictly increasing and there is a function* $\mathsf{G} : \mathbb{I}^n \to \mathbb{I}$ *such that* $\mathsf{F} = \delta_\mathsf{F} \circ \mathsf{G}$. *Moreover,* G *is idempotent and is given by* $\mathsf{G} = \delta_\mathsf{F}^{-1} \circ \mathsf{F}$.

Example 6.34. (i) Applying Proposition 6.33 to the sum function Σ defined on $[0, \infty]$ (or on $[-\infty, 0]$, $[-\infty, \infty]$) we obtain the standard arithmetic mean AM. Indeed, we have $\delta_\Sigma(x) = nx$, and thus $\mathsf{G} = \delta_\Sigma^{-1} \circ \Sigma = \mathsf{AM}$.

(ii) Similarly, starting from the product function Π defined either on $[0, 1]$ or $[0, \infty]$, by the described procedure we get the geometric mean GM.

(iii) The idempotization of the function Q given by $\mathsf{Q}(\mathbf{x}) := \prod_{i=1}^{n} x_i^i$ leads to the weighted geometric mean

$$\mathsf{GM}_\Delta : [0, 1]^n \to [0, 1], \quad \mathsf{GM}_\Delta(\mathbf{x}) = \prod_{i=1}^{n} x_i^{w_{in}},$$

with weights $w_{in} = \frac{2i}{n(n+1)}$, $i \in [n]$, $n \in \mathbb{N}$.

(iv) From the nonstandard examples take, e.g., the Einstein sum $\mathsf{S}_2^\mathbf{H}$ (see Example 3.103), whose binary form is

$$\mathsf{S}_2^\mathbf{H}(x, y) = \frac{x + y}{1 + xy}.$$

Applying Proposition 6.33, we obtain an idempotent aggregation function A, whose binary form is

$$\mathsf{A}(x, y) = \frac{1 + xy - \sqrt{(1 - x^2)(1 - y^2)}}{x + y}, \quad (x, y) \neq (0, 0). \qquad (6.21)$$

Observe that this function is the quasi-arithmetic mean (see Section 4.2) generated by $f(x) = \log \frac{1+x}{1-x}$.

6.5.2 *Augmenting*

There may be several reasons for augmenting (or decreasing) the output given by a given aggregation function. For a deeper discussion of this topic we recommend [86]. Basically two approaches can be used. In the first one, we try to get the desired effect by means of some additional aggregation functions and some arithmetic operations.

Proposition 6.35. *Let* $A, B : \cup_{n \in \mathbb{N}} [0,1]^n \to [0,1]$ *be two extended aggregation functions on* $[0,1]$, *and let a nonnegative constant* b *be given. Define* $A_{bB}, A^{bB} :$ $[0,1]^n \to [0,1]$ *by*

$$A_{bB}(\mathbf{x}) := \mathsf{Max}\,\big(A(\mathbf{x}) - b(1 - B(\mathbf{x})), 0\big) \qquad (6.22)$$

and

$$A^{bB}(\mathbf{x}) := \mathsf{Min}(A(\mathbf{x}) + bB(\mathbf{x}), 1). \qquad (6.23)$$

Then $(A_{bB})_{b \in [0,\infty[}$ *is a nonincreasing family of extended aggregation functions with* $A_{0B} = A, \lim_{b \to \infty} A_{bB} = A_{\perp}$. *For positive* b, A_{bB} *is called a decreased* A. *Similarly, the family* $(A^{bB})_{b \in [0,\infty[}$ *is nondecreasing,* $A^{0B} = A$ *and* $\lim_{b \to \infty} A^{bB} = A_{\top}$. *For positive* b, A^{bB} *is called an augmented* A.

Proof is straightforward and therefore omitted.

Example 6.36. (i) Take the aggregation function Π and decrease it by means of its dual function Π^d. In the binary form we have for $A_\beta := \Pi_{\beta \Pi^d} :$

$$A_\beta(x, y) = \mathsf{Max}(0, xy - \beta(1 - x - y + xy))$$
$$= \mathsf{Max}(0, \beta(x + y - 1) + (1 - \beta)xy). \qquad (6.24)$$

A_β is a Sugeno–Weber t-norm with $\lambda = \frac{1 - \beta}{\beta}$ (Example 3.27(iii); see also [220]).

(ii) When augmenting Π^d by means of Π, for $B_\beta = \left(\Pi^d\right)^{\beta \Pi}$ we obtain:

$$B_\beta(x, y) = \mathsf{Min}(1, x + y - xy + \beta xy) = \mathsf{Min}(1, x + y + (\beta - 1)xy), \quad (6.25)$$

i.e., B_β is a Sugeno–Weber t-conorm (Sugeno λ-addition) for $\lambda = \beta - 1$; see Example 3.91(iii). Note that this means that B_β is a continuous Archimedean t-conorm; see Remark 3.92(ii). For more examples and applications of these aggregation functions we refer the reader to [85].

Remark 6.37. An alternative approach was proposed in [233]. In this approach, first the inputs are augmented (decreased) by means of some transformations and then the transformed inputs are aggregated by an aggregation function A, i.e.,

$$A_{\mathcal{F}}(\mathbf{x}) := A\big(f_1^{(n)}(x_1), \ldots, f_n^{(n)}(x_n)\big),$$

where $\mathcal{F} = \big(f_i^{(n)} \mid n \in \mathbb{N}, i \in [n]\big)$ is a family of $[0,1] \to [0,1]$ nondecreasing mappings with fixed points 0 and 1.

Example 6.38. Put $f_i^{(n)} : [0,1] \to [0,1], f_i^{(n)}(x) = x^{1/n}, n \in \mathbb{N}, i \in [n]$. As $f_i^{(n)}(x) \geqslant x$, we augment the input values. For example, the product will be transformed into the geometric mean, i.e., $\Pi_{\mathcal{F}} = \mathrm{GM}$.

6.5.3 Method of flying parameter

Having a parameterized family $(A_\alpha)_{\alpha \in [0,1]}$ of aggregation functions, the crucial task for application is the choice of a parameter α. If this choice depends on input values to be aggregated, we get *the method of flying parameter*. This idea has appeared already in [443], and can be formalized as follows.

Proposition 6.39. *Let* $(A_\alpha)_{\alpha \in [0,1]}$ *be a family of extended aggregation functions on* $[0,1]$, *nondecreasing with respect to* α, *and* B *be any extended aggregation function on* $[0,1]$. *Then* $A_B : \cup_{n \in \mathbb{N}}[0,1]^n \to [0,1]$ *given by*

$$A_B(\mathbf{x}) := A_{B(\mathbf{x})}(\mathbf{x}) \tag{6.26}$$

is an extended aggregation function.

Proof. The boundary conditions can be verified directly. To see the monotonicity, observe that $x_1 \leqslant y_1, \ldots, x_n \leqslant y_n$ implies $B(\mathbf{x}) \leqslant B(\mathbf{y})$ and due to the nondecreasing monotonicity of the family $(A_\alpha)_{\alpha \in [0,1]}$ we have

$$A_B(\mathbf{x}) = A_{B(\mathbf{x})}(\mathbf{x}) \leqslant A_{B(\mathbf{y})}(\mathbf{x}) \leqslant A_{B(\mathbf{y})}(\mathbf{y}) = A_B(\mathbf{y}). \qquad \square$$

Example 6.40. For the family of extended root-mean-power aggregation functions $(A_{\mathrm{id}^\alpha})_{\alpha \in [0,1]}$, where $A_{\mathrm{id}^0} = \mathrm{GM}$ and for $\alpha > 0$,

$$A_{\mathrm{id}^\alpha}(\mathbf{x}) = \left(\frac{1}{n} \sum_{i=1}^n x_i^\alpha \right)^{1/\alpha},$$

let $B = \mathrm{AM}$. Then A_{AM} is an idempotent symmetric extended aggregation function on $[0,1]$ which is incomparable with all $A_\alpha, \alpha \in \,]0,1[$, and

$$\mathrm{GM} < A_{\mathrm{AM}} < \mathrm{AM}.$$

For $n = 2$,

$$A_{\mathrm{AM}}(x,y) = \left(\frac{x^{\frac{x+y}{2}} + y^{\frac{x+y}{2}}}{2} \right)^{\frac{2}{x+y}}$$

whenever $(x,y) \neq (0,0)$.

6.5.4 Constraining

As the last construction method in this section we introduce a method inspired by conditioning in probability theory. This method was originally proposed in [230].

Proposition 6.41. *Let* A *be an extended aggregation function on* $[0,1]$ *such that for a given constant* $u \in [0,1]$ *it satisfies* $A^{(n+1)}(u, n \cdot 0) < A^{(n+1)}(u, n \cdot 1)$. *Then the extended function* $_uA : \cup_{n\in\mathbb{N}}[0,1]^n \to [0,1]$ *defined by*

$$_uA(\mathbf{x}) := \frac{A^{(n+1)}(u, x_1, \ldots, x_n) - A^{(n+1)}(u, 0, \ldots, 0)}{A^{(n+1)}(u, 1, \ldots, 1) - A^{(n+1)}(u, 0, \ldots, 0)} \tag{6.27}$$

is also an extended aggregation function.

Proof. The nondecreasing monotonicity of $_uA$ is a direct consequence of the nondecreasing monotonicity of A. Moreover, applying (6.27) we obtain $_uA(n \cdot 0) = 0$ and $_uA(n \cdot 1) = 1$.   □

Remark 6.42. Symmetric functions invariant under constraining (6.27), i.e., with the property $_uA = A$ for all considered u, are appropriate functions for evaluating information with possible collapse of some of the inputs, for instance if the ith sensor is broken (with unknown i). Such functions form a parameterized class $(K_\alpha)_{\alpha\in]0,1[}$ where

$$K_\alpha(\mathbf{x}) := \frac{\prod_{i=1}^{n}(\alpha + (1 - 2\alpha)x_i) - \alpha^n}{(1-\alpha)^n - \alpha^n}, \quad \text{for } \alpha \neq 0.5, \tag{6.28}$$

and $K_{0.5} = \text{AM}$. The limit members of this class are functions $K_0 = \Pi$ and $K_1 = \Pi^d$, where Π^d is the probabilistic sum, i.e., the dual function to Π, and they are constrained invariant for all $u \in [0,1]$ up to 0 or 1, respectively. Observe that for each $\alpha \in [0,1]$, $\alpha = K_\alpha(0,1) = K_\alpha(1,0)$, that is, the parameter α corresponds to the aggregation output when aggregating the contradictory inputs 0 and 1.

Example 6.43. (i) Aggregation functions Min and Max fulfill requirements of Proposition 6.41 for any $u \in]0,1[$, and then

$$_u\text{Min}(\mathbf{x}) = \text{Min}\left(\frac{\text{Min}(\mathbf{x})}{u}, 1\right) \text{ and } _u\text{Max}(\mathbf{x}) = \text{Max}\left(\frac{\text{Max}(\mathbf{x}) - u}{1 - u}, 0\right).$$

(ii) For the harmonic mean HM and the constant $u = 1/k, k \in \mathbb{N}$,

$$\frac{1}{\frac{1}{k}\text{HM}(\mathbf{x})} = \text{HM}(k \cdot 1, \mathbf{x}).$$

6.6 Aggregation functions based on minimal dissimilarity

For the Euclidean metric d on $\mathbb{R}^n$ (L_2 metric),

$$d(\mathbf{x}, \mathbf{y}) := \sqrt{\sum_{i=1}^{n} (x_i - y_i)^2},$$

it is well known that for each $\mathbf{x} \in \mathbb{R}^n$ there exists a unique $s \in \mathbb{R}$ such that

$$d(\mathbf{x}, n \cdot s) = \inf\{d(\mathbf{x}, n \cdot r) \mid r \in \mathbb{R}\},$$

and that $s = \mathsf{AM}(\mathbf{x})$. Hence the arithmetic mean can be understood as a solution of a minimization problem (projection, in fact). Similarly, the Chebyshev metric c on $\mathbb{R}^n$ (L_∞ metric),

$$c(\mathbf{x}, \mathbf{y}) := \|\mathbf{x} - \mathbf{y}\|_\infty,$$

yields the arithmetic mean of Min and Max,

$$s = \frac{\mathsf{Min}(\mathbf{x}) + \mathsf{Max}(\mathbf{x})}{2}$$

(observe that this is an ordered weighted averaging function; see (1.19)). On the other hand, for the "Manhattan distance" (L_1 metric) l on $\mathbb{R}^n$,

$$l(\mathbf{x}, \mathbf{y}) := \|\mathbf{x} - \mathbf{y}\|_1,$$

the set of all points minimizing the expression $l(\mathbf{x}, n \cdot r)$ can be a closed interval, and taking as s the middle point of this interval (in the case when a single real number is the minimizer, it also can be understood as a closed real interval), the median is obtained, $s = \mathsf{Med}(\mathbf{x})$. We modify this minimization problem replacing the metrics (distance functions) by dissimilarity functions and thus proposing a new method for constructing aggregation functions.

Definition 6.44. Let $K : \mathbb{R} \to \mathbb{R}$ be a convex function with unique minimum $K(0) = 0$. Then K is called a *shape function* and for any real interval $\mathbb{I}$, the function $D_K : \mathbb{I}^2 \to \mathbb{R}$ given by

$$D_K(x, y) := K(x - y)$$

is called a *dissimilarity function* on $\mathbb{I}$.

Remark 6.45. If the function K in Definition 6.44 is even, then, taking $L : [0, \infty[\to [0, \infty[$ the inverse function of $K|_{[0,\infty[}$, and defining $d_K : \mathbb{R}^n \to \mathbb{R}$ by

$$d_K(\mathbf{x}, \mathbf{y}) := L\left(\sum_{i=1}^{n} K(x_i - y_i)\right),$$

one can show that d_K is a metric on $\mathbb{R}^n$. The above-mentioned Euclidean metric d is related to K given by $K(x) = x^2$, while the "Manhattan metric" l is related to $K(x) = |x|$. Similarly, the L_p-distance for $p \in [1, \infty[$ is related to $K_{(p)}(x) := |x|^p$.

Example 6.46. (i) For the shape function $K(x) = \exp(|x|) - 1$, the corresponding dissimilarity function D_K is given by $D_K(x, y) = \exp(|x - y|) - 1$.

(ii) Shape functions need not be even. For any $\gamma \in]0, \infty[$ different from 1, the function $K_{<\gamma>} : \mathbb{R} \to \mathbb{R}$ given by

$$K_{<\gamma>}(x) := \begin{cases} x & \text{if } x \geqslant 0 \\ -\gamma x & \text{otherwise} \end{cases}$$

is a shape function which is not even.

Proposition 6.47. *For a given $n \in \mathbb{N}$, let $K_1, \dots, K_n : \mathbb{R} \to \mathbb{R}$ be given shape functions. For an arbitrary real interval $\mathbb{I}$ define a function $\mathsf{A}_{K_1, \dots, K_n} : \mathbb{I}^n \to \mathbb{I}$ by*

$$\mathsf{A}_{K_1, \dots, K_n}(\mathbf{x}) := \frac{s_* + s^*}{2}, \tag{6.29}$$

where

$$[s_*, s^*] = \left\{ u \in \mathbb{I} \,\middle|\, \sum_{i=1}^{n} D_{K_i}(x_i, u) = \inf \left\{ \sum_{i=1}^{n} D_{K_i}(x_i, r), r \in \mathbb{I} \right\} \right\}.$$

Then $\mathsf{A}_{K_1, \dots, K_n}$ is an idempotent aggregation function on $\mathbb{I}$.

Proof. Each function $D_{K_i}(x_i, \cdot) : \mathbb{I} \to \mathbb{R}$ is a convex function with unique minimum 0 at the point $r = x_i$. Then also the function $F : \mathbb{I} \to \mathbb{R}$ given by

$$F(r) := \sum_{i=1}^{n} D_{K_i}(x_i, r)$$

is convex. Moreover, for each $r > \mathsf{Max}(\mathbf{x})$,

$$F(r) > F(\mathsf{Max}(\mathbf{x})).$$

Similarly, if $r < \mathsf{Min}(\mathbf{x})$, then

$$F(r) > F(\mathsf{Min}(\mathbf{x})).$$

Thus we have to look for the set of points minimizing the function F on interval $[\mathsf{Min}(\mathbf{x}), \mathsf{Max}(\mathbf{x})]$. The convexity of F ensures that the set of its minimizing points is a closed interval $[s_*, s^*]$, proving that the function $\mathsf{A}_{K_1, \dots, K_n}$ is well defined. The idempotency of $\mathsf{A}_{K_1, \dots, K_n}$ follows from the fact that for $\mathbf{x} = (n \cdot x)$ the convex function

F has unique minimum 0 in point $s = x$. To see the nondecreasing monotonicity of $A_{K_1,...,K_n}$, recall first that for each convex function $K : \mathbb{R} \to \mathbb{R}$ we have

$$K(x) - K(y) \leqslant K(x+z) - K(y+z)$$

for all $x \geqslant y$ and all $z \geqslant 0$. Let $\mathbf{x} \in \mathbb{I}^n$ be given so that for a fixed coordinate $j \in [n], x_j + \varepsilon \in \mathbb{I}$ for some positive constant $\varepsilon > 0$. Let $u \in \mathbb{I}$ be a point minimizing F. Then for each $v \in \mathbb{I}, v < u$,

$$F(u) = \sum_{i=1}^{n} K_i(x_i - u) \leqslant \sum_{i=1}^{n} K_i(x_i - v) = F(v). \tag{6.30}$$

Moreover, the convexity of K_j ensures that

$$K_j(x_j + \varepsilon - u) - K_j(x_j - u) \leqslant K_j(x_j + \varepsilon - v) - K_j(x_j - v) \tag{6.31}$$

whenever $v < u$. Summing the inequalities (6.30) and (6.31) we obtain

$$\sum_{i=1, i \neq j}^{n} K_i(x_i - u) + K_j(x_j + \varepsilon - u) \leqslant \sum_{i=1, i \neq j}^{n} K_i(x_i - v) + K_j(x_j + \varepsilon - v)$$

for all $v \in \mathbb{I}, v < u$. Consequently, if $[s_*, s^*]$ is the set of points minimizing $\sum_{i=1}^{n} D_{K_i}(x_i, r)$ and $[t_*, t^*]$ is the set of points minimizing

$$\sum_{i=1, i \neq j}^{n} D_{K_i}(x_i, r) + D_{K_j}(x_j + \varepsilon, r),$$

we have $s_* \leqslant t_*$ and $s^* \leqslant t^*$. Thus $\frac{s_* + s^*}{2} \leqslant \frac{t_* + t^*}{2}$, proving the nondecreasing monotonicity of $A_{K_1,...,K_n}$ in the jth coordinate. $\qquad\square$

The next result easily follows from the above proposition and thus its proof is omitted.

Corollary 6.48. *For any fixed shape function $K : \mathbb{R} \to \mathbb{R}$ and any real interval $\mathbb{I}$, the extended function $A_K : \cup_{n \in \mathbb{N}} \mathbb{I}^n \to \mathbb{I}$ given by*

$$A_K(\mathbf{x}) := A_{K,...,K}(\mathbf{x}), \tag{6.32}$$

see (6.29), is a symmetric idempotent extended aggregation function on $\mathbb{I}$.

Remark 6.49. If a shape function $K : \mathbb{R} \to \mathbb{R}$ is positively homogeneous for some order $p \geqslant 1$, i.e., $K(cx) = c^p K(x)$ for all $x \in \mathbb{R}$ and $c \in]0, \infty[$, then the extended aggregation function A_K given in Corollary 6.48 is positively homogeneous (ratio scale invariant), $A_K(c\mathbf{x}) = cA_K(\mathbf{x})$ for all $c \in [0, \infty[$ and $\mathbf{x} \in \cup_{n \in \mathbb{N}} \mathbb{R}^n$. Moreover, the eveness of such shape K means that K is a multiple of $K_{(p)}$ (see Remark 6.45), and then the corresponding aggregation function A_K is homogeneous, $A_K(c\mathbf{x}) = cA_K(\mathbf{x})$ for all $c \in \mathbb{R}$ and $\mathbf{x} \in \cup_{n \in \mathbb{N}}\mathbb{R}^n$.

Example 6.50. (i) For $n = 2$, and for $x \in \mathbb{R}$, take $K_1(x) = |x|$ and $K_2(x) = x^2$, i.e., $K_1 = K_{(1)}$ and $K_2 = K_{(2)}$ are shape functions. Then $A_{K_1,K_2} : \mathbb{R}^2 \to \mathbb{R}$ is given by

$$A_{K_1,K_2}(x,y) = \mathsf{Med}\left(x, y - \frac{1}{2}, y + \frac{1}{2}\right).$$

(ii) For $K_{<\gamma>}$ given in Example 6.46(ii), the extended aggregation function $A_{<\gamma>} : \cup_{n \in \mathbb{N}}\mathbb{R}^n \to \mathbb{R}$ is the $\frac{1}{1+\gamma}$ 100%-quantile from the uniformly distributed sample $(x_1, \ldots, x_n)$, well known in statistics.

For each shape function K, wK is also a shape function for any positive weight w. This fact allows one to easily incorporate weights into the $A_{K_1,\ldots,K_n}$ introduced in Proposition 6.47, simply dealing with the aggregation function $A_{w_1K_1,\ldots,w_nK_n}$. For any $w > 0$,

$$A_{K_1,\ldots,K_n} = A_{wK_1,\ldots,wK_n},$$

and thus it suffices to deal with normalized weight vectors $\mathbf{w} \in [0,1]^n$, $\sum_{i=1}^n w_i = 1$, only.

Example 6.51. (i) For $\mathbf{w} \in [0,1]^n$ and $K = K_{(2)}$, we have $A_{K_{(2)}} = \mathsf{AM}$ and

$$(A_K)_\mathbf{w} = A_{w_1K_{(2)},\ldots,w_nK_{(2)}}$$

is the weighted arithmetic mean with weights $w_1, \ldots, w_n$.

(ii) $A_{K_{(1)}}$ is the median function, i.e., $A_K = \mathsf{Med}$, and then $A_{w_1K_{(1)},\ldots,w_nK_{(1)}}$ is the *weighted median*. In particular, if all weights are integers, then

$$A_{w_1K_{(1)},\ldots,w_nK_{(1)}}(\mathbf{x}) = \mathsf{Med}(w_1 \cdot x_1, \ldots, w_n \cdot x_n)$$

(i.e., the median of $\sum_{i=1}^n w_i$ elements).

(iii) By our approach, we can introduce weights in nonsymmetric aggregation, too. Continuing Example 6.50(i), we have

$$(A_{w_1K_{(1)},w_2K_{(2)}})(x,y) = \mathsf{Med}\left(x, y - \frac{w_1}{w_2}, y + \frac{w_1}{w_2}\right)$$

(if $w_2 = 0$, formally $\mathsf{Med}(x, y - \infty, y + \infty) = x$).

Remark 6.52. The fixed weights w_i in the above approach (independent of input values x_i) can be replaced by input-dependent weights $w(x_i)$ for some weighting function $w : \mathbb{I} \to [0, \infty[$, i.e., we have to minimize the expression

$$\sum_{i=1}^n w(x_i)D_{K_i}(x_i,r). \tag{6.33}$$

Based on minimization of (6.33), we can introduce the (extended) function $\mathsf{A}_{K_1,\dots,K_n;w} : \mathbb{I}^n \to \mathbb{I}$ (respectively, $\mathsf{A}_{K;w} : \cup_{n \in \mathbb{N}} \mathbb{I}^n \to \mathbb{I}$) in the same way as we have introduced the function $\mathsf{A}_{K_1,\dots,K_n}$ in (6.29). However, the monotonicity (and even idempotency) of these functions may fail, in general. Some more details on this topic can be found in [311, 313].

Example 6.53. For $K = K_{(2)}$ and $w : \mathbb{I} \to]0, \infty[$, the extended function $\mathsf{A}_{K;w} : \cup_{n \in \mathbb{N}} \mathbb{I}^n \to \mathbb{I}$ is given by

$$\mathsf{A}_{K;w}(\mathbf{x}) = \frac{\sum_{i=1}^{n} w(x_i) x_i}{\sum_{i=1}^{n} w(x_i)}$$

(see Section 4.3.2) and it is called a mixture operator in [293]; see also [23]. On $\mathbb{I} = [0, 1]$, if a smooth nondecreasing function w satisfies $w(x) \geqslant w'(x)$, then $\mathsf{A}_{K;w}$ is an idempotent symmetric extended aggregation function. The above condition can be relaxed to $w(x) \geqslant w'(x)(1 - x)$ for all $x \in [0, 1]$; see [311].

Remark 6.54. We can modify a dissimilarity function D_K on an interval $\mathbb{I}$ by a continuous strictly monotone function $f : \mathbb{I} \to \mathbb{R}$ (this function is often called a scale) to

$$D_{K,f}(x, y) := K(f(x) - f(y)).$$

However, the minimization problem $\sum_{i=1}^{n} D_{K_i,f}(x_i, r)$ leads then to an aggregation function $\mathsf{A}_{K_1,\dots,K_n;f} : \mathbb{I}^n \to \mathbb{I}$ (or an extended aggregation function $\mathsf{A}_{K;f} : \cup_{n \in \mathbb{N}} \mathbb{I}^n \to \mathbb{I}$) which is an f-transform of the aggregation function $\mathsf{A}_{K_1,\dots,K_n}$ (extended aggregation function A_K), i.e., we can look on this approach as a combination of two construction methods. As a typical example recall the extended aggregation function $\mathsf{A}_{K_{(2)};f}$ based on the shape function $K_{(2)}(x) = x^2$ which is, in fact, the quasi-arithmetic mean based on the generator f; see Definition 4.4.

6.7 Ordinal sums of aggregation functions

The idea of ordinal sums has its roots in extension of algebraic structures, namely of posets and lattices [44], and of semigroups [63, 64]. In the framework of special aggregation functions, namely t-norms, this method is studied in detail in [220]. In general, ordinal sums extend functions defined on $\mathbb{I}$. We restrict our considerations to the case $\mathbb{I} = [0, 1]$ only, from which the case of a general real interval can be straightforwardly obtained. Depending on the properties which have to be preserved, several types of ordinal sums of aggregation functions can be introduced. From well-known types of ordinal sums recall ordinal sums of t-norms and t-conorms [220, 384], or copulas [332, 384]. Our aim is to discuss the construction methods for constructing new aggregation functions from given ones, hence the crucial point is the monotonicity and the boundary conditions of resulting functions. From given aggregation functions $\mathsf{A}_i, i = 1, \dots, n$ defined on nonoverlapping domains $[a_i, b_i] \subseteq [0, 1]$, $i = 1, \dots, k$, several possible extensions of $\mathsf{A}_i's$ to an aggregation function A defined on $[0, 1]$ can be introduced, in general. We introduce only some distinguished (and unique in some sense) possible extensions. The next results are shown in detail in [306].

Proposition 6.55. *Let* $(A_i : \cup_{n \in \mathbb{N}}[a_i, b_i]^n \to [a_i, b_i], i = 1, \ldots, k)$, *be a family of aggregation functions defined on nonoverlapping domains* $[a_i, b_i], i = 1, \ldots, k$, $0 \leqslant a_1 < b_1 \leqslant a_2 < b_2 \leqslant \ldots < b_k \leqslant 1$. *Define two functions*

$$A^{(\ell)} = \left(\left(< a_i, b_i, A_i >\right)_{i \in \{1,\ldots,k\}}\right)_\ell : \cup_{n \in \mathbb{N}}[0, 1]^n \to [0, 1]$$

and

$$A^{(u)} = \left(\left(< a_i, b_i, A_i >\right)_{i \in \{1,\ldots,k\}}\right)_u : \cup_{n \in \mathbb{N}}[0, 1]^n \to [0, 1]$$

by

$$A^{(\ell)}(\mathbf{x}) := \begin{cases} 0 & \text{if } \mathsf{Min}(\mathbf{x}) < a_1 \\ A_i(\mathsf{Min}(x_1, b_1), \ldots, \mathsf{Min}(x_n, b_n)) & \text{if } a_i \leqslant \mathsf{Min}(\mathbf{x}) < a_{i+1} \quad (6.34) \\ 1 & \text{if } \mathsf{Min}(\mathbf{x}) = 1, \end{cases}$$

where $a_{k+1} = 1$ *by convention, and*

$$A^{(u)}(\mathbf{x}) := \begin{cases} 0 & \text{if } \mathsf{Max}(\mathbf{x}) = 0 \\ A_i\left(\mathsf{Max}(x_1, a_i), \ldots, \mathsf{Max}(x_n, a_i)\right) & \text{if } b_{i-1} < \mathsf{Max}(\mathbf{x}) \leqslant b_i \quad (6.35) \\ 1 & \text{if } b_k < \mathsf{Max}(\mathbf{x}), \end{cases}$$

where $b_0 = 0$ *by convention.*

Then $A^{(\ell)}$ *and* $A^{(u)}$ *are the smallest and the greatest aggregation functions, respectively, such that the corresponding restrictions to the inputs from* $[a_i, b_i]$ *coincide with aggregation functions* $A_i, i = 1, \ldots, k$.

Proof. Easily we can check that both $A^{(\ell)}$ and $A^{(u)}$ are extended aggregation functions on $[0, 1]$. By direct computation we see that

$$A^{(\ell)}|_{\cup_{n \in \mathbb{N}}[a_i, b_i]^n} = A^{(u)}|_{\cup_{n \in \mathbb{N}}[a_i, b_i]^n} = A_i.$$

The rest of the proof follows from the monotonicity of all extended aggregation functions coinciding on $[a_i, b_i]$ with $A_i, i = 1, \ldots, k$. □

Remark 6.56. (i) The function $A^{(\ell)}$ is called *the lower ordinal sum* (of aggregation functions A_i), while $A^{(u)}$ is called *the upper ordinal sum* (of aggregation functions A_i).

(ii) The case $k = 0$ can be formally accepted also, and then (6.34) gives $A_\perp$, and (6.35) leads to $A_\top$.

Example 6.57. To illustrate Proposition 6.55, suppose that $A_1 = GM$ is defined on $[a_1, b_1] = [0, 0.5]$ while $A_2 = AM$ is defined on $[a_2, b_2] = [0.7, 1]$. Then

$$A^{(\ell)}(x, y) = \begin{cases} AM(x, y) = \frac{x+y}{2} & \text{if } (x, y) \in [0.7, 1]^2 \\ \\ GM(Min(x, 0.5), Min(y, 0.5)) \\ \quad = \sqrt{Min(xy, x/2, y/2, 1/4)} & \text{otherwise.} \end{cases}$$

Further,

$$A^{(u)}(x, y) = \begin{cases} GM(x, y) = \sqrt{xy} & \text{if } (x, y) \in [0, 0.5]^2 \\ \\ AM(Max(x, 0.7), Max(y, 0.7)) \\ \quad = Max(AM(x, y), AM(x, 0.7), AM(y, 0.7), 0.7) & \text{otherwise.} \end{cases}$$

The lower and upper ordinal sums preserve the symmetry of incoming summands A_i; however, they may violate other properties, in general. To preserve the idempotency of the incoming summands A_i by the constructed extension, we have the next result introduced in [306].

Proposition 6.58. *Let all aggregation functions A_i from Proposition 6.55 be idempotent. Then the smallest idempotent aggregation function $A^{(i\ell)}$ and the greatest idempotent aggregation function $A^{(iu)}$ defined on $[0, 1]$ and extending all functions A_i, $i = 1, \ldots, k$, are given by*

$$A^{(i\ell)}(\mathbf{x}) := \begin{cases} A_i\left(Min(x_1, b_i), \ldots, Min(x_n, b_i)\right) & \text{if } a_i \leqslant Min(\mathbf{x}) < b_i \\ Min(\mathbf{x}) & \text{otherwise,} \end{cases} \quad (6.36)$$

and

$$A^{(iu)}(\mathbf{x}) := \begin{cases} A_i\left(Max(x_1, a_i), \ldots, Max(x_n, a_i)\right) & \text{if } a_i < Max(\mathbf{x}) \leqslant b_i \\ Max(\mathbf{x}) & \text{otherwise.} \end{cases} \quad (6.37)$$

Proof. The result follows from Proposition 6.55 in the case when $\cup_{i=1}^k [a_i, b_i] = [0, 1]$. In the general case, we can introduce into "gaps" of the form $[b_i, a_{i+1}]$ the smallest idempotent aggregation function Min (the greatest idempotent aggregation function Max) and again apply Proposition 6.55. □

Remark 6.59. Admitting $k = 0$ (i.e., an empty family of idempotent aggregation functions) in Proposition 6.58 leads to $A^{(i\ell)} = Min$ and $A^{(iu)} = Max$. Moreover, constructions (6.36) and (6.37) can be applied to any aggregation functions A_i defined on $[a_i, b_i]$, $i = 1, \ldots, k$.

Example 6.60. Under the specifications of Example 6.57 we have

$$\mathsf{A}^{(i\ell)}(x,y) = \begin{cases} \mathsf{Min}(x,y) & \text{if } \mathsf{Min}(x,y) \in [0.5, 0.7[\\ \mathsf{A}^{(\ell)}(x,y) & \text{otherwise,} \end{cases}$$

and

$$\mathsf{A}^{(iu)}(x,y) = \begin{cases} \mathsf{Max}(x,y) & \text{if } \mathsf{Max}(x,y) \in]0.5, 0.7] \\ \mathsf{A}^{(u)}(x,y) & \text{otherwise.} \end{cases}$$

The standard ordinal sums of t-norms (see Section 3.3.7) or copulas, as introduced in [220, 384], are just our $\mathsf{A}^{(i\ell)}$ ordinal sum, while $\mathsf{A}^{(iu)}$ describes exactly the standard ordinal sum of t-conorms or of dual copulas, see [220, 332, 384] (though neither t-norms nor copulas are idempotent functions, in general).

We have that $\mathsf{A}^{(\ell)} = \mathsf{A}^{(i\ell)}$ and $\mathsf{A}^{(iu)} = \mathsf{A}^{(u)}$ if and only if $\cup_{i=1}^{k}[a_i, b_i] = [0, 1]$.

Evidently, each extension $\mathsf{A} : \cup_{n \in \mathbb{N}}[0, 1]^n \to [0, 1]$ of aggregation functions A_i defined on nonoverlapping intervals $[a_i, b_i] \subset [0, 1]$, $i = 1, \ldots, k$, is characterized by the inequalities

$$\mathsf{A}^{(\ell)} \leqslant \mathsf{A} \leqslant \mathsf{A}^{(u)}.$$

Moreover, $\mathsf{A}^{(\ell)} = \mathsf{A}^{(u)}$, i.e., there is a unique extension, only if $k = 2$, A_1 is defined on $[0, a]$ and A_2 is defined on $[a, 1]$, where a is the annihilator of both functions A_1 and A_2. Then this unique extension is given by

$$\mathsf{A}(\mathbf{x}) = \begin{cases} \mathsf{A}_1(\mathbf{x}) & \text{if all } x_i \in [0, a] \\ \mathsf{A}_2(\mathbf{x}) & \text{if all } x_i \in [a, 1] \\ a & \text{otherwise.} \end{cases}$$

As an example recall the a-median Med_a introduced in [131] for a fixed element $a \in [0, 1]$ as $\mathsf{Med}_a : [0, 1]^2 \to [0, 1]$ by

$$\mathsf{Med}_a(x,y) := \mathsf{Med}(x, y, a)$$

(see (1.15) for the general definition). Then, $\mathsf{A}_1 = \mathsf{Max}$ on $[0, a]$ and $\mathsf{A}_2 = \mathsf{Min}$ on $[a, 1]$.

An important property for technical applications is continuity. But neither $\mathsf{A}^{(\ell)}$, $\mathsf{A}^{(u)}$ nor $\mathsf{A}^{(i\ell)}$, $\mathsf{A}^{(iu)}$ need be continuous though all summands are continuous functions. Therefore we propose a method resulting in a continuous extension.

Suppose that all the functions A_i in Proposition 6.55 are continuous, and $\cup_{i=1}^{k}[a_i, b_i] = [0, 1]$, $a_1 = 0, b_k = 1$. If the latter condition is not satisfied we can add any continuous summands such as Min, Max, AM, GM, etc., to act on occurring gaps.

Proposition 6.61. *Suppose that all functions A_i satisfying conditions from Proposition 6.55 are continuous, and $\cup_{i=1}^{k}[a_i, b_i] = [0, 1]$, $a_1 = 0, b_k = 1$. Let*

$f : [0,1] \to \overline{\mathbb{R}}$ be any continuous strictly monotone function with $\mathrm{ran}(f) \neq \overline{\mathbb{R}}$. Then the mapping $\mathsf{A}^{(f)} : \bigcup_{n \in \mathbb{N}}[0,1]^n \to [0,1]$ given by

$$\mathsf{A}^{(f)}(\mathbf{x}) := f^{-1}\left(\sum_{i=1}^{k} f\left(\mathsf{A}_i(x_1^{(i)}, \ldots, x_n^{(i)})\right) - \sum_{i=2}^{k} f(a_i)\right), \qquad (6.38)$$

where $x^{(i)} = \mathsf{Max}(a_i, \mathsf{Min}(b_i, x))$, is a continuous aggregation function such that for $i = 1, \ldots, k$ we have

$$\mathsf{A}^{(f)}|_{\bigcup_{n \in \mathbb{N}}[a_i, b_i]^n} = \mathsf{A}_i.$$

Proof. The continuity of $\mathsf{A}^{(f)}$ follows from the continuity of all involved members and operations in (6.38). Similarly, monotonicity and fulfillment of boundary conditions of $\mathsf{A}^{(f)}$ is straightforward, and thus $\mathsf{A}^{(f)}$ is a continuous extended aggregation function. Suppose that $\mathbf{x} \in [a_i, b_i]^n$. Then for $j = 1, \ldots, i-1$ we have

$$f(\mathsf{A}_j(x_1^{(j)}, \ldots, x_n^{(j)})) = f(b_j) = f(a_{j+1}).$$

Similarly, for $j \in \{i+1, \ldots, k\}$ we have

$$f(\mathsf{A}_j(x_1^{(j)}, \ldots, x_n^{(j)})) = f(a_j) = f(b_{j-1}),$$

and obviously

$$f(\mathsf{A}_i(x_1^{(i)}, \ldots, x_n^{(i)})) = f(\mathsf{A}_i(x_1, \ldots, x_n)).$$

Then

$$\mathsf{A}^{(f)}(x) = f^{-1}(f(\mathsf{A}_i(x))) = \mathsf{A}_i(x). \qquad \square$$

Remark 6.62. (i) $x^{(i)}$ is a point from $[a_i, b_i]$ closest to x.
(ii) If $f(x) = \mathrm{id}(x) = x$, we get

$$\mathsf{A}^{(\mathrm{id})}(\mathbf{x}) = \sum_{i=1}^{k}\left(\mathsf{A}_i(x_1^{(i)}, \ldots, x_n^{(i)}) - a_i\right),$$

while for $f(x) = \log x$ we have

$$\mathsf{A}^{(\log)}(\mathbf{x}) = \prod_{i=1}^{k} \frac{\mathsf{A}_i(x_1^{(i)}, \ldots, x_n^{(i)})}{b_i}.$$

(iii) Remarkably, if all functions A_i are t-norms (respectively, t-conorms, copulas, quasi-copulas, conjunctors, dual copulas) then for any f, $\mathsf{A}^{(f)}$ is the standard ordinal sum of t-norms (respectively, t-conorms, copulas, quasi-copulas, conjunctors, dual copulas).

Formula (6.38) is a special case of the D-based ordinal sum construction [306], given in the following definition.

Definition 6.63. Let $D : \cup_{n \in \mathbb{N}}[0, 1]^n \to [0, 1]$ be a symmetric continuous idempotent aggregation function which is strictly monotone (i.e., cancellative) on $\cup_{n \in \mathbb{N}}]0, 1[^n$. Then the D-*ordinal sum* $A^D : \cup_{n \in \mathbb{N}}[0, 1]^n \to [0, 1]$ of aggregation functions $A_i : \cup_{n \in \mathbb{N}}[a_{i-1}, a_i]^n \to [a_{i-1}, a_i]$, $i = 1, \ldots, k$, $0 = a_0 < a_1 \ldots < a_k = 1$, is given as a (unique) solution of the equation

$$D\left(A^D(x_1, \ldots, x_n), a_1, \ldots, a_{k-1}\right) =$$
$$D\left(A_1(x_1^{(1)}, \ldots, x_n^{(1)}), \ldots, A_k(x_1^{(k)}, \ldots, x_n^{(k)})\right), \tag{6.39}$$

where $x^{(i)} = \text{Max}(a_{i-1}, \text{Min}(a_i, x))$, $i = 1, \ldots, k$.

In particular, if

$$D(\mathbf{x}) = f^{-1}\left(\frac{1}{n}\sum_{i=1}^{n} f(x_i)\right)$$

for some continuous strictly monotone function $f : [0, 1] \to [-\infty, \infty]$, that is, if D is a quasi-arithmetic mean, then (6.39) results in (6.38).

6.8 Extensions to aggregation functions

In Section 6.7, we have discussed the extension of aggregation functions defined on some subintervals of an interval $\mathbb{I}$ to a full aggregation function on $\mathbb{I}$ by means of several types of ordinal sums. In this section we discuss several other types of extensions to aggregation functions when only partial knowledge is available. For n-ary aggregation functions with specific properties, minor information about their values is often sufficient to completely determine the relevant aggregation function. For example, additive aggregation functions on interval $[0, 1]$ (or $[0, \infty[$) are just the weighted arithmetic means and they are completely determined by the values at points corresponding to the characteristic functions of singletons, i.e., at points $\mathbf{1}_i \mathbf{0}$. Similarly, the comonotone additive n-ary aggregation functions on $[0, 1]$ (on $[0, \infty[$) are completely determined by the values at points from $\{0, 1\}^n$ (Choquet integral-based aggregation functions; see Section 5.4). Another special example are strict t-norms, which are completely characterized by their values on the diagonal $(T(x, x))$ and opposite diagonal $(T(x, 1 - x))$ sections; see [220, Prop. 7.13].

In most cases, the partial knowledge about an aggregation function only restricts our choice of an appropriate aggregation function, and leads to a class of aggregation functions satisfying the prescribed information. This was the case of ordinal sums discussed in Section 6.7. In this section we restrict our considerations to the binary aggregation functions on the unit interval $\mathbb{I} = [0, 1]$, and discuss some other extension techniques. Mostly we look for some distinguished aggregation functions satisfying the given properties and having the prescribed values on certain subdomains on $[0, 1]^2$, for example the smallest and the greatest one, or some with a simple formula.

The smallest possible nonempty piece of information about an aggregation function $A : [0, 1]^2 \to [0, 1]$ is the information about its value in some (one) fixed point (u, v) not covered by the boundary conditions, i.e., the knowledge about $A(u, v)$ for some $(u, v) \in [0, 1]^2 \setminus \{(0, 0), (1, 1)\}$.

Proposition 6.64. *Let some $(u, v) \in [0, 1]^2 \setminus \{(0, 0), (1, 1)\}$, and $a \in [0, 1]$ be given. The class of all aggregation functions $A : [0, 1]^2 \to [0, 1]$ such that $A(u, v) = a$ is a convex compact (in the uniform convergence topology) subclass of the class of all binary aggregation functions on $[0, 1]$, with the smallest element $A_{(u,v,a)}$ and the greatest element $A^{(u,v,a)}$ given by*

$$A_{(u,v,a)}(x, y) := \begin{cases} 1 & \text{if } (x, y) = (1, 1) \\ a & \text{if } (x, y) \in [u, 1] \times [v, 1] \setminus \{(1, 1)\} \\ 0 & \text{otherwise,} \end{cases} \quad (6.40)$$

and

$$A^{(u,v,a)}(x, y) := \begin{cases} 0 & \text{if } (x, y) = (0, 0) \\ a & \text{if } (x, y) \in [0, u] \times [0, v] \setminus \{(0, 0)\} \\ 1 & \text{otherwise.} \end{cases} \quad (6.41)$$

The proof follows directly from the definition of binary aggregation functions.

Remark 6.65. We have that $A_{(u,v,0)} = A_\perp$ and $A^{(u,v,1)} = A_\top$ for any $(u, v) \in [0, 1]^2 \setminus \{(0, 0), (1, 1)\}$.

The above proposition can be easily extended for an arbitrary number of points with known output values preserving the nondecreasing monotonicity whenever applicable.

Corollary 6.66. *Let $((u_k, v_k))_{k \in K}$ be a family of points in $[0, 1]^2 \setminus \{(0, 0), (1, 1)\}$ and let $(a_k)_{k \in K}$ be a family of values from $[0, 1]$ such that $a_k \leqslant a_i$ whenever $k, i \in K$ and $u_k \leqslant u_i, v_k \leqslant v_i$. Then the class of all aggregation functions $A : [0, 1]^2 \to [0, 1]$ such that $A(u_k, v_k) = a_k$ for all $k \in K$ is convex and compact, and its smallest element A_* and the greatest element A^* are given by*

$$A_*(x, y) := \sup \left\{ A_{(u_k, v_k, a_k)}(x, y) \mid k \in K \right\}$$

and

$$A^*(x, y) := \inf \left\{ A^{(u_k, v_k, a_k)}(x, y) \mid k \in K \right\}.$$

Proof. Due to Proposition 6.64, for each aggregation function A having values a_k in points $(u_k, v_k), k \in K$, we have

$$A_{(u_k, v_k, a_k)} \leqslant A \leqslant A^{(u_k, v_k, a_k)},$$

and thus also $A_* \leqslant A \leqslant A^*$. Moreover, both functions A_* and A^* are binary aggregation functions on $[0, 1]$. Due to the consistency requirement $a_k \leqslant a_i$ whenever $k, i \in K$ and $u_k \leqslant u_i, v_k \leqslant v_i$ it also follows that

$$a_k = A_{(u_k, v_k, a_k)}(u_k, v_k) \geqslant A_{(u_j, v_j, a_j)}(u_k, v_k)$$

for all $j \in K$, i.e., $A_*(u_k, v_k) = a_k$. Similarly, $A^*(u_k, v_k) = a_k$, which concludes the proof. $\qquad \square$

Some additional requirements on A can essentially reduce the possible choice of appropriate aggregation functions. For example, binary aggregation functions on $[0, 1]$ possessing the minimal Chebyshev norm (i.e., this norm is 1) with prescribed value at one point (in some subdomains of $[0, 1]^2$) are discussed in [235]. We focus on 1-Lipschitzian aggregation functions and their special case quasi-copulas; see Section 3.4.4.

Proposition 6.67. *Let some* $(u, v) \in [0, 1]^2 \setminus \{(0, 0), (1, 1)\}$ *and* $a \in [0, 1]$ *be given. The class of all 1-Lipschitzian aggregation functions* $L : [0, 1]^2 \rightarrow [0, 1]$ *(respectively, of all quasi-copulas* $Q : [0, 1]^2 \rightarrow [0, 1]$*) such that* $L(u, v) = a$ *(respectively,* $Q(u, v) = a$*) is nonempty if and only if* $u + v - 1 \leqslant a \leqslant u + v$ *(respectively,* $u + v - 1 \leqslant a \leqslant \text{Min}(u, v)$*), and then it is a convex compact subclass of the class of all binary aggregation functions on* $[0, 1]$*, with the smallest element* $L_{(u,v,a)}$ *(respectively,* $Q_{(u,v,a)}$*) and the greatest element* $L^{(u,v,a)}$ *(respectively,* $Q^{(u,v,a)}$*) given by*

$$L_{(u,v,a)}(x, y) := \text{Max}\left(0, x + y - 1, a + \text{Min}(0, x - u) + \text{Min}(0, y - v)\right),$$

$$L^{(u,v,a)}(x, y) := \text{Min}(1, x + y, a + \text{Max}(0, x - u) + \text{Max}(0, y - v)),$$

$$Q_{(u,v,a)}(x, y) := L_{(u,v,a)}(x, y),$$

$$Q^{(u,v,a)}(x, y) := \text{Min}\left(x, y, a + \text{Max}(0, x - u) + \text{Max}(0, y - v)\right).$$

Proof. The results follow directly from the properties of 1-Lipschitzian aggregation functions (respectively, quasi-copulas), and the fact that an arbitrary 1-Lipschitzian aggregation function L (respectively, arbitrary quasi-copula Q) fulfills $T_L \leqslant L \leqslant S_L$ (respectively, $T_L \leqslant Q \leqslant \text{Min}$; see Section 3.4.4). $\qquad \square$

We can extend Proposition 6.67 for an arbitrary set of points with consistently given values.

Corollary 6.68. *Let* $((u_k, v_k))_{k \in K}$ *be a family of points in* $[0, 1]^2 \setminus \{(0, 0), (1, 1)\}$ *and let* $(a_k)_{k \in K}$ *be a family of values from* $[0, 1]$ *such that:*

(i) $a_k \leqslant a_i$ *whenever* $k, i \in K$ *and* $u_k \leqslant u_i, v_k \leqslant v_i$*;*

(ii) $u_k + v + k - 1 \leqslant a_k \leqslant u_k + v_k$ *(respectively,* $u_k + v_k - 1 \leqslant a_k \leqslant \text{Min}(u_k, v_k)$*) for all* $k \in K$*;*

(iii) $|a_k - a_i| \leqslant |u_k - u_i| + |v_k - v_i|$ *for all* $k, i \in K$*.*

Then the class of all 1-Lipschitzian aggregation functions $\mathsf{L} : [0, 1]^2 \to [0, 1]$ *such that* $\mathsf{L}(u_k, v_k) = a_k$ *for all* $k \in K$ *(respectively, of all quasi-copulas* $\mathsf{Q} : [0, 1]^2 \to [0, 1]$ *such that* $\mathsf{Q}(u_k, v_k) = a_k$ *for all* $k \in K$*) is convex and compact, and its smallest element* L_* *and the greatest element* L^* *(respectively,* Q_* *and* Q^**) are given by*

$$\mathsf{L}_*(x, y) = \sup\{\mathsf{L}_{(u_k, v_k, a_k)}(x, y) \mid k \in K\},$$
$$\mathsf{L}^*(x, y) = \inf\{\mathsf{L}^{(u_k, v_k, a_k)}(x, y) \mid k \in K\},$$
$$\mathsf{Q}_*(x, y) = \sup\{\mathsf{Q}_{(u_k, v_k, a_k)}(x, y) \mid k \in K\} = \mathsf{L}_*(x, y),$$
$$\mathsf{Q}^*(x, y) = \inf\{\mathsf{Q}^{(u_k, v_k, a_k)}(x, y) \mid k \in K\}.$$

Though Corollaries 6.66 and 6.68 can be applied to any subdomain of $[0, 1]^2$ with known values of an unknown aggregation function A (respectively, L, Q), in some cases more transparent formulas for the smallest and the greatest aggregation functions satisfying the given information can be found.

Proposition 6.69. *Let* $\delta_\mathsf{A} : [0, 1] \to [0, 1]$ *be the diagonal section of an aggregation function* $\mathsf{A} : [0, 1]^2 \to [0, 1]$. *Then the smallest and the greatest aggregation functions* A_δ *and* A^δ, *respectively, such that* $\delta_{\mathsf{A}_\delta} = \delta_{\mathsf{A}^\delta} = \delta_\mathsf{A}$ *are given by*

$$\mathsf{A}_\delta(x, y) := \delta_\mathsf{A}(\mathsf{Min}(x, y)) \quad \text{and} \quad \mathsf{A}^\delta(x, y) := \delta_\mathsf{A}(\mathsf{Max}(x, y)).$$

Proof. This follows from the nondecreasing monotonicity of aggregation functions. ☐

Proposition 6.70. *Let* $\delta_\mathsf{L} : [0, 1] \to [0, 1]$ *be the diagonal section of a 1-Lipschitzian aggregation function* $\mathsf{L} : [0, 1]^2 \to [0, 1]$ *(respectively,* δ_Q *for a quasi-copula* $\mathsf{Q} : [0, 1]^2 \to [0, 1]$*), i.e.,* δ_L *is nondecreasing, 2-Lipschitzian and* $\delta_\mathsf{L}(0) = 0, \delta_\mathsf{L}(1) = 1$ *(respectively, for* δ_Q, *and* $\delta_\mathsf{Q}(x) \leqslant x$ *for all* $x \in [0, 1]$*). Then the smallest and the greatest 1-Lipschitzian aggregation function* L_δ *and* L^δ *(respectively, quasi-copulas* Q_δ *and* Q^δ*), such that*

$$\mathsf{L}(x, x) = \delta_\mathsf{L}(x) \quad \left(\text{respectively, } \mathsf{Q}(x, x) = \delta_\mathsf{Q}(x)\right), \quad x \in [0, 1],$$

are given by

$$\mathsf{L}_\delta(x, y) = \mathsf{Min}(x, y) + \sup\{\delta_\mathsf{L}(z) - z \mid z \in [\mathsf{Min}(x, y), \mathsf{Max}(x, y)]\}, \quad (6.42)$$

$$\mathsf{L}^\delta(x, y) = \mathsf{Max}(x, y) + \inf\{\delta_\mathsf{L}(z) - z \mid z \in [\mathsf{Min}(x, y), \mathsf{Max}(x, y)]\} \quad (6.43)$$

and $\mathsf{Q}_\delta(x, y) = \mathsf{L}_\delta(x, y)$,

$$\mathsf{Q}^\delta(x, y) = \mathsf{Min}\left(x, y, \mathsf{L}^\delta(x, y)\right). \quad (6.44)$$

Proof. Suppose that $0 \leqslant u < \mathsf{Min}(x,y)$. Then due to Proposition 6.67 we have

$$\mathsf{L}_{(u,u,\delta_\mathsf{L}(u))}(x,y) = \mathsf{Max}(0, x+y-1, \delta_\mathsf{L}(u))$$

$$= \delta(u)$$

$$\leqslant \delta_\mathsf{L}(\mathsf{Min}(x,y))$$

$$= \mathsf{Max}(0, x+y-1, \delta_\mathsf{L}(\mathsf{Min}(x,y)))$$

$$= \mathsf{L}_{(\mathsf{Min}(x,y),\mathsf{Min}(x,y),\delta_\mathsf{L}(\mathsf{Min}(x,y)))}(x,y).$$

Similarly, for each $v \in \,]\mathsf{Max}(x,y), 1]$,

$$\mathsf{L}^{(v,v,\delta(v))}(x,y) \leqslant \mathsf{L}^{(\mathsf{Max}(x,y),\mathsf{Max}(x,y),\delta_\mathsf{L}(\mathsf{Max}(x,y)))}(x,y)$$

and thus

$$\mathsf{L}_\delta(x,y) = \sup \left\{ \mathsf{L}_{(z,z,\delta_\mathsf{L}(z))}(x,y) \mid z \in [\mathsf{Min}(x,y), \mathsf{Max}(x,y)] \right\}.$$

Moreover, for $z \in [\mathsf{Min}(x,y), \mathsf{Max}(x,y)]$,

$$\mathsf{L}_{(z,z,\delta(z))}(x,y) = \mathsf{Max}(0, x+y-1, \delta_\mathsf{L}(z) + \mathsf{Min}(x,y) - z)$$

$$= \mathsf{Min}(x,y) + (\delta_\mathsf{L}(z) - z).$$

Summarizing all these facts, the formula (6.42) for L_δ follows. Similarly, the formula (6.43) can be shown. Moreover, for any 1-Lipschitzian aggregation function $\mathsf{L} : [0,1]^2 \to [0,1]$, the function $\mathsf{Q} : [0,1]^2 \to [0,1]$ given by

$$\mathsf{Q}(x,y) = \mathsf{Min}(x,y,\mathsf{L}(x,y))$$

is a quasi-copula, which concludes the rest of the proof. $\qquad\qquad\square$

Remark 6.71. Functions given by formulas (6.43) and (6.44) are symmetric. Moreover, the smallest quasi-copula Q_δ given by (6.42) is also a copula (and thus the smallest copula C satisfying $\mathsf{C}(x,x) = \delta_\mathsf{C}(x)$ for all $x \in [0,1]$). The copula Q_δ is also called the Bertino copula [41, 123]. On the other hand, the greatest quasi-copula Q^δ given by (6.44) need not be a copula, in general. Observe that the greatest symmetric copula C^δ with the given diagonal function δ was introduced in [123], and it is given by

$$\mathsf{C}^\delta(x,y) = \mathsf{Min}\left(x, y, \frac{\delta_\mathsf{C}(x) + \delta_\mathsf{C}(y)}{2}\right).$$

There may exist nonsymmetric copulas with diagonal section δ_C which are incomparable with C, and the greatest copula with given diagonal δ_C exists if and only if $\mathsf{Q}^\delta = \mathsf{C}^\delta$ (and then it is C^δ; this happens only if δ_C is the diagonal section of an ordinal sum t-norm (see Section 3.3.7 and Section 6.7), with all involved summands being T_L [332]).

Example 6.72. Let $\delta : [0,1] \rightarrow [0,1]$ be the quadratic function $\delta(x) = x^2$. Evidently, the product $\Pi : [0,1]^2 \rightarrow [0,1]$ satisfies $\Pi(x,x) = x^2$ (recall that the product is a copula, and thus also a quasi-copula and a 1-Lipschitzian aggregation function). The smallest 1-Lipschitzian aggregation function (quasi-copula, Bertino copula) related to δ is given by

$$L_\delta(x,y) = \begin{cases} (\mathrm{Min}(x,y))^2 & \text{if } x+y \leqslant 1 \\ (\mathrm{Max}(x,y))^2 - |x-y| & \text{otherwise.} \end{cases}$$

The greatest 1-Lipschitzian aggregation function L^δ is given by

$$L^\delta(x,y) = \begin{cases} (\mathrm{Max}(x,y))^2 & \text{if } x+y \leqslant 1 \\ (\mathrm{Min}(x,y))^2 + |x-y| & \text{otherwise.} \end{cases}$$

In this case, the greatest quasi-copula Q^δ, given by

$$Q^\delta(x,y) = \mathrm{Min}(x,y,L^\delta(x,y)),$$

is not a copula. The greatest copula does not exist for this δ; however, the greatest symmetric copula C^δ is given by

$$C^\delta(x,y) = \mathrm{Min}\left(x, y, \frac{x^2 + y^2}{2}\right).$$

Similar results can be obtained in the case when the values of an aggregation function $A : [0,1]^2 \rightarrow [0,1]$ on a horizontal section $A(\cdot, c)$ and/or on a vertical section $A(d, \cdot)$ are known; see, e.g., [106, 214, 215].

7

Aggregation on specific scale types

7.1 Introduction

This chapter is devoted to the study of meaningful n-ary functions $\mathsf{F} : \mathbb{I}^n \to \mathbb{R}$ mapping specific scales into a scale in the sense of measurement theory, all the scales considered being of the same type. In many practical problems, individual measurements are merged into one dependent variable and further exploited for decision purposes, demanding the exclusion of the influence of the applied scales (both in independent and dependent variables). The scale types are defined through admissible transformations, whose consideration may significantly reduce the number of acceptable aggregation functions. For a detailed introduction we recommend Section 2.4 of this book. The relevant literature can be found in [6, 12, 13, 238, 256, 257, 364, 365].

Though it is possible to combine scales of different types, too (see for instance Aczél and Roberts [12] and Aczél et al. [13]), we focus in this chapter on the case when the independent and dependent variables define scales of the same type. Namely, we discuss ratio scales, difference scales, interval scales, and log-ratio scales. The case of ordinal scales will be discussed in Chapter 8. Note that the majority of results in the literature deal with admissible transformations which are (increasing) bijections on $\mathbb{I}$, and thus the choice of $\mathbb{I}$ is restricted, too. For example, for ratio scales supposing $rx \in \mathbb{I}$ for each $r > 0$ and $x \in \mathbb{I}$ means that a nondegenerate interval $\mathbb{I}$ is either $]0, \infty[$, or $] - \infty, 0]$, or $\mathbb{R}$. Similarly, for difference scales, $\mathbb{I} = \mathbb{R}$ is usually supposed.

Meaningfulness properties introduced in Section 2.4 are more general, allowing one to take into account any interval $\mathbb{I}$ (however, then only transformations with restricted domain are taken into account). As a prototypical example we will often deal with $\mathbb{I} = [0, 1]$.

Note also that general solutions of discussed meaningfulness properties need not be aggregation functions (mostly, monotonicity is not taken into account). However, for each discussed scale type we present also the set of solutions belonging to the class of aggregation functions, which can then be dramatically reduced.

For the convenience of the reader, we recall the basic meaningfulness properties introduced in Section 2.4 whenever we need them. Note also that we include proofs for the majority of the results on ratio scales, i.e., in Section 7.2, while on the other types of scales we omit them, to avoid bothering readers with repeating similar arguments (but always indicating the relevant sources).

7.2 Ratio scales

We recall the meaningfulness properties for ratio scales as introduced in Definitions 2.86–2.88.

A function $F : \mathbb{I}^n \to \mathbb{R}$ is

(i) *ratio scale invariant* (positively homogeneous) if, for any $r > 0$, we have

$$F(r\mathbf{x}) = r\,F(\mathbf{x})$$

for all $\mathbf{x} \in \mathbb{I}^n$ such that $r\mathbf{x} \in \mathbb{I}^n$;

(ii) *meaningful on a single ratio scale* if, for any $r > 0$, there exists $R(r) > 0$ such that

$$F(r\mathbf{x}) = R(r)\,F(\mathbf{x})$$

for all $\mathbf{x} \in \mathbb{I}^n$ such that $r\mathbf{x} \in \mathbb{I}^n$;

(iii) *meaningful on independent ratio scales* if, for any $\mathbf{r} \in\,]0, \infty[^n$, there exists $R(\mathbf{r}) > 0$ such that

$$F(\mathbf{r}\mathbf{x}) = R(\mathbf{r})\,F(\mathbf{x})$$

for all $\mathbf{x} \in \mathbb{I}^n$ such that $\mathbf{r}\mathbf{x} \in \mathbb{I}^n$.

Clearly, each function F that is meaningful on independent ratio scales is also meaningful on a single ratio scale (take, for example, the product Π), but not vice-versa (take, e.g., the function Max on $[0, 1]$). Similarly, ratio scale invariant functions are meaningful on a single ratio scale, but not vice-versa (again the product Π illustrates this fact). Relationships among the above ratio scale properties are illustrated in Figure 7.1.

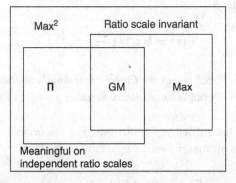

Figure 7.1 Relationships among ratio scale properties for functions in $[0, 1]^n$

7.2.1 General descriptions

The most specific situation of meaningful functions (on $[0, \infty[$) on independent ratio scales was already described in Example 2.85. For details see [12, 13], where also other results summarized in this subsection can be found.

Proposition 7.1. *A function* $\mathsf{F} : [0, \infty[^n \to [0, \infty[$ *is meaningful on independent ratio scales if and only if*

$$\mathsf{F}(\mathbf{x}) = a \prod_{i=1}^{n} f_i(x_i), \tag{7.1}$$

where $a > 0$ *and* $f_i : [0, \infty[\to [0, \infty[$ *satisfy the Cauchy equation*

$$f_i(xy) = f_i(x) f_i(y)$$

for $i = 1, \ldots, n.$

Proof. The sufficiency of (7.1) is evident, and then $R(\mathbf{r}) = \prod_i f_i(r_i)$. To see the necessity, by induction we obtain for any function $\mathsf{F} : [0, \infty[^n \to [0, \infty[$, which is meaningful on independent ratio scales, that

$$\mathsf{F}(\mathbf{x}) = R(x_1, 1, \ldots, 1)\, R(1, x_2, \ldots, 1) \cdots R(1, \ldots, 1, x_n)\, \mathsf{F}(\mathbf{1}).$$

Putting $f_i(x) = R(1, \ldots, 1, x, 1, \ldots, 1)$ (x is at the ith position), it is easy to see that f_i satisfies $f_i(xy) = f_i(x) f_i(y)$. If $\mathsf{F}(\mathbf{1}) > 0$ then it is enough to put $a = \mathsf{F}(\mathbf{1})$ to get (7.1). In the remaining case when $\mathsf{F}(\mathbf{1}) = 0$ one can take an arbitrary positive constant as then each f_i and F are constant 0 functions. $\qquad \square$

Remark 7.2. We observe that (7.1) solves the problem of meaningfulness on independent ratio scales for functions $\mathsf{F} : \mathbb{I}^n \to [0, \infty[$ for an arbitrary interval $\mathbb{I}$.

Proposition 7.3. *A function* $\mathsf{F} :]0, \infty[^n \to]0, \infty[$, $n \geqslant 2$, *is meaningful on a single ratio scale if and only if*

$$\mathsf{F}(\mathbf{x}) = h(x_1) f\left(\frac{x_2}{x_1}, \ldots, \frac{x_n}{x_1}\right), \tag{7.2}$$

where $h :]0, \infty[\to]0, \infty[$ *solves the Cauchy functional equation* $h(xy) = h(x)h(y)$ *and* $f :]0, \infty[^{n-1} \to]0, \infty[$ *is an arbitrary function.*

Proof. Here again, the sufficiency is obvious. For the necessity, suppose that $\mathsf{F} :]0, \infty[^n \to]0, \infty[$ is meaningful on a single ratio scale. Then

$$\mathsf{F}(\mathbf{x}) = R(x_1)\, \mathsf{F}\left(1, \frac{x_2}{x_1}, \ldots, \frac{x_n}{x_1}\right).$$

Putting $h = R$ and $f(u_1, \ldots, u_{n-1}) = \mathsf{F}(1, u_1, \ldots, u_{n-1})$ we get (7.2). Moreover,

$$\mathsf{F}(n \cdot xy) = h(xy)f(\mathbf{1}) = h(x)\mathsf{F}(n \cdot y) = h(x)h(y)f(\mathbf{1}),$$

and hence, h solves the Cauchy functional equation $h(xy) = h(x)h(y)$. $\qquad \square$

Remark 7.4. Again, we can extend Proposition 7.3 to any interval $\mathbb{I}$ including $\mathbb{I} = [0, 1]$. Note that if $0 \in \mathbb{I}$, then the structure of all solutions is more complicated. Take, e.g., $\mathbb{I} = [0, 1]$. Then, for $n \geqslant 2$, a function $\mathsf{F} : [0, 1]^n \to [0, \infty[$ is meaningful on a single ratio scale if and only if there are functions $h_1, \ldots, h_n : [0, 1] \to [0, \infty[$ satisfying the Cauchy functional equation

$$h_i(xy) = h_i(x)h_i(y)$$

and functions $f_i : [0, 1]^{n-i} \to [0, \infty[, i = 2, \ldots, n - 1$, such that

$$\mathsf{F}(\mathbf{x}) = \begin{cases} h_1(x_1)f_1(\frac{x_2}{x_1}, \ldots, \frac{x_n}{x_1}) & \text{if } x_1 > 0 \\ h_2(x_2)f_2(\frac{x_3}{x_2}, \ldots, \frac{x_n}{x_2}) & \text{if } x_1 = 0, x_2 > 0 \\ \qquad \vdots \\ h_{n-1}(x_{n-1})f_{n-1}(\frac{x_n}{x_{n-1}}) & \text{if } x_1 = \cdots = x_{n-2} = 0, x_{n-1} > 0 \\ h_n(x_n) & \text{if } x_1 = \cdots x_{n-1} = 0, \end{cases}$$

and $F(\mathbf{0}) = c$ is a nonnegative constant.

Finally, we characterize all ratio scale invariant (positively homogeneous) functions on $]0, \infty[$.

Proposition 7.5. *A function* $\mathsf{F} :]0, \infty[^n \to]0, \infty[, n \geqslant 2$, *is ratio scale invariant if and only if*

$$\mathsf{F}(\mathbf{x}) = x_1 f\left(\frac{x_2}{x_1}, \ldots, \frac{x_n}{x_1}\right), \tag{7.3}$$

where $f :]0, \infty[^{n-1} \to]0, \infty[$ *is an arbitrary function.*

Proof. The sufficiency is obvious. The necessity follows from Proposition 7.3. Indeed, ratio scale invariance implies meaningfulness on a single ratio scale with $R = \text{id} = h$, and thus (7.2) is then equivalent to (7.3). $\qquad \square$

Remark 7.6. A similar conclusion to that in the case of meaningful functions on a single ratio scale concerning their domain is valid also in this case.

Example 7.7. Consider $f(u, v) = \exp(u - 2v)$ and define the 3-ary function $\mathsf{F}(x, y, z) = xf(\frac{y}{x}, \frac{z}{x}) = x \exp(\frac{y-2z}{x})$. Due to Proposition 7.5, F is ratio scale invariant.

Considering the possible peculiar solutions of the classical Cauchy equation related to characterizations (7.1), (7.2), and (7.3), one can introduce rather peculiar examples of functions which are meaningful on ratio scales or ratio scale invariant. We omit such examples having in mind our main focus, namely aggregation functions.

7.2.2 Aggregation functions on ratio scales

The nondecreasing monotonicity of aggregation functions is reflected in the non-decreasing monotonicity of solutions of Cauchy's equation $h(xy) = h(x)h(y)$ in the description of meaningful functions on ratio scales. However, then each such solution has the form $h(x) = x^c$, where c is a nonnegative constant, and $h(0) \in \{0, 1\}$; see Aczél [3]. This observation drastically reduces the choice of aggregation functions possessing some of the discussed properties on ratio scales. As an easy corollary of Proposition 7.1 we have the next characterization of all aggregation functions on a specified $\mathbb{I}$ which are meaningful on independent ratio scales.

Proposition 7.8. *Let* $\mathbb{I} = [0, b[$, *with* $b \in]0, \infty]$. *A function* $\mathsf{F} : \mathbb{I}^n \to \mathbb{I}$ *is a meaningful aggregation function on independent ratio scales if and only if*

$$\mathsf{F}(\mathbf{x}) = a \prod_{i=1}^{n} x_i^{a_i}, \tag{7.4}$$

where $a_1, \ldots, a_n \in [0, \infty[$, $\sum_{i=1}^{n} a_i > 0$, *and* $a > 0$ *if* $b = \infty$, *while* $a = b \prod_{i=1}^{n} b^{-a_i}$ *if* $b < \infty$.

Obviously, each aggregation function F described in (7.4) is continuous. Moreover, it is symmetric whenever $a_i = \cdots = a_n = c$, i.e., if $\mathsf{F}(\mathbf{x}) = a \prod_{i=1}^{n} x_i^c$. Similarly, F is idempotent whenever $\sum_{i=1}^{n} a_i = 1$ (and $a = 1$) and then F is the weighted geometric mean, $\mathsf{F}(\mathbf{x}) = \prod_{i=1}^{n} x_i^{a_i}$. Roberts [365, §6] showed that functions of the form (7.4), and particularly the weighted geometric means, are appropriate aggregation functions to merge relative values, such as relative prices or relative performance scores.

On $]0, \infty[$, meaningful functions on a single ratio scale and possessing some regularity (monotonicity, boundedness, etc.) were characterized in Aczél and Roberts [12] and Aczél *et al.* [13] in the form (7.2) with $h(x) = x^c$, $c > 0$, i.e.,

$$\mathsf{F}(\mathbf{x}) = x_1^c f\left(\frac{x_2}{x_1}, \ldots, \frac{x_n}{x_1}\right).$$

Then $\mathsf{F}^{1/c}$ is a ratio scale invariant function, and it is nondecreasing if and only if F is nondecreasing. Therefore the complete description of ratio scale invariant aggregation functions enables us to complete the description of the meaningful aggregation functions on a single ratio scale.

Proposition 7.9. *An aggregation function* $\mathsf{A} : \mathbb{I}^n \to \mathbb{I}$, *with* $\mathbb{I} = [0, b[$, $b \in]0, \infty]$, *is meaningful on a single ratio scale if and only if*

- *we have*

$$\frac{A(n \cdot x)}{A(n \cdot x_0)} = \left(\frac{x}{x_0}\right)^c$$

for some $c > 0$, $x_0 \in \mathbb{I}$ and all $x \in \mathbb{I}$, and
- *the function $a A^{1/c} : \mathbb{I}^n \to \mathbb{I}$, where $a > 0$ if $\sup \mathbb{I} = \infty$ and $a = b^{\frac{c-1}{c}}$ if $\sup \mathbb{I} = b < \infty$, is a ratio scale invariant aggregation function.*

Moreover, if $\mathbb{I} = [a, b] \subset]0, \infty[$, then an aggregation function $A : \mathbb{I}^n \to \mathbb{I}$ is meaningful on a single ratio scale if and only if A is ratio scale invariant.

For ratio scale invariant aggregation functions we introduce their complete description on $[0, \infty[$ derived from Aczél *et al.* [10, Th. 8], where also the case $\mathbb{I} = \mathbb{R}$ is discussed, and which can be extended also for $\mathbb{I} = |0, \infty|$.

Proposition 7.10. *An aggregation function $A : [0, \infty[^n \to [0, \infty[$, $n \geqslant 2$, is ratio scale invariant if and only if $A(\mathbf{0}) = 0$ and*

$$A(\mathbf{x}) = x_i f_i\left(\frac{x_{i+1}}{x_i}, \ldots, \frac{x_n}{x_i}\right)$$

if $x_1 = \cdots = x_{i-1} = 0$, $x_i > 0$, where

(i) *$f_i : [0, \infty[^{n-i} \to [0, \infty[$ is nondecreasing for $i = 1, \ldots, n-1$ and f_n is a positive constant;*
(ii) *$f_i(c\mathbf{y}) \geqslant c f_i(\mathbf{y})$ for all $i = 1, \ldots, n-1$, all $c \in]0, 1[$ and all $\mathbf{y} \in [0, \infty[^{n-i}$;*
(iii) *$f_i(0, \ldots, 0, t) \geqslant t f_n$ for all $t \in]0, \infty[$;*
(iv) *$f_i(0, \ldots, 0, t, z_1, \ldots, z_k) \geqslant t f_{n-k}(z_1, \ldots, z_k)$ for all $t \in]0, \infty[$ and all $(z_1, \ldots, z_k) \in [0, \infty[^k$, $1 \leqslant k < n - i$.*

Proof. The proof follows from Remark 7.4 in a similar manner to the way Proposition 7.5 follows from Proposition 7.3, keeping in mind the nondecreasing monotonicity of aggregation functions. For example, requirement (ii) is equivalent to the nondecreasing monotonicity of $F(0, \ldots, 0, x_i, x_{i+1}, \ldots, x_n)$ in the ith coordinate. □

Example 7.11. Consider the binary aggregation function

$$A(x, y) = \begin{cases} x f\left(\frac{y}{x}\right) & \text{if } x > 0 \\ ay & \text{otherwise,} \end{cases}$$

where $f(u) \geqslant au$, so taking $f(u) = u^2 + 1$ and $a = 1$, we have

$$A(x, y) = \begin{cases} \frac{x^2 + y^2}{x} & \text{if } x > 0 \\ y & \text{if } x = 0 \end{cases}$$

is a ratio scale invariant aggregation function.

Adding some specific properties we can further limit the appropriate choice of ratio scale invariant functions.

Corollary 7.12. *An aggregation function* $\mathsf{A} : [0, \infty[^n \to [0, \infty[$ *with an annihilator* $a = 0$ *is ratio scale invariant if and only if*

$$\mathsf{A}(\mathbf{x}) = \begin{cases} 0 & \text{if } x_1 = 0 \\ x_1 f(\frac{x_2}{x_1}, \ldots, \frac{x_n}{x_1}) & \text{otherwise,} \end{cases}$$

where $f : [0, \infty[^{n-1} \to [0, \infty[$ *is a nondecreasing function such that*

$$f(c\mathbf{y}) \geqslant cf(\mathbf{y})$$

for all $c \in \,]0, 1[$ *and all* $\mathbf{y} \in [0, \infty[^{n-1}$, *and* $f(\mathbf{y}) = 0$ *whenever* $0 \in \{y_1, \ldots, y_{n-1}\}$.

We also have the next result (see Aczél *et al.* [10, Prop. 9]).

Proposition 7.13. *An aggregation function* $\mathsf{A} : [0, \infty[^n \to [0, \infty[$ *is ratio scale invariant and differentiable at* $\mathbf{0}$ *if and only if* A *is a weighted sum, i.e.,*

$$\mathsf{A}(\mathbf{x}) = \sum_{i=1}^{n} w_i x_i$$

for $\mathbf{w} = (w_1, \ldots, w_n) \in [0, \infty[^n$, $\mathbf{w} \neq \mathbf{0}$.

Ratio scale invariant aggregation functions on $[0, \infty[$ are closely related to ratio scale invariant aggregation functions on $[0, 1]$. Indeed, if $\mathsf{A} : [0, \infty[^n \to [0, \infty[$ is a ratio scale invariant aggregation function, then the function $\mathsf{B} : [0, 1]^n \to [0, 1]$ given by $\mathsf{B}(\mathbf{x}) := \frac{\mathsf{A}(\mathbf{x})}{\mathsf{A}(\mathbf{1})}$ is a ratio scale invariant aggregation function, too.[1] Conversely, for any ratio scale invariant aggregation function $\mathsf{C} : [0, 1]^n \to [0, 1]$ and any constant $c > 0$, $\mathsf{D} : [0, \infty[^n \to [0, \infty[$ given by $\mathsf{D}(\mathbf{0}) := 0$ and

$$\mathsf{D}(\mathbf{x}) := c\, \mathsf{Max}(\mathbf{x})\, \mathsf{C}\Big(\frac{\mathbf{x}}{\mathsf{Max}(\mathbf{x})}\Big), \qquad \text{if } \mathbf{x} \neq \mathbf{0}, \tag{7.5}$$

is also a ratio scale invariant aggregation function. Note that (7.5) can be applied to an arbitrary aggregation function C, but then the resulting function D need not be monotone, though it is ratio scale invariant. Construction (7.5) was discussed in Rückschlossová and Rückschloss [370, Th. 1].

Proposition 7.14. *Let* $\mathsf{C} : [0, 1]^n \to [0, 1]$ *be an aggregation function and let* $\mathsf{D} : [0, \infty[^n \to [0, \infty[$ *be given by (7.5). Then* D *is a ratio scale invariant aggregation function if and only if*

$$\frac{\mathsf{C}(\mathbf{x})}{\mathsf{C}(\mathbf{y})} \geqslant \mathsf{Min}\Big(\frac{\mathbf{x}}{\mathbf{y}}\Big) \tag{7.6}$$

---

[1] The fact that $\mathsf{B}(\mathbf{x})$ lies in $[0, 1]$ follows trivially from the fact that A is an aggregation function and that $\mathsf{A}(\mathbf{1}) > 0$.

(recall that $\frac{x}{y}$ is defined componentwise) with convention $\frac{0}{0} = 1$ for all $x, y \in [0, 1]^n$ such that $x \leqslant y$ and $x_i = y_i = 1$ for some $i \in [n]$.

Proof. Evidently, D fulfills the boundary conditions for aggregation functions. Suppose that (7.6) holds. We show the nondecreasing monotonicity of D in the first coordinate (the case of the remaining coordinates is similar). Fix $x \in [0, \infty[^n$ such that $x \neq 0$. If $x_1 < \mathsf{Max}(x)$ then the monotonicity of C ensures $D(x_1 + \varepsilon, x_2, \ldots, x_n) \geqslant D(x_1, \ldots, x_n)$ for all $0 < \varepsilon \leqslant \mathsf{Max}(x) - x_1$. If $x_1 = \mathsf{Max}(x)$, then (7.6) ensures for all $\varepsilon > 0$ that

$$\frac{C\left(1, \frac{x_2}{x_1+\varepsilon}, \ldots, \frac{x_n}{x_1+\varepsilon}\right)}{C\left(1, \frac{x_2}{x_1}, \ldots, \frac{x_n}{x_1}\right)} \geqslant \frac{x_1}{x_1 + \varepsilon},$$

and hence

$$D(x) = c x_1 C\left(1, \frac{x_2}{x_1}, \ldots, \frac{x_n}{x_1}\right)$$

$$\leqslant c(x_1 + \varepsilon) C\left(1, \frac{x_2}{x_1 + \varepsilon}, \ldots, \frac{x_n}{x_1 + \varepsilon}\right)$$

$$= D(x_1 + \varepsilon, x_2, \ldots, x_n).$$

To see the necessity, assume that (7.6) is violated. That is, there is $i \in [n]$ and $u, v \in [0, 1]^n$, $u \leqslant v$, $u_i = v_i = 1$, such that

$$\frac{C(u)}{C(v)} < \mathsf{Min}\left(\frac{u}{v}\right) \leqslant 1.$$

Define $w \in [0, 1]^n$ by $w_i = v_i \, \mathsf{Min}(\frac{u}{v})$. Then evidently $w \leqslant u$, but

$$D(w) = \mathsf{Min}\left(\frac{u}{v}\right) D(v) = c \, \mathsf{Min}\left(\frac{u}{v}\right) C(v) > c \, C(u) = D(u),$$

thus violating the nondecreasing monotonicity of D in the ith coordinate. $\qquad \square$

Remark 7.15. (i) Property (7.6) of an aggregation function $C : [0, 1]^n \to [0, 1]$ is crucial for the monotonicity of the function $D : [0, \infty[^n \to [0, \infty[$ constructed by means of (7.5) (and thus inducing a ratio scale invariant function $B : [0, 1]^n \to [0, 1]$, $B(x) = \mathsf{Max}(x)C\left(\frac{x}{\mathsf{Max}(x)}\right)$ for $x \neq 0$). Actually, by using the logarithmic transformation of C into $L : [0, \infty]^n \to [0, \infty]$, namely

$$L(x) := -\log(C(\exp(-x_1), \ldots, \exp(-x_n))), \qquad (7.7)$$

property (7.6) can be rewritten as

$$\|L(x) - L(y)\| \leqslant \|x - y\|_\infty, \qquad (7.8)$$

where $\|.\|_\infty$ is the standard Chebyshev norm (i.e., L_∞-norm).

(ii) The function D in (7.5) is idempotent if and only if $c = 1$, that is, if $D(x) = \mathsf{Max}(x) \, C(x/\mathsf{Max}(x))$ whenever $x \neq 0$.

Due to the monotonicity of L, it is enough to deal with $\mathbf{x}, \mathbf{y} \in [0, \infty]^n$ such that $x_i = y_i = 0$ for some $i \in [n]$. Note that aggregation functions satisfying (7.8) for all $\mathbf{x}, \mathbf{y} \in [0, \infty]^n$ are equivalently characterized by[2]

$$L(\mathbf{x} + s\mathbf{1}) \leqslant L(\mathbf{x}) + s$$

for all $\mathbf{x} \in]0, \infty[^n$ and $s \in [0, \infty]$, and as a prominent example we recall the Choquet integral-based aggregation functions (related to a normalized capacity; see Section 5.2.2).

Example 7.16. For $n = 2$, a general form of the Choquet integral $L : [0, \infty]^2 \to [0, \infty]$ related to a normalized capacity is given by

$$L(x, y) = \begin{cases} ax + (1 - a)y & \text{if } x \geqslant y \\ (1 - b)x + by & \text{otherwise,} \end{cases}$$

where $a, b \in [0, 1]$ are given constants. Then the corresponding aggregation function $C : [0, 1]^2 \to [0, 1]$ related to L by (7.7) is given by

$$C(x, y) = \begin{cases} x^a y^{1-a} & \text{if } x \leqslant y \\ x^{1-b} y^b & \text{otherwise.} \end{cases}$$

Observe that C is a ratio scale invariant aggregation function. Moreover, the function $D : [0, \infty[^2 \to [0, \infty[$ constructed by means of (7.5) is given by

$$D(x, y) = \begin{cases} cx^a y^{1-a} & \text{if } x \leqslant y \\ cx^{1-b} y^b & \text{otherwise,} \end{cases}$$

where $c > 0$, and then D is a ratio scale invariant aggregation function.

7.3 Difference scales

We first recall the meaningfulness properties for difference scales as introduced in Definitions 2.89–2.91. Namely, a function $F : \mathbb{I}^n \to \mathbb{R}$ is

(i) *difference scale invariant* if, for any $s \in \mathbb{R}$, we have

$$F(\mathbf{x} + s\mathbf{1}) = F(\mathbf{x}) + s$$

for all $\mathbf{x} \in \mathbb{I}^n$ such that $\mathbf{x} + s\mathbf{1} \in \mathbb{I}^n$;

---

[2] Indeed, the equivalence follows from the monotonicity of L (note that C is an aggregation function). For any $\mathbf{x}, \mathbf{y}$, we have

$$|L(\mathbf{x}) - L(\mathbf{y})| \leqslant L(\text{Max}(\mathbf{x}, \mathbf{y})) - L(\text{Min}(\mathbf{x}, \mathbf{y})) \leqslant L(\text{Min}(\mathbf{x}, \mathbf{y}) + s\mathbf{1}) - L(\text{Min}(\mathbf{x}, \mathbf{y})) \leqslant s,$$

where $s = \|\mathbf{x} - \mathbf{y}\|_\infty$, which is exactly (7.8).

(ii) *meaningful on a single difference scale* if, for any $s \in \mathbb{R}$, there exists $S(s) \in \mathbb{R}$ such that

$$F(\mathbf{x} + s\mathbf{1}) = F(\mathbf{x}) + S(s)$$

for all $\mathbf{x} \in \mathbb{I}^n$ such that $\mathbf{x} + s\mathbf{1} \in \mathbb{I}^n$;

(iii) *meaningful on independent difference scales* if, for any $\mathbf{s} \in \mathbb{R}^n$, there exists $S(\mathbf{s}) \in \mathbb{R}$ such that

$$F(\mathbf{x} + \mathbf{s}) = F(\mathbf{x}) + S(\mathbf{s})$$

for all $\mathbf{x} \in \mathbb{I}^n$ such that $\mathbf{x} + \mathbf{s} \in \mathbb{I}^n$.

In formula (7.7) we have seen a transformation relating an (aggregation) function C reflecting the ratio scales properties to an (aggregation) function L reflecting the difference scales properties.

Proposition 7.17. *Let* $F : \mathbb{I}^n \to \mathbb{R}$ *be a given function and let* $G : \mathbb{J}^n \to \mathbb{R}$ *be given by*

$$G(\mathbf{x}) := \exp(-F(-\log x_1, \ldots, -\log x_n)), \tag{7.9}$$

where $\mathbb{J} = \{\exp(-t) \mid t \in \mathbb{I}\}$. *Then*

(i) F *is meaningful on a single difference scale if and only if* G *is meaningful on a single ratio scale.*

(ii) F *is meaningful on independent difference scales if and only if* G *is meaningful on independent ratio scales.*

(iii) F *is difference scale invariant if and only if* G *is ratio scale invariant.*

The proof of the above proposition is only a matter of basic calculus. However, Proposition 7.17 gives a hint on how to describe meaningfulness properties on difference scales by means of the corresponding properties on ratio scales discussed in Section 7.2. Observe that in the literature, the case of ratio scales is discussed mostly independently of the case of difference scales; see for example Aczél *et al.* [10]. For the convenience of the reader, we summarize in the next subsection the results concerning the difference scales (the relation with the corresponding results on the ratio scales is not always immediate).

7.3.1 General descriptions

Recall that each meaningful function F on independent difference scales is also meaningful on a single difference scale. Moreover, each difference scale invariant function F is also meaningful on a single difference scale. Functions on $\mathbb{R}$ that are meaningful on independent difference scales are characterized in the next proposition.

Proposition 7.18. *A function* $F : \mathbb{R}^n \to \mathbb{R}$ *is meaningful on independent difference scales if and only if*

$$F(\mathbf{x}) = c + \sum_{i=1}^{n} f_i(x_i), \tag{7.10}$$

where $c \in \mathbb{R}$ and $f_i : \mathbb{R} \to \mathbb{R}$ satisfy the Cauchy equation

$$f_i(x + y) = f_i(x) + f_i(y)$$

for $i = 1, \ldots, n$.

Remark 7.19. Note that (7.10) gives a general solution of the meaningfulness on independent difference scales also for functions $\mathsf{F} : \mathbb{I}^n \to \mathbb{R}$, where $\mathbb{I}$ is an arbitrary fixed interval.

For meaningful functions on a single difference scale we have the next description.

Proposition 7.20. *A function $\mathsf{F} : \mathbb{R}^n \to \mathbb{R}$, $n \geqslant 2$, is meaningful on a single difference scale if and only if*

$$\mathsf{F}(\mathbf{x}) = h(x_1) + f(x_2 - x_1, \ldots, x_n - x_1), \tag{7.11}$$

where $h : \mathbb{R} \to \mathbb{R}$ solves the Cauchy equation $h(x+y) = h(x) + h(y)$ and $f : \mathbb{R}^{n-1} \to \mathbb{R}$ is an arbitrary function.

Remark 7.21. Again the formula (7.11) yields a complete description of functions $\mathsf{F} : \mathbb{I}^n \to \mathbb{R}$, which are meaningful on a single difference scale, where $\mathbb{I} \subset \mathbb{R}$ is an arbitrary real interval. In the case when ∞ or $-\infty$ are elements of $\mathbb{I}$, the structure of meaningful functions on a single difference scale may be much more complicated; see Remark 7.4 (for ratio scales).

Proposition 7.22. *A function $\mathsf{F} : \mathbb{R}^n \to \mathbb{R}$, $n \geqslant 2$, is difference scale invariant if and only if*

$$\mathsf{F}(\mathbf{x}) = x_1 + f(x_2 - x_1, \ldots, x_n - x_1), \tag{7.12}$$

where $f : \mathbb{R}^{n-1} \to \mathbb{R}$ is an arbitrary function.

Formula (7.12) provides a hint on how to construct difference scale invariant functions not only defined on $\mathbb{R}^n$, but also on $\mathbb{I}^n$ for an arbitrary real interval $\mathbb{I}$.

7.3.2 Aggregation functions on difference scales

As we have seen in Section 7.3.1, an important role in the description of functions related to difference scales is played by the solutions of the Cauchy functional equation $h(x + y) = h(x) + h(y)$. By Proposition 2.115, the only nondecreasing solutions of this functional equation have the form $h(x) = cx$, where $c \geqslant 0$ is a given constant. This observation has the following impact on the description of aggregation functions related to difference scales.

Proposition 7.23. *A function* $F : \mathbb{I}^n \to \mathbb{I}$ *is a meaningful aggregation function on independent difference scales if and only if*

$$F(\mathbf{x}) = d + \sum_{i=1}^{n} c_i\, x_i, \qquad (7.13)$$

where

(i) $c_1, \ldots, c_n \in [0, \infty[,\ \sum_{i=1}^{n} c_i > 0,\ d \in \mathbb{R};$
(ii) $d + a \sum_{i=1}^{n} c_i = a,\ d + b \sum_{i=1}^{n} c_i = b,$ *where* $a = \inf \mathbb{I}$ *and* $b = \sup \mathbb{I}.$

Each aggregation function $A : \mathbb{I}^n \to \mathbb{I}$, which is meaningful on independent difference scales, is also continuous. It is symmetric whenever $c_1 = \cdots = c_n = c$, i.e., $A(\mathbf{x}) = d + c \sum_{i=1}^{n} x_i$. Moreover, it is idempotent whenever $d = 0$ and $\sum_{i=1}^{n} c_i = 1$, i.e., $A(\mathbf{x}) = \sum_{i=1}^{n} c_i x_i$ is a weighted arithmetic mean.

Proposition 7.24. *An aggregation function* $A : \mathbb{I}^n \to \mathbb{I}$, *with* $\mathbb{I} \subseteq \mathbb{R}$, *is meaningful on a single difference scale if and only if*

(i) $A(n \cdot x) - A(n \cdot y) = c(x - y)$ *for some* $c > 0$ *and all* $x, y \in \mathbb{R};$
(ii) *the function* $B : \mathbb{I}^n \to \mathbb{I}$, *given by* $B(\mathbf{x}) := \frac{A(\mathbf{x})}{c}$, *is a difference scale invariant aggregation function.*

Moreover, if $\mathbb{I} = [a, b] \subset \mathbb{R}$, *then an aggregation function* $A : \mathbb{I}^n \to \mathbb{I}$ *is meaningful on a single difference scale if and only if* A *is difference scale invariant.*

Due to Proposition 7.24, meaningful aggregation functions on a single difference scale are completely determined by the difference scale invariant aggregation functions (up to an affine transformation). Note also that if $\mathbb{I}$ is a bounded real interval then aggregation functions which are meaningful on a single difference scale coincide with those which are difference scale invariant. Following the ideas of Lázaro *et al.* [245] and Rückschlossová [369], one can derive the next results.

Proposition 7.25. *A function* $F : \mathbb{R}^n \to \mathbb{R}$, $n \geqslant 2$, *is a difference scale invariant aggregation function if and only if*

$$F(\mathbf{x}) = x_1 + f(x_2 - x_1, \ldots, x_n - x_1)$$

where $f : \mathbb{R}^{n-1} \to \mathbb{R}$ *is a nondecreasing function such that* $f(\mathbf{0}) = 0$ *and*

$$|f(\mathbf{u}) - f(\mathbf{v})| \leqslant \|\mathbf{u} - \mathbf{v}\|_\infty, \qquad (7.14)$$

(i.e., the Chebyshev norm of f, *namely* $\sup\{|f(\mathbf{x})| \mid \mathbf{x} \in \mathrm{dom}(f)\}$, *does not exceed 1).*

Observe that if F (or, equivalently, f) is differentiable, then (7.14) can be rewritten as $\sum_{i=1}^{n-1} \frac{\partial f}{\partial u_i} \leqslant 1$; see Aczél *et al.* [10]. The specific case $\mathbb{I} = [0, 1]$ was discussed in Lázaro *et al.* [245] and Rückschlossová [369], and it can be easily extended to $\mathbb{I} = [a, b] \subset \mathbb{R}$.

Proposition 7.26. *A function* $\mathsf{F} : [0, 1]^n \to [0, 1]$, $n \geqslant 2$, *is a difference scale invariant aggregation function if and only if*

$$\mathsf{F}(\mathbf{x}) = \mathrm{Min}(\mathbf{x}) + \mathsf{F}(\mathbf{x} - \mathrm{Min}(\mathbf{x})\mathbf{1})$$

and

$$0 \leqslant \mathsf{F}(\mathbf{x}) - \mathsf{F}(\mathbf{y}) \leqslant \mathrm{Max}(\mathbf{x} - \mathbf{y}),$$

for all $\mathbf{x}, \mathbf{y} \in [0, 1]^n$ *such that* $x_i = y_i = 0$ *for some* $i \in [n]$ *and* $\mathbf{x} \geqslant \mathbf{y}$.

Proposition 7.26 also gives a hint on how to construct difference scale invariant aggregation functions on $[0, 1]$. Indeed, for any aggregation function $\mathsf{B} : [0, 1]^n \to [0, 1]$ with Chebyshev norm equal to 1 (i.e., due to boundary conditions such B possesses the minimal possible Chebyshev norm), it is enough to define $\mathsf{A} : [0, 1]^n \to [0, 1]$ by

$$\mathsf{A}(\mathbf{x}) = \mathrm{Min}(\mathbf{x}) + \mathsf{B}(\mathbf{x} - \mathrm{Min}(\mathbf{x})\mathbf{1}). \tag{7.15}$$

Example 7.27. Let $\mathsf{B} : [0, 1]^2 \to [0, 1]$ be given by

$$\mathsf{B}(x, y) = \sqrt{\frac{x^2 + y^2}{2}},$$

i.e., B is the quadratic mean. Then B has Chebyshev norm equal to 1 and, applying (7.15), we can construct a difference scale invariant aggregation function $\mathsf{A} : [0, 1]^2 \to [0, 1]$ given by

$$\mathsf{A}(x, y) = \frac{\sqrt{2} - 1}{\sqrt{2}} \, \mathrm{Min}(x, y) + \frac{1}{\sqrt{2}} \, \mathrm{Max}(x, y),$$

i.e., A is an ordered weighted averaging function; see (1.19).

7.4 Interval scales

We first recall the meaningfulness properties for interval scales as introduced in Definitions 2.92–2.94.

A function $\mathsf{F} : \mathbb{I}^n \to \mathbb{R}$ is

(i) *interval scale invariant* if, for any $r > 0$ and any $s \in \mathbb{R}$, we have

$$\mathsf{F}(r\mathbf{x} + s\mathbf{1}) = r\,\mathsf{F}(\mathbf{x}) + s$$

for all $\mathbf{x} \in \mathbb{I}^n$ such that $r\mathbf{x} + s\mathbf{1} \in \mathbb{I}^n$;

(ii) *meaningful on a single interval scale* if, for any $r > 0$ and any $s \in \mathbb{R}$, there exists $R(r, s) > 0$ and $S(r, s) \in \mathbb{R}$ such that

$$\mathsf{F}(r\mathbf{x} + s\mathbf{1}) = R(r, s)\,\mathsf{F}(\mathbf{x}) + S(r, s)$$

for all $\mathbf{x} \in \mathbb{I}^n$ such that $r\mathbf{x} + s\mathbf{1} \in \mathbb{I}^n$;

(iii) *meaningful on independent interval scales* if, for any $\mathbf{r} \in\,]0, \infty[^n$ and any $\mathbf{s} \in \mathbb{R}^n$, there exists $R(\mathbf{r}, \mathbf{s}) > 0$ and $S(\mathbf{r}, \mathbf{s}) \in \mathbb{R}$ such that

$$\mathsf{F}(\mathbf{r}\mathbf{x} + \mathbf{s}) = R(\mathbf{r}, \mathbf{s})\,\mathsf{F}(\mathbf{x}) + S(\mathbf{r}, \mathbf{s})$$

for all $\mathbf{x} \in \mathbb{I}^n$ such that $\mathbf{r}\mathbf{x} + \mathbf{s} \in \mathbb{I}^n$.

It is evident that each interval scale invariant function $\mathsf{F} : \mathbb{I}^n \to \mathbb{R}$ is both ratio scale invariant (it is enough to put $s = 0$) and difference scale invariant (when fixing $r = 1$). Also the opposite claim is true, as well as similar claims for the other types of interval scales properties.

Proposition 7.28. *For a function $\mathsf{F} : \mathbb{I}^n \to \mathbb{R}$ we have:*

(i) *F is interval scale invariant if and only if F is ratio scale invariant and difference scale invariant.*

(ii) *F is meaningful on a single interval scale if and only if F is meaningful on a single ratio scale and on a single difference scale.*

(iii) *F is meaningful on independent interval scales if and only if F is meaningful on independent ratio scales and on independent difference scales.*

Proposition 7.28 indicates that the class of all (aggregation) functions $\mathsf{F} : \mathbb{I}^n \to \mathbb{R}$ possessing one of the interval scale properties is just the intersection of the class of all functions $\mathsf{G} : \mathbb{I}^n \to \mathbb{R}$ possessing the corresponding ratio scale property, and of the class of all functions $\mathsf{H} : \mathbb{I}^n \to \mathbb{R}$ possessing the corresponding difference scale property. Note that in the literature, the interval scale properties are mostly discussed separately and therefore we also summarize the characterizations of functions possessing some of the above-described interval scale properties independently of the corresponding results for ratio scales (see Section 7.2) and for difference scales (see Section 7.3). For more specific results, we recommend Aczél and Roberts [12] and Aczél *et al.* [13].

Table 7.1 indicates, for some basic aggregation functions, those which are ratio scale invariant (r.s.i.), meaningful on a single ratio scale (s.r.s.), meaningful on independent ratio scales (i.r.s.), difference scale invariant (d.s.i.), meaningful on a single difference scale (s.d.s.), meaningful on independent difference scales (i.d.s.), interval scale invariant (i.s.i.), meaningful on a single interval scale (s.i.s.), and meaningful on independent interval scales (i.i.s.).

Table 7.1. *Meaningfulness of some aggregation functions*

	r.s.i.	s.r.s.	i.r.s.	d.s.i.	s.d.s.	i.d.s.	i.s.i.	s.i.s.	i.i.s.
AM	Yes	Yes	No	Yes	Yes	Yes	Yes	Yes	No
GM	Yes	Yes	Yes	No	No	No	No	No	No
P_k	Yes	Yes	Yes	Yes	Yes	Yes	Yes	Yes	Yes
OS_k	Yes	Yes	No	Yes	Yes	No	Yes	Yes	No
WAM_w	Yes	Yes	No	Yes	Yes	Yes	Yes	Yes	No
WGM_w	Yes	Yes	Yes	No	No	No	No	No	No
OWA_w	Yes	Yes	No	Yes	Yes	No	Yes	Yes	No
Σ	Yes	Yes	No	No	Yes	Yes	No	Yes	No
Π	No	Yes	Yes	No	No	No	No	No	No
Max^2	No	Yes	No	No	No	No	No	No	No
$Med_{0.5}$	No	No	No	No	No	No	No	No	No

7.4.1 General descriptions

Meaningfulness on independent interval scales is a strong property significantly restricting the possible choice of acceptable functions.

Proposition 7.29. *A function* $F : \mathbb{I}^n \to \mathbb{R}$ *is meaningful on independent interval scales if and only if*

$$F(\mathbf{x}) = ax_i + b$$

for some $i \in [n]$, $a, b \in \mathbb{R}$.

Obviously, the structure of meaningful functions on a single interval scale is much richer.

Proposition 7.30. *Let* $n \geqslant 2$. *A function* $F : \mathbb{I}^n \to \mathbb{R}$ *is meaningful on a single interval scale if and only if*

$$F(\mathbf{x}) = \begin{cases} ax + b & \text{if } x_1 = \cdots = x_n = x \\ S(\mathbf{x}) f\left(\frac{\mathbf{x} - AM(\mathbf{x})\mathbf{1}}{S(\mathbf{x})}\right) + aAM(\mathbf{x}) + b & \text{otherwise,} \end{cases}$$

or

$$F(\mathbf{x}) = \begin{cases} b & \text{if } x_1 = \cdots = x_n \\ h(S(\mathbf{x})) f\left(\frac{\mathbf{x} - AM(\mathbf{x})\mathbf{1}}{S(\mathbf{x})}\right) + b & \text{otherwise,} \end{cases}$$

where $a, b \in \mathbb{R}$, $AM(\mathbf{x}) = \frac{1}{n} \sum_{i=1}^n x_i$ *is the arithmetic mean, and* $S(\mathbf{x}) = \sqrt{\sum_i (x_i - AM(\mathbf{x}))^2}$, $f : \mathbb{R}^n \to \mathbb{R}$ *is an arbitrary function, and* $h :]0, \infty[\to]0, \infty[$ *is a solution of the Cauchy functional equation* $h(xy) = h(x)h(y)$.

The structure of interval scale invariant functions is rather complicated, compare with Aczél *et al.* [10] for $\mathbb{I} = \mathbb{R}$.

Proposition 7.31. *A function* $\mathsf{F} : \mathbb{R}^n \to \mathbb{R}$ *is interval scale invariant if and only if*

$$\mathsf{F}(\mathbf{x}) = x_1 + (x_i - x_1) f_i^{\operatorname{sign}(x_i - x_1)} \left(\frac{x_{i+1} - x_1}{x_i - x_1}, \ldots, \frac{x_n - x_1}{x_i - x_1} \right)$$

if $x_1 = \cdots = x_{i-1}$ *and* $x_1 \neq x_i$ *and*

$$\mathsf{F}(n \cdot x_1) = x_1,$$

where $f_i^{+1}, f_i^{-1} : \mathbb{R}^{n-i} \to \mathbb{R}$, $i = 2, \ldots, n-1$ *are arbitrary functions, and* f_n^{+1}, f_n^{-1} *are arbitrary real constants.*

Observe that for $n = 2$, the only interval scale invariant functions $\mathsf{F} : \mathbb{R}^2 \to \mathbb{R}$ are given by

$$\mathsf{F}(x, y) = \begin{cases} x + a(y - x) = (1 - a)x + ay & \text{if } x \leqslant y \\ x + b(y - x) = (1 - b)x + by & \text{if } x > y, \end{cases}$$

where $a, b \in \mathbb{R}$ are arbitrary constants. Observe that, if $a, b \in [0, 1]$, then F is the Choquet integral; see Section 5.4.

We observe that the description given in Proposition 7.31 is not the only way to represent interval scale invariant functions. In Aczél *et al.* [10, 12], we also have the following description:

Proposition 7.32. *Let* $n \geqslant 2$. *A function* $\mathsf{F} : \mathbb{I}^n \to \mathbb{R}$ *is interval scale invariant if and only if*

$$\mathsf{F}(\mathbf{x}) = \begin{cases} x & \text{if } x_1 = \cdots = x_n = x \\ S(\mathbf{x}) f \left(\frac{\mathbf{x} - \mathsf{AM}(\mathbf{x}) \mathbf{1}}{S(\mathbf{x})} \right) + \mathsf{AM}(\mathbf{x}) & \text{otherwise,} \end{cases}$$

where AM *and* S *are defined as in Proposition 7.30, and* $f : \mathbb{R}^n \to \mathbb{R}$ *is an arbitrary function.*

For bounded intervals $\mathbb{I} = [a, b]$, we also have the following description (see Marichal *et al.* [284, Prop. 3.3]):

Proposition 7.33. *Let* $n \geqslant 2$. *A function* $\mathsf{F} : [a, b]^n \to \mathbb{R}$ *is interval scale invariant if and only if*

$$\mathsf{F}(\mathbf{x}) = \begin{cases} x & \text{if } x_1 = \cdots = x_n = x \\ (\mathsf{Max}(\mathbf{x}) - \mathsf{Min}(\mathbf{x})) f \left(\frac{\mathbf{x} - \mathsf{Min}(\mathbf{x}) \mathbf{1}}{\mathsf{Max}(\mathbf{x}) - \mathsf{Min}(\mathbf{x})} \right) + \mathsf{Min}(\mathbf{x}) & \text{otherwise,} \end{cases}$$

where $f : [a, b]^n \to \mathbb{R}$ *is an arbitrary function.*

7.4.2 Aggregation functions on interval scales

Boundary conditions and nondecreasing monotonicity of aggregation functions significantly limit the possible choice of aggregation functions possessing some of the discussed properties on interval scales.

Proposition 7.34. *An aggregation function* $A : \mathbb{I}^n \to \mathbb{I}$ *is meaningful on independent interval scales if and only if*

$$A(\mathbf{x}) = cx_i + d$$

for some $i \in [n]$, *where* $c > 0$ *and* $d \in \mathbb{R}$ *satisfy* $ca + d = a$, $cb + d = b$, *where* $a = \inf \mathbb{I}, b = \sup \mathbb{I}$ *(i.e., on any bounded interval, the only aggregation functions which are meaningful on independent interval scales are the projections onto single coordinates).*

Meaningfulness on a single interval scale reduces in the case of aggregation functions to invariance on interval scales.

Proposition 7.35. *An aggregation function* $A : \mathbb{I}^n \to \mathbb{I}$ *is meaningful on a single interval scale only if it is interval scale invariant.*

Interval scale invariance is a rather strong property. However, it admits a rich class of acceptable aggregation functions, in general; see for instance Aczél and Roberts [12] and Aczél *et al.* [13].

Proposition 7.36. *Under the notation of Proposition 7.31, a function* $F : \mathbb{R}^n \to \mathbb{R}$, $n \geqslant 2$ *is an interval scale invariant aggregation function if and only if the following are satisfied:*

(i) $f_i^\varepsilon(u\mathbf{y}) \geqslant u f_i^\varepsilon(\mathbf{y})$ *for all* $\mathbf{y} \in \mathbb{R}^{n-i}$, $u \in {]}0,1{[}$ *and* $\varepsilon \in \{-1,+1\}$, $i = 2,\ldots,n$;

(ii) $f_j^\varepsilon(0,\ldots,0,t,z_1,\ldots,z_{n-i}) \geqslant t f_i^\sigma(z_1,\ldots,z_{n-i})$ *for* $z_1 = \cdots = z_{n-i} = 0$, $\varepsilon \in \{-1,+1\}$, $2 \leqslant j < i \leqslant n$, $t \neq 0$, $\sigma = \varepsilon \operatorname{sign}(t)$;

(iii) $f_i^\varepsilon(\mathbf{0}) \geqslant 0$ *for* $\varepsilon \in \{-1,+1\}$, $2 \leqslant i \leqslant n$;

(iv) $f_2^\varepsilon(u\mathbf{y} + (1-u)\mathbf{1}) \leqslant u f_2^\varepsilon(\mathbf{y}) + (1-u)$ *for all* $\varepsilon \in \{-1,+1\}, u \in {]}0,1{[}$ *and* $\mathbf{y} \in \mathbb{R}^{n-2}$;

(v) $f_2^\varepsilon(t(0,\ldots,0,1,z_1,\ldots,z_{n-m}) + \mathbf{1}) \leqslant t f_m^\sigma(z_1,\ldots,z_{n-m})$ *for* $2 < m \leqslant n$, $(z_1,\ldots,z_{n-m}) \in \mathbb{R}^{n-m}$, $t \neq 0$, $\sigma = \varepsilon \operatorname{sign}(t)$;

(vi) $f_2^\varepsilon(\mathbf{1}) \leqslant 1$ *for* $\varepsilon \in \{-1,+1\}$.

For the interval $\mathbb{I} = [0,1]$ (and also by isomorphism for any interval $\mathbb{I} = [a,b] \subset \mathbb{R}$) we have the next result, which can be understood also as a construction method.

Proposition 7.37. *A function* $F : [0,1]^n \to [0,1]$, $n \geqslant 2$ *is an interval scale invariant aggregation function if and only if*

$$F(\mathbf{x}) = (\operatorname{Max}(\mathbf{x}) - \operatorname{Min}(\mathbf{x})) \, F\left(\frac{\mathbf{x} - \operatorname{Min}(\mathbf{x})\mathbf{1}}{\operatorname{Max}(\mathbf{x}) - \operatorname{Min}(\mathbf{x})}\right) + \operatorname{Min}(\mathbf{x}), \qquad (7.16)$$

whenever $\mathrm{Max}(\mathbf{x}) \neq \mathrm{Min}(\mathbf{x})$, *and*

$$F(x,\ldots,x) = x$$

for all $x \in [0,1]$, *and*

(i) $F(\mathbf{x}) - F(\mathbf{y}) \leqslant \mathrm{Max}(\mathbf{x} - \mathbf{y})$ *for all* $\mathbf{x}, \mathbf{y} \in [0,1]^n$ *such that* $\mathbf{x} \geqslant \mathbf{y}$ *and* $x_i = y_i = 0$
   for some $i \in [n]$;
(ii) $\frac{F(\mathbf{x})}{F(\mathbf{y})} \geqslant \mathrm{Min}(\frac{\mathbf{x}}{\mathbf{y}})$ *for all* $\mathbf{x}, \mathbf{y} \in [0,1]^n$ *such that* $\mathbf{x} \leqslant \mathbf{y}$ *and* $x_j = y_j = 1$ *for some*
   $j \in [n]$, *with convention* $\frac{0}{0} = 1$.

Remark 7.38. (i) Formula 7.16 gives a hint on how to construct interval scale invariant aggregation functions. Indeed, it is enough to take a nondecreasing function F defined on the boundary of the hypercube $[0,1]^n$ (i.e., defined on $[0,1]^n \setminus]0,1[^n$) and satisfying the requirements (i) and (ii) of Proposition 7.37. Then formula (7.16) allows us to extend F to the whole domain $[0,1]^n$.

(ii) For $n = 2$, one can easily see [284] that the only interval scale invariant aggregation function $\mathsf{A} : [0,1]^2 \to [0,1]$ is the Choquet integral, namely

$$A(x,y) = \begin{cases} A(1,0)\,x + (1 - A(1,0))\,y, & \text{if } x \leqslant y, \\ (1 - A(0,1))\,x + A(0,1)\,y, & \text{otherwise.} \end{cases}$$

Example 7.39. The quadratic mean $\mathsf{B} : [0,1]^3 \to [0,1]$ satisfies (i) and (ii) of Proposition 7.37. The corresponding interval scale invariant aggregation function $\mathsf{A} : [0,1]^3 \to [0,1]$ constructed by means of (7.16) is given by

$$A(\mathbf{x}) = \mathrm{Min}(\mathbf{x}) + \left(\frac{(\mathrm{Med}(\mathbf{x}) - \mathrm{Min}(\mathbf{x}))^2 + (\mathrm{Max}(\mathbf{x}) - \mathrm{Min}(\mathbf{x}))^2}{3} \right)^{1/2}.$$

Interval scale invariant functions have also been investigated and described under additional assumptions such as bisymmetry and autodistributivity. Extended versions (in the sense of extended functions) have also been considered under associativity, decomposability, strong decomposability, and strong bisymmetry. The reader will find some results in Corollary 4.16 and Theorems 4.24 and 4.25. For more results and proofs, see Marichal *et al.* [284].

7.5 Log-ratio scales

Log-ratio scales are related to power transformations of single variables; see Definitions 2.96–2.98.

For $\mathbb{I} \subseteq [0,\infty]$, a function $F : \mathbb{I}^n \to [0,\infty]$ is

(i) *log-ratio scale invariant* if, for any $r > 0$, we have

$$F(\mathbf{x}^{r\mathbf{1}}) = F(\mathbf{x})^r$$

for all $\mathbf{x} \in \mathbb{I}^n$ such that $\mathbf{x}^{r\mathbf{1}} \in \mathbb{I}^n$;

(ii) *meaningful on a single log-ratio scale* if, for any $r > 0$, there exists $R(r) > 0$ such that

$$F(\mathbf{x}^{r\mathbf{1}}) = F(\mathbf{x})^{R(r)}$$

for all $\mathbf{x} \in \mathbb{I}^n$ such that $\mathbf{x}^{r\mathbf{1}} \in \mathbb{I}^n$;

(iii) *meaningful on independent log-ratio scales* if, for any $\mathbf{r} \in]0, \infty[^n$, there exists $R(\mathbf{r}) > 0$ such that

$$F(\mathbf{x}^{\mathbf{r}}) = F(\mathbf{x})^{R(\mathbf{r})}$$

for all $\mathbf{x} \in \mathbb{I}^n$ such that $\mathbf{x}^{\mathbf{r}} \in \mathbb{I}^n$.

Log-ratio scales are closely related to ratio scales.

Proposition 7.40. *A function* $F : \mathbb{I}^n \to [0, \infty]$, $\mathbb{I} \subseteq [0, \infty]$, *is meaningful on a single log-ratio scale (respectively, meaningful on independent log-ratio scales, log-ratio scale invariant) if and only if the function* $G : \mathbb{J}^n \to [-\infty, \infty]$ *given by*

$$G(\mathbf{x}) = \log(F(\exp(x_1), \dots, \exp(x_n)))$$

is meaningful on a single ratio scale (respectively, meaningful on independent ratio scales, ratio scale invariant), where $\mathbb{J} = \{\log x \mid x \in \mathbb{I}\}$.

Due to Proposition 7.40, all results for ratio scales given in Section 7.2 can be transformed to the corresponding results for log-ratio scales and thus we will not formulate them explicitly. We focus here on specific results for log-ratio invariant aggregation functions on $[0, 1]$ dealing with special classes of aggregation functions. Note first of all that in the class of copulas (see Section 3.4 and Nelsen [332]), log-ratio scale invariant copulas are called *extreme values copulas*, in short EV-copulas, or Max-attractors; see section 3.4. For a deeper study of EV-copulas and their description for $n > 2$ we recommend Joe [200].

Proposition 7.41. *A function* $C : [0, 1]^2 \to [0, 1]$ *is an EV-copula (i.e., log-ratio scale invariant copula) if and only if*

$$C(x, y) = (xy)^{D\left(\frac{\log x}{\log xy}\right)}, \tag{7.17}$$

where $D : [0, 1] \to [0, 1]$ *is a convex function (called a dependence function) such that* $\text{Max}(u, 1 - u) \leqslant D(u) \leqslant 1$, $u \in [0, 1]$, *and the convention* $\frac{\infty}{\infty} = \frac{0}{0} = 1$ *is used whenever needed.*

In the class of all t-norms (see Chapter 3), the only log-ratio scale invariant t-norms are the greatest t-norm Min and the smallest t-norm T_D, and the members of the Aczél–Alsina family $(T_\lambda^{AA})_{\lambda \in]0,\infty[}$, where each T_λ^{AA} is a strict t-norm generated by an additive generator $t_\lambda : [0, 1] \to [0, \infty]$, $t_\lambda(x) = (-\log x)^\lambda$; see also Durante and Mesiar [107, Ex. 3].

Example 7.42. The EV-copula C related to a dependence function D is symmetric if and only if $D(u) = D(1 - u)$ for all $u \in [0, 1]$. Due to Durante and Mesiar [107], the maximal difference $|D(u) - D(1-u)| = \frac{1}{6}$ is attained only for dependence functions $D_1, D_2 : [0, 1] \to [0, 1]$ given by $D_1(u) = \mathsf{Max}(1-u, \frac{u+1}{2})$, and $D_2(u) = D_1(1-u)$, and for $u = \frac{1}{3}$ (or $u = \frac{2}{3}$). The corresponding EV-copulas $C_1, C_2 : [0, 1]^2 \to [0, 1]$ are given by $C_1(x, y) = \mathsf{Min}(x\sqrt{y}, y) = C_2(y, x)$, and they attain the maximal asymmetry in the class of all EV-copulas. Indeed the value $\sup\{|C(x, y) - C(y, x)| \mid (x, y) \in [0, 1]^2, C \text{ is EV-copula}\} = (\frac{4}{5})^4$ is attained by C_1, C_2 at the points $((\frac{4}{5})^2, (\frac{4}{5})^4)$ and $((\frac{4}{5})^4, (\frac{4}{5})^2)$.

8

Aggregation on ordinal scales

8.1 Introduction

In the present chapter we investigate meaningful n-ary functions $\mathsf{F} : \mathbb{I}^n \to \mathbb{R}$ mapping ordinal scales into an ordinal scale in the sense of measurement theory. More precisely, we present a catalog of all the possible *ordinal scale invariant functions*, all the possible *comparison meaningful functions on a single ordinal scale*, and all the possible *comparison meaningful functions on independent ordinal scales*, as defined in Section 2.4. We also present subfamilies of those functions fulfilling further assumptions such as continuity, symmetry, idempotency, and nondecreasing monotonicity.

Let us briefly recall how those special functions are defined (for a detailed introduction to invariance properties, see Section 2.4).

Let $\Phi[\mathbb{I}]$ denote the set of all increasing bijections of $\mathbb{I}$ onto itself. As each function $\varphi \in \Phi[\mathbb{I}]$ preserves the ordinal structure of $\mathbb{I}$, the set $\Phi[\mathbb{I}]$ is actually the order automorphism group, under composition, of $\mathbb{I}$.

Let $x_1, \ldots, x_n$ be independent variables defining the same ordinal scale, with domain $\mathbb{I}$ and suppose that, when aggregating these variables by a function $\mathsf{F} : \mathbb{I}^n \to \mathbb{R}$, we require that the dependent variable

$$x_{n+1} = \mathsf{F}(x_1, \ldots, x_n) \tag{8.1}$$

defines the same scale. As equation (8.1) should represent a meaningful relation between the independent and dependent variables, the function F should be invariant under actions from $\Phi[\mathbb{I}]$. That is,

$$\varphi(x_{n+1}) = \mathsf{F}\big(\varphi(x_1), \ldots, \varphi(x_n)\big)$$

for all $\varphi \in \Phi[\mathbb{I}]$. Thus, such a function F must be *ordinal scale invariant*, that is, it must satisfy $\mathrm{ran}(\mathsf{F}) \subseteq \mathbb{I}$ and

$$\mathsf{F}\big(\varphi(x_1), \ldots, \varphi(x_n)\big) = \varphi\big(\mathsf{F}(x_1, \ldots, x_n)\big) \tag{8.2}$$

for all $\varphi \in \Phi[\mathbb{I}]$.

292

In a more general setting, when x_{n+1} defines an ordinal scale, possibly different from that defined by the dependent variables, with an arbitrary domain in $\mathbb{R}$, then the function F must be a *comparison meaningful function on a single ordinal scale*, which means that, for any $\varphi \in \Phi[\mathbb{I}]$, there is a strictly increasing mapping $\psi_\varphi : \text{ran}(F) \to \text{ran}(F)$ such that

$$F\big(\varphi(x_1),\ldots,\varphi(x_n)\big) = \psi_\varphi\big(F(x_1,\ldots,x_n)\big). \tag{8.3}$$

Finally, if the independent variables define independent ordinal scales, with a common domain $\mathbb{I}$, and if the dependent variable also defines an ordinal scale, with an arbitrary domain in $\mathbb{R}$, then the function F must be a *comparison meaningful function on independent ordinal scales*, which means that, for any $\boldsymbol{\varphi} = (\varphi_1,\ldots,\varphi_n) \in \Phi[\mathbb{I}]^n$, there is a strictly increasing mapping $\psi_\varphi : \text{ran}(F) \to \text{ran}(F)$ such that

$$F\big(\varphi_1(x_1),\ldots,\varphi_n(x_n)\big) = \psi_\varphi\big(F(x_1,\ldots,x_n)\big). \tag{8.4}$$

The outline of this chapter is as follows. In Section 8.2 we introduce the concept of order invariant subsets, which will play a key role in the description of the functions considered in this chapter. In Section 8.3 we recall and discuss the concept of lattice polynomial functions, which represent most of the regular (e.g., nondecreasing) solutions of (8.2) and (8.3). In Section 8.4 we present and discuss all the ordinal scale invariant functions. In Sections 8.5 and 8.6 we present respectively the comparison meaningful functions on a single ordinal scale and the comparison meaningful functions on independent ordinal scales. Finally in Section 8.7 we provide interpretations of equations (8.2)–(8.4) in the setting of aggregation on finite chains.

Throughout this chapter we denote by $B[\mathbb{I}]$ the set of *included boundaries* of $\mathbb{I}$, that is,

$$B[\mathbb{I}] := \{\inf \mathbb{I}, \sup \mathbb{I}\} \cap \mathbb{I} = \mathbb{I} \setminus \text{int}(\mathbb{I}).$$

Also, for any $\mathbf{x} \in \mathbb{I}^n$ and any $\boldsymbol{\varphi} \in \Phi[\mathbb{I}]^n$, the symbol $\boldsymbol{\varphi}(\mathbf{x})$ denotes the vector $(\varphi_1(x_1),\ldots,\varphi_n(x_n))$.

To keep the exposition as concise as possible the proofs of the results from this chapter have been omitted.

8.2 Order invariant subsets

The domain $\mathbb{I}^n$ can be partitioned into *order invariant subsets*, which are very useful in describing the general solutions of the functional equations (8.2)–(8.4). Those subsets were introduced first by Ovchinnikov (see [337, §3] and [338, §2]) in the general framework of ordered sets and then independently by Bartłomiejczyk and Drewniak [27] for closed real intervals; see also [285, 286, 309]. In this section we introduce them through the concept of group orbit.

Consider the product set

$$\Phi[\mathbb{I}]^n = \big\{(\varphi_1,\ldots,\varphi_n) \mid \varphi_1,\ldots,\varphi_n \in \Phi[\mathbb{I}]\big\}$$

and its *diagonal restriction*

$$\Phi_n[\mathbb{I}] := \big\{\underbrace{(\varphi,\ldots,\varphi)}_{n} \mid \varphi \in \Phi[\mathbb{I}]\big\}.$$

As $\Phi_n[\mathbb{I}]$ is clearly a subgroup of $\Phi[\mathbb{I}]^n$, we can define the orbit of any element $\mathbf{x} \in \mathbb{I}^n$ under the action of $\Phi_n[\mathbb{I}]$, that is,

$$\Phi_n[\mathbb{I}](\mathbf{x}) := \{\varphi(\mathbf{x}) \mid \varphi \in \Phi_n[\mathbb{I}]\}.$$

The set of orbits of $\mathbb{I}^n$ under $\Phi_n[\mathbb{I}]$ forms a partition of $\mathbb{I}^n$ into equivalence classes, where $\mathbf{x}, \mathbf{y} \in \mathbb{I}^n$ are equivalent if their orbits are the same, that is, if there exists $\varphi \in \Phi_n[\mathbb{I}]$ such that $\mathbf{y} = \varphi(\mathbf{x})$.

The orbits of $\mathbb{I}^n$ under $\Phi_n[\mathbb{I}]$ are *order invariant subsets* in the following sense (see Bartłomiejczyk and Drewniak [27]):

Definition 8.1. A nonempty subset I of $\mathbb{I}^n$ is called *order invariant* if

$$\mathbf{x} \in I \quad \Rightarrow \quad \varphi(\mathbf{x}) \in I$$

for all $\varphi \in \Phi_n[\mathbb{I}]$.[1] An order invariant subset of $\mathbb{I}^n$ is *minimal* if it has no proper order invariant subset.

It is easy to see that the set $\mathcal{I}_n[\mathbb{I}] := \mathbb{I}^n/\Phi_n[\mathbb{I}]$ of orbits of $\mathbb{I}^n$ under $\Phi_n[\mathbb{I}]$ is identical to the set of minimal order invariant subsets of $\mathbb{I}^n$. Moreover, any order invariant subset is a union of those orbits.

The following proposition (for closed $\mathbb{I}$, see [27,309]) yields a complete description of the orbits under $\Phi_n[\mathbb{I}]$:

Proposition 8.2. *We have $I \in \mathcal{I}_n[\mathbb{I}]$ if and only if there exists a permutation σ on $[n]$ and a sequence $\{\lhd_i\}_{i=0}^n$ of symbols $\lhd_i \in \{<,=\}$, containing at least one symbol $<$ if $\inf \mathbb{I} \in \mathbb{I}$ and $\sup \mathbb{I} \in \mathbb{I}$, such that*

$$I = \{\mathbf{x} \in \mathbb{I}^n \mid \inf \mathbb{I} \lhd_0 x_{\sigma(1)} \lhd_1 \cdots \lhd_{n-1} x_{\sigma(n)} \lhd_n \sup \mathbb{I}\},$$

where $\lhd_0$ is $<$ if $\inf \mathbb{I} \notin \mathbb{I}$ and $\lhd_n$ is $<$ if $\sup \mathbb{I} \notin \mathbb{I}$.

Example 8.3. The unit square $[0,1]^2$ contains exactly 11 minimal order invariant subsets, namely the open triangles $\{(x_1,x_2) \mid 0 < x_1 < x_2 < 1\}$ and $\{(x_1,x_2) \mid 0 < x_2 < x_1 < 1\}$, the open diagonal $\{(x_1,x_2) \mid 0 < x_1 = x_2 < 1\}$, the four square vertices, and the four open line segments joining neighboring vertices.

---

[1] Equivalently, I is order invariant if $\varphi(I) \subseteq I$ for all $\varphi \in \Phi_n[\mathbb{I}]$. Actually, since $\Phi_n[\mathbb{I}]$ is a group, we can even write $\varphi(I) = I$.

Remark 8.4. From Proposition 8.2 we can easily derive an alternative way to characterize the membership of given vectors $\mathbf{x}, \mathbf{y} \in \mathbb{I}^n$ in the same orbit. Let $\mathfrak{S}_K$ be the set of permutations on $K := \{0, 1, \ldots, n + 1\}$ and, for any $\mathbf{x} \in \mathbb{I}^n$, define

$$\mathfrak{S}(\mathbf{x}) := \{\sigma \in \mathfrak{S}_K \mid x_{\sigma(0)} \leqslant x_{\sigma(1)} \leqslant \cdots \leqslant x_{\sigma(n+1)}\},$$

where $x_0 := \inf \mathbb{I}$ and $x_{n+1} := \sup \mathbb{I}$. Then, for any $\mathbf{x}, \mathbf{y} \in \mathbb{I}^n$, there exists $I \in \mathcal{I}_n[\mathbb{I}]$ such that $\mathbf{x}, \mathbf{y} \in I$ if and only if $\mathfrak{S}(\mathbf{x}) = \mathfrak{S}(\mathbf{y})$.[2]

Since $\Phi[\mathbb{I}]^n$ is itself a group, we can also define the orbit of any element $\mathbf{x} \in \mathbb{I}^n$ under the action of $\Phi[\mathbb{I}]^n$, that is,

$$\Phi[\mathbb{I}]^n(\mathbf{x}) := \{\varphi(\mathbf{x}) \mid \varphi \in \Phi[\mathbb{I}]^n\}.$$

Just as for the subgroup $\Phi_n[\mathbb{I}]$, the set of orbits of $\mathbb{I}^n$ under $\Phi[\mathbb{I}]^n$ forms a partition of $\mathbb{I}^n$ into equivalence classes, where $\mathbf{x}, \mathbf{y} \in \mathbb{I}^n$ are equivalent if there exists $\varphi \in \Phi[\mathbb{I}]^n$ such that $\mathbf{y} = \varphi(\mathbf{x})$.

The orbits of $\mathbb{I}^n$ under $\Phi[\mathbb{I}]^n$ are *strongly order invariant subsets* in the following sense (see Marichal *et al.* [286]):

Definition 8.5. A nonempty subset I of $\mathbb{I}^n$ is called *strongly order invariant* if

$$\mathbf{x} \in I \quad \Rightarrow \quad \varphi(\mathbf{x}) \in I$$

for all $\varphi \in \Phi[\mathbb{I}]^n$.[3] A strongly order invariant subset of $\mathbb{I}^n$ is *minimal* if it has no proper strongly order invariant subset.

The set $\mathcal{I}_n^*[\mathbb{I}] := \mathbb{I}^n / \Phi[\mathbb{I}]^n$ of orbits of $\mathbb{I}^n$ under $\Phi[\mathbb{I}]^n$ is identical to the set of minimal strongly order invariant subsets of $\mathbb{I}^n$. Moreover, any strongly order invariant subset is a union of those orbits.

The following proposition [286] yields a complete description of the orbits under $\Phi[\mathbb{I}]^n$:

Proposition 8.6. *We have*

$$\mathcal{I}_n^*[\mathbb{I}] = \left\{ \underset{i=1}{\overset{n}{\times}} I_i : I_i \in \mathcal{I}_1[\mathbb{I}] \right\} = (\mathcal{I}_1[\mathbb{I}])^n,$$

with cardinality $|\mathcal{I}_n^*[\mathbb{I}]| = (1 + |B[\mathbb{I}]|)^n$.

Example 8.7. The unit square $[0, 1]^2$ contains exactly nine minimal strongly order invariant subsets, namely the open square $]0, 1[^2$, the four square vertices, and the four open line segments joining neighboring vertices.

---

[2] This condition is more restrictive than *comonotonicity* of vectors $\mathbf{x}$ and $\mathbf{y}$ (cf. Definition 2.123), which simply means that $\mathfrak{S}(\mathbf{x})$ and $\mathfrak{S}(\mathbf{y})$ overlap.

[3] Equivalently, I is strongly order invariant if $\varphi(I) \subseteq I$ for all $\varphi \in \Phi[\mathbb{I}]^n$. Once again, since $\Phi[\mathbb{I}]^n$ is a group, we can even write $\varphi(I) = I$.

Let us now show that the set $\mathcal{I}_n^*[\mathbb{I}]$ can be described by means of the set $\mathcal{I}_n[\mathbb{I}]$. Recall that, for any $i \in [n]$, $\mathsf{P}_i : \mathbb{I}^n \to \mathbb{I}$ is the projection function onto the ith coordinate, that is, $\mathsf{P}_i(\mathbf{x}) = x_i$; see Section 1.2. We can easily see that, for any $I \in \mathcal{I}_n[\mathbb{I}]$, we have $\mathsf{P}_i(I) \in \mathcal{I}_1[\mathbb{I}]$. Define an equivalence relation $\sim$ on $\mathcal{I}_n[\mathbb{I}]$ as

$$I \sim J \quad \Leftrightarrow \quad \mathsf{P}_i(I) = \mathsf{P}_i(J), \quad \forall i \in [n].$$

Then, it is easy to see that

$$\mathcal{I}_n^*[\mathbb{I}] = \Big\{ \bigcup_{\substack{J \in \mathcal{I}_n[\mathbb{I}] \\ J \sim I}} J : I \in \mathcal{I}_n[\mathbb{I}] \Big\} = \Big\{ \underset{i=1}{\overset{n}{\times}} \mathsf{P}_i(I) : I \in \mathcal{I}_n[\mathbb{I}] \Big\}.$$

Now, to easily describe certain nondecreasing aggregation functions, it is useful to consider partial orders on $\mathcal{I}_n[\mathbb{I}]$ and $\mathcal{I}_n^*[\mathbb{I}]$. Starting from the natural order

$$\{\inf \mathbb{I}\} \prec \mathrm{int}(\mathbb{I}) \prec \{\sup \mathbb{I}\}$$

on $\mathcal{I}_1[\mathbb{I}]$, we can straightforwardly derive a partial order $\preccurlyeq$ on $\mathcal{I}_n[\mathbb{I}]$, namely

$$I \preccurlyeq J \quad \Leftrightarrow \quad \mathsf{P}_i(I) \preccurlyeq \mathsf{P}_i(J), \quad \forall i \in [n].$$

The corresponding partial order on $\mathcal{I}_n^*[\mathbb{I}]$ is defined similarly.

Remark 8.8. Consider again the set $\mathfrak{S}_K$ of permutations on $K = \{0, 1, \ldots, n+1\}$; see Remark 8.4. For any $\mathbf{x} \in \mathbb{I}^n$, we can define

$$\mathfrak{S}^*(\mathbf{x}) := \{\sigma \in \mathfrak{S}_K \mid \sigma(i) \leqslant \ell(\mathbf{x}) \Leftrightarrow x_i = \inf \mathbb{I}$$
$$\text{and } \sigma(j) \geqslant n+1 - u(\mathbf{x}) \Leftrightarrow x_j = \sup \mathbb{I}\},$$

where $x_0 := \inf \mathbb{I}$, $x_{n+1} := \sup \mathbb{I}$ and $\ell(\mathbf{x}) = \{i \in [n] \mid x_i = \inf \mathbb{I}\}$, $u(\mathbf{x}) = \{j \in [n] \mid x_j = \sup \mathbb{I}\}$. Then, for any $\mathbf{x}, \mathbf{y} \in \mathbb{I}^n$, there exists $I \in \mathcal{I}_n^*[\mathbb{I}]$ such that $\mathbf{x}, \mathbf{y} \in I$ if and only if $\mathfrak{S}^*(\mathbf{x}) = \mathfrak{S}^*(\mathbf{y})$.[4]

8.3 Lattice polynomial functions and some of their properties

As we will see in subsequent sections, certain solutions of equations (8.2) and (8.3) are constructed from *lattice polynomial functions*. In this section we briefly recall the basic material about these functions (for more details, see Section 5.5.1). As we are concerned with aggregation functions defined in real domains, we do not consider lattice polynomial functions on a general lattice, but simply on $\mathbb{R}$, which is a particular

---

[4] The following alternative characterization is also worth mentioning: For any $\mathbf{x}, \mathbf{y} \in \mathbb{I}^n$, there exists $I \in \mathcal{I}_n^*[\mathbb{I}]$ such that $\mathbf{x}, \mathbf{y} \in I$ if and only if, for all $i \in [n]$,

$$x_i = \inf I \Leftrightarrow y_i = \inf I \quad \text{and} \quad x_i = \sup I \Leftrightarrow y_i = \sup I.$$

lattice. The lattice operations $\wedge$ and $\vee$ then represent the minimum and maximum operations, respectively.

8.3.1 Lattice polynomial functions

Let us first recall an important representation result on lattice polynomial functions; see Proposition 5.55.

Proposition 8.9. *Let $p : \mathbb{R}^n \to \mathbb{R}$ be any lattice polynomial function. Then there are nonconstant set functions $\alpha : 2^{[n]} \to \{0, 1\}$ and $\beta : 2^{[n]} \to \{0, 1\}$, with $\alpha(\varnothing) = 0$ and $\beta(\varnothing) = 1$, such that*

$$p(\mathbf{x}) = \bigvee_{\substack{K \subseteq [n] \\ \alpha(K)=1}} \bigwedge_{i \in K} x_i = \bigwedge_{\substack{K \subseteq [n] \\ \beta(K)=0}} \bigvee_{i \in K} x_i. \tag{8.5}$$

As already observed in Remark 5.56, the set functions α and β that disjunctively and conjunctively define the polynomial function p in Proposition 8.9 are not unique. For example, we have

$$x_1 \vee (x_1 \wedge x_2) = x_1 = x_1 \wedge (x_1 \vee x_2).$$

However, it can be shown [272] (see also Proposition 5.58) that, from among all the possible set functions that disjunctively define a given lattice polynomial function, only one is nondecreasing. Similarly, from among all the possible set functions that conjunctively define a given lattice polynomial function, only one is nonincreasing. These particular set functions are given by

$$\alpha(K) = p(\mathbf{1}_K) \quad \text{and} \quad \beta(K) = p(\mathbf{1}_{[n]\setminus K}),$$

where, as usual, $\mathbf{1}_K$ denotes the characteristic vector of the subset K in $\{0, 1\}^n$. Thus, a lattice polynomial function $p : \mathbb{R}^n \to \mathbb{R}$ can always be written as

$$p(\mathbf{x}) = \bigvee_{\substack{K \subseteq [n] \\ p(\mathbf{1}_K)=1}} \bigwedge_{i \in K} x_i = \bigwedge_{\substack{K \subseteq [n] \\ p(\mathbf{1}_{[n]\setminus K})=0}} \bigvee_{i \in K} x_i.$$

Remark 8.10. Now it becomes evident that any n-ary lattice polynomial function is a nondecreasing and continuous ordinal scale invariant function in $\mathbb{R}^n$. We will see in Proposition 8.13 that the converse is also true: a nondecreasing (or continuous) ordinal scale invariant function in $\mathbb{R}^n$ is a lattice polynomial function; see also Theorem 6.4.

Denote by $p_\alpha^\vee$ (respectively, $p_\beta^\wedge$) the lattice polynomial function disjunctively (respectively, conjunctively) defined by a given set function α (respectively, β) as defined in Proposition 8.9. Let $f : \{0, 1\}^n \to \{0, 1\}$ be a nonconstant and nondecreasing Boolean function. Then the lattice polynomial function $p_\alpha^\vee$, where

$\alpha : 2^{[n]} \rightarrow \{0, 1\}$ is defined by $\alpha(K) = f(1_K)$ for all $K \subseteq [n]$, is an extension to $\mathbb{R}^n$ of f. Indeed, we immediately have

$$f(1_K) = \alpha(K) = p_\alpha^\vee(1_K)$$

for all $K \subseteq [n]$. Consequently, any n-ary lattice polynomial function is an extension to $\mathbb{R}^n$ of a nonconstant and nondecreasing Boolean function.

The set function $\alpha : 2^{[n]} \rightarrow \{0, 1\}$ defined by $\alpha(K) = f(1_K)$ is nothing other than a 0–1 capacity on $[n]$; see Section 5.2.2. Recall that $\mathcal{F}_{0-1}(n)$ denotes the set of 0–1 capacities on $[n]$ (i.e., $\{0, 1\}$-valued nonconstant and nondecreasing set functions on $[n]$). By definition, this set is equipollent to the set of n-ary lattice polynomial functions, as well as to the set of nonconstant and nondecreasing Boolean functions.[5]

Now, regard the lattice polynomial function p as a function from $\mathbb{I}^n$ to $\mathbb{I}$. If $\mathbb{I} = [a, b]$ is a bounded lattice,

$$\bigvee_{x \in \varnothing} x = \inf \mathbb{I} \quad \text{and} \quad \bigwedge_{x \in \varnothing} x = \sup \mathbb{I}.$$

Then, from (8.5), we clearly have $p \equiv \inf \mathbb{I}$ if $\alpha \equiv 0$, and $p \equiv \sup \mathbb{I}$ if $\alpha \equiv 1$. Thus we can extend the definition of lattice polynomial functions by allowing the set function α to be constant.

Let $\mathcal{F}_{0-1}^{\mathbb{I}}(n)$ denote the set $\mathcal{F}_{0-1}(n)$ completed with the constant set function $\alpha \equiv 0$, if $\inf \mathbb{I} \in \mathbb{I}$, and the constant set function $\alpha \equiv 1$, if $\sup \mathbb{I} \in \mathbb{I}$. Evidently $\mathcal{F}_{0-1}^{\mathbb{I}}(n)$ can be partially ordered by the standard partial order on set functions, namely $\alpha_1 \preccurlyeq \alpha_2$ if and only if $\alpha_1(K) \leqslant \alpha_2(K)$ for all $K \subseteq [n]$. We will refer to this partial order in the subsequent sections.

8.3.2 Special lattice polynomial functions

We now consider the important special case of symmetric lattice polynomial functions. Denote by $x_{(1)}, \ldots, x_{(n)}$ the *order statistics* resulting from reordering the variables $x_1, \ldots, x_n$ in nondecreasing order, that is, $x_{(1)} \leqslant \cdots \leqslant x_{(n)}$. As Ovchinnikov [337, §7] observed, any order statistic is a symmetric lattice polynomial function. More precisely, for any $k \in [n]$, we have

$$x_{(k)} = \bigvee_{\substack{K \subseteq [n] \\ |K| = n-k+1}} \bigwedge_{i \in K} x_i = \bigwedge_{\substack{K \subseteq [n] \\ |K| = k}} \bigvee_{i \in K} x_i.$$

Conversely, Marichal [272, §2] showed that any symmetric lattice polynomial function is an order statistic; see also Proposition 5.50.

---

[5] The problem of enumerating the number of distinct nondecreasing Boolean functions of n variables is known as Dedekind's problem [211, 212] (Sloane's integer sequence A000372). Although Dedekind first considered this question in 1897, there is still no concise closed-form expression for this sequence.

Recall that $OS_k : \mathbb{R}^n \to \mathbb{R}$ denotes the kth *order statistic function*, that is, $OS_k(\mathbf{x}) := x_{(k)}$; see Chapter 1. It is then easy to see that, for any $K \subseteq [n]$, we have $OS_k(1_K) = 1$ if and only if $|K| \geqslant n - k + 1$ and, likewise, we have $OS_k(1_{[n] \setminus K}) = 0$ if and only if $|K| \geqslant k$.

Note that when n is odd, $n = 2k - 1$, the particular order statistic $x_{(k)}$ is the well-known *median* function

$$\mathsf{Med}(x_1, \ldots, x_{2k-1}) = x_{(k)}.$$

Another special case of lattice polynomial functions is given by the projection functions, already used in Section 8.2; see also Section 1.2. Recall that, for any $k \in [n]$, the *projection* function $P_k : \mathbb{R}^n \to \mathbb{R}$ associated with the kth argument is defined by $P_k(\mathbf{x}) := x_k$. Thus, the projection function P_k merely consists in projecting $\mathbf{x} \in \mathbb{R}^n$ onto the kth coordinate axis.

8.3.3 Properties of lattice polynomial functions

Lattice polynomial functions $p : \mathbb{I}^n \to \mathbb{I}$ are clearly continuous, nondecreasing, and ordinal scale invariant functions. As they are also idempotent and hence internal, they are means and average functions (as defined in Chapter 4). Thus, the internality property makes it possible to define means even on ordinal scales; see, e.g., Ovchinnikov [337]. For example, as a particular lattice polynomial, the classical median function (see Section 8.3.2), which gives the middle value of an odd-length sequence of ordered values, is a continuous, nondecreasing, and symmetric mean defined on ordinal scales. To give a second example, consider the classical *mode* function, $\mathsf{Mode} : \mathbb{I}^n \to \mathbb{I}$, defined by

$$\mathsf{Mode}(\mathbf{x}) = \underset{r \in \mathbb{I}}{\mathrm{argmax}} \sum_{i=1}^{n} 1_{\{0\}}(x_i - r) \tag{8.6}$$

(in case of multiple values for argmax, take the smallest one). This function, which gives the (lowest) most repeated value of a sequence of values, is a symmetric mean defined on ordinal scales, and even on nominal scales.[6] However, since the mode function is not nondecreasing, it is not a lattice polynomial.

We can also observe that any lattice polynomial is *discretizable* in the sense that it always yields the value of one of its variables. This property was actually introduced in the framework of t-norms (see for instance [76, 115]) but is easily extended to any function as follows:

Definition 8.11. $F : \mathbb{I}^n \to \mathbb{I}$ is said to be a *discretizable* function if

$$F(\mathbf{x}) \in \{x_1, \ldots, x_n\} \cup B[\mathbb{I}]$$

for all $\mathbf{x} \in \mathbb{I}^n$.

---

[6] The admissible transformations associated with a nominal scale are one-to-one transformations (injections) of $\mathbb{I}$ into itself; see Roberts [364, p. 66].

We can readily prove [304] that $F : \mathbb{I}^n \to \mathbb{I}$ is a discretizable function if and only if, for any nonempty finite subset $C \subset \mathbb{I}$ and any $\mathbf{x} \in (C \cup B[\mathbb{I}])^n$, we have

$$F(\mathbf{x}) \in C \cup B[\mathbb{I}].$$

Thus, this property means that the domain and range of F can be restricted to a countable chain.

Assume that $B[\mathbb{I}]$ is not a singleton and let $\alpha \in \mathcal{F}_{0-1}(n)$. We can straightforwardly show that the lattice polynomial function $p_\alpha^\vee : \mathbb{I}^n \to \mathbb{I}$ is weakly self-dual (see Definition 2.104) if and only if $\overline{\alpha} = \alpha$, where $\overline{\alpha} \in \mathcal{F}_{0-1}(n)$ is the conjugate (dual) of α, defined by $\overline{\alpha}(K) = 1 - \alpha([n] \setminus K)$. This result was already observed in the more general case of Sugeno integrals; see Proposition 5.80.

The special case of order statistics is dealt with in the next immediate result (see Marichal [272, §5]), which characterizes the median as the only weakly self-dual order statistic.

Proposition 8.12. *Assume that n is odd and that $B[\mathbb{I}]$ is not a singleton. The kth order statistic function $OS_k : \mathbb{I}^n \to \mathbb{I}$ is weakly self-dual if and only if $n = 2k - 1$. In this case $OS_k = \mathsf{Med}$ is the median function.*

8.4 Ordinal scale invariant functions

The first meaningful aggregation functions we consider are the *ordinal scale invariant functions* (cf. Definition 2.99), which were first investigated (as ordinally stable functions) by Marichal and Roubens [289], and then by many other authors; see [27, 113, 203, 262, 272, 281, 285, 286, 304, 309, 337, 338, 341, 342].

The following result (see Propositions 8.19 and 8.25 below) shows that the lattice polynomial functions are the most prominent ordinal scale invariant functions (however see Theorem 8.17 for a full description of ordinal scale invariant functions):

Proposition 8.13. *Assume that $\mathbb{I}$ is open and consider a function $F : \mathbb{I}^n \to \mathbb{I}$. Then the following three assertions are equivalent:*

   (i) F is a nondecreasing ordinal scale invariant function.
   (ii) F is a continuous ordinal scale invariant function.
   (iii) F is a lattice polynomial function.

Proposition 8.13 poses the interesting question of how we can interpret the continuity property for ordinal scale invariant functions. Let $\Phi'[\mathbb{I}]$ be the superset of $\Phi[\mathbb{I}]$ consisting of the continuous nondecreasing surjections $\varphi : \mathbb{I} \to \mathbb{I}$. The following result [285, §5.2], inspired from [45, Prop. 2], shows that the conjunction of continuity and ordinal scale invariance is equivalent to requiring that the admissible transformations belong to $\Phi'[\mathbb{I}]$.

Proposition 8.14. $\mathsf{F} : \mathbb{I}^n \to \mathbb{I}$ *is a continuous ordinal scale invariant function if and only if*

$$\mathsf{F}(\varphi(x_1), \ldots, \varphi(x_n)) = \varphi(\mathsf{F}(x_1, \ldots, x_n))$$

for all $\mathbf{x} \in \mathbb{I}^n$ *and all* $\varphi \in \Phi'[\mathbb{I}]$.

Let $\Phi''[\mathbb{I}]$ be the superset of $\Phi[\mathbb{I}]$ consisting of all the monotone bijections of $\mathbb{I}$ onto itself (assuming that $B[\mathbb{I}]$ is not a singleton). It is clear (for bounded $\mathbb{I}$, see for instance [309, §3]) that the conjunction of weak self-duality (cf. Definition 2.104) and ordinal scale invariance is equivalent to requiring that the admissible transformations belong to $\Phi''[\mathbb{I}]$. The independent and dependent variables then define a *nominal* scale.

Proposition 8.15. *Assume that* $B[\mathbb{I}]$ *is not a singleton.* $\mathsf{F} : \mathbb{I}^n \to \mathbb{I}$ *is a weakly self-dual ordinal scale invariant function if and only if*

$$\mathsf{F}(\varphi(x_1), \ldots, \varphi(x_n)) = \varphi(\mathsf{F}(x_1, \ldots, x_n))$$

for all $\mathbf{x} \in \mathbb{I}^n$ *and all* $\varphi \in \Phi''[\mathbb{I}]$.

8.4.1 General descriptions

When $\mathbb{I}$ is open we have the following description (see Ovchinnikov [338, Th. 5.1]):

Proposition 8.16. *Assume that* $\mathbb{I}$ *is open. Then* $\mathsf{F} : \mathbb{I}^n \to \mathbb{I}$ *is an ordinal scale invariant function if and only if there exists a mapping* $\zeta : \mathcal{I}_n[\mathbb{I}] \to [n]$ *such that* $\mathsf{F}|_I = \mathsf{P}_{\zeta(I)}|_I$ *for all* $I \in \mathcal{I}_n[\mathbb{I}]$.

This result shows that, when $\mathbb{I}$ is open, the restriction of F to any minimal order invariant subset is a projection function onto one coordinate. That is, for any $I \in \mathcal{I}_n[\mathbb{I}]$, there exists $k_I \in [n]$ such that $\mathsf{F}|_I = \mathsf{P}_{k_I}|_I$. Clearly, such a function is internal and hence idempotent.

As an example, any nonconstant lattice polynomial function is a continuous, nondecreasing, idempotent, and ordinal scale invariant function. On the other hand, the mode function (8.6) is an idempotent and ordinal scale invariant function that is neither continuous nor nondecreasing.

When $\mathbb{I}$ is not open, the restriction of F to any minimal order invariant subset reduces to a constant function or a projection function onto one coordinate; see [286, 309].

Theorem 8.17. $\mathsf{F} : \mathbb{I}^n \to \mathbb{I}$ *is an ordinal scale invariant function if and only if there exists a mapping* $\zeta : \mathcal{I}_n[\mathbb{I}] \to [n]$ *such that, for any* $I \in \mathcal{I}_n[\mathbb{I}]$,

(i) either $\mathsf{F}|_I \equiv c \in B[\mathbb{I}]$ *(assuming* $B[\mathbb{I}] \neq \varnothing$*),*
(ii) or $\mathsf{F}|_I = \mathsf{P}_{\zeta(I)}|_I$.

Remark 8.18. It was proved in [272, Prop. 3.1] (see [203, 337, 338] for preliminary results), that any ordinal scale invariant function is discretizable, and hence it is internal whenever $\mathbb{I}$ is open; it is clear that this follows from Theorem 8.17. For instance, the mode function (8.6) is ordinal scale invariant and hence discretizable. The converse is not true. For example, the function $F :]0, 1[^2 \to]0, 1[$ defined by

$$F(x_1, x_2) = \begin{cases} x_1 & \text{if } x_1 + x_2 < 1 \\ x_2 & \text{otherwise} \end{cases}$$

is discretizable but not ordinal scale invariant.

When an ordinal scale invariant function is idempotent, clearly it must be a projection on the open diagonal of $\mathbb{I}^n$, also on $I = \{(\inf \mathbb{I}, \dots, \inf \mathbb{I})\}$ (if $\inf \mathbb{I} \in \mathbb{I}$), and on $I = \{(\sup \mathbb{I}, \dots, \sup \mathbb{I})\}$ (if $\sup \mathbb{I} \in \mathbb{I}$).

8.4.2 The nondecreasing case

We now present descriptions of ordinal scale invariant functions which are nondecreasing. The following result (see Marichal [272, Cor. 4.4]) shows that, when $\mathbb{I}$ is open, the family of nondecreasing ordinal scale invariant functions in $\mathbb{I}^n$ is identical to that of lattice polynomial functions in $\mathbb{I}^n$. Recall that the lattice polynomial function in $\mathbb{I}^n$ disjunctively defined by $\alpha \in \mathcal{F}_{0-1}^{\mathbb{I}}(n)$ is denoted $p_\alpha^\vee$; see Section 8.3.1.

Proposition 8.19. *Assume that $\mathbb{I}$ is open. Then $F : \mathbb{I}^n \to \mathbb{I}$ is a nondecreasing ordinal scale invariant function if and only if there exists $\alpha \in \mathcal{F}_{0-1}(n)$ such that $F = p_\alpha^\vee$.*

Corollary 8.20. *Assume that $\mathbb{I}$ is open. Then $F : \mathbb{I}^n \to \mathbb{I}$ is a symmetric, nondecreasing, and ordinal scale invariant function if and only if there exists $k \in [n]$ such that $F = OS_k$.*

Combining Proposition 8.12 with Corollary 8.20 immediately yields the following axiomatization of the median function:

Corollary 8.21. *Assume that n is odd and that $\mathbb{I}$ is open. Then $F : \mathbb{I}^n \to \mathbb{I}$ is a symmetric, weakly self-dual, nondecreasing, and ordinal scale invariant function if and only if $F = \text{Med}$.*

A complete description of nondecreasing ordinal scale invariant functions in $\mathbb{I}^n$, with open or non-open interval $\mathbb{I}$, is given in the following theorem; see [286, 309]. It shows that discontinuities of F may occur only on the border of $\mathbb{I}^n$.

Theorem 8.22. *$F : \mathbb{I}^n \to \mathbb{I}$ is a nondecreasing ordinal scale invariant function if and only if there exists a nondecreasing mapping $\zeta : \mathcal{I}_n^*[\mathbb{I}] \to \mathcal{F}_{0-1}^{\mathbb{I}}(n)$ such that $F|_I = p_{\zeta(I)}^\vee|_I$ for all $I \in \mathcal{I}_n^*[\mathbb{I}]$.*

Example 8.23. Consider the semiopen interval $\mathbb{I} = [a, b[$.[7] The function $\mathsf{F} : [a, b[^3 \to [a, b[$ defined by

$$\mathsf{F}(x_1, x_2, x_3) = \begin{cases} a & \text{if } x_1 = a \\ x_3 & \text{if } x_1 \neq a \text{ and } x_2 = a \\ x_1 \vee x_2 \vee x_3 & \text{otherwise} \end{cases}$$

is a nondecreasing ordinal scale invariant aggregation function in $[a, b[^3$.

Corollary 8.24. $\mathsf{F} : \mathbb{I}^n \to \mathbb{I}$ *is a nondecreasing, idempotent, and ordinal scale invariant function if and only if there exists a nondecreasing mapping* $\zeta : \mathcal{I}_n^*[\mathbb{I}] \to \mathcal{F}_{0-1}^{\mathbb{I}}(n)$, *where* $\zeta((\text{int}(\mathbb{I}))^n)$ *is nonconstant, such that* $\mathsf{F}|_I = p_{\zeta(I)}^\vee|_I$ *for all* $I \in \mathcal{I}_n^*[\mathbb{I}]$.

8.4.3 The continuous case

We now consider the family of continuous ordinal scale invariant functions. It was shown in [272, Cor. 4.2] that, when $\mathbb{I}$ is open, this family is identical to the family of lattice polynomial functions in $\mathbb{I}^n$; see also [262, §3.4.2].

Proposition 8.25. *Assume that* $\mathbb{I}$ *is open. Then* $\mathsf{F} : \mathbb{I}^n \to \mathbb{I}$ *is a continuous ordinal scale invariant function if and only if there exists* $\alpha \in \mathcal{F}_{0-1}(n)$ *such that* $\mathsf{F} = p_\alpha^\vee$.

Remark 8.26. Note that this result was independently stated and proved earlier by Ovchinnikov [339, Th. 5.3] in the more general setting where the range of variables is a doubly homogeneous simple order, that is, a simple order X satisfying the following property:

For any $x_1, x_2, y_1, y_2 \in X$, with $x_1 < x_2$ and $y_1 < y_2$, there is an automorphism $\varphi : X \to X$ such that $\varphi(x_1) = y_1$ and $\varphi(x_2) = y_2$.

As any open interval $\mathbb{I}$ of the real line is clearly a doubly homogeneous simple order, Ovchinnikov's result encompasses that of Proposition 8.25.[8]

A complete description of continuous ordinal scale invariant function in $\mathbb{I}^n$ was stated in [272, Cor. 4.3] as follows (see also [286]):

Theorem 8.27. $\mathsf{F} : \mathbb{I}^n \to \mathbb{I}$ *is a continuous ordinal scale invariant function if and only if there exists* $\alpha \in \mathcal{F}_{0-1}^{\mathbb{I}}(n)$ *such that* $\mathsf{F} = p_\alpha^\vee$.

Theorem 8.27 actually says that a continuous ordinal scale invariant function $\mathsf{F} : \mathbb{I}^n \to \mathbb{I}$ is either the constant function $\mathsf{F} \equiv \inf \mathbb{I}$ if $\inf \mathbb{I} \in \mathbb{I}$, or the constant function $\mathsf{F} \equiv \sup \mathbb{I}$ if $\sup \mathbb{I} \in \mathbb{I}$, or any lattice polynomial function in $\mathbb{I}^n$ (any order statistic function in $\mathbb{I}^n$ if F is symmetric).

---

[7] Here the poset $\mathcal{I}_n^*[\mathbb{I}]$ contains eight elements (a point, three open line segments, three open square facets, and an open cube).

[8] Note that the extension of this result to the (infinite) case of functional operators was described by Ovchinnikov and Dukhovny [341]; see also [342].

Remark 8.28. From Theorems 8.17 and 8.27 it follows that a function $F : \mathbb{I}^n \to \mathbb{I}$ is a lattice polynomial function if and only if its restriction to each closed simplex of the standard triangulation of $\mathbb{I}^n$ is a projection function onto one coordinate; see also Marichal [272, Prop. 2.1].

Corollary 8.29. $F : \mathbb{I}^n \to \mathbb{I}$ *is a continuous, idempotent, and ordinal scale invariant function if and only if there exists* $\alpha \in \mathcal{F}_{0-1}(n)$ *such that* $F = p_\alpha^\vee$.

Corollary 8.30. $F : \mathbb{I}^n \to \mathbb{I}$ *is a symmetric, continuous, idempotent, and ordinal scale invariant function if and only if there exists* $k \in [n]$ *such that* $F = OS_k$.

Corollary 8.31. *Assume that n is odd and that $B[\mathbb{I}]$ is not a singleton. Then* $F : \mathbb{I}^n \to \mathbb{I}$ *is a symmetric, weakly self-dual, continuous, idempotent, and ordinal scale invariant function if and only if* $F = \text{Med}$.

Remark 8.32. By combining Proposition 8.12 with Theorem 8.27, we immediately see that idempotency is not necessary in Corollary 8.31. Indeed, a weak self-dual lattice polynomial function cannot be constant and hence it is necessarily idempotent.

8.5 Comparison meaningful functions on a single ordinal scale

We now present the class of *comparison meaningful functions on a single ordinal scale* (cf. Definition 2.100). These functions were introduced first by Orlov [335] and then investigated by many other authors; see [203, 262, 269, 272, 281, 285, 286, 337, 446].

   Comparison meaningful functions on a single ordinal scale were originally defined as those functions preserving the comparison of aggregated values when changing the scale defined by the independent variables.[9] We paraphrase from Orlov [335]:

When one compares two sets of objects according to a criterion, it is sometimes required to evaluate each object on the same ordinal scale (e.g., by means of measurement or expert estimate). The aggregated values of the evaluations corresponding to each set of objects are computed by a certain aggregation function, and then compared together. It is natural to require that the inferences made from this comparison are meaningful, that is, depend only on the initial information, but not on the scale used.[10]

The equivalence between Definition 2.100 and Orlov's original definition was formulated mathematically in Proposition 2.102 as follows:

Proposition 8.33. $F : \mathbb{I}^n \to \mathbb{R}$ *is a comparison meaningful function on a single ordinal scale if and only if*

$$F(\mathbf{x}) \leqslant F(\mathbf{x}') \quad \Leftrightarrow \quad F\big(\varphi(\mathbf{x})\big) \leqslant F\big(\varphi(\mathbf{x}')\big)$$

for all $\mathbf{x}, \mathbf{x}' \in \mathbb{I}^n$ *and all* $\varphi \in \Phi_n[\mathbb{I}]$.

---

[9] A general study on meaningfulness of ordinal comparisons can be found in Roberts and Rosenbaum [363].

[10] More generally, a statement using scales of measurement is said to be *meaningful* if its truth or falsity is invariant when every scale is replaced by another acceptable version of it; see Roberts [364, p. 59].

Remark 8.34. Although the condition in Proposition 8.33 is natural and even manda-tory to aggregate ordinal values, it severely restricts the allowable operations for defining a meaningful aggregation function. For example, the comparison of two arithmetic means is meaningless on an ordinal scale. Indeed, considering the pairs of values $(3, 5)$ and $(1, 8)$, we have

$$\frac{3 + 5}{2} < \frac{1 + 8}{2}$$

and, using any admissible transformation φ such that $\varphi(1) = 1, \varphi(3) = 4, \varphi(5) = 7$, and $\varphi(8) = 8$, we have

$$\frac{\varphi(3) + \varphi(5)}{2} > \frac{\varphi(1) + \varphi(8)}{2}.$$

Ordinal scale invariant functions and comparison meaningful functions on a single ordinal scale can actually be related through the idempotency property. Indeed, when a comparison meaningful function on a single ordinal scale is idempotent then the output scale must coincide with the input scale. This result is stated in the next proposition; see [272, Prop. 3.3] and preliminary work in [203, 337].

Proposition 8.35. *Consider a function* $\mathsf{F} : \mathbb{I}^n \to \mathbb{I}$.

 (i) *If* F *is idempotent and comparison meaningful on a single ordinal scale then it is ordinal scale invariant.*
 (ii) *If* F *is ordinal scale invariant then it is comparison meaningful on a single ordinal scale.*
(iii) *If* $\mathbb{I}$ *is open then* F *is idempotent and comparison meaningful on a single ordinal scale if and only if it is ordinal scale invariant.*

Just as for ordinal scale invariant functions, continuity of comparison meaningful functions on a single ordinal scale can be interpreted by means of the set $\Phi'[\mathbb{I}]$ of continuous nondecreasing surjections from $\mathbb{I}$ onto $\mathbb{I}$; see Marichal and Mesiar [285, §5.2]. Denote by $\Phi_n'[\mathbb{I}]$ the diagonal restriction of $\Phi'[\mathbb{I}]^n$ (see Section 8.2).

Proposition 8.36. $\mathsf{F} : \mathbb{I}^n \to \mathbb{I}$ *is a continuous and comparison meaningful function on a single ordinal scale if and only if, for any* $\varphi \in \Phi_n'[\mathbb{I}]$, *there is a continuous and nondecreasing mapping* $\psi_\varphi : \mathrm{ran}(\mathsf{F}) \to \mathrm{ran}(\mathsf{F})$ *such that* $\mathsf{F}(\varphi(\mathbf{x})) = \psi_\varphi(\mathsf{F}(\mathbf{x}))$ *for all* $\mathbf{x} \in \mathbb{I}^n$.

8.5.1 General descriptions

The class of comparison meaningful functions on a single ordinal scale can be described as follows (see Marichal *et al.* [286, Th. 3.1]):

Theorem 8.37. $\mathsf{F} : \mathbb{I}^n \to \mathbb{I}$ *is a comparison meaningful function on a single ordinal scale if and only if, for any* $I \in \mathcal{I}_n[\mathbb{I}]$, *there exist an index* $k_I \in [n]$ *and a strictly* *monotonic or constant function* $g_I : \mathsf{P}_{k_I}(I) \to \mathbb{R}$ *such that* $\mathsf{F}|_I = (g_I \circ \mathsf{P}_{k_I})|_I$, *where, for any* $I, I' \in \mathcal{I}_n[\mathbb{I}]$,

  (i) *either* $g_I = g_{I'}$,
 (ii) *or* $\mathrm{ran}(g_I) = \mathrm{ran}(g_{I'})$ *is a singleton,*
(iii) *or* $\mathrm{ran}(g_I) < \mathrm{ran}(g_{I'})$,
 (iv) *or* $\mathrm{ran}(g_I) > \mathrm{ran}(g_{I'})$.[11]

Thus, a comparison meaningful function on a single ordinal scale reduces, on each minimal order invariant subset of $\mathbb{I}^n$, to a constant or a transformed projection onto a coordinate.

Example 8.38. We have seen in Example 8.3 that there are 11 minimal order invariant subsets in the unit square $[0,1]^2$, namely

  (i) $I_1 = \{(0,0)\}, I_2 = \{(1,0)\}, I_3 = \{(1,1)\}, I_4 = \{(0,1)\}$,
 (ii) $I_5 = (0,1) \times \{0\}, I_6 = \{1\} \times (0,1), I_7 = (0,1) \times \{1\}, I_8 = \{0\} \times (0,1)$,
(iii) $I_9 = \{(x_1,x_2) \mid 0 < x_1 = x_2 < 1\}, I_{10} = \{(x_1,x_2) \mid 0 < x_1 < x_2 < 1\}$,
       $I_{11} = \{(x_1,x_2) \mid 0 < x_2 < x_1 < 1\}$.

Let $k_{I_j} = 1$ and $g_{I_j}(x) = 1-x$ if $j \in \{1,2,3,5,6,9,11\}$, and $k_{I_j} = 2$ and $g_{I_j}(x) = 2x-3$ if $j \in \{4,7,8,10\}$, where always $x \in \mathsf{P}_{k_{I_j}}(I_j)$. Then the corresponding comparison meaningful function $\mathsf{F} : [0,1]^2 \to \mathbb{R}$ is given by

$$\mathsf{F}(x_1,x_2) = \begin{cases} 1 - x_1 & \text{if } x_1 \geqslant x_2 \\ 2x_2 - 3 & \text{if } x_1 < x_2. \end{cases}$$

When a comparison meaningful function on a single ordinal scale is idempotent, it must satisfy, for all $x \in \mathsf{P}_{k_I}(I)$,

$$g_I(x) = x,$$

whenever either I is the open diagonal of $\mathbb{I}^n$, or $I = \{(\inf \mathbb{I}, \ldots, \inf \mathbb{I})\}$ (if $\inf \mathbb{I} \in \mathbb{I}$), or $I = \{(\sup \mathbb{I}, \ldots, \sup \mathbb{I})\}$ (if $\sup \mathbb{I} \in \mathbb{I}$).

8.5.2 The nondecreasing case

The following result [286] yields, when $\mathbb{I}$ is open, a description of all nondecreasing comparison meaningful functions $\mathsf{F} : \mathbb{I}^n \to \mathbb{R}$ on a single ordinal scale.

Proposition 8.39. *Assume that* $\mathbb{I}$ *is open. Then* $\mathsf{F} : \mathbb{I}^n \to \mathbb{R}$ *is a nondecreasing comparison meaningful function on a single ordinal scale if and only if there exist* $\alpha \in \mathcal{F}_{0-1}(n)$ *and a strictly increasing or constant function* $g : \mathbb{I} \to \mathbb{R}$ *such that* $\mathsf{F} = g \circ p_\alpha^\vee$.

---

[11] Note that $\mathrm{ran}(g_I) < \mathrm{ran}(g_{I'})$ means that for all $r \in \mathrm{ran}(g_I)$ and all $r' \in \mathrm{ran}(g_{I'})$, we have $r < r'$.

As we can see, all the functions described in Proposition 8.39 are continuous up to possible discontinuities of the function g.

The following corollaries [272, Th. 4.4] (see [281, Th. 3.1] for preliminary results) immediately follow from Proposition 8.39:

Corollary 8.40. *Assume that $\mathbb{I}$ is open. Then $\mathsf{F} : \mathbb{I}^n \to \mathbb{R}$ is a nondecreasing, idempotent, and comparison meaningful function on a single ordinal scale if and only if there exists $\alpha \in \mathcal{F}_{0-1}(n)$ such that $\mathsf{F} = p_\alpha^\vee$.*

Corollary 8.41. *Assume that $\mathbb{I}$ is open. Then $\mathsf{F} : \mathbb{I}^n \to \mathbb{R}$ is a symmetric, nondecreasing, idempotent, and comparison meaningful function on a single ordinal scale if and only if there exists $k \in [n]$ such that $\mathsf{F} = \mathsf{OS}_k$.*

Corollary 8.42. *Assume that n is odd and that $\mathbb{I}$ is open. Then $\mathsf{F} : \mathbb{I}^n \to \mathbb{R}$ is a symmetric, weakly self-dual, nondecreasing, idempotent, and comparison meaningful function on a single ordinal scale if and only if $\mathsf{F} = \mathsf{Med}$.*

A complete description of nondecreasing comparison meaningful functions F : $\mathbb{I}^n \to \mathbb{R}$ on a single ordinal scale is given in the next theorem [286, Cor. 4.1]. Let $\mathcal{G}(\mathbb{I})$ be the set of all strictly increasing or constant real functions g defined either on $\mathrm{int}(\mathbb{I})$, or on the singleton $\{\inf \mathbb{I}\} \cap \mathbb{I}$, or on the singleton $\{\sup \mathbb{I}\} \cap \mathbb{I}$ (if these singletons exist). This set is partially ordered as follows: $g_1 \preccurlyeq g_2$ if either $g_1 = g_2$, or $\mathrm{ran}(g_1) = \mathrm{ran}(g_2)$ is a singleton, or $\mathrm{ran}(g_1) < \mathrm{ran}(g_2)$.

Theorem 8.43. *$\mathsf{F} : \mathbb{I}^n \to \mathbb{R}$ is a nondecreasing comparison meaningful function on a single ordinal scale if and only if there exist nondecreasing mappings $\gamma : \mathcal{I}_n^*[\mathbb{I}] \to \mathcal{G}(\mathbb{I})$ and $\zeta : \mathcal{I}_n^*[\mathbb{I}] \to \mathcal{F}_{0-1}^{\mathbb{I}}(n)$ such that $\mathsf{F}|_I = (\gamma(I) \circ p_{\zeta(I)}^\vee)|_I$ for all $I \in \mathcal{I}_n^*[\mathbb{I}]$.*

If furthermore F is idempotent, then by nondecreasing monotonicity, we have $\mathrm{ran}(\mathsf{F}) = \mathbb{I}$ and, by Proposition 8.35, F is ordinal scale invariant. Hence we have the following corollary:

Corollary 8.44. *$\mathsf{F} : \mathbb{I}^n \to \mathbb{R}$ is a nondecreasing, idempotent, and comparison meaningful function on a single ordinal scale if and only if there exists a nondecreasing mapping $\zeta : \mathcal{I}_n^*[\mathbb{I}] \to \mathcal{F}_{0-1}^{\mathbb{I}}(n)$, where $\zeta[(\mathrm{int}(\mathbb{I}))^n]$ is nonconstant, such that $\mathsf{F}|_I = p_{\zeta(I)}^\vee|_I$ for all $I \in \mathcal{I}_n^*[\mathbb{I}]$.*

8.5.3 The continuous case

Based on a preliminary result [281, §4] (see also [262, §3.4.2]), a full description of continuous comparison meaningful functions on a single ordinal scale was given by Marichal [272, Th. 4.2] as follows:

Theorem 8.45. *$\mathsf{F} : \mathbb{I}^n \to \mathbb{R}$ is a continuous comparison meaningful function on a single ordinal scale if and only if there exist $\alpha \in \mathcal{F}_{0-1}(n)$ and a continuous and strictly monotonic or constant function $g : \mathbb{I} \to \mathbb{R}$ such that $\mathsf{F} = g \circ p_\alpha^\vee$.*

Corollary 8.46. $F : \mathbb{I}^n \to \mathbb{R}$ *is a continuous, idempotent, and comparison meaningful function on a single ordinal scale if and only if there exists* $\alpha \in \mathcal{F}_{0-1}(n)$ *such that* $F = p_\alpha^\vee$.

Remark 8.47. The result in Corollary 8.46 was stated and proved first in social choice theory by Yanovskaya [446, Th. 1] when $\mathbb{I} = \mathbb{R}$.

Corollary 8.48. $F : \mathbb{I}^n \to \mathbb{R}$ *is a symmetric, continuous, and comparison meaningful function on a single ordinal scale if and only if there exist* $k \in [n]$ *and a continuous strictly monotonic or constant function* $g : \mathbb{I} \to \mathbb{R}$ *such that* $F = g \circ \mathsf{OS}_k$.

Corollary 8.49. $F : \mathbb{I}^n \to \mathbb{R}$ *is a symmetric, continuous, idempotent, and comparison meaningful function on a single ordinal scale if and only if there exists* $k \in [n]$ *such that* $F = \mathsf{OS}_k$.

Remark 8.50. A slightly stronger version of the result in Corollary 8.49, consisting in replacing idempotency with internality, was actually proved first by Orlov [335] in $\mathbb{R}^n$, then by Marichal and Roubens [289, Th. 1] in $\mathbb{I}^n$ (see also Marichal [262, Th. 3.4.13]), and finally by Ovchinnikov [337, Th. 4.3] in the more general framework where the range of variables is a simple order whose open intervals are homogeneous and nonempty; see also Ovchinnikov [339, §6].

Corollary 8.51. *Assume that n is odd and that* $B[\mathbb{I}]$ *is not a singleton. Then* $F : \mathbb{I}^n \to \mathbb{R}$ *is a symmetric, weakly self-dual, continuous, idempotent, and comparison meaningful function on a single ordinal scale if and only if* $F = \mathsf{Med}$.

8.6 Comparison meaningful functions on independent ordinal scales

In this section we present the class of *comparison meaningful functions on independent ordinal scales* (cf. Definition 2.101), which were introduced by Aczél and Roberts [12, Case #21] and studied by Kim [209] (see preliminary work in Osborne [336]) and then investigated by some other authors; see [272, 281, 285, 286].

Remark 8.52. As observed in Proposition 2.103, comparison meaningful functions on independent ordinal scales can also be defined as those functions preserving the comparison of aggregated values when changing the scales defined by the independent variables; see Marichal and Mesiar [285].

Comparison meaningfulness on independent ordinal scales is a very strong condition, much stronger than comparison meaningfulness on a single ordinal scale. For example, it was proved [272, Lem. 5.2] that this condition reduces any lattice polynomial function to a projection function onto one coordinate.

Regarding continuity of comparison meaningful functions on independent ordinal scales, it can be interpreted in the same way as for comparison meaningful functions on a single ordinal scale; see Marichal and Mesiar [285, §5.2]. Consider again the set $\Phi'[\mathbb{I}]$ of continuous nondecreasing surjections from $\mathbb{I}$ onto $\mathbb{I}$.

Proposition 8.53. $F : \mathbb{I}^n \to \mathbb{R}$ *is a continuous and comparison meaningful function on independent ordinal scales if and only if, for any* $\varphi \in \Phi'[\mathbb{I}]^n$, *there is a continuous and nondecreasing mapping* $\psi_\varphi : \mathrm{ran}(F) \to \mathrm{ran}(F)$ *such that* $F(\varphi(\mathbf{x})) = \psi_\varphi(F(\mathbf{x}))$ *for all* $\mathbf{x} \in \mathbb{I}^n$.

8.6.1 General descriptions

The description of comparison meaningful functions on independent ordinal scales is very similar to that of comparison meaningful functions on a single ordinal scale. The result can be formulated as follows [286, Cor. 3.1]:

Theorem 8.54. $F : \mathbb{I}^n \to \mathbb{R}$ *is a comparison meaningful function on independent ordinal scales if and only if, for any* $I \in \mathcal{I}_n^*[\mathbb{I}]$, *there exist an index* $k_I \in [n]$ *and a strictly monotonic or constant function* $g_I : \mathsf{P}_{k_I}(I) \to \mathbb{R}$ *such that* $F|_I = (g_I \circ \mathsf{P}_{k_I})|_I$, *where, for any* $I, I' \in \mathcal{I}_n^*[\mathbb{I}]$,

(i) *either* $g_I = g_{I'}$,
(ii) *or* $\mathrm{ran}(g_I) = \mathrm{ran}(g_{I'})$ *is a singleton*,
(iii) *or* $\mathrm{ran}(g_I) < \mathrm{ran}(g_{I'})$,
(iv) *or* $\mathrm{ran}(g_I) > \mathrm{ran}(g_{I'})$.

Thus, a comparison meaningful function on independent ordinal scales reduces, on each minimal strongly order invariant subset of $\mathbb{I}^n$, to a constant or a transformed projection onto a coordinate.

When a comparison meaningful function on independent ordinal scales is idempotent, it must satisfy, for all $x \in \mathsf{P}_{k_I}(I)$,

$$g_I(x) = x,$$

whenever either $I = (\mathrm{int}(\mathbb{I}))^n$, or $I = \{(\inf \mathbb{I}, \dots, \inf \mathbb{I})\}$ (if $\inf \mathbb{I} \in \mathbb{I}$), or $I = \{(\sup \mathbb{I}, \dots, \sup \mathbb{I})\}$ (if $\sup \mathbb{I} \in \mathbb{I}$).

When $\mathbb{I}$ is open, the family $\mathcal{I}_n^*[\mathbb{I}]$ reduces to $\{\mathrm{int}(\mathbb{I})\}$, thus considerably simplifying Theorem 8.54 as follows:

Proposition 8.55. *Assume that* $\mathbb{I}$ *is open. Then* $F : \mathbb{I}^n \to \mathbb{R}$ *is a comparison meaningful function on independent ordinal scales if and only if there exist* $k \in [n]$ *and a strictly monotonic or constant function* $g : \mathbb{I} \to \mathbb{R}$ *such that* $F = g \circ \mathsf{P}_k$.

Corollary 8.56. *Assume that* $\mathbb{I}$ *is open. Then* $F : \mathbb{I}^n \to \mathbb{R}$ *is an idempotent and comparison meaningful function on independent ordinal scales if and only if there exists* $k \in [n]$ *such that* $F = \mathsf{P}_k$.

It follows from Proposition 8.55 that, when $\mathbb{I}$ is open and $n \geqslant 2$, any symmetric and comparison meaningful function on independent ordinal scales is necessarily a constant function. In this case, it cannot be idempotent.

8.6.2 The nondecreasing case

Starting from Proposition 8.55 we deduce immediately the following characterizations:

Proposition 8.57. *Assume that* $\mathbb{I}$ *is open. Then* $\mathsf{F} : \mathbb{I}^n \to \mathbb{R}$ *is a nondecreasing comparison meaningful function on independent ordinal scales if and only if there exist* $k \in [n]$ *and a strictly increasing or constant function* $g : \mathbb{I} \to \mathbb{R}$ *such that* $\mathsf{F} = g \circ \mathsf{P}_k$.

When $\mathbb{I}$ is not open, we have the following (see Marichal *et al.* [286, Cor. 4.2]):

Theorem 8.58. $\mathsf{F} : \mathbb{I}^n \to \mathbb{R}$ *is a nondecreasing comparison meaningful function on independent ordinal scales if and only if there exists a mapping* $\zeta : \mathcal{I}_n^*[\mathbb{I}] \to [n]$ *and a nondecreasing mapping* $\gamma : \mathcal{I}_n^*[\mathbb{I}] \to \mathcal{G}(\mathbb{I})$ *such that* $\mathsf{F}|_I = (\gamma(I) \circ \mathsf{P}_{\zeta(I)})|_I$ *for all* $I \in \mathcal{I}_n^*[\mathbb{I}]$, *where if* $\gamma(I) = \gamma(I')$ *then also* $\zeta(I) = \zeta(I')$ *(unless* $\gamma(I) = \gamma(I')$ *is constant).*

8.6.3 The continuous case

As we already mentioned above, comparison meaningfulness on independent ordinal scales reduces any lattice polynomial function to a projection function onto one coordinate. From this result we deduce immediately the following characterizations; see Marichal [272, §5].

Theorem 8.59. $\mathsf{F} : \mathbb{I}^n \to \mathbb{R}$ *is a continuous and comparison meaningful function on independent ordinal scales if and only if there exist* $k \in [n]$ *and a continuous and strictly monotonic or constant function* $g : \mathbb{I} \to \mathbb{R}$ *such that* $\mathsf{F} = g \circ \mathsf{P}_k$.

Corollary 8.60. $\mathsf{F} : \mathbb{I}^n \to \mathbb{R}$ *is a continuous, idempotent, and comparison meaningful function on independent ordinal scales if and only if there exists* $k \in [n]$ *such that* $\mathsf{F} = \mathsf{P}_k$.

Remark 8.61. The result in Theorem 8.59 was proved first by Kim [209, Cor. 1.2] in $\mathbb{R}^n$; see Osborne [336] for preliminary results.

It follows from Theorem 8.59 that, if $n \geqslant 2$, any symmetric, continuous, and comparison meaningful function on independent ordinal scales is necessarily a constant function.

8.7 Aggregation on finite chains by chain independent functions

In this final section, mainly based on a paper by Marichal and Mesiar [285], we give interpretations of ordinal scale invariance and comparison meaningfulness properties in the setting of aggregation on finite chains (i.e., totally ordered finite sets). These interpretations show that the ordinal scale invariant functions and comparison meaningful functions always have isomorphic discrete representatives defined on finite chains. These discrete functions do not depend on the chains on which they are defined.

8.7.1 Introduction

Let A be a set of *alternatives* (objects, individuals, etc.) and consider an open real interval $\mathbb{I}$, possibly unbounded.[12] In representational measurement theory [364,365], a *scale of measurement* can be seen as a mapping $h : A \to \mathbb{I}$ that assigns a real number to each element of A according to some attribute or criterion.[13] As already mentioned in the introduction, such a scale is an ordinal scale if any other acceptable version of it is of the form $\varphi \circ h$ for some strictly increasing function $\varphi : \mathbb{I} \to \mathbb{I}$.

An ordinal scale is finite if $\mathrm{ran}(h)$ is a finite subset of $\mathbb{I}$, that is of the form

$$\mathrm{ran}(h) = \{b_1, b_2, \ldots, b_k\},$$

where the values $b_1, b_2, \ldots, b_k$ represent the possible rating benchmarks defined along some ordinal criterion, and $b_1 < b_2 < \cdots < b_k$. We assume throughout that $|\mathrm{ran}(h)| = k \geqslant 2$.

Since the values $b_1, b_2, \ldots, b_k$ of the scale are defined up to order, that is, within a strictly increasing function $\varphi : \mathbb{I} \to \mathbb{I}$, we can simply consider $\mathrm{ran}(h)$ as a finite chain $(S, \preccurlyeq)$ of k elements, that is,

$$S = \{s_1 \prec s_2 \prec \cdots \prec s_k\},$$

where $\preccurlyeq$ represents a total order on S and $\prec$ represents its asymmetric part. In this representation we denote by $s_* = s_1$ (respectively, $s^* = s_k$) the bottom element (respectively, top element) of the chain.

Example 8.62. Consider the problem of evaluating a commodity by a consumer according to a given ordinal criterion. Typically this evaluation is done by rating the product on a finite ordinal scale. For instance we could consider the following rating benchmarks:

$$1 = \text{Bad}, \ 2 = \text{Weak}, \ 3 = \text{Fair}, \ 4 = \text{Good}, \ 5 = \text{Excellent}.$$

Since the scale values are determined only up to order, this scale can be replaced with a finite chain

$$S = \{\text{B} \prec \text{W} \prec \text{F} \prec \text{G} \prec \text{E}\}$$

whose elements B, W, F, G, E refer to the following linguistic terms: *bad, weak, fair, good, excellent.*

---

[12] Without loss of generality, we can assume that $\mathbb{I} = \,]0, 1[$ or $\mathbb{I} = \mathbb{R}$.
[13] A criterion is an attribute defined in a preference-ordered domain.

It is well known (see Krantz *et al.* [238, Chap. 1]) that the total order $\preccurlyeq$ defined on S can always be numerically represented in $\mathbb{I}$ by means of an isomorphism $f : S \to \mathbb{I}$ such that

$$s_i \preccurlyeq s_j \quad \Leftrightarrow \quad f(s_i) \leqslant f(s_j)$$

for all $s_i, s_j \in S$. Moreover, just as for the mapping h, the isomorphism f is defined up to a strictly increasing function $\varphi : \mathbb{I} \to \mathbb{I}$. That is, with f all isomorphisms $f' = \varphi \circ f$ (and only these) represent the same order on S.

By choosing f so that $f(s_i) = b_i$ for $i = 1, \ldots, k$, we immediately see that the elements of A can be ordinally evaluated not only by means of the numerical mapping $h : A \to \mathrm{ran}(h)$ but also by the nonnumerical mapping $h_S : A \to S$, defined by $h_S = f^{-1} \circ h$. The following diagram illustrates the relationship among the mappings, where h and f are defined within a strictly increasing function $\varphi : \mathbb{I} \to \mathbb{I}$:

We may also consider nonopen intervals $\mathbb{I}$ with the natural condition that if $f(s) = \inf \mathbb{I} \in \mathbb{I}$ for some $s \in S$ then $s = s_*$, and similarly, if $f(s) = \sup \mathbb{I} \in \mathbb{I}$ for some $s \in S$ then $s = s^*$. In that case, the isomorphism f is required to be *endpoint preserving*, that is, if $\inf \mathbb{I} \in \mathbb{I}$ (respectively, $\sup \mathbb{I} \in \mathbb{I}$) then $f(s_*) = \inf \mathbb{I}$ (respectively, $f(s^*) = \sup \mathbb{I}$), regardless of the chain $(S, \preccurlyeq)$ considered.[14] Consequently also all the functions $\varphi : \mathbb{I} \to \mathbb{I}$ must be endpoint preserving in the sense that $\varphi(x) = x$ for all $x \in B[\mathbb{I}]$. Due to the finiteness of the ordinal scales, we may even assume that the functions φ are continuous, which amounts to assuming that they all belong to $\Phi[\mathbb{I}]$.

The endpoint preservation assumption of f (and hence of φ) clarifies why we consider numerical representations in an interval $\mathbb{I}$ of $\mathbb{R}$, possibly nonopen, rather than $\mathbb{R}$ itself.[15]

In this section, the set of all endpoint preserving isomorphisms $f : S \to \mathbb{I}$ is denoted $F[S, \mathbb{I}]$. The diagonal restriction of $F[S, \mathbb{I}]^n$ is the set

$$F_n[S, \mathbb{I}] := \{ \underbrace{(f, \ldots, f)}_{n} \mid f \in F[S, \mathbb{I}] \}.$$

Finally, for any $\mathbf{a} \in S^n$ and any $\mathbf{f} \in F[S, \mathbb{I}]^n$, the symbol $\mathbf{f}(\mathbf{a})$ denotes the vector $(f_1(a_1), \ldots, f_n(a_n))$.

[14] This amounts to assuming that all the chains considered have a common bottom element s_* (resp. a common top element s^*) whose numerical representation is $\inf \mathbb{I}$ (resp. $\sup \mathbb{I}$).

[15] If $\mathbb{I}$ is closed, one typically chooses $\mathbb{I} = [0, 1]$ or $\mathbb{I} = \mathbb{R}$.

8.7.2 Aggregation by ordinal scale invariant functions

Suppose we have n evaluations expressed in a finite chain $(S, \preccurlyeq)$, with $|S| = k \geqslant 2$. To aggregate these evaluations and obtain an overall evaluation in the same chain, we can use a discrete aggregation function $G : S^n \to S$, which is a ranking function sorting k^n n-tuples into k classes. (Here, "discrete" means that the domain of the function G is a discrete set.)

Among all the possible aggregation functions, we could choose one that is "independent" of the chain used.[16] Such a *chain independent* aggregation function is necessarily based on a numerical function $\mathsf{F} : \mathbb{I}^n \to \mathbb{I}$ that can be represented in any finite chain $(S, \preccurlyeq)$ by a discrete analog $G : S^n \to S$ in the sense that the following identity:

$$\mathsf{F}(x_1, \ldots, x_n) = f\big(G(f^{-1}(x_1), \ldots, f^{-1}(x_n))\big), \qquad \forall \mathbf{x} \in \mathbb{I}^n,$$

holds for all isomorphisms $f \in \mathsf{F}[S, \mathbb{I}]$.

As the following theorem shows [285, Prop. 4.1], this condition completely characterizes the ordinal scale invariant functions.

Theorem 8.63. $\mathsf{F} : \mathbb{I}^n \to \mathbb{I}$ *is an ordinal scale invariant function if and only if, for any finite chain $(S, \preccurlyeq)$, there exists an aggregation function $G : S^n \to S$ such that, for any $f \in \mathsf{F}[S, \mathbb{I}]$, we have*

$$\mathsf{F}\big(f(a_1), \ldots, f(a_n)\big) = f\big(G(a_1, \ldots, a_n)\big) \tag{8.7}$$

for all $\mathbf{a} \in S^n$.

Thus, an ordinal scale invariant function is characterized by the fact that it can always be represented by a discrete aggregation function $G : S^n \to S$ on any finite chain $(S, \preccurlyeq)$, regardless of the cardinality of this chain.[17] It is informative to represent (8.7) by the following commutative diagram, where $\mathbf{f} = (f, \ldots, f)$:

$$
\begin{array}{ccc}
\mathbb{I}^n & \xrightarrow{\ \mathsf{F}\ } & \mathbb{I} \\
{\scriptstyle \mathbf{f}}\big\uparrow & & \big\uparrow{\scriptstyle f} \\
S^n & \xrightarrow[\ G\ ]{} & S
\end{array}
$$

---

[16] For example, we could use any lattice polynomial function, which does not depend on the chain used.

[17] It is important to remember that considering a discrete function $G : S^n \to S$, where $(S, \preccurlyeq)$ is a given chain, is not equivalent to considering an ordinal scale invariant function $\mathsf{F} ; \mathbb{I}^n \to \mathbb{I}$. Indeed, defining an ordinal scale invariant function is much more restrictive since such a function should be independent of any scale. For instance, if $n = 2$ and $\mathbb{I}$ is open, we see by Proposition 8.16 that there are only four invariant functions, namely

$$\mathsf{F}(x_1, x_2) = x_1 \quad \text{or} \quad x_2 \quad \text{or} \quad x_1 \wedge x_2 \quad \text{or} \quad x_1 \vee x_2,$$

while the number of possible discrete functions $G : S^2 \to S$ is clearly k^{k^2}, where $k = |S|$.

It is clear from (8.7) that the discrete function G representing F in $(S, \preccurlyeq)$ is uniquely determined and, in some sense, is isomorphic to the "restriction" of F to S^n. For example, if $n = 2$ and $\mathsf{F}(\mathbf{x}) = x_1 \wedge x_2$ (respectively, $\mathsf{F}(\mathbf{x}) = \inf \mathbb{I}$) then the unique representative G of F is defined by $G(\mathbf{a}) = a_1 \wedge a_2$ (respectively, $G(\mathbf{a}) = s_*$).

Evidently an ordinal scale invariant function is nondecreasing if and only if its discrete representative is nondecreasing. Another property that might be required on ordinal scale invariant functions is continuity (see Section 8.4.3) whose discrete counterpart, called *smoothness*, is defined as follows [140].[18]

Definition 8.64. Consider $(n + 1)$ finite chains $(S_0, \preccurlyeq_{S_0}), \ldots, (S_n, \preccurlyeq_{S_n})$. A discrete function $G : \times_{i=1}^{n} S_i \to S_0$ is said to be *smooth* if, for any $\mathbf{a}, \mathbf{b} \in \times_{i=1}^{n} S_i$, the elements $G(\mathbf{a})$ and $G(\mathbf{b})$ are equal or neighboring whenever there exists $j \in [n]$ such that a_j and b_j are neighboring and $a_i = b_i$ for all $i \neq j$.

The following important result [285, Prop. 5.1] relates the continuity property of ordinal scale invariant functions to the smoothness condition of its discrete representatives, thus making continuity sensible and even appealing for ordinal scale invariant functions.

Proposition 8.65. *An ordinal scale invariant function* $\mathsf{F} : \mathbb{I}^n \to \mathbb{I}$ *is continuous if and only if it is represented only by smooth discrete aggregation functions.*

8.7.3 Aggregation by comparison meaningful functions on a single ordinal scale

Consider the more general situation where the evaluations to be aggregated are expressed in the same finite chain $(S, \preccurlyeq_S)$ and the overall evaluation is expressed in a finite chain $(T, \preccurlyeq_T)$, possibly different from $(S, \preccurlyeq_S)$. Again, we can consider aggregation functions $G : S^n \to T$ and, among them, we might want to choose aggregation functions that are independent of the chains used.

As the following theorem shows [285, Prop. 4.3], such chain-independent functions are constructed from numerical functions $\mathsf{F} : \mathbb{I}^n \to \mathbb{R}$ that are exactly the comparison meaningful functions on a single ordinal scale.

Theorem 8.66. $\mathsf{F} : \mathbb{I}^n \to \mathbb{R}$ *is a comparison meaningful function on a single ordinal scale if and only if, for any finite chain* $(S, \preccurlyeq_S)$, *there exists a finite chain* $(T, \preccurlyeq_T)$ *and a surjective aggregation function* $G : S^n \to T$ *such that, for any* $\mathbf{f} \in F_n[S, \mathbb{I}]$, *there is a isomorphism* $g_{\mathbf{f}} : T \to \mathbb{R}$ *such that, for all* $\mathbf{a} \in S^n$,

$$\mathsf{F}(\mathbf{f}(\mathbf{a})) = g_{\mathbf{f}}(G(\mathbf{a})). \tag{8.8}$$

Thus, a comparison meaningful function on a single ordinal scale is characterized by the fact that it can always be represented by a discrete aggregation function

---

[18] Fodor [115, Th. 2] (see [285] for the general case) showed that the smoothness condition is equivalent to the discrete version of the intermediate value theorem [131, Lem. 1].

$G : S^n \to T$ on any finite chain $(S, \preccurlyeq)$, regardless of the cardinality of this chain. Equation (8.8) can be graphically represented by the following commutative diagram:

$$
\begin{array}{ccc}
\mathbb{I}^n & \xrightarrow{\ \ F\ \ } & \mathbb{R} \\
{\scriptstyle f}\uparrow & & \uparrow{\scriptstyle g_f} \\
S^n & \xrightarrow[\ \ G\ \ ]{} & T
\end{array}
$$

It can easily be shown [285, §4.2] that, given a comparison meaningful function $F : \mathbb{I}^n \to \mathbb{R}$ on a single ordinal scale and a finite chain $(S, \preccurlyeq_S)$, the output chain $(T, \preccurlyeq_T)$ and the functions $G : S^n \to T$ and $g_f : T \to \mathbb{R}$ are uniquely determined.

The analog of Proposition 8.65 can be stated as follows [285, Prop. 5.2]. Unfortunately here we no longer have a necessary and sufficient condition.

Proposition 8.67. *A continuous comparison meaningful function* $F : \mathbb{I}^n \to \mathbb{R}$ *on a single ordinal scale is represented only by smooth discrete aggregation functions.*

8.7.4 Aggregation by comparison meaningful functions on independent ordinal scales

We now assume that the n evaluations are expressed in independent finite chains $(S_i, \preccurlyeq_{S_i})$, $i = 1, \ldots, n$, and that the overall evaluation is expressed in a finite chain $(T, \preccurlyeq_T)$. We can consider aggregation functions

$$
G : \underset{i=1}{\overset{n}{\times}} S_i \to T
$$

and, among them, we might want to choose aggregation functions that are independent of the chains used.

As the following theorem shows [285, Prop. 4.6], such chain-independent functions are constructed from numerical functions $F : \mathbb{I}^n \to \mathbb{R}$ that are exactly the comparison meaningful functions on independent ordinal scales.

Theorem 8.68. $F : \mathbb{I}^n \to \mathbb{R}$ *is a comparison meaningful function on independent ordinal scales if and only if, for any finite chains* $(S_i, \preccurlyeq_{S_i})$, $i = 1, \ldots, n$, *there exists a finite chain* $(T, \preccurlyeq_T)$ *and a surjective aggregation function* $G : \times_{i=1}^{n} S_i \to T$ *such that, for any* $f \in F[S, \mathbb{I}]^n$, *there is an isomorphism* $g_f : T \to \mathbb{R}$ *such that, for all* $a \in \times_{i=1}^{n} S_i$,

$$
F\big(f(a)\big) = g_f\big(G(a)\big).
$$

Thus, a comparison meaningful function on independent ordinal scales is characterized by the fact that it can always be represented by a discrete aggregation function

$G : \times_{i=1}^{n} S_i \rightarrow T$, regardless of the cardinality of the chains considered. Here the commutative diagram is given by

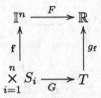

Here again, it can easily be shown [285, §4.3] that, given a comparison meaningful function $F : \mathbb{I}^n \rightarrow \mathbb{R}$ on independent ordinal scales and n finite chains $(S_i, \preccurlyeq_{S_i})$, $i = 1, \ldots, n$, the output chain $(T, \preccurlyeq_T)$ and the functions $G : \times_{i=1}^{n} S_i \rightarrow T$ and $g_{\mathfrak{f}} : T \rightarrow \mathbb{R}$ are uniquely determined.

Regarding continuous comparison meaningful functions, we have the following result [285, Prop. 5.3]:

Proposition 8.69. *A continuous comparison meaningful function* $F : \mathbb{I}^n \rightarrow \mathbb{R}$ *on independent ordinal scales is represented only by smooth discrete aggregation functions.*

9

Aggregation on bipolar scales

9.1 Introduction

So far, we have mainly considered aggregation functions whose variables lie in $[0, 1]$ or some similar structure, i.e., a closed interval of some linearly ordered set. The lower and upper bounds of this interval represent the lowest and highest scores (or utility values, outcomes, etc.) along each dimension.

We may desire to consider a third particular point of the interval, say e, which will play a particular role, for example a neutral value (in some sense) or an annihilator value. We have already encountered this situation when dealing with uninorms (cf. Section 3.6): $e \in]0, 1[$ is a neutral element in the sense that $U(e, x) = x$ for any $x \in [0, 1]$. For convenience, up to a rescaling, we may always consider that we work on $[-1, 1]$, and 0 corresponds to our particular point, denoted e before. In the more general case of bounded linearly ordered sets, we apply a symmetrization procedure; see Section 9.3.

The motivation for such a study is not only mathematical. There is psychological evidence that in many cases, scores or utilities manipulated by humans lie on a *bipolar scale*, that is to say, a scale with a neutral value making the frontier between good or satisfactory scores, and bad or unsatisfactory scores. With our convention, good scores are positive ones, while negative scores reflect bad scores. Most of the time, our behavior with positive scores is not the same as with negative ones: for example, a conjunctive attitude may be turned into a disjunctive attitude when changing the sign of the scores. So, it becomes important to define aggregation functions that are able to reflect the variety of aggregation behaviors on bipolar scales. By contrast, intervals without neutral value are called *unipolar scales*.

Let A be an aggregation function defined in $[-1, 1]^n$, such that 0 is an idempotent element. Clearly, the restriction of A to nonnegative numbers corresponds to some (usual) aggregation function A^+ on $[0, 1]^n$. Similarly, the symmetric version of its restriction to $[-1, 0]^n$ corresponds to a (possibly different) function A^-, after some suitable symmetrization. However, this does not suffice to define the value of A for the mixed case, when positive and negative scores coexist. The exact way to do this is dependent on the nature of A and the meaning of 0. We shall distinguish several cases.

317

Let us consider first the case when A is associative, so we need to consider only two arguments. For the meaning of the 0 point, apart from the fact that it should be an idempotent element, we can think of two cases of interest: either 0 is a neutral element in the sense that $A(0, x) = A(x, 0) = x$ for any $x \in [-1, 1]$, or 0 is an annihilator element, i.e., $A(0, x) = A(x, 0) = 0$, for any $x \in [-1, 1]$. The first case leads naturally to pseudo-additions, while the second one leads to pseudo-multiplications. This is the topic of Section 9.2. The particular case of the definition of the bipolar version of minimum and maximum on $[-1, 1]^n$ will be addressed in Section 9.3, where we deal with symmetrized linearly ordered sets.

Let us consider now (possibly) nonassociative aggregation functions. A first important class of functions are those in the form

$$A(\mathbf{x}) := \psi(A^+(\mathbf{x}^+), A^-(\mathbf{x}^-)), \tag{9.1}$$

where $\mathbf{x} \in [-1, 1]^n$ for some n, and $\mathbf{x}^+ := \mathbf{x} \vee \mathbf{0}$, $\mathbf{x}^- := (-\mathbf{x})^+$, A^+, A^- are given aggregation functions on $[0, 1]^n$, and ψ is a pseudo-difference (see below). We call such aggregation functions *separable*. A more general case is defined as follows. We say that $\mathbf{x}$ is a *ternary vector* if $\mathbf{x} \in \{-1, 0, 1\}^n$ for some n. Let us suppose that the value of A for each ternary vector is given. Then we define A for every $\mathbf{x} \in [-1, 1]^n$ by some interpolation rule between the known values. The separable case is recovered only when A^+ and A^- are also obtained by some interpolation rule. As in the usual unipolar case, we will show that this type of aggregation function is based on an integral (Section 9.5).

Before entering the topic, we introduce the fundamental concept of pseudo-difference.

Definition 9.1. Let S be a t-conorm.

(i) The S-*difference* is defined by

$$a \overset{S}{-} b := \inf\{c \in [0, 1] \mid S(b, c) \geqslant a\}$$

for any (a, b) in $[0, 1]^2$.

(ii) The *pseudo-difference associated to* S is defined by

$$a \ominus_S b := \begin{cases} a \overset{S}{-} b & \text{if } a \geqslant b \\ -(b \overset{S}{-} a) & \text{if } a < b \\ 0, & \text{if } a = b, \end{cases}$$

for any (a, b) in $[0, 1]^2$. Equivalently

$$a \ominus_S b = \text{sign}\,(a - b)\big(\text{Max}(a, b) \overset{S}{-} \text{Min}(a, b)\big).$$

Remark 9.2. S-differences have been proposed by Weber [429]; see also Section 5.6. From a logical point of view, they are extensions of the binary coimplication, the logical dual of implication (in the sense of de Morgan) [73]. S-differences are dual to residual implicators of t-norms.

Example 9.3. (i) If $S = \vee$ then for $a, b \in [0, 1]^2$

$$a \ominus_\vee b = \begin{cases} a & \text{if } a > b \\ -b & \text{if } a < b \\ 0 & \text{otherwise.} \end{cases}$$

(ii) If $S = S_L$ then $a \ominus_L b = a - b$, $(a, b) \in [0, 1]^2$.

Proposition 9.4. *If* S *is a continuous Archimedean t-conorm with additive generator* s, *then*

$$a \overset{S}{-} b = s^{-1}(0 \vee (s(a) - s(b)))$$

$$a \ominus_S b = g^{-1}(g(a) - g(b)),$$

with $g(x) := s(x)$ *for* $x \geqslant 0$, *and* $g(x) := -s(-x)$ *for* $x \leqslant 0$.

Proof. $S(b, c) \geqslant a$ is equivalent to $(s(b) + s(c)) \wedge s(1) \geqslant s(a)$. Denote by c^* the lowest value c such that $S(b, c) \geqslant a$ (it exists by continuity of S). Suppose S is strict. Then $S(b, c) \geqslant a$ becomes equivalent to $s(c) \geqslant s(a) - s(b)$. If $a \geqslant b$, then $s(a) - s(b) \geqslant 0$, and since S is strict, $c^* = s^{-1}(s(a) - s(b))$. If $a < b$, then $s(a) - s(b) < 0$, hence $c^* = 0$.

Next suppose that S is nilpotent. Note that the above solution still works since $s(c^*) + s(b) = s(a) \leqslant s(1)$.

Now, $a \ominus_S b$ is merely a symmetrization of $a \overset{S}{-} b$, hence the formula. $\square$

Remark 9.5. We do not need to specify here the result of $\infty - \infty$ which happens with $a = b = 1$ and any strict t-conorm, because later the case $a = b = 1$ is treated separately; see (9.3).

Throughout this chapter, we set $\mathbb{I} := [-1, 1]$, except in Section 9.3.

9.2 Associative bipolar operators

In this section, we want to define associative and commutative operators where 0 is either a neutral element or an annihilator element, which we call respectively *(symmetric) pseudo-addition* and *(symmetric) pseudo-multiplication*, the term "symmetric" stressing the fact that we deal with both positive and negative numbers. By contrast, definitions of similar operators in Section 5.6 are for positive numbers only. However we will often drop the term "symmetric" since it is implicit in the whole chapter. This section is mainly based on [157].

We denote respectively by $\oplus, \otimes : [-1,1]^2 \to [-1,1]$ these operators, and adopt an infix notation.

9.2.1 Pseudo-additions

Our basic requirements are the following, for any $x, y, z \in [-1, 1]$:

A1 Commutativity: $x \oplus y = y \oplus x$.
A2 Associativity: $x \oplus (y \oplus z) = (x \oplus y) \oplus z$.
A3 Neutral element $x \oplus 0 = 0 \oplus x = x$.

Endowing $[-1, 1]$ with the usual ordering, we may require in addition that $\oplus$ is nondecreasing in each argument. As observed by Fuchs [126], under the assumption of nondecreasing or nonincreasing monotonicity of $\oplus$, associativity implies that $\oplus$ cannot be decreasing. Indeed, suppose without loss of generality that $\oplus$ is decreasing in the first place and take $x' \leqslant x$. Then $x' \oplus (y \oplus z) \geqslant x \oplus (y \oplus z) = (x \oplus y) \oplus z \geqslant (x' \oplus y) \oplus z = x' \oplus (y \oplus z)$, a contradiction unless $\oplus$ is degenerate. Hence we are led to assume **A4**.

A4 Nondecreasing monotonicity: $x \oplus y \leqslant x' \oplus y'$, for any $x \leqslant x', y \leqslant y'$.

The above requirements mean that we recognize $\oplus$ as a t-conorm when restricted to $[0, 1]$, which we denote by S. Since $[-1, 1]$ is a symmetric interval, and if 0 plays the role of a neutral element, then we should have

A5 Symmetry: $x \oplus (-x) = 0$, for all $x \in]-1, 1[$.

Remark 9.6.   (i) Excluding $x = 1$ or -1 above comes from associativity and from the fact that 1 is an annihilator element on $[0, 1]^2$. Indeed, letting $1 \oplus (-1) = 0$ leads to

$$1 = 0 \oplus 1 = ((-1) \oplus 1) \oplus 1 = (-1) \oplus (1 \oplus 1) = (-1) \oplus 1 = 0,$$

a contradiction. If we suppose $(-1) \oplus 1 = x > 0$, then as above

$$1 = x \oplus 1 = (-1) \oplus (1 \oplus 1) = x.$$

Similarly, if we suppose $x < 0$, we are led to $x = -1$. In summary, $1 \oplus (-1) \in \{-1, +1\}$.

(ii) Each $x \in]-1, 1[$ has a unique symmetric element, i.e., $x \oplus y = 0$ if and only if $y = -x$. Indeed, assume there exist x', x'' being symmetric elements of x. Then by **A1**, **A2** and **A3**

$$x' = 0 \oplus x' = (x \oplus x'') \oplus x' = x'' \oplus (x \oplus x') = x'' \oplus 0 = x''.$$

Let us show that under axioms **A1** to **A5**, the structure of $\oplus$ is completely determined on $[-1, 1]^2$. A first fact is the following.

Proposition 9.7. *Under* **A1**, **A2**, *and* **A5**

$$(-x) \oplus (-y) = -(x \oplus y), \quad \forall (x, y) \in]-1, 0]^2 \cup [0, 1[^2.$$

Proof. $0 = (x \oplus (-x)) \oplus (y \oplus (-y)) = (x \oplus y) \oplus ((-x) \oplus (-y))$, which implies the result by uniqueness of the symmetric element. $\qquad \square$

Suppose now that $0 \leqslant y \leqslant x < 1$, and let us compute $x \oplus (-y)$. By **A3**, **A4**, and **A5** we have

$$x \oplus y \geqslant x \geqslant x \oplus (-y) \geqslant 0.$$

By associativity,

$$(x \oplus (-y)) \oplus y = x$$

hence, $x \oplus (-y)$ is a solution of the equation $z \oplus y = x$ for $0 \leqslant z \leqslant x$. In case of nonuniqueness or no solution, **A4** implies that taking

$$x \oplus (-y) := \inf\{z \mid \mathsf{S}(y, z) \geqslant x\} = x \overset{\mathsf{S}}{-} y \qquad (9.2)$$

ensures $0 \leqslant x \oplus (-y) \leqslant x$, and $x \oplus (-y) \oplus y = x$ whenever the equation $z \oplus y = x$ has a solution (which is the case if S is continuous). This shows how we are naturally led to pseudo-differences. In summary, we can always adopt, for continuous t-conorms

$$x \oplus y = \begin{cases} \mathsf{S}(x, y) & \text{if } x, y \in [0, 1] \\ -\mathsf{S}(-x, -y) & \text{if } x, y \in [-1, 0] \\ x \ominus_{\mathsf{S}} (-y) & \text{if } x \in [0, 1[, y \in]-1, 0] \\ 1 \text{ or } -1 & \text{if } x = 1, y = -1, \end{cases} \qquad (9.3)$$

with the remaining cases being determined by commutativity. We distinguish several cases for S. We write for convenience $x \oplus (-y) = x \ominus y$ for any $x, y \in [-1, 1]^2$.

S is a strict t-conorm with additive generator s. Let us rescale $\oplus$ on $[0, 1]^2$, calling U the result:

$$\mathsf{U}(z, t) := \frac{((2z - 1) \oplus (2t - 1)) + 1}{2}. \qquad (9.4)$$

We introduce $g : [-1, 1] \to [-\infty, \infty]$ as follows:

$$g(x) := s(x) \text{ for positive } x, \quad g(x) := -s(-x) \text{ for negative } x, \qquad (9.5)$$

i.e., g is a symmetrization of s, and is clearly a strictly increasing function. We introduce also another function $u : [0, 1] \to [-\infty, \infty]$ defined by $u(x) = g(2x - 1)$ that is strictly increasing and satisfies $u(\frac{1}{2}) = 0$.

Proposition 9.8. *Let* S *be a strict t-conorm with additive generator s,* $\oplus$ *the corresponding pseudo-addition defined by (9.3), and g, u defined as above. Then:*

(i) $x \oplus y = g^{-1}(g(x) + g(y))$ *for any* $x, y \in [-1, 1]$;
(ii) $U(z, t) = u^{-1}(u(z) + u(t))$ *for any* $z, t \in [0, 1]$,

with the convention $\infty - \infty = \infty$ *or* $-\infty$.

Proof. The two cases for $\infty - \infty$ arise with $1 \oplus (-1)$, and correspond to the last line of (9.3).

(i) Clearly $x \oplus y = s^{-1}(s(x) + s(y)) = g^{-1}(g(x) + g(y))$ when $x, y \in [0, 1]$. When x, y are negative, we have

$$x \oplus y = -g^{-1}(g(|x|) + g(|y|))$$
$$= g^{-1}(-(g(|x|) + g(|y|)))$$
$$= g^{-1}(g(x) + g(y)).$$

When x is positive and y is negative, we write $x \oplus y = x \ominus (-y)$ and use Proposition 9.4. The result then follows from the symmetry of g.

(ii) Using (9.4) and (i), we get for any $z, t \in [0, 1]$

$$U(z, t) = \frac{g^{-1}(g(2z - 1) + g(2t - 1)) + 1}{2}$$
$$= \frac{g^{-1}(u(z) + u(t)) + 1}{2}.$$

Now observe that for any $x, y \in [-1, 1]$, the equality $g^{-1}(y) = x$ is equivalent to $y = g(x) = u(\frac{1}{2}x + \frac{1}{2})$, which in turn is equivalent to $u^{-1}(y) = \frac{1}{2} + \frac{1}{2}x = \frac{1}{2} + \frac{1}{2}g^{-1}(y)$. This shows that $U(z, t) = u^{-1}(u(z) + u(t))$. $\square$

This result was originally established in [177]; see also [75, 217].

Corollary 9.9. *Under the assumptions of Proposition 9.8,* U *is a generated uninorm (see Theorem 3.100) that is continuous (except at* $(0, 1)$ *and* $(1, 0)$*), strictly increasing on* $]0, 1[^2$*, has neutral element* $\frac{1}{2}$*, and is conjunctive (respectively, disjunctive) when the convention* $\infty - \infty = -\infty$ *(respectively,* $\infty - \infty = \infty$*) is taken in Proposition 9.8. Moreover, the t-norm* T_U *induced is the dual of* S*.*

By T_U and S_U we mean the t-norm and the t-conorm defined by

$$T_U(x, y) := \frac{1}{e}U(ex, ey),$$

$$S_U(x, y) := \frac{1}{1 - e}(U(e + (1 - e)x, e + (1 - e)y) - e),$$

where e is the neutral element of U (here $e = \frac{1}{2}$), and S_U coincides with S above; see (3.40) and (3.41). We denote their additive generators respectively by t_U and s_U, given by

$$t_\mathsf{U}(x) = -u(ex), \qquad s_\mathsf{U}(x) = u(e + (1 - e)x) \qquad (9.6)$$

(see (3.50) and (3.51)).

Proof. Since u is strictly increasing, Theorem 3.100 applies, hence U is a (generated) uninorm, continuous except at $(0,1)$ and $(1,0)$, and $u(\frac{1}{2}) = 0$. Now, using (9.6) with $e = \frac{1}{2}$, we obtain $t(x) = -s(x - 1)$, so that T_U and S are dual. $\qquad\square$

Now we can state the main result [157]; see also [177].

Theorem 9.10. *Let S be a strict t-conorm with additive generator s and $\oplus$ the corresponding pseudo-addition. Then $(]-1, 1[, \oplus)$ is an Abelian group.*

Proof. Since $\oplus$ is a uninorm with neutral element $\frac{1}{2}$ transposed in $[-1, 1]^2$, commutativity and associativity hold, and the neutral element is 0. Moreover, symmetry holds since for any $x \in {]-1, 1[}$ we have by (9.4) and Proposition 9.8(ii)

$$x \oplus (-x) = 2\mathsf{U}\left(\frac{1}{2}x + \frac{1}{2}, -\frac{1}{2}x + \frac{1}{2}\right) - 1$$

$$= 2u^{-1}(u(z) + u(1 - z)) - 1 = 2u^{-1}(u(z) - u(z)) - 1 = 0$$

with $z := \frac{1}{2}x + \frac{1}{2}$ and using $u(z) = -u(1 - z)$, for all $z \in [0, 1]$. $\qquad\square$

S is a nilpotent t-conorm with additive generator s. For a nilpotent t-conorm with additive generator s, it is easy to see that statement (i) in Proposition 9.8 is still valid. However, the construction does not lead to an associative operator, as is easily seen in the following example. Consider the Łukasiewicz t-conorm $\mathsf{S}_\mathsf{L}(x, y) = (x + y) \wedge 1$ with additive generator $s_\mathsf{L}(x) = x$. Then $x \ominus y = x - y$. Let $x = -0.3$, $y = 0.6$, and $z = 0.6$, then we obtain:

$$x \oplus (y \oplus z) = -0.3 \oplus (0.6 \oplus 0.6) = -0.3 \oplus 1 = 0.7,$$

$$(x \oplus y) \oplus z = (-0.3 \oplus 0.6) \oplus 0.6 = 0.3 \oplus 0.6 = 0.9.$$

S is the maximum operator This case will be treated in Section 9.3.

S is an ordinal sum of continuous Archimedean t-conorms Suppose that $a \in {]0, 1[}$ is an idempotent element of S, that is, $\mathsf{S}(x, y) = x \vee y$ whenever $x \wedge y \leqslant a \leqslant x \vee y$. Consider b, c such that $0 < b < a < c < 1$. We have $(b \oplus c) \ominus_\mathsf{S} c = (b \vee c) \ominus_\mathsf{S} c = c \ominus_\mathsf{S} c = 0$. However, $b \oplus (c \ominus_\mathsf{S} c) = b$. Hence associativity cannot hold everywhere. We conclude that ordinal sums cannot lead to associative functions.

Remark 9.11. Under axioms **A1** to **A5**, the problem of defining $\oplus$ amounts to defining an *ordered Abelian group (OAG)* on $[-1, 1]$; see Fuchs [126] and [178, 179]. In fact no group can exist on $[-1, 1]$. Either extremal elements have to be discarded, or some convention for them has to be defined, which leads to the notion of extended group. A classical result in the theory of OAGs says that a completely ordered, dense (i.e., with no least positive element), extended (i.e., including extremal elements) OAG is necessarily isomorphic to the usual Abelian group of extended real numbers, endowed with the usual ordering. But this means precisely that $\oplus$ has the following form:

$$x \oplus y = \varphi^{-1}\big(\varphi(x) + \varphi(y)\big) \tag{9.7}$$

where $\varphi : [-1, 1] \to \overline{\mathbb{R}}$ is one-to-one, odd, increasing, and satisfies $\varphi(0) = 0$. This is exactly Proposition 9.8(i).

9.2.2 Pseudo-multiplications

From the introductory discussion, our first requirements are, for any $x, y, z \in [-1, 1]$

M0 0 is an annihilator element: $x \otimes 0 = 0 \otimes x = 0$.
M1 Commutativity: $x \otimes y = y \otimes x$.
M2 Associativity: $x \otimes (y \otimes z) = (x \otimes y) \otimes z$.

Let us require for the moment that $\otimes$ is nondecreasing only on $[0, 1]^2$:

M3 Nondecreasing monotonicity on $[0, 1]^2$: $x \otimes y \leqslant x' \otimes y'$, for any $0 \leqslant x \leqslant x' \leqslant 1$, $0 \leqslant y \leqslant y' \leqslant 1$.

If we adopt the following:

M4 Neutral element for positive elements: $x \otimes 1 = 1 \otimes x = x$, for all $x \in [0, 1]$,

then axioms **M1** to **M4** make $\otimes$ a t-norm on $[0, 1]^2$; see Section 3.3. Recall that **M0** on $[0, 1]^2$ is implied by **M3** and **M4**. If pseudo-addition and pseudo-multiplication are used conjointly, a natural requirement is then distributivity.

M5 Distributivity of $\otimes$ with respect to $\oplus$: $x \otimes (y \oplus z) = (x \otimes y) \oplus (x \otimes z)$ and $(x \oplus y) \otimes z = (x \otimes z) \oplus (y \otimes z)$ for all $x, y, z \in [-1, 1]$.

From Proposition 3.117, we deduce immediately that under **A1** to **A4**, and **M1** to **M4**, axiom **M5** can be satisfied on $[0, 1]^2$ if and only if $\oplus = \vee$.

Let us show that under axioms **M1** to **M5**, supposing $\otimes$ to be known on $[0, 1]^2$, the structure of $\otimes$ is completely determined on $[-1, 1]^2$.

Proposition 9.12. *Under axioms* **M1** *to* **M5** *and* **A3**, **A5**, $\otimes$ *obeys the rule of sign of the usual product, i.e., for any $x, y \in [-1, 1]$, $(-x) \otimes y = -(x \otimes y)$.*

Proof. We have $0 = (x \oplus (-x)) \otimes y = (x \otimes y) \oplus ((-x) \otimes y)$, which entails $(-x) \otimes y = -(x \otimes y)$. □

This case corresponds to ordered rings and fields; see Fuchs [126]. Then $\otimes$ is not monotone on $[-1, 1]^2$, and is uniquely determined by its values on $[0, 1]^2$, where it is a t-norm T. In summary:

Proposition 9.13. *Under* **M1** *to* **M5** *and* **A3**, **A5**, $\otimes$ *has the following form:*

$$x \otimes y = \text{sign}(x \cdot y)\mathsf{T}(|x|, |y|),$$

for some t-norm T.

Since distributivity is a strong condition, one may require only restricted distributivity.

If distributivity is not needed, nothing prevents us from imposing monotonicity of $\otimes$ on the whole domain $[-1, 1]^2$:

M3' Nondecreasing monotonicity for $\otimes$: $x \otimes y \leqslant x' \otimes y'$, $-1 \leqslant x \leqslant x' \leqslant 1$, $-1 \leqslant y \leqslant y' \leqslant 1$.

Then, if we impose in addition

M4' Neutral element for negative numbers: $(-1) \otimes x = x$ for all $x \leqslant 0$,

up to a rescaling in $[0, 1]^2$, $\otimes$ is then a nullnorm with $a = 1/2$, since $\otimes$ is associative, commutative, nondecreasing, and -1 is neutral on $[-1, 0]^2$, 1 is neutral on $[0, 1]^2$; see Section 3.7. In summary, we have shown the following.

Proposition 9.14. *Under* **M1**, **M2**, **M3'**, **M4** *and* **M4'**, $\otimes$ *has the following form:*

$$x \otimes y = \begin{cases} \mathsf{T}(x, y) & \text{if } x, y \geqslant 0 \\ \mathsf{S}(x + 1, y + 1) - 1 & \text{if } x, y \leqslant 0 \\ 0 & \text{otherwise} \end{cases}$$

for some t-norm T *and t-conorm* S.

9.3 Minimum and maximum on symmetrized linearly ordered sets

The previous section has shown that except for strict t-conorms, there was no way to build a pseudo-addition fulfilling requirements **A1** to **A5**. Hence extending the maximum on $[-1, 1]^2$ in this way is not possible. However, we will show that this is in fact almost possible. Also, since our construction works on any linearly ordered set, this section addresses the construction of aggregation functions on ordinal bipolar scales. We mainly follow Grabisch [156]; see also Baccelli *et al.* [22, §3.4] for max-plus algebra.

We consider a linearly ordered set $(L^+, \leqslant)$, with bottom and top denoted by $\mathbb{O}$, $\mathbb{1}$ respectively, and we define $L := L^+ \cup L^-$, where L^- is a reversed copy of L^+, i.e., for any $a, b \in L^+$, we have $a \leqslant b$ if and only if $-b \leqslant -a$, where $-a, -b$ are the copies of a, b in L^-. Moreover, we make $\mathbb{O}$ and $-\mathbb{O}$ coincide.

Our aim is to define extensions of minimum and maximum operations on L^2, denoted by $\oslash$, $\varovee$, and called respectively *symmetric minimum* and *symmetric maximum*, following a procedure similar to that for symmetric pseudo-additions and pseudo-multiplications.

9.3.1 The symmetric maximum

Our first requirement is by definition

SM1 $\varovee$ coincide with $\vee$ on $(L^+)^2$.

Then we require usual group properties:

SM2 Commutativity.
SM3 Associativity.
SM4 $\mathbb{O}$ is a neutral element.
SM5 $-x$ is the symmetric image of x, i.e., $x \varovee (-x) = \mathbb{O}$.

These requirements are already contradictory. In fact, **SM1** and **SM5** imply that **SM3** cannot hold. Indeed, let us take $\mathbb{O} < x < y$. Then $((-y) \varovee y) \varovee x = \mathbb{O} \varovee x = x \neq (-y) \varovee (y \varovee x) = (-y) \varovee y = \mathbb{O}$. Since for bipolar operators, symmetry is a basic requirement, we are forced to abandon associativity for $\varovee$. As associativity is needed to infer the rule of signs $(-x) \varovee (-y) = -(x \varovee y)$, we are also forced to consider this property as an axiom. Thus we require

SM6 $-(x \varovee y) = (-x) \varovee (-y), \forall x, y \in L^+$.

The following proposition shows further properties of this exotic algebra. In particular, **SM4** can be deduced from **SM1** and **SM6**.

Proposition 9.15. *(i) Under **SM1** and **SM6**, $\mathbb{O}$ is neutral for $\varovee$.*

*(ii) Under **SM1**, **SM6** and **SM3**, $|x \varovee (-x)| \geqslant |x|$, where $| \cdot |$ is the absolute value, defined in the obvious way. Further, if we require nondecreasing monotonicity of $\varovee$, then $|x \varovee (-x)| = |x|$.*

Proof. (i) If $x > \mathbb{O}$, then $x \varovee \mathbb{O} = x$, and $-(x \varovee \mathbb{O}) = (-x) \varovee \mathbb{O} = -x$.

(ii) If associativity holds, then taking $x > \mathbb{O}$, we have $((-x) \varovee x) \varovee x = (-x) \varovee (x \varovee x)$, which gives $((-x) \varovee x) \varovee x = (-x) \varovee x \neq \mathbb{O}$ since associativity is imposed. If $(-x) \varovee x > \mathbb{O}$, then to satisfy the above equality we must have $(-x) \varovee x \geqslant x$. If it is negative, a similar argument using (**SM6**) shows that $(-x) \varovee x \leqslant -x$. Lastly, if $\varovee$ is nondecreasing, we have $x \varovee (-x) \leqslant x \varovee \mathbb{O} = x$, and similarly for the negative case. $\qquad\square$

From **SM1** and **SM6**, we know that on $(L^+)^2$ and $(L^-)^2$, $\varovee$ coincides respectively with the maximum and the minimum operators. Indeed, taking $x, y \in L^-$, we have

$$x \varovee y = -((-x) \varovee (-y)) = -(|x| \vee |y|) = x \wedge y.$$

It remains to determine $\oslash$ for mixed positive and negative arguments. Due to the lack of associativity, it is not possible to follow the same procedure as for pseudo-additions and to come up with the associated pseudo-difference. Let us take nevertheless the pseudo-difference associated to $\vee$ (see Example 9.3) as the definition for the mixed case. Proposition 9.16 will justify that this choice is the best possible. In summary, we define

$$
x \oslash y := \begin{cases} x \vee y & \text{if } x, y \in L^+ \\ x \wedge y & \text{if } x, y \in L^- \\ x \ominus_{\vee} (-y) & \text{if } x \in L^+, y \in L^-, \end{cases} \tag{9.8}
$$

the remaining case being determined by commutativity. A more convenient form is

$$
x \oslash y = \begin{cases} -(|x| \vee |y|) & \text{if } y \neq -x \text{ and } |x| \vee |y| = -x \text{ or } = -y \\ \mathbb{O} & \text{if } y = -x \\ |x| \vee |y| & \text{otherwise.} \end{cases} \tag{9.9}
$$

Except for the case $y = -x$, $x \oslash y$ equals the absolutely larger one of the two elements x and y; see Figure 9.1. The following result [156] shows that there is no "better" definition of $\oslash$ under the given conditions.

Proposition 9.16. *Under conditions* **SM1**, **SM5** *and* **SM6**, *no operation is associative on a larger domain than* $\oslash$ *as given by* (9.8).

Proof. The only degree of freedom is the definition of $x \oslash y$ when x, y have different signs. We know that the only nonassociative case (see Proposition 9.18(v)) happens

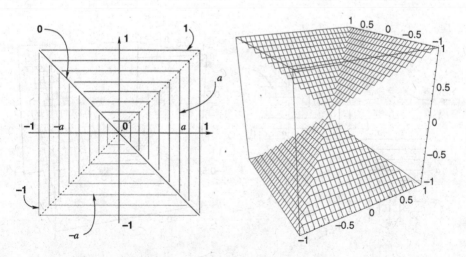

Figure 9.1 Constant level curves (left: reproduced from [153, p. 477], with permission of Elsevier) and output (right) of the symmetric maximum ($L = [-1, 1]$)

in expressions like $-x \oslash (x \oslash y), x, y > \mathbb{O}$. Since $\oslash \equiv \vee$ on $[\mathbb{O}, \mathbb{1}]^2$, we get:

$$-x \oslash (x \oslash y) = -x \oslash (x \vee y) = \begin{cases} -x \oslash x = \mathbb{O} & \text{if } x \geqslant y \\ -x \oslash y & \text{if } x \leqslant y. \end{cases}$$

Observing that $(-x \oslash x) \oslash y = y$, clearly the first case can never lead to associativity. Let us examine the second case. It leads to associativity if and only if $-x \oslash y = y$. Discarding the case $x = y$, we see that we have in fact the definition of the symmetric maximum. Hence only it can lead to associativity in this case, and any other operation would not. □

9.3.2 Symmetric minimum

The case of the symmetric minimum is less problematic. The following requirements determine it uniquely.

Sm1 $\oslash$ coincides with $\wedge$ on $(L^+)^2$.
Sm2 Rule of signs: $-(x \oslash y) = (-x) \oslash y = x \oslash (-y)$, for all $x, y \in L$.

Under **Sm1** and **Sm2**, we get

$$x \oslash y := \begin{cases} -(|x| \wedge |y|) & \text{if sign}(x) \neq \text{sign}(y) \\ |x| \wedge |y| & \text{otherwise.} \end{cases} \tag{9.10}$$

The absolute value of $x \oslash y$ equals $|x| \wedge |y|$ and $x \oslash y < \mathbb{O}$ if and only if the two elements x and y have opposite signs; see Figure 9.2.

Remark 9.17. As for pseudo-multiplications, we could as well impose a different rule of signs, namely $-(x \oslash y) = (-x) \oslash (-y)$, and impose monotonicity on the whole

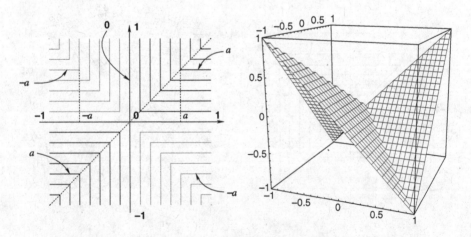

Figure 9.2 Constant level curves (left: reproduced from [153, p. 478], with permission of Elsevier) and output (right) of the symmetric minimum ($L = [-1, 1]$)

domain. This would give, up to a rescaling, a nullnorm, namely $\mathrm{Med}_{0.5}(x,y) := \mathrm{Med}(x,y,0.5)$.

Algebraic properties of the symmetric minimum and maximum are given next.

Proposition 9.18. *The structure* $(L, \varovee, \varowedge)$ *has the following properties.*

   (i) $\varovee$ *is commutative (SM2).*
   (ii) $\mathbb{O}$ *is the neutral element of* $\varovee$ *(SM4), and the annihilator element of* $\varowedge$.
   (iii) $x \varovee (-x) = \mathbb{O}$, *for all* $x \in L$ *(SM5).*
   (iv) $-(x \varovee y) = (-x) \varovee (-y)$, *for all* $x,y \in L$.
   (v) $\varovee$ *is associative for any expression involving* $x_1, \ldots, x_n$, $x_i \in L$, *such that* $\bigvee_{i=1}^{n} x_i \neq - \bigwedge_{i=1}^{n} x_i$.
   (vi) $\varowedge$ *is commutative.*
   (vii) $\mathbb{1}$ *is the neutral element of* $\varowedge$, *and the annihilator element of* $\varovee$ *on* $] - \mathbb{1}, \mathbb{1}]$, *while* $-\mathbb{1}$ *is the annihilator element of* $\varovee$ *on* $[-\mathbb{1}, \mathbb{1}[$.
   (viii) $\varowedge$ *is associative on* L^2.
   (ix) $\varowedge$ *is distributive with respect to* $\varovee$ *in* $(L^+)^2$ *and* $(L^-)^2$ *separately.*
   (x) $\varovee$ *is nondecreasing on* L^2, *i.e.,* $x \leqslant x', y \leqslant y'$ *implies* $x \varovee y \leqslant x' \varovee y'$.

Proof. All results are almost clear from the construction. We just detail (v) and (ix).

(v) Let us study what happens if the equality $(x \varovee y) \varovee z = x \varovee (y \varovee z)$ holds supposing there is no pair of symmetric elements, such as $(x, -x)$. This implies $|x \varovee y| = |x| \vee |y|$; see (9.9). Hence

$$|(x \varovee y) \varovee z| = |x \varovee y| \vee |z| = |x| \vee |y| \vee |z| = |x| \vee |y \varovee z| = |x \varovee (y \varovee z)|.$$

Thus, $(x \varovee y) \varovee z$ and $x \varovee (y \varovee z)$ have the same absolute value. It remains to prove that they have the same sign. The sign of $x \varovee y$ is the sign of the largest term in absolute value. Hence, the sign of $(x \varovee y) \varovee z$ is the sign of the largest in absolute value among $x \varovee y$ and z, so it is the sign of the largest in absolute value among x, y, z. Doing the same with $x \varovee (y \varovee z)$, we conclude that the two expressions have the same sign.

Suppose now $x = -y$. Then $(x \varovee y) \varovee z = z$. Clearly, $x \varovee (y \varovee z) = z$ if $|z| > |x|$. This coincides with the condition given in (v).

(ix) Distributivity is clearly satisfied on $(L^+)^2$. For any $x, y, z \in L^-$:

$$(x \varovee y) \varowedge z = (x \wedge y) \varowedge |z| = |x \wedge y| \wedge |z|$$

$$(x \varowedge z) \varovee (y \varowedge z) = (|x| \wedge |z|) \vee (|y| \wedge |z|)$$

$$= (|x| \vee |y|) \wedge |z|$$

$$= |x \wedge y| \wedge |z|. \qquad \square$$

9.3.3 *Nonassociative calculus*

The problem of nonassociativity may be a severe limitation if $\oslash$ is used as a grouping operation to perform computation, like $\oslash_{i=1}^{n} x_i$. To overcome this difficulty, we propose several *computation rules* [156], which amount to eliminating situations where nonassociativity occurs, as given in Proposition 9.18.

Let us consider a sequence $(x_i)_{i \in I}$ of terms $x_i \in L$, with $I \subseteq \mathbb{N}$. We say that the sequence *fulfills associativity* if either $|I| \leqslant 2$ or $\vee_{i \in I} x_i \neq - \wedge_{i \in I} x_i$. Hence, from Proposition 9.18(v), $\oslash_{i \in I} x_i$ is well defined if and only if the sequence $(x_i)_{i \in I}$ fulfills associativity. If a sequence does not fulfill associativity, it necessarily has at least three terms and contains a pair of maximal opposite terms $(a, -a)$, with $a := \vee_{i \in I} x_i$. Discarding all occurrences of $a, -a$ in the sequence, we may still find (new) maximal opposite terms $b, -b$, which can be discarded, etc., until no more such terms remain, which means that the new sequence fulfills associativity. We call the sequence of all deleted terms the *sequence of maximal opposite terms*, whose index set is denoted $I_=$. Taking for example with $L = \mathbb{Z}$ the sequence $3, 3, 3, 2, 1, 0, -2, -3, -3$, the sequence of maximal opposite terms is $3, 3, 3, 2, -2, -3, -3$.

Another way to fulfill associativity is obtained by discarding in the sequence the pair $(a, -a)$, with $a := \vee_{i \in I} x_i$, and if the new sequence $(x_i)_{i \in I} \setminus (a, -a)$ does not fulfill associativity, then discard the pair of maximal opposite terms in this new sequence, etc., until associativity is fulfilled. We call the sequence of all deleted terms the *restricted sequence of maximal opposite terms*, and we denote its index set by I_0. In the previous example, the restricted sequence of maximal opposite terms is $3, -3, 3, -3$. Note that we always have $I_0 \subseteq I_=$, and that I_0 is minimal in the sense that no proper subset of it can ensure associativity.

We denote the set of all (at most countable) sequences, including the empty one, by $\mathfrak{L} := \bigcup_{i=1}^{\infty} L^i \cup \{\varnothing\}$. From now on, we make the convention $\oslash_\varnothing x_i = \mathbb{O}$.

Definition 9.19. A *computation rule* is a systematic way to delete terms in a sequence $(x_i)_{i \in I}$, so that it satisfies associativity, provided the way they are deleted can be obtained as the result of a suitable arrangement of parentheses in $\oslash_{i \in I} x_i$.

For example, deleting 3 in the sequence $3, 1, -3$ makes the sequence associative, but does not correspond to some arrangement of parentheses, and so is not a computation rule. Formally, we denote a computation rule by the infix notation:

$$\langle \cdot \rangle : \quad \begin{array}{ccc} \mathfrak{L} & \longrightarrow & \mathfrak{L} \\ (x_i)_{i \in I} & \mapsto & \langle (x_i)_{i \in I} \rangle := (x_i)_{i \in I \setminus J} \end{array}$$

where $J \subseteq I$ is the index set of deleted terms. To avoid cumbersome notation, we denote $\oslash_{i \in I \setminus J} \langle (x_i)_{i \in I} \rangle$ by $\langle \oslash_{i \in I} x_i \rangle$.

Let us give some basic examples of computation rule.

(i) The *weak rule* $\langle \cdot \rangle_=$, where the index set of deleted terms is $J = I_=$. It obviously corresponds to a particular arrangement of parentheses, as shown in the following example:

$$\langle 3 \oslash 3 \oslash 3 \oslash 2 \oslash 1 \oslash 0 \oslash -2 \oslash -3 \oslash -3 \rangle_= =$$
$$((3 \oslash 3 \oslash 3) \oslash (-3 \oslash -3)) \oslash (2 \oslash -2) \oslash (1 \oslash 0) = 1. \quad (9.11)$$

(ii) The *strong rule* $\langle \cdot \rangle_0$, whose index set of deleted terms is I_0. It obviously corresponds to a particular arrangement of parentheses. Our example gives

$$\langle 3 \oslash 3 \oslash 3 \oslash 2 \oslash 1 \oslash 0 \oslash -2 \oslash -3 \oslash -3 \rangle_0 =$$
$$(3 \oslash -3) \oslash (3 \oslash -3) \oslash (3 \oslash 2 \oslash 1 \oslash 0 \oslash -2) = 3. \quad (9.12)$$

(iii) The *splitting rule* $\langle \cdot \rangle_-^+$, whose index set of deleted terms is $J = \varnothing$ if the sequence fulfills associativity, and $J = I$ if not. Then in the latter case, $\langle \oslash_{i \in I} x_i \rangle_-^+ = \mathbb{O}$, due to our convention $\oslash_{\varnothing} x_i = 0$. The corresponding arrangement of parentheses is

$$\langle \oslash_{i \in I} x_i \rangle_-^+ := \left(\oslash_{x_i \geq 0} x_i \right) \oslash \left(\oslash_{x_i < 0} x_i \right),$$

hence the name of the rule (splitting positive and negative terms).

Remark 9.20. (i) These rules have a clear meaning in decision making. Assume that $(x_i)_{i \in I}$ is a sequence of scores assigned to some alternative. The quantity $\oslash_{i \in I} x_i$ is the overall score of the alternative. If the splitting rule is used, the overall score is $\mathbb{O}$ whenever best and worse scores are opposite. This way of computing the overall score is not very discriminating since many alternatives get $\mathbb{O}$ as overall score, even if the scores assigned to them are very different. The two other rules are more discriminating since they discard maximal opposite scores: if best and worst scores are opposite, then look at second best and second worst scores, etc.

(ii) The strong rule coincides with the limit of some family of uninorms proposed by Mesiar and Komorníková [307].

We give several simple properties of these computation rules.

Lemma 9.21. *(i) All computation rules satisfy the following boundary property for any sequence $x_1, \ldots, x_n$:*

$$\bigwedge_{i=1}^n x_i \leq \langle \oslash_{i=1}^n x_i \rangle \leq \bigvee_{i=1}^n x_i.$$

(ii) The rules $\langle \cdot \rangle_-^+$ and $\langle \cdot \rangle_0$ are isotone, i.e., they satisfy

$$x_i \leqslant x_i', \quad i = 1, \ldots, n \text{ implies } \langle \overset{n}{\underset{i=1}{\oslash}} x_i \rangle \leqslant \langle \overset{n}{\underset{i=1}{\oslash}} x_i' \rangle.$$

Proof. (i) Clear from definition.

(ii) It suffices to show the result for one argument, say x_j. Let us consider the rule $\langle \cdot \rangle_-^+$. If $x_j \geqslant \mathbb{O}$, then by Proposition 9.18(x), $\oslash_{x_i \geqslant \mathbb{O}} x_i$ does not decrease when x_j is replaced by x_j', so that $\oslash_{i \in I} x_i$ does not decrease too (similarly if $x_j < \mathbb{O}$).

We turn to the rule $\langle \cdot \rangle_0$. We consider the sequence $(x_i)_{i \in I}$, and the index set of deleted terms J. If $j \in I \setminus J$, then the expression $\oslash_{i \in I \setminus J} x_i$ is isotone provided associativity still holds when x_j is replaced by x_j'; see Proposition 9.18(x). Since $x_j' \geqslant x_j$, the only case where associativity is lost is when $\oslash_{i \in I \setminus J} x_i = x_k$ with $x_k < \mathbb{O}$, and $x_j' = -x_k$. In this case x_k, x_j' are deleted, and the result is the second largest in absolute value, which is greater than or equal to x_k, hence the rule is still isotone.

Let us consider the case when $j \in J$, and suppose that $\oslash_{i \in I \setminus J} x_i = x_k$. If $x_j > \mathbb{O}$, then for $x_j' > x_j$, the pair $(x_j', -x_j)$ is no longer deleted, and the result of computation is x_j'. Since $x_j' > x_j \geqslant x_k$, the rule is isotone. Now, if $x_j < \mathbb{O}$, for $x_j' > x_j$, the pair $(x_j', -x_j)$ is no longer deleted, and the result becomes $-x_j$. Since $-x_j \geqslant x_k$, isotonicity holds in this case too. □

Computation rule $\langle \cdot \rangle_=$ is not isotone, as shown by the following example: take the sequence $-3, 3, 1$ in $\mathbb{Z}$. Applying the weak rule leads to 1. Now, if 1 is raised to 3, the result becomes 0.

The sequence $x_1, \ldots, x_n$ in L is said to be a *cancelling sequence for the rule* $\langle \cdot \rangle$ if $\langle \oslash_{i=1}^n x_i \rangle = \mathbb{O}$. We denote by $\mathcal{O}_{\langle \cdot \rangle}$ the set of cancelling sequences of $\langle \cdot \rangle$.

We say that computation rule $\langle \cdot \rangle_1$ is more *discriminating* than rule $\langle \cdot \rangle_2$ if $\mathcal{O}_{\langle \cdot \rangle_1} \subset \mathcal{O}_{\langle \cdot \rangle_2}$.

Lemma 9.22.

$$\mathcal{O}_{\langle \cdot \rangle_0} \subseteq \mathcal{O}_{\langle \cdot \rangle_=} \subseteq \mathcal{O}_{\langle \cdot \rangle_-^+}.$$

(See [156] for a proof.)

9.4 Separable aggregation functions

We consider here not necessarily associative functions A, in the spirit of means. We assume in this section that $\mathbb{I} = [-1, 1]$ and that all aggregation functions have n arguments, unless otherwise specified.

A simple way to build bipolar aggregation functions is the following. Let A^+, A^- be given aggregation functions on $[0, 1]^n$. A^+ defines the aggregation for positive values, while A^- defines the aggregation of negative values:

$$A(\mathbf{x}) = A^+(\mathbf{x}) \text{ if } \mathbf{x} \geqslant 0, \quad A(\mathbf{x}) = -A^-(-\mathbf{x}) \text{ if } \mathbf{x} \leqslant 0.$$

For any $\mathbf{x} \in [-1,1]^n$, we recall that $\mathbf{x}^+ := \mathbf{x} \vee \mathbf{0}$ and $\mathbf{x}^- := (-\mathbf{x})^+$. Note that $\mathbf{x} = \mathbf{x}^+ - \mathbf{x}^-$, which suggests the following construction:

$$A(\mathbf{x}) := \psi(A^+(\mathbf{x}^+), A^-(\mathbf{x}^-)), \quad \forall \mathbf{x} \in [-1,1]^n, \tag{9.13}$$

where ψ is a pseudo-difference (Definition 9.1).

A bipolar aggregation function defined by (9.13) is called *separable*.

We give as illustration three cases of interest.

$A^+ = A^-$ is a strict t-conorm S If $A^+ = A^-$ is a strict t-conorm S with generator s, and $\ominus_S$ is taken as pseudo-difference, we recover the construction of Section 9.2. Indeed, taking $n = 2$ (which is sufficient by associativity), and g being the generator of $\ominus_S$:

$$\begin{aligned}
A(x,y) &= S(x^+, y^+) \ominus_S S(x^-, y^-) \\
&= g^{-1}(g(S(x^+, y^+)) - g(S(x^-, y^-))) \\
&= g^{-1}(g(x^+) + g(y^+) - g(x^-) - g(y^-)) \\
&= g^{-1}(g(x) + g(y))
\end{aligned}$$

which is Proposition 9.8(i), and indeed g is odd, strictly increasing, and $g(0) = 0$. Note that for computing $A(1, -1)$, the convention $\infty - \infty$ has to be fixed.

$A^+ = A^-$ is a continuous t-conorm S We know by Section 9.2 that associativity is lost if S is not strict. Restricting to the binary case, it is always possible to apply the definition of $\oplus$ given by (9.3), taking the associated pseudo-difference operator $\ominus_S$. For example, considering $S = S_L$, we easily obtain $A(x,y) = ((x+y) \wedge 1) \vee (-1)$.

If an additive generator s exists, the extension to n-ary functions is immediate. Using Proposition 9.4, we get for any $\mathbf{x} \in [-1,1]^n$

$$A(\mathbf{x}) = g^{-1}\left(\left(g(1) \wedge \sum_{i=1}^{n} g(x_i^+)\right) - \left(g(-1) \vee \sum_{i=1}^{n} g(-x_i^-)\right) \right)$$

with $g(x) := s(x)$ for $x \geqslant 0$, and $g(x) := -s(-x)$ for $x \leqslant 0$.

A^+, A^- are integral-based aggregation functions An interesting case is when A^+, A^- are integral-based aggregation functions, such as the Choquet or Sugeno integrals (Definitions 5.19 and 5.59). Applying (9.13) with suitable pseudo-differences, we recover various definitions of integrals for real-valued functions. Specifically, let us take A^+, A^- to be Choquet integrals with respect to capacities μ^+, μ^-, and ψ is the usual difference $\ominus_L$. Then:

- Taking $\mu^+ = \mu^-$ we obtain the *symmetric Choquet integral* or Šipoš integral (Definition 5.23):

$$\check{C}_\mu(\mathbf{x}) := C_\mu(\mathbf{x}^+) - C_\mu(\mathbf{x}^-).$$

- Taking $\mu^- = \overline{\mu^+}$ we obtain the *asymmetric Choquet integral* (Definition 5.23):

$$C_\mu(\mathbf{x}) := C_\mu(\mathbf{x}^+) - C_{\overline{\mu}}(\mathbf{x}^-).$$

- For the general case, we obtain what is called in decision-making theory the *Cumulative Prospect Theory (CPT)* model [413]:

$$\mathrm{CPT}_{\mu^+,\mu^-}(\mathbf{x}) := C_{\mu^+}(\mathbf{x}^+) - C_{\mu^-}(\mathbf{x}^-).$$

We consider now that $\mathsf{A}^+, \mathsf{\check{A}}^-$ are Sugeno integrals, with respect to capacities μ^+, μ^-, and ψ is the pseudo-difference associated to the maximum, i.e., $\psi(x,y) := x \oslash (-y)$. Then as above,

- Taking $\mu^+ = \mu^-$ we obtain the *symmetric Sugeno integral* (Definition 5.69):

$$\check{S}_\mu(\mathbf{x}) := S_\mu(\mathbf{x}^+) \oslash (-S_\mu(\mathbf{x}^-)).$$

- For the general case, we obtain what corresponds to the CPT model in an ordinal version:

$$\mathrm{OCPT}_{\mu^+,\mu^-}(\mathbf{x}) := S_{\mu^+}(\mathbf{x}^+) \oslash (-S_{\mu^-}(\mathbf{x}^-)). \tag{9.14}$$

Remark 9.23. Taking the greatest normalized capacity $\mu_{\max}$ and $n = 2$, we have that $\check{S}_{\mu_{\max}}$ is the symmetric maximum. This suggests another way to define the symmetric maximum, by taking the symmetric Choquet integral instead. Denoting by $\overset{C}{\oslash}$ this "modified" symmetric maximum, we have $x \overset{C}{\oslash} y = \mathsf{Max}(x,y)$ if $x,y \geqslant 0$, $x \overset{C}{\oslash} y = \mathsf{Min}(x,y)$ if $x,y \leqslant 0$, and $x \overset{C}{\oslash} y = x + y$ otherwise. Note that it satisfies **SM1**, **SM5** and **SM6**, hence due to Proposition 9.16, it is less associative than $\oslash$. Indeed, $((-0.5) \overset{C}{\oslash} 0.5) \overset{C}{\oslash} 0.7 = 0.7$, and $(-0.5) \overset{C}{\oslash} (0.5 \overset{C}{\oslash} 0.7) = 0.2$; however $((-0.5) \oslash 0.5) \oslash 0.7 = 0.7 = (-0.5) \oslash (0.5 \oslash 0.7)$.

9.5 Integral-based aggregation functions

Let us study the case of integral-based aggregation functions (see Chapter 5), and we will limit ourselves to the Choquet and Sugeno integrals, which are the most representative.

9.5.1 Bicapacities

As explained in Section 5.4.2, the Choquet integral can be defined as a parsimonious linear interpolation between vertices of $[0, 1]^n$. Extending the domain to $[-1, 1]^n$, let us try to take a similar approach.

The basic ingredient of the interpolative view is that $\mathcal{C}_\mu(\mathbf{1}_A) = \mathcal{S}_\mu(\mathbf{1}_A) = \mu(A)$. Let us call *binary vectors* those of the form $\mathbf{1}_A \mathbf{0}$ (equivalently $\mathbf{1}_A$). In the unipolar case, coordinates of binary vectors are the boundaries of the interval $[0, 1]$. In the bipolar case, apart from boundaries, we should also consider 0, as this value plays a particular role. We thus consider *ternary vectors* $\mathbf{1}_A(-\mathbf{1})_B\mathbf{0}$, whose components are either 1, 0 or -1. Obviously, $A \cap B = \varnothing$, so that the set of ternary vectors is obtained when the pair (A, B) belongs to $\mathcal{Q}([n]) := \{(A, B) \mid A, B \subseteq [n], A \cap B = \varnothing\}$. The basic idea is to produce an aggregation function A which coincides with a set of fixed quantities $w(A, B)$, for $(A, B) \in \mathcal{Q}([n])$. The first argument A refers to the positive part $(+1)$, while the second argument refers to the negative part (-1).

Since we need nondecreasing monotonicity for an aggregation function, it should hold in particular for ternary vectors. Noting that $(\mathbf{1}_A(-\mathbf{1})_B\mathbf{0}) \leqslant (\mathbf{1}_{A'}(-\mathbf{1})_{B'}\mathbf{0})$ if and only if $A \subseteq A'$ and $B \supseteq B'$, we are led to the following definition.

Definition 9.24. A *bicapacity* w on $[n]$ is a function $w : \mathcal{Q}([n]) \to \mathbb{R}$ satisfying $w(\varnothing, \varnothing) = 0$, and $w(A, B) \leqslant w(C, D)$ whenever $A \subseteq C$ and $B \supseteq D$ (monotonicity).

A bicapacity is *normalized* if $w([n], \varnothing) = 1$, $w(\varnothing, [n]) = -1$. Dropping monotonicity from the definition of bicapacities leads to the so-called *bicooperative games*. We denote by $\mathcal{F}_2(n)$ and $\mathcal{F}_2^*(n)$ the set of bicapacities and normalized bicapacities respectively.

Definition 9.25. Let w be a bicapacity on $[n]$. We say that w is

(i) *Additive* if for every $(A, B), (C, D) \in \mathcal{Q}([n])$ such that $(A \cup C, B \cup D) \in \mathcal{Q}([n])$, $A \cap C = B \cap D = \varnothing$, we have

$$w(A \cup C, B \cup D) = w(A, \varnothing) + w(C, \varnothing) + w(\varnothing, B) + w(\varnothing, D).$$

(ii) *Symmetric* if for any $(A, B), (C, D) \in \mathcal{Q}([n])$, $|A| = |C|$ and $|B| = |D|$ imply $w(A, B) = w(C, D)$.

A useful example of bicapacity is given next.

Definition 9.26. A bicapacity w on $[n]$ is of the *CPT type* if there exist two capacities v_+, v_- on $[n]$ such that, for all $(A, B) \in \mathcal{Q}([n])$,

$$w(A, B) = v_+(A) - v_-(B).$$

Remark 9.27. (i) An equivalent definition of additivity is $w(A \cup C, B \cup D) = w(A, B) + w(C, D)$ (with the notation of Definition 9.25(i)). Indeed, since $A \cap \varnothing = \varnothing \cap B = \varnothing$, the above equality implies

$$w(A, B) = w(A \cup \varnothing, \varnothing \cup B) = w(A, \varnothing) + w(\varnothing, B).$$

Considering A, B, C, D as in Definition 9.25(i), we get

$$w(A \cup C, B \cup D) = w(A, B) + w(C, D)$$
$$= w(A, \varnothing) + w(\varnothing, B) + w(C, \varnothing) + w(\varnothing, D).$$

(ii) Bicooperative games have been proposed by Bilbao [43] in the spirit of cooperative game theory defined on combinatorial structures, while bicapacities have been proposed independently by Grabisch and Labreuche [161] in a context of multicriteria decision making. In this domain, another generalization of capacities for bipolar scales has been proposed independently by Greco *et al.* [175].

(iii) An additive bicapacity is a CPT-type bicapacity where $v^+(\cdot) := w(\cdot, \varnothing)$ and $v^-(\cdot) := -w(\varnothing, \cdot)$ are additive capacities.

(iv) CPT stands for "Cumulative Prospect Theory"; see Section 9.4. The reason for this name proposed in [161] is that w treats independently the "positive" argument A and the "negative" argument B, and will be fully justified in Proposition 9.36.

We address now the definition of the Möbius transform.

Definition 9.28. Let w be a bicapacity on $[n]$. Its *Möbius transform* b is the unique solution of the equation

$$w(A_1, A_2) = \sum_{(B_1, B_2) \in \mathcal{Q}([n]) | B_1 \subseteq A_1, B_2 \subseteq A_2} b(B_1, B_2)$$

for all $(A_1, A_2) \in \mathcal{Q}([n])$, and is given by

$$b(A_1, A_2) = \sum_{\substack{B_1 \subseteq A_1 \\ B_2 \subseteq A_2}} (-1)^{|A_1 \setminus B_1| + |A_2 \setminus B_2|} w(B_1, B_2)$$

for all $(A_1, A_2) \in \mathcal{Q}([n])$.

Accordingly, *biunanimity games* are defined by

$$u_{(A_1, A_2)}(B_1, B_2) := \begin{cases} 1 & \text{if } B_1 \supseteq A_1, B_2 \supseteq A_2 \\ 0 & \text{otherwise,} \end{cases}$$

for all $(A_1, A_2) \in \mathcal{Q}([n])$, and form a basis of bicooperative games.

Remark 9.29. (i) Looking at the general definition of the Möbius transform (see (5.2)), one can note that the above definition supposes that the underlying order relation on $\mathcal{Q}([n])$ is the product order on $2^{[n]} \times 2^{[n]}$:

$$(A_1, A_2) \leqslant (B_1, B_2) \Leftrightarrow [A_1 \subseteq B_1 \text{ and } A_2 \subseteq B_2].$$

However, with this definition, bicapacities are no longer monotone functions from $\mathcal{Q}([n])$ to $\mathbb{R}$. To preserve this, the following order should be taken:

$$(A_1, A_2) \sqsubseteq (B_1, B_2) \Leftrightarrow [A_1 \subseteq B_1 \text{ and } A_2 \supseteq B_2].$$

This order was proposed by Grabisch and Labreuche [161, 163], leading to a different definition of the Möbius transform. It turns out that the Möbius transform b, proposed by Fujimoto [127] and called by him *bipolar Möbius transform*, is more appropriate, especially for expressing the Choquet integral. The reason is that the point $(\varnothing, \varnothing)$, which is the bottom of $(\mathcal{Q}([n]), \leqslant)$, is a kind of center of symmetry in the Choquet integral with respect to a bicapacity (see below), while in $(\mathcal{Q}([n]), \sqsubseteq)$ this point does not play any special role. A careful study of this topic, together with a general definition of bipolar structures and their associated Choquet integral, has been done by Grabisch and Labreuche [165].

(ii) As for capacities, other transformations can be defined as well, like the interaction transform. However, we will not address this topic here.

9.5.2 The Choquet integral for bicapacities

Let us turn to the definition of the Choquet integral for bicapacities. Applying an interpolative approach between ternary vectors, we are led to the following. First we examine in detail the case $n = 2$ (Figure 9.3). Let us take any point $\mathbf{x}$ such that

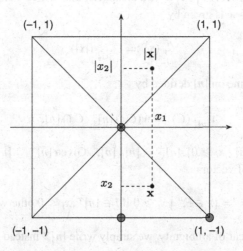

Figure 9.3 Interpolation for the case of bicapacities

$x_1 \geqslant 0$, $x_2 \leqslant 0$ and $|x_1| \leqslant |x_2|$. Then, for $|\mathbf{x}|$ which is in the first (positive) quadrant, we already know that the best linear interpolation is the Choquet integral. It suffices to use the formula with the appropriate vertices:

$$A(x_1, x_2) := |x_1|A(1, -1) + (|x_2| - |x_1|)A(0, -1).$$

This is the Choquet integral with respect to a game v_1 defined by:

$$v_1(\{1, 2\}) = A(1, -1),$$
$$v_1(\{2\}) = A(0, -1).$$

Let us consider now the general case. Defining $[n]_\mathbf{x}^+ := \{i \in [n] \mid x_i \geqslant 0\}$, $[n]_\mathbf{x}^- = [n] \setminus [n]_\mathbf{x}^+$, with similar considerations of symmetry, we obtain:

$$A(\mathbf{x}) = |x_{\sigma(1)}|A(1_{[n]_\mathbf{x}^+}(-1)_{[n]_\mathbf{x}^-}0)$$

$$+ \sum_{i=2}^{n}(|x_{\sigma(i)}| - |x_{\sigma(i-1)}|)A(1_{\{\sigma(i),\dots,\sigma(n)\}\cap[n]_\mathbf{x}^+}(-1)_{\{\sigma(i),\dots,\sigma(n)\}\cap[n]_\mathbf{x}^-}0)$$

where σ is a permutation on $[n]$ such that $|x_{\sigma(1)}| \leqslant \cdots \leqslant |x_{\sigma(n)}|$. This expression is the Choquet integral of $|\mathbf{x}|$ with respect to a game $v_{[n]_\mathbf{x}^+}$ defined by:

$$v_{[n]_\mathbf{x}^+}(A) := A(1_{A\cap[n]_\mathbf{x}^+}(-1)_{A\cap[n]_\mathbf{x}^-}0).$$

Recalling that $A(1_A(-1)_B0) =: w(A, B)$, we finally come up with the following definition.

Definition 9.30. [161, 164] Let w be a bicapacity and $\mathbf{x} \in \mathbb{R}^n$. The *Choquet integral* of $\mathbf{x}$ with respect to w is given by

$$\mathcal{C}_w(\mathbf{x}) := \mathcal{C}_{v_{[n]_\mathbf{x}^+}}(|\mathbf{x}|)$$

where $v_{[n]_\mathbf{x}^+}$ is a game on $[n]$ defined by

$$v_{[n]_\mathbf{x}^+}(C) := w(C \cap [n]_\mathbf{x}^+, C \cap [n]_\mathbf{x}^-),$$

and $[n]_\mathbf{x}^+ := \{i \in [n] \mid x_i \geqslant 0\}$, $[n]_\mathbf{x}^- = [n] \setminus [n]_\mathbf{x}^+$. Given $[n]^+ \subseteq [n]$, the cone induced by $[n]^+$ is the set of vectors

$$\Sigma_{[n]^+} := \{\mathbf{x} \in \mathbb{R}^n \mid x_i \geqslant 0 \text{ if } i \in [n]^+, x_i \leqslant 0 \text{ otherwise}\}.$$

When there is no fear of ambiguity, we simply write $[n]^+$ instead of $[n]_\mathbf{x}^+$.

For the sake of clarity, let us give a numerical example.

Example 9.31. We consider $n = 3$, and $\mathbf{x} := (-1, 3, 2)$. Then $[n]^+ = \{2, 3\}$, $[n]^- = \{1\}$, so that $v_{[n]^+}(C) = w(C \cap \{2, 3\}, C \cap \{1\})$. We obtain:

$$
\begin{aligned}
\mathcal{C}_w(\mathbf{x}) &= \mathcal{C}_{v_{[n]^+}}(|\mathbf{x}|) \\
&= |x_1|v_{[n]^+}([n]) + (|x_3| - |x_1|)v_{[n]^+}(\{2, 3\}) + (|x_2| - |x_3|)v_{[n]^+}(\{2\}) \\
&= w(\{2, 3\}, \{1\}) + w(\{2, 3\}, \varnothing) + w(\{2\}, \varnothing).
\end{aligned}
$$

Remark 9.32. (i) Using Definition 5.19, an explicit expression of $\mathcal{C}_w(\mathbf{x})$ is:

$$
\mathcal{C}_w(\mathbf{x}) = \sum_{i=1}^{n}(|x_{\sigma(i)}| - |x_{\sigma(i-1)}|)w(A_{\sigma(i)} \cap [n]^+, A_{\sigma(i)} \cap [n]^-) \tag{9.15}
$$

$$
= \sum_{i=1}^{n}|x_{\sigma(i)}|\Big(w(A_{\sigma(i)} \cap [n]^+, A_{\sigma(i)} \cap [n]^-) - w(A_{\sigma(i+1)} \cap [n]^+,
$$

$$
A_{\sigma(i+1)} \cap [n]^-\Big) \tag{9.16}
$$

where $A_{\sigma(i)} := \{\sigma(i), \dots, \sigma(n)\}$, $A_{\sigma(n+1)} = \varnothing$, and σ is a permutation on $[n]$ so that $|x_{\sigma(1)}| \leqslant \cdots \leqslant |x_{\sigma(n)}|$, $x_{\sigma(0)} := 0$.

(ii) The definition of $[n]^+$ can be turned into $[n]^+ := \{i \in [n] \mid x_i > 0\}$ without any change in the definition of the Choquet integral. Indeed, if $x_i = 0$, we can put $\sigma(1) = i$, so that $A_{\sigma(j)}$ contains i if and only if $j = 1$, hence either the term is null $(j = 1)$ or it does not depend on i; see (9.15). Consequently, whether i is put in $[n]^+$ or $[n]^-$ is unimportant. A similar reasoning holds if there are several such i.

Consequently, each formula $\mathcal{C}_{v_{[n]^+}}$ can be extended to the whole cone $\Sigma_{[n]^+}$, and they coincide at the intersection of these cones. This proves the continuity of $\mathcal{C}_w$.

Let us give the expression of the Choquet integral with respect to the Möbius transform.

Proposition 9.33. *Let w be a bicapacity, b its Möbius transform, and $\mathbf{x} \in \mathbb{R}^n$. Then*

$$
\mathcal{C}_w(\mathbf{x}) = \sum_{(A_1, A_2) \in \mathcal{Q}([n])} b(A_1, A_2)\Big(\bigwedge_{i \in A_1} x_i^+ \wedge \bigwedge_{j \in A_2} x_j^-\Big).
$$

Proof. Recall that for any 0–1 capacity μ on $2^{[n]}$ we have (see Proposition 5.36(v)):

$$
\mathcal{C}_\mu(\mathbf{x}) = \bigvee_{A \mid \mu(A)=1} \bigwedge_{i \in A} x_i, \quad \forall \mathbf{x} \in \mathbb{R}^n.
$$

Observe that for any biunanimity game $u_{(A,B)}$, $\mathcal{C}_{u_{(A,B)}}(\mathbf{x}) = \mathcal{C}_\mu(|\mathbf{x}|)$, where μ is a 0–1 capacity defined by $\mu(C) := u_{(A,B)}(C \cap [n]_\mathbf{x}^+, C \cap [n]_\mathbf{x}^-)$, using previous notations. By definition of biunanimity games, we have that $\mu(C) = 1$ if and only if $C \cap [n]_{\mathbf{x}}^+ \supseteq A$ and $C \cap [n]_{\mathbf{x}}^- \supseteq B$. This yields:

$$\mathcal{C}_\mu(|\mathbf{x}|) = \bigvee_{\substack{C \supseteq A \cup B \\ A \subseteq [n]_{\mathbf{x}}^+ \\ B \subseteq [n]_{\mathbf{x}}^-}} \bigwedge_{i \in C} |x_i|$$

$$= \bigwedge_{i \in A} x_i^+ \wedge \bigwedge_{i \in B} x_i^- .$$

Using linearity of the Choquet integral with respect to capacities (see Proposition 5.36(ii)) and the decomposition of any w in the basis of biunanimity games, we get the desired result.   □

We give several basic properties, similar to those of Propositions 5.36, 5.38, and 5.41. The following definition is needed.

Definition 9.34. Two vectors $\mathbf{x}, \mathbf{y} \in \mathbb{R}^n$ are said to be *cosigned* if for all $i \in [n]$, $x_i y_i \geqslant 0$.

Proposition 9.35. *The Choquet integral satisfies the following properties:*

 (i) *For any $(A, B) \in \mathcal{Q}([n])$ and any bicooperative game w on $[n]$, we have*
     $$\mathcal{C}_w(1_A(-1)_B 0) = w(A, B).$$
 (ii) *The Choquet integral is linear with respect to bicooperative games, that is, for any bicooperative games w_1, w_2 on $[n]$, and any $\lambda_1, \lambda_2 \in \mathbb{R}$,*

$$\mathcal{C}_{\lambda_1 w_1 + \lambda_2 w_2} = \lambda_1 \mathcal{C}_{w_1} + \lambda_2 \mathcal{C}_{w_2}.$$

 (iii) *Let w, w' be two bicooperative games on $[n]$. Then $w \leqslant w'$ if and only if $\mathcal{C}_w \leqslant \mathcal{C}_{w'}$.*
 (iv) *Let $\mathbf{x}, \mathbf{y} \in \mathbb{R}^n$. If $\mathbf{x}, \mathbf{y}$ are cosigned and $|\mathbf{x}|, |\mathbf{y}|$ are comonotonic, then for any bicapacity w*
     $$\mathcal{C}_w(\mathbf{x} + \mathbf{y}) = \mathcal{C}_w(\mathbf{x}) + \mathcal{C}_w(\mathbf{y}).$$

Proof. (i), (ii), (iii) are clear.
    (iv) [164] Let us suppose for the moment that $x_i, y_i \neq 0$, for all $i \in [n]$. Let us denote $[n]_{\mathbf{x}}^+ := \{i \in [n] \mid x_i \geqslant 0\}$. Due to our assumptions, we have $[n]_{\mathbf{x}+\mathbf{y}}^+ = [n]_{\mathbf{x}}^+ = [n]_{\mathbf{y}}^+$, and $|\mathbf{x} + \mathbf{y}| = |\mathbf{x}| + |\mathbf{y}|$. Then, by comonotonic additivity of the Choquet integral:

$$\mathcal{C}_w(\mathbf{x} + \mathbf{y}) = \mathcal{C}_{v_{[n]_{\mathbf{x}+\mathbf{y}}^+}}(|\mathbf{x} + \mathbf{y}|) = \mathcal{C}_{v_{[n]_{\mathbf{x}+\mathbf{y}}^+}}(|\mathbf{x}| + |\mathbf{y}|)$$

$$= \mathcal{C}_{v_{[n]_{\mathbf{x}}^+}}(|\mathbf{x}|) + \mathcal{C}_{v_{[n]_{\mathbf{y}}^+}}(|\mathbf{y}|)$$

$$= \mathcal{C}_w(\mathbf{x}) + \mathcal{C}_w(\mathbf{y}).$$

Now suppose that $\mathbf{x}$ or $\mathbf{y}$ have zero components for some $i \in [n]$. Define $\mathbf{x}', \mathbf{y}'$ which are identical to $\mathbf{x}, \mathbf{y}$, except on those $i \in [n]$, where we put, if $x_i = 0$,

$$x_i' = \begin{cases} \varepsilon & \text{if } y_i \geqslant 0 \\ -\varepsilon & \text{otherwise,} \end{cases}$$

and, if $y_i = 0$,

$$y_i' = \begin{cases} \varepsilon & \text{if } x_i \geqslant 0 \\ -\varepsilon & \text{otherwise,} \end{cases}$$

where ε is a positive number. Then we are back to our previous case, where the above result holds. Now the result holds for $\mathbf{x}, \mathbf{y}$ too by continuity of the Choquet integral since we can obtain $\mathbf{x}, \mathbf{y}$ as limits of $\mathbf{x}', \mathbf{y}'$. □

The following result is a straightforward consequence of definitions. It shows that the Choquet integral is indeed a generalization of the CPT model.

Proposition 9.36. *If w is of the CPT type, with $w(A, B) = v_+(A) - v_-(B)$, the Choquet integral reduces to*

$$\mathcal{C}_w(\mathbf{x}) = \sum_{i=1}^{n} x_{\sigma(i)}^{+} \left(v_+(A_{\sigma(i)} \cap [n]^+) - v_+(A_{\sigma(i+1)} \cap [n]^+) \right)$$

$$- \sum_{i=1}^{n} x_{\sigma(i)}^{-} \left(v_-(A_{\sigma(i)} \cap [n]^-) - v_-(A_{\sigma(i+1)} \cap [n]^-) \right)$$

$$= \mathcal{C}_{v_+}(\mathbf{x}^+) - \mathcal{C}_{v_-}(\mathbf{x}^-).$$

Remark 9.37. Refering to Definition 5.23, we see that by putting $v_+ = v_- =: v$, we recover the symmetric Choquet integral, and by putting $v_+ = \overline{v_-} =: v$, we recover the asymmetric Choquet integral.

Proposition 9.38. *Let w be a bicapacity on $[n]$, and $\mathbb{I} := \mathbb{R}$. The Choquet integral satisfies the following properties:*

(i) *Continuity.*
(ii) *Nondecreasing monotonicity.*
(iii) *Strict increasing monotonicity if and only if w is strictly monotone, i.e., $(A_1, A_2) \sqsubset (B_1, B_2)$ implies $w(A_1, A_2) < w(B_1, B_2)$.*
(iv) *Idempotency if w is normalized.*
(v) *Internality if w is normalized.*

Proof. Since these properties are fulfilled by the Choquet integral with respect to a capacity (see Proposition 5.38), it is plain that they hold for any $\mathbf{x}$ in a given cone $\Sigma_{[n]^+}$. Difficulties may occur only when crossing cones. Hence we have to check only (i), (ii), and (iii).

(i) See Remark 9.32.

Properties (ii) and (iii) hold by continuity. □

Proposition 9.39. *Let* $\mathbb{I} := \mathbb{R}$. *The Choquet integral with respect to a bicapacity satisfies the following properties:*

(i) Symmetry (or neutrality, commutativity) if and only if w is symmetric.
(ii) Additivity if and only if w is additive.

Proof. (i) For an arbitrary $\mathbf{x} \in \mathbb{R}^n$, we have

$$\mathcal{C}_w(\mathbf{x}) = \sum_{i=1}^{n}(|x_{\sigma(i)}| - |x_{\sigma(i-1)}|)w(A_{\sigma(i)} \cap [n]^+, A_{\sigma(i)} \cap [n]^-).$$

For any permutation τ, we have

$$\mathcal{C}_w([\mathbf{x}]_\tau) = \sum_{i=1}^{n}(|x_{\sigma(i)}| - |x_{\sigma(i-1)}|)w(\tau^{-1}(A_{\sigma(i)}) \cap \tau^{-1}([n]^+), \tau^{-1}(A_{\sigma(i)}) \cap \tau^{-1}([n]^-))$$

$$= \sum_{i=1}^{n}(|x_{\sigma(i)}| - |x_{\sigma(i-1)}|)w(\tau^{-1}(A_{\sigma(i)} \cap [n]^+), \tau^{-1}(A_{\sigma(i)} \cap [n]^-)).$$

Equality $\mathcal{C}_w(\mathbf{x}) = \mathcal{C}_w([\mathbf{x}]_\tau)$ holds for every $\mathbf{x} \in \mathbb{R}^n$ and every permutation τ if and only if $w(A_{\sigma(i)} \cap [n]^+, A_{\sigma(i)} \cap [n]^-) = w(\tau^{-1}(A_{\sigma(i)} \cap [n]^+), \tau^{-1}(A_{\sigma(i)} \cap [n]^-))$, which is possible if and only if $w(A, B)$ depends only on the cardinality of A and B.

(ii) Suppose $\mathcal{C}_w$ is additive. Taking $(A, B), (C, D) \in \mathcal{Q}([n])$ such that $A \cap C = B \cap D = \varnothing$ and $(A \cup C, B \cup D) \in \mathcal{Q}([n])$, we have by Proposition 9.35(i) $\mathcal{C}_w(\mathbf{1}_A + \mathbf{1}_C - \mathbf{1}_B - \mathbf{1}_D) = \mathcal{C}_w(\mathbf{1}_{A \cup C}(-\mathbf{1}_{B \cup D})\mathbf{0}) = w(A \cup C, B \cup D)$. The integral being additive, we get $\mathcal{C}_w(\mathbf{1}_A + \mathbf{1}_C - \mathbf{1}_B - \mathbf{1}_D) = \mathcal{C}_w(\mathbf{1}_A) + \mathcal{C}_w(-\mathbf{1}_B) + \mathcal{C}_w(\mathbf{1}_C) + \mathcal{C}_w(-\mathbf{1}_D) = w(A, \varnothing) + w(\varnothing, B) + w(C, \varnothing) + w(\varnothing, D)$. This proves the additivity of v.

Conversely, if w is additive, it is of the CPT type with v_+, v_- being additive; see Remark 9.27(iii). By Proposition 9.36 and Remark 9.37, this corresponds to symmetric and asymmetric Choquet integrals, which are additive by Proposition 5.41. □

We present a characterization result similar to Theorem 5.48, where the aggregation function is supposed beforehand to depend on a bicapacity, hence the notation $\mathbf{F}_w$, w being any normalized bicapacity on $[n]$. Let us introduce for convenience $\mathcal{G}_2(n)$ the set of all bicooperative games on $[n]$. We recall that $\mathcal{F}_2^*(n)$ is the set of all normalized bicapacities. Let us introduce first some definitions.

For $A \subseteq [n]$, consider the following application $\Pi_A : \mathbb{R}^n \to \mathbb{R}^n$ defined by

$$(\Pi_A(\mathbf{x}))_i := \begin{cases} x_i & \text{if } i \in A \\ -x_i & \text{otherwise.} \end{cases}$$

Supposing that F_w is an extension of w (see below), $w(B, B')$ corresponds to the vector $(1_B(-1)_{B'}0)$. Define $\Pi_A \circ w(B, B')$ as the term of the bicapacity associated with the vector

$$\Pi_A(1_B(-1)_{B'}0) = (1_{(B\cap A)\cup(B'\cap A^c)}(-1)_{(B\cap A^c)\cup(B'\cap A)}0).$$

Hence we set

$$\Pi_A \circ w(B, B') := w((B \cap A) \cup (B' \cap A^c), (B \cap A^c) \cup (B' \cap A)).$$

Theorem 9.40. *Let us consider* $\mathbb{I} = \mathbb{R}$ *and a family of functions* $\{F_w : \mathbb{I}^n \to \mathbb{I} \mid w \in \mathcal{G}_2^*(n)\}$. *Then* $F_w = \mathcal{C}_w$ *for all* $w \in \mathcal{F}_2^*(n)$, *if and only if the family satisfies the following properties:*

(i) Each function F_w *satisfies linearity with respect to* w *in the cone* $[0, \infty[^n$: *consider* $w, w_1, \ldots, w_p \in \mathcal{G}_2(n)$ *such that* $w(B, \varnothing) = \sum_{i=1}^{p} \alpha_i w_i(B, \varnothing)$ *with* $\alpha_1, \ldots, \alpha_p \in \mathbb{R}$, *for all* $B \subseteq [n]$. *Then for all* $\mathbf{x} \in [0, \infty[^n$,*

$$F_w(\mathbf{x}) = \sum_{i=1}^{p} \alpha_i F_{w_i}(\mathbf{x}).$$

(ii) For any $w \in \mathcal{F}_2^*(n)$, F_w *is nondecreasing in each place.*

(iii) For any $w \in \mathcal{F}_2^*(n)$, F_w *is stable for the same positive affine transformations with positive shift for any nonnegative* $\mathbf{x} \in \mathbb{I}^n$:*

$$F_w(\alpha\mathbf{x} + \beta\mathbf{1}) = \alpha F_w(\mathbf{x}) + \beta, \quad \forall \alpha > 0, \forall \beta \geqslant 0.$$

(iv) For any $w \in \mathcal{G}_2(n)$, *for any* $A \subseteq [n]$ *and any* $\mathbf{x} \in \mathbb{I}^n$,

$$F_w(\mathbf{x}) = F_{\Pi_A \circ w}(\Pi_A(\mathbf{x})).$$

(v) For any $w \in \mathcal{F}_2^*(n)$, F_w *is an extension of* w: $F_w(1_A(-1)_B 0) = w(A, B)$.

This result is due to Labreuche and Grabisch [244].

Proof. ($\Leftarrow$) Property (i) is obvious, and (ii) and (v) are immediate from previous propositions. Property (iii) holds since under the restrictions given in (iii), we recover the Choquet integral with respect to capacities, which satisfies stability for positive affine transformations; see Proposition 5.42(i).

We prove (iv). Let $A, [n]^+ \subseteq [n]$, $w \in \mathcal{G}_2(n)$ and $\mathbf{x} \in \Sigma_{[n]^+}$. Put as before $[n]^- := [n] \setminus [n]^+$. Let us check that $F_w(\mathbf{x}) = F_{\Pi_A \circ w}(\Pi_A(\mathbf{x}))$. On the one hand,

$$F_w(\mathbf{x}) = \mathcal{C}_{v_{[n]^+}}(|\mathbf{x}|).$$

On the other hand, $\Pi_A(\mathbf{x}) \in \Sigma_D$ with $D := ([n]^+ \cap A) \cup ([n]^- \cap A^c)$. Hence $\Pi_D(\Pi_A(\mathbf{x})) \in \Sigma_{[n]}$ and

$$\mathsf{F}_{\Pi_A \circ w}(\Pi_A(\mathbf{x})) = \mathcal{C}_{\nu'}(\Pi_D(\Pi_A(\mathbf{x}))) = \mathcal{C}_{\nu'}(|\mathbf{x}|),$$

where $\nu' = \nu_{\Pi_A \circ w, D}$ is given by

$$
\begin{aligned}
\nu'(C) &= \Pi_A \circ w(C \cap D, C \cap D^c) \\
&= w\big((C \cap D \cap A) \cup (C \cap D^c \cap A^c), (C \cap D \cap A^c) \cup (C \cap D^c \cap A)\big) \\
&= w\big((C \cap [n]^+ \cap A) \cup (C \cap [n]^+ \cap A^c), (C \cap [n]^- \cap A^c) \cup (C \cap [n]^- \cap A)\big) \\
&= w(C \cap [n]^+, C \cap [n]^-) = \nu_{[n]^+}(C),
\end{aligned}
$$

with D^c indicating the complement of D, etc. Finally, we get

$$\mathsf{F}_{\Pi_A \circ w}(\Pi_A(\mathbf{x})) = \mathcal{C}_{\nu'}(|\mathbf{x}|) = \mathcal{C}_{[n]^+}(|\mathbf{x}|) = \mathsf{F}_w(\mathbf{x}).$$

As a consequence, (iv) holds.

($\Rightarrow$) We consider F_w satisfying the above conditions. Let $w \in \mathcal{F}_2^*(n)$ be fixed. To any game ν on $[n]$, we associate a bicooperative game w_ν by

$$
\nu_\nu(B, B') = \begin{cases} \nu(B) & \text{if } B' = \varnothing \\ \mathrm{Min}(\nu(B, B'), \nu(B)) & \text{otherwise.} \end{cases}
$$

Define $\mathsf{G}_\nu(\mathbf{x}) := \mathsf{F}_{w_\nu}(\mathbf{x})$ for any $\mathbf{x} \in [0, \infty[^n$, and let us prove that G_ν is the Choquet integral. For this, we use the following result, which is a slight generalization of Theorem 5.48; see [244].

Proposition 9.41. *Let us consider* $\mathbb{I} := \mathbb{R}_+$, *and a family of functions* $\{\mathsf{G}_\nu : \mathbb{I}^n \to \mathbb{I} \mid \nu \in \mathcal{G}(n)\}$, *where* $\mathcal{G}(n)$ *is the set of games on* $[n]$. *Then* $\mathsf{G}_\nu = \mathcal{C}_\nu$ *for all* $\nu \in \mathcal{G}(n)$ *if and only if the family satisfies the following properties:*

(i) *Each function* F_ν *is a linear expression of* ν, *that is, for any* $\nu, \nu_1 \ldots, \nu_p \in \mathcal{G}(n)$ *such that* $\nu = \sum_{i=1}^p \alpha_i \nu_i$ *with* $\alpha_1, \ldots, \alpha_p \in \mathbb{R}$, *we have* $\mathsf{G}_\nu = \sum_{i=1}^p \alpha_i \mathsf{G}_{\nu_i}$.

(ii) *For any* $\nu \in \mathcal{F}^*(n)$, G_ν *is nondecreasing in each place.*

(iii) *For any* $\nu \in \mathcal{F}^*(n)$, G_ν *is stable under the same positive affine transformation with positive shift, for any* $\mathbf{x} \in \mathbb{I}^n$:

$$\mathsf{G}_\nu(\alpha \mathbf{x} + \beta) = \alpha \mathsf{G}_\nu(\mathbf{x}) + \beta, \forall \alpha, \beta > 0.$$

(iv) *For any* $\nu \in \mathcal{F}^*(n)$, G_ν *is an extension of* ν.

Let $\nu, \nu_1, \ldots, \nu_p \in \mathcal{G}(n)$ such that $\nu = \sum_{i=1}^p \alpha_i \nu_i$, with $\alpha_1, \ldots, \alpha_p \in \mathbb{R}$. We have $w_\nu(B, \varnothing) = \sum_{i=1}^p \alpha_i w_{\nu_i}(B, \varnothing)$ for all $B \subseteq [n]$, where $w_\nu, w_{\nu_1}, \ldots, w_{\nu_p} \in \mathcal{G}_2(n)$. Then by (i), for all $\mathbf{x} \in [0, \infty[^n$

$$G_v(\mathbf{x}) = F_{w_v}(\mathbf{x}) = \sum_{i=1}^{p} \alpha_i F_{w_{v_i}}(\mathbf{x}) = \sum_{i=1}^{p} \alpha_i G_{v_i}(\mathbf{x}).$$

Hence G_v satisfies (i) of Proposition 9.41.

Consider $v \in \mathcal{F}^*(n)$. By construction, w_v is monotone and normalized so that $w_v \in \mathcal{F}_2^*(n)$. Therefore, we have by (v) for all $C \subseteq [n]$

$$G_v(\mathbf{1}_C \mathbf{0}) = F_{w_v}(\mathbf{1}_C \mathbf{0}) = w_v(C, \varnothing) = v(C).$$

Hence G_v satisfies (iv) of Proposition 9.41.

Now, G_v satisfies (ii) of Proposition 9.41 since $w_v \in \mathcal{F}_2^*(n)$ and F_{w_v} satisfies (ii). By (iii), and since $w_v \in \mathcal{F}_2^*(n)$, we have for any $\mathbf{x} \in [0, \infty[^n$, $\alpha > 0$ and $\beta \geqslant 0$,

$$G_v(\alpha \mathbf{x} + \beta) = F_{w_v}(\alpha \mathbf{x} + \beta) = \alpha F_{w_v}(\mathbf{x}) + \beta$$
$$= \alpha G_v(\mathbf{x}) + \beta.$$

Hence G_v satisfies (iii) of Proposition 9.41, and we conclude by Proposition 9.41 that G_v is the Choquet integral with respect to v. We apply this result to $v_{w,\varnothing}$ defined by $v_{w,\varnothing}(B) := w(B, \varnothing)$. We have $w_{v_{w,\varnothing}}(B, B') = w(B, B')$ for all $(B, B') \in \mathcal{Q}([n])$. We conclude that for all $\mathbf{x} \in [0, \infty[^n$,

$$F_w(\mathbf{x}) = F_{w_{v_{w,\varnothing}}}(\mathbf{x}) = G_{v_{w,\varnothing}}(\mathbf{x}) = \mathcal{C}_{v_{w,\varnothing}}(\mathbf{x}) = \mathcal{C}_w(\mathbf{x}). \qquad (9.17)$$

Consider now $w \in \mathcal{G}_2(n)$. Let $v \in \mathcal{G}(n)$ be defined by $v(B) := w(B, \varnothing)$, $B \subseteq [n]$. Using the decomposition into unanimity games (see (5.8)), we write $v = \sum_{C \subseteq [n]} m_C u_C$, where m_C are the Möbius coefficients, and u_C the unanimity games. Define w_C by

$$w_C(B, B') := u_C(B) - u_C(B').$$

Clearly, $w_C \in \mathcal{F}_2^*(n)$. Moreover, $w(B, \varnothing) = \sum_{C \subseteq [n]} m_C w_C(B, \varnothing)$ for all $B \subseteq [n]$. By (i), for all $\mathbf{x} \in [0, \infty[^n$

$$F_w(\mathbf{x}) = \sum_{C \subseteq [n]} m_C F_{w_C}(\mathbf{x}).$$

Since $w_C \in \mathcal{F}_2^*(n)$, one has $F_{w_C}(\mathbf{x}) = \mathcal{C}_{u_C}(\mathbf{x})$ by (9.17). Hence for all $\mathbf{x} \in [0, \infty[^n$

$$F_w(\mathbf{x}) = \sum_{C \subseteq [n]} m_C \mathcal{C}_{u_C}(\mathbf{x}) = \mathcal{C}_{\sum_{C \subseteq [n]} m_C u_C}(\mathbf{x}) = \mathcal{C}_v(\mathbf{x}).$$

This proves that (9.17) holds also for $w \in \mathcal{G}_2(n)$.

Consider finally $w \in \mathcal{F}_2^*(n)$ and $[n]^+ \subseteq N$. By (iv), we have for $\mathbf{x} \in \Sigma_{[n]^+}$, $F_w(\mathbf{x}) = F_{\Pi_{[n]^+} \circ w}(\Pi_{[n]^+}(\mathbf{x}))$. Applying (9.17) to $\Pi_{[n]^+} \circ w \in \mathcal{G}_2(n)$, and to $\Pi_{[n]^+}(\mathbf{x}) \in [0, \infty[^n$, we get $F_{\Pi_{[n]^+} \circ w}(\Pi_{[n]^+}(\mathbf{x})) = \mathcal{C}_{\nu_{\Pi_{[n]^+} \circ w, \varnothing}}(\Pi_{[n]^+}(\mathbf{x}))$, where

$$\nu_{\Pi_{[n]^+} \circ w, \varnothing}(B) = \Pi_{[n]^+} \circ w(B, \varnothing) = w(B \cap [n]^+, B \setminus [n]^+) = \nu_{[n]^+}(B).$$

Therefore $F_w(\mathbf{x}) = \mathcal{C}_{\nu_{[n]^+}}(\Pi_{[n]^+}(\mathbf{x}))$, so that $F_w \equiv \mathcal{C}_w$. □

9.5.3 The Sugeno integral for bicapacities

By analogy, a definition can be proposed for the Sugeno integral with respect to a bicapacity:

$$\mathcal{S}_w(\mathbf{x}) := \mathcal{S}_{\nu_{[n]_{\mathbf{x}}^+}}(|\mathbf{x}|)$$

with the same notations as above. However, since $\nu_{[n]_{\mathbf{x}}^+}$ may assume negative values, it is necessary to extend the definition of Sugeno integral as follows:

$$\mathcal{S}_\nu(\mathbf{x}) := \Big\langle \overset{n}{\underset{i=1}{\otimes}} \big(x_{\sigma(i)} \oslash \nu(\{\sigma(i), \ldots, \sigma(n)\})\big)\Big\rangle_-^+$$

where $\mathbf{x} \in [0,1]^n$, ν is any real-valued set function such that $\nu(\varnothing) = 0$, and σ is a permutation on $[n]$ such that $\mathbf{x}$ becomes nondecreasing. The notation $\langle \cdot \rangle_-^+$ indicates the splitting rule defined in Section 9.3.3. Then, the Sugeno integral for bicapacities can be rewritten as

$$\mathcal{S}_w(\mathbf{x}) = \Big\langle \overset{n}{\underset{i=1}{\otimes}} \big(|x_{\sigma(i)}| \oslash w(\{\sigma(i), \ldots, \sigma(n)\} \cap [n]^+, \{\sigma(i), \ldots, \sigma(n)\} \cap [n]^-)\big)\Big\rangle_-^+.$$

$$(9.18)$$

This formula is similar to the one proposed by Greco *et al.* [175].

One would expect that the Sugeno integral with respect to a bicapacity encompasses the OCPT model; see (9.14). Unfortunately, this is not true as shown in the following example.[1]

Example 9.42. Let $n = 2$ and $w(A, B) := \mu^+(A) \oslash (-\mu^-(B))$, where $\mu^+(\varnothing) = 0$, $\mu^+(\{1\}) = \mu^+(\{2\}) = \frac{1}{2}$, $\mu^+(\{1,2\}) = 1$, and $\mu^- = \mu^+$. Consider $\mathbf{x} \in [-1,1]^2$ such that $x_1 = -\frac{1}{2}$ and $x_2 = 1$. Then, since $\sigma(1) = 1$, $\sigma(2) = 2$, and $[n]^+ = \{2\}$, $[n]^- = \{1\}$, it follows that

$$\mathcal{S}_w(\mathbf{x}) = \Big(\Big| -\frac{1}{2}\Big| \oslash w(\{2\}, \{1\})\Big) \oslash (|1| \oslash w(\{2\}, \varnothing))$$

$$= \Big(\frac{1}{2} \oslash 0\Big) \oslash \Big(1 \oslash \frac{1}{2}\Big) = \frac{1}{2}.$$

---

[1] This example has been communicated by T. Murofushi.

On the other hand, we have

$$\mathcal{S}_{\mu^+}(\mathbf{x}^+) = 1 \wedge \frac{1}{2} = \frac{1}{2}$$
$$\mathcal{S}_{\mu^-}(\mathbf{x}^-) = \frac{1}{2} \wedge \frac{1}{2} = \frac{1}{2},$$

so that

$$\mathcal{S}_{\mu^+}(\mathbf{x}^+) \oslash (-\mathcal{S}_{\mu^-}(\mathbf{x}^-)) = \frac{1}{2} \oslash \left(-\frac{1}{2}\right) = 0.$$

Hence, it is not true that $\mathcal{S}_w(\mathbf{x}) = \mathcal{S}_{\mu^+}(\mathbf{x}^+) \oslash (-\mathcal{S}_{\mu^-}(\mathbf{x}^-)) =: \text{OCPT}_{\mu^+,\mu^-}(\mathbf{x})$.

Remark 9.43. The OCPT model has been characterized by Pap and Mihailović by the property of comonotonic $\oslash$-additivity, $\oslash$-homogeneity, and monotonicity [352].

10

Behavioral analysis of aggregation functions

10.1 Introduction

Given a function $F : \mathbb{I}^n \to \mathbb{R}$, possibly an aggregation function, it is useful to define values or indices that offer a better understanding of the general behavior of F with respect to its variables. These indices may constitute a kind of identity card of F and enable one to classify the aggregation functions according to their behavioral properties.

For example, given an internal aggregation function A (recall that "internal" means $\mathsf{Min} \leqslant A \leqslant \mathsf{Max}$), it might be convenient to appraise the degree to which A is conjunctive, that is, close to Min. Similarly, it might be very instructive to know which variables, among $x_1, \ldots, x_n$, have the greatest influence on the output value $A(\mathbf{x})$.

In this chapter we present various indices, such as: andness and orness degrees of internal functions, idempotency degrees of conjunctive and disjunctive functions, importance and interaction indices, tolerance indices, and dispersion indices.

Sometimes different indices can be considered to measure the same behavior. In that case it is often needed to choose an appropriate index according to the nature of the underlying aggregation problem.

To keep the exposition concise the proofs of many results from this chapter have been omitted.

10.2 Expected values and distribution functions

A very informative treatment of a given function $F : \mathbb{I}^n \to \mathbb{R}$ consists in applying it to a random input vector and examining the behavior of the output signal by computing its distribution function. However, as we will see at the end of this section, determining an explicit form of the distribution remains very difficult in general.

Instead, we can calculate the expected value or, more generally, the moments of the output variable and derive indices that would provide information on the location of the output values within the range of the function.

10.2.1 Expected values

Given a function $F : \mathbb{I}^n \to \mathbb{R}$, it is interesting to appraise its average value (if it exists) when the input values are chosen at random in $\mathbb{I}^n$. That average value may be very relevant, especially if we want to estimate the conjunctive or disjunctive character of an internal aggregation function; see Section 10.2.2.

Definition 10.1. Let $F : \mathbb{I}^n \to \mathbb{R}$ be a measurable function and let X be a continuous random vector with (joint) probability density function $h : \mathbb{R}^n \to \mathbb{R}$. The *expected value* of $F(X)$ with respect to h, when it exists, is given by

$$E(F(X)) := \int_{\mathbb{I}^n} F(x)h(x) \, dx.$$

The choice of the probability density function may vary from one context to another. If the interval $\mathbb{I}$ is bounded, it might be convenient (at least from a computational viewpoint) to consider the uniform distribution on the domain $\mathbb{I}^n$. In that case, the expected value of $F(X)$ is simply called the *average value* of F (over $\mathbb{I}^n$).

Definition 10.2. Let $a, b \in \mathbb{R}$ such that $a < b$. The *average value* over $|a, b|^n$ of any integrable function $F : |a, b|^n \to \mathbb{R}$ is defined as

$$\overline{F} := \frac{1}{(b - a)^n} \int_{|a,b|^n} F(x) \, dx. \tag{10.1}$$

By means of a simple linear change of variables, we can even consider the uniform distribution over the unit hypercube $|0, 1|^n$. In that case, we have

$$\overline{F} = \int_{|0,1|^n} F(x) \, dx.$$

Unless otherwise specified, $\overline{F}$ will always be understood in this section as the average value of F over the unit hypercube, with uniform distribution.

Table 10.1 provides the average values of some aggregation functions over the domain $|0, 1|^n$. As far as Choquet and Sugeno integrals are concerned, we have the following result; see Marichal [273, 277].

Proposition 10.3. *For any normalized capacity μ on $[n]$, we have*

$$\overline{\mathcal{C}}_\mu = \sum_{K \subseteq [n]} \mu(K) \int_0^1 x^{n-|K|}(1 - x)^{|K|} \, dx$$

$$= \sum_{K \subseteq [n]} \frac{1}{(n + 1)\binom{n}{|K|}} \mu(K) = \sum_{K \subseteq [n]} \frac{1}{|K| + 1} m^\mu(K)$$

Table 10.1. *Average values of some aggregation functions over* $]0, 1[^n$

A	Name	$\overline{A}$
$\text{WAM}_\mathbf{w}$	weighted arithmetic mean	$\dfrac{1}{2}$
$\text{WGM}_\mathbf{w}$	weighted geometric mean	$\displaystyle\prod_{i=1}^{n} \dfrac{1}{w_i + 1}$
$\text{M}_{\text{id}^{1/2}}$	root-mean-power with $r = 1/2$	$\dfrac{8n + 1}{18n}$
OS_k	order statistic	$\dfrac{k}{n + 1}$
$\text{T}_\mathbf{L}$	Łukasiewicz t-norm	$\dfrac{1}{(n + 1)!}$
Π	product	$\dfrac{1}{2^n}$

and

$$\overline{S}_\mu = \sum_{K \subseteq [n]} \int_0^{\mu(K)} x^{n-|K|}(1 - x)^{|K|} \, dx$$

$$= \sum_{K \subseteq [n]} \sum_{i=0}^{|K|} \binom{|K|}{i} \frac{(-1)^{|K|-i}}{n - i + 1} \mu(K)^{n-i+1}.$$

Recall that, when $\mathbb{I} = [0, 1]$ or $]0, 1[$, the *dual* $\mathsf{F}^d : \mathbb{I}^n \to \mathbb{R}$ of a function $\mathsf{F} : \mathbb{I}^n \to \mathbb{R}$ is defined as $\mathsf{F}^d(\mathbf{x}) = 1 - \mathsf{F}(1 - \mathbf{x})$. We then have the following immediate result:

Proposition 10.4. *Consider a function* $\mathsf{F} : \mathbb{I}^n \to \mathbb{R}$, *where* $\mathbb{I} = [0, 1]$ *or* $\mathbb{I} =]0, 1[$. *Then* $\overline{\mathsf{F}}$ *exists if and only if* $\overline{\mathsf{F}^d}$ *exists, and in this case we have* $\overline{\mathsf{F}^d} = 1 - \overline{\mathsf{F}}$.

In the case of an extended function $\mathsf{F} : \cup_{n \in \mathbb{N}}]0, 1[^n \to \mathbb{R}$, it may be informative to calculate, when it exists, the limiting average value of $\mathsf{F}^{(n)}$ as the arity grows, that is,

$$\lim \overline{\mathsf{F}} := \lim_{n \to \infty} \overline{\mathsf{F}^{(n)}}. \tag{10.2}$$

For instance, using l'Hospital's rule, we obtain

$$\lim \overline{\text{GM}} = \lim_{n \to \infty} \left(\frac{n}{n + 1} \right)^n = \frac{1}{e}.$$

Even if the limit (10.2) exists, it may sometimes be difficult to calculate it. In this case, an alternative approach consists in calculating the limit

$$m(\mathsf{F}) := \lim_{n \to \infty} \frac{1}{n!} \sum_{\sigma \in \mathfrak{S}_{[n]}} \mathsf{F}^{(n)} \left(\frac{\sigma(1)}{n}, \frac{\sigma(2)}{n}, \ldots, \frac{\sigma(n)}{n} \right)$$

which, when F is symmetric, reduces to

$$m(\mathsf{F}) = \lim_{n \to \infty} \mathsf{F}^{(n)} \left(\frac{1}{n}, \frac{2}{n}, \ldots, \frac{n}{n} \right).$$

For many extended aggregation functions $\mathsf{A} : \cup_{n \in \mathbb{N}} |0, 1|^n \to \mathbb{R}$, including certain quasi-arithmetic means (see Section 4.2), we have $\lim \overline{\mathsf{A}} = m(\mathsf{A})$. Finding conditions on A for both limits to coincide remains an interesting question.

Example 10.5. Considering the root-mean-power

$$\mathsf{M}_{\mathrm{id}^r}(\mathbf{x}) = \left(\frac{1}{n} \sum_{i=1}^{n} x_i^r \right)^{1/r},$$

where $r \in \mathbb{Z}$, we have

$$m(\mathsf{M}_{\mathrm{id}^r}) = \begin{cases} (r+1)^{-1/r} & \text{if } r \in \mathbb{N} \\ 1/e & \text{if } r = 0 \\ 0 & \text{if } -r \in \mathbb{N}. \end{cases}$$

10.2.2 Andness and orness degrees of internal functions

Consider the average value (10.1) of an integrable function $\mathsf{F} : |0, 1|^n \to \mathbb{R}$. If F is internal, i.e., $\mathsf{Min} \leqslant \mathsf{F} \leqslant \mathsf{Max}$, then we always have

$$\overline{\mathsf{Min}} \leqslant \overline{\mathsf{F}} \leqslant \overline{\mathsf{Max}}.$$

For those internal functions F, it seems convenient to locate the position of $\overline{\mathsf{F}}$ within the interval $[\overline{\mathsf{Min}}, \overline{\mathsf{Max}}]$. More precisely, we define the *conjunction degree* or the *global andness value* of F as the relative position of $\overline{\mathsf{F}}$ with respect to the lower bound of the interval $[\overline{\mathsf{Min}}, \overline{\mathsf{Max}}]$.

Remark 10.6. This idea was proposed in 1974 by Dujmović [104] for the special case of root-mean-powers, but it actually applies to any internal function.

Definition 10.7. The *global andness value* of an internal and integrable function $\mathsf{F} : |0, 1|^n \to \mathbb{R}$ is defined by

$$\mathrm{andness}(\mathsf{F}) := \frac{\overline{\mathsf{Max}} - \overline{\mathsf{F}}}{\overline{\mathsf{Max}} - \overline{\mathsf{Min}}}.$$

This value clearly represents the degree to which the average value of F is close to that of Min. In some sense, it also reflects the extent to which F behaves like a minimum or has a conjunctive behavior.

Similarly, we can define the relative position of $\overline{F}$ with respect to $\overline{Max}$ as the *disjunction degree* or the *global orness value* of F. It measures the degree to which F behaves like a maximum or has a disjunctive behavior.

Definition 10.8. The *global orness value* of an internal and integrable function F : $]0, 1]^n \to \mathbb{R}$ is defined by

$$\text{orness}(F) := \frac{\overline{F} - \overline{Min}}{\overline{Max} - \overline{Min}}.$$

Clearly, the global orness and andness values are normalized and mutually complementary values in the sense that

$$0 \leqslant \text{andness}(F) \leqslant 1,$$
$$0 \leqslant \text{orness}(F) \leqslant 1,$$
$$\text{andness}(F) + \text{orness}(F) = 1.$$

The computation of these values requires the knowledge of $\overline{Min}$ and $\overline{Max}$. To this end, we go through the following lemma.

Lemma 10.9. *The following holds:*

$$\int_{[0,1]^n} \bigwedge_{i \in K} x_i \, d\mathbf{x} = \frac{1}{|K| + 1}, \qquad \forall K \subseteq [n].$$

Proof. Observe first that we can assume $K = [n]$. Next, defining the *n*-simplices

$$[0, 1]^n_\sigma := \{\mathbf{x} \in [0, 1]^n \mid x_{\sigma(1)} \leqslant \cdots \leqslant x_{\sigma(n)}\}$$

for all $\sigma \in \mathfrak{S}_{[n]}$, we obtain

$$\int_{[0,1]^n} \bigwedge_{i \in [n]} x_i \, d\mathbf{x} = \sum_{\sigma \in \mathfrak{S}_{[n]}} \int_{[0,1]^n_\sigma} x_{\sigma(1)} \, d\mathbf{x}$$

$$= \sum_{\sigma \in \mathfrak{S}_{[n]}} \int_0^1 \int_0^{x_{\sigma(n)}} \cdots \int_0^{x_{\sigma(2)}} x_{\sigma(1)} \, dx_{\sigma(1)} \cdots dx_{\sigma(n)}$$

$$= \sum_{\sigma \in \mathfrak{S}_{[n]}} \frac{1}{(n+1)!} = \frac{1}{n+1},$$

which completes the proof. $\qquad\qquad\square$

Table 10.2. *Global orness values of some internal aggregation functions*

A	Name	orness(A)
WAM$_\mathbf{w}$	weighted arithmetic mean	$\dfrac{1}{2}$
WGM$_\mathbf{w}$	weighted geometric mean	$-\dfrac{1}{n-1} + \dfrac{n+1}{n-1} \displaystyle\prod_{i=1}^{n} \dfrac{1}{w_i+1}$
OWA$_\mathbf{w}$	ordered weighted averaging	$\dfrac{1}{n-1} \displaystyle\sum_{i=1}^{n} (i-1)w_i$
M$_{\mathrm{id}^{1/2}}$	root-mean-power with $r = 1/2$	$\dfrac{8n-1}{18n}$
OS$_k$	order statistic	$\dfrac{k-1}{n-1}$

By Lemma 10.9 we have $\overline{\mathsf{Min}} = \frac{1}{n+1}$. Since Max is the dual of Min, that is,

$$\mathsf{Max}(\mathbf{x}) = 1 - \mathsf{Min}(1 - \mathbf{x}),$$

from Proposition 10.4 we immediately obtain $\overline{\mathsf{Max}} = 1 - \overline{\mathsf{Min}} = \frac{n}{n+1}$. Therefore, we obtain the explicit formulas:

$$\mathrm{andness}(\mathsf{F}) = \frac{n}{n-1} - \frac{n+1}{n-1}\overline{\mathsf{F}}, \tag{10.3}$$

$$\mathrm{orness}(\mathsf{F}) = -\frac{1}{n-1} + \frac{n+1}{n-1}\overline{\mathsf{F}}. \tag{10.4}$$

As andness(F) and orness(F) render more or less the same information, we can restrict ourselves to the computation of orness(F). Table 10.2 provides the global orness values of some internal aggregation functions over the domain $]0, 1[^n$. Regarding the Choquet integral, we have the following result (see Marichal [264, 273]):

Proposition 10.10. *For any normalized capacity μ on $[n]$, we have*

$$\mathrm{orness}(\mathcal{C}_\mu) = \sum_{\substack{K \subseteq [n] \\ 0 < |K| < n}} \frac{1}{(n-1)\binom{n}{|K|}} \mu(K)$$

$$= \sum_{K \subseteq [n]} \frac{n - |K|}{(n-1)(|K|+1)} m^\mu(K).$$

Using Proposition 10.4, we derive the following straightforward result, which implies that the global orness value of any self-dual function (i.e., a function F such that $F^d = F$) is $1/2$.

Proposition 10.11. *Consider an integrable and internal function* $F : \mathbb{I}^n \to \mathbb{R}$, *where* $\mathbb{I} = [0, 1]$ *or* $\mathbb{I} = {]0, 1[}$. *Then*

$$\mathrm{orness}(F^d) = \mathrm{andness}(F) = 1 - \mathrm{orness}(F).$$

Remark 10.12. If two integrable and internal functions $F : {]0, 1[}^n \to \mathbb{R}$ and $G : {]0, 1[}^n \to \mathbb{R}$ fulfill $F \leqslant G$, then we clearly have $\overline{F} \leqslant \overline{G}$ and hence $\mathrm{orness}(F) \leqslant \mathrm{orness}(G)$. For example, if F is k-conjunctive (i.e., $F \leqslant OS_k$), then $\mathrm{orness}(F) \leqslant \mathrm{orness}(OS_k) = (k - 1)/(n - 1)$.

On the basis of Proposition 2.55, Dujmović [103] (see also Dujmović [105]) introduced the following concepts of *local andness function* and *local orness function*, rediscovered independently by Fernández Salido and Murakami [111] as *orness distribution function* and *andness distribution function*, respectively.

Definition 10.13. The *local andness* (respectively, *orness*) *function* associated with an internal function $F : \mathbb{I}^n \to \mathbb{R}$, where $\mathbb{I} = {]0, 1[}$, is a function laf_F (respectively, lof_F) from $\mathbb{I}^n \setminus \mathrm{diag}(\mathbb{I}^n)$ to $[0, 1]$, defined as

$$\mathrm{laf}_F(\mathbf{x}) := \frac{\mathrm{Max}(\mathbf{x}) - F(\mathbf{x})}{\mathrm{Max}(\mathbf{x}) - \mathrm{Min}(\mathbf{x})} \qquad \left(\text{respectively, } \mathrm{lof}_F(\mathbf{x}) := \frac{F(\mathbf{x}) - \mathrm{Min}(\mathbf{x})}{\mathrm{Max}(\mathbf{x}) - \mathrm{Min}(\mathbf{x})}\right).$$

(For future needs, we also formally define $\mathrm{laf}_F(n \cdot x) = \mathrm{lof}_F(n \cdot x) = 1/2$ for all $x \in \mathbb{I}$.)

Thus defined, the local andness (respectively, orness) function associated with an internal function $F : {]0, 1[}^n \to \mathbb{R}$ measures, at each $\mathbf{x} \in {]0, 1[}^n \setminus \mathrm{diag}([0, 1]^n)$, the extent to which $F(\mathbf{x})$ is close to $\mathrm{Min}(\mathbf{x})$ (respectively, $\mathrm{Max}(\mathbf{x})$), that is, the extent to which $F(\mathbf{x})$ has a conjunctive (respectively, disjunctive) or "andlike" (respectively, "orlike") behavior. To measure the average andness or orness quality of an internal function over its domain, Dujmović [103] also introduced the concepts of *mean local andness* and *mean local orness*, later called *andness average value* and *orness average value*, respectively, by Fernández Salido and Murakami [111].

Definition 10.14. The *mean local andness* (respectively, *orness*) of an internal and integrable function $F : {]0, 1[}^n \to \mathbb{R}$ is defined as $\overline{\mathrm{laf}}_F$ (respectively, $\overline{\mathrm{lof}}_F$).

As an immediate property, we note that

$$\mathrm{laf}_F(\mathbf{x}) + \mathrm{lof}_F(\mathbf{x}) = 1,$$

which entails $\overline{\mathrm{laf}}_F + \overline{\mathrm{lof}}_F = 1$. Thus, as expected, we can restrict ourselves to the computation of $\overline{\mathrm{lof}}_F$.

We also have the following straightforward result, from which we deduce that the mean local orness of any self-dual function is $1/2$.

Proposition 10.15. *Consider an internal function* $\mathsf{F} : \mathbb{I}^n \to \mathbb{R}$*, where* $\mathbb{I} = [0, 1]$ *or* $\mathbb{I} =]0, 1[$*. Then*

$$\mathrm{lof}_{\mathsf{F}^d}(\mathbf{x}) = \mathrm{laf}_{\mathsf{F}}(1 - \mathbf{x}) = 1 - \mathrm{lof}_{\mathsf{F}}(1 - \mathbf{x})$$

for all $\mathbf{x} \in \mathbb{I}^n$*. In particular, if* F *is integrable,* $\overline{\mathrm{lof}}_{\mathsf{F}^d} = 1 - \overline{\mathrm{lof}}_{\mathsf{F}}$*.*

The mean local orness plays more or less the same role as the global orness value. By definition, the global orness value of an internal function $\mathsf{F} :]0, 1[^n \to \mathbb{R}$ measures the relative position of $\overline{\mathsf{F}}$ with respect to the upper bound of the interval $[\mathsf{Min}, \mathsf{Max}]$ while the mean local orness measures the average relative position, over $]0, 1[^n$, of $\mathsf{F}(\mathbf{x})$ with respect to the upper bound of the interval $[\mathsf{Min}(\mathbf{x}), \mathsf{Max}(\mathbf{x})]$. As we will see below, these values are generally different even though they coincide for some internal functions F.

For most of the internal functions F, the exact computation of $\overline{\mathrm{lof}}_{\mathsf{F}}$ remains much more difficult than that of $\mathrm{orness}(\mathsf{F})$. However, the following formula (see Marichal [276]) proved to be useful in the computation of $\overline{\mathrm{lof}}_{\mathsf{F}}$. We have

$$\overline{\mathrm{lof}}_{\mathsf{F}} = \sum_{\substack{j,k=1 \\ j \neq k}}^{n} \int_0^1 dv \int_0^v du \int_{|u,v|^{n-2}} \frac{\mathsf{F}(u_{\{j\}} v_{\{k\}} \mathbf{x}) - u}{v - u} \prod_{i \in [n] \setminus \{j,k\}} dx_i, \qquad (10.5)$$

which reduces for $n = 2$ to

$$\overline{\mathrm{lof}}_{\mathsf{F}^{(2)}} = \int_0^1 dv \int_0^v \frac{\mathsf{F}(u, v) + \mathsf{F}(v, u) - 2u}{v - u} \, du. \qquad (10.6)$$

Example 10.16. Let us calculate the mean local orness of the geometric mean GM. The case $n = 2$ is straightforward. Using (10.6) we immediately obtain $\overline{\mathrm{lof}}_{\mathsf{GM}^{(2)}} = \ln 4 - 1$.

Assume now that $n \geqslant 3$. As the integrand is a symmetric function, we can write

$$\mathsf{GM}^{(n)}(u_{\{j\}} v_{\{k\}} \mathbf{x}) = \mathsf{GM}^{(n)}(x_1, \ldots, x_{n-2}, u, v)$$

and hence, we have

$$\int_{|u,v|^{n-2}} \mathsf{GM}^{(n)}(u_{\{j\}} v_{\{k\}} \mathbf{x}) \prod_{i \in [n] \setminus \{j,k\}} dx_i$$

$$= \left(\frac{n}{n+1}\right)^{n-2} \left(v^{1+1/n} - u^{1+1/n}\right)^{n-2} u^{1/n} v^{1/n}.$$

Then, using the binomial theorem and observing that $\frac{1}{v-u} = \frac{1}{v}\sum_{i=0}^{\infty}(\frac{u}{v})^i$, we obtain

$$\int_0^1 dv \int_0^v \frac{(v^{1+1/n} - u^{1+1/n})^{n-2}u^{1/n}v^{1/n}}{v - u} \, du$$

$$= \sum_{i=0}^{\infty}\sum_{k=0}^{n-2}\binom{n-2}{k}\frac{(-1)^k}{ni + (k+1)(n+1)}$$

$$= \sum_{i=0}^{\infty}\sum_{k=0}^{n-2}\binom{n-2}{k}(-1)^k \int_0^1 x^{ni+kn+k+n} \, dx$$

$$= \int_0^1 \frac{x^n(1 - x^{n+1})^{n-2}}{1 - x^n} \, dx.$$

Finally, using formula (10.5), we obtain

$$\overline{\text{lof}}_{\text{GM}^{(n)}} = n(n - 1)\Big(\frac{n}{n+1}\Big)^{n-2} \int_0^1 \frac{x^n(1 - x^{n+1})^{n-2}}{1 - x^n} \, dx - \frac{1}{n-2},$$

which is to be compared with

$$\text{orness}(\text{GM}^{(n)}) = -\frac{1}{n-1} + \frac{n+1}{n-1}\Big(\frac{n}{n+1}\Big)^n.$$

Regarding the discrete Choquet integral, we have the following result (see Marichal [276]):

Proposition 10.17. *For any normalized capacity μ on $[n]$, we have*

$$\overline{\text{lof}}_{\mathcal{C}_\mu} = \sum_{K\subseteq[n]} \frac{n - |K|}{(n - 1)(|K| + 1)} m^\mu(K).$$

Remark 10.18. Comparing Propositions 10.10 and 10.17, we observe that, for any normalized capacity μ on $[n]$, we have

$$\overline{\text{lof}}_{\mathcal{C}_\mu} = \text{orness}(\mathcal{C}_\mu),$$

that is, for any discrete Choquet integral, the mean local orness is identical to the global orness value. This result was already obtained by Fernández Salido and Murakami [111] for the special case of symmetric Choquet integrals, that is, the class of ordered weighted averaging functions OWA_w. The interesting question of determining those internal functions $F : |0, 1|^n \to \mathbb{R}$ fulfilling the equation $\overline{\text{lof}}_F = \text{orness}(F)$ remains open.

Table 10.3. *Global idempotency value of some conjunctive aggregation functions over* $[0, 1]^n$

A	Name	idemp(A)
$\mathsf{T_L}$	Łukasiewicz t-norm	$\dfrac{1}{n!}$
Π	product	$\dfrac{n+1}{2^n}$

10.2.3 Idempotency degrees of conjunctive and disjunctive functions

Recall that a function $\mathsf{F} : \mathbb{I}^n \to \mathbb{R}$ is conjunctive (respectively, disjunctive) if

$$\inf \mathbb{I} \leqslant \mathsf{F} \leqslant \mathsf{Min} \qquad (\text{respectively, } \mathsf{Max} \leqslant \mathsf{F} \leqslant \sup \mathbb{I}).$$

If F is integrable, we can write

$$\inf \mathbb{I} \leqslant \overline{\mathsf{F}} \leqslant \overline{\mathsf{Min}} \qquad (\text{respectively, } \overline{\mathsf{Max}} \leqslant \overline{\mathsf{F}} \leqslant \sup \mathbb{I}).$$

Based on this observation, the following concept of *global idempotency value* was introduced by Kolesárová [232] for t-norms as an idempotency measure:

Definition 10.19. Let $a, b \in \mathbb{R}$ such that $a < b$. The *global idempotency value* of a conjunctive (respectively, disjunctive) and integrable function $\mathsf{F} : |a, b|^n \to \mathbb{R}$ is defined as

$$\mathrm{idemp}(\mathsf{F}) = \frac{\overline{\mathsf{F}} - a}{\overline{\mathsf{Min}} - a} \qquad \left(\text{respectively, } \mathrm{idemp}(\mathsf{F}) = \frac{b - \overline{\mathsf{F}}}{b - \overline{\mathsf{Max}}} \right).$$

Similarly to the global orness and andness values, the global idempotency value of a conjunctive (respectively, disjunctive) function $\mathsf{F} : |a, b|^n \to \mathbb{R}$ measures the extent to which the average value of F is close to that of Min (respectively, Max) or, equivalently, the extent to which F is idempotent.

Here again, we restrict ourselves to functions $\mathsf{F} : |0, 1|^n \to \mathbb{R}$ defined on the unit hypercube. In this case, if F is conjunctive (respectively, disjunctive), we obtain immediately the explicit formula:

$$\mathrm{idemp}(\mathsf{F}) = (n + 1) \overline{\mathsf{F}} \qquad (\text{respectively, } \mathrm{idemp}(\mathsf{F}) = (n + 1)(1 - \overline{\mathsf{F}})).$$

Table 10.3 provides the global idempotency value of some conjunctive aggregation functions over $[0, 1]^n$.

Just as for the local andness and orness functions, we can naturally define the concept of *local idempotency function* associated with a conjunctive (respectively, disjunctive) function $\mathsf{F} : |0, 1|^n \to \mathbb{R}$ as a measure, at each $\mathbf{x} \in |0, 1|^n$, of the extent to which $\mathsf{F}(\mathbf{x})$ is close to $\mathsf{Min}(\mathbf{x})$ (respectively, $\mathsf{Max}(\mathbf{x})$); see Marichal [276].

Definition 10.20. The *local idempotency function* associated with a conjunctive (respectively, disjunctive) function $F : |0, 1|^n \to \mathbb{R}$ is a function $\mathrm{lif}_F :]0, 1[^n \to [0, 1]$, defined as

$$\mathrm{lif}_F(\mathbf{x}) := \frac{F(\mathbf{x})}{\mathrm{Min}(\mathbf{x})} \qquad \left(\text{respectively, } \mathrm{lif}_F(\mathbf{x}) := \frac{1 - F(\mathbf{x})}{1 - \mathrm{Max}(\mathbf{x})} \right).$$

The concept of *mean local idempotency* can then be defined as follows.

Definition 10.21. The *mean local idempotency* of a conjunctive or disjunctive and integrable function $F : |0, 1|^n \to \mathbb{R}$ is defined as the average value $\overline{\mathrm{lif}}_F$ of the local idempotency function associated with F.

From these definitions, we derive the following straightforward result, which shows that we can confine ourselves to conjunctive functions.

Proposition 10.22. *Consider a conjunctive function* $F : \mathbb{I}^n \to \mathbb{R}$, *where* $\mathbb{I} = [0, 1]$ *or* $\mathbb{I} =]0, 1[$. *Then its dual* $F^d : \mathbb{I}^n \to \mathbb{R}$ *is a disjunctive function and we have*

$$\mathrm{lif}_{F^d}(\mathbf{x}) = \mathrm{lif}_F(1 - \mathbf{x})$$

for all $\mathbf{x} \in \mathbb{I}^n$. *In particular, if* F *is integrable,* $\overline{\mathrm{lif}}_{F^d} = \overline{\mathrm{lif}}_F$.

For most of the conjunctive functions F, the exact computation of $\overline{\mathrm{lif}}_F$ remains much more difficult than that of $\mathrm{idemp}(F)$. However, the following formula (see Marichal [276]) proved to be useful in the computation of $\overline{\mathrm{lif}}_F$. We have

$$\overline{\mathrm{lif}}_F = \sum_{j=1}^n \int_0^1 du \int_{|u,1|^{n-1}} \frac{F(u_{\{j\}}\mathbf{x})}{u} \prod_{i \in [n] \setminus \{j\}} dx_i, \qquad (10.7)$$

which reduces for $n = 2$ to

$$\overline{\mathrm{lif}}_{F^{(2)}} = \int_0^1 du \int_u^1 \frac{F(u, v) + F(v, u)}{u} \, dv. \qquad (10.8)$$

Example 10.23. Let us calculate the mean local idempotency over $[0, 1]^n$ of the product $\Pi^{(n)}$, which is a conjunctive function. Using formula (10.7), we immediately obtain

$$\overline{\mathrm{lif}}_{\Pi^{(n)}} = n \int_0^1 du \int_{|u,1|^{n-1}} \left(\prod_{i=1}^{n-1} x_i \right) dx_1 \cdots dx_{n-1}$$

$$= \frac{n}{2^{n-1}} \int_0^1 (1 - u^2)^{n-1} \, du.$$

Setting $u = v^{1/2}$ and then using the classical beta function

$$B(a, b) = \int_0^1 t^{a-1}(1 - t)^{b-1} \, dt,$$

we obtain

$$\overline{\text{lif}}_{\Pi^{(n)}} = \frac{n}{2^n} \int_0^1 v^{-1/2}(1-v)^{n-1} \, dv$$

$$= \frac{n}{2^n} \, \text{B}(1/2, n) = \frac{n}{2^n} \frac{\Gamma(1/2)\Gamma(n)}{\Gamma(n+1/2)}$$

$$= \frac{2^{n-1}}{\binom{2n-1}{n}}.$$

10.2.4 Distribution functions and moments

Let $\mathsf{F} : \mathbb{I}^n \to \mathbb{R}$ be a measurable function, and let $\mathbf{X}$ be a continuous random vector with distribution function $H : \mathbb{R}^n \to [0, 1]$ and probability density function $h : \mathbb{R}^n \to \mathbb{R}$. We assume that the function h is supported on $\mathbb{I}^n$, that is, $h(\mathbf{x}) = 0$ if $\mathbf{x} \notin \mathbb{I}^n$. An interesting but generally difficult problem is to provide explicit expressions for the distribution function of the aggregated random variable $Y = \mathsf{F}(\mathbf{X})$, namely

$$H_Y(y) := \text{P}(Y \leqslant y) = \text{P}(\mathsf{F}(\mathbf{X}) \leqslant y) = \int_{\{\mathbf{x} \in \mathbb{I}^n : \mathsf{F}(\mathbf{x}) \leqslant y\}} dH(\mathbf{x}).$$

If $H_Y(y)$ is absolutely continuous we can even consider the probability density function of Y, that is,

$$h_Y(y) = \frac{d}{dy} H_Y(y).$$

Example 10.24. Consider the Łukasiewicz t-norm of n independent variables $Y = \mathsf{T_L}(\mathbf{X})$, where $\mathsf{T_L}(\mathbf{x}) = \text{Max}(0, \sum_i x_i - (n - 1))$. In this case, we have

$$H_Y(y) = \text{P}(\text{Max}(0, \textstyle\sum_i X_i - (n-1)) \leqslant y)$$

$$= \text{P}(0 \leqslant y \text{ and } \textstyle\sum_i X_i - (n-1) \leqslant y)$$

$$= \text{Ind}(y \geqslant 0) \, \text{P}(\textstyle\sum_i X_i \leqslant y + n - 1)$$

$$= \mathbf{1}_{[0,\infty[}(y) \, H_{\mathsf{AM}}(\tfrac{y+n-1}{n}),$$

where $H_{\mathsf{AM}}(y)$ is the distribution function of the arithmetic mean of n independent variables; see Example 10.27 below. We observe here that $H_Y(y)$ is discontinuous at $y = 0$ and hence $h_Y(y)$ does not exist.

For any measurable function $g : \mathbb{R} \to \mathbb{R}$, we can consider the expectation of $g(Y)$, when it exists. It is defined by

$$\text{E}(g(Y)) = \int_{\mathbb{R}} g(y) \, dH_Y(y) = \int_{\mathbb{R}} g(y) h_Y(y) \, dy, \tag{10.9}$$

or, equivalently, by the following n-dimensional integrals

$$E(g(Y)) = \int_{\mathbb{I}^n} g(\mathsf{F}(\mathbf{x})) \, dH(\mathbf{x}) = \int_{\mathbb{I}^n} g(\mathsf{F}(\mathbf{x})) h(\mathbf{x}) \, d\mathbf{x}. \qquad (10.10)$$

The special cases $g(y) = y$, y^r, $(y - E(Y))^r$, and e^{ty} give, respectively, the expected value, the raw moments, the central moments, and the moment-generating function of Y.

Remark 10.25. We note that the distribution function of Y can also be calculated from $E(g(Y))$ by choosing for $g(y)$ the indicator function $\mathrm{Ind}(y \leqslant z) = \mathbf{1}_{]-\infty,z]}(y)$, for any fixed $z \in \mathbb{R}$. In fact,

$$H_Y(z) = P(Y \leqslant z) = P(g(Y) = 1) = E(g(Y)).$$

If the variables $X_1, \ldots, X_n$ are independent, each X_i ($i \in [n]$) having distribution function $H_i(x)$ and density function $h_i(x)$, then (10.10) becomes

$$E(g(Y)) = \int_{\mathbb{I}^n} g(\mathsf{F}(\mathbf{x})) \prod_{i=1}^n dH_i(x_i) = \int_{\mathbb{I}^n} g(\mathsf{F}(\mathbf{x})) \prod_{i=1}^n h_i(x_i) \, d\mathbf{x}. \qquad (10.11)$$

When F satisfies certain regularity conditions, the distribution function $H_Y(y)$ can sometimes be calculated by using the next result, which is a direct consequence of the multivariate transformation theorem; see for instance McColl [301, §7.2] and Weiss [431, §9.7].

Proposition 10.26. *Let* $\mathsf{F} : \mathbb{R}^n \to \mathbb{R}$ *be a measurable function and let* $\mathbf{X}$ *be a continuous random vector, with probability density function* $h : \mathbb{R}^n \to \mathbb{R}$. *Assume*

$$(x_1, \ldots, x_n) \mapsto \big(\mathsf{F}(x_1, \ldots, x_n), x_2, \ldots, x_n\big)$$

is a continuously differentiable bijection from $\mathbb{R}^n$ *onto* $\mathbb{R}^n$, *with inverse bijection*

$$(y_1, \ldots, y_n) \mapsto \big(\mathsf{G}(y_1, \ldots, y_n), y_2, \ldots, y_n\big).$$

Then the random variable $Y = \mathsf{F}(\mathbf{X})$ *is continuous and its probability density function is given by*

$$h_Y(y) = \int_{\mathbb{R}^{n-1}} f\big(\mathsf{G}(y, y_2, \ldots, y_n), y_2, \ldots, y_n\big) \left| \frac{\partial \mathsf{G}}{\partial y_1}(y, y_2, \ldots, y_n) \right| dy_2 \cdots dy_n.$$

We can easily see that, under the assumptions of Proposition 10.26, with the condition $\frac{\partial \mathsf{G}}{\partial y_1} \geqslant 0$ on $\mathbb{R}^n$, and assuming additionally that the variables $X_1, \ldots, X_n$ are independent, with distribution functions $H_1, \ldots, H_n$, we have

$$H_Y(y) = \int_{\mathbb{R}^{n-1}} H_1(\mathsf{G}(y, y_2, \ldots, y_n)) \, dH_2(y_2) \cdots dH_n(y_n).$$

Example 10.27. Consider the arithmetic mean of n independent variables $Y = \text{AM}(\mathbf{X})$. Then, the distribution function of Y is given by the convolution product

$$H_Y(y) = \int_{\mathbb{R}^{n-1}} H_1(ny - y_2 - \cdots - y_n) \, dH_2(y_2) \cdots dH_n(y_n).$$

Finding explicit expressions for the distribution function and the raw moments of the variable $Y = \mathsf{F}(\mathbf{X})$ remains a hard problem in general, even under the assumptions of Proposition 10.26.

However, in the special case when $\mathbf{X}$ is uniformly distributed on $[0, 1]^n$, this problem has been completely solved for certain aggregation functions, especially piecewise linear functions such as weighted sums [26] (see also [288]), linear and convex combinations of order statistics [14, 299, 430] (see also [72, §6.5] for an overview), lattice polynomial functions [274], discrete Choquet integrals [278], and discrete Sugeno integrals [277].

Example 10.28. If $\mathcal{S}_\mu$ denotes the Sugeno integral defined from a normalized capacity μ on $[n]$, and if $\mathbf{X}$ is uniformly distributed on $[0, 1]^n$, then the distribution function of $Y = \mathcal{S}_\mu(\mathbf{X})$ is given by [277]

$$H_Y(y) = 1 - \sum_{K \subseteq [n]} \mathbf{1}_{]-\infty, \mu(K)[}(y) \, H(y)^{n-|K|} [1 - H(y)]^{|K|},$$

where $H(y) := \text{Med}(0, y, 1)$. Also, the kth raw moment of Y is

$$E(Y^k) = k \sum_{K \subseteq [n]} \int_0^{\mu(K)} t^{n-|K|+k} (1 - t)^{|K|} \, dt.$$

10.3 Importance indices

When using a given aggregation function A of n variables, one may wonder which are the most influential variables in the computation of $\mathsf{A}(\mathbf{x})$, if any. We may say that no such variable exists if A is symmetric. In case symmetry does not hold, e.g., for weighted aggregation functions (see Section 6.4) and for integral-based ones, it is very instructive to know the level or percentage of contribution of each variable in the computation of the result. Let us call this level of contribution or influential power the *importance index*, postponing its precise definition.

For weighted aggregation functions, a naive answer to the above question is to take as importance index simply the weight of each variable. A first simple reason to discard this idea is that the definition, meaning and normalization of weights differ from one aggregation function to another: just consider the weighted arithmetic mean, with weights in $[0, 1]$ summing up to 1, and the weighted maximum, whose weights are in $[0, 1]$ with no summation condition, but whose maximum value is 1. A second reason is that intuitively, a weight value, say 0.5, does not have the same effect in a weighted arithmetic mean as in a weighted geometric mean.

A natural approach when $\mathbb{I}$ is a bounded closed interval $[a, b]$ is to compute an average of the marginal contribution of variable x_i as follows:

Definition 10.29. Let $a, b \in \mathbb{R}$ such that $a < b$, let A be an integrable aggregation function in $[a, b]^n$, and consider $i \in [n]$.

(i) The *(total) variation of A with respect to coordinate i* is the function $\Delta_i A :$ $[a, b]^n \to \mathbb{R}$ defined by

$$\Delta_i A(\mathbf{x}) := A(b_{\{i\}}\mathbf{x}) - A(a_{\{i\}}\mathbf{x}).$$

(ii) The *importance index of coordinate i on A* is defined by

$$\phi_i(A) := \frac{1}{(b-a)^n} \int_{[a,b]^n} \frac{\Delta_i A(\mathbf{x})}{b-a} \, d\mathbf{x}.$$

(iii) The *normalized importance index of coordinate i on A* is

$$\overline{\phi}_i(A) := \frac{\phi_i(A)}{\sum_{i=1}^n \phi_i(A)}.$$

Thus defined, the importance index of coordinate i on A is the average relative amplitude of the range of A that variable x_i may control when assigning random values to the other variables (assuming a uniform distribution on $[a, b]^n$). Thus it is an index of influence or contribution of variable x_i in the computation of $A(\mathbf{x})$. The normalized importance index of i represents the percentage of contribution of variable x_i in the computation of $A(\mathbf{x})$. Clearly, its value is $1/n$ for all $i \in [n]$ if A is symmetric.

The importance index is invariant to duality, as shown in the next proposition.

Proposition 10.30. *Let A be an aggregation function in $[0, 1]^n$. Then for any $i \in [n]$,*

$$\phi_i(A^d) = \phi_i(A).$$

Proof. For any $\mathbf{x} \in \mathbb{I}^n$, we have

$$\Delta_i A^d(\mathbf{x}) = A^d(1_{\{i\}}\mathbf{x}) - A^d(0_{\{i\}}\mathbf{x})$$

$$= 1 - A(0_{\{i\}}(1 - \mathbf{x})) - 1 + A(1_{\{i\}}(1 - \mathbf{x}))$$

$$= \Delta_i A(1 - \mathbf{x}).$$

This implies $\phi_i(A^d) = \phi_i(A)$. $\square$

Proposition 10.31. *Consider the Choquet integral C_μ as an aggregation function in* $[0, 1]^n$, *with μ a normalized capacity on $[n]$. Then, for any $i \in [n]$, the importance index $\phi_i(C_\mu)$ is the Shapley value ϕ_i^μ for i associated to μ, that is,*

$$\phi_i(C_\mu) = \phi_i^\mu = \sum_{K \subseteq [n] \setminus \{i\}} \frac{(n - |K| - 1)!|K|!}{n!} \left(\mu(K \cup \{i\}) - \mu(K) \right). \qquad (10.12)$$

Proof. See Proposition 10.43. □

Remark 10.32. The Shapley value [388] (see (5.18)) is a well-known concept in cooperative game theory. For any game $v : 2^{[n]} \to \mathbb{R}$, it represents a way of sharing the total worth of the game, $v([n])$, among the players in a fair and rational way. Denoting by $\mathcal{G}(n)$ the set of games on $[n]$, and $\Phi := (\phi_1, \dots, \phi_n)$, it is the unique sharing $\Phi : \mathcal{G}(n) \to \mathbb{R}^n, v \mapsto \Phi^v$ satisfying the following set of natural axioms (see, e.g., Weber [427]):

(i) Linearity: for any games $u, v \in \mathcal{G}(n)$, $\Phi^{u+v} = \Phi^u + \Phi^v$.
(ii) Null player: if i is a null player (that is, if $v(K \cup \{i\}) = v(K)$ for all $K \subseteq [n] \setminus \{i\}$), then $\phi_i^v = 0$. The axiom says that a player who has a null contribution in any situation should not be rewarded.
(iii) Symmetry: $\phi_{\sigma(i)}^{v \circ \sigma} = \phi_i^v$, for all $i \in [n]$, all $\sigma \in \mathfrak{S}_{[n]}$, and all $v \in \mathcal{G}(n)$. This axiom says that the labeling of the players has no influence on the sharing. This depicts fairness.
(iv) Efficiency: $\sum_{i \in [n]} \phi_i^v = v([n])$. This axiom says that the "whole cake" is shared.

The first to have advocated the use of the Shapley value to model the importance of criteria in a multicriteria decision model based on the Choquet integral seems to have been Murofushi [322].

Remark 10.33. Since it is a very natural concept, the Shapley value was discovered also in other domains, in particular in artificial intelligence. In Dempster–Shafer theory [387], it is the so-called *pignistic transform*, which transforms a belief measure (capacity whose Möbius transform is nonnegative) into a probability distribution. It was proposed by Smets [395].

Proposition 10.34. *Consider the multilinear extension* MLE_μ *(see (5.30)) as an aggregation function in* $[0, 1]^n$, *with μ a normalized capacity on $[n]$. Then, for any $i \in [n]$, the importance index $\phi_i(\mathsf{MLE}_\mu)$ is the Banzhaf value B_i^μ for i associated to μ, that is,*

$$\phi_i(\mathsf{MLE}_\mu) = B_i^\mu := \frac{1}{2^{n-1}} \sum_{K \subseteq [n] \setminus \{i\}} \left(\mu(K \cup \{i\}) - \mu(K) \right). \qquad (10.13)$$

Proof. See Proposition 10.46. □

Table 10.4. *Importance index of some nonsymmetric aggregation functions over* $[0,1]^n$

A	Name	$\phi_i(A)$
$\text{WAM}_\mathbf{w}$	weighted arithmetic mean	w_i
$\text{WGM}_\mathbf{w}$	weighted geometric mean	$\displaystyle\prod_{j\in[n]\setminus\{i\}} \frac{\text{sign}(w_i)}{w_j + 1}$
$\mathcal{C}_\mu$	Choquet integral	ϕ_i^μ
MLE_μ	multilinear extension	B_i^μ

Remark 10.35. The Banzhaf value [25] is well known in voting games (0–1 valued games), where it is more commonly called the *Banzhaf power index*. It satisfies linearity, the null axiom, and symmetry, but fails to satisfy efficiency (see Remark 10.32).

Table 10.4 provides the importance index of some aggregation functions over the domain $[0,1]^n$.

The normalized importance index of a given integrable and internal aggregation function can be used as a weight vector to define a weighted arithmetic mean, which could represent a kind of linear approximation of the aggregation function.

Definition 10.36. Given an integrable and internal aggregation function $\mathsf{A} : \mathbb{I}^n \to \mathbb{I}$, let $\text{WAM}_{\overline{\phi}(\mathsf{A})}$ be the weighted arithmetic mean defined from A by

$$\text{WAM}_{\overline{\phi}(\mathsf{A})}(\mathbf{x}) = \sum_{i=1}^{n} \overline{\phi}_i(\mathsf{A})\, x_i.$$

As an example, from the Choquet integral $\mathcal{C}_\mu$ we define the so-called "Shapley integral" (see Marichal [263, Def. 5.1])

$$\text{WAM}_{\overline{\phi}(\mathcal{C}_\mu)}(\mathbf{x}) = \sum_{i=1}^{n} \phi_i^\mu\, x_i.$$

From Remark 10.33, the Shapley integral can be seen as the expected value of some random variable with respect to the pignistic transform.

The concept of importance index straightforwardly generalizes to subsets of coordinates, giving rise to the following definition:

Definition 10.37. Let $a, b \in \mathbb{R}$ such that $a < b$, let A be an integrable aggregation function in $[a,b]^n$, and consider $K \subseteq [n]$. The *importance index of coordinates in K*

Table 10.5. *Importance index of $\{i,j\}$ on some aggregation functions over $[0,1]^n$*

A	Name	$\phi_{\{i,j\}}(A)$
WAM$_\mathbf{w}$	weighted arithmetic mean	$w_i + w_j$
WGM$_\mathbf{w}$	weighted geometric mean	$\displaystyle\prod_{k \in [n]\backslash\{i,j\}} \frac{\text{sign}\,(w_i + w_j)}{w_k + 1}$
OWA$_\mathbf{w}$	ordered weighted average	$\displaystyle\sum_{i=1}^{n} w_i \frac{\text{Min}(i, 2, n-i+1, n-1)}{n-1}$

on A is defined by

$$\phi_K(A) := \frac{1}{(b-a)^n} \int_{[a,b]^n} \frac{A(b_K\mathbf{x}) - A(a_K\mathbf{x})}{b-a} \; d\mathbf{x}.$$

Thus defined, $\phi_K(A)$ represents the average relative amplitude of the range of A that variables x_i $(i \in K)$ may control when assigning random values to the other variables. For a detailed exposition on this concept, see [265, 279].

Table 10.5 provides the importance index of $\{i,j\}$ on some aggregation functions over the domain $[0,1]^n$.

We also introduce the following definitions:

Definition 10.38. Let $a, b \in \mathbb{R}$ such that $a < b$, let A be an integrable aggregation function in $[a,b]^n$, and consider $k \in [n]$.

(i) The *(total) variation of* A *with respect to rank* k is the function $\Psi_{(k)}A : [a,b]^n \to \mathbb{R}$ defined by

$$\Psi_{(k)}A(\mathbf{x}) := A(\mathbf{x} \mid x_{(k)} = b) - A(\mathbf{x} \mid x_{(k)} = a)$$
$$= A\big(b_{\{(k),\dots,(n)\}}\mathbf{x}\big) - A\big(a_{\{(1),\dots,(k)\}}\mathbf{x}\big),$$

where, as usual, $(\cdot)$ is a permutation on $[n]$ such that $x_{(1)} \leqslant \cdots \leqslant x_{(n)}$.

(ii) The *lowest relative variation of* A *with respect to rank* k is defined by

$$\Theta_{(k)}A(\mathbf{x}) := \frac{A\big(b_{\{(k),\dots,(n)\}}a\big) - A\big(a_{\{(1),\dots,(k)\}}b\big)}{b-a}.$$

Because A is nondecreasing, we observe that, for any permutation $\sigma \in \mathfrak{S}_{[n]}$, we have

$$\Theta_{(k)}A\big|_{[a,b]^n_\sigma} = \inf_{\mathbf{x} \in [a,b]^n_\sigma} \frac{\Psi_{(k)}A(\mathbf{x})}{b-a},$$

which justifies the name "lowest relative variation". We thus see that the function $\Theta_{(k)}A|_{[a,b]_\sigma^n}$ is a constant for each $\sigma \in \mathfrak{S}_{[n]}$.

It it worth comparing the two functions $\Theta_{(k)}A(\mathbf{x})$ and $\Delta_i A(\mathbf{x})/(b-a)$. By definition, $\Delta_i A(\mathbf{x})/(b-a)$ gives the relative variation of A with respect to coordinate i, that is, the (local) importance or contribution of coordinate i at each $\mathbf{x} \in [a,b]^n$. The function $\Theta_{(k)}A(\mathbf{x})$ somehow yields the minimal importance of the kth smallest component for each ordering of the components of $\mathbf{x}$.

Now, the average value of $\Theta_{(k)}A$ can be calculated by dividing $[a,b]^n$ into the simplices $[a,b]_\sigma^n$ ($\sigma \in \mathfrak{S}_{[n]}$), each having volume $(b-a)^n/n!$. Thus, we have successively

$$\overline{\Theta_{(k)}A} = \frac{1}{(b-a)^n} \sum_{\sigma \in \mathfrak{S}_{[n]}} \int_{[a,b]_\sigma^n} \Theta_{(k)}A(\mathbf{x}) \, d\mathbf{x}$$

$$= \frac{1}{n!} \sum_{\sigma \in \mathfrak{S}_{[n]}} \frac{A\big(b_{\{\sigma(k),\dots,\sigma(n)\}}a\big) - A\big(a_{\{\sigma(1),\dots,\sigma(k)\}}b\big)}{b-a}$$

$$= \frac{1}{b-a}\left(\frac{1}{\binom{n}{k-1}} \sum_{\substack{K \subseteq [n] \\ |K|=n-k+1}} A(b_K a) - \frac{1}{\binom{n}{k}} \sum_{\substack{K \subseteq [n] \\ |K|=n-k}} A(b_K a) \right).$$

We also observe that the functions $\Theta_{(k)}A$ ($k \in [n]$) are mutually normalized:

$$\sum_{k=1}^n \Theta_{(k)}A(\mathbf{x}) = \sum_{k=1}^n \frac{A\big(a_{\{(1),\dots,(k-1)\}}b\big) - A\big(a_{\{(1),\dots,(k)\}}b\big)}{b-a}$$

$$= \frac{A(n \cdot b) - A(n \cdot a)}{b-a}$$

$$= 1.$$

Clearly, for any weight vector $\mathbf{w}$, we have $\Theta_{(k)}\mathrm{OWA}_\mathbf{w}(\mathbf{x}) = w_k$. Also, one can easily prove that $\Theta_{(k)}\mathrm{WAM}_\mathbf{w}(\mathbf{x}) = w_{(k)}$, where $w_{(k)}$ is the coefficient of $x_{(k)}$ in $\mathrm{WAM}_\mathbf{w}(\mathbf{x})$. More generally, we have the following result:

Proposition 10.39. *For any capacity μ on $[n]$, we have*

$$\mathcal{C}_\mu(\mathbf{x}) = \sum_{i=1}^n x_{(i)} \Theta_{(i)} \mathcal{C}_\mu(\mathbf{x}).$$

Proof. For any capacity μ on $[n]$ and any $K \subseteq [n]$, we have

$$\mathcal{C}_\mu(b_K a) = (b-a)\,\mu(K) + a\,\mu([n])$$

(immediate from Proposition 5.42(i) and $\mathcal{C}_\mu(\mathbf{1}_K) = \mu(K)$, Proposition 5.36(i)). It follows that

$$\Theta_{(k)}\mathcal{C}_\mu(\mathbf{x}) = \frac{\mathcal{C}_\mu\big(b_{\{(k),\ldots,(n)\}}a\big) - \mathcal{C}_\mu\big(b_{\{(k+1),\ldots,(n)\}}a\big)}{b-a}$$

$$= \mu(A_{(k)}) - \mu(A_{(k+1)}),$$

where $A_{(k)} = \{(k), \ldots, (n)\}$. $\qquad\square$

Remark 10.40. For a given aggregation function $\mathbf{A} : [a,b]^n \to [a,b]$, it seems that the numbers $\overline{\Theta_{(k)}}\mathbf{A}$ and $\overline{\phi}_i(\mathbf{A})$ somehow have orthogonal behaviors. This can be observed by comparing $\overline{\Theta_{(k)}}\mathsf{OWA_w} = w_k$ and $\overline{\Theta_{(k)}}\mathsf{WAM_w} = 1/n$ together with $\overline{\phi}_i(\mathsf{OWA_w}) = 1/n$ and $\overline{\phi}_i(\mathsf{WAM_w}) = w_i$. Moreover, for any capacity μ on $[n]$, we have

$$\overline{\Theta_{(k)}\mathcal{C}_\mu} = \frac{1}{\binom{n}{k-1}} \sum_{\substack{K \subseteq [n] \\ |K| = n-k+1}} \mu(K) - \frac{1}{\binom{n}{k}} \sum_{\substack{K \subseteq [n] \\ |K| = n-k}} \mu(K),$$

which is in some sense the orthogonal counterpart of ϕ_i^μ.

10.4 Interaction indices

Although the notion of importance index is useful to analyze a given aggregation function, the description it provides is still very primitive. Take for example the arithmetic mean, the minimum, and the maximum. Since they are symmetric, they have the same importance index for all coordinates, yet they are extremely different aggregation functions, because the minimum operator is a conjunctive aggregation function, the maximum operator is disjunctive, and the arithmetic mean is neither conjunctive nor disjunctive.

The question is how to quantify or describe the difference between these aggregation functions, which are indistinguishable by the importance index. Since andness and orness are reserved to internal aggregation functions (see Section 10.2), other indices have to be found.

The key of the problem lies in the interrelation between variables. The notion of importance index is based on the variation of the aggregated value vs. the total variation of a given variable, the others being fixed. We may consider the variation induced by the mixed variation of two variables, or more. Considering again the bounded close interval $\mathbb{I} := [a,b]$, this is expressed by

$$\Delta_i(\Delta_j\mathbf{A})(\mathbf{x}) = \Delta_j(\Delta_i\mathbf{A})(\mathbf{x})$$

$$= \mathbf{A}(b_{\{i\}}b_{\{j\}}\mathbf{x}) - \mathbf{A}(b_{\{i\}}a_{\{j\}}\mathbf{x}) - \mathbf{A}(a_{\{i\}}b_{\{j\}}\mathbf{x}) + \mathbf{A}(a_{\{i\}}a_{\{j\}}\mathbf{x}).$$

We call this function the *second-order (total) variation of* $\mathbf{A}$ *with respect to coordinates i and j*, and we denote it by $\Delta_{ij}\mathbf{A}(\mathbf{x})$.

Applied to the minimum, maximum, and arithmetic mean in $[0, 1]^n$, we get

$$\Delta_{ij}\mathsf{Min}(\mathbf{x}) = \bigwedge_{k \in [n] \setminus \{i,j\}} x_k \geqslant 0,$$

$$\Delta_{ij}\mathsf{Max}(\mathbf{x}) = -1 + \bigvee_{k \in [n] \setminus \{i,j\}} x_k \leqslant 0,$$

$$\Delta_{ij}\mathsf{AM}(\mathbf{x}) = 0.$$

Clearly, the three aggregation functions are well distinguished, and we remark that a positive (respectively, negative) value is given to the conjunctive (respectively, disjunctive) aggregation function, while the arithmetic mean receives a zero value.

Going further, one can define higher-order variations of A. For any $\varnothing \neq K \subseteq [n]$, and $i \in [n] \setminus K$, we define inductively the *(total) variation of* A *at* $\mathbf{x}$ *with respect to* $K \cup \{i\}$ by $\Delta_{K \cup \{i\}}\mathsf{A}(\mathbf{x}) := \Delta_i(\Delta_K\mathsf{A})(\mathbf{x})$. An explicit formula is

$$\Delta_K\mathsf{A}(\mathbf{x}) = \sum_{L \subseteq K} (-1)^{|L|}\mathsf{A}(a_L b_{K \setminus L}\mathbf{x}). \tag{10.14}$$

Note that with $K := \{i\}$, we recover our definition of Δ_i. Also, for mathematical convenience we may allow $K = \varnothing$, putting $\Delta_\varnothing\mathsf{A} := \mathsf{A}$.

As for the importance index, we take the average of the relative variation over $\mathbb{I}^n$, and we call it the interaction index.

Definition 10.41. Let $a, b \in \mathbb{R}$ such that $a < b$, let A be an integrable aggregation function in $[a, b]^n$, and consider any subset $K \subseteq [n]$. The *interaction index of* K *on* A is defined by

$$I_K(\mathsf{A}) := \frac{1}{(b-a)^n} \int_{[a,b]^n} \frac{\Delta_K\mathsf{A}(\mathbf{x})}{b-a} \, d\mathbf{x}.$$

Taking $K = \{i\}$, the importance index of coordinate i is recovered; see Definition 10.29. Taking $K = \varnothing$, the (relative) average value $\overline{\mathsf{A}}/(b-a)$ is recovered; see Definition 10.2.

Proposition 10.42. *Let* A *be an aggregation function in* $\mathbb{I} := [0, 1]$. *Then for any* $\varnothing \neq K \subseteq [n]$,

$$I_K(\mathsf{A}^d) = (-1)^{|K|+1}I_K(\mathsf{A}).$$

Proof. It suffices to prove that $\Delta_K\mathsf{A}^d = (-1)^{|K|+1}\Delta_K\mathsf{A}$. We proceed by induction. By Proposition 10.30, it is true for $|K| = 1$. Suppose it holds up to $|K| = k$, $1 \leqslant k < n$, and consider $i \in [n] \setminus K$. Then

$$\Delta_{K \cup \{i\}}\mathsf{A}^d(\mathbf{x}) = \Delta_i(\Delta_K\mathsf{A}^d)(\mathbf{x})$$

$$= \Delta_i((-1)^{|K|+1}\Delta_K\mathsf{A})(1 - \mathbf{x})$$

$$= -(-1)^{|K|+1}(\Delta_{K \cup \{i\}}\mathsf{A})(1 - \mathbf{x}). \qquad \square$$

For $K = \varnothing$, see Proposition 10.4.

The reader may have noticed that the term "interaction" is already used in Chapter 5 for capacities; see Definition 5.13. The next proposition justifies this use.

Proposition 10.43. *Consider the Choquet integral $\mathcal{C}_\mu$ as an aggregation function in $[0,1]^n$, with μ a normalized capacity on $[n]$. Then, for any $K \subseteq [n]$, the interaction index $I_K(\mathcal{C}_\mu)$ is precisely the interaction transform $I^\mu(K)$, that is,*

$$I_K(\mathcal{C}_\mu) = I^\mu(K) = \sum_{L \subseteq [n] \setminus K} \frac{(n - |L| - |K|)! |L|!}{(n - |K| + 1)!} \sum_{L' \subseteq K} (-1)^{|K| - |L'|} \mu(L' \cup L). \quad (10.15)$$

Proof. For any $\mathbf{x} \in [0,1]^n$, by (5.27), we have

$$\mathcal{C}_\mu(\mathbf{x}) = \sum_{L \subseteq [n]} m^\mu(L) \bigwedge_{i \in L} x_i,$$

with m^μ the Möbius transform of μ, which gives

$$\Delta_K \mathcal{C}_\mu(\mathbf{x}) = \sum_{L \supseteq K} m^\mu(L) \bigwedge_{i \in L \setminus K} x_i.$$

Using Lemma 10.9 and then (5.15), we finally obtain

$$I_K(\mathcal{C}_\mu) = \int_{[0,1]^n} \Delta_K \mathcal{C}_\mu(\mathbf{x}) \, d\mathbf{x} = \sum_{L \supseteq K} \frac{1}{|L| - |K| + 1} m^\mu(L) = I^\mu(K),$$

which completes the proof. ☐

Remark 10.44. The interaction index $I^\mu(S)$ when $S = \{i, j\}$ was proposed by Murofushi and Soneda [329] in multicriteria decision making for the description of capacities, and even earlier by Owen [343] in game theory, under the name of *co-value*. It has a very useful interpretation since it depicts a kind of synergy between players or criteria. Specifically, considering the domain of multicriteria decision making:

(i) If criteria i, j have a positive interaction, the contribution of i, j to the overall score (value of the Choquet integral) is high only if both scores on i and j are high. This can easily be seen in (5.37), which is the Choquet integral for 2-additive capacities, that is, whose interaction index $I(S)$ is nonzero only for $|S| \leqslant 2$. Indeed, terms corresponding to positive interaction aggregate scores by Min. Criteria with a positive interaction are said to be *complementary*, since both criteria need to be satisfied (this term is borrowed from multiattribute utility theory; see [207]). Lastly, note that for Min, we have seen above that Δ_{ij}Min $\geqslant 0$.

(ii) If criteria i, j have a negative interaction, their contribution to the overall score is high if one of the scores on i, j is high. Again, this is clear from (5.37), since criteria with a negative interaction are aggregated by Max. These criteria are

Table 10.6. *Interaction index I_{ij} of some aggregation functions over $[0,1]^n$*

A	Name	$I_{ij}(A)$
$\text{WAM}_\mathbf{w}$	weighted arithmetic mean	0
$\text{WGM}_\mathbf{w}$	weighted geometric mean	$\displaystyle\prod_{k\in[n]\setminus\{i,j\}}\frac{\text{sign}\,(w_i w_j)}{w_k+1}$
$\mathcal{C}_\mu$	Choquet integral	$I^\mu(\{i,j\})$
MLE_μ	multilinear extension	$I_B^\mu(\{i,j\})$
$\text{OWA}_\mathbf{w}$	ordered weighted average	$\dfrac{w_1-w_n}{n-1}$
Min	minimum	$\dfrac{1}{n-1}$
Max	maximum	$-\dfrac{1}{n-1}$

said to be *substitutive* [207], which means that they play the same role. Finally, note that for Max, we have seen above that $\Delta_{ij}\text{Max}\leqslant 0$.

(iii) A null interaction means that the contribution of i,j is simply the sum of contributions of i and j, without any interaction between them. Such criteria are said to be *independent*. Note that in the above, $\Delta_{ij}\text{AM}(\mathbf{x})=0$ for all $\mathbf{x}$, hence its interaction index is null.

A more detailed interpretation of interaction indices can be found in [167].

Remark 10.45. As for the Shapley value, the interaction has been axiomatized by several authors, mainly by Grabisch and Roubens [172], and Fujimoto *et al.* [128].

Proposition 10.46. *Consider the multilinear extension* MLE_μ *as an aggregation function in* $[0,1]^n$, *with* μ *a normalized capacity on* $[n]$. *Then, for any* $K\subseteq[n]$, *the interaction index* $I_K(\text{MLE}_\mu)$ *is the Banzhaf interaction index* $I_B^\mu(K)$, *that is,*

$$I_K(\text{MLE}_\mu)=I_B^\mu(K):=\frac{1}{2^{n-|K|}}\sum_{L\subseteq[n]\setminus K}\sum_{L'\subseteq K}(-1)^{|K|-|L'|}\mu(L'\cup L).\qquad(10.16)$$

The proof is similar to that of Proposition 10.43. Propositions 10.43 and 10.46 were shown by Grabisch *et al.* [168].

Table 10.6 provides the interaction index I_{ij} of some aggregation functions over the domain $[0,1]^n$.

10.5 Maximum improving index

Another natural question arises in practical situations, concerning the influence of each variable on the output. Given an aggregation function $\text{A}:[0,1]^n\to[0,1]$, which coordinate(s) should we augment so as to get the maximum increase on the output value, considering all possible input vectors on the average?

For any $\varnothing \neq K \subseteq [n]$, let us denote by $W_K(\mathsf{A})$ the index quantifying the interest one has to augment the value of coordinates belonging to K in order to get a maximum augmentation on the output value of A. We construct this index step by step.

First, we suppose that W_K is linear and continuous, and we consider a family of *threshold aggregation functions* $\delta_{\mathbf{t}} : [0, 1]^n \to \{0, 1\}$, $\mathbf{t} \in [0, 1]^n$, defined by

$$\delta_{\mathbf{t}}(\mathbf{x}) = \begin{cases} 1 & \text{if } x_i \geqslant t_i, \quad i = 1, \ldots, n \\ 0 & \text{otherwise.} \end{cases}$$

Intuitively, $W_K(\delta_{\mathbf{t}})$ should be proportional to the number of vectors $\mathbf{x}$ of $[0, 1]^n$ such that the value $\delta_{\mathbf{t}}(\mathbf{x})$ goes from 0 to 1 if only the scores on coordinates in K are augmented. Specifically, let us introduce $T_{\mathbf{t}}$ the set of situations $(\mathbf{x}, \mathbf{y}) \in [0, 1]^n \times [0, 1]^n$ such that $\mathbf{y} \geqslant \mathbf{x}$, $\mathbf{x}$ and $\mathbf{y}$ coincide on $[n] \setminus K$, and $\delta_{\mathbf{t}}(\mathbf{x}) = 0$, $\delta_{\mathbf{t}}(\mathbf{y}) = 1$. The value $W_K(\delta_{\mathbf{t}})$ should be proportional to the Lebesgue measure of $T_{\mathbf{t}}$.

It remains to add a normalization axiom, saying that if A is the weighted arithmetic mean $\mathsf{WAM}_{\mathbf{w}}$, then $W_K(\mathsf{A}) = \sum_{i \in K} w_i$. These four simple and natural axioms uniquely determine W_K, which is

$$W_K(\mathsf{A}) = 3 \cdot 2^{|K|} \int_{\mathbf{x} \in [0,1]^n} \int_{\mathbf{y}_K \in [\mathbf{x}_K, 1]} (\mathsf{A}(\mathbf{y}_K \mathbf{x}) - \mathsf{A}(\mathbf{x})) \; d\mathbf{y}_K \, d\mathbf{x}$$

where $\mathbf{y}_K \in [\mathbf{x}_K, 1]$ is a shorthand for $y_i \in [x_i, 1]$ for all $i \in K$. When A is the Choquet integral, one obtains for $K = \{i\}$:

$$W_i(\mathcal{C}_\mu) = 6 \sum_{L \subseteq [n] \setminus \{i\}} \frac{(n - |L|)!(|L| + 1)!}{(n + 2)!} \left(\mu(L \cup \{i\}) - \mu(L) \right).$$

For $K = \{i, j\}$, one obtains in general

$$W_{ij}(\mathsf{A}) = W_i(\mathsf{A}) + W_j(\mathsf{A}),$$

but this additivity property fails once $|K| > 2$.

Remark 10.47. (i) This index has been proposed by Grabisch and Labreuche [160]. It is similar to, although different from the importance index of Section 10.3, and hence from the Shapley value. It can be shown that $W_i(\mathcal{C}_\mu) \leqslant 3\phi_i^\mu$.

(ii) It is possible to build in an analogous way an index which is specific to a given input $\mathbf{x} \in [0, 1]^n$, and not to an average over all possible inputs; see [243].

(iii) Marichal and Mathonet [282, Cor. 19] have shown that the $W_i(\mathcal{C}_\mu)$ coefficients are also exactly the dominant coefficients in the best approximation of the Choquet integral by a linear function.

10.6 Tolerance indices

Some internal aggregation functions are more or less intolerant (respectively, tolerant) in the sense that they are bounded from above (respectively, below) by one of the input values or by a function of these values.

In this section, we mainly deal with internal aggregation functions having veto and/or favor coordinates as well as k-conjunctive and k-disjunctive internal aggregation functions. Starting from the properties of these functions, we define indices that provide degrees to which an internal aggregation function is intolerant or tolerant.

10.6.1 Veto and favor indices

Grabisch [147] introduced in multicriteria decision making the following concepts of *veto* and *favor* criteria. To be context-free, we talk in terms of coordinates instead of criteria.

Definition 10.48. Let $A : \mathbb{I}^n \to \mathbb{I}$ be an internal aggregation function. A coordinate $j \in [n]$ is said to be a *veto* (respectively, a *favor*) for A if $A \leqslant P_j$ (respectively, $A \geqslant P_j$).

An internal aggregation function having a veto coordinate is intolerant in the sense that a low input value on that coordinate entails a low aggregated value. Similarly, an internal aggregation function having a favor coordinate is tolerant in the sense that a high input value on that coordinate entails a high aggregated value.

A consequence of these definitions is that no internal aggregation function can model simultaneously a veto on a coordinate and a favor on another one. Indeed, we clearly have

$$P_j \leqslant A \leqslant P_k \quad \Rightarrow \quad j = k.$$

However, if the same coordinate $j \in [n]$ is both a veto and a favor, then we obtain $A = P_j$.

Remark 10.49. The intolerance (respectively, tolerance) character of an internal aggregation function A having a veto (respectively, favor) coordinate can be interpreted through the concepts of andness and orness degrees; see Section 10.2.2. Indeed, it is clear from (10.3) and (10.4) that if a coordinate $j \in [n]$ is a veto (respectively, favor) for A then

$$\text{orness}(A) \leqslant \tfrac{1}{2} \quad (\text{respectively, orness}(A) \geqslant \tfrac{1}{2})$$

and

$$\overline{\text{lof}}_A \leqslant \tfrac{1}{2} \quad (\text{respectively, } \overline{\text{lof}}_A \geqslant \tfrac{1}{2}).$$

The following immediate result shows that we can restrict our investigation to the concept of veto coordinates.

Proposition 10.50. *Let* $\mathsf{A} : [0,1]^n \to [0,1]$ *be an internal aggregation function. A coordinate* $j \in [n]$ *is a veto (respectively, favor) for* A *if and only if it is a favor (respectively, veto) for* A^d.

Let $\mathsf{A} : [0,1]^n \to [0,1]$ be an internal aggregation function. It is clear that if $j \in [n]$ is a veto for A, then

$$\mathsf{A}(0_{\{j\}}\mathbf{x}) = 0 \tag{10.17}$$

for all $\mathbf{x} \in [0,1]^n$. Similarly, if $j \in [n]$ is a favor for A, then

$$\mathsf{A}(1_{\{j\}}\mathbf{x}) = 1 \tag{10.18}$$

for all $\mathbf{x} \in [0,1]^n$. The converse is not always true. For instance, the geometric mean GM on $[0,1]^n$ fulfills property (10.17) but has no veto coordinate.

Interestingly, it can be shown [273, 275] that, for any discrete Choquet integral on $[0,1]^n$ whose capacity is normalized, property (10.17) implies that j is a veto and property (10.18) implies that j is a favor.

Since they present rather extreme behaviors, veto and favor coordinates rarely occur in practical applications. It is then natural to define indices measuring the intensity (between 0 and 1) with which a given coordinate $j \in [n]$ behaves like a veto or a favor for a given internal aggregation function $\mathsf{A} : [0,1]^n \to \mathbb{R}$.

We consider a first definition.

Definition 10.51. Let $\mathsf{A} : [0,1]^n \to [0,1]$ be an internal aggregation function. The *probability-based veto* (respectively, *favor*) *index* of coordinate $j \in [n]$ for A is defined as

$$\text{pveto}(\mathsf{A},j) := P(\mathsf{A}(\mathbf{X}) \leqslant X_j) \qquad (\text{respectively, pfavor}(\mathsf{A},j) := P(\mathsf{A}(\mathbf{X}) \geqslant X_j)),$$

assuming that the random vector $\mathbf{X}$ is uniformly distributed on $[0,1]^n$.

Even though the indices introduced in Definition 10.51 are rather natural, they often lead to tedious computations.

An alternative approach consists in introducing indices measuring the extent to which properties (10.17) and (10.18) are satisfied. Of course, these indices should be used only with aggregation functions for which property (10.17) (respectively, (10.18)) implies that j is a veto (respectively, favor). For example, as we have already observed, the Choquet integral can be considered but not the geometric mean.

We first observe that properties (10.17) and (10.18) can respectively be rewritten as

$$\mathsf{A}(0_{\{j\}}\mathbf{x}) = \text{Min}(0_{\{j\}}\mathbf{x}), \qquad \forall \mathbf{x} \in [0,1]^n,$$

$$\mathsf{A}(1_{\{j\}}\mathbf{x}) = \text{Max}(1_{\{j\}}\mathbf{x}), \qquad \forall \mathbf{x} \in [0,1]^n.$$

This observation suggests the following approach; see Marichal [275]. For any internal aggregation function $\mathsf{A} : [0,1]^n \to [0,1]$ and any $j \in [n]$, we introduce the indices

$$\text{andness}(\mathsf{A} \mid X_j = 0) := \frac{E(\text{Max}(0_{\{j\}}\mathbf{X})) - E(\mathsf{A}(0_{\{j\}}\mathbf{X}))}{E(\text{Max}(0_{\{j\}}\mathbf{X})) - E(\text{Min}(0_{\{j\}}\mathbf{X}))},$$

$$\text{orness}(\mathsf{A} \mid X_j = 1) := \frac{E(\mathsf{A}(1_{\{j\}}\mathbf{X})) - E(\text{Min}(1_{\{j\}}\mathbf{X}))}{E(\text{Max}(1_{\{j\}}\mathbf{X})) - E(\text{Min}(1_{\{j\}}\mathbf{X}))},$$

where the random vector $\mathbf{X}$ is assumed to be uniformly distributed on $[0,1]^n$. By using Lemma 10.9, we can immediately rewrite these indices as

$$\text{andness}(\mathsf{A} \mid X_j = 0) = 1 - \frac{n}{n-1} E(\mathsf{A}(0_{\{j\}}\mathbf{X})), \tag{10.19}$$

$$\text{orness}(\mathsf{A} \mid X_j = 1) = \frac{n}{n-1} E(\mathsf{A}(1_{\{j\}}\mathbf{X})) - \frac{1}{n-1}. \tag{10.20}$$

Definition 10.52. Let $\mathsf{A} : [0,1]^n \to [0,1]$ be an internal aggregation function. The *veto* (respectively, *favor*) *index* of coordinate $j \in [n]$ for A is defined as

$$\text{veto}(\mathsf{A},j) := \text{andness}(\mathsf{A} \mid X_j = 0)$$

$$(\text{respectively, favor}(\mathsf{A},j) := \text{orness}(\mathsf{A} \mid X_j = 1)).$$

Considering the Choquet integral, we have the following result [273, 275]:

Proposition 10.53. *For any normalized capacity μ on $[n]$, we have*

$$\text{veto}(\mathcal{C}_\mu, j) = 1 - \sum_{K \subseteq [n] \setminus \{j\}} \frac{1}{(n-1)\binom{n-1}{|K|}} \mu(K)$$

$$= 1 - \sum_{K \subseteq [n] \setminus \{j\}} \frac{n}{(n-1)(|K|+1)} m^\mu(K),$$

$$\text{favor}(\mathcal{C}_\mu, j) = \sum_{K \subseteq [n] \setminus \{j\}} \frac{1}{(n-1)\binom{n-1}{|K|}} \mu(K \cup \{j\}) - \frac{1}{n-1}$$

$$= \sum_{K \subseteq [n] \setminus \{j\}} \frac{n}{(n-1)(|K|+1)} (m^\mu(K \cup \{j\}) + m^\mu(K)) - \frac{1}{n-1},$$

$$\frac{1}{n} \sum_{i=1}^{n} \text{veto}(\mathcal{C}_\mu, j) = \text{andness}(\mathcal{C}_\mu),$$

$$\frac{1}{n} \sum_{i=1}^{n} \text{favor}(\mathcal{C}_\mu, j) = \text{orness}(\mathcal{C}_\mu).$$

Table 10.7 provides the favor index of some Choquet integrals.

Let us now examine some properties of the veto and favor indices.

Table 10.7. *Favor index of some Choquet integrals*

$\mathcal{C}_\mu$	Name	favor$(\mathcal{C}_\mu, j)$
WAM$_\mathbf{w}$	weighted arithmetic mean	$\dfrac{1}{2} + \dfrac{nw_j - 1}{2(n-1)}$
OWA$_\mathbf{w}$	ordered weighted averaging	$\dfrac{1}{n-1}\displaystyle\sum_{i=1}^{n}(i-1)w_i$
OS$_k^-$	order statistic	$\dfrac{k-1}{n-1}$

Proposition 10.54. *Let* $A : [0,1]^n \to [0,1]$ *be an internal aggregation function and let* $j \in [n]$. *Then* $\text{veto}(A^d, j) = \text{favor}(A, j)$ *and* $\text{favor}(A^d, j) = \text{veto}(A, j)$.

Proof. We have $A^d(0_{\{j\}}\mathbf{x}) = 1 - A(1_{\{j\}}(1 - \mathbf{x}))$ and hence, using (10.19),

$$\text{veto}(A^d, j) = 1 - \frac{n}{n-1}\, E(A^d(0_{\{j\}}X))$$

$$= -\frac{1}{n-1} + \frac{n}{n-1}\, E(A(1_{\{j\}}X)) = \text{favor}(A, j).$$

The other identity follows immediately from $A^{dd} = A$. □

Proposition 10.55. *Let* $A : [0,1]^n \to [0,1]$ *be an internal aggregation function and let* $j \in [n]$. *Then we have*

$$\text{veto}(A, j) + \text{favor}(A, j) = 1 + \frac{n\phi_j(A) - 1}{n-1}.$$

Proof. Using (10.19) and (10.20), we obtain

$$\text{veto}(A, j) + \text{favor}(A, j)$$

$$= 1 + \frac{n}{n-1}\big(E(A(1_{\{j\}}X)) - E(A(0_{\{j\}}X))\big) - \frac{1}{n-1}$$

$$= 1 + \frac{n\phi_j(A) - 1}{n-1}.$$

□

The following corollary makes use of the weighted arithmetic mean defined from the concept of normalized importance index of an aggregation function; see Definition 10.36.

Corollary 10.56. *For any integrable and internal aggregation function* $A : [0, 1]^n \to \mathbb{R}$, *we have*

$$\frac{\text{veto}(A, j) + \text{favor}(A, j)}{2} = \text{veto}(\text{WAM}_{\overline{\phi}(A)}, j) = \text{favor}(\text{WAM}_{\overline{\phi}(A)}, j).$$

Proof. Since $\text{WAM}_{\overline{\phi}(A)}$ is merely a weighted arithmetic mean, we immediately have (see also Table 10.7)

$$\text{veto}(\text{WAM}_{\overline{\phi}(A)}, j) = \text{favor}(\text{WAM}_{\overline{\phi}(A)}, j) = \frac{1}{2}\left(1 + \frac{n\phi_j(A) - 1}{n - 1}\right).$$

We then conclude by Proposition 10.55. $\qquad\qquad\square$

10.6.2 *k-conjunction and k-disjunction indices*

Recall that an internal aggregation function $A : \mathbb{I}^n \to \mathbb{I}$ is k-conjunctive (respectively, k-disjunctive) for some $k \in [n]$ if $A \leqslant OS_k$ (respectively, $A \geqslant OS_{n-k+1}$); see Definitions 2.49 and 2.50.

From this definition and the concepts introduced in this section, we can immediately derive the following facts:

 (i) If an internal aggregation function $A : \mathbb{I}^n \to \mathbb{I}$ is k-conjunctive and l-disjunctive for some $k, l \in [n]$, then necessarily $k + l \geqslant n + 1$.
 (ii) If an internal aggregation function $A : [0, 1]^n \to [0, 1]$ is k-conjunctive (respectively, k-disjunctive) for some $k \in [n]$, then A^d is k-disjunctive (respectively, k-conjunctive).
 (iii) If an internal aggregation function $A : [0, 1]^n \to [0, 1]$ is k-conjunctive for some $k \in [n]$ then $\overline{A} \leqslant \overline{OS}_k$, andness$(A) \geqslant$ andness(OS_k), orness$(A) \leqslant$ orness(OS_k), veto$(A, j) \geqslant$ veto(OS_k, j), favor$(A, j) \leqslant$ favor(OS_k, j), and similarly if A is k-disjunctive.

It is clear that, for any internal aggregation function $A : [0, 1]^n \to [0, 1]$, k-conjunctiveness implies

$$A(\mathbf{x}) = 0 \text{ for all } \mathbf{x} \in [0, 1]^n \text{ such that } x_{(k)} = 0, \qquad (10.21)$$

and, similarly, k-disjunctiveness implies

$$A(\mathbf{x}) = 1 \text{ for all } \mathbf{x} \in [0, 1]^n \text{ such that } x_{(n-k+1)} = 1. \qquad (10.22)$$

The converse is not always true. For instance, the geometric mean GM on $[0, 1]^n$ satifies property (10.21) but for each k it is not k-conjunctive (compare the values of GM and OS_k at the point $x_{[n-1]}1$). However, it can be shown [275] that, for any discrete Choquet integral on $[0, 1]^n$ whose capacity is normalized, k-conjunctiveness is equivalent to (10.21) and, similarly, k-disjunctiveness is equivalent to (10.22).

Just as for veto and favor indices, it seems interesting to introduce indices measuring the degree to which a given internal aggregation function is k-conjunctive or k-disjunctive. Again, we can think of a probability-based approach.

Definition 10.57. Let $A : [0, 1]^n \to [0, 1]$ be an internal aggregation function and let $k \in [n]$. The *probability-based k-conjunctiveness* (respectively, *k-disjunctiveness*) *index* for A is defined as

$$\text{pconj}_k(A) := P(A(\mathbf{X}) \leqslant X_{(k)})$$

$$(\text{respectively}, \text{pdisj}_k(A) := P(A(\mathbf{X}) \geqslant X_{(n-k+1)})),$$

assuming that $\mathbf{X}$ is uniformly distributed on $[0, 1]^n$.

Similarly to the probability-based veto and favor indices, the probability-based k-conjunctiveness and k-disjunctiveness indices, although rather natural, lead to tedious computations. Instead, we define indices measuring the extent to which conditions (10.21) and (10.22) are fulfilled.

First define the following conditional expectations:

$$E(A \mid X_{(k)} = 0) := \frac{1}{\binom{n}{k}} \sum_{\substack{K \subseteq [n] \\ |K|=k}} E(\mathbf{0}_K \mathbf{X}),$$

$$E(A \mid X_{(n-k+1)} = 1) := \frac{1}{\binom{n}{k}} \sum_{\substack{K \subseteq [n] \\ |K|=k}} E(\mathbf{1}_K \mathbf{X}).$$

Now, proceeding as for veto and favor indices, we introduce (assuming $k < n$)

$$\text{andness}(A \mid X_{(k)} = 0) := \frac{n-k+1}{n-k} E(A \mid X_{(k)} = 0),$$

$$\text{orness}(A \mid X_{(n-k+1)} = 1) := \frac{n-k+1}{n-k} E(A \mid X_{(n-k+1)} = 1) - \frac{1}{n-k}.$$

Definition 10.58. Let $A : [0, 1]^n \to [0, 1]$ be an internal aggregation function and let $k \in [n - 1]$. The *k-conjunctiveness* (respectively, *k-disjunctiveness*) *index* for A is defined as

$$\text{conj}_k(A) := \text{andness}(A \mid X_{(k)} = 0)$$

$$(\text{respectively}, \text{disj}_k(A) := \text{orness}(A \mid X_{(n-k+1)} = 1)).$$

Proposition 10.59. *Let $A : [0, 1]^n \to [0, 1]$ be an internal aggregation function and let $k \in [n - 1]$. Then* $\text{conj}_k(A^d) = \text{disj}_k(A)$ *and* $\text{disj}_k(A^d) = \text{conj}_k(A)$.

Table 10.8. *k-conjunctiveness index of some Choquet integrals*

$\mathcal{C}_\mu$	Name	$\mathrm{conj}_k(\mathcal{C}_\mu)$
$\mathrm{WAM_w}$	weighted arithmetic mean	$\dfrac{n+k-1}{2n}$
$\mathrm{OWA_w}$	ordered weighted averaging	$1 - \displaystyle\sum_{i=k}^{n} \dfrac{i-k}{n-k}\, w_i$
OS_i	order statistic	$1 - \dfrac{(i-k)^+}{n-k}$

Considering the Choquet integral, we have the following result [275]:

Proposition 10.60. *For any normalized capacity μ on $[n]$ and $k \in [n-1]$, we have*

$$\mathrm{conj}_k(\mathcal{C}_\mu) = 1 - \frac{1}{n-k} \sum_{j=0}^{n-k} \frac{1}{\binom{n}{j}} \sum_{\substack{J \subseteq [n] \\ |J|=j}} \mu(J),$$

$$\mathrm{disj}_k(\mathcal{C}_\mu) = \frac{1}{n-k} \sum_{j=k}^{n} \frac{1}{\binom{n}{j}} \sum_{\substack{J \subseteq [n] \\ |J|=j}} \mu(J) - \frac{1}{n-k}.$$

Table 10.8 provides the k-conjunctiveness index of some Choquet integrals.

10.7 Measures of arguments contribution and involvement

Given an aggregation function $\mathsf{A} : [a,b]^n \to [a,b]$, we consider in this section the following two indices:

 (i) *The index of uniformity of arguments contribution*, which measures the uniformity of contribution of the n components of $\mathbf{x} \in \mathbb{I}^n$ in the computation of the aggregated value $\mathsf{A}(\mathbf{x})$.
 (ii) *The index of arguments involvement*, which measures the proportion of arguments among $x_1, \ldots, x_n$ that are involved in the computation of the aggregated value $\mathsf{A}(\mathbf{x})$.

10.7.1 Index of uniformity of arguments contribution

To better illustrate what we mean by uniformity of the contribution of the arguments, let us consider the classical weighted arithmetic mean $\mathsf{WAM_w}$. When $\mathbf{w} = \mathbf{1}_{\{1\}}$, we get the projection onto the first argument, that is, $\mathsf{WAM_w} = \mathsf{P}_1$. When $\mathbf{w} = \frac{1}{n}\mathbf{1}$, we get the symmetric arithmetic mean $\mathsf{WAM_w} = \mathsf{AM}$.

Both P_1 and AM have the same expected and orness values; see Section 10.2. However, they strongly differ by the fact that only the first argument x_1 is utilized in the calculation of $P_1(x)$, whereas all the arguments in x contribute evenly in the calculation of $AM(x)$.

To measure the degree of uniformity of contribution of the arguments in x to produce $WAM_w(x)$, it is natural to consider the normalized *Shannon entropy* of the weight vector w, that is,

$$H_S(w) = -\frac{1}{\ln n} \sum_{i=1}^{n} w_i \ln w_i,$$

with the convention that $0 \ln 0 := 0$. Thus defined, $H_S(w)$ lies in the unit interval $[0, 1]$ and measures the *uniformity* (or *evenness*, *regularity*, *dispersion*) of the components of w. In the extreme cases, we have $H_S(1_{\{i\}}) = 0$ for all $i \in [n]$ and $H_S(\frac{1}{n}1) = 1$.

This motivates the following definition.

Definition 10.61. Let $a, b \in \mathbb{R}$ such that $a < b$. Given an integrable aggregation function A in $[a, b]^n$, the *index of uniformity of arguments contribution*, associated with A, is defined as

$$AC(A) := H_S(\overline{\phi}_1(A), \ldots, \overline{\phi}_n(A)),$$

where $\overline{\phi}_i(A)$ is the normalized importance index of coordinate i on A; see Definition 10.29.

Thus defined, the index $AC(A)$ somehow measures the uniformity of the increasing monotonicity of the aggregation function A. Clearly, when A is symmetric, the index of uniformity of arguments contribution is maximum, that is, $AC(A) = 1$.

Remark 10.62. This index was already proposed in 1999 by Yager [439, 440] in the special case where A is the Choquet integral C_μ. More precisely, for any normalized capacity μ on $[n]$, Yager considered the value $H_S(\phi_1^\mu, \ldots, \phi_n^\mu)$ as an uncertainty index associated with the capacity μ, where ϕ_i^μ is the Shapley value for i associated with μ. Now, we can observe from Proposition 10.31 and Definition 10.61 that this value is exactly $AC(C_\mu)$.

The following result immediately follows from Proposition 10.30.

Proposition 10.63. *For any aggregation function* A *in* $[0, 1]^n$, *we have* $AC(A^d) = AC(A)$.

10.7.2 Index of arguments involvement

Consider the ordered weighted averaging function $OWA_w(x) = \sum_i w_i x_{(i)}$. When $w = 1_{\{1\}}$, we get the minimum function $OWA_w = Min$. When $w = \frac{1}{n}1_{[n]}$, we get the symmetric arithmetic mean $OWA_w = AM$. Since both functions are symmetric, we immediately have $AC(Min) = AC(AM) = 1$, which means that all the arguments contribute with the same strength in the calculation of the aggregated value.

However, we can observe that Min renders only one argument (the smallest) whereas AM renders a uniform combination of all the arguments. Thus, it seems interesting to define an index measuring the proportion of arguments involved in the computation of the aggregated value.

For the function $\mathsf{OWA}_\mathbf{w}$, it is natural to consider the normalized Shannon entropy of the weight vector $\mathbf{w}$, that is, $H_S(\mathbf{w})$. Using this index, we get 0 for Min and 1 for AM, which reflects the degree of involvement of the arguments in the aggregated value.

To build an appropriate index for a given aggregation function A in $[a, b]^n$, we make use of the "lowest relative variations of A with respect to ranks" (see Definition 10.38):

Definition 10.64. Let $a, b \in \mathbb{R}$ such that $a < b$. Given an aggregation function A in $[a, b]^n$, the *index of arguments involvement*, associated with A, is defined as

$$\mathrm{AI}(\mathsf{A}) := \frac{1}{(b-a)^n} \int_{[a,b]^n} H_S\big(\Theta_{(1)}\mathsf{A}(\mathbf{x}), \ldots, \Theta_{(n)}\mathsf{A}(\mathbf{x})\big) \, d\mathbf{x},$$

where, for any $k \in [n]$, $\Theta_{(k)}\mathsf{A}(\mathbf{x})$ is the lowest relative variation of A with respect to rank k; see Definition 10.38.

Again, by dividing $[a, b]^n$ into the simplices $[a, b]_\sigma^n$ ($\sigma \in \mathfrak{S}_{[n]}$), we can write

$$\mathrm{AI}(\mathsf{A}) = \frac{1}{(b-a)^n} \sum_{\sigma \in \mathfrak{S}_{[n]}} \int_{[a,b]_\sigma^n} H_S\big(\Theta_{(1)}\mathsf{A}(\mathbf{x}), \ldots, \Theta_{(n)}\mathsf{A}(\mathbf{x})\big) \, d\mathbf{x}$$

$$= \frac{1}{n!} \sum_{\sigma \in \mathfrak{S}_{[n]}} H_S\big(\Theta_{\sigma(1)}\mathsf{A}, \ldots, \Theta_{\sigma(n)}\mathsf{A}\big).$$

When A is the Choquet integral $\mathcal{C}_\mu$ with respect to a capacity μ, we simply have (see also Kojadinovic *et al.* [228])

$$\mathrm{AI}(\mathcal{C}_\mu) = \frac{1}{n!} \sum_{\sigma \in \mathfrak{S}_{[n]}} H_S(p_\sigma^\mu), \tag{10.23}$$

where p_σ^μ is a vector in $[0, 1]^n$ whose ith component is

$$p_\sigma^\mu(i) = \mu(\{\sigma(i), \ldots, \sigma(n)\}) - \mu(\{\sigma(i+1), \ldots, \sigma(n)\}).$$

It is noteworthy that this index can also be rewritten as

$$\mathrm{AI}(\mathcal{C}_\mu) = \frac{1}{\ln n} \sum_{i \in [n]} \sum_{K \subseteq [n] \setminus \{i\}} \frac{(n - |K| - 1)! \, |K|!}{n!} h\big(\mu(K \cup \{i\}) - \mu(K)\big), \tag{10.24}$$

where $h(x) = -x \ln x$, with the convention that $h(0) = 0$.

Table 10.9 provides the index of uniformity of arguments contribution and the index of arguments involvement for some Choquet integrals.

Table 10.9. *Index of uniformity of arguments contribution and index of arguments involvement for some Choquet integrals*

A	Name	AC(A)	AI(A)
AM	arithmetic mean	1	1
WAM$_\mathbf{w}$	weighted arithmetic mean	$H_S(\mathbf{w})$	$H_S(\mathbf{w})$
OWA$_\mathbf{w}$	ordered weighted averaging	1	$H_S(\mathbf{w})$
P$_i$	projection	0	0
OS$_k$	order statistic	1	0

Remark 10.65. The index AI($\mathcal{C}_\mu$), as given in (10.23) and (10.24), was introduced in 1998 by Marichal [262, 271] as the entropy of a Choquet capacity. This index proved to have very nice properties extending those of the classical Shannon entropy; see Marichal and Roubens [291]. For instance, if $\mathcal{C}_\mu(\mathbf{x}) \in \{x_1, \ldots, x_n\}$ for all $\mathbf{x} \in [a, b]^n$, then AI($\mathcal{C}_\mu$) $= 0$, which means that the involvement of the arguments in the aggregated value is minimum. A comparative study between Marichal's entropy AI($\mathcal{C}_\mu$) and Yager's entropy AC($\mathcal{C}_\mu$) (see Remark 10.62 above) can also be found in [291]. For example, using the concavity property of $h(x) = -x \ln x$, it was proved therein that AI($\mathcal{C}_\mu$) $\leqslant$ AC($\mathcal{C}_\mu$), for any capacity μ.

11

Identification of aggregation functions

11.1 Introduction

The major part of this book is devoted to studying the main classes of aggregation functions, their properties and their construction. A deep understanding of them is necessary to tackle applications, in order to choose – in some sense fixed by the user – the best aggregation function. Yet, it is unlikely that this will suffice to determine in a unique way the aggregation function that best fits a given problem. Properties are merely guidelines to select a family of suitable aggregation functions, e.g., we could deduce that we need a t-norm of the Frank family, an ordered weighted averaging (OWA) function, or a Choquet integral with respect to a capacity exhibiting a positive interaction between criteria 1 and 3. What remains unreachable is the knowledge of the best individual(s) in this family for our problem of interest, that is, the best parameter $\lambda \in [0, \infty]$ of the Frank family, the best weights of the OWA function, and the best capacity for the Choquet integral. By *identification*, we mean precisely this process of complete determination of the best aggregation function.

The identification can be achieved only if one has at hand a sufficient amount of information, as pairs of input/output data, and some criterion or objective function (e.g., minimize the total squared error). In some cases, the identification is not perfect, in the sense that a unique aggregation function is not produced, but a (usually infinite and convex) set of possible aggregation functions. Then, a choice in this set can be achieved on the basis of some additional criterion, for example by maximizing the entropy of the parameters of the aggregation function.

Defined in such a way, identification amounts to an optimization problem. Since optimization is a vast area by itself, clearly out of our scope in this book, we will not go deeply into the details. Our aim is merely to show the different ways the identification problem can be written, for different classes of aggregation functions, and to which type of optimization problem it refers. Further details can be found in the references and in classical books on optimization.

11.2 General formulation

11.2.1 The identification problem

Let us denote by $\mathsf{A} : \mathbb{I}^n \to \mathbb{I}$ the aggregation function which has to be identified. For simplicity, we assume that A has a fixed arity, say n. This is the most common case in practice. Considering extended aggregation functions could make the problem much more complex, especially if the aggregation function is weighted. Also, we consider that $\mathbb{I} := [0, 1]$.

The identification problem is defined by three ingredients:

(i) The kind of information used for the identification of A.
(ii) The variables or parameters to be identified.
(iii) The criterion or objective function to be minimized/maximized with respect to these variables, and most often a set of inequalities to be satisfied (constraints).

In most cases, it is assumed that the information is given in the form of pairs of input/output values $(\mathbf{x}^k, y^k)$, $k = 1, \ldots, l$, where y^k is the desired result of the aggregation when the input is $\mathbf{x}^k$.

Remark 11.1. This assumption is not so natural in the context of decision making, more precisely, in preference representation (see Appendix B, Section B.1), where typically the information is of ordinal nature. Specifically, let $\mathbf{x}, \mathbf{x}' \in \mathbb{R}^n$ be vectors of scores of two alternatives $\mathbf{a}, \mathbf{a}'$ evaluated on n criteria. It is assumed that the decision maker is only able to tell whether $\mathbf{a}$ is preferable to $\mathbf{a}'$, or the converse, or both. More precise information, such as an overall score for $\mathbf{a}, \mathbf{a}'$ (which would constitute the desired output value for aggregation) is considered as unreliable. Hence, if $\mathbf{a}$ is preferred to $\mathbf{a}'$, the available information is merely $\mathsf{A}(\mathbf{x}) \geqslant \mathsf{A}(\mathbf{x}')$.

Additional information is possible, which specifies the kind of "behavior" of A. Here, indices presented in Chapter 10 can be used, which leads for example to the following kind of information: the andness of A, importance of coordinate i, interaction between i and j, veto index of coordinate i, etc., should be greater than some specified threshold or lie within some interval. Clearly, this information translates into constraints in the optimization problem.

The variables or parameters to be identified are those of the chosen family of aggregation functions, which uniquely determine an element of this family. For example, if the Frank family of t-norms is chosen, then the only parameter is $\lambda \in [0, \infty]$; see Example 3.27(i). If the family of continuous Archimedean t-norms is considered, then we have to identify an additive generator. Identification of a function can be turned into an optimization problem with a finite number of variables if the function is approximated by a given family of functions, such as linear functions, or spline functions. The same holds for any aggregation function with a generator, like quasi-arithmetic means, uninorms and nullnorms, etc. Note that in the latter cases, the values of the neutral element e of the uninorm, and of the annihilator a of the nullnorm, are also variables, unless fixed beforehand. Lastly, if A is the Choquet integral, the set of variables is the set of values of the capacity for the different subsets.

The criterion or objective function depends on the kind of information which is available. If pairs of input/output values $(\mathbf{x}^k, y^k)$, $k = 1, \ldots, l$, are given,[1] the most natural criterion is to minimize the L_p-norm of the difference between the desired output y^k and the actual output $\mathbf{A}(\mathbf{x}^k)$ (error):

$$J_p := \Big(\sum_{k=1}^{l} |\mathbf{A}(\mathbf{x}^k) - y^k|^p \Big)^{\frac{1}{p}} \tag{11.1}$$

for some $p \geqslant 1$. If $p = 1$, we obtain the least absolute deviation problem, which is often used in robust regression, since it is less sensitive to outliers. If $p = 2$, we get the classical least squares problem. Taking $p = \infty$ amounts to minimizing the maximal absolute deviation:

$$J_\infty = \max_{k=1}^{l} |\mathbf{A}(\mathbf{x}^k) - y^k|.$$

The case $p = 2$ leads to a quadratic program, while the cases $p = 1$ and $p = \infty$ can be turned into a linear program. Indeed, for $p = 1$, it suffices to use the auxiliary nonnegative variables z_+^k, z_-^k defined by $z_+^k - z_-^k = \mathbf{A}(\mathbf{x}^k) - y^k$, $z_+^k + z_-^k = |\mathbf{A}(\mathbf{x}^k) - y^k|$, $k = 1, \ldots, l$. For $p = \infty$, the criterion is to minimize ε under the constraints

$$\varepsilon \geqslant \mathbf{A}(\mathbf{x}^k) - y^k, \quad k = 1, \ldots, l,$$

$$\varepsilon \geqslant -\mathbf{A}(\mathbf{x}^k) + y^k, \quad k = 1, \ldots, l.$$

Such error criteria cannot be used if the available information is only ordinal, e.g., coming from preference representation problems; see Remark 11.1. In such cases, other objective functions have to be found, such as the maximum separation between alternatives, dispersion criteria, etc. This case will be addressed in Section 11.5, devoted to the Choquet integral.

The set of constraints should contain all requirements proper to the given family of aggregation functions, as well as those coming from some additional information related to the desired behavior of the aggregation function. Concerning the former, one should not forget to express as constraints the basic requirements of any aggregation function, that is, nondecreasing monotonicity with respect to each coordinate, as well as $\mathbf{A}(\mathbf{0}) = 0$ and $\mathbf{A}(\mathbf{1}) = 1$.

11.2.2 Least squares regression

Before detailing the most important particular cases in the sequel, we recall basic results on least squares estimation, since this is a central tool in this chapter. These can be found in many textbooks, e.g., [21].

---

[1] By commodity, in the whole chapter, the superscript on input/output values $\mathbf{x}$, y, etc., indicates the numbering.

First, we consider the simple (one-dimensional) linear regression problem. Data are pairs (x^k, y^k), $k = 1, \ldots, l$, and the model is assumed to be

$$y = \beta_0 + \beta_1 x + \varepsilon \tag{11.2}$$

with β_1, β_0 two unknown real constants, and ε is the error term. Least squares linear regression gives the best constants β_1, β_0 which minimize the total squared error $J_2^2 = \sum_{k=1}^{l} (\varepsilon^k)^2$, with

$$\varepsilon^k := y^k - \beta_0 - \beta_1 x^k, \quad k = 1, \ldots, l.$$

Solving $\partial J_2^2 / \partial \beta_1 = 0$ and $\partial J_2^2 / \partial \beta_0 = 0$ yields

$$\hat{\beta}_1 = \frac{\sum_k x^k y^k - (\sum_k x^k)(\sum_k y^k)/l}{\sum_k (x^k)^2 - (\sum_k x^k)^2 / l}, \tag{11.3}$$

$$\hat{\beta}_0 = \bar{y} - \hat{\beta}_1 \bar{x}, \tag{11.4}$$

with $\bar{x} := \frac{1}{l} \sum_k x^k$, and $\bar{y} := \frac{1}{l} \sum_k y^k$. When $\beta_0 = 0$ in the model, the above formula reduces to

$$\hat{\beta}_1 = \frac{\sum_k x^k y^k}{\sum_k (x^k)^2}. \tag{11.5}$$

We now consider the multiple linear regression problem. The model reads

$$y = \beta_0 + \beta_1 x_1 + \cdots + \beta_n x_n + \varepsilon.$$

We use the following matrix-like notation for the data:

$$\mathbf{y}^T := \begin{bmatrix} y^1 & \cdots & y^l, \end{bmatrix}$$

$$\mathbf{X}^T := \begin{bmatrix} \mathbf{x}_1^T & \cdots & \mathbf{x}_l^T, \end{bmatrix}$$

with $\mathbf{x}_k := \begin{bmatrix} 1 & x_1^k & \cdots & x_n^k \end{bmatrix}$, $k = 1, \ldots, l$. We introduce also

$$\boldsymbol{\beta}^T := \begin{bmatrix} \beta_0 & \beta_1 & \cdots & \beta_n \end{bmatrix}, \quad \boldsymbol{\epsilon}^T := \begin{bmatrix} \varepsilon^1 & \cdots & \varepsilon^l \end{bmatrix}.$$

Then we have

$$\mathbf{y} = \mathbf{X}\boldsymbol{\beta} + \boldsymbol{\epsilon}.$$

We minimize $\boldsymbol{\epsilon}^T \boldsymbol{\epsilon} = (\mathbf{y} - \mathbf{X}\boldsymbol{\beta})^T (\mathbf{y} - \mathbf{X}\boldsymbol{\beta})$ versus $\boldsymbol{\beta}$, which amounts to minimizing

$$J_2^2 = \boldsymbol{\beta}^T \mathbf{X}^T \mathbf{X} \boldsymbol{\beta} - 2\boldsymbol{\beta}^T \mathbf{X}^T \mathbf{y}. \tag{11.6}$$

Because the quadratic function defined by (11.6) is convex, a necessary and sufficient condition for optimality is that the gradient vanishes. Differentiating J_2^2 with respect to β and equating $\partial J_2^2 / \partial \beta$ to zero, we get the normal equation

$$\mathbf{X}^T \mathbf{X} \boldsymbol{\beta} = \mathbf{X}^T \mathbf{y}. \qquad (11.7)$$

If $\mathbf{X}$ is of rank $n + 1$, then $\mathbf{X}^T \mathbf{X}$ is positive definite, and so is nonsingular. Then the unique solution to (11.7) is

$$\hat{\boldsymbol{\beta}} = (\mathbf{X}^T \mathbf{X})^{-1} \mathbf{X}^T \mathbf{y}. \qquad (11.8)$$

If the parameter vector β is subject to some linear equality contraint $\mathbf{A}\boldsymbol{\beta} = \mathbf{c}$, by using the Lagrangian multiplier technique, it is still possible to find an explicit solution. However, if there is some inequality constraint on β, like nonnegativity, then it is no longer possible to get an explicit solution. Unfortunately, this is most often the case when identifying aggregation functions. Then quadratic programming algorithms have to be used. A quadratic program has the following form:

$$\text{Minimize } \frac{1}{2} \boldsymbol{\beta}^T \mathbf{D} \boldsymbol{\beta} + \mathbf{c}^T \boldsymbol{\beta}$$

$$\text{Subject to } \mathbf{A}\boldsymbol{\beta} \leqslant \mathbf{b}$$

where the objective function is $\frac{1}{2} J_2^2$, and constraints are linear inequalities. We indicate in Section 11.6 some available algorithms.

11.3 The case of parametrized families of aggregation functions

We suppose that a certain family of aggregation functions, depending on a vector of parameters $\theta \in \Theta$, has been chosen beforehand (e.g., a Frank t-norm (see Example 3.27(i)), a gamma operator of Zimmermann and Zysno (see Section 3.8), an ordered weighted averaging (OWA) function (see (1.19)) or some other weighted aggregation function). Let us denote this family by $\{\mathsf{A}_\theta\}_{\theta \in \Theta}$.

We also suppose that our information is given by pairs of input/output data $(\mathbf{x}^k, y^k)$, $k = 1, \ldots, l$, and that the criterion is the L_2-norm (least squared error). Then the optimization problems reads

$$\text{Minimize } \sum_{k=1}^{l} \left(\mathsf{A}_\theta(\mathbf{x}^k) - y^k \right)^2 \qquad (11.9)$$

$$\text{Subject to } \theta \in \Theta.$$

The exact type of optimization problem depends of course on the family, and may be often nonlinear and difficult to solve in an exact way. We give some simple examples, borrowed from Beliakov [30].

Linear convex T–S-operators   (see Section 3.8(iii)) This family is defined by

$$\mathsf{L}_{\mathsf{T},\mathsf{S},\gamma}(\mathbf{x}) := (1 - \gamma)\mathsf{T}(\mathbf{x}) + \gamma \mathsf{S}(\mathbf{x}),$$

the parameter being $\gamma \in [0, 1]$, and T, S are a t-norm and a t-conorm, respectively. This is a simple linear regression problem (see (11.2)) with $\beta_0 = 0$, $\beta_1 = \gamma$, $x = \mathsf{S}(\mathbf{x}^k) - \mathsf{T}(\mathbf{x}^k)$ and $y = y^k - \mathsf{T}(\mathbf{x}^k)$. Hence by (11.5), we immediately get

$$\hat{\gamma} = \frac{\sum_{k=1}^{l} \left(y^k - \mathsf{T}(\mathbf{x}^k)\right)\left(\mathsf{S}(\mathbf{x}^k) - \mathsf{T}(\mathbf{x}^k)\right)}{\sum_{k=1}^{l} \left(\mathsf{S}(\mathbf{x}^k) - \mathsf{T}(\mathbf{x}^k)\right)^2}. \tag{11.10}$$

However, $\hat{\gamma}$ must belong to $[0, 1]$. If this is not the case, γ is chosen as either 0 or 1, whichever gives the smallest error.

Of course, the above technique can be generalized to any convex combination of aggregation functions, with weights $\gamma_1, \ldots, \gamma_p \in [0, 1]$, $\sum_{j=1}^{p} \gamma_j = 1$, using the solution (11.8) of the multiple linear regression model. However, the constraints on the γ_i's can no longer be handled as simply as in the one-dimensional case. It is necessary to use quadratic programming algorithms to get the solution.

Taking the n projections as aggregation functions, we recover the case of the weighted arithmetic mean. This shows that even for one of the simplest and most common aggregation functions, no explicit formula can be found, and mathematical programming techniques have to be employed.

Exponential convex T–S-operators   (see Section 3.8(ii)) This family is defined by

$$\mathsf{E}_{\mathsf{T},\mathsf{S},\gamma}(\mathbf{x}) := (\mathsf{T}(\mathbf{x}))^{1-\gamma}(\mathsf{S}(\mathbf{x}))^{\gamma},$$

the parameter being $\gamma \in [0, 1]$. The same process can be applied to the family after taking the logarithm. Hence the solution becomes[2]

$$\hat{\gamma} = \frac{\sum_{k=1}^{l} \left(\log y^k - \log(\mathsf{T}(\mathbf{x}^k))\right)\left(\log(\mathsf{S}(\mathbf{x}^k)) - \log(\mathsf{T}(\mathbf{x}^k))\right)}{\sum_{k=1}^{l} \left(\log(\mathsf{S}(\mathbf{x}^k)) - \log(\mathsf{T}(\mathbf{x}^k))\right)^2}. \tag{11.11}$$

Note that taking $\mathsf{T} = \Pi$ and $\mathsf{S} = \mathsf{S}_P$, we recover the gamma operator of Zimmermann and Zysno; see Section 3.8(i).

As above, the process can be generalized to any number of terms. This in particular permits solving the case of the weighted geometric mean.

Ordered weighted averaging (OWA) functions   (see (11.2)) This family is defined by

$$\mathsf{OWA}_{\mathbf{w}}(\mathbf{x}) := \sum_{i=1}^{n} w_i x_{\sigma(i)},$$

with $\mathbf{w} \in [0, 1]^n$, $\sum_{i=1}^{n} w_i = 1$, and σ is a permutation on $[n]$ such that $x_{\sigma(1)} \leqslant \cdots \leqslant x_{\sigma(n)}$. By introducing $z_i^k := x_{\sigma(i)}^k$ for $i = 1, \ldots, n$ and $k = 1, \ldots, l$, the identification of

---

[2] Note however that $\hat{\gamma}$ minimizes the squared additive error on $\log y$. Hence it is only an approximation of the optimal solution for y, in the least squares sense.

the ordered weighted averaging function amounts to the identification of a weighted arithmetic mean with data $(\mathbf{z}^k, y^k)_{k=1,\ldots,l}$.

11.4 The case of generated aggregation functions

We choose Archimedean continuous t-norms (see Section 3.3.5) as representatives of this class of functions. We will address the other cases more briefly.

Also in this section, we assume that the available information is given by pairs of input/output data $(\mathbf{x}^k, y^k)$, $k = 1, \ldots, l$, and that the criterion is the L_2-norm (least squares error).

We know from Theorem 3.36 that any continuous Archimedean t-norm T has an additive generator $t : [0, 1] \to [0, \infty]$, which is continuous and strictly decreasing with $t(1) = 0$, i.e.,

$$\mathsf{T}(\mathbf{x}) = t^{-1}\Big(\mathrm{Min}\big(t(0), \sum_{i=1}^{n} t(x_i)\big)\Big). \tag{11.12}$$

Moreover, t is unique up to a multiplicative constant, and T is strict if $t(0) = \infty$, otherwise it is nilpotent. Hence, it is enough to consider $t(0) := 1$ if the t-norm is nilpotent, otherwise we set $t(\varepsilon) := 1$, with ε defined later on.

Since the convergence of a sequence of additive generators on $]0, 1]$ is equivalent to the convergence of the corresponding t-norms (see Theorem 3.57), it is possible to fit continuous Archimedean t-norms to data by approximating their generators on $]0, 1]$.

Beliakov has proposed using splines to approximate the additive generator; see [29–31] for details, as well as the monograph [32]. Specifically, t is approximated by a spline S, given as a linear combination of some basis functions B_j:

$$S(x) = \sum_{j=1}^{m} c_j B_j(x).$$

It is enough to use linear splines (i.e., piecewise linear functions) in general, although higher-order splines can be used if some smoothness condition has to be satisfied. Also, the knots (places where the linear pieces are joined together) are fixed beforehand. It remains to determine the coefficients c_j so as to minimize the error criterion.

It is shown in [29] that in order to get a strictly decreasing function, this amounts to choosing negative coefficients $c_j, j = 1, \ldots, m$, if the basis $\{B_j\}_{j=1,\ldots,m}$ is suitably chosen: it suffices to take

$$B_j(x) := \sum_{l=j}^{m} N_l^{k+1}(x), \quad j = 1, \ldots, m.$$

where $N_1^{k+1}, \ldots, N_m^{k+1}$ are the B-splines of order $k + 1$. Boundary requirements for t translate into

$$\sum_{j=1}^{m} c_j B_j(1) = 0,$$

$$\sum_{j=1}^{m} c_j B_j(0) = 1 \quad \text{(for nilpotent t-norms)}, \quad \sum_{j=1}^{m} c_j B_j(\varepsilon) = 1 \quad \text{(for strict t-norms)}.$$

Beliakov takes the following definition for the error of the kth datum:

$$e^k := \sum_{i=1}^{n} t(x_i^k) - t(y^k),$$

for $k = 1, \ldots, l$. Note that this is not the error $\mathsf{T}(\mathbf{x}^k) - y^k$ which is used in (11.1), but its transform by t, up to the fact that we may have $\sum_{i=1}^{n} t(x_i^k) > t(0) = 1$. Replacing t by its spline approximation, we get

$$e'^k := \sum_{i=1}^{n} \left(\sum_{j=1}^{m} c_j B_j(x_i^k) \right) - \sum_{j=1}^{m} c_j B_j(y^k)$$

$$= \sum_{j=1}^{m} c_j \left(\sum_{i=1}^{n} B_j(x_i^k) - B_j(y^k) \right),$$

for $k = 1, \ldots, l$. Finally, the optimization problem is

Minimize $\displaystyle\sum_{k=1}^{l} (e'^k)^2$

Subject to $\displaystyle\sum_{j=1}^{m} c_j B_j(1) = 0$

$$\sum_{j=1}^{m} c_j B_j(0) = 1 \quad \text{(nilpotent case)}, \quad \sum_{j=1}^{m} c_j B_j(\varepsilon) = 1 \quad \text{(strict case)}$$

$$c_j \leqslant 0, \quad j = 1, \ldots m.$$

This is a constrained quadratic program with linear inequalities and equalities.

It remains to choose ε in an appropriate way for the case of strict t-norms, the only problem being that no spline approximation can lead to an infinite value at 0. It suffices to take

$$\varepsilon < \min_{k=1}^{l} \min_{i=1}^{n} \{x_i^k, y^k \mid x_i^k > 0, \quad y^k > 0\},$$

i.e., any positive value strictly smaller than any positive datum. Then the values of t on $[0, \varepsilon]$ are irrelevant to the data, and we can take on this interval any arbitrary continuous function tending to infinity at 0, and to $S(\varepsilon) = 1$ at ε, e.g.,

$$t(x) := \frac{1}{x} + 1 - \frac{1}{\varepsilon}$$

for all $x \in [0, \varepsilon]$.

A slight modification of the above program permits identifying Archimedean copulas. It suffices to add the constraints

$$c_{j+1} - c_j \geqslant 0, \quad j = 1, \ldots m - 1,$$

which force S to be convex; see Proposition 3.73.

We briefly address the case of uninorms and nullnorms. Let U be a generated uninorm, with additive generator u which is a monotone bijection from $[0, 1]$ to $[-\infty, \infty]$. Hence by Theorem 3.100, U is continuous and cancellative (see Definition 3.99) on $]0, 1[^n$. Clearly, the same technique as above can be applied, except for the difference that an additional parameter defining U is the neutral element $e \in [0, 1]$, satisfying $u(e) = 0$. If e is known or arbitrarily fixed, the boundary conditions become

$$\sum_{j=1}^{m} c_j B_j(e) = 0$$

$$\sum_{j=1}^{m} c_j B_j(\varepsilon) = 1 \text{ (disjunctive uninorm)}, \quad \sum_{j=1}^{m} c_j B_j(\varepsilon) = -1 \text{ (conjunctive uninorm)}.$$

If e is unknown, then we get a bilevel optimization problem: at the outer level it is a nonlinear problem with respect to e, and at the inner level it is the previous constrained least squares problem. The objective function is

$$\min_{e} \left(\min_{c_1, \ldots, c_m} \sum_{k=1}^{l} \left(\sum_{j=1}^{m} c_j \left(\sum_{i=1}^{n} B_j(x_i^k) - B_j(y^k) \right) \right)^2 \right).$$

Since a nullnorm V is a median between a t-norm T, a t-conorm S, and a constant a, which acts as an annihilator (see Proposition 3.107), the above technique can be applied if T, S are continuous and Archimedean. If a is known or arbitrarily fixed, then it suffices to cut the data set into three parts: data in $[0, a]^2$ are used to identify the generator of S, data in $[a, 1]^2$ are used for identifying T, while other data are simply not used since in this domain, $U(x) = a$. If a is unknown, just proceed in the same way as for uninorms, ending up with a bilevel optimization problem.

The case of quasi-arithmetic means, with generator g being a bijection on $[0, 1]$, proceeds exactly in the same way. The boundary conditions are, if g is increasing,

$$\sum_{j=1}^{m} c_j B_j(0) = 0,$$

$$\sum_{j=1}^{m} c_j B_j(1) = 1.$$

11.5 The case of integral-based aggregation functions

In this section we mostly consider the case of the Choquet integral.

Once the type of integral has been chosen, an integral-based aggregation function is completely determined by its capacity. Hence, the identification problem here is of the same type as for a parametrized family of operators; see Section 11.3. However, the peculiar nature of these aggregation functions deserves a particular treatment. Also, since the Choquet and Sugeno integrals are widely used in decision making, many developments suited to this field have been done. In particular, as remarked in the introduction, it is rarely the case in decision making that the available information is in the form of pairs of input/output data, but is rather of ordinal nature. This inevitably leads to other types of objective functions. In the sequel, we will develop three main types of objective functions. Also, it is interesting to discuss in detail the kinds of constraints which can be used; see Section 11.5.1.

As in previous sections, we consider a fixed number of arguments, say n, for the aggregation function.

An original feature of the identification problem for integral-based aggregation functions is that a capacity μ can be represented in different equivalent ways, essentially by the values $\{\mu(A)\}_{A \subseteq [n]}$, but also by the values of its Möbius transform $\{m(A)\}_{A \subseteq [n]}$, or of its interaction transform $\{I(A)\}_{A \subseteq [n]}$, or others; see Section 5.3. Practically, only the first two representations are used. The Möbius transform is very well suited to encode k-additive capacities, since the size of the vector can be reduced to $\binom{n}{1} + \ldots + \binom{n}{k}$, and permits simple expressions of the monotonicity contraints and of the Choquet integral.

Since $\mu(\varnothing) = 0 = m(\varnothing)$, the number of variables in both representations is $2^n - 1$. We denote the vectors of variables by $\mathbf{u}$ and $\mathbf{m}$ in the representation by μ and by m respectively.

Remark 11.2. A practical question arises with the precise definition of vectors $\mathbf{u}$ and $\mathbf{m}$. Indeed, an ordering of these $2^n - 1$ variables should be chosen. A natural ordering would be to take the lexicographic ordering subordinated to cardinality. This gives for $n = 4$:

$$\varnothing, 1, 2, 3, 4, 12, 13, 14, 23, 24, 34, 123, 124, 134, 234, 1234.$$

Although simple, this ordering does not lead to nicely structured matrices. Also, when passing from $[n]$ to $[n+1]$, the whole list has to be rebuilt. We prefer the *binary order*, where the subsets of $[n]$ are enumerated as the natural order on the natural numbers if one represents a subset by the binary number corresponding to its indicator function. For example, with $n = 5$, subset $\{1, 4\}$ is the integer 01001, i.e., 9. Then the ordering of subsets is induced by the natural ordering of integers. This gives for $n = 4$:

$$\varnothing, 1, 2, 12, 3, 13, 23, 123, 4, 14, 24, 124, 34, 134, 234, 1234.$$

The fundamental property of this ordering is that to get the list for $[n+1]$, we add to the list obtained for $[n]$ a duplicate of it, where to each subset the element $n + 1$ is added. This recursive feature gives matrices with "fractal" structures, i.e., built from the growth of an initial pattern; see [168] for full details.

11.5.1 Constraints

The first set of constraints is due to monotonicity of μ, i.e., $\mu(A) \leqslant \mu(B)$ whenever $A \subseteq B$. These are mandatory, otherwise the resulting function may not be monotone nondecreasing; see Proposition 5.38(ii). Since many of the above inequalities are redundant, it suffices to consider as constraints:

$$\mu(A) \leqslant \mu(A \cup \{i\}), \quad \forall A \subset [n], \forall i \notin A. \tag{11.13}$$

This gives a set of $n2^{n-1}$ constraints; see [170, §10.2.2]. Note however that the n constraints obtained for $A = \varnothing$ are just nonnegativity of variables $\mu(\{i\})$. If the Möbius representation is used, then the monotonicity constraints (11.13) become

$$\sum_{i \in B \subseteq A} m(B) \geqslant 0, \quad \forall A \subseteq [n], A \neq \varnothing, \forall i \in A$$

(see Proposition 5.15(ii)(b)). If one restricts to k-additive capacities, which can be represented through **m** with much fewer coefficients, the number of monotonicity constraints remains the same as soon as $k > 1$; see [319].

If the capacity is normalized, we add the constraint $\mu([n]) = 1$, or $\sum_{A \subseteq [n]} m(A) = 1$ if the Möbius representation is used.

Various constraints stemming from information given by the decision maker can be added. We give some examples:

(i) The Shapley value for coordinate i lies in a given interval.
(ii) The Shapley value for coordinate i is greater than or equal to the Shapley value for coordinate j.
(iii) The interaction between i and j lies in a given interval.
(iv) The interaction between i, j is greater than or equal to the interaction between k, l.
(v) The Choquet integral of datum $\mathbf{x}^k$ is greater than or equal to that of datum $\mathbf{x}^{k'}$.

These constraints can be easily expressed using the appropriate formulas from Sections 5.3 and 5.4, for both representations μ and m. They are all linear constraints.

11.5.2 Least mean squares criterion

We suppose that the information is given in the form of pairs of input/output data $(\mathbf{x}^k, y^k)_{k=1,\dots,l}$, and that we use as objective function the least squares error:

$$J_2 := \left(\sum_{k=1}^{l} \left(\mathcal{C}_\mu(\mathbf{x}^k) - y^k \right)^2 \right)^{\frac{1}{2}}.$$

This can be put into a quadratic form. We detail the case where $\mathbf{u}$ is used as a variable. From Definition 5.19, we have

$$\mathcal{C}_\mu(\mathbf{x}^k) = \mathbf{c}_k^T \mathbf{u},$$

where $\mathbf{c}_k$ is a $(2^n - 1)$-dimensional vector containing the differences $x^k_{\sigma(i)} - x^k_{\sigma(i-1)}$, $i = 1, \dots, n$ (hence it has at most n nonzero components), and σ is a permutation on $[n]$ such that $x^k_{\sigma(1)} \leqslant \cdots \leqslant x^k_{\sigma(n)}$. Minimizing J_2^2 is a multiple least squares regression (see Section 11.2.2), where the parameter vector $\boldsymbol{\beta}$ is $\mathbf{u}$, the vector $\mathbf{x}_k$ is $\mathbf{c}_k^T$, and $\mathbf{y} = \begin{bmatrix} y^1 & \cdots & y^l \end{bmatrix}$. Hence from (11.6) we immediately get

$$J_2^2 = \mathbf{u}^t \mathbf{C}^T \mathbf{C} \mathbf{u} - 2\mathbf{u}^T \mathbf{C}^T \mathbf{y}$$

with $\mathbf{C}^T := \begin{bmatrix} \mathbf{c}_1 & \cdots & \mathbf{c}_l \end{bmatrix}$, up to the constant term. Note that the symmetric square matrix $\mathbf{C}^T \mathbf{C}$ of dimension $2^n - 1$ could be very sparse, in particular if there are few data or if few different permutations are used by the data.

The expression with $\mathbf{m}$ can be obtained in the same way, replacing $\mathbf{c}_k$ by a vector $\mathbf{a}_k$ defined by

$$\mathcal{C}_\mu(\mathbf{x}^k) = \sum_{A \subseteq [n]} m(A) \bigwedge_{i \in A} x_i^k = \mathbf{a}_k^T \mathbf{m}$$

(see (5.27)). Components of $\mathbf{a}^k$ are the terms $\bigwedge_{i \in A} x_i^k$, in general all different from zero.

If $\mathbf{m}$ is the Möbius transform of a general capacity, the dimensions of the matrices are identical to those of the representation with $\mathbf{u}$. If one restricts to k-additive capacities, then one gets much smaller matrices and vectors, since $2^n - 1$ is replaced by $\binom{n}{1} + \dots + \binom{n}{k}$.

The minimization of J_2^2 under the monotonicity constraints (11.13) and possibly the normalization constraint leads to a quadratic program. An important question is whether this program has a unique solution. We can write J_2^2 as $J_2 = d(\mathbf{Cu}, \mathbf{y})$, where d is the Euclidian distance, so that the minimization of J_2^2 amounts to finding $\mathbf{u}_0$ such that

$$d(\mathbf{Cu_0}, \mathbf{y}) = \inf_{\mathbf{u} \in \mathcal{F}(n)} \{d(\mathbf{Cu}, \mathbf{y})\},$$

where $\mathcal{F}(n)$ is the set of capacities on $[n]$. Since $\mathcal{F}(n)$ is a closed convex set, so is $\{\mathbf{Cu}\}_{\mathbf{u} \in \mathcal{F}(n)}$, and by standard results on convexity, there exists a unique $\mathbf{z} \in \{\mathbf{Cu}\}_{\mathbf{u} \in \mathcal{F}(n)}$ such that

$$d(\mathbf{z}, \mathbf{y}) = \inf_{\mathbf{u} \in \mathcal{F}(n)} \{d(\mathbf{Cu}, \mathbf{y})\}.$$

However, the linear system $\mathbf{Cu_0} = \mathbf{z}$ has a unique solution if and only if $\mathbf{C}$ has full rank, i.e., $2^n - 1$. Otherwise, the set of solutions is a vector space of dimension $\mathrm{Ker}(\mathbf{C})$ (the same result can be obtained through (11.7), but this equation applies to the unconstrained case only).

Remark 11.3. (i) The question of uniqueness was examined in [319], where more details can be found. In particular, the authors give several surprising examples about uniqueness. For example, there exist situations where a unique solution can be attained with $l = 2$, n being arbitrary. On the other hand, one may intuitively think that in order to have a unique solution, the data must be such that all possible permutations σ on $[n]$ are used, or all variables $\mu(A)$, $A \subseteq [n]$ must be used. But there exist counterexamples showing that this is false.

(ii) In [145], Grabisch has proposed a heuristic algorithm called HLMS (Heuristic Least Mean Squares) minimizing J_2 under the monotonicity and normalization constraints; see also an improved version in [171]. HLMS is a gradient descent-type algorithm tailored for the Choquet integral. Although suboptimal, it has the advantage of being very fast and using little memory (of order $2^n - 1$, instead of 2^{2n-2}). Also it is able to work with very few learning data (a situation which causes very sparse matrices for the quadratic programming), and provide "less extremal" solutions (i.e., closer to the uniform capacity μ_{unif}; see Example 5.4(vi)). However, the algorithm uses the values of μ as variables, and only constraints of monotonicity can be taken into account, hence it is not possible to handle k-additive models. An empirical comparison of HLMS and the quadratic approach is described in [171], which shows its robustness against lack of data.

(iii) There exist numerous algorithms based on genetic algorithms, most of them being restricted to λ-measures; see Remark 5.7. A good representative of such a family, not restricted to λ-measures, is given by Wang *et al.* [426]. Grabisch has proposed a version handling k-additive capacities [152], while Combarro and Miranda have proposed an original approach exploiting the convexity of the set of capacities [65].

(iv) Kwon and Sugeno [242, 406] propose, in order to avoid the exponential complexity, to replace the Choquet integral with respect to a single capacity μ by a sum of p Choquet integrals with respect to $\mu_1, \ldots, \mu_p$ defined on subsets $C_1, \ldots, C_p$ of $[n]$, such that $C_1, \ldots, C_p$ form a covering of $[n]$. The idea stems from the work of Fujimoto about inclusion–exclusion covering [129].

(v) In [31], Beliakov *et al.* propose a method of identification for the Choquet integral for an unfixed number of inputs, considering universal capacities (i.e., a kind of sequence of capacities on $[n]$, for all $n \in \mathbb{N}$). The particular case of ordered weighted averaging functions is considered.

11.5.3 Case of ordinal information

We suppose that instead of pairs of input/output data, we have only ordinal information, i.e., a set of input data $\mathbf{x}^k$, $k = 1, \ldots, l$, and a ranking from worst to best preferred vectors. For convenience, let us write $\mathbf{x}^k \preceq \mathbf{x}^{k'}$ if $\mathbf{x}^{k'}$ is preferred or indifferent to $\mathbf{x}^k$. If $\mathbf{x}^k \prec \mathbf{x}^{k'}$ (with strict preference), then the capacity μ must be such that $C_\mu(\mathbf{x}^k) < C_\mu(\mathbf{x}^{k'})$.

Clearly, this defines a set of (in general strict) linear constraints (hence open half-spaces), and together with the monotonicity constraints, the set of solutions is a convex (but not closed) bounded polyhedron. There exist several ways to turn this into an optimization problem; let us describe two of them (more can be found in [159,287]).

Maximum separation criterion   The idea is to maximize the difference between $C_\mu(\mathbf{x}^k)$ and $C_\mu(\mathbf{x}^{k'})$ when $\mathbf{x}^k \prec \mathbf{x}^{k'}$. This leads to the following linear program:

Maximize ε

Subject to $C_\mu(\mathbf{x}^k) \leqslant C_\mu(\mathbf{x}^{k'}) + \varepsilon, \quad \forall k, k'$ s.t. $\mathbf{x}^k \prec \mathbf{x}^{k'}$

monotonicity constraints (11.13)

others (normalization, Shapley value, interaction, etc.).

Remark 11.4. This method was proposed by Marichal and Roubens [290], and has the advantage of using linear programming, for which very efficient algorithms exist. However, as with the least squares approach, this method does not necessarily give a unique solution. Moreover, the solution can be sometimes considered as too extreme.

Minimum distance and variance approaches   The idea is to produce a "least specific" capacity (i.e., closest to the uniform capacity μ_{unif}) compatible with the preference of the decision maker. The objective function is similar to a variance:

$$J = \frac{1}{n} \sum_{i \in [n]} \sum_{A \subseteq [n] \setminus \{i\}} \frac{(n - |A| - 1)! |A|!}{n!} \left(\sum_{B \subseteq A} m^\mu(B \cup \{i\}) - \frac{1}{n} \right)^2,$$

and the constraints are the same as above. Minimizing J amounts to maximizing the extended Havrda and Charvat entropy of order 2. It is a strictly convex quadratic program, with a unique solution. It has features similar to HLMS, since it can work with very few learning data (here, these are preferences over alternatives), and does not produce extreme solutions. This approach has been proposed by Kojadinovic [227].

11.5.4 The case of the Sugeno integral

The Sugeno integral (see Definition 5.59) involves nonlinear, nondifferentiable oper-ations $\vee, \wedge$. In such cases, only meta-heuristic methods can be used, such as genetic algorithms, simulated annealing, etc. There exist some applications of these methods to the case of the Sugeno integral, although most of the time they are used in fact for the Choquet integral, which is questionable since optimal classical methods work there [152, 426]. If the problem is convex (which is the case if monotonicity con-straints are used), then also classical nonsmooth convex optimization methods can be used.

An alternative to this option which can be applied when the information is ordinal, is to find the set of capacities (possibly empty) which enable the representation of the ranking of vectors $\mathbf{x}^k$, $k = 1, \ldots, l$ by the Sugeno integral, as explained above (Section 11.5.3). A detailed study of this problem has been done in [362].

11.6 Available software

We conclude this chapter by indicating some available software for the identification of aggregation functions; see [32] for a more complete list.

(i) As we have shown, it is useful to have a solver for quadratic programming with linear constraints, and most of the software for the identification of aggregation functions uses such solvers. We may indicate Algorithm 587 from netlib (see http://www.netlib.org/toms/), the quadprog and kernlab rou-tines of the R environment for statistics http://www.r-project.org/, the QL routine of Schittkowsky http://www.old.uni-bayreuth.de/departments/math/~kschittkowski/software.htm, the CPLEX program www.ILOG.com, Xpress-MP of Matlab (see, e.g., http://tomopt.com/tomlab/products/xpress/), but the latter three are not free.

(ii) The AOTool developed by G. Beliakov is a toolbox for general problems of identifying aggregation functions. It is available at http://www.deakin.edu.au/~gleb/aotool.html, and includes methods described in Sections 11.3 and 11.4.

(iii) The Kappalab package of the R environment is dedicated to the treatment of capacities, and the Choquet and Sugeno integrals. It contains several routines for the identification of capacities when the model is a Choquet integral. All meth-ods described in Section 11.5 are implemented there. It is available at http://www.stat.auckland.ac.nz/~ivan/kappalab, and one can find a description of its usage in [159].

Appendix A

Aggregation of infinitely many arguments

A.1 Introduction

Aggregation of infinitely but still countably many inputs is important in several mathematical areas, such as discrete probability theory, but also in non-mathematical areas, such as decision problems with an infinite jury, game theory with infinitely many players, etc. Though these theoretical tasks seem to be far from reality, they enable a better understanding of decision problems with extremely huge juries, game theoretical problems with extremely many players, etc.; see [333, 368, 416].

In Section A.2, based on [308], we discuss infinitary aggregation functions on sequences possessing some *a priori* given properties, such as additivity, comonotone additivity, symmetry, etc. On the other side we discuss infinitary aggregation functions $A^{(\infty)} \colon [0, 1]^{\mathbb{N}} \to [0, 1]$ related to a given extended aggregation function $A \colon \cup_{n \in \mathbb{N}} [0, 1]^n \to [0, 1]$, where special attention is paid to t-norms, t-conorms, and weighted arithmetic means. Note that the discussion of the infinitary arithmetic mean $AM^{(\infty)} \colon [0, 1]^{\mathbb{N}} \to [0, 1]$ can be found in [141, 142].

General infinitary aggregation is discussed in Section A.3, thus extending the results from Section A.2. Note that in such case, some restrictions on the domain of aggregation functions is usually necessary. For example, to apply Lebesgue, Choquet or Sugeno integrals one should require the measurability of the input function to be aggregated.

A.2 Infinitary aggregation functions on sequences

We extend the notion of the usual aggregation function to the case of infinite inputs. We consider the set $[0, 1]^{\mathbb{N}}$ of all sequences $\mathbf{x} = (x_1, x_2, \ldots, x_i, \ldots)$, where $x_i \in [0, 1]$ $(i \in \mathbb{N})$. The input space $[0, 1]^{\mathbb{N}}$ equipped with standard Cartesian ordering (i.e., $\mathbf{x} \leqslant \mathbf{y}$ means $x_i \leqslant y_i, i \in \mathbb{N}$) is a complete lattice with bottom element $\mathbf{0} = \{0\}^{\mathbb{N}}$ and top element $\mathbf{1} = \{1\}^{\mathbb{N}}$. We equip $[0, 1]^{\mathbb{N}}$ with coordinatewise convergence, i.e., a sequence $\mathbf{x}^{(n)} = (x_1^{(n)}, x_2^{(n)}, \ldots, x_i^{(n)}, \ldots)$ from $[0, 1]^{\mathbb{N}}$ converges to $\mathbf{x} = (x_1, x_2, \ldots, x_n, \ldots) \in [0, 1]^{\mathbb{N}}$ if and only if $\lim_{n \to \infty} x_i^{(n)} = x_i$ for all $i \in \mathbb{N}$.

Definition A.1. A function $A^{(\infty)}: [0,1]^{\mathbb{N}} \to [0,1]$ is an *(infinitary) aggregation function* if it satisfies the following conditions:

(i) Nondecreasing monotonicity, i.e., $\mathbf{x} \leqslant \mathbf{y}$ implies $A^{(\infty)}(\mathbf{x}) \leqslant A^{(\infty)}(\mathbf{y})$.

(ii) $A^{(\infty)}(\mathbf{0}) = 0$ and $A^{(\infty)}(\mathbf{1}) = 1$.

Properties of these functions are defined similarly to the corresponding properties of *n*-ary aggregation functions; see Chapter 2.

Definition A.2. An aggregation function $A^{(\infty)}: [0,1]^{\mathbb{N}} \to [0,1]$ is said to be

(i) *additive* whenever $A^{(\infty)}(\mathbf{x}+\mathbf{y}) = A^{(\infty)}(\mathbf{x}) + A^{(\infty)}(\mathbf{y})$ for all $\mathbf{x}, \mathbf{y} \in [0,1]^{\mathbb{N}}$ such that $\mathbf{x} + \mathbf{y} \in [0,1]^{\mathbb{N}}$;

(ii) *comonotonic additive* whenever $A^{(\infty)}(\mathbf{x}+\mathbf{y}) = A^{(\infty)}(\mathbf{x}) + A^{(\infty)}(\mathbf{y})$ for all $\mathbf{x}, \mathbf{y} \in [0,1]^{\mathbb{N}}$ such that $\mathbf{x}+\mathbf{y} \in [0,1]^{\mathbb{N}}$ and $(x_i - x_j)(y_i - y_j) \geqslant 0$ for all $i, j \in \mathbb{N}$;

(iii) (positively) *homogeneous* whenever $A^{(\infty)}(c\mathbf{x}) = cA^{(\infty)}(\mathbf{x})$ for all $\mathbf{x} \in [0,1]^{\mathbb{N}}$ and $c \in [0, \infty[$ such that $c\mathbf{x} \in [0,1]^{\mathbb{N}}$;

(iv) *symmetric* whenever $A^{(\infty)}((x_n)_{n\in\mathbb{N}}) = A^{(\infty)}((x_{\sigma(n)})_{n\in\mathbb{N}})$ for all $(x_n)_{n\in\mathbb{N}} \in [0,1]^{\mathbb{N}}$ and any bijective mapping (i.e., permutation) $\sigma: \mathbb{N} \to \mathbb{N}$;

(v) *continuous* whenever $\lim_{k\to\infty} A^{(\infty)}(\mathbf{x}^{(k)}) = A^{(\infty)}(\mathbf{x})$ for any coordinatewise convergent sequence $(\mathbf{x}^{(k)})_{k\in\mathbb{N}} \in ([0,1]^{\mathbb{N}})^{\mathbb{N}}$ such that $\lim_{k\to\infty} \mathbf{x}^{(k)} = \mathbf{x}$ (i.e., $\lim_{k\to\infty} x_i^{(k)} = x_i$ for each $i \in \mathbb{N}$);

(vi) *idempotent* whenever $A^{(\infty)}(\mathbf{c}) = c$ for each $c \in [0,1]$, $\mathbf{c} = \{c\}^{\mathbb{N}}$.

Additive aggregation functions. Additivity of the aggregation function implies its comonotone additivity, which yields its idempotence. On the other hand, there are no aggregation functions $A^{(\infty)}: [0,1]^{\mathbb{N}} \to [0,1]$ which are both additive and symmetric; see Remark A.5(i). Additivity is a strong property which forces positive homogeneity and nondecreasing monotonicity of functions in $[0,1]$.

Proposition A.3. *An additive function* $F: [0,1]^{\mathbb{N}} \to [0,1]$ *is homogeneous and nondecreasing. If* F *satisfies additionally* $F(\mathbf{0}) = 0$ *and* $F(\mathbf{1}) = 1$, *then it is an (infinitary) aggregation function.*

The additivity together with the continuity of an aggregation function A forces A to be an extended weighted arithmetic mean.

Proposition A.4. *An aggregation function* $A^{(\infty)}: [0,1]^{\mathbb{N}} \to [0,1]$ *is additive and continuous if and only if* $A^{(\infty)}(\mathbf{x}) = \sum_{n=1}^{\infty} w_n x_n$ *for all* $\mathbf{x} = (x_n)_{n\in\mathbb{N}} \in [0,1]^{\mathbb{N}}$, *where* $(w_n)_{n\in\mathbb{N}} \in [0,1]^{\mathbb{N}}$, $\sum_{n=1}^{\infty} w_n = 1$.

Remark A.5. (i) The arithmetic mean $AM^{(n)}: [0,1]^n \to [0,1]$ is characterized as the unique *n*-ary additive symmetric aggregation function. Symmetry forces the equality of weights $w_1 = \cdots = w_n = \frac{1}{n}$. However, requiring similar properties on $[0,1]^{\mathbb{N}}$ can be reduced to looking for a sequence of weights $(w_n)_{n\in\mathbb{N}} \in [0,1]^{\mathbb{N}}$ such that all weights are equal and $\sum_{n=1}^{\infty} w_n = 1$. Evidently, such a sequence of weights cannot exist.

(ii) There are additive aggregation functions $\mathbf{A}^{(\infty)}: [0,1]^{\mathbb{N}} \to [0,1]$ which are not continuous and thus not determined by a sequence of weights $(w_n)_{n \in \mathbb{N}}$. In this case, they possess some peculiar properties. Take for example the aggregation function $\mathbf{A}^{(\infty)}: [0,1]^{\mathbb{N}} \to [0,1]$ discussed in [34], which is a Choquet integral-based aggregation function with respect to a $\{0,1\}$-valued additive capacity μ on $\mathbb{N}$, introduced by Tarski [408], which is vanishing on finite subsets of $\mathbb{N}$. Then

$$\mathbf{A}^{(\infty)}(\mathbf{1}_{\{n\}}\mathbf{0}) = 0 \quad \text{and} \quad \mathbf{A}^{(\infty)}\left(\sum_{i=1}^{n} \mathbf{1}_{\{i\}}\mathbf{0}\right) = 0$$

for all $n \in \mathbb{N}$. This aggregation function (capacity) is introduced in an existential manner, based on the Zorn lemma, and thus it is impossible to describe it by a closed form.

Comonotonic additive aggregation function. The next result is derived from [35]; see also [349].

Proposition A.6. *An aggregation function* $\mathbf{A}^{(\infty)}: [0,1]^{\mathbb{N}} \to [0,1]$ *is comonotonic additive and lower semicontinuous if and only if there is a lower semicontinuous capacity* $\mu: 2^{\mathbb{N}} \to [0,1]$ *(for each nondecreasing sequence* $(A_n)_{n \in \mathbb{N}}$ *in* $2^{\mathbb{N}}$ *and for each* $A \in 2^{\mathbb{N}}$, *with* $(A_n)_{n \in \mathbb{N}}$ *increasing to* A, *we have* $\lim_{n \to \infty} \mu(A_n) = \mu(\cup_{n \in \mathbb{N}} A_n))$, *such that*

$$\mathbf{A}^{(\infty)}(\mathbf{x}) = (C)\int_{\mathbb{N}} \mathbf{x}\, d\mu = \int_0^1 \mu(\{i \in \mathbb{N} \mid x_i \geqslant t\})\, dt, \qquad (A.1)$$

where the last term in (A.1) *is the standard Riemann integral, i.e.,* $\mathbf{A}^{(\infty)}$ *is the Choquet integral with respect to* μ. *Note that for any* $E \subset \mathbb{N}$ *we then have*

$$\mu(E) = \mathbf{A}(\mathbf{1}_E).$$

Remark A.7. Due to the duality properties of the Choquet integral, a similar result is valid for the upper semi-continuous case, and thus also for the continuous case.

Example A.8. The supremum on $[0,1]^{\mathbb{N}}$ can be seen as an infinitary aggregation function, and it is related through (A.1) to the greatest normalized capacity $\mu_{\max}: 2^{\mathbb{N}} \to [0,1]$, given by

$$\mu_{\max}(A) := \begin{cases} 0 & \text{if } A = \varnothing \\ 1 & \text{otherwise.} \end{cases}$$

Evidently, $\mu_{\max}$ is a lower semi-continuous capacity which is not continuous (take, e.g., $A_k = \{k, k+1, \ldots\}$, then $\lim_{k \to \infty} A_k = \varnothing$ but $\lim_{k \to \infty} \mu_{\max}(A_k) = 1 \neq 0 = \mu_{\max}(\varnothing)$). Similarly, the infimum on $[0,1]^{\mathbb{N}}$ is a comonotone additive aggregation function which is upper semi-continuous but not continuous. As an example of a continuous comonotonic additive aggregation function $\mathbf{A}^{(\infty)}: [0,1]^{\mathbb{N}} \to [0,1]$ which is not additive (for the additive case, see Proposition A.4), define a capacity $\mu: 2^{\mathbb{N}} \to [0, 1]$ by

$$\mu(A) := \left(\sum_{n \in A} \frac{1}{2^n} \right)^2.$$

Then μ is a continuous nonadditive capacity, and thus the corresponding Choquet integral satisfies our requirements. Observe that then $\mathbf{A}^{(\infty)}$ is given by

$$\mathbf{A}^{(\infty)}((x_n)_{n \in \mathbb{N}}) = \sum_{n=1}^{\infty} \sum_{m=1}^{\infty} \frac{\mathrm{Min}(x_n, x_m)}{2^{n+m}}.$$

Symmetric aggregation function. The symmetry of $\mathbf{A}^{(\infty)}: [0, 1]^{\mathbb{N}} \to [0, 1]$ when it is a Choquet integral-based aggregation function is related to the symmetry of the corresponding capacity $\mu: 2^{\mathbb{N}} \to [0, 1]$, i.e.,

$$\mu(A) = \mu(\{\sigma(n) \mid n \in A\})$$

for all $A \subset \mathbb{N}$ and any bijective mapping $\sigma: \mathbb{N} \to \mathbb{N}$. However, this means that for any $n \in \mathbb{N}_0$ there exists a weight $a_n \in [0, 1]$ such that $\mu(A) = a_n$ whenever $|A| = n$ (evidently, $a_0 = 0 \leqslant a_1 \leqslant a_2 \leqslant \cdots$). Similarly, there are weights $b_n \in [0, 1]$ such that $\mu(A) = b_n$ whenever $\mathrm{card}(A^c) = n$, and $b_0 = 1 \geqslant b_1 \geqslant b_2 \geqslant \cdots$. Finally, there exists $c \in [0, 1]$, $\lim_{n \to \infty} a_n \leqslant c \leqslant \lim_{n \to \infty} b_n$ such that $\mu(A) = c$ whenever both A and A^c are infinite subsets on $\mathbb{N}$.

Example A.9. For $c \in [0, 1]$, define a symmetric capacity $\mu_c: 2^{\mathbb{N}} \to [0, 1]$ putting $a_n = 0$ and $b_n = 1$ for all $n \in \mathbb{N} \cup \{0, 1\}$, i.e., by

$$\mu_c(A) := \begin{cases} 0 & \text{if } A \text{ is finite} \\ 1 & \text{if } A^c \text{ is finite} \\ c & \text{otherwise.} \end{cases}$$

Then the corresponding symmetric Choquet integral $\mathbf{A}_{(c)}^{(\infty)}: [0, 1]^{\mathbb{N}} \to [0, 1]$ is given by

$$\mathbf{A}_{(c)}^{(\infty)}((x_n)_{n \in \mathbb{N}}) = (1 - c) \lim \inf x_n + c \lim \sup x_n, \tag{A.2}$$

where $\lim \inf x_n := \lim_{n \to \infty} \inf_{k \geqslant n} x_k$ and $\lim \sup x_n := \lim_{n \to \infty} \sup_{k \geqslant n} x_k$.

All above examples of aggregation functions are idempotent.

Example A.10. (i) As a nonidempotent aggregation function on $[0, 1]^{\mathbb{N}}$, we mention the product $\Pi^{(\infty)}: [0, 1]^{\mathbb{N}} \to [0, 1]$ given by

$$\Pi^{(\infty)}((x_n)_{n \in \mathbb{N}}) := \prod_{n=1}^{\infty} x_n.$$

Clearly, for any constant $c \in [0, 1[$, $\Pi^{(\infty)}(\mathbf{c}) = 0$, hence, $\Pi^{(\infty)}$ is not continuous on $[0, 1]^{\mathbb{N}}$. However, it is symmetric.

(ii) Another example of a noncontinuous symmetric aggregation function on $[0, 1]^{\mathbb{N}}$ which is not idempotent is the bounded sum $S_L^{(\infty)} : [0, 1]^{\mathbb{N}} \to [0, 1]$ given by

$$S_L^{(\infty)}((x_n)_{n \in \mathbb{N}}) := \mathrm{Min}\left(\sum_{n=1}^{\infty} x_n, 1\right).$$

Note that $S_L^{(\infty)}(\mathbf{c}) = 1$ for any constant $c \in\ ]0, 1]$ but $S_L^{(\infty)}(\mathbf{0}) = 0$, thus violating the continuity of $S_L^{(\infty)}$.

Countably extendable aggregation functions. For a given extended aggregation function $A: \cup_{n \in \mathbb{N}} [0, 1]^n \to [0, 1]$, we look for an appropriate aggregation function $A^{(\infty)} : [0, 1]^{\mathbb{N}} \to [0, 1]$ somehow linked to A. A natural approach is to define $A^{(\infty)}$ as a limit of $(A^{(n)})_{n \in \mathbb{N}}$,

$$A^{(\infty)}((x_n)_{n \in \mathbb{N}}) := \lim_{n \to \infty} A^{(n)}(x_1, \ldots, x_n). \tag{A.3}$$

If this limit exists, for any $(x_n)_{n \in \mathbb{N}} \in [0, 1]^{\mathbb{N}}$, we accept $A^{(\infty)}$ given by (A.3) as an extension of A to the domain $[0, 1]^{\mathbb{N}}$, and we keep the notation A also for $A^{(\infty)}$ whenever appropriate. The aggregation function A is called *countably extendable*.

A sufficient condition for the extendability is the downwards (upwards) attitude of extended aggregation functions as introduced in [443].

Definition A.11. An extended aggregation function $A: \cup_{n \in \mathbb{N}} [0, 1]^n \to [0, 1]$ is said to have a *downwards* (respectively, an *upwards*) *attitude* whenever, for any $n \in \mathbb{N}$ and any $x_1, \ldots, x_{n+1} \in [0, 1]$,

$$A(x_1, \ldots, x_n, x_{n+1}) \leqslant A(x_1, \ldots, x_n)$$

(respectively, $A(x_1, \ldots, x_n, x_{n+1}) \geqslant A(x_1, \ldots, x_n)$).

Lemma A.12. *Each downwards (respectively, upwards) extended aggregation function* $A: \cup_{n \in \mathbb{N}} [0, 1]^n \to [0, 1]$ *is countably extendable.*

Corollary A.13. *Let* $T: \cup_{n \in \mathbb{N}} [0, 1]^n \to [0, 1]$ *(respectively,* $S: \cup_{n \in \mathbb{N}} [0, 1]^n \to [0, 1]$*) be an extended t-norm (respectively, extended t-conorm). Then* T *(respectively,* S*) is countably extendable.*

Observe that t-norms and t-conorms are associative aggregation functions (in their binary form) and thus their extension to extended aggregation functions is unique. Moreover, $T^{(\infty)} : [0, 1]^{\mathbb{N}} \to [0, 1]$ is given by

$$T^{(\infty)}(\mathbf{x}) = \inf\{T^{(n)}(x_1, \ldots, x_n) \mid n \in \mathbb{N}\}.$$

Similarly, $S^{(\infty)}: [0, 1]^{\mathbb{N}} \to [0, 1]$ is given by

$$S^{(\infty)}(\mathbf{x}) = \sup\{S^{(n)}(x_1, \ldots, x_n) \mid n \in \mathbb{N}\}.$$

Example A.14. Countable extensions $\Pi^{(\infty)}$ and $S_L^{(\infty)}$ are aggregation functions introduced in Example A.10(i) and (ii), respectively.

Properties of the original t-norms (respectively, t-conorms) may be lost when extending them to infinite sequences. As already observed in Example A.10, when discussing the product $\Pi^{(\infty)}$, the continuity of $T^{(\infty)}$ (respectively, $S^{(\infty)}$) need not be preserved (in fact, $T^{(\infty)}$ is continuous only if $T = \mathsf{Min}$ and then $T^{(\infty)} = \inf$). Similarly, we can lose the associativity (compare with similar defects when extending the standard addition on $\mathbb{R}$ to infinite series). A deep discussion of another possible extension of t-norms and t-conorms to infinitary functions can be found in [314].

Example A.15. (i) In [49], an extended aggregation function $Q: \bigcup_{n\in\mathbb{N}} [0, 1]^n \to [0, 1]$ given by $Q^{(n)}(\mathbf{x}) := \prod_{i=1}^{n} x_i^i$ was introduced. Evidently, Q possesses the downwards attitude and thus it is countably extendable to $[0, 1]^{\mathbb{N}}$, $Q^{(\infty)}(\mathbf{x}) = \prod_{n=1}^{\infty} x_n^n$.

(ii) Other countably extendable extended aggregation functions are special weighted arithmetic means and ordered weighted averaging functions (see [49, 435]), determined by a weight triangle $\triangle = (w_{i,n})$, where $n \in \mathbb{N}$, $i \in [n]$, and $w_{i,n} \geqslant 0$, $\sum_{i=1}^{n} w_{i,n} = 1$ for all $n \in \mathbb{N}$; see Definition 4.52. Indeed, if for each $i \in \mathbb{N}$, $\lim_{n\to\infty} w_{i,n} = w_i$ exists and $\sum_{i=1}^{\infty} w_i = 1$, then the weighted arithmetic mean $\mathsf{WAM}_{\triangle}: \bigcup_{n\in\mathbb{N}} [0, 1]^n \to [0, 1]$ given by

$$\mathsf{WAM}_{\triangle}^{(n)}(\mathbf{x}) = \sum_{i=1}^{n} w_{i,n} x_i$$

is countably extendable, and $\mathsf{WAM}_{\triangle}^{(\infty)}: [0, 1]^{\mathbb{N}} \to [0, 1]$ is given by

$$\mathsf{WAM}_{\triangle}^{(\infty)}(\mathbf{x}) := \sum_{n=1}^{\infty} w_n x_n.$$

For example, reversing the Sierpiński carpet given in Example 4.54, i.e., for the weight triangle $\triangle_S$ given by

$$w_{i,n} = a(1 - a)^{i-1}$$

for $i = 1, \ldots, n-1$ and $w_{n,n} = (1-a)^{n-1}$ (with convention $0^0 = 1$), we obtain

$$\mathsf{WAM}_{\triangle_S}^{(\infty)}(\mathbf{x}) = a \sum_{n=1}^{\infty} x_n (1 - a)^{n-1},$$

whenever $a \in]0, 1]$. Note that if $a = 0$ then $\mathsf{WAM}_{\Delta_S}^{(n)}(\mathbf{x}) = x_n$ is not countably extendable.

(iii) The ordered weighting averaging function $\mathsf{OWA}_\Delta \colon \cup_{n \in \mathbb{N}} [0, 1]^n \to [0, 1]$ is given by

$$\mathsf{OWA}_\Delta^{(n)}(\mathbf{x}) := \sum_{i=1}^n w_{i,n} x_{\sigma(i)},$$

where $\sigma \colon [n] \to [n]$ is a permutation such that $x_{\sigma(1)} \leqslant x_{\sigma(2)} \leqslant \cdots \leqslant x_{\sigma(n)}$, and it is countably extendable whenever all limits $a_k = \lim_{n \to \infty} w_{k,n}$ and $b_k = \lim_{n \to \infty} w_{n-k+1,n}$, $k \in \mathbb{N}$, exist, they equal 0 up to a finite number of indices, and $\sum_{k=1}^\infty (a_k + b_k) = 1$. Then $\mathsf{OWA}_\Delta^{(\infty)} \colon [0, 1]^{\mathbb{N}} \to [0, 1]$ is given by

$$\mathsf{OWA}_\Delta^{(\infty)}(\mathbf{x}) = \sum_{k=1}^\infty a_k y_k + \sum_{k=1}^\infty b_k z_k,$$

where y_k is the kth smallest element of $\mathbf{x}$ if it exists, and $y_k = \liminf x_n$ otherwise, and z_k is the kth largest element of $\mathbf{x}$ if it exists, and $z_k = \limsup x_n$ otherwise. As an example take Δ given by $w_{1,n} = w_{n,n} = \frac{1}{2}$ and $w_{i,n} = 0$, otherwise. Then

$$\mathsf{OWA}_\Delta^{(\infty)}((x_n)_{n \in \mathbb{N}}) = \frac{1}{2}(\inf x_n + \sup x_n).$$

(iv) Recall that for a fixed $\mathbf{x} \in [0, 1]^{\mathbb{N}}$, $\lim_{n \to \infty} \mathsf{AM}^{(n)}(x_1, \ldots, x_n)$, if it exists, is called the Cesaro mean of $\mathbf{x}$. Evidently, AM is not countably extendable; see [141, 142]. Take, for example $\mathbf{x} \in [0, 1]^{\mathbb{N}}$ given by

$$x_1 = 1, x_2 = \cdots = x_{10} = 0, x_{11} = \cdots = x_{100} = 1, \cdots.$$

Then $\limsup \mathsf{AM}^{(n)}(\mathbf{x}) = \frac{10}{11}$ and $\liminf \mathsf{AM}^{(n)}(\mathbf{x}) = \frac{1}{11}$. However, this means that $\lim \mathsf{AM}^{(n)}(\mathbf{x})$ does not exist.

When trying to extend AM on $[0, 1]^{\mathbb{N}}$ by means of some settings of properties which determine AM as an extended aggregation function (or n-ary aggregation function), we can either see the impossibility of this approach (see Remark A.5(i), Example A.15(iv)), or we can obtain different aggregation functions. For example, we can put

$$\mathsf{AM}_*(\mathbf{x}) := \sup \left\{ c \in [0, 1] \,\middle|\, \sum_{n=1}^\infty (x_n - c) \geqslant 0 \right\} = \liminf \mathsf{AM}^{(n)}(\mathbf{x})$$

and

$$\mathsf{AM}^*(\mathbf{x}) := \inf \left\{ c \in [0, 1] \,\middle|\, \sum_{n=1}^\infty (x_n - c) \leqslant 0 \right\} = \limsup \mathsf{AM}^{(n)}(\mathbf{x}).$$

For more details we recommend [141, 142].

Countable extension. To obtain the uniqueness of the countable extension of the extended aggregation function $A: \bigcup_{n \in \mathbb{N}} [0,1]^n \to [0,1]$ to $[0,1]^{\mathbb{N}}$, we propose the following definition.

Definition A.16. The *countable extension* $A^{(\infty)}: [0,1]^{\mathbb{N}} \to [0,1]$ of an extended aggregation function $A: \bigcup_{n \in \mathbb{N}} [0,1]^n \to [0,1]$ to $[0,1]^{\mathbb{N}}$, is given by

$$A^{(\infty)}(\mathbf{x}) := \frac{1}{2} \left(\liminf A^{(n)}(\mathbf{x}) + \limsup A^{(n)}(\mathbf{x}) \right). \qquad (A.4)$$

In the case of countably extendable aggregation functions this definition is consistent with (A.3).

Example A.17. (i) The nonextendable projection on the last coordinate $P_L: \bigcup_{n \in \mathbb{N}} [0,1]^n \to [0,1]$ (i.e., weighted arithmetic mean WAM_{Δ_S} related to the reversed Sierpiński carpet with $a = 0$ (see Example A.15(ii))) yields via (A.4) the extension $(P_L)^{(\infty)}$ which is exactly $A^{(\infty)}_{(0.5)}$; see (A.2).

(ii) As an interesting example recall the symmetric extended aggregation function $\mathsf{Med}: \bigcup_{n \in \mathbb{N}} [0,1]^n \to [0,1]$, which is not countably extendable. Then $\mathsf{Med}^{(\infty)}: [0,1]^{\mathbb{N}} \to [0,1]$ given by (A.4) leads to

$$\mathsf{Med}^{(\infty)}(0,1,0,1,\ldots) = \frac{1}{4}$$

and

$$\mathsf{Med}^{(\infty)}(1,0,1,0,\ldots) = \frac{3}{4},$$

i.e., $\mathsf{Med}^{(\infty)}$ is not symmetric.

Means and averages. Averaging aggregation functions (means) are characterized by their boundedness by Min and Max, $\mathsf{Min} \leqslant A \leqslant \mathsf{Max}$. Then also Min and Max are means, though our intuitive feeling is disturbed by such observation. Based on the infinitary extension (A.4) of extended averaging aggregation functions, we propose the next characterization of the averaging property.

Definition A.18. Let $A: \bigcup_{n \in \mathbb{N}} [0,1]^n \to [0,1]$ be an extended mean. It is called a *pure mean* whenever its extension $A^{(\infty)}: [0,1]^{\mathbb{N}} \to [0,1]$ given by (A.4) satisfies

$$A^{(\infty)}(\mathbf{x}) = x$$

for all $\mathbf{x} = (x_n)_{n \in \mathbb{N}}$ from the subspace of all convergent sequences such that $\lim_{n \to \infty} x_n = x$.

Example A.19. (i) Evidently, Min and Max with countable extensions $\mathsf{Min}^{(\infty)} = \inf$ and $\mathsf{Max}^{(\infty)} = \sup$, respectively, are not pure means.

(ii) The arithmetic mean AM and the median Med are pure means.

We have a more general result.

Theorem A.20. *For the weighted arithemic mean* $\mathsf{WAM}_\triangle : \cup_{n\in\mathbb{N}}[0,1]^n \to [0,1]$ *its countable extension* $\mathsf{WAM}_\triangle^{(\infty)} : [0,1]^{\mathbb{N}} \to [0,1]$ *given by (A.4) is a pure mean if and only if* $\lim_{n\to\infty} w_{i,n} = 0$ *for* $i \in \mathbb{N}$.

Remark A.21. By Theorem A.20 and Example A.15(ii) the countable extension of the weighted arithmetic mean, which is a pure mean, never satisfies (A.3) on $[0,1]^{\mathbb{N}}$.

A.3 General aggregation of infinite number of inputs

For theoretical purposes, also aggregation of uncountably many inputs is sometimes necessary. Suppose that J is an (uncountable) index set, and that $\mathbf{x} = (x_j)_{j\in J}$ is an input vector to be aggregated, where $\mathbf{x} \in \mathbb{I}^J$.

Definition A.22. A mapping $\mathsf{A}^{(J)} : \mathbb{I}^J \to \mathbb{I}$ is called a *J-aggregation function* whenever it is nondecreasing, i.e.,

$$\mathsf{A}^{(J)}(\mathbf{x}) \leqslant \mathsf{A}^{(J)}(\mathbf{y}) \text{ if } x_j \leqslant y_j \text{ for all } j \in J,$$

and

$$\inf\{\mathsf{A}^{(J)}(\mathbf{x}) \mid \mathbf{x} \in \mathbb{I}^{(J)}\} = \inf \mathbb{I}, \quad \sup\{\mathsf{A}^{(J)}(\mathbf{x}) \mid \mathbf{x} \in \mathbb{I}^{(J)}\} = \sup \mathbb{I}.$$

We can introduce properties of these functions in a way similar to what we did in Definition A.2. We give examples of *J*-aggregation functions (observe that the formulas below can be applied also for aggregation of sequences, discussed in Section A.2).

Two aggregation functions defined for any index set J and any closed interval $\mathbb{I}$ are the standard supremum and infimum on the extended real line. The functions sup and inf are comonotonic additive, homogeneous, symmetric, continuous and idempotent, but not additive.

Proposition A.23. *Let* $\mathsf{T} : \cup_{n\in\mathbb{N}}[0,1]^n \to [0,1]$ *be a continuous t-norm characterized by the ordinal sum structure* $(< a_k, b_k, \mathsf{T}_k >)_{k\in K}$ *such that for each summand* $< a_k, b_k, \mathsf{T}_k >, k \in K$, *the corresponding additive generator is denoted by* $t_k : [a_k, b_k] \to [0,\infty], t_k(b_k) = 0$ *(see Section 3.3.7), i.e.,*

$$\mathsf{T}(\mathbf{x}) = \begin{cases} t_k^{-1}\left(\mathrm{Min}\left(t_k(a_k), \sum_{i=1}^n t_k(\mathrm{Min}(x_i, b_k))\right)\right) & \text{if } \mathrm{Min}\, x_i \in \,]a_k, b_k[\\ \mathrm{Min}(\mathbf{x}) & \text{otherwise.} \end{cases}$$

Let J be an arbitrary index set. Then the functions $\mathsf{T}_1^{(J)}, \mathsf{T}_2^{(J)} : [0,1]^J \to [0,1]$ defined by

$$
\mathsf{T}_1^{(J)}(\mathbf{x}) := \begin{cases} t_k^{-1}\left(\text{Min}\left(t_k(a_k), \sum_{x_j \in]a_k, b_k[} t_k(\text{Min}(x_j, b_k))\right)\right) & \text{if inf } \mathbf{x} \in]a_k, b_k[\\ \inf(\mathbf{x}) & \text{otherwise,} \end{cases}
$$

and

$$
\mathsf{T}_2^{(J)}(\mathbf{x}) := \begin{cases} a_k & \text{if inf } \mathbf{x} \in]a_k, b_k[\text{ and} \\ & |\{j \in J \mid x_j \in]a_k, b_k[\}| \text{ is infinite} \\ \mathsf{T}_1^{(J)}(\mathbf{x}) & \text{otherwise,} \end{cases}
$$

are symmetric (conjunctive) J-aggregation functions on $[0,1]$. The sum of uncountably many positive reals is ∞ by convention.

Remark A.24. (i) Both J-aggregation functions $\mathsf{T}_1^{(J)}$ and $\mathsf{T}_2^{(J)}$ coincide with the standard n-ary form of the t-norm T whenever $|J| = n$. If $J = \mathbb{N}$, then $\mathsf{T}_1^{(\mathbb{N})} = \mathsf{T}^{(\infty)}$ (see Corollary A.13), while $\mathsf{T}_2^{(\mathbb{N})}$ differs from $\mathsf{T}^{(\infty)}$. Indeed, take $\mathsf{T} = \mathsf{T}_P$ the standard product. Then $\mathsf{T}^{(\infty)}(\mathbf{x}) = \prod_{i=1}^{\infty} x_i$ while

$$
\mathsf{T}_2^{(\mathbb{N})}(\mathbf{x}) = \begin{cases} \prod_{i=1}^{\infty} x_i & \text{if } |\{i \in \mathbb{N} \mid x_i < 1\}| \text{ is finite} \\ 0 & \text{otherwise.} \end{cases}
$$

(ii) We can extend the concept of $\mathsf{T}_1^{(J)}$ to any t-norm T, putting

$$
\mathsf{T}_1^{(J)} = \inf\{\mathsf{T}(\mathbf{x}|_L) \mid L \text{ is a finite subset of } J\}, \tag{A.5}
$$

see [314].

(iii) $\mathsf{T}_2^{(J)}$ was introduced in [314] as a general quantifier.

The concept of J–t-norms can be straightforwardly extended to t-conorms, uninorms and nullnorms (see Chapter 3), for both $\mathsf{T}_1^{(J)}$ and $\mathsf{T}_2^{(J)}$ cases.

Proposition A.25. *Let $\mathsf{S} : \cup_{n \in \mathbb{N}}[0,1]^n \to [0,1]$ be a continuous t-conorm which is dual to a t-norm T. Let J be a given index set. Then the functions $\mathsf{S}_1^{(J)}, \mathsf{S}_2^{(J)} : [0,1]^n \to [0,1]$ given by*

$$
\mathsf{S}_i^{(J)}(\mathbf{x}) := 1 - \mathsf{T}_i^{(J)}(1 - \mathbf{x}), \quad i = 1, 2,
$$

are symmetric (disjunctive) J-aggregation functions.

Remark A.26. For $\mathsf{T}_1^{(J)}$ we can apply formula (A.5) to any t-norm T, while in the case of $\mathsf{T}_2^{(J)}$ we need continuity of T, i.e., continuity of its dual S should be considered.

Proposition A.27. *Let* $\mathsf{U} : \cup_{n\in\mathbb{N}}[0,1]^n \to [0,1]$ *be a uninorm with an extended neutral element* $e \in]0,1[$ *such that for any* $\mathbf{x} \in \cup_{n\in\mathbb{N}}[0,1]^n$ *we have*

$$\mathsf{U}(\mathbf{x}) = \mathsf{U}(\mathsf{T}(\mathbf{e} \wedge \mathbf{x})), \mathsf{S}(\mathbf{e} \vee \mathbf{x})),$$

where $\mathbf{e} = (e,\dots,e)$, T *is a t-norm given by (3.40), and* S *is a t-conorm given by (3.41). Let* J *be an index set. Then the functions* $\mathsf{U}_1^{(J)}, \mathsf{U}_2^{(J)} : [0,1]^J \to [0,1]$ *given by*

$$\mathsf{U}_i^{(J)}(\mathbf{x}) := \mathsf{U}(\mathsf{T}_i^{(J)}(\mathbf{e} \wedge \mathbf{x}), \mathsf{S}_i^{(J)}(\mathbf{e} \vee \mathbf{x})), \quad i = 1, 2$$

(in the case $i = 2$, *we suppose the continuity of* T *and* S) *are symmetric J-aggregation functions.*

Proposition A.28. *Let* $\mathsf{V} : \cup_{n\in\mathbb{N}}[0,1]^n \to [0,1]$ *be a nullnorm with annihilator* $a \in]0,1[$ *(see Definition 3.105) such that for any* $\mathbf{x} \in \cup_{n\in\mathbb{N}}[0,1]^n$ *we have*

$$\mathsf{V}(\mathbf{x}) = \mathsf{Med}(a, \mathsf{T}(\mathbf{x}), \mathsf{S}(\mathbf{x})),$$

where T *is a t-norm given by (3.55) and* S *is a t-conorm given by (3.54). Let* J *be an index set. Then the functions* $\mathsf{V}_1^{(J)}, \mathsf{V}_2^{(J)} : [0,1]^J \to [0,1]$ *given by*

$$\mathsf{V}_i^{(J)}(\mathbf{x}) := \mathsf{Med}\left(a, \mathsf{T}_i^{(J)}(\mathbf{x}), \mathsf{S}_i^{(J)}(\mathbf{x})\right), \quad i = 1, 2$$

(in the case $i = 2$, *we suppose the continuity of* T *and* S) *are symmetric J-aggregation functions.*

The above examples show that we can apply several construction methods discussed in Chapter 6 also in the case of J-aggregation functions. As another typical example of this nature we introduce the function $\mathsf{A}^{(J)} : \mathbb{I}^J \to \mathbb{I}$, where $\mathbb{I}$ is a closed interval, given by

$$\mathsf{A}^{(J)}(\mathbf{x}) = \frac{\sup \mathbf{x} + \inf \mathbf{x}}{2},$$

which is a simple application of the arithmetic mean to sup and inf aggregation functions ($\mathsf{A}^{(J)}$ can be considered as a special OWA J-aggregation function; see Chapter 4, and compare with Example A.8). A related method of constructing J-aggregation functions is based on an *a priori* given vector $\mathbf{z} \in \mathbb{I}^J$, where $\mathbb{I}$ is a closed interval, $\mathbb{I} = [a,b]$, and a binary aggregation function $\mathsf{B} : \mathbb{I}^2 \to \mathbb{I}$ (further generalizations are also possible).

Proposition A.29. *Let* $\mathbb{I} = [a,b]$, J *be an index set,* $\mathsf{A}^{(J)} : \mathbb{I}^J \to \mathbb{I}$ *a J-aggregation function,* $\mathsf{B} : \mathbb{I}^2 \to \mathbb{I}$, *and let* $\mathbf{z} \in \mathbb{I}^J$ *be a fixed vector such that*

$$\mathsf{A}^{(J)}\left((\mathsf{B}(z_j, a))_{j\in J}\right) = \alpha < \beta = \mathsf{A}^{(J)}\left((\mathsf{B}(z_j, b))_{j\in J}\right).$$

If we define $A_{B,z}^{(J)} : \mathbb{I}^J \to \mathbb{I}$ *by*

$$A_{B,z}^{(J)}(\mathbf{x}) := a + (b-a)\frac{A^{(J)}\big((B(z_j,x_j))_{j\in J}\big) - \alpha}{\beta - \alpha},$$

then $A_{B,z}^{(J)}$ *is a* J-*aggregation function.*

Example A.30. A typical example is related to $B = \mathsf{Min}$ and $\mathbb{I} = [0,1]$. Suppose $z_j = 1$ for at least one $j \in J$. Then for $A^{(J)} = \sup$ we have $\alpha = 0, \beta = 1$, and $A_{\mathsf{Min},z}^{(J)} =: \mathcal{S}_\mu^{(J)}$, where the J-aggregation function $\mathcal{S}_\mu^{(J)}$ is the Sugeno integral on $(J, 2^J)$ with respect to a possibility measure $\mu : 2^J \to [0,1]$ given by

$$\mu(K) := \sup\{z_k \mid k \in K\}$$

for all $K \subseteq J$. For more details on the Sugeno integral, see Section 5.5.

Remark A.31. (i) All introduced J-aggregation functions reduce to standard n-ary aggregation functions whenever $|J| = n$, and to (∞)-aggregation functions discussed in Section A.2 if $J = \mathbb{N}$.

(ii) Similarly to what was done in Section A.2, one can introduce $\limsup$ and $\liminf$ as J-aggregation functions also if J is infinite and differs from $\mathbb{N}$ (there is no increasing bijection mapping from J into $\mathbb{N}$). Namely, for any closed interval $\mathbb{I}$ we can define for $\mathbf{x} \in \mathbb{I}^J$ two J-aggregation functions as follows:

$$\liminf \mathbf{x} := \inf\{t \in [a,b] \text{ such that } |\{j \in J \mid x_j \geqslant t\}| \text{ is infinite}\}$$
$$= \sup\{t \in [a,b] \text{ such that } |\{j \in J \mid x_j \leqslant t\}| \text{ is finite}\}$$

and

$$\limsup \mathbf{x} := \sup\{t \in [a,b] \text{ such that } |\{j \in J \mid x_j \leqslant t\}| \text{ is infinite}\}$$
$$= \inf\{t \in [a,b] \text{ such that } |\{j \in J \mid x_j \geqslant t\}| \text{ is finite}\}.$$

Evidently, if $J = \mathbb{N}$ the above definitions coincide with the standard $\liminf$ and $\limsup$. Moreover, for any $\mathbf{x} \in \mathbb{I}^J$ we have

$$\inf \mathbf{x} \leqslant \liminf \mathbf{x} \leqslant \limsup \mathbf{x} \leqslant \sup \mathbf{x}.$$

All J-aggregation functions discussed till now were defined for all input vectors $\mathbf{x} \in \mathbb{I}^J$. However, this is not the case for J-counterparts of several distinguished classes of standard aggregation functions. Even one of the oldest infinitary aggregation methods – the Riemann integral, which is fundamental for calculus and has numerous applications, cannot be applied to any input function. For real applications it often suffices to aggregate only some of the possible input vectors from $\mathbb{I}^J$. Not going deeper into details, we recall only that for $J = [c,d]$ and $\mathbb{I} = [0, \infty[$, the Riemann integral can be applied to any integrable function $f : J \to \mathbb{I}$, i.e., for $f \in \mathbb{I}^J$ we have $\mathsf{Rie}(f) := \int_c^d f(x)\, dx$. For a possibly larger class of all J-(Borel-)measurable functions $f : J \to [0, \infty]$, one can apply the Choquet integral with respect to a capacity μ on $(J, \mathcal{J})$, where J is an arbitrary (infinite) index set and $\mathcal{J}$ a σ-algebra of subsets of J (for more details see Section 5.4). Similarly, one can introduce the Sugeno integral, or several other types of integrals defined on an arbitrary measurable space $(J, \mathcal{J})$; see Sections 5.5 and 5.6.

In some cases, one can introduce idempotent infinitary aggregation functions. For example, in the case $\mathbb{I} = [c, d] \subset \mathbb{R}$, the mean value of a Riemann integrable function $f : J \to [0, \infty[$ is given by

$$\mathsf{M}_{\mathsf{Rie}}(f) := \frac{\int_c^d f(x)\, dx}{d - c}.$$

Similarly, in the case of the Choquet integral, it is enough to deal with a normalized capacity μ, i.e., $\mu(J) = 1$, on $(J, \mathcal{J})$, and then

$$\mathcal{C}_\mu^{(J)}(f) := (C) \int_J f\, d\mu$$

defines an idempotent aggregation function on the class of all nonnegative $\mathcal{J}$-measurable functions. Observe that sup and inf can be understood also as special Choquet integrals. Namely, we have on $(J, 2^J)$ and with respect to the capacity $\mu_{\max} : 2^J \to [0, 1]$ given by

$$\mu_{\max}(K) := \begin{cases} 0 & \text{for } K = \varnothing \\ 1 & \text{if } \varnothing \neq K \subseteq J, \end{cases}$$

that $\mathcal{C}_{\mu_{\max}}^{(J)}(f) = \sup f$. Similarly, for the capacity $\mu_{\min} : 2^J \to [0, 1]$ given by

$$\mu_{\min}(K) := \begin{cases} 1 & \text{for } K = J \\ 0 & \text{if } K \subsetneq J, \end{cases}$$

we have $\mathcal{C}_{\mu_{\min}}^{(J)}(f) = \inf f$.

Observe that also lim inf and lim sup on infinite J can be obtained by means of a Choquet integral. Indeed, for the capacity $\mu^\square : 2^J \to [0, 1]$ given by

$$\mu^\square(K) := \begin{cases} 0 & \text{for } |K| \text{ finite} \\ 1 & \text{otherwise}, \end{cases}$$

we have $\mathcal{C}_{\mu^\square}^{(J)}(f) = \limsup f$. Similarly, for the capacity $\mu_\square : 2^J \to [0, 1]$ given by

$$\mu_\square(K) := \begin{cases} 1 & \text{for } |J \setminus K| \text{ finite} \\ 0 & \text{otherwise}, \end{cases}$$

we have $\mathcal{C}_{\mu_\square}^{(J)}(f) = \liminf f$.

Appendix B

Examples and applications

B.1 Main domains of applications

We give here a commented list of application domains, with references for further study. We do not pretend to be exhaustive, and the reader may consult more application-oriented books on aggregation, e.g., [411].

A first group of applications comes from decision theory. Making decisions often amounts to aggregating scores or preferences on a given set of alternatives, the scores or preferences being obtained from several decision makers, voters, experts, etc., or representing different points of view, criteria, objectives, etc. This concerns decision under multiple criteria or multiple attributes, multiperson decision making, and multiobjective optimization.

A second group is rooted in information or data fusion. The aim is to refine the information on a given set of objects, by fusing several sources. Often, this amounts to making some kind of decision, as in the first group of applications. Typical applications here are pattern recognition and classification, as well as image analysis.

A third group comes from artificial intelligence and fuzzy logic. Aggregation functions are essentially used there as a generalization of logical connectives in rule-based systems (automated reasoning).

Lastly, we mention but do not detail applications related to probability theory. Obviously, copulas play a prominent role there.

Decision making under multiple criteria or attributes Let X represent a set of alternatives (objects of interest on which a decision or selection has to be made, like candidates to hire, projects to fund, apartments to rent, etc.). Each alternative $x \in X$ is described by a set of attributes (e.g., for the apartment example, rent, size, location, etc.), and is evaluated with respect to these attributes. The evaluation gives rise to a score on each attribute, reflecting the preference of the decision maker among the possible values taken by the attribute (e.g., low rent, large size, close to a shopping mall, etc.). An attribute equipped with such a preference is called a criterion. A final score is computed by an aggregation function, representing the overall assessment of the decision maker concerning the alternative in question, taking into account all criteria.

This very rough and narrow presentation of multicriteria decision making (MCDM) follows the spirit of multiattribute utility theory (MAUT), whose classical reference is [207]. A much wider exposition, presenting many different approaches, can be found in [355].

Whatever the method used, a central step in multicriteria decision making is the aggregation step, where quantities to be aggregated are most often scores on criteria for a given alternative. By far the most widely used aggregation function is the weighted arithmetic mean. However, in principle any aggregation function being internal could be used as well, like means and averages, and in particular integral-based aggregation functions. The Choquet integral must be especially mentioned here, since it has given rise to many applications; see the surveys [146, 166], which contain many references and examples of applications, as well as several chapters in the edited book [169]. The reason for this is that the notions of importance index, interaction index, tolerance, veto and favor, etc., presented in Chapter 10, can be adequately handled by capacities and the Choquet integral. Moreover, all these notions are very important in multicriteria decision making, since they reflect the language used by the decision maker.

Multiobjective optimization The situation is similar for multiobjective optimization (MOP), although the domain has its specificities. In MOP, contrarily to MCDM, there is a huge number of alternatives (called solutions), most often an uncountable set. The problem is to find a best solution maximizing a set of objective functions $f_1, \ldots, f_n$. Each solution $x \in X$ is adequately represented by the vector $\mathbf{f}(x) := (f_1(x), \ldots, f_n(x))$ of values of the objective functions for that solution. The key notion is Pareto dominance: x is Pareto optimal if there is no $y \in X$ such that $\mathbf{f}(y) > \mathbf{f}(x)$, i.e., $f_i(y) \geqslant f_i(x)$ for all $i = 1, \ldots, n$, and strict inequality holds for at least one i. Methods in MOP more or less amount to exploring in an efficient way the set of Pareto optimal solutions. An exhaustive exploration being most of the time intractable, one popular method is to use a parametrized aggregation function A, replacing the vector $\mathbf{f}(x)$ by its aggregated value, $\mathsf{A}(\mathbf{f}(x))$. However, the aggregation function has to satisfy two "efficiency" conditions. The first one says that maximizing $\mathsf{A}(\mathbf{f}(x))$ always gives solutions that are Pareto optimal. The second one, much more difficult to fulfill, is that any Pareto optimal solution must correspond to the maximization of $\mathsf{A}(\mathbf{f}(x))$, for some parameter vector θ of A. A classical result says that the weighted arithmetic mean satisfies these two conditions if the domain $\{\mathbf{f}(x)\}_{x \in X}$ is convex. For nonconvex domains, the Chebyshev norm used with respect to a reference point x_0 as follows:

$$\psi_{\mathbf{w}, x_0}(x) = \max_{i=1}^{n} \{w_i | f_i(x) - f_i(x_0) | \},$$

where $\mathbf{w}$ is a weight vector, satisfies the two conditions. The Choquet integral can also be used for nonconvex domains, but this topic has hardly been explored till now. For a thorough reference on MOP, we recommend the book of Ehrgott [109].

Multiperson decision making The theoretical framework for decisions with several persons is social choice theory, which has its roots back in the French revolution, when voting procedures were studied. Well-known procedures from this time are universal suffrage in two rounds, the Borda count, and the Condorcet rule. The classical way to build voting procedures is to consider that each voter gives his/her preference on the set of candidates, in the form of a total order. Then some aggregation of these orders has to be performed, to get a final total order, which points out the best candidate. The famous Arrow's theorem [19, pp. 96–100] has ruined any hope of choosing a candidate using this approach in a rational way. It shows that if one wants as a result of aggregation a total order (i.e., a preference relation without cycles – the Condorcet rule may produce cycles), wants to avoid dictators, to satisfy the unanimity rule, and the independence of irrelevant alternatives condition, then no aggregation function fulfilling these conditions exists.

This surprising result concerns aggregation of total orders, not of numerical scores, as we deal with in this book. It shows once again that the nature of "objects" to be aggregated heavily conditions the existence of aggregation functions, a phenomenon well illustrated in Chapters 7, 8, and 9. Considering that voters give scores to candidates, representing in some sense the intensity of their preference, permits us to escape Arrow's theorem, but formally amounts to using methods of multicriteria decision making, up to the difference that most often, voters are anonymous, and thus symmetric aggregation functions have to be chosen. In this respect, it is interesting to note that the usual way to score sportsmen in Olympic games, is to take an arithmetic mean after having discarded the two extremal scores (min and max) to avoid a biased evaluation. But this is a particular case of an ordered weighted averaging (OWA) function; see (1.19) and Corollary 2.61. Giving scores to candidates instead of just ordering them is a recent (at the time we are writing) although controversial tendency in social choice theory; see the works of Balinski, e.g., [24].

Another approach to social choice theory is to use valued-preference relations (or fuzzy preferences), a kind of mix of the two previous approaches. An account of this can be found in, e.g., [202]. For a thorough introduction to social choice theory, we recommend the classical paper by Sen [386], and the more recent books [20, 133].

Pattern recognition and classification One popular approach to classification of objects and pattern recognition is data or sensor fusion. Typically, let us denote again by X the set of objects of interest (flowers, animals, planes, words, diseases, etc.), to be eventually classified in some set of predefined classes $\{C_1, \ldots, C_p\}$. Each object being a complex structure, it is described by a set of attributes, which can be very large, or, depending on the domain of applications, it can be "measured" by a set of sensors, each of them bringing a partial description of the object. Refering to the above examples, attributes of flowers are colors of petals, leaves and stamens, height, number of petals, shape, etc., while a plane can be detected by several radars or observed with binoculars. In the first case, classes are the different species of flowers, like *iris versicolor* or *iris virginica*, and in the second case, classes could be either the different types of planes, or in a military context, only two classes may be considered: *friend* or *foe*.

To classify a given (unknown) object, one transforms the measurements given by the sensors $S_1, \ldots, S_n$ or the values of the attributes into confidence degrees of belonging to some class. Specifically, $d(S_i, C_j, x)$ is the confidence degree that $x \in X$ belongs to class C_j according to sensor S_i (or attribute i). Finally, an aggregation of the confidence degrees $d(S_1, C_j, x), \ldots, d(S_n, C_j, x)$ is performed, giving an overall confidence degree for x belonging to class C_j. Strictly speaking, the aggregation function should depend on the class, that is, p different aggregation functions are used. This is because some sensors may be more discriminative for certain classes, and unable to distinguish some others. Hence, the weight given to sensors should depend on the classes.

Internal weighted (nonsymmetric) aggregation functions are the most natural choice in this situation, like in MCDM. The Choquet integral, due to its versatility, has often been used with success in practical applications; see a survey in [149], an application where the Choquet integral is used to combine several classifiers [61], and an application to handwritten character recognition [132]. With this approach, computing the Shapley value (importance index) permits one to perform feature extraction.

Image analysis   This domain is highly related to the previous one, and similar approaches are used. Image analysis is such a difficult task that often sensor (or method) fusion is used. Here also, the Choquet integral has been widely used; see a survey in [208].

The second place where aggregation functions appear in image processing is filtering. Let us consider for simplicity a gray level image, that is, an integer-valued function h defined on a subinterval I of $\mathbb{Z}^2$, and a pixel (picture element) x of I. We denote by $h(x)$ the gray level of pixel x. Filtering consists in modifying the value $h(x)$, taking into account the gray level of neighbors of x. Denoting by W_x the set of neighbors (window) of x, we compute $h'(x) = \mathsf{A}(y \mid y \in W_x)$, using some aggregation function A. Linear filters (i.e., weighted arithmetic means) are popular, but most robust to noise are order statistic filters, weighted arithmetic means applied on the ordered set of neighbors (in our terminology, these are ordered weighted averaging (OWA) functions), and once again, Choquet integrals; see a survey in [208]. Choquet integral filters have been used also for texture recognition [158].

Rule-based systems   In classical (binary) logic, an inference rule has the form

$$\text{IF } p_1 \text{ AND } p_2 \text{ AND } \cdots \text{ AND } p_n, \text{ THEN } q,$$

where $p_1, \ldots, p_n, q$ are predicates, being true or false. The IF–THEN implication is the material implication $p \rightarrow q$ defined by $\neg p \vee q$, where $\vee$ denotes the logical OR. If "false" and "true" are coded by 0 and 1 respectively, the truth value of the rule is computed by

$$t = \mathsf{Max}(1 - \mathsf{Min}(p_1, \ldots, p_n), q).$$

If, like in fuzzy logic, the truth value of a predicate is allowed to lie in $[0, 1]$, the above formula contains an aggregation of the truth values of $p_1, \ldots, p_n$ by the minimum, which is an aggregation function modeling conjunction. Note that the implication $\mathsf{Max}(1 - \cdot, \cdot)$ is not an aggregation function since it is decreasing in the first place, but Max is an aggregation function modeling disjunction. In fuzzy logic, conjunction and disjunction are more generally modeled by a t-norm and a t-conorm [143, 178, 220]. The use of t-conorms for disjunction and various negations leads to a wide family of implications.

The so-called fuzzy inference rules have been used in many applications, especially in fuzzy control. For a rigorous treatment of rule-based systems in fuzzy logic we recommend [100].

B.2 A specific application: mixture of uncertainty measures

Utility theory is based on the notion of mathematical expectation. Its axiomatic foundations, following von Neumann and Morgenstern [423], are based on the notion of probabilistic mixtures. It has been shown by Dubois *et al.* [89] that the notion of mixtures can be extended to S-capacities.

The aim of the paper [92] was to present the answer to the following question: *what else remains possible beyond idempotent (possibilistic) and probabilistic mixtures?*

The solution obtained in [92] takes advantage of a result obtained in [220, Th. 5.21], presented in Theorem 3.120, on the restricted distributivity of a t-norm over a t-conorm. This result has a drastic consequence on the notion of mixtures. Beyond possibilistic (see [90]) and probabilistic mixtures, only a form of hybridization is possible such that the mixture is possibilistic under a certain threshold, and probabilistic above. The same distributivity property must be satisfied between the t-conorm characterizing the pseudo-additive measure, and the t-norm expressing separability (independence); see [92, 93, 351].

S-measures and independence   Let S be a continuous t-conorm, and X be a given nonempty finite set. Recall that a capacity $\mu : 2^X \to [0, 1]$ is called an S-capacity if for every $A, B \subseteq X$ such that $A \cap B = \varnothing$, we have

$$\mu(A \cup B) = \mathsf{S}(\mu(A), \mu(B)),$$

see Definition 5.6.

Remark B.1. If $\mu : 2^X \to [0, 1]$ is an S-capacity and $\psi : [0, 1] \to [0, 1]$ an increasing bijection, then $\psi^{-1} \circ \mu : 2^X \to [0, 1]$ is an S_ψ-capacity, where S_ψ is defined by

$$\mathsf{S}_\psi(x, y) = \psi^{-1}\left(\mathsf{S}(\psi(x), \psi(y))\right).$$

In [92] the following problem was investigated: Which continuous t-norms T can be used for extending the notion of independence for an S-capacity? Namely, commutativity and associativity of T reflect the corresponding properties for conjunctions and it is natural that T be nondecreasing in each place and continuous. Since the term independence has a precise meaning in probability theory, we shall speak of separability instead.

Definition B.2. Two events A and B are said to be T-*separable* if and only if

$$\mu(A \cap B) = T(\mu(A), \mu(B))$$

for a t-norm T.

The only "reasonable" S-capacities according to [92] are

(i) probability measures (then $T = $ product);
(ii) Max-capacity (then T is any t-norm);
(iii) hybrid Max–probability capacity μ such that there exists $a \in]0, 1[$ which gives for A and B disjoint

$$\mu(A \cup B) := \begin{cases} \mu(A) + \mu(B) - a & \text{if } \mu(A) > a, \mu(B) > a \\ \\ \text{Max}(\mu(A), \mu(B)) & \text{otherwise,} \end{cases}$$

and for independence:

$$\mu(A \cap B) = \begin{cases} a + \dfrac{(\mu(A) - a)(\mu(B) - a)}{1 - a} & \text{if } \mu(A) > a, \mu(B) > a \\ \\ aT_1\left(\dfrac{\mu(A)}{a}, \dfrac{\mu(B)}{a}\right) & \text{if } \mu(A) \leqslant a, \mu(B) \leqslant a \\ \\ \text{Min}(\mu(A), \mu(B)) & \text{otherwise,} \end{cases}$$

where T_1 is from Theorem 3.120, and the normalization condition reads

$$\sum_{\{x\},\mu(\{x\})>a} \mu(\{x\}) = 1 + (|\{x \mid \mu(\{x\}) > a\}| - 1)a.$$

Any probability distribution on a finite set X can be represented as a sequence of binary lotteries. A binary lottery is a quadruple (A, α, x, y) where $A \subset X$ and $\alpha \in [0, 1]$ such that $P(A) = \alpha$, and it represents the random event that yields x if A occurs and y otherwise. More generally, suppose μ is an S-capacity on, e.g., $X = \{x_1, x_2, x_3\}$, and $\mu_i = \mu(\{x_i\})$. Suppose we want to decompose the ternary tree into the binary tree so that they are equivalent; see Figure B.1. Then following the calculations from [92], the reduction of lottery property enforces the following equations for given μ_2 and μ_3:

$$S(v_1, v_2) = 1, \quad T(w, v_1) = \mu_2, \quad T(w, v_2) = \mu_3,$$

where T is the t-norm that expresses separability for S-measures. The complete calculation is given in [92].

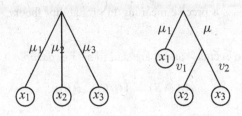

Figure B.1 S-capacity tree (left) and the corresponding binary tree (right)

Hybrid mixtures   Let (S, T) be a pair consisting of a continuous t-conorm and t-norm, respectively, which satisfy the condition (RD); see Definition 3.118. Then by Theorem 3.120 we have the form of this restricted distributive pair of continuous t-conorm $S = (< a, 1, S^* >)$ and t-norm $T = (< 0, a, T_1 >, < a, 1, T^* >)$ (see Figure 3.24), where S^* is a nilpotent t-conorm, T_1 an arbitrary continuous t-norm and T^* a strict t-norm. We define the set Φ_S of ordered pairs (α, β) in the following way:

$$\Phi_S := \{(\alpha, \beta) \mid (\alpha, \beta) \in [0, 1], S(\alpha, \beta) = 1\}.$$

Based on the classical framework of the utility theory related to the mixture [187], the following notion was introduced in [89].

Definition B.3. An *extended mixture set* is a quadruple $(\mathcal{G}, M, T, S)$ where $\mathcal{G}$ is a set, $M : \mathcal{G}^2 \times \Phi_S \to \mathcal{G}$ is a function (extended mixture operation), and (S, T) is a pair consisting of a continuous t-conorm and t-norm, respectively, which satisfy the condition (RD), such that the following conditions are satisfied:

Mix1. $M(x, y; 1, 0) = x$.
Mix2. $M(x, y; \alpha, \beta) = M(y, x; \beta, \alpha)$.
Mix3. $M(M(x, y; \alpha, \beta), y; \gamma, \delta) = M(x, y; T(\alpha, \gamma), S(T(\beta, \gamma), T(\delta, 1)))$.

The conditions **Mix1–Mix3** imply the following condition:

Mix4. $M(x, x; \alpha, \beta) = x$.

The following lemma is proved in [89].

Lemma B.4. *Suppose M is an extended mixture, i.e.,* **Mix1–Mix3** *holds for M. Then the condition* **Mix5***:*

$$M(M(x, y; \alpha, \beta), M(x, y; \gamma, \delta); \lambda, \mu) = M(x, y; S(T(\alpha, \lambda), T(\gamma, \mu)),$$
$$S(T(\beta, \lambda), T(\delta, \mu))$$

holds for all $x, y \in \mathcal{G}$ *and all* $(\alpha, \beta), (\gamma, \delta), (\lambda, \mu) \in \Phi'$, *where* Φ' *is a nonempty subset of* Φ_S, *if and only if*

$$T(\gamma, S(\alpha, \beta)) = S(T(\gamma, \alpha), T(\gamma, \beta)),$$

i.e., T *is distributive over* S *on* Φ'.

Let (S, T) be a pair consisting of a continuous t-conorm and a t-norm, respectively, such that they satisfy the condition (RD), with $a \in [0, 1]$. We restrict ourselves to the canonical situation, where $S = (< a, 1, S_L >)$ and the t-norm $T = (< 0, a, T_1 >, < a, 1, \Pi >)$, since this is the most important case, and other cases can be obtained by isomorphisms; see Theorem 3.39, and the dual theorem for t-conorms.

We define the set $\Phi' = \Phi_{S,a}$ of ordered pairs (α, β) in the following way:

$$\Phi_{S,a} := \{(\alpha, \beta) \mid (\alpha, \beta) \in]a, 1[^2, \alpha + \beta = 1 + a\}$$
$$\cup \{(\alpha, \beta) \mid \mathsf{Min}(\alpha, \beta) \leqslant a, \mathsf{Max}(\alpha, \beta) = 1\}.$$

We have $\Phi_{S,a} \subset \Phi_S$, and we have that for every $(\alpha, \beta), (\alpha, \gamma) \in \Phi_{S,a}$ the distributivity holds.

We define now hybrid mixture sets.

Definition B.5. A *hybrid mixture set* is a quadruple $(\mathcal{G}, M, T, S)$ where $\mathcal{G}$ is a set, (S, T) is a pair consisting of a continuous t-conorm and a t-norm, respectively, satisfying the condition (RD) with $a \in [0, 1]$, and $M : \mathcal{G}^2 \times \Phi_S' \to \mathcal{G}$ is a function (hybrid mixture operation) given by

$$M(x, y; \alpha, \beta) = S(T(\alpha, x), T(\beta, y)).$$

As we said, we shall restrict ourselves to the case $(< S_M, S_L >, < T_1, T_P >)_a$. Then it is easy to verify that M satisfies axioms **Mix1–Mix5** on $\Phi_{S,a}$. This kind of mixture exhausts the possible solutions to **Mix1–Mix5**.

Hybrid possibilistic–probabilistic utility function Let (S, T) be a pair consisting of a continuous t-conorm and a t-norm, respectively, of the form $S = (< a, 1, S_L >)$ and $T = (< 0, a, T_1 >, < a, 1, \Pi >)$. Let u_1, u_2 be two utility values in $[0, 1]$, and let w_1, w_2 be two degrees of plausibility from $\Phi_{S,a}$. Then we define the *optimistic hybrid utility function* by means of the hybrid mixture as

$$U(u_1, u_2; w_1, w_2) = S(T(u_1, w_1), T(u_2, w_2)).$$

We shall examine in detail this utility function.

Case I. Let $w_1 > a, w_2 > a$, i.e., $w_1 + w_2 = 1 + a$. Then we have the following subcases:

(a) Let $u_1 > a, u_2 > a$. Then we have

$$U(u_1, u_2; w_1, w_2) = S\left(a + \frac{(u_1 - a)(w_1 - a)}{1 - a}, a + \frac{(u_2 - a)(w_2 - a)}{1 - a}\right).$$

(B.1)

Then $a + \frac{(u_i - a)(w_i - a)}{1 - a} > a$ for $i = 1, 2$. Hence by (B.1)

$$U(u_1, u_2; w_1, w_2) = \frac{u_1(w_1 - a) + u_2(1 - w_1)}{1 - a}.$$

(b) Let $u_1 \leqslant a, u_2 > a$. Then we have

$$U(u_1, u_2; w_1, w_2) = S\left(u_1, a + \frac{(u_2 - a)(w_2 - a)}{1 - a}\right)$$

$$= a + \frac{(u_2 - a)(w_2 - a)}{1 - a}.$$

In a quite analogous way it follows for $u_1 > a, u_2 \leqslant a$ that

$$U(u_1, u_2; w_1, w_2) = a + \frac{(u_1 - a)(w_1 - a)}{1 - a}.$$

(c) Let $u_1 \leqslant a, u_2 \leqslant a$. Then

$$U(u_1, u_2; w_1, w_2) = \mathsf{Max}(u_1, u_2).$$

Case II. Let $w_1 \leqslant a, w_2 = 1$ (in a quite analogous way we can consider the case $w_2 \leqslant a, w_1 = 1$). Then we have the following subcases, where $S = \mathsf{Max}$:

(a) Let $u_1 > a, u_2 > a$. Then we have

$$U(u_1, u_2; w_1, w_2) = S(w_1, u_2) = u_2.$$

(b) Let $u_1 \leqslant a, u_2 > a$. Then we have

$$U(u_1, u_2; w_1, w_2) = S\left(aT_1\left(\frac{u_1}{a}, \frac{w_1}{a}\right), u_2\right) = u_2.$$

(c) Let $u_1 > a, u_2 \leqslant a$. Then we have

$$U(u_1, u_2; w_1, w_2) = S(w_1, u_2) = \mathsf{Max}(w_1, u_2).$$

(d) Let $u_1 \leqslant a, u_2 \leqslant a$. Then we have

$$U(u_1, u_2; w_1, w_2) = \mathsf{Max}\left(a\mathsf{T}_1\left(\frac{u_1}{a}, \frac{w_1}{a}\right), u_2\right).$$

For $\mathsf{T}_1 = \mathsf{Min}$, cases II and Ic are exactly idempotent (possibilistic) utility.

Although the above description of optimistic hybrid utility is rather complex, it can be easily explained, including the name optimistic.

Case I is when the decision maker is very uncertain about the state of nature: both w_1 and w_2 are high and the two involved states have high plausibility. Case Ia is when the reward is high in both states: then the behavior of utility is probabilistic. Case Ib is when the reward is low in state $x_1 (u_1 \leqslant a)$, but high in the other state. Then the decision maker looks forward to the best outcome and the utility is a function of u_2 and w_2 only. In case Ic when both rewards are low, the decision maker is possibilistic and again focuses on the best outcome. Case II is when state x_1 is unlikely. In case IIa,b when the plausible reward is good, then the decision maker looks forward to this reward. In case IIc where the most plausible reward is low then the decision maker still keeps some hope that state x_1 will prevail if u_2 is really bad, but weakens the utility of state x_1, because of its lack of plausibility. This phenomenon subsides when the least plausible outcome is also bad, but the (bad) utility of x_1 participates in the calculation of the resulting utility, by discounting w_1 even further. From the analysis, the optimistic attitude of an agent ranking decisions using the hybrid utility is patent.

It remains as a problem to find a corresponding axiomatization for hybrid utility as was done for classical utility theory and possibility utility theory. One possible axiomatization is given in [353].

Symbols

$\mu_{\min}$	smallest normalized capacity	174
μ_{unif}	uniform capacity	174
$\mu(x,y)$	Möbius function	177
ξ	set function	173
$\overline{\xi}$	conjugate of ξ	173
τ_k	threshold measure	174
$\varphi(\mathbf{x})$	vector constructed from $\varphi = (\varphi_1, \ldots, \varphi_n)$ and a vector $\mathbf{x}$	10
ϕ^ξ	Shapley value of set function ξ	179
$\phi_i(\mathbf{A})$	importance index of i on $\mathbf{A}$	362
$\overline{\phi}_i(\mathbf{A})$	normalized importance index of i on $\mathbf{A}$	362
$\phi_K(\mathbf{A})$	importance index of K on $\mathbf{A}$	365
Γ_γ	gamma operator	120
Δ_i	total variation of $\mathbf{A}$ w.r.t. i	362
$\Delta_{ij}\mathbf{A}$	second-order total variation of $\mathbf{A}$ w.r.t. i and j	367
$\Delta_K\mathbf{A}$	total variation of $\mathbf{A}$ w.r.t. K	368
$\Theta_{(k)}\mathbf{A}$	lowest relative variation of $\mathbf{A}$ w.r.t. rank k	365
Π	product function	8
$\Pi^{(\infty)}$	product function for infinite number of arguments	400
Σ	sum function	8
$\Phi[\mathbb{I}]$	set of increasing bijections of $\mathbb{I}$ onto itself	46
$\Phi'[\mathbb{I}]$	set of continuous nondecreasing surjections of $\mathbb{I}$ onto $\mathbb{I}$	300
$\Phi''[\mathbb{I}]$	set of monotone bijections of $\mathbb{I}$ onto $\mathbb{I}$	301
$\Phi_n[\mathbb{I}]$	diagonal restriction of $\Phi[\mathbb{I}]^n$	46
$\Phi'_n[\mathbb{I}]$	diagonal restriction of $\Phi'[\mathbb{I}]^n$	305
$\Psi_{(k)}\mathbf{A}$	total variation of $\mathbf{A}$ w.r.t. rank k	365
$(< a_k, b_k, \mathsf{T}_k >)_{k \in K}$	ordinal sum of t-norms	82
andness(F)	global andness value of function F	352
b	Möbius transform of a bicapacity	336
$\text{conj}_k(\mathbf{A})$	k-conjunctiveness index for $\mathbf{A}$	377
d_K	distance related to even function K	257
$\text{diag}(\mathbb{I}^n)$	diagonal section of $\mathbb{I}^n$	10
$\text{disj}_k(\mathbf{A})$	k-disjunctiveness index for $\mathbf{A}$	377
$\text{dom}(f)$	domain of f	10
$f^{(-1)}$	pseudo-inverse of function f	61
favor($\mathbf{A},j$)	favor index of coordinate j for $\mathbf{A}$	374
id	identity function	10
idemp(F)	global idempotency value of F	357
$\text{int}(\mathbb{I})$	interior of $\mathbb{I}$	2
$k \cdot x$	concatenation of k copies of element x	9
$k \cdot \mathbf{x}$	concatenation of k copies of vector $\mathbf{x}$	10

$\mathcal{B}_\mu^{\oplus,\odot}$	Benvenuti integral	231
$\mathcal{C}_\mu$	(asymmetric) Choquet integral	181
$\check{\mathcal{C}}_\mu$	symmetric Choquet integral	182
$\mathcal{C}_\mu^{(J)}$	Choquet integral for infinite number of arguments	409
$\mathcal{D}_{a,b,\theta}$	special class of decomposable means	156
$\mathcal{F}(n)$	set of capacities on $[n]$	173
$\mathcal{F}^*(n)$	set of normalized capacities on $[n]$	173
$\mathcal{F}_{0\text{-}1}(n)$	set of 0–1 capacities on $[n]$	173
$\mathcal{F}_{0\text{-}1}^{\mathbb{I}}(n)$	set $\mathcal{F}_{0\text{-}1}(n)$ completed with the constant set functions 0, 1	298
$\mathcal{F}_2(n)$	set of bicapacities on $[n]$	335
$\mathcal{F}_2^*(n)$	set of normalized bicapacities on $[n]$	335
$\mathcal{G}(n)$	set of games on $[n]$	344
$\mathcal{G}_2(n)$	set of bicooperative games on $[n]$	342
$\mathcal{G}(\mathbb{I})$	set of strictly increasing or constant functions defined on int($\mathbb{I}$) 307	
$\mathcal{I}_n[\mathbb{I}]$	set of orbits of $\mathbb{I}^n$ under $\Phi_n[\mathbb{I}]$	294
$\mathcal{I}_n^*[\mathbb{I}]$	set of orbits of $\mathbb{I}^n$ under $\Phi[\mathbb{I}]^n$	295
$\mathcal{M}_\mu^{\mathcal{S}}$	Murofushi integral	230
$\mathcal{O}_{\langle\cdot\rangle}$	set of cancelling sequences of computation rule $\langle\cdot\rangle$	332
$\mathcal{Q}([n])$	set of pairs of disjoint subsets of $[n]$	335
$\mathcal{S}_\mu$	Sugeno integral	210
$\check{\mathcal{S}}_\mu$	symmetric Sugeno integral	214
$\mathcal{S}_\mu^{(J)}$	Sugeno integral with infinite number of arguments	408
$\mathbb{I}, \mathbb{J}$	intervals of $\mathbb{R}$ (or $\overline{\mathbb{R}}$)	2
$\overline{\mathbb{I}}$	(set) closure of $\mathbb{I}$	2
$\mathbb{I}_\sigma^n$	subset of $\mathbb{I}^n$ constructed from permutation σ	10
$\mathbb{N}$	set of strictly positive integers	9
$\mathbb{N}_0$	set of nonnegative integers	9
$\mathbb{Q}$	set of rational numbers	9
$\mathbb{R}$	set of real numbers	2
$\overline{\mathbb{R}}$	extended set of real numbers	2
$\mathbb{Z}$	set of integers	9
$\mathfrak{L}$	set of all at most countable sequences	330
$\mathfrak{S}_K$	set of all permutations on K	10

References

[1] J. Aczél. On mean values. *Bull. Amer. Math. Soc.*, 54:392–400, 1948.

[2] J. Aczél. Sur les opérations définies pour des nombres réels. *Bull. Soc. Math. France*, 1949.

[3] J. Aczél. *Lectures on Functional Equations and their Applications*. Mathematics in Science and Engineering, Vol. 19. Academic Press, New York, 1966.

[4] J. Aczél. *Lectures on Functional Equations and their Applications*. Academic Press, New York, 1966.

[5] J. Aczél. On weighted synthesis of judgements. *Aequationes Math.*, 27(3):288–307, 1984.

[6] J. Aczél. *A Short Course on Functional Equations*. Theory and Decision Library. Series B: Mathematical and Statistical Methods. D. Reidel Publishing Co., Dordrecht, 1987.

[7] J. Aczél and C. Alsina. Synthesizing judgements: a functional equations approach. *Math. Modelling*, 9(3–5):311–320, 1987.

[8] J. Aczél and Z. Daróczy. Über verallgemeinerte quasilineare Mittelwerte, die mit Gewichtsfunktionen gebildet sind. *Publ. Math. Debrecen*, 10:171–190, 1963.

[9] J. Aczél and J. Dhombres. *Functional Equations in Several Variables*, volume 31 of *Encyclopedia of Mathematics and its Applications*. Cambridge University Press, Cambridge, 1989.

[10] J. Aczél, D. Gronau, and J. Schwaiger. Increasing solutions of the homogeneity equation and of similar equations. *J. Math. Anal. Appl.*, 182(2):436–464, 1994.

[11] J. Aczél and M. Kuczma. On two mean value properties and functional equations associated with them. *Aequationes Math.*, 38(2–3):216–235, 1989.

[12] J. Aczél and F. S. Roberts. On the possible merging functions. *Math. Social Sci.*, 17(3):205–243, 1989.

[13] J. Aczél, F. S. Roberts, and Z. Rosenbaum. On scientific laws without dimensional constants. *J. Math. Anal. Appl.*, 119(1–2):389–416, 1986.

[14] G. G. Agarwal, R. J. Dalpatadu, and A. K. Singh. Linear functions of uniform order statistics and B-splines. *Comm. Statist. Theory Methods*, 31(2):181–192, 2002.

[15] C. Alsina, M. J. Frank, and B. Schweizer. *Associative Functions: Triangular Norms and Copulas*. World Scientific Publishing Co. Pte. Ltd, Hackensack, NJ, 2006.

[16] C. Alsina, R. B. Nelsen, and B. Schweizer. On the characterization of a class of binary operations on distribution functions. *Statist. Probab. Lett.*, 17(2):85–89, 1993.

[17] C. Antoine. *Les Moyennes*, volume 3383 of *Que Sais-Je? [What Do I Know?]*. Presses Universitaires de France, Paris, 1998.

[18] V. Arnold. Concerning the representability of functions of two variables in the form $x[\phi(x) + \psi(y)]$. *Uspekhi Mat. Nauk*, 12:119–121, 1957.

[19] K. Arrow. *Social Choice and Individual Values*. Wiley, 2nd edition, 1963.

[20] K. Arrow, A. Sen, and K. Suzumura, editors. *Handbook of Social Choice and Welfare*. Handbooks in Economics 19. Elsevier/North Holland, Amsterdam, 2002.

[21] T. S. Arthanari and Y. Dodge. *Mathematical Programming in Statistics*. John Wiley & Sons Inc., New York, 1981.

[22] F. L. Baccelli, G. Cohen, G. J. Olsder, and J.-P. Quadrat. *Synchronization and Linearity*. Wiley Series in Probability and Mathematical Statistics: Probability and Mathematical Statistics. John Wiley & Sons Ltd, Chichester, 1992.

[23] M. Bajraktarević. Sur une équation fonctionnelle aux valeurs moyennes. *Glasnik Mat.-Fiz. Astronom. Društvo Mat. Fiz. Hrvatske. Ser. II*, 13:243–248, 1958.

[24] M. Balinski and R. Laraki. A theory of measuring, electing, and ranking. *Proc. Natl. Acad. Sci. USA*, 104(21):8720–8725 (electronic), 2007.

[25] J. F. Banzhaf. Weighted voting doesn't work: A mathematical analysis. *Rutgers Law Review*, 19:317–343, 1965.

[26] D. L. Barrow and P. W. Smith. Classroom notes: Spline notation applied to a volume problem. *Amer. Math. Monthly*, 86(1):50–51, 1979.

[27] L. Bartłomiejczyk and J. Drewniak. A characterization of sets and operations invariant under bijections. *Aequationes Math.*, 68(1):1–9, 2004.

[28] E. F. Beckenbach and R. Bellman. *Inequalities*. Second revised printing. Ergebnisse der Mathematik und ihrer Grenzgebiete. Neue Folge, Band 30. Springer-Verlag, New York, Inc., 1965.

[29] G. Beliakov. Monotone approximation of aggregation operators using least squares splines. *Int. J. Uncertain. Fuzziness Knowledge-Based Systems*, 10(6):659–676, 2002.

[30] G. Beliakov. How to build aggregation operators from data? *Int. J. Intelligent Systems*, 18:903–923, 2003.

[31] G. Beliakov, R. Mesiar, and L. Valášková. Fitting generated aggregation operators to empirical data. *Int. J. Uncertain. Fuzziness Knowledge-Based Systems*, 12(2):219–236, 2004.

[32] G. Beliakov, A. Pradera, and T. Calvo. *Aggregation Functions: a Guide for Practitioners*. Springer, 2007.

[33] G. Bemporad. Sul principio della media aritmetica. (Italian). *Atti Accad. Naz. Lincei*, 3(6):87–91, 1926.

[34] P. Benvenuti and R. Mesiar. On Tarski's contribution to the additive measure theory and its consequences. *Ann. Pure Appl. Logic*, 126(1–3):281–286, 2004.

[35] P. Benvenuti, R. Mesiar, and D. Vivona. Monotone set functions-based integrals. In E. Pap, editor, *Handbook of Measure Theory, Vol. II*, pages 1329–1379. North-Holland, Amsterdam, 2002.

[36] C. Berge. *Principles of Combinatorics*. Translated from the French. Mathematics in Science and Engineering, Vol. 72. Academic Press, New York, 1971.

[37] E. Berkson and T. A. Gillespie. Absolutely continuous functions of two variables and well-bounded operators. *J. London Math. Soc.*, (2) 30:305–321, 1984.

[38] L. R. Berrone. Decreasing sequences of means appearing from non-decreasing functions. *Publ. Math. Debrecen*, 55(1–2):53–72, 1999.

[39] L. R. Berrone and J. Moro. Lagrangian means. *Aequationes Math.*, 55(3):217–226, 1998.

[40] L. R. Berrone and J. Moro. On means generated through the Cauchy mean value theorem. *Aequationes Math.*, 60(1–2):1–14, 2000.

[41] S. Bertino. On dissimilarity between cyclic permutations. *Metron*, 35(1–2):53–88 (1979), 1977.

[42] R. Bhatia. *Positive Definite Matrices*. Princeton Series in Applied Mathematics. Princeton University Press, Princeton, NJ, 2007.

[43] J. M. Bilbao. *Cooperative Games on Combinatorial Structures*, volume 26 of *Theory and Decision Library. Series C: Game Theory, Mathematical Programming and Operations Research*. Kluwer Academic Publishers, Boston, MA, 2000.

[44] G. Birkhoff. *Lattice Theory*, 3rd edition. American Mathematical Society Colloquium Publications, Vol. XXV. American Mathematical Society, Providence, RI, 1967.

[45] D. Bouyssou and M. Pirlot. Choosing and ranking on the basis of fuzzy preference relations with the "min in favor". In *Multiple Criteria Decision Making (Hagen, 1995)*, volume 448 of *Lecture Notes in Econom. and Math. Systems*, pages 115–127. Springer, Berlin, 1997.

[46] M. Budinčević and M. S. Kurilić. A family of strict and discontinuous triangular norms. *Fuzzy Sets and Systems*, 95(3):381–384, 1998.

[47] P. S. Bullen. *Handbook of Means and their Inequalities*, volume 560 of *Mathematics and its Applications*. Kluwer Academic Publishers Group, Dordrecht, 2003.

[48] P. S. Bullen, D. S. Mitrinović, and P. M. Vasić. *Means and their Inequalities*, volume 31 of *Mathematics and its Applications (East European Series)*. D. Reidel Publishing Co., Dordrecht, 1988.

[49] T. Calvo, A. Kolesárová, M. Komorníková, and R. Mesiar. Aggregation operators: properties, classes and construction methods. In *Aggregation Operators*, volume 97 of *Stud. Fuzziness Soft Comput.*, pages 3–104. Physica, Heidelberg, 2002.

[50] T. Calvo and R. Mesiar. Criteria importances in median-like aggregation. *IEEE Trans. Fuzzy Syst.*, 9(4):662–666, 2001.

[51] T. Calvo and R. Mesiar. Stability of aggregation operators. In *Proc. Int. Conf. in Fuzzy Logic and Technology (EUSFLAT 2001)*, Leicester, England, September 2001.

[52] T. Calvo and R. Mesiar. Weighted triangular norms-based aggregation operators. *Fuzzy Sets and Systems*, 137:3–10, 2003.

[53] T. Calvo, R. Mesiar, and R. R. Yager. Quantitative weights and aggregation. *IEEE Trans. Fuzzy Syst.*, 12(1):62–69, 2004.

[54] T. Calvo and A. Pradera. Double aggregation operators. *Fuzzy Sets and Systems*, 142(1):15–33, 2004.

[55] P. Capéraà, A.-L. Fougères, and C. Genest. Bivariate distributions with given extreme value attractor. *J. Multivariate Anal.*, 72(1):30–49, 2000.

[56] A. L. Cauchy. *Cours d'analyse de l'Ecole Royale Polytechnique, Vol. I. Analyse algébrique*. Debure, Paris, 1821.

[57] A. Chateauneuf and J.-Y. Jaffray. Some characterizations of lower probabilities and other monotone capacities through the use of Möbius inversion. *Math. Social Sci.*, 17:263–283, 1989.

[58] C.-P. Chen and F. Qi. A new proof for monotonicity of the generalized weighted mean values. *Adv. Stud. Contemp. Math. (Kyungshang)*, 6(1):13–16, 2003.

[59] C.-P. Chen and F. Qi. New proofs of monotonicities of generalized weighted mean values. *Tamkang J. Math.*, 35(4):301–304, 2004.

[60] O. Chisini. Sul concetto di media. (Italian). *Periodico di matematiche*, 9(4):106–116, 1929.

[61] S.-B. Cho and J. Kim. Combining multiple neural networks by fuzzy integral for robust classification. *IEEE Trans. Systems, Man, Cybernetics*, 25(2):380–384, 1995.

[62] G. Choquet. Theory of capacities. *Ann. Inst. Fourier, Grenoble*, 5:131–295, 1953–1954.

[63] A. H. Clifford. Naturally totally ordered commutative semigroups. *Amer. J. Math.*, 76:631–646, 1954.

[64] A. C. Climescu. Sur l'équation fonctionnelle de l'associativité. *Bull. École Polytech. Jassy [Bul. Politehn. Gh. Asachi. Iași]*, 1:211–224, 1946.

[65] E. Combarro and P. Miranda. A genetic algorithm for the identification of fuzzy measures from sample data. In *Int. Fuzzy Systems Association World Congress (IFSA 2003)*, pages 163–166, Istanbul, Turkey, June 2003.

[66] R. Craigen and Z. Páles. The associativity equation revisited. *Aequationes Math.*, 37(2–3):306–312, 1989.

[67] I. Cuculescu and R. Theodorescu. Extreme value attractors for star unimodal copulas. *C. R. Math. Acad. Sci. Paris*, 334(8):689–692, 2002.

[68] I. Curiel. *Cooperative. Game Theory and Applications*, volume 16 of *Theory and Decision Library. Series C: Game Theory, Mathematical Programming and Operations Research.* Kluwer Academic Publishers, Boston, MA, 1997.

[69] V. Cutello and J. Montero. Recursive connective rules. *Int. J. Intelligent Systems*, 14:3, 1999.

[70] E. Czogała and J. Drewniak. Associative monotonic operations in fuzzy set theory. *Fuzzy Sets and Systems*, 12(3):249–269, 1984.

[71] W. F. Darsow, B. Nguyen, and E. T. Olsen. Copulas and Markov processes. *Illinois J. Math.*, 36(4):600–642, 1992.

[72] H. A. David and H. N. Nagaraja. *Order Statistics.* Wiley Series in Probability and Statistics. Wiley-Interscience [John Wiley & Sons], Hoboken, NJ, 3rd edition, 2003.

[73] B. De Baets. Coimplicators, the forgotten connectives. *Tatra Mt. Math. Publ.*, 12:229–240, 1997.

[74] B. De Baets. Idempotent uninorms. *European J. Oper. Res.*, 118:631–642, 1999.

[75] B. De Baets and J. Fodor. Van Melle's combining function in MYCIN is a representable uninorm: an alternative proof. *Fuzzy Sets and Systems*, 104(1):133–136, 1999.

[76] B. De Baets and R. Mesiar. Discrete triangular norms. In *Topological and Algebraic Structures in Fuzzy Sets*, pages 389–400. Kluwer Academic Publishers, 2003.

[77] L. M. de Campos and M. J. Bolaños. Characterization and comparison of Sugeno and Choquet integrals. *Fuzzy Sets and Systems*, 52(1):61–67, 1992.

[78] L. M. de Campos, M. T. Lamata, and S. Moral. A unified approach to define fuzzy integrals. *Fuzzy Sets and Systems*, 39(1):75–90, 1991.

[79] B. de Finetti. Sul concetto di media. (Italian). *Giorn. Ist. Ital. Attuari*, 2(3):369–396, 1931.

[80] C. Dellacherie. Quelques commentaires sur les prolongements de capacités. In *Séminaire de Probabilités, V (Univ. Strasbourg, année universitaire 1969-1970)*, pages 77–81. Lecture Notes in Math., Vol. 191. Springer, Berlin, 1971.

[81] A. P. Dempster. Upper and lower probabilities induced by a multivalued mapping. *Ann. Math. Statist.*, 38:325–339, 1967.

[82] D. Denneberg. *Non-additive Measure and Integral*, volume 27 of *Theory and Decision Library. Series B: Mathematical and Statistical Methods.* Kluwer Academic Publishers Group, Dordrecht, 1994.

[83] D. Denneberg and M. Grabisch. Interaction transform of set functions over a finite set. *Inform. Sci.*, 121(1–2):149–170, 1999.

[84] D. Denneberg and M. Grabisch. Measure and integral with purely ordinal scales. *J. Math. Psych.*, 48(1):15–27, 2004.

[85] M. Detyniecki. *Mathematical Aggregation Operators and their Applications to Video Querying*. PhD thesis, University Paris VI, 2000.

[86] M. Detyniecki, R. R. Yager, and B. Bouchon-Meunier. Reducing t-norms and augmenting t-conorms. *Int. J. Gen. Syst.*, 31(3):265–276, 2002.

[87] E. L. Dodd. The substitutive mean and certain subclasses of this general mean. *Ann. Math. Statistics*, 11:163–176, 1940.

[88] T. Driessen. *Cooperative Games, Solutions and Applications*. Kluwer Academic Publishers, 1988.

[89] D. Dubois, J. C. Fodor, H. Prade, and M. Roubens. Aggregation of decomposable measures with application to utility theory. *Theory and Decision*, 41(1):59–95, 1996.

[90] D. Dubois, L. Godo, H. Prade, and A. Zapico. Making decision in a qualitative setting: from decision under uncertainty to case-based decision. In A. Cohn, L. Schubert, and S. Shapiro, editors, *Proceedings of the 6th International Conference on Principles of Knowledge Representation and Reasoning KR'98*, pages 594–605, 1998.

[91] D. Dubois and J.-L. Koning. Social choice axioms for fuzzy set aggregation. *Fuzzy Sets and Systems*, 43(3):257–274, 1991.

[92] D. Dubois, E. Pap, and H. Prade. Hybrid probabilistic–possibilistic mixtures and utility functions. In *Preferences and Decisions under Incomplete Knowledge*, volume 51 of *Stud. Fuzziness Soft Comput.*, pages 51–73. Physica, Heidelberg, 2000.

[93] D. Dubois, E. Pap, and H. Prade. Pseudo-additive measures and the independence of events. In B. Bouchon-Meunier, J. Gutiérrez-Rios, L. Magdalena, and R. R. Yager, editors, *Technologies for Constructing Intelligent Systems 1, Studies in Fuzziness and Soft Computing*, volume 89, pages 179–191. Springer-Verlag, 2001.

[94] D. Dubois and H. Prade. A class of fuzzy measures based on triangular norms. A general framework for the combination of uncertain information. *Int. J. Gen. Systems*, 8(1):43–61, 1982.

[95] D. Dubois and H. Prade. Criteria aggregation and ranking of alternatives in the framework of fuzzy set theory. In *Fuzzy Sets and Decision Analysis*, volume 20 of *Stud. Management Sci.*, pages 209–240. North-Holland, Amsterdam, 1984.

[96] D. Dubois and H. Prade. A review of fuzzy set aggregation connectives. *Inform. Sci.*, 36:85–121, 1985.

[97] D. Dubois and H. Prade. Weighted minimum and maximum operations in fuzzy set theory. *Inform. Sci.*, 39:205–210, 1986.

[98] D. Dubois and H. Prade. *Possibility Theory*. Plenum Press, 1988.

[99] D. Dubois and H. Prade. Aggregation of possibility measures. In *Multiperson Decision Making Models using Fuzzy Sets and Possibility Theory*, volume 18

of *Theory Decis. Lib. Ser. B Math. Statist. Methods*, pages 55–63. Kluwer Academic Publishers, Dordrecht, 1990.

[100] D. Dubois and H. Prade. Fuzzy sets in approximate reasoning, part 1: inference with possibility distributions. *Fuzzy Sets and Systems*, 40:143–202, 1991.

[101] D. Dubois and H. Prade. Possibility theory: qualitative and quantitative aspects. In *Quantified Representation of Uncertainty and Imprecision*, volume 1 of *Handb. Defeasible Reason. Uncertain. Manag. Syst.*, pages 169–226. Kluwer Academic Publishers, Dordrecht, 1998.

[102] D. Dubois, H. Prade, and C. Testemale. Weighted fuzzy pattern matching. *Fuzzy Sets and Systems*, 28:313–331, 1988.

[103] J. J. Dujmović. A generalization of some functions in continuous mathematical logic – Evaluation function and its applications, (in Serbo-Croatian). In *Proc. Informatica Conference*, Bled, Yugoslavia, 1973.

[104] J. J. Dujmović. Weighted conjunctive and disjunctive means and their application in system evaluation. *J. Univ. Belgrade EE Dept., Series Mathematics and Physics*, (461–497):147–158, 1974.

[105] J. J. Dujmović. Seven flavors of andness/orness. In B. De Baets, J. Fodor, and D. Radojević, editors, *Proc. Eurofuse 2005*, pages 81–92, Belgrade, 2005.

[106] F. Durante, A. Kolesárová, R. Mesiar, and C. Sempi. Copulas with given values on a horizontal and a vertical section. *Kybernetika (Prague)*, 43(2):209–220, 2007.

[107] F. Durante and R. Mesiar. Maximally non-exchangeable bivariate extreme values copulas. Submitted.

[108] F. Durante and C. Sempi. Semicopulæ. *Kybernetika (Prague)*, 41(3):315–328, 2005.

[109] M. Ehrgott. *Multicriteria Optimization*, volume 491 of *Lecture Notes in Economics and Mathematical Systems*. Springer-Verlag, Berlin, 2000.

[110] K. Fan. Entfernung zweier zufälligen Grössen und die Konvergenz nach Wahrscheinlichkeit. *Math. Z.*, 49:681–683, 1944.

[111] J. M. Fernández Salido and S. Murakami. Extending Yager's orness concept for the OWA aggregators to other mean operators. *Fuzzy Sets and Systems*, 139(3):515–542, 2003.

[112] J. Fodor, J.-L. Marichal, and M. Roubens. Characterization of the ordered weighted averaging operators. *IEEE Trans. Fuzzy Syst.*, 3(2):236–240, 1995.

[113] J. Fodor and M. Roubens. On meaningfulness of means. *J. Comput. Appl. Math.*, 64(1–2):103–115, 1995.

[114] J. C. Fodor. An extension of Fung–Fu's theorem. *Int. J. Uncertain. Fuzziness Knowledge-Based Systems*, 4(3):235–243, 1996.

[115] J. C. Fodor. Smooth associative operations on finite ordinal scales. *IEEE Trans. Fuzzy Syst.*, 8(6):791–795, 2000.

[116] J. C. Fodor and J.-L. Marichal. On nonstrict means. *Aequationes Math.*, 54(3):308–327, 1997.

[117] J. C. Fodor and J.-L. Marichal. Erratum to: "On nonstrict means" [Aequationes Math. **54** (1997), no. 3, 308–327; mr1476032]. *Aequationes Math.*, 71(3):318–320, 2006.

[118] J. C. Fodor, J.-L. Marichal, and M. Roubens. Characterization of some aggregation functions arising from MCDM problems. In *Fuzzy Logic and Soft Computing*, pages 194–201. World Scientific Publishing, River Edge, NJ, 1995.

[119] J. C. Fodor and M. Roubens. *Fuzzy Preference Modelling and Multicriteria Decision Support*. Kluwer, Dordrecht, 1994.

[120] J. C. Fodor and M. Roubens. Characterization of weighted maximum and some related operations. *Inform. Sci.*, 84(3–4):173–180, 1995.

[121] J. C. Fodor, R. R. Yager, and A. Rybalov. Structure of uninorms. *Int. J. Uncertain. Fuzziness Knowledge-Based Systems*, 5(4):411–427, 1997.

[122] M. J. Frank. On the simultaneous associativity of $F(x, y)$ and $x + y - F(x, y)$. *Aequationes Math.*, 19(2–3):194–226, 1979.

[123] G. A. Fredricks and R. B. Nelsen. The Bertino family of copulas. In *Distributions with Given Marginals and Statistical Modelling*, pages 81–91. Kluwer Academic Publishers, Dordrecht, 2002.

[124] V. Frosini. Averages. In *Italian Contributions to the Methodology of Statistics*, pages 1–17. Cleup, Padova, 1987.

[125] L. Fuchs. On mean systems. *Acta Math. Acad. Sci. Hungar.*, 1:303–320, 1950.

[126] L. Fuchs. *Partially Ordered Algebraic Systems*. Pergamon Press, Oxford, 1963.

[127] K. Fujimoto. Some characterizations of k-monotonicity through the bipolar Möbius transform in bi-capacities. *J. Advanced Computational Intelligence and Intelligent Informatics*, 9(5):484–495, 2005.

[128] K. Fujimoto, I. Kojadinovic, and J.-L. Marichal. Axiomatic characterizations of probabilistic and cardinal-probabilistic interaction indices. *Games Econom. Behav.*, 55(1):72–99, 2006.

[129] K. Fujimoto and T. Murofushi. Hierarchical decomposition of the Choquet integral. In M. Grabisch, T. Murofushi, and M. Sugeno, editors, *Fuzzy Measures and Integrals*, volume 40 of *Stud. Fuzziness Soft Comput.*, pages 94–103. Physica, Heidelberg, 2000.

[130] K. Fujimoto, T. Murofushi, and M. Sugeno. Canonical hierarchical decomposition of Choquet integral over finite set with respect to null additive fuzzy measure. *Int. J. Uncertain. Fuzziness Knowledge-Based Systems*, 6(4):345–363, 1998.

[131] L. W. Fung and K. S. Fu. An axiomatic approach to rational decision making in a fuzzy environment. In *Fuzzy Sets and their Applications to Cognitive and Decision Processes (Proc. U.S.-Japan Sem., Univ. Calif., Berkeley, Calif., 1974)*, pages 227–256. Academic Press, New York, 1975.

[132] P. Gader, M. Mohamed, and J. Keller. Fusion of handwritten word classifiers. *Pattern Recognition Letters*, 17(6):577–584, 1996.

[133] W. Gaertner. *A Primer in Social Choice Theory*. LSE Perspectives in Economic Analysis. Oxford: Oxford University Press, 2006.

[134] T. Gajdos. Measuring inequalities without linearity in envy: Choquet integrals for symmetric capacities. *J. Econom. Theory*, 106(1):190–200, 2002.

[135] J. Galambos. *The Asymptotic Theory of Extreme Order Statistics*. Robert E. Krieger Publishing Co. Inc., Melbourne, FL, 2nd edition, 1987.

[136] J. L. García-Lapresta and R. A. Marques Pereira. The self-dual core and the anti-self-dual remainder of an aggregation operator. *Fuzzy Sets and Systems*, 159(1):47–62, 2008.

[137] M. Gehrke, C. Walker, and E. Walker. Averaging operators on the unit interval. *International Journal of Intelligent Systems*, 14(9):883–898, 1999.

[138] C. Genest, J. J. Quesada Molina, J. A. Rodríguez Lallena, and C. Sempi. A characterization of quasi-copulas. *J. Multivariate Anal.*, 69(2):193–205, 1999.

[139] D. Głazowska and J. Matkowski. An invariance of geometric mean with respect to Lagrangian means. *J. Math. Anal. Appl.*, 331(2):1187–1199, 2007.

[140] L. Godo and C. Sierra. A new approach to connective generation in the framework of expert systems using fuzzy logic. In *Proc. 18th Int. Symposium on Multiple-Valued Logic*, pages 157–162, Palma de Mallorca, Spain, 24–26 May 1988.

[141] L. González, E. Muel, and R. Mesiar. A remark on the arithmetic mean of an infinite sequence. *Int. J. Uncertain. Fuzziness Knowledge-Based Systems*, 10(suppl.):51–58, 2002.

[142] L. González, E. Muel, and R. Mesiar. What is the arithmetic mean of an infinite sequence? In *Proc. ESTYLF'2002*, pages 183–187, 2002.

[143] S. Gottwald. *A Treatise on Many-valued Logics*, volume 9 of *Studies in Logic and Computation*. Research Studies Press Ltd, Baldock, 2001.

[144] M. Grabisch. Fuzzy integral in multicriteria decision making. *Fuzzy Sets and Systems*, 69(3):279–298, 1995.

[145] M. Grabisch. A new algorithm for identifying fuzzy measures and its application to pattern recognition. In *Int. Joint Conf. of the 4th IEEE Int. Conf. on Fuzzy Systems and the 2nd Int. Fuzzy Engineering Symposium*, pages 145–150, Yokohama, Japan, March 1995.

[146] M. Grabisch. The application of fuzzy integrals in multicriteria decision making. *European J. Oper. Res.*, 89:445–456, 1996.

[147] M. Grabisch. Alternative representations of discrete fuzzy measures for decision making. *Int. J. Uncertain. Fuzziness Knowledge-Based Systems*, 5(5):587–607, 1997.

[148] M. Grabisch. k-order additive discrete fuzzy measures and their representation. *Fuzzy Sets and Systems*, 92(2):167–189, 1997.

[149] M. Grabisch. Fuzzy integral for classification and feature extraction. In M. Grabisch, T. Murofushi, and M. Sugeno, editors, *Fuzzy Measures and Integrals – Theory and Applications*, pages 415–434. Physica Verlag, 2000.

[150] M. Grabisch. A graphical interpretation of the Choquet integral. *IEEE Trans. on Fuzzy Systems*, 8:627–631, 2000.

[151] M. Grabisch. Symmetric and asymmetric fuzzy integrals: the ordinal case. In *6th Int. Conf. on Soft Computing (Iizuka'2000)*, Iizuka, Japan, October 2000.

[152] M. Grabisch. Modelling data by the Choquet integral. In V. Torra, editor, *Information Fusion in Data Mining*, pages 135–148. Physica Verlag, 2003.

[153] M. Grabisch. The symmetric Sugeno integral. *Fuzzy Sets and Systems*, 139(3):473–490, 2003.

[154] M. Grabisch. The symmetric Sugeno integral. *Fuzzy Sets and Systems*, 139(3):473–490, 2003.

[155] M. Grabisch. The Choquet integral as a linear interpolator. In *10th Int. Conf. on Information Processing and Management of Uncertainty in Knowledge-Based Systems (IPMU 2004)*, pages 373–378, Perugia, Italy, July 2004.

[156] M. Grabisch. The Möbius transform on symmetric ordered structures and its application to capacities on finite sets. *Discrete Math.*, 287(1–3):17–34, 2004.

[157] M. Grabisch, B. de Baets, and J. Fodor. The quest for rings on bipolar scales. *Int. J. Uncertain. Fuzziness Knowledge-Based Systems*, 12(4):499–512, 2004.

[158] M. Grabisch and F. Huet. Texture recognition by Choquet integral filters. In *6th Int. Conf. on Information Processing and Management of Uncertainty in Knowledge-Based Systems (IPMU)*, pages 1325–1330, Granada, Spain, July 1996.

[159] M. Grabisch, I. Kojadinovic, and P. Meyer. A review of capacity identification methods for Choquet integral based multi-attribute utility theory – applications of the Kappalab R package. *European J. Oper. Res.*, 186:766–785, 2008.

[160] M. Grabisch and C. Labreuche. How to improve acts: an alternative representation of the importance of criteria in MCDM. *Int. J. Uncertain. Fuzziness Knowledge-Based Systems*, 9(2):145–157, 2001.

[161] M. Grabisch and C. Labreuche. Bi-capacities for decision making on bipolar scales. In *EUROFUSE Workshop on Informations Systems*, pages 185–190, Varenna, Italy, September 2002.

[162] M. Grabisch and C. Labreuche. The symmetric and asymmetric Choquet integrals on finite spaces for decision making. *Statist. Papers*, 43(1):37–52, 2002.

[163] M. Grabisch and C. Labreuche. Bi-capacities. I. Definition, Möbius transform and interaction. *Fuzzy Sets and Systems*, 151(2):211–236, 2005.

[164] M. Grabisch and C. Labreuche. Bi-capacities. II. The Choquet integral. *Fuzzy Sets and Systems*, 151(2):237–259, 2005.

[165] M. Grabisch and C. Labreuche. Bipolarization of posets and natural interpolation. *J. Math. Anal. Appl.*, 343:1080–1097, 2008.

[166] M. Grabisch and C. Labreuche. A decade of application of the Choquet and Sugeno integrals in multi-criteria decision aid. *4OR*, 6:1–44, 2008.

[167] M. Grabisch, C. Labreuche, and J.-C. Vansnick. On the extension of pseudo-Boolean functions for the aggregation of interacting criteria. *European J. Oper. Res.*, 148(1):28–47, 2003.

[168] M. Grabisch, J.-L. Marichal, and M. Roubens. Equivalent representations of set functions. *Math. Oper. Res.*, 25(2):157–178, 2000.

[169] M. Grabisch, T. Murofushi, and M. Sugeno, editors. *Fuzzy Measures and Integrals*, volume 40 of *Studies in Fuzziness and Soft Computing*. Physica-Verlag, Heidelberg, 2000.

[170] M. Grabisch, H. Nguyen, and E. Walker. *Fundamentals of Uncertainty Calculi, with Applications to Fuzzy Inference*. Kluwer Academic, 1995.

[171] M. Grabisch and E. Raufaste. An empirical study of statistical properties of Choquet and Sugeno integrals. *IEEE Trans. on Fuzzy Systems*, to appear.

[172] M. Grabisch and M. Roubens. An axiomatic approach to the concept of interaction among players in cooperative games. *Int. J. Game Theory*, 28(4):547–565, 1999.

[173] M. Grabisch and M. Sugeno. Fuzzy integrals and dual measures : application to pattern classification. In *Sino-Japan Joint Meeting on Fuzzy Sets and Systems*, Beijing, China, October 1990.

[174] G. Grätzer. *General Lattice Theory*. Birkhäuser Verlag, Basel, 2nd edition, 1998.

[175] S. Greco, B. Matarazzo, and R. Słowiński. Bipolar Sugeno and Choquet integrals. In *EUROFUSE, Workshop on Informations Systems*, pages 191–196, Varenna, Italy, September 2002.

[176] O. Hadžić and E. Pap. *Fixed Point Theory in Probabilistic Metric Spaces*, volume 536 of *Mathematics and its Applications*. Kluwer Academic Publishers, Dordrecht, 2001.

[177] P. Hájek. Combining functions for certainty degrees in consulting systems. *Int. J. Man-Machine Studies*, 22(1):59–76, 1985.

[178] P. Hájek. *Metamathematics of Fuzzy Logic*, volume 4 of *Trends in Logic – Studia Logica Library*. Kluwer Academic Publishers, Dordrecht, 1998.

[179] P. Hájek, T. Havránek, and R. Jiroušek. *Uncertain Information Processing in Expert Systems*. CRC Press, Boca Raton, FL, 1992.

[180] P. R. Halmos. *Measure Theory*. D. Van Nostrand Company, Inc., New York, NY, 1950.

[181] H. Hamacher. *Über logische Aggregationen nicht-binär explizierter Entscheidungskriterien*. Rita G. Fischer Verlag, 1978.

[182] P. L. Hammer and R. Holzman. On approximations of pseudo-Boolean functions. *ZOR – Methods and Models of Operations Research*, 36:3–21, 1992.

[183] P. L. Hammer and S. Rudeanu. *Boolean Methods in Operations Research and Related Areas*. Springer, 1968.

[184] G. H. Hardy. On double Fourier series. *Quart. J. Math.*, 37:53–79, 1906.

[185] G. H. Hardy, J. E. Littlewood, and G. Pólya. *Inequalities*. Cambridge, University Press, 1952, 2nd edition.

[186] J. C. Harsanyi. A simplified bargaining model for the *n*-person cooperative game. *International Economic Review*, 4:194–220, 1963.

[187] I. N. Herstein and J. Milnor. An axiomatic approach to measurable utility. *Econometrica*, 21:291–297, 1953.

[188] E. Hewitt and K. Stromberg. *Real and Abstract Analysis. A modern treatment of the theory of functions of a real variable.* Springer-Verlag, New York, 1965.

[189] E. W. Hobson. *The Theory of Functions of a Real Variable and the Theory of Fourier's Series, Vol. 1,* 3rd edition. University Press, Cambridge (1927); Dover, New York, 1957.

[190] J. Horváth. Sur le rapport entre les systèmes de postulats caractérisant les valeurs moyennes quasi arithmétiques symétriques. *C. R. Acad. Sci. Paris*, 225:1256–1257, 1947.

[191] A. Horwitz. Means and divided differences. *J. Math. Anal. Appl.*, 191(3):618–632, 1995.

[192] A. Horwitz. Invariant means. *J. Math. Anal. Appl.*, 270(2):499–518, 2002.

[193] H. Imaoka. On a subjective evaluation model by a generalized fuzzy integral. *Int. J. Uncertain. Fuzziness Knowledge-Based Systems*, 5(5):517–529, 1997.

[194] H. Imaoka. Comparison between three fuzzy integrals. In M. Grabisch, T. Murofushi, and M. Sugeno, editors, *Fuzzy Measures and Integrals*, volume 40 of *Stud. Fuzziness Soft Comput.*, pages 273–286. Physica, Heidelberg, 2000.

[195] M. Inuiguchi, H. Ichihashi, and H. Tanaka. Fuzzy linear programming using multiattribute value function. *J. Oper. Res. Soc. Japan*, 31(1):121–141, 1988. In Japanese.

[196] S. Jenei. On Archimedean triangular norms. *Fuzzy Sets and Systems*, 99(2):179–186, 1998.

[197] S. Jenei. Fibred triangular norms. *Fuzzy Sets and Systems*, 103(1):67–82, 1999.

[198] S. Jenei. Structure of left-continuous triangular norms with strong induced negations. II. Rotation-annihilation construction. *J. Appl. Non-Classical Logics*, 11(3–4):351–366, 2001.

[199] S. Jenei and J. C. Fodor. On continuous triangular norms. *Fuzzy Sets and Systems*, 100(1–3):273–282, 1998.

[200] H. Joe. *Multivariate Models and Dependence Concepts*, volume 73 of *Monographs on Statistics and Applied Probability*. Chapman & Hall, London, 1997.

[201] D. Jočić. Uninorms and distributivity. *J. Elec. Eng.*, 12:101–103, 2005.

[202] J. Kacprzyk and H. Nurmi. Group decision making under fuzziness. In *Fuzzy Sets in Decision Analysis, Operations Research and Statistics*, volume 1 of *Handb. Fuzzy Sets Ser.*, pages 103–136. Kluwer Academic Publishers, Boston, MA, 1998.

[203] Y. Kamen and S. Ovchinnikov. Meaningful means on ordered sets. In B. Bouchon-Meunier, R. R. Yager, and L. A. Zadeh, editors, *Fuzzy Logic*

and Soft Computing, pages 189–193. World Scientific Publishing, River Edge, NJ, 1995.

[204] A. Kandel and W. Byatt. Fuzzy sets, fuzzy algebra, and fuzzy statistics. *Proc. of the IEEE*, 66:1619–1639, 1978.

[205] U. Kaymak and H. R. van Nauta Lemke. A sensitivity analysis approach to introducing weight factors into decision functions in fuzzy multicriteria decision making. *Fuzzy Sets and Systems*, 97(2):169–182, 1998.

[206] U. Kaymak, H. R. van Nauta Lemke, and T. den Boer. A sensitivity-based analysis of weighted fuzzy aggregation. In *Proc. IEEE World Congress on Computational Intelligence*, pages 755–760, Anchorage, Alaska, May 1998.

[207] R. L. Keeney and H. Raiffa. *Decisions with Multiple Objectives: Preferences and value tradeoffs*. John Wiley & Sons, New York, 1976.

[208] J. M. Keller, P. D. Gader, and A. K. Hocaoğlu. Fuzzy integrals in image processing and recognition. In M. Grabisch, T. Murofushi, and M. Sugeno, editors, *Fuzzy Measures and Integrals – Theory and Applications*, pages 435–466. Physica Verlag, 2000.

[209] S.-R. Kim. On the possible scientific laws. *Math. Social Sci.*, 20(1):19–36, 1990.

[210] C. H. Kimberling. A probabilistic interpretation of complete monotonicity. *Aequationes Math.*, 10:152–164, 1974.

[211] D. Kleitman. On Dedekind's problem: The number of monotone Boolean functions. *Proc. Amer. Math. Soc.*, 21:677–682, 1969.

[212] D. Kleitman and G. Markowsky. On Dedekind's problem: the number of isotone Boolean functions. II. *Trans. Amer. Math. Soc.*, 213:373–390, 1975.

[213] E. P. Klement. Construction of fuzzy σ-algebras using triangular norms. *J. Math. Anal. Appl.*, 85(2):543–565, 1982.

[214] E. P. Klement and A. Kolesárová. Extension to copulas and quasi-copulas as special 1-Lipschitz aggregation operators. *Kybernetika (Prague)*, 41(3):329–348, 2005.

[215] E. P. Klement, A. Kolesárová, R. Mesiar, and C. Sempi. Copulas constructed from horizontal sections. *Comm. Stat. Theory Meth.*, 36:2901–2911, 2007.

[216] E. P. Klement and R. Mesiar, editors. *Logical, Algebraic, Analytic, and Probabilistic Aspects of Triangular Norms*. Elsevier B. V., Amsterdam, 2005.

[217] E. P. Klement, R. Mesiar, and E. Pap. On the relationship of associative compensatory operators to triangular norms and conorms. *Int. J. Uncertain. Fuzziness Knowledge-Based Systems*, 4(2):129–144, 1996.

[218] E. P. Klement, R. Mesiar, and E. Pap. Quasi- and pseudo-inverses of monotone functions, and the construction of t-norms. *Fuzzy Sets and Systems*, 104(1):3–13, 1999.

[219] E. P. Klement, R. Mesiar, and E. Pap. Integration with respect to decomposable measures, based on a conditionally distributive semiring on the unit interval. *Int. J. Uncertain. Fuzziness Knowledge-Based Systems*, 8(6):701–717, 2000.

[220] E. P. Klement, R. Mesiar, and E. Pap. *Triangular Norms*, volume 8 of *Trends in Logic – Studia Logica Library*. Kluwer Academic Publishers, Dordrecht, 2000.

[221] E. P. Klement, R. Mesiar, and E. Pap. Triangular norms as ordinal sums of semigroups in the sense of A. H. Clifford. *Semigroup Forum*, 65(1):71–82, 2002.

[222] E. P. Klement, R. Mesiar, and E. Pap. Measure-based aggregation operators. *Fuzzy Sets and Systems*, 142(1):3–14, 2004.

[223] E. P. Klement, R. Mesiar, and E. Pap. Archimax copulas and invariance under transformations. *C. R. Math. Acad. Sci. Paris*, 340(10):755–758, 2005.

[224] E. P. Klement, R. Mesiar, and E. Pap. Archimedean components of triangular norms. *J. Aust. Math. Soc.*, 78(2):239–255, 2005.

[225] E. P. Klement, R. Mesiar, and E. Pap. Transformations of copulas. *Kybernetika (Prague)*, 41(4):425–434, 2005.

[226] E. P. Klement, R. Mesiar, and E. Pap. A universal integral. In *Proc. 5th EUSFLAT Conf.*, pages 253–259, Ostrava, Czech Republic, September 2007.

[227] I. Kojadinovic. Minimum variance capacity identification. *Eur. J. Oper. Res.*, 177:498–514, 2007.

[228] I. Kojadinovic, J.-L. Marichal, and M. Roubens. An axiomatic approach to the definition of the entropy of a discrete Choquet capacity. *Inform. Sci.*, 172:131–153, 2005.

[229] A. Kolesárová. Comparison of quasi-arithmetic means. In *Proc. EUROFUSE-SICÂ'99*, pages 237–240, Budapest, 1999.

[230] A. Kolesárová. Limit properties of quasi-arithmetic means. *Fuzzy Sets and Systems*, 124(1):65–71, 2001.

[231] A. Kolesárová. Möbius fitting aggregation operators. *Kybernetika (Prague)*, 38(3):259–273, 2002.

[232] A. Kolesárová. Revision of parametric evaluation of aggregation functions. In *Proc. 13th Zittau Fuzzy Colloquium*, pages 202–211, Zittau, Germany, September 2006.

[233] A. Kolesárová and M. Komorníková. Triangular norm-based iterative compensatory operators. *Fuzzy Sets and Systems*, 104(1):109–120, 1999.

[234] A. Kolesárová and J. Mordelová. 1-Lipschitz and kernel aggregation operators. In *Proceedings of AGOP'2001*, pages 71–76, Oviedo, Spain, 2001.

[235] A. Kolesárová, J. Mordelová, and E. Muel. Kernel aggregation operators and their marginals. *Fuzzy Sets and Systems*, 142:35–50, 2004.

[236] A. N. Kolmogoroff. Sur la notion de la moyenne. (French). *Atti Accad. Naz. Lincei*, 12(6):388–391, 1930.

[237] M. Komorníková. Aggregation operators and additive generators. *Int. J. Uncertain. Fuzziness Knowledge-Based Systems*, 9(2):205–215, 2001.

[238] D. H. Krantz, R. D. Luce, P. Suppes, and A. Tversky. *Foundations of measurement. Vol. I: Additive and polynomial representations*. Academic Press, New York, 1971.

[239] R. Kruse. Fuzzy integrals and conditional fuzzy measures. *Fuzzy Sets and Systems*, 10(3):309–313, 1983.

[240] M. Kuczma. On the quasiarithmetic mean in a mean value property and the associated functional equation. *Aequationes Math.*, 41(1):33–54, 1991.

[241] M. Kuczma, B. Choczewski, and R. Ger. *Iterative Functional Equations*, volume 32 of *Encyclopedia of Mathematics and its Applications*. Cambridge University Press, Cambridge, 1990.

[242] S. H. Kwon and M. Sugeno. A hierarchical subjective evaluation model using non-monotonic fuzzy measures and the Choquet integral. In M. Grabisch, T. Murofushi, and M. Sugeno, editors, *Fuzzy Measures and Integrals – Theory and Applications*, pages 375–391. Physica Verlag, 2000.

[243] C. Labreuche. Determination of the criteria to be improved first in order to improve as much as possible the overall evaluation. In *10th Int. Conf. on Information Processing and Management of Uncertainty in Knowledge-Based Systems (IPMU 2004)*, pages 609–616, Perugia, Italy, July 2004.

[244] C. Labreuche and M. Grabisch. Generalized Choquet-like aggregation functions for handling bipolar scales. *European J. Oper. Res.*, 172(3):931–955, 2006.

[245] J. Lázaro, T. Rückschlossová, and T. Calvo. Shift invariant binary aggregation operators. *Fuzzy Sets and Systems*, 142(1):51–62, 2004.

[246] C. Ling. Representation of associative functions. *Publ. Math. Debrecen*, 12:189–212, 1965.

[247] R. Lipschitz. De explicatione per series trigonometricas instuenda functionum unius variables arbitrariarum et praecipue earum, quae per variablis spatium finitum valorum maximorum et minimorum numerum habent infinitum disquisitio. *J. Reine Angew. Math.*, 63:296–308, 1864.

[248] G. Lorenzen. Why means in two arguments are special. *Elem. Math.*, 49(1):32–37, 1994.

[249] L. Losonczi. Über eine neue Klasse von Mittelwerten. *Acta Sci. Math. (Szeged)*, 32:71–81, 1971.

[250] L. Losonczi. General inequalities for nonsymmetric means. *Aequationes Math.*, 9:221–235, 1973.

[251] L. Losonczi. Homogeneous Cauchy mean values. In *Functional Equations – Results and Advances*, volume 3 of *Adv. Math. (Dordr.)*, pages 209–218. Kluwer Academic Publishers, Dordrecht, 2002.

[252] L. Losonczi. Equality of two variable means revisited. *Aequationes Math.*, 71(3):228–245, 2006.

[253] L. Losonczi and Z. Páles. Comparisons of means generated by two functions and a measure. *J. Math. Anal. Appl.*, 345:135–146, 2008.

[254] L. Lovász. Submodular functions and convexity. In *Mathematical Programming: The state of the art (Bonn, 1982)*, pages 235–257. Springer, Berlin, 1983.

[255] R. Lowen. *Fuzzy Set Theory*. Kluwer Academic Publishers, Dordrecht, 1996.

[256] R. D. Luce. On the possible psychophysical laws. *Psych. Rev.*, 66:81–95, 1959.

[257] R. D. Luce, D. H. Krantz, P. Suppes, and A. Tversky. *Foundations of Measurement. Vol. III: Representation, Axiomatization, and Invariance.* Academic Press Inc., San Diego, CA, 1990.

[258] M. K. Luhandjula. Compensatory operators in fuzzy linear programming with multiple objectives. *Fuzzy Sets and Systems*, 8(3):245–252, 1982.

[259] X. Luo and N. R. Jennings. A spectrum of compromise aggregation operators for multi-attribute decision making. *Artificial Intelligence*, 171(2–3):161–184, 2007.

[260] K. C. Maes, S. Saminger, and B. De Baets. Representation and construction of self-dual aggregation operators. *European J. Oper. Res.*, 177(1):472–487, 2007.

[261] J.-L. Marichal. Weighted lattice polynomials. *Discrete Math.*, to appear. http://arxiv.org/abs/0706.0570.

[262] J.-L. Marichal. *Aggregation Operators for Multicriteria Decision Aid*. PhD thesis, Institute of Mathematics, University of Liège, Liège, Belgium, December 1998.

[263] J.-L. Marichal. An axiomatic approach of the discrete Choquet integral as a tool to aggregate interacting criteria. *IEEE Trans. Fuzzy Syst.*, 8(6):800–807, 2000.

[264] J.-L. Marichal. Behavioral analysis of aggregation in multicriteria decision aid. In *Preferences and Decisions under Incomplete Knowledge*, pages 153–178. Physica, Heidelberg, 2000.

[265] J.-L. Marichal. The influence of variables on pseudo-Boolean functions with applications to game theory and multicriteria decision making. *Discrete Appl. Math.*, 107(1–3):139–164, 2000.

[266] J.-L. Marichal. On an axiomatization of the quasi-arithmetic mean values without the symmetry axiom. *Aequationes Math.*, 59(1–2):74–83, 2000.

[267] J.-L. Marichal. On Sugeno integral as an aggregation function. *Fuzzy Sets and Systems*, 114(3):347–365, 2000.

[268] J.-L. Marichal. On the associativity functional equation. *Fuzzy Sets and Systems*, 114(3):381–389, 2000.

[269] J.-L. Marichal. An axiomatic approach of the discrete Sugeno integral as a tool to aggregate interacting criteria in a qualitative framework. *IEEE Trans. Fuzzy Syst.*, 9(1):164–172, 2001.

[270] J.-L. Marichal. Aggregation of interacting criteria by means of the discrete Choquet integral. In T. Calvo, G. Mayor, and R. Mesiar, editors, *Aggregation Operators: New trends and Applications*, pages 224–244. Physica, Heidelberg, 2002.

[271] J.-L. Marichal. Entropy of discrete Choquet capacities. *European J. Oper. Res.*, 137(3):612–624, 2002.

[272] J.-L. Marichal. On order invariant synthesizing functions. *J. Math. Psych.*, 46(6):661–676, 2002.

[273] J.-L. Marichal. Tolerant or intolerant character of interacting criteria in aggregation by the Choquet integral. *European J. Oper. Res.*, 155(3):771–791, 2004.

[274] J.-L. Marichal. Cumulative distribution functions and moments of lattice polynomials. *Stat. Prob. Lett.*, 76(12):1273–1279, 2006.

[275] J.-L. Marichal. *k*-intolerant capacities and Choquet integrals. *European J. Oper. Res.*, 177(3):1453–1468, 2007.

[276] J.-L. Marichal. Multivariate integration of functions depending explicitly on the minimum and the maximum of the variables. *J. Math. Anal. Appl.*, 341(1):200–210, 2008.

[277] J.-L. Marichal. Weighted lattice polynomials of independent random variables. *Discrete Appl. Math.*, 156(5):685–694, 2008.

[278] J.-L. Marichal and I. Kojadinovic. Distribution functions of linear combinations of lattice polynomials from the uniform distribution. *Stat. Prob. Lett.*, 78(8):985–991, 2008.

[279] J.-L. Marichal, I. Kojadinovic, and K. Fujimoto. Axiomatic characterizations of generalized values. *Discrete Appl. Math.*, 155(1):26–43, 2007.

[280] J.-L. Marichal and P. Mathonet. A characterization of the ordered weighted averaging functions based on the ordered bisymmetry property. *IEEE Trans. Fuzzy Syst.*, 7(1):93–96, 1999.

[281] J.-L. Marichal and P. Mathonet. On comparison meaningfulness of aggregation functions. *J. Math. Psych.*, 45(2):213–223, 2001.

[282] J.-L. Marichal and P. Mathonet. Approximations of Lovász extensions and their induced interaction index. *Discrete Appl. Math.*, 156(1):11–24, 2008.

[283] J.-L. Marichal, P. Mathonet, and E. Tousset. Mesures floues définies sur une échelle ordinale. Working paper, 1996.

[284] J.-L. Marichal, P. Mathonet, and E. Tousset. Characterization of some aggregation functions stable for positive linear transformations. *Fuzzy Sets and Systems*, 102(2):293–314, 1999.

[285] J.-L. Marichal and R. Mesiar. Aggregation on finite ordinal scales by scale independent functions. *Order*, 21(2):155–180, 2004.

[286] J.-L. Marichal, R. Mesiar, and T. Rückschlossová. A complete description of comparison meaningful functions. *Aequationes Math.*, 69(3):309–320, 2005.

[287] J.-L. Marichal, P. Meyer, and M. Roubens. Sorting multi-attribute alternatives: the TOMASO method. *Comp. Oper. Res.*, 32:861–877, 2005.

[288] J.-L. Marichal and M. J. Mossinghoff. Slices, slabs, and sections of the unit hypercube. *Online J. Anal. Comb.*, (3):Art. 1, 11, 2008.

[289] J.-L. Marichal and M. Roubens. Characterization of some stable aggregation functions. In *Proc. 1st Int. Conf. on Industrial Engineering and Production Management (IEPM'93)*, pages 187–196, Mons, Belgium, June 1993.

[290] J.-L. Marichal and M. Roubens. Determination of weights of interacting criteria from a reference set. *Eur. J. Oper. Res.*, 124:641–650, 2000.

[291] J.-L. Marichal and M. Roubens. Entropy of discrete fuzzy measures. *Int. J. Uncertain. Fuzziness Knowledge-Based Systems*, 8(6):625–640, 2000.

[292] M. Marinacci. Vitali's early contribution to nonadditive integration. *Rivista di Matematici per le Scienze Economiche e Sociali*, 20(2):153–158, 1997.

[293] R. A. Marques Pereira and R. A. Ribeiro. Aggregation with generalized mixture operators using weighting functions. *Fuzzy Sets and Systems*, 137(1):43–58, 2003.

[294] M. Mas, G. Mayor, and J. Torrens. t-operators. *Int. J. Uncertain. Fuzziness Knowledge-Based Systems*, 7(1):31–50, 1999.

[295] M. Mas, R. Mesiar, M. Monserrat, and J. Torrens. Aggregation operators with annihilator. *Int. J. Gen. Syst.*, 34(1):17–38, 2005.

[296] V. P. Maslov and S. N. Samborskiĭ. Idempotent Analysis (in place of an intro-duction). In *Idempotent Analysis*, volume 13 of *Adv. Soviet Math.*, pages vii–xi. Amer. Math. Soc., Providence, RI, 1992.

[297] J. Matkowski. Mean value property and associated functional equations. *Aequationes Math.*, 58(1–2):46–59, 1999.

[298] J. Matkowski. On invariant generalized Beckenbach–Gini means. In *Functional Equations – Results and Advances*, volume 3 of *Adv. Math. (Dordr.)*, pages 219–230. Kluwer Academic Publishers, Dordrecht, 2002.

[299] T. Matsunawa. The exact and approximate distributions of linear combinations of selected order statistics from a uniform distribution. *Ann. Inst. Statist. Math.*, 37(1):1–16, 1985.

[300] G. Mayor and J. Torrens. On a class of operators for expert systems. *Int. J. Intelligent Systems*, 8:771–778, 1993.

[301] J. H. McColl. *Multivariate Probability*. Arnold Texts in Statistics. London: Arnold, 2004.

[302] R. Mesiar. k-order pan-additive discrete fuzzy measures. In *7th IFSA World Congress*, pages 488–490, Prague, Czech Republic, June 1997.

[303] R. Mesiar. Generated conjunctors and related operators in MV-logic as a basis for AI applications. In *ECAI'98, Workshop 17*, pages 1–5, Brighton, 1998.

[304] R. Mesiar. Scale invariant operators. In *Proc. Int. Conf. in Fuzzy Logic and Technology (EUSFLAT'2001)*, pages 479–481, Leicester, September 5–7 2001.

[305] R. Mesiar. Triangular norms – an overview. In *Computational Intelligence in Theory and Practice*, Adv. Soft Comput., pages 35–54. Physica, Heidelberg, 2001.

[306] R. Mesiar and B. D. Baets. New construction methods for aggregation operators. In *Proceedings IPMU'2000*, pages 701–706, Madrid, 2000.

[307] R. Mesiar and M. Komorníková. Triangular norm-based aggregation of evi-dence under fuzziness. In *Aggregation and Fusion of Imperfect Information*, volume 12 of *Stud. Fuzziness Soft Comput.*, pages 11–35. Physica, Heidelberg, 1998.

[308] R. Mesiar and E. Pap. Aggregation of infinite sequences. *Inform. Sci.*, 178:3557–3564, 2008.

[309] R. Mesiar and T. Rückschlossová. Characterization of invariant aggregation operators. *Fuzzy Sets and Systems*, 142(1):63–73, 2004.

[310] R. Mesiar and C. Sempi. Ordinal sums and idempotents of copulas. *Aequationes Math.*

[311] R. Mesiar and J. Špirková. Weighted means and weighting functions. *Kybernetika (Prague)*, 42(2):151–160, 2006.

[312] R. Mesiar and J. Špirková. Weighted aggregation operators based on minimization. In *Proc. Int. Summer School on Aggregation Operators and their Applications (AGOP'2007)*, pages 203–206, Ghent, Belgium, July 2007.

[313] R. Mesiar, J. Špirková, and L. Vavríková. Weighted aggregation operators based on minimization. *Inform. Sci.*, 178(4):1133–1140, 2008.

[314] R. Mesiar and H. Thiele. On T-quantifiers and S-quantifiers. In V. Novák and I. Perfilieva, editors, *Discovering the World with Fuzzy Logic*, volume 57 of *Stud. Fuzziness Soft Comput.*, pages 310–326. Physica, Heidelberg, 2000.

[315] R. Mesiar and D. Vivona. Two-step integral with respect to fuzzy measure. *Tatra Mt. Math. Publ.*, 16(part II):359–368, 1999.

[316] A. Mesiarová. Continuous triangular subnorms. *Fuzzy Sets and Systems*, 142(1):75–83, 2004.

[317] A. Mesiarová. Generators of triangular norms. In E. P. Klement, R. Mesiar, editors, *Logical, Algebraic, Analytic, and Probabilistic Aspects of Triangular Norms*, pages 95–111. Elsevier B. V., Amsterdam, 2005.

[318] T. Micháliková-Rückschlossová. Some constructions of aggregation operators. *J. Electrical Engin.*, 12:29–32, 2000.

[319] P. Miranda and M. Grabisch. Optimization issues for fuzzy measures. *Int. J. Uncertain. Fuzziness Knowledge-Based Systems*, 7(6):545–560, 1999.

[320] P. S. Mostert and A. L. Shield. On the structure of semigroups on a compact manifold with boundary. *Ann. of Math.*, 65:117–143, 1957.

[321] R. Moynihan. Infinite τ_T products of distribution functions. *J. Austral. Math. Soc. Ser. A*, 26(2):227–240, 1978.

[322] T. Murofushi. A technique for reading fuzzy measures (I): the Shapley value with respect to a fuzzy measure. In *2nd Fuzzy Workshop*, pages 39–48, Nagaoka, Japan, October 1992. In Japanese.

[323] T. Murofushi. Lexicographic use of Sugeno integrals and monotonicity conditions. *IEEE Trans. on Fuzzy Systems*, 9(6):783–794, 2001.

[324] T. Murofushi. Multilevel Choquet integral. *J. of Japan Soc. for Fuzzy Theory and Intelligent Informatics*, 16(4):319–327, in Japanese, 2004.

[325] T. Murofushi and S. Soneda. Techniques for reading fuzzy measures (III): interaction index. In *9th Fuzzy System Symposium*, pages 693–696, Sapporo, Japan, May 1993. In Japanese.

[326] T. Murofushi and M. Sugeno. An interpretation of fuzzy measures and the Choquet integral as an integral with respect to a fuzzy measure. *Fuzzy Sets and Systems*, 29(2):201–227, 1989.

[327] T. Murofushi and M. Sugeno. Fuzzy t-conorm integral with respect to fuzzy measures: generalization of Sugeno integral and Choquet integral. *Fuzzy Sets and Systems*, 42(1):57–71, 1991.

[328] T. Murofushi and M. Sugeno. A theory of fuzzy measures: representations, the Choquet integral, and null sets. *J. Math. Anal. Appl.*, 159(2):532–549, 1991.

[329] T. Murofushi and M. Sugeno. Some quantities represented by the Choquet integral. *Fuzzy Sets and Systems*, 56(2):229–235, 1993.

[330] M. Nagumo. Über eine klasse der mittelwerte. (German). *Japanese J. Math.*, 7:71–79, 1930.

[331] Y. Narukawa and T. Murofushi. The n-step Choquet integral on finite spaces. In *Proc. of the 9th Int. Conf. on Information Proc. and Management of Uncertainty in Knowledge-Based Systems*, pages 539–543, Annecy, France, July 2002.

[332] R. B. Nelsen. *An Introduction to Copulas*, volume 139 of *Lecture Notes in Statistics*. Springer-Verlag, New York, 1999.

[333] A. Neyman. Values of games with infinitely many players. In R. Aumann and S. Hart, editors, *Handbook of Game Theory with Economic Applications, Volume 3*, pages 2121–2167. Elsevier, 2002.

[334] H. T. Nguyen and E. A. Walker. *A First Course in Fuzzy Logic*. CRC Press, Boca Raton, FL, 1997.

[335] A. I. Orlov. The connection between mean values and the admissible transformations of scale. *Math. Notes*, 30:774–778, 1981.

[336] D. K. Osborne. Further extensions of a theorem of dimensional analysis. *J. Math. Psych.*, 7:236–242, 1970.

[337] S. Ovchinnikov. Means on ordered sets. *Math. Social Sci.*, 32(1):39–56, 1996.

[338] S. Ovchinnikov. Invariant functions on simple orders. *Order*, 14(4):365–371, 1998.

[339] S. Ovchinnikov. On ordinal OWA operators. In *Proc. 7th Int. Conf. on Information Processing and Management of Uncertainty in Knowledge-Based Systems (IPMU'98)*, pages 511–514, Paris, 1998.

[340] S. Ovchinnikov. Max-min representation of piecewise linear functions. *Beiträge Algebra Geom.*, 43(1):297–302, 2002.

[341] S. Ovchinnikov and A. Dukhovny. Integral representation of invariant functionals. *J. Math. Anal. Appl.*, 244(1):228–232, 2000.

[342] S. Ovchinnikov and A. Dukhovny. On order invariant aggregation functionals. *J. Math. Psych.*, 46(1):12–18, 2002.

[343] G. Owen. Multilinear extensions of games. *Management Sci.*, 18:P64–P79, 1972.

[344] G. Owen. Multilinear extensions of games. In *The Shapley Value*, pages 139–151. Cambridge University Press, Cambridge, 1988.

[345] G. Owen. *Game Theory*. Academic Press Inc., San Diego, CA, 3rd edition, 1995.

[346] Z. Páles. On the characterization of quasi-arithmetic means with weight function. *Aequationes Math.*, 32(2–3):171–194, 1987.

[347] E. Pap. An integral generated by a decomposable measure. *Zb. Rad. Prirod.-Mat. Fak. Ser. Mat.*, 20(1):135–144, 1990.

[348] E. Pap. On nonadditive set functions. *Atti Sem. Mat. Fis. Univ. Modena*, 39(1):345–360, 1991.

[349] E. Pap. *Null-additive Set Functions*, volume 337 of *Mathematics and its Applications*. Kluwer Academic Publishers Group, Dordrecht, 1995.

[350] E. Pap, editor. *Handbook of Measure Theory. Vol. I, II*. North-Holland, Amsterdam, 2002.

[351] E. Pap. A generalization of the utility theory using a hybrid idempotent-probabilistic measure. In *Proceedings of the Conference on Idempotent Mathematics and Mathematical Physics*, pages 261–274. American Mathematical Society, 2005.

[352] E. Pap and B. Mihailović. A representation of a comonotone-$\oslash$-additive and monotone functional by two Sugeno integrals. *Fuzzy Sets and Systems*, 155:77–88, 2005.

[353] E. Pap and M. Roca. An axiomatization of the hybrid probabilistic-possibilistic utility theory. In *4th Serbian-Hungarian Joint Symposium on Intelligent Systems*, pages 229–235, Subotica, Serbia, 2006.

[354] B. Peleg and P. Sudhölter. *Introduction to the Theory of Cooperative Games*, volume 34 of *Theory and Decision Library. Series C: Game Theory, Mathematical Programming and Operations Research*. Kluwer Academic Publishers Group, Dordrecht, 2003.

[355] J.-C. Pomerol and S. Barba-Romero. *Multicriterion Decision in Management: Principles and Practice*. Kluwer Academic Publishers, 2000.

[356] F. Qi. Generalized weighted mean values with two parameters. *R. Soc. Lond. Proc. Ser. A Math. Phys. Eng. Sci.*, 454(1978):2723–2732, 1998.

[357] F. Qi, J.-Q. Mei, D.-F. Xia, and S.-L. Xu. New proofs of weighted power mean inequalities and monotonicity for generalized weighted mean values. *Math. Inequal. Appl.*, 3(3):377–383, 2000.

[358] F. Qi and S.-Q. Zhang. Note on monotonicity of generalized weighted mean values. *R. Soc. Lond. Proc. Ser. A Math. Phys. Eng. Sci.*, 455(1989):3259–3260, 1999.

[359] D. Radojević. Logical interpretation of discrete Choquet integral defined by general measure. *Int. J. Uncertain. Fuzziness Knowledge-Based Systems*, 7(6):577–588, 1999.

[360] A. L. Ralescu and D. A. Ralescu. Extensions of fuzzy aggregation. *Fuzzy Sets and Systems*, 86(3):321–330, 1997.

[361] A. Rico. *Modélisation des préférences pour l'aide à la décision par l'intégrale de Sugeno*. PhD thesis, Université Paris I, 2002.

[362] A. Rico, M. Grabisch, C. Labreuche, and A. Chateauneuf. Preference modeling on totally ordered sets by the Sugeno integral. *Discrete Appl. Math.*, 147(1):113–124, 2005.

[363] F. Roberts and Z. Rosenbaum. The meaningfulness of ordinal comparisons for general order relational systems. In P. Humphreys, editor, *Patrick Suppes: Scientific Philosopher, Vol. 2*, pages 251–274. Kluwer, The Netherlands, 1994.

[364] F. S. Roberts. *Measurement Theory, with Applications to Decision-making, Utility and the Social Sciences*, volume 7 of *Encyclopedia of Mathematics and its Applications*. Addison-Wesley Publishing Co., Reading, MA, 1979.

[365] F. S. Roberts. Limitations on conclusions using scales of measurement. In S. M. Pollock, M. H. Rothkopf, and A. Barnett, editors, *Operations Research and the Public Sector*, pages 621–671. Elsevier, Amsterdam, 1994.

[366] G.-C. Rota. On the foundations of combinatorial theory. I. Theory of Möbius functions. *Z. Wahrscheinlichkeitstheorie und Verw. Gebiete*, 2:340–368 (1964), 1964.

[367] J. J. Rotman. *An Introduction to the Theory of Groups*, volume 148 of *Graduate Texts in Mathematics*. Springer-Verlag, New York, 4th edition, 1995.

[368] R. Rovatti and C. Fantuzzi. s-norm aggregation of infinite collections. *Fuzzy Sets and Systems*, 84(3):255–269, 1996.

[369] T. Rückschlossová. *Aggregation operators and invariantness*. PhD thesis, Slovak University of Technology, Bratislava, Slovakia, June 2003.

[370] T. Rückschlossová and R. Rückschloss. Homogeneous aggregation operators. *Kybernetika (Prague)*, 42(3):279–286, 2006.

[371] W. Rudin. *Real and Complex Analysis*. McGraw-Hill Book Co., New York, 1966.

[372] C. Ryll-Nardzewski. Sur les moyennes. *Studia Math.*, 11:31–37, 1949.

[373] M. Šabo, A. Kolesárová, and Š. Varga. RET operators generated by triangular norms and copulas. *Int. J. Uncertain. Fuzziness Knowledge-Based Systems*, 9(2):169–181, 2001.

[374] P. K. Sahoo and T. Riedel. *Mean Value Theorems and Functional Equations*. World Scientific Publishing Co. Inc., River Edge, NJ, 1998.

[375] W. Sander. Associative aggregation operators. In T. Calvo, G. Mayor, and R. Mesiar, editors, *Aggregation Operators*, volume 97 of *Stud. Fuzziness Soft Comput.*, pages 124–158. Physica, Heidelberg, 2002.

[376] W. Sander and J. Siedekum. Multiplication, distributivity and fuzzy-integral. I. *Kybernetika (Prague)*, 41(3):397–422, 2005.

[377] W. Sander and J. Siedekum. Multiplication, distributivity and fuzzy-integral. II. *Kybernetika (Prague)*, 41(4):469–496, 2005.

[378] W. Sander and J. Siedekum. Multiplication, distributivity and fuzzy-integral. III. *Kybernetika (Prague)*, 41(4):497–518, 2005.

[379] J. Sándor. On the identric and logarithmic means. *Aequationes Math.*, 40(2-3):261–270, 1990.

[380] D. Schmeidler. Integral representation without additivity. *Proc. Amer. Math. Soc.*, 97(2):255–261, 1986.

[381] B. Schweizer and A. Sklar. Statistical metric spaces. *Pacific J. Math.*, 10:313–334, 1960.

[382] B. Schweizer and A. Sklar. Associative functions and statistical triangle inequalities. *Publ. Math. Debrecen*, 8:169–186, 1961.

[383] B. Schweizer and A. Sklar. Associative functions and abstract semigroups. *Publ. Math. Debrecen*, 10:69–81, 1963.

[384] B. Schweizer and A. Sklar. *Probabilistic Metric Spaces*. North-Holland Series in Probability and Applied Mathematics. North-Holland Publishing Co., New York, 1983.

[385] B. Schweizer and A. Sklar. *Probabilistic Metric Spaces*. Dover Publications, New York, 2005.

[386] A. Sen. Social choice theory. In *Handbook of Mathematical Economics, Vol. III*, volume 1 of *Handbooks in Econom.*, pages 1073–1181. North-Holland, Amsterdam, 1986.

[387] G. Shafer. *A Mathematical Theory of Evidence*. Princeton University Press, Princeton, NJ, 1976.

[388] L. S. Shapley. A value for n-person games. In *Contributions to the Theory of Games, Vol. 2*, Annals of Mathematics Studies, no. 28, pages 307–317. Princeton University Press, Princeton, NJ, 1953.

[389] H. Sherwood and M. D. Taylor. Some PM structures on the set of distribution functions. *Rev. Roumaine Math. Pures Appl.*, 19:1251–1260, 1974.

[390] N. Shilkret. Maxitive measure and integration. *Nederl. Akad. Wetensch. Proc. Ser. A 74 = Indag. Math.*, 33:109–116, 1971.

[391] W. Silvert. Symmetric summation: a class of operations on fuzzy sets. *IEEE Trans. on Systems, Man, and Cybernetics*, 9:657–659, 1979.

[392] I. Singer. Extensions of functions of 0-1 variables and applications to combinatorial optimization. *Numer. Funct. Anal. Optim.*, 7(1):23–62, 1984/85.

[393] J. Šipoš. Integral with respect to a pre-measure. *Math. Slovaca*, 29(2):141–155, 1979.

[394] M. Sklar. Fonctions de répartition à n dimensions et leurs marges. *Publ. Inst. Statist. Univ. Paris*, 8:229–231, 1959.

[395] P. Smets. The combination of evidence in the transferable belief model. *IEEE Tr. Pattern Anal. Machine Intelligence*, 12(5):447–458, 1990.

[396] D. Smutná. On a peculiar t-norm. *Busefal*, 75:60–67, 1998.

[397] J.-P. Soublin. Étude algébrique de la notion de moyenne. *J. Math. Pure Appl.*, 50(9):53–264, 1971.

[398] J. M. Steele. *The Cauchy–Schwarz Master Class*. MAA Problem Books Series. Mathematical Association of America, Washington, DC, 2004.

[399] K. B. Stolarsky. Generalizations of the logarithmic mean. *Math. Mag.*, 48:87–92, 1975.

[400] P. Struk. Extremal fuzzy integrals. *Soft Computing*, 10:502–505, 2006.

[401] F. Suárez García and P. Gil Álvarez. Two families of fuzzy integrals. *Fuzzy Sets and Systems*, 18(1):67–81, 1986.

[402] M. Sugeno. Fuzzy measures and fuzzy integrals. *Trans. S.I.C.E. (Keisoku Jidoseigyo Gakkai)*, 8(2):218–226, 1972. In Japanese.

[403] M. Sugeno. Construction of fuzzy measures and evaluation of similarity patterns by fuzzy integral. *Trans. S.I.C.E. (Keisoku Jidōseigyō Gakkai)*, 9:361–368, 1973. In Japanese.

[404] M. Sugeno. *Theory of Fuzzy Integrals and its Applications*. PhD thesis, Tokyo Institute of Technology, 1974.

[405] M. Sugeno. Fuzzy measures and fuzzy integrals – a survey. In M. M. Gupta, G. N. Saridis, and B. R. Gaines, editors, *Fuzzy Automata and Decision Processes*, pages 89–102. North-Holland, New York, 1977.

[406] M. Sugeno and S. H. Kwon. A clusterwise regression-type model for subjective evaluation. *J. of Japan Society for Fuzzy Theory and Systems*, 7(2):291–310, 1995.

[407] M. Sugeno and T. Murofushi. Pseudo-additive measures and integrals. *J. Math. Anal. Appl.*, 122:197–222, 1987.

[408] A. Tarski. Une contribution a la théorie de la measure. *Fund. Math.*, 15:42–50, 1930.

[409] J. A. Tawn. Bivariate extreme value theory: models and estimation. *Biometrika*, 75(3):397–415, 1988.

[410] B. S. Thomson. *Symmetric Properties of Real Functions*, volume 183 of *Monographs and Textbooks in Pure and Applied Mathematics*. Marcel Dekker Inc., New York, 1994.

[411] V. Torra and Y. Narukawa. *Modeling Decisions: Information Fusion and Aggregation Operators*. Cognitive Technologies. Springer, 2007.

[412] E. Trillas. Negation functions in the theory of fuzzy sets. *Stochastica*, 3(1):47–60, 1979.

[413] A. Tversky and D. Kahneman. Advances in prospect theory: cumulative representation of uncertainty. *J. Risk Uncertain.*, 5:297–323, 1992.

[414] M. Urbański and J. Wąsowski. Fuzzy arithmetic based on boundary weak T-norms. *Int. J. Uncertain. Fuzziness Knowledge-Based Systems*, 13(1):27–37, 2005.

[415] M. K. Urbański and J. Wąsowski. Boundary weak triangular norms. *Inform. Sci.*

[416] P. Vallentyne and S. Kagan. Infinite value and finitely additive value theory. *J. Philos.*, 94(1):5–26, 1997.

[417] L. Valverde and S. Ovchinikov. Representation of T-similarity relations. *Fuzzy Sets and Systems*, 159:2211–2220, 2008.

[418] P. Viceník. Additive generators and discontinuity. *Busefal*, 76:25–28, 1998.

[419] P. Viceník. A note on generators of t-norms. *Busefal*, 75:33–38, 1998.

[420] P. Viceník. A note to a construction of t-norms based on pseudo-inverses of monotone functions. *Fuzzy Sets and Systems*, 104(1):15–18, 1999.

[421] P. Viceník. Additive generators of non-continuous triangular norms. In S. Rodabaugh and P. Klement, editors, *Topological and Algebraic Structures in Fuzzy Sets: A Handbook of Recent Developments in the Mathematics of Fuzzy Sets*, pages 441–454. Kluwer Academic Publishers, 2000.

[422] G. Vitali. Sulla definizione di integrale delle funzioni di una variabile. *Ann. Mat. Pura Appl.*, 2(1):111–121, 1925. English translation: On the definition of integral of functions of one variable, *Rivista di Matematica per le Scienze Sociali*, 20:159–168, 1997.

[423] J. von Neumann and O. Morgenstern. *Theory of Games and Economic Behaviour*. Princeton University Press, Princeton, NJ, 1944.

[424] P. Walley. Coherent lower (and upper) probabilities. Technical Report 22, University of Warvick, Coventry, 1981.

[425] Z. Wang and G. J. Klir. *Fuzzy Measure Theory*. Plenum, 1992.

[426] Z. Wang, K.-S. Leung, and J. Wang. A genetic algorithm for determining nonadditive set functions in information fusion. *Fuzzy Sets and Systems*, 102(3):463–469, 1999.

[427] R. J. Weber. Probabilistic values for games. In A. E. Roth, editor, *The Shapley Value*, pages 101–119. Cambridge University Press, Cambridge, 1988.

[428] S. Weber. A general concept of fuzzy connectives, negations and implications based on t-norms and t-conorms. *Fuzzy Sets and Systems*, 11(2):115–134, 1983.

[429] S. Weber. $\perp$-decomposable measures and integrals for Archimedean t-conorms $\perp$. *J. Math. Anal. Appl.*, 101(1):114–138, 1984.

[430] H. Weisberg. The distribution of linear combinations of order statistics from the uniform distributions. *Ann. Math. Statist.*, 42:704–709, 1971.

[431] N. A. Weiss. *A Course in Probability*. Pearson International Edition. Addison Wesley, 2006.

[432] J. Wimp. Quadrature with generalized means. *Amer. Math. Monthly*, 93(6):466–468, 1986.

[433] A. Witkowski. Monotonicity of generalized weighted mean values. *Colloq. Math.*, 99(2):203–206, 2004.

[434] R. R. Yager. On a general class of fuzzy connectives. *Fuzzy Sets and Systems*, 4(3):235–242, 1980.

[435] R. R. Yager. On ordered weighted averaging aggregation operators in multi-criteria decisionmaking. *IEEE Trans. Systems Man Cybernet.*, 18(1):183–190, 1988.

[436] R. R. Yager. Aggregation operators and fuzzy systems modeling. *Fuzzy Sets and Systems*, 67(2):129–145, 1994.

[437] R. R. Yager. Criteria importances in OWA aggregation: an application of fuzzy modeling. In *Proc. of the 6th IEEE Int. Conf. on Fuzzy Systems (FUZZ'IEEE'97)*, pages 1677–1682, vol. 3, Barcelona, July 1997.

[438] R. R. Yager. Fusion of ordinal information using weighted median aggregation. *Int. J. Approx. Reason.*, 18(1–2):35–52, 1998.

[439] R. R. Yager. A class of fuzzy measures generated from a Dempster–Shafer belief structure. *Int. J. Intell. Syst.*, 14(12):1239–1247, 1999.

[440] R. R. Yager. On the entropy of fuzzy measures. *IEEE Trans. on Fuzzy Systems*, 8:453–461, 2000.

[441] R. R. Yager. The power average operator. *IEEE Trans. Systems Man Cybernet.*, 31(6):724–731, 2001.

[442] R. R. Yager. Using importances in group preference aggregation to block strategic manipulation. In *Aggregation Operators: New trends and applications*, pages 177–191. Physica, Heidelberg, 2002.

[443] R. R. Yager and D. Filev. *Essentials of Fuzzy Modelling and Control*. J. Wiley & Sons, New York, 1994.

[444] R. R. Yager and J. Kacprzyk, editors. *The Ordered Weighted Averaging operators*. Kluwer Academic Publishers, USA, 1997.

[445] R. R. Yager and A. Rybalov. Uninorm aggregation operators. *Fuzzy Sets and Systems*, 80:111–120, 1996.

[446] E. B. Yanovskaya. Group choice rules in problems with interpersonal preference comparisons. *Automat. Remote Control*, 50(6):822–830, 1989.

[447] L. A. Zadeh. Fuzzy sets as a basis for a theory of possibility. *Fuzzy Sets and Systems*, 1(1):3–28, 1978.

[448] H. Zimmermann and P. Zysno. Latent connectives in human decision making. *Fuzzy Sets and Systems*, 4:37–51, 1980.

[449] H. Zimmermann and P. Zysno. Decisions and evaluations by hierarchical aggregation of information. *Fuzzy Sets and Systems*, 10:243–260, 1983.

[450] A. Zygmund. *Trigonometric Series. Vol. I, II*. Cambridge Mathematical Library. Cambridge University Press, Cambridge, 1988.

Index